——THE——

FOUNDERS OF ANNE ARUNDEL

——AND——

HOWARD COUNTIES,

MARYLAND.

A Genealogical and Biographical Review from wills, deeds and church records.

——BY——

J. D. WARFIELD, A. M.

Formerly Professor of English Literature in the Maryland Agricultural College, genealogist and author of "The Warfields of Maryland."

KOHN & POLLOCK,
PUBLISHERS,
BALTIMORE, MD.
1905.

COPYRIGHT
1905.

Facsimile Reprint
Published 1995 By

HERITAGE BOOKS, INC.
1540E Pointer Ridge Place, Bowie, MD 20716
(301) 390-7709

ISBN 0-7884-0217-X

A Complete Catalog Listing Hundreds of Titles
On History, Genealogy, and Americana
Available Free Upon Request

INTRODUCTION.

I have searched the record for their good deeds and have herein handed them down to our children.

To master Maryland history we must know the biography of its founders. That biography has never before been written. Bozman, McMahan, McSherry, Davis and Scharf, content to accept the biased opinions of contemporary partisans, have been lavish in their criticisms of our "Early Settlers."

At this distance from that crucial era, under our broad ideas of toleration, it is difficult to judge the men and measures of an age of limited privileges.

For the first time in all history an ideal government had been organized in Maryland; a benevolent lord with knightly powers was at its head.

An act of toleration had just been passed. It was the joint product of liberal men of all faiths, but it was at a time when the mother country was involved in religious controversies, which, of necessity, were just as bitter here. Hence the act of toleration was for a season obscured in Maryland; but its influence, once felt, continued to grow until it became a leaven of enlightenment, ending finally in complete revolution.

Having searched the record of our "Early Settlers," the historian of to-day can see our early men as they were.

Judging them by their records, herein brought to light for the first time, their interested descendants will endorse the sentiment of a young historian who has recently recorded:

"In no other place upon the American Continent is there to be found so good an example of a people, who, after a struggle of nearly a century and a half, made the transition from a monarchical government to a 'government of the people, for the people, by the people,' as in Maryland."

(Mereness.)

Another Maryland historian, who has given us glances at some of the founders herein recorded, in the face of the harsh criticisms of his contemporaries, has left us this record:

"Between the morals of the past and those of the present, it would be impossible to draw a full or fair contrast, but injustice in this particular has certainly been done to the memory of our ancestors. Without wishing to draw a veil over the sins of the past, or excuse in the least its rudeness or its violence, I have no hesitation in expressing the opinion for whatever it may be worth, that in the sincerity of their friendships, in the depth of their religious convictions, in the strength of their domestic affections, and a general reverence for things sacred, our forefathers far outshine the men of this generation with all its pomp and pride of civilization."

(Davis.)

FRONTISPIECE.

"At the beginning of this new century we are going to the garrets, bringing out the portraits of our forefathers, brushing off the dust,—putting them into new frames and handing them down to our children. Search the records for their good deeds."

CHAPTER 1.

OUR EARLY SETTLERS.

All authorities pretty generally agree that our first Anne Arundel settlers came up from Virginia.

In 1620 Edward Bennett, a rich merchant of England, interested in Virginia trade, had organized a company consisting of his nephews Richard Bennett, Robert Bennett, Thomas Ayres, Richard and Thomas Wiseman, to send two hundred settlers to Virginia.

Many of those sent were murdered by the Indians in 1622. Robert Bennett and John Howard were among the number.

Richard Bennett, in 1642, came over in person to revive the company's efforts. He brought with him members of an Independent Church in England, who sought a more favorable field for building up their church.

Upon organizing in their new homes surrounding Edward Bennett's plantation upon the Elizabeth river, in Nansemond County, Philip Bennett, a nephew, was sent to Boston to secure ministers. He carried with him a letter written by John Hill. Rev. William Thompson, a graduate of Oxford, John Knowles, of Immanuel College, Cambridge, and Thomas James were induced to come. Upon their arrival in Virginia, they were coldly received by Governor Berkeley and his chaplain, Rev. Thomas Harrison. Through the Governor's influence, an act was passed by the Virginia legislature forbidding any minister, who did not use the "Book of Common Prayer," to officiate in the churches of Virginia.

The ministers from Boston soon retired from this unpromising field, but to the disgust and surprise of the Governor, his own chaplain, Mr. Harrison, announced his determination to take up the work just laid down.

The church had been built in 1638 upon "Sewell's Point," on the Elizabeth river. It was near Richard Bennett's two thousand acre plantation. It has recently been selected as the site of our coming Jamestown exposition.

HERE ARE SOME OF ITS RECORDS.

"At a meeting of the inhabitants of Lower Norfolk County, May 25th, 1640, Mr. Henry Sewell and Lieutenant Francis Mason, both of whom had been appointed by Governor Berkeley to hold monthly courts, to induce Mr. Harrison to continue service at Sewells Point, agreed to pay for themselves and the inhabitants of the parish from Captain Willoughby's plantation to Daniel Tanner's Creek, the sum of £32. Cornelius Lloyd, Henry Catlin and John Hill, agreed to pay for themselves and the Western Branch, £33. And Thomas Meeres, John Gatear (Gaither) and John Watkins, agreed to pay £36 for themselves and the inhabitants of Daniel Tanners Creek." All the members signed this agreement. From the Virginia Rent Rolls we find other early settlers, who later came to Maryland.

There was a grant to John Chew, gentleman, of five hundred acres, in the County of Charles River, due said Chew for the adventure of himself and nine persons on July 6th, 1636. The record shows that John Chew came to Virginia in 1622, and again in 1623.

John Gatear (Gaither) received 300 acres in Elizabeth City County, a neck of land on the eastern branch of Elizabeth River. Fifty acres of which were due him on his own personal adventure, and 250 acres for the transportation of his wife Jane and five persons in 1636. He received 200 acres more on the south of Elizabeth River for the transportation of four persons, the names not given.

Cornelius Lloyd received 800 acres in the County of Elizabeth River, due him for the transportation of sixteen persons in 1665. He was also one of the London merchants who received 8,000 acres in Berkeley Hundred in 1636.

Richard Preston was a justice of Nansemond County, in 1636.

William Ayres secured a plantation on Nansemond River for transporting five persons. Ann Ayres, wife of Samuel Chew, was his sole heiress.

Thomas Meeres held 300 acres in the Upper County of New Norfolk in 1644-5-6-7; he was a justice in 1645, and a churchwarden. There is a record which states "that Edward Lloyd was acting for Thomas Meeres, of Providence, Maryland, in 1645."

Thomas Davis held 300 acres in the Upper County of New Norfolk on the south side of Elizabeth River, five or six miles up, due him for transporting six persons on May, 1637. He was a justice of Nansemond, 1654.

In 1648, the vestry of Elizabeth River Church were Francis Mason, John Hill, Cornelius Lloyd, Henry Catlin. The following order was then passed: "And the sheriff is desired to give notice and summon John Norwood to appear before said vestry to account or the profits of the "Glebe Land' ever since Parson Harrison hath deserted his ministerial office and denied to administer ye sacrements with those of the Church of England." That was Captain John Norwood, the first sheriff of Anne Arundel.

Mr. Thomas Browne became a member of the vestry in 1648, and John Hill and William Crouch were elected wardens.

Wm. Durand having been banished in 1648, Thomas Marsh was ordered to pay the tax upon Durand's property.

The vestry in 1649 consisting of Thomas Browne, John Hill, Cornelius Lloyd, Henry Catlin, employed Mr. Sampson Calvert as minister. Mr. James Warner was church warden. He came to Maryland.

At the County Court of 1649, (the same year these parties left for Maryland), the following record reads: "Whereas, Mr. Edward Lloyd and Mr. Thomas Meeres, commissioners, with Edward Selby, Richard Day, Richard Owens, Thomas Marsh, George Kemp and

John Norwood were presented to ye board by the sheriff, for seditious sectuaries for not repairing to their church, and for refusing to hear common prayer—liberty is granted till October next, to inform their judgements, and to conform themselves to the established law."

Before that probation had expired all of the above were in Maryland. Edward Lloyd was both burgess and justice of Lower Norfolk. There is a deed on record from Francis Watkins, late wife of John Watkins, of Virginia, then wife of Edward Lloyd, in which she surrendered her dower to Edward Lloyd in consideration for his payment of a certain sum to her son, John Watkins. This agreement was carried out by Edward Lloyd when commander of the Severn. He surveyed a tract for his "son-in-law," (stepson) "John Watkins."

Edward and Cornelius Lloyd were near neighbors in Virginia, in 1635, of Matthew Howard and Ann, his wife. The latter named his son Cornelius in honor of Colonel Cornelius Lloyd.

Two more prominent Virginia officials, Colonel Obedience Robins and his brother, Edward Robins, sent representatives to Maryland. The former was the brother-in-law of Captain George Puddington. The latter was the father-in-law of Colonel William Burgess and Richard Beard, all settlers of South River, Maryland, in 1650.

Mr. Harrison's persistence had increased the independent church in Virginia to a membership of one hundred and eighteen, and when the order of banishment was issued, we have Mr. Harrison's statement that he and Elder William Durand left Virginia because they were ordered to go. This statement was supported by the record that "the lands of William Durand in Virginia were confiscated because of his banishment." At this crisis in Virginia a protestant Virginian had just been appointed Governor of Maryland. Governor Wm. Stone knew many of the independent exiles, and having promised Lord Baltimore to bring to his new province a large number of settlers, he naturally sought an interview with them.

Calvert's previous attempts to induce immigrants from England had not been successful.

He had even written a letter to Captain Gibbons, of Boston, offering land to any people of Massachusetts, who would transport themselves to his province; but "the Captain had no mind to further his desire, nor had any of our people temptation that way."

Governor Stone sought out William Durand. The evidence is the following records.

"Captain Wm. Stone, of Hungers Creek on eastern shore of Virginia, was born in Northamptonshire, England in 1603. He was the nephew of Thomas Stone, a haberdasher of London.

"In 1648 he conducted the negotiation for the removal of a party of non-conformists from Virginia to Maryland; and in August of that year Lord Baltimore commissioned him governor of that colony.

"William Durand, in 1648, came to Maryland with his wife, his daughter Elizabeth, and four other children, two freemen, Pell and Archer, and servants, Thomas Marsh, Margaret Marsh, William Warren, Wm. Hogg and Ann Coles." This is what our "Rent Rolls" show upon his coming: "William Durand demanded 800 acres of land for transporting himself, two male servants, one female servant, and two freemen into the province in 1648."

The grant was located in "Durands' Place," on the north side of the Severn.

Richard Bennett, the same year, took another grant of 250 acres, to be divided into small lots for a number of settlers who wished to be close together. This was located at "Towne Neck," a point now known as "Greenberry Point."

They then returned to Virginia, with the terms upon which their followers could obtain homes in Maryland. John Hammond, the historian, thus records that agreement.

"Upon the express assurance that there would be a modification of the oaths of the office and fidelity, an enjoyment of liberty of conscience, and the privilege of choice in officers, the Virginia Non-Conformists agreed to remove to the banks of the Severn."

Hammond was a strong advocate of Governor Stone's administration. Other historians differ as to the exact promises made at that interview, but our "Rent Rolls" undoubtedly show that Governor Stone and Lord Baltimore were both anxious to have settlers upon the modified terms offered in the "Condition of Plantation" of 1648.

Hammond declares, "Maryland was considered by the Puritans as a refuge. The lord proprietor and his governor solicited, and several addresses made for their admittance and entertainment into that province, under the conditions that they should have convenient portions of land assigned, the liberty of conscience and privilege to choose their own officers."

"After their arrival," continues Hammond, "an assembly was called throughout the whole county, consisting as well of themselves as the rest, and because there were some few papists that first inhabited, these themselves, and others, being different judgements, an act was passed that all professing Jesus Christ should have equal justice." And, "At the request of the Virginia Puritans," the oath of fidelity was overhauled and this clause added to it: "Provided it infringe not the liberty of conscience."

This was confirmed in 1650.

In confirmation of Hammond's statement, our "Rent Rolls" show that Edward Lloyd, in 1649, was granted a permit to lay out one thousand acres on the western side of the Chesapeake Bay to the northward of the Patuxent River, and a small creek, about the middle of "The Cliffs,' adjoining the lands of Richard Owens, there and to the northward of the Patuxent, not formally taken up yet."

He was so desirable an immigrant that he easily secured another grant of 570 acres on the north side of the Severn, just opposite

Annapolis. There he seated himself and was soon surrounded by many neighbors. Colonel William Burgess, that same year, brought up his colony to South River.

As there has been considerable discussion upon the exact location of the first settlement of the Severn, I will give the best light that comes from our Record Office. Read this grant of 1654.

"Cecilius, Absolute Lord and Proprietary of the Province of Maryland. To all persons to whom these presents come, greeting: Whereas, William Pell, George Saphir, Robert Rockhould, William Penny, Christopher Oatley, Oliver Sprye, John Lordking, and Richard Bennett, Esq., did in the 1649 and 1650, transport themselves into this province, here to inhabit and for their mutual security, did several small parcels of land then take upon a place called the "Towne Neck," to the intent they might seat close together, and whereas, the said several parcels are since by lawful purchase from the said (persons named), become the sole right of the said Richard Bennett, and whereas, the said Richard Bennett hath since alienated, and for a valuable consideration, sould the said several parcels unto our trusty and well beloved counselor, Nathaniel Utie, Esq. Now know ye, that we hereby grant unto said Nathaniel Utie all that parcel called Towne Neck, on the west side of Chesapeak Bay, and on the east side of Anne Arundel River, now again surveyed to the said Nathaniel Utie, beginning at Towne Creek, and running for breath northeast 140 perches, to a creek called Ferry Creeke, bounding on the east by a line drawn south, for length by the said creeke and bay 320 perches; on the south by a line drawn west from the end of the south line 110 perches, unto Anne Arundel River; on the west by a line drawn north from the end of the west line unto the marked line; on the north by the first northeast line—containing 250 acres," (There is no evidence from our "Rent Rolls" that any of these people were ever seated at "Towne Neck.")

Nathaniel Utie held this Towne Neck from 1654 to 1661, when he sold it to Wm. Pennington, who, that same year, sold it to Ralph Williams, of Bristol, England. It descended to his daughters, Mrs. Elizabeth Molling and Mrs. Rebecca Barber, who sold the same to Edward Perrin, of Bristol, England. It was then transferred to Edward Deaver and finally to Colonel Nicholas Greenberry, who did not come over until 1674. It was not secured by him until 1685. It then became known as "Greenberry Point." The deeds of transfers cover some thirty pages, and the time of transfers some thirty years.

Adjoining "Towne Neck," on the west, extensive tracts were taken up and held, as our "Rent Rolls" show.

Edward Lloyd, in 1650, had laid out 570 acres on the north side of the Severn, adjoining "Harrards' Line," (this may have been Howards), running with the river for a length of fifty-five perches.

In 1659, he also took up "Pendenny," upon which stands, to-day, the house of Captain John Worthington, now held by the late Mr. R. Tilghman Brice's family, just opposite the Naval Academy.

There are many evidences in the old foundation relics at "Pen-denny Heights," to show that here dwelt Edward Lloyd, when in 1650, Governor Stone and his secretary, Nathaniel Utie, came up to the Severn and organized the new settlement.

By Governor Stone's appointment, Edward Lloyd was made commander of Providence, a title kindred to that of deputy-governor; with power to name his own Council, who, with him, were empowered to grant certificates of surveys of lands, organize courts, and direct that settlement.

Edward Lloyd's commissioners were James Homewood, Thomas Meeres, Thomas Marsh, George Puddington, Matthew Hawkins, James Merryman, and Henry Catlyn.

He built his home on the north side of the Severn, in the neck, just opposite the city of Annapolis; Henry Catlyn and James Merryman were his immediate neighbors.

These two settlers did not long remain. Their combined estates were later embraced in the Greenberry and Worthington surveys, now held by Messrs. R. Tilghman Brice and Charles E. Remson.

James Homewood and Matthew Hawkins were upon the Magothy River; George Puddington was upon South River; Thomas Marsh and Thomas Meeres were first upon Herring Creek, but later resided on the Severn.

Edward Lloyd's house was the Council Chamber. His immediate neighbors were William Crouch, on the Severn; Richard Young, on the Magothy; Ralph Hawkins, of the Magothy; Richard Ewen, of the Magothy; William Hopkins, Thomas Browne, John Browne, Henry Catlyn, John Clarke were all near the Commander upon North Severn.

George Goldsmith and Nathaniel Proctor held lands adjoining Lloyd's "Swan Neck," upon the bay.

Captain William Fuller located on "Fuller's Survey," which is now known as "White Hall." Leonard Strong, the first historian of the Anne Arundel settlers, and his daughter Elizabeth, held 800 acres adjoining Captain Fuller.

Thomas Meeres adjoined them, holding 500 acres. This North Severn settlement was "Broad Neck," and included Colonel Greenberry's "Towne Neck."

Rev. Ethan Allen, in his historical notes of St. Annes, records: "There was a meeting house at Towne Neck; there is still to be seen the place where the chapel and burying ground was. Among the ruins is a massive slab with this inscription: 'Here lies interred the body of Mr. Roger Newman, merchant, born at London, who dwelt at Palip, in Talbot, in Maryland, twenty-five years, and departed this life the 14th of May, 1704.

"There was at this time a dissenting minister, a Mr. Davis, in the neighborhood."

MIDDLE NECK HUNDRED.

In 1650, there were three known settlers on the site of Annapolis, as the following grant to Thomas Todd, the shipwright, shows. "Laid out for Thomas Todd 100 acres, commencing at Oyster Shell Point, running up the river northwest 160 perches to Deep Cove, bounding on said creek 140 perches to a marked line; on the west unto the bounds of Richard Acton's land at a marked oak; on the south with a line drawn northwest by north unto the bounds of Thomas Hall's land, being a marked poplar; and with the same for thirty-five perches. Then from the end of a former line unto a creek called Todd's Creek; on the east with said river; containing one hundred acres."

One more surveyor, destined to be better known in history, was Robert Proctor, who took up "Proctor's Chance," in 1679, at a beginning tree of "Intact," on the west side of the Severn River. This tract became "Proctor's Landing," and was his residence in 1681, when he then designated his place as "town." Major Dorsey was there and had built a row of houses on "Bloombury Square," near the present new post-office. He also held houses and lots on High Street, which his widow, Margaret Israel, sold to William Bladen, in 1706.

Another survey of Todd's tract seems to locate a town there in 1651. It reads: "bounding on Thomas Hall's land and on Todd's Creek, beginning at ye northeast point of "Town" and extending along the river to ye first creek to ye west and then with back lines to ye beginning." "Todd's Range" extended along the south side of the Severn, west to the head of Dorsey's Creek.

The south-side settlers followed the Severn back to Round Bay. They were James Horner, who held "Locust Neck"; Peter Porter at "Bustions Point," adjoining James Warner.

Captain John Norwood held 200 acres of "Norwood's Fancy," adjoining Thos. Meeres.

Nicholas Wyatt surveyed "Wyatt's Harbor" and "Wyatts' Hills," upon which "Belvoir" now stands, just south of, and in sight of Round Bay. Adjoining it was Thomas Gates, upon "Dorsey's Creek," near "Dorsey," taken up by the first Edward Dorsey, in partnership with Captain John Norwood.

James Warner and John Freeman were both near by; William Galloway and Thomas Browne were further west, but touching upon Round Bay.

Lawrence Richardson and the first Matthew Howard surveyed also near Round Bay.

John Collier was on "Todd's Creek," near the present site of Annapolis.

The Middle Neck settlers along the bay, north of South River were Philip Thomas, of "Thomas Point;" Captain William Fuller Leonard Strong, Thomas Meeres, Thomas Tolley and William James

Upon their surveys stand, to-day, Bay Ridge and Arundel-on-the-Bay.

At the head of South River on the north side,, were John Baldwin, James Warner and Henry Ridgely.

SOUTH RIVER HUNDRED.

In 1650, Colonel William Burgess, the merchant whose vessels brought 150 settlers, was the central figure around whom settled a band of large land-holders.

Joseph Morely held "Morely's Grove."

John Freeman, son-in-law and heir of Joseph Morely, took up at the head of South River, "Freeman's Fancy," "Freeman's Stone," "Freeman's Landing." Adjoining him were John Gaither and Robert Proctor, both heirs of Joseph Morely. They were surveyors of "Abbington," and final heirs of Freeman's and Morely's lands.

Mareen Duval, the Huguenot immigrant from Nantes, France, held a large estate around South River, viz: "Middle Plantation" and "Great Marsh." He came with Colonel William Burgess.

Captain George Puddington surveyed "Puddington Harbor," and "West Puddington." Richard Beard, brother-in-law of Colonel William Burgess, held "Beard's Habitation" on "Beard's Creek," near the site of Londontown. Neal Clarke, related to both Puddington and Beard, was an adjoining neighbor near the head of South River.

Thos. Besson, the younger, adjoined Colonel William Burgess on the south side of South River. Ellis Brown was on the south side, near Edward Selbys. Captain John Welsh held lands first upon South River and afterwards on the Severn.

RHODE RIVER HUNDRED.

Robert Harwood took up "Harwood," in 1657, which later descended to Abel Browne. Walter Mansfield adjoined him. Captain Thomas Besson settled on the west side. His neighbors were Thomas Sparrow, George Nettlefield, John Brewer, Edward Townhill and Colonel Nicholas Gassaway, son-in-law of Captain Thomas Besson, Sr. Captain Thomas Francis "The Ranger," was another large land-holder of Rhode River.

THE WEST RIVER HUNDRED.

Roger Grosse, the popular representative, whose widow married Major John Welsh, held a large estate upon West River. His neighbors were Thomas Miles, John Watkins, Hugh and Emanuel Drew, Richard Talbott, John Browne and John Clarke. Still later the West River meeting-house of Quakers attracted a large settlement of leading Quakers, among whom were the Galloways.

HERRING CREEK HUNDRED.

Samuel Chew laid out Herrington.

Thomas Marsh took up lands on the west side of Herring Creek, beginning at Parker's Branch, and running to Selby's Cove; he also held a thousand acres adjoining Richard Bennett, running up the bay. He held a tract adjoining John Norwood, running down the bay, 600 acres more. He gave the name to Marshe's Creek, so difficult to locate in the division of the two counties. Edward Selby held lands on Selby's Cove, adjoining Thomas Marsh. He also adjoined Thomas Meeres on the west side of South River, next to John Watkins; in all some 1000 acres. William Parker adjoined Thomas Marsh on Herring Creek, and also, Richard Bennett, Sampson Warring, and Thomas Davis on the bay, holding 1200 acres. William Durand adjoined Edward Selby, running down the bay; John Covell adjoined William Durand; Thomas Emerson adjoined William Parker; Captain Edward Carter, near Herring Creek, adjoined William Ayers, whose lands were assigned him by Thomas Marsh. Richard Ewen adjoined Richard Bennett and Richard Talbott, on Herring Creek. Richard Wells, Chirurgeon, was on the west side of Herring Bay, adjoining Stockett's Creek, holding 600 arces. The three Stockett brothers were on Stockett's Run; they did not come from Virginia. Back on the Patuxent, Colonel Richard Preston held 500 acres, and built a house which still stands; it is the oldest house in Maryland. He was an important man, in both Maryland and Virginia. Commander Robert Brooke, with his body guard of forty, was still below on the Patuxent, holding at first a whole county. Richard Bennett held thousands of acres at Herring Creek, and later as many more upon the Eastern Shore.

From these surveys, running form 100 to 1000 acres, we get a list of the most prominent settlers in 1649-50. The leaders took up land in several sections. The largest land-holders were in the southern section, where the soil was remarkably rich.

As soon as these settlers were well-seated, Governor Stone by proclamation, called a legislature in which he used these words: "and for the Puri— to give them particular notice." This referred to the settlers just enumerated; the term "Puritan" was then a reproach, and from policy perhaps, Governor Stone left the word incomplete. About the time for assemblying the legislature, Governor Stone paid a visit to these settlers; he succeeded in getting a representation. Upon his return he made this report: "By the Lieutenant of Maryland, The Freemen of that part of this province now called Providence, being by my appointment duly summoned to this present assembly, did unanimously make choice of Mr. George Puddington and Mr. James Cox for their burgesses, I being there in person at that time." Upon the organization of the assembly, a high compliment was paid to that settlement, in the election of Mr. James Cox speaker of the house. There were fourteen members, eight of whom were Protestants who threw their influence to

Mr. Cox for speaker. The assembly passed an order that the governor issue writs to summon three or four inhabitants of Anne Arundel, to meet him and the council, to consider what is necessary to be added to the levies of this year, besides those already brought in by the committee. An act was passed for fixing surveyors' charges at one pound of tobacco per acre; if above 100 are surveyed, then one-half pound per acre be charged. The expenses for the assembly to be levied from Anne Arundel County, in 1650, were:

To Mr. Puddington and Mr. James Cox, for

37 days, apiece at 50 pounds per day . . .3,700 pounds

Boate, hand and wages . . . . 600 pounds

4,300 pounds

An order was passed providing for a march upon the Indians for murdering an English inhabitant in Anne Arundel—to press men to make war. The charge of such war to be laid by an equal assessment on the person and estate of the inhabitants of the province. An order was passed for a levy of half a bushel of corn per poll upon every freeman in Anne Arundel, to be disposed of by the governor as he shall see fit. During that session, was passed an act for erecting Providence into a county by the name of Anne Arundel. This was the first and almost only legislative provision for erecting any county in the province. It's name was in honor of Lady Anne Arundel, daughter of Lord Arundel, of Wardour, wife of Cecilius Lord Baltimore. Induced by the murder of some English in that section, an act was passed prohibiting Indians from coming into the new county of Anne Arundel. The last important act of the session of 1650, was the oath of fidelity to Lord Baltimore.

The Protestants were in the majority in the assembly, yet they joined Governor Stone in his declaration setting forth that they enjoyed fitting freedom of conscience in Lord Baltimore's province. This act was signed by speaker Cox, George Puddington and even by William Durand, the Virginia elder who attested Leonard Strong's pamphlet. This Protestant assembly enacted that an oath of fidelity should be taken. John Langford recorded the following: "No one was banished under that law for refusing to take it." Up to this period it was evident that a judicial administration of govermental affairs had, to a certain extent, conciliated the cautious non-conformist element, which had looked with suspicion upon the oath of fidelity

Let us now look at the government to which these people had just come. Cecilius Calvert, the second Lord Baltimore, held by charter rights, a territory with almost unrestricted privileges. All office, title, honor were in his hands; head of the church, of the military, executive and judicial powers, he could control all legislative acts. Yet the charter granted him secured to the people of Maryland "all the privileges, franchises and liberties" which other English subjects enjoyed.

Granted by a king who held to "the divine right"; modeled after the established institutions of an absolute monarch, William, the Norman, the charter of Maryland, though giving a long list of sovereign rights which made the lord proprietor absolute in his domain, contained three words above quoted, which, viewed under the light of the Magna Charta and the English Bill of Rights, were destined to put the people in control of the province even upon the Charta basis.

The ruling motive of the more influential settlers in Maryland, was a desire for greater political and religious liberty.

Others of the more restless nature were attracted by the easy and favorable terms on which land was offered.

Both classes were opposed to the extensive sovereign rights granted the lord proprietary, and were only brought into subjection by concessions to prevent uprisings. Back of these storm signals serious trouble had already threatened the proprietary of Maryland. William Clayborne, of a distinguished English family, a man of marked ability, had made a prior claim to the very territory over which Cecilius Calvert was now lord. Further than this, a war was at hand in the mother country between the king and parliament.

There were, in Maryland, influential settlers ready then to take the side of parliament; and when, at last, the parliamentary forces were victorious, and King Charles had been sacrificed in the triumph of popular rights over "divine right," the contest was to be fought out in the province of Maryland.

Parliament had declared it to be treason for any one to acknowledge Charles, the son, king, yet in the face of that declaration, Governor Green, acting for Governor Stone, had already acknowledged Charles, the Second, "the rightful heir of all his father's dominions." This unfortunate proclamation, not intended by the Lord Proprietary, gave much trouble in Maryland, ending finally in its reduction.

LEGISLATURE OF 1651.

Governor Stone called an assembly in 1651; to this the people of Anne Arundel sent no delegates. News had reached them that Parliament had, in 1650, passed an ordinance for the reduction of Lord Baltimore's province. Instead of sending delegates to the assembly of 1651, Commander Lloyd sent a message explaining the reason for not answering the call. That message, when forwarded to Lord Baltimore in England, gave offence.

Though not a matter of record, its tenor may be seen in the following proclamation of Lord Baltimore.

"To Governor Wm. Stone, and the Upper and Lower Houses, and all the other officers and inhabitants of the Province:

Greeting:—We can but much wonder at a message which we understand has lately been sent by one Mr. Lloyd from some lately seated at Anne Arundel, to our general assembly at St. Maries, in

March last; but are unwilling to impute either to the sender or deliverer thereof, so malign a sense of ingratitude as it may seem to bear, conceiving rather that it proceeded from some apprehension in them at that time grounded upon some reports of a dissolution or resignation of our patent and right to that province, which might, perhaps, for the present, make them doubtful what to do till they had more certain intelligence thereof." Thus in a very temperate, conciliatory spirit, he continued to review the necessity for all settlers to conform to the rules and usages already established, urging that a government, divided in itself, must needs bring confusion and misery upon all. "If such divisions continue, which God forbid, then we must use our authority to compel all factious spirits to a better compliance with the lawful government; requiring you, our said lieutenant, to proceed against such disturbers, and, if continued after admunition, then to be declared enemies to the public peace.

"And, whereas, we understand that in the late rebellion of 1644, most of the records of that province being then lost, or embezzled, no enrollment remains now of divers patents of land formerly granted by us, we therefore require you to issue a proclamation requiring all persons within a certain time therein fixed, to produce to our surveyor-general, or his deputy, all such patents by which they claim land in our province; and to require our secretary to give you a list of all such patents now on record, and to require all such persons as claim land to cause them to be enrolled in our secretary's office within some convenient time, to be limited by you. And, whereas, by the third article of our last "Conditions of Plantation," dated 1649, there is allowed one hundred acres to every adventurer, or planter, for every person of British or Irish descent, transported thither, we understand that it may be prejudicial to the general good of the colony, in case so great allowance shall be long continued, causing the people to be too remote from each other; inasmuch as a few persons may take up large tracts, leaving but little opportunity for others to come, therefore, we proclaim that, after the 20th day of June, 1652, only fifty acres shall be assigned, instead of one hundred acres.

"The proportionate rents and oath of fidelity to stand as already expressed, in 1650." Dated 1651.

Following that proclamation, Governor Stone issued his call for all settlers to come forward and demand grants. As the returns from Commander Lloyd, of Anne Arundel, and Robert Vaughan, of Kent Island, were both unsatisfactory, their commissions to issue land grants were revoked.

The year 1651 ended without much change in the condition of the settlers. Parliament, however, had determined to take in hand the struggling provinces of Virginia and Maryland. Commissioners were appointed to take control. Virginia readily acquiesced and soon after, in 1652, the Virginia commissioners came to Maryland to subdue it.

Mr. John Langford states, "that Richard Bennett, who was active in procuring preachers from Boston for the Puritans of Virginia, was one of those, who, when driven out of Virginia, came and settled in Providence." Bennett, however, still retained his residence in Virginia when appointed one of the commissioners for the reduction of Maryland. In his proclamation he proposed, "that the settlers should all remain in their places, but only conform to the laws of the commonwealth of England, and not infringe the Lord Baltimore's just rights. That all the inhabitants, including the governor and council, should subscribe the test called 'the engagement.' "

Governor Stone and the rest of the officers readily assented to a portion of the requirements, but having refused to accept the proposition "that all writs should be issued in the name of 'The Keepers of the Liberty of England,' "commissioners Bennett and Claiborne demanded Stone's commission from Lord Baltimore. This they detained, and dismissing him, appointed other officers. Issuing their proclamation that all writs, warrants and other processes be made in the name of the Keepers of the Liberty of England, by authority of parliament, they named the following commissioners, one or more of whom should sign them, viz: Robert Brooke, Colonel Francis Yardley, Mr. Job. Chandler, Captain Edmund Winder, Colonel Richard Preston and Lieutenant Richard Banks. These were authorized to take in hand the government of the province. The acts of Governor Stone and his council were declared null and void.

All the records were then ordered to be placed into the hands of the above council, at Richard Preston's, where the proceedings were to be held.

Lord Baltimore's power was thus quietly obliterated. The commissioners returned to Virginia, where Bennett became governor, and Claiborne, secretary of state.

Robert Brooke was now head of the province. He was not one of the Virginia settlers, but came with his household of forty persons direct from England, bearing in his pocket the following grant from the proprietor, then in London.

"We appoint him, the said Robert Brooke, to be commander under us, and our lieutenant of our whole county, to be newly set forth next adjoining the place he shall so settle and plant in, giving him all the perquisites of a county commander, with power to appoint six or more inhabitants to advise with him."

The county thus set off was the present county of Calvert, but then named Charles County.

The location of Robert Brooke, was first at "Dela Brooke," but still later at "Brooke Place," upon Battle Creek, about forty miles from the mouth of the Patuxent. Two years from his landing he, too, was acting with opposing settlers. Governor Bennett and Secretary Claiborne, of Virginia, soon returned to Maryland to watch the progress of their revolution. Knowing that Governor

Stone was popular with the people, they sought him and offered the office of governor, which Stone accepted under certain conditions.

Thomas Hatton, his late secretary, was also accepted, who, with Robert Brooke, Captain John Price, Job. Chandler, Colonel Francis Yardley, Colonel Richard Preston, were declared the governor's council. Colonel Claiborne renewed his claim to Kent Island. Governor Stone next issued a commission to Captain William Fuller, purporting to be in the name of "The Keepers of the Liberty of England," as commander-in-chief under him of all forces for a speedy march against the Eastern Shore Indians, giving him full power to levy forces in Anne Arundel County. The people of Anne Arundel were not in favor of going against the Eastern Shore Indians. Their reasons were given in Commander Fuller's letter to Governor Stone. "Sir, I find the inhabitants of these parts wholly disaffected, not to the thing, but the time of year, on account of a want of vessels and the frozen waters."

In 1652, Governor Stone issued his proclamation that information from Captain William Fuller of the want of soldiers, apparel and the unseasonable time induced him to relinquish the movement and discharge the forces raised." In the meantime, an important treaty was that year made "at the River of Severn" with the Susquehannock Indians, by which Richard Bennett, Edward Lloyd, Thomas Marsh, William Fuller and Leonard Strong, commissioners upon the part of the English settlers, had secured all the land lying on the west side of the Chesapeak Bay, from the Patuxent River unto Palmer's Island, which island was recorded as belonging to William Claiborne, along with the Isle of Kent. That treaty was pointedly indicative that the two chief owners of the land of the Province, were by those commissioners, considered to be the Susquehannock Indians, and Captain William Claiborne, of Virginia. This treaty was made under the big popular on College Green. These men preferred to secure their rights and protection by means of a treaty rather than through the hazards of war.

This act showed wisdom in an age when might generally secured right. That treaty also shows the cause of their delay in taking up grants from the proprietary. They were already seated upon lands which their Commander Edward Lloyd, had been authorized to have surveyed for them. The claim to the province was known to be in dispute. Parliament was in control in England, and they were more in sympathy with the parliamentary leaders than with the faith and requirements of the proprietary. They saw the coming conflict and awaited its results, believing that the final issues would be more favorable to them.

These are the unwritten reasons that actuated the settlers of Anne Arundel. Whether they were right or wrong, the history of succeeding events showed that their judgment was well founded, for even though the proprietary held his patent under Cromwell, his son and successor was destined to lose it, by rebellions still more active.

We come now to a clash of arms for the mastery of contending claims. Leonard Strong, the settler's historian, and John Langford, the historian of Lord Baltimore, in their respective publications, give us some contemporary records of that contest. Strong's pamphlet was "Babylon's Fall", and Langford's was "A Refutation of Babylon's Fall."

Strong declared that John Langford, and not Governor Stone, had invited them to come. "They were received and protected, but an oath to Lord Baltimore was urged upon them soon after their coming up from Virginia, which, if they did not take, they must have no land or abiding place in the Province." This was the oath of fidelity attached to the "Conditions of Plantation," issued by the proprietary in 1648. Strong further adds, "That they must swear to uphold that government and those officers who were sworn to countenance and uphold the Roman Catholic Church."

John Langford in answer wrote, in 1655: "That there was nothing promised by my lord or Captain Stone to them, but what was performed. They were first acquainted by Captain Stone before they came there, with that oath of fidelity, which was to be taken by those who would have any land there from his lordship. That the terms were well known, and they were not forced to come or stay. He denied that the oath "was to uphold the Roman Catholic Church," but urged that the officers were Protestants, and that the oath of fidelity bound no man to maintain any other jurisdiction of my lord's than what is granted in the patent. He boldly charged Mr. Strong's people with a desire "to exercise more absolute dominion than my Lord Baltimore ever did. Not content to enjoy, as they did, freedom of conscience for themselves, they were anxious for the liberty to debar others from like freedom."

The next witnesses are the settlers themselves, under their own names, in 1653, in formal and dignified appeal, as follows:

PETITIONS TO THE COMMISSIONERS OF THE COMMONWEALTH 1653.

To Hon. Richard Bennett and Colonel Wm. Claiborne, Esqs., Commissioners of the Commonwealth of England, from Virginia and Maryland." It was styled, "The Humble Petition of the Commissioners and Inhabitants of Severne, alias Anne Arundel County, Showwith," and reads: "That, whereas, we were invited and encouraged by Captain Stone, the Lord Baltimore's Governor of Maryland, to remove ourselves and estates into the province, with promise of enjoying the liberty of conscience in matter of religion, and all other privileges of English subjects. And your petitioners did, upon this ground, with great cost, labor and danger, remove ourselves, and have been at great charges in building and clearing. Now the Lord Baltimore imposeth an oath upon us by proclamation, which, if we do not take in three months, all of our lands are to be seized, for his lordship's use. This oath, we conceive not agreeable to the terms on which we came hither. We have complained of this grievance to the late Hon. Council of State, which never received an answer, such as might clear the lawlessness of such, but an aspersion cast upon us of being factious fellows. In consideration whereof, we humbly tend to our condition intreating your honors to relieve us according to the power, wherewith you are intrusted by the Commonwealth of England. Severn River, January 3rd, 1663."

This petition was signed by Edward Lloyd, and seventy-seven others of the house-keepers, freemen, and inhabitants of the Severn.

The people of North Patuxent sent a similar petition, dated March the 1st, 1653, signed by Richard Preston and sixty others.

On March the 12th, 1653, Bennett and Claiborne returned an answer, encouraging the petitioners of the Severn and Patuxent, "to continue in your due obedience to the Commonwealth of England and not to be drawn aside by any pretense of power from Lord Baltimore's agents, or any other, whatsoever to the contrary."

PROCLAMATION OF 1653.

Governor Stone, in 1653, issued his final call for taking up lands under the conditions of plantations, as then existing.

In that proclamation, in the face of his promise to the Parliamentary Commissioners, he declared that the oath of fidelity and writs "*must be in the proprietor's name.*" During that year the Little Parliament had surrendered its powers to Cromwell, the Protector. Governor Stone issued his proclamation in compliance with the change. The next strike at the settlers of Anne Arundel was in 1654, when Robert Brooke, the commander of Charles County, because of his support of them, was deprived of his command by the erection of Calvert County out of the territory of Charles County. This change was intended to cripple the power of Robert Brooke, the commander. Governor Stone next charged the settlers of Anne Arundel with drawing away the people, and leading them into faction, rebellion, and sedition against Lord Baltimore.

This charge caused Bennett and Claiborne to return to Maryland, to look after Governor Stone. They claimed to come under authority of the Lord Protector. But Leonard Strong, even, did not state that they bore an order from Cromwell, and Mr. Langford denied that they had any authority from the Protector. They, however, went before Governor Stone and his Council, who returning uncivil answers, called together his men, to surprise said Commissioners. The latter "in a quiet and peaceable manner, with some people of Patuxent and Severn, went over on the Calvert side of the Patuxent, and then proceeded into St. Mary's, meeting no opposition. There Captain Stone sent a message that he would treat with them in the woods; fearful of the coming of a party from Virginia, Stone condescended to lay down his power, and submit again to such a government as the commissioners should appoint under the authority of the protector." On July 22nd, 1654, the commissioners, then at Patuxent, issued this order: "For the public administration of justice, Captain William Fuller, Mr. Richard Preston, Mr. William Durand, Mr. Edward Lloyd, Captain John Smith, Mr. Leonard Strong, Mr. John Lawson, Mr. John Hatch, Mr. Richard Wells and Mr. Richard Ewen—with the first three of the Quorum. They were empowered to call an assembly at the Patuxent, the home of Colonel Preston, but all who bore arms, against parliament, or were of the Roman Catholic faith, were to be deprived of vote. William Durand was made Secretary of State, and Mr. Thomas Hatton was ordered to deliver to him the papers of his office.

The assembly met at Patuxent, October 20th, 1654, and sat as one house. Colonel Richard Preston was made speaker; Thomas Hatten and Job. Chandler, delegates from St. Mary's, refused to sit because they had taken an oath to Lord Baltimore. They were taxed with the necessary expense to elect their successors. It was then declared that "henceforth all power in this province is held by the protector and parliament." Further, "that no Catholic can be protected in his faith, but be restrained from the exercise thereof."

This assembly further enacted that "all those that transport themselves or others into this province, have a right to land by virtue of their transportation. That all may enter their rights of land in their respective courts, and also, may enter caveat for such a particular tract of land as they shall take up."

This revolt culminated in an act making "null and void" the proclamation of Lord Baltimore which read, "that all who would not submit to his authority should be declared rebels."

This act meant war, and war was now at hand.

CHAPTER II.

THE BATTLE OF THE SEVERN.

An important letter now arrived. It was written by Lord Baltimore, and was addressed to Governor Stone. It was in care of Wm. Eltonhead, a messenger, who came in Captain Tilghman's "Golden Fortune."

That letter censured Governor Stone for yielding up his authority without a struggle, and renewed his instructions for action.

Eltonhead further announced that Lord Baltimore still held his patent, and that his Highness, the Protector, had neither taken the patent nor land.

This letter and the assured support of Eltonhead gave Governor Stone new life. He at once organized a military company. Sending Hammond, the historian, and others to the house of Colonel Richard Preston, the provencial records were seized and brought back.

John Hammond thus describes his venture: "Governor Stone sent me to fetch the records. I went unarmed amongst these sons of Thunder, only three or four to row me, and despite all their braves of raising the country, calling in his servants to apprehend me, threatened me with the severity of their new made law, myself alone seized and carried away the records in defiance."

Governor Stone now started for the Severn. He had gathered two hundred men and eleven vessels. They marched along the bay coast, using the vessels to ferry them across the rivers.

Before arriving at Herring Creek, they were met by two sets of messengers, sent in boats by the people of Providence. The first messenger was to demand his power and the ground of such proceedings. The Governor's reply was not satisfactory, as shown by the following letter from Secretary William Durand.

"For Captain Wm. Stone, Esq. Sir,—The people of these parts have met together and considered the present transactions on your part, and have not a little marvelled that no other answer of the last message hath been made than what tended rather to make men desperate than conformable. Yet, being desirous of peace, do once again present to your serious consideration these ensuing proposals as the mind of the people. 1st. If you will govern us so as we will enjoy the liberty of English subjects. 2nd. And that we be and remain indemnified in respect of our engagement, and all former acts relating to the reducement and government. 3rd. That those who are minded to depart the province may freely do it without any prejudice to themselves or their estates. We are content to own yourself as governor, and submit to your government. If not, we are resolved to submit ourselves into the hands of God, and rather die like men than be made slaves.—William Durand, Secretary."

Roger Heamans records: "But no answer to this was returned, but the same paper in scorn, sent back again."

Governor Stone not only made no answer, but detained the messengers in order to surprise the settlers.

Leonard Strong records: "Governor Stone, on his arrival at Herring Creek, captured one of Captain Fuller's commissioners and forced another man of quality to fly for his life, having threatened to hang him up to his door, and not finding the man, frightened his wife and plundered the house of amunition and provision, threatening still what they would do to the people of Providence and that they would force the factious Roundheads to submit, and then they would show their power."

Governor Stone later sent Dr. Luke Barber and Mr. Coursey to go on before to Providence, bearing a proclamation to the people of Anne Arundel, in which he declared, "in the presence of Almighty God, that he came not in the hostile way to do them any hurt, but sought all means possible to reclaim them by faire meanes."

Dr. Barber adds: "He gave strict command that if they met any Anne Arundel men, they should not fire the first gun, nor upon pain of death, plunder any upon the march."

Strong records: "The messengers having no other treaty to offer, they were quietly dismissed to their own company, to whom they might have gone if they would." They did not, however, return. After sending another messenger and none returning, on the evening of the same day, the Governor with his fleet, made his appearance in the Severn.

Captain Fuller in command of the Anne Arundel forces, called a council together and dispatched Secretary Durand to the merchant-ship, Golden Lyon, Roger Heamans master, then lying in the harbor. Durand, by proclamation in the name of the Lord Protector and Commonwealth of England, summoned Heamans to aid in this service of maintaining the lives, liberties and estates of the free subjects thereof.

Heamans, in his defense, confirmed Strong's mission, and adds: "After seeing the equity of the cause and the groundless proceedings of the enemy, I offered myself, ship and men for that service, to be directed by said councilors."

Hammond declares that there is not a syllable of truth in Heaman's pamphlet, and charges that he was "hired." Heamans was, without doubt, a sympathizing friend, and he gives, from his commanding position, the following intelligent review of the contest:

"In the very shutting up of the daylight, the ship's company descried off, a company of sloops and boats, making toward the ship. Whereupon the Council on board, and the ship's company would have made shot at them, but this relator commanded them to forbear, and went himself upon the poop in the stern of the ship, and hailed them several times, and no answer was made; he then ordered them not to come nearer the ship. His mates and company, having had information of their threatenings, as well against the ship as the poor distressed people, resolved to fire upon them without their commander's consent, rather than hazard all by the enemy's nearer approach; whereupon, he ordered them to fire a gun at random, to divert their course from the ship, but the enemy kept still its course right with the ship, and took no notice of any warning given. He then commanded his gunner to fire at them, but one of his mates, Mr. Robert Morris, who knew the country very well, the malice of the adversary against the people, who were then near worn out with fears and watchings, made a shot at them, which came fairly with them. Whereupon they suddenly altered their course from the ship, and rowed into the creek, calling the ship's company, rogues, roundhead rogues, and dogs, and with many execrations and railings, threatened to fire them on the morning."

"Governor Stone," says Bozman, "did not think it proper to pay any attention to this signal of war, as it appeared; but having arrived within the mouth of the creek, which forms the southern boundary of the peninsula on which the city of Annapolis now stands, proceeded to land his men on a peninsular which lies on the southern side of both the River Severn, and the before mentioned creek, nearly opposite to, and in an eastern direction from what is called the dock, or inner harbor of Annapolis; and on which point a small fortress called 'Fort Horn,' was afterwards built during the Revolutionary War. During the landing of the governor's men, the Golden Lyon repeated its fire. Whereupon, Governor Stone sent a messenger on board to inform the captain that he (Governor Stone) thought 'the captain of the ship had been satisfied.' To which Heamans replied, 'Satisfied with what? I never saw any power Captain Stone had, to do as he hath done, but the superscription of a letter; I must and will appear for these in a good cause.' "

Heamans continues: "The same night came further intelligence from the enemy in the harbor, that they were making fire-works against the ship. Whereupon, the governor (Fuller, whose prudence and valor in this business deserves very much honor), commanded a small ship of Captain Cuts, of New England, to lye in the mouth of the creek, to prevent the enemy's coming forth in the night, to work any mischief against the ship.

The next morning, by break of day, being the Lord's day, the 25th of March last, the Relator, himself, and company discovered Captain Stone, with his whole body drawn out and coming toward the water's side; marching with drums beating, colors flying—the colors were black and yellow, appointed by the Lord Proprietary.

"There was not the least token of any subjugation in Stone and his company, or acknowledgement of the Lord Protector of England, but God bless the Lord Proprietary; and their rayling against his ship's company was rogues, and roundheaded rogues, etc."

When Stone had reached the shore, the Golden Lyon and Captain Cut's vessel opened fire upon them, killing one man and compelling Stone to retire up the neck. Dr. Barber and Mrs. Stone, both confirmed this statement. Mrs. Stone added: "the gunner's mate of Heamans, since coming down from Anne Arundel to Patuxent, hath boasted that he shot the first man that was shot of our party."

In the meantime Captain Fuller with 170 men, embarked in boats; going "over the river some six miles from the enemy," he landed and made a circuit round the creek in order to get in the rear of Stone's forces. Upon Fuller's approach, a sentry of Stone's army fired a gun, which brought on an engagement, thus described by Leonard Strong.

"Captain Fuller still expecting that, then at last, possibly Governor Stone might give a reason of his coming, commanded his men, upon pain of death, not to shoot a gun, or give the first onset. Setting up the Standard of the Commonwealth of England, against which the enemy shot five or six guns, they killed one man in the front before a shot was made by the other." (That man was William Ayers, the standard bearer.) "Then the word was given, 'In the name of God fall on'; 'God is our strength'—that was the word of Providence. The Maryland word was, 'Hey! for St. Maries.'

"The charge was fierce and sharp for a time; but through the glorious presence of the Lord of Hosts the enemy could not endure, but gave back and were so effectually charged home, that they were all routed, turned their backs, threw down their arms, and begged for mercy. After the first shot a small company of the enemy from behind a great tree fallen, galled us, and wounded divers of our men, but were soon beaten off. Of the whole company of Marylanders there escaped only four or five, who ran away out of the army to carry the news to their confederates. Captain Stone, Colonel Peirce, Captain Gerrard, Captain Lewis, Captain Fendall, Captain Guyther Major Chandler and all the rest of the councillors, officers and soldiers of the Lord Baltimore, among whom were a great number of Papists, were taken; and so were all their vessels, arms, ammunition, provisions. About fifty men were slain and wounded. (Mr. Thomas Hatton, late secretary of the province, was one of the slain). We lost only two in the field, but two died since of their wounds. God did appear wonderful in the field and in the hearts of the people; all confessing him to be the worker of this victory and deliverance."

Heamans adds: "All the arms, bag and baggage was taken, together with the boats that brought them; wherein was the preparations and fuses for the firing of the ship 'Golden Lyon.' And amongst the rest of their losses, all their consecrated ware was taken, viz: their pictures, crucifixes, and rows of beads, with a great store of reliques and trash they trusted in."

Dr. Barber records: "After the skirmish, the governor, upon quarter given him and all his company in the field, yielded to be prisoners; but two or three days after, the victors condemned ten to death, and executed four, and had executed all had not the incessant petitioning and begging of some good women saved them, and the soldiers, others. The governor himself being condemned by them, and since begged by the soldiers; some being saved just as they were leading out to execution."

The four who were shot were William Eltonhead, of Governor Stones' council, Captain William Lewis, John Legatt and John Pedro. Governor Stone was wounded. His wife, Virlinda Stone, wrote a confirmatory letter of the above contest to Lord Baltimore, in which she called Heamans of the "Golden Lyon," "a very knave, for he hath abused my husband most grossly."

The deposition of Henry Coursey, one of Governor Stone's messengers, sheds this further light on the contest: "Governor Stone and most of his party, (after their surrender), were transported over the river to a fort at Anne Arundel, where they were all kept prisoners, and about three days after, the said Captain Fuller, William Burgess, Richard Ewen, Leonard Strong, William Durand, Roger Heamans, John Browne, John Cuts, Richard Smith, one Thomas, and one Besson, Samson Warren, Thomas Mears, and one Crouch, sat in a council of war, and there condemned the said Governor, Captain Stone, Colonel John Price, Mr. Job. Chandler, Mr. William Eltonhead, Mr. Robert Clark, Nicholas Geyther, Captain William Evans, Captain Wm. Lewis, Mr. John Legat and John Pedro to die, and not long afterward they sequestered all the estates of those of Lord Baltimore's council and other officers there."

Mr. Coursey further adds, in opposition to Strong's statement: "When Mr. Barber and said deponent went up to the Severn with Governor Stone's proclamation, the said Captain Fuller would not suffer them to read it. They found the people all in arms, and refusing to give any obedience thereto they were dismissed; but suddenly, before they could get away, were taken prisoners, whereby Governor Stone was prevented of any answer."

The Severn men being thus masters of the province, the dominion of the proprietary seemed now at an end. The pretensions of Virginia were renewed. Documents in opposition of the restoration poured in upon the Protector, but the committee on trade and plantations, to which Cromwell had referred Lord Baltimore's claim, reported in his favor in 1656. A strong party in Maryland were still loyal to him. Among these advocates was Josias Fendall, who received, in 1656, a commission from Lord Baltimore as Governor of Maryland, to be aided by the following councilors: Captain Wm. Stone, Mr. Thomas Gerald, Colonel John Price, Mr. Job. Chandler and Mr. Luke Barber. Before Fendall could organize his government, the Severn's Provincial Council, composed of Captain William Fuller, Edward Lloyd, Richard Wells, Captain Richard Ewen, Thomas Marsh, and Thomas Meeres, in August, 1656, caused Fendall's arrest on the charge "of dangerousness to the public peace." He denied the power of the court to try him. The verdict of the court was: "Whereas Josias Fendall, gent, hath been charged, contrary to his oath, with disturbance of public peace, for assuming a pretended power from Captain William Stone, he the said Josias Fendall, shall go to the place from whence he came a prisoner, and there abide in safe custody until the matters of government in the Province of Maryland be further settled by his Highness Lord Protector." Fendall, tired of imprisonment, took an oath that he would abide by the present government until there be a full determination of the matter."

Each party was now anxious to defend itself before the Protector. Dr. Luke Barber, who stood well with both Lord Baltimore and the Protector, though detained by the Puritans, wrote a letter to the Protector, but when released, carried it with him and delivered it in person. It, no doubt, had its effect in the subsequent fair treatment of Lord Baltimore's claim by the Protector. Bennett went to England to settle matters with Cromwell and labored hard by a recital of all the provocations, to defend the action of his associates in their abuse of the law of nations. He gave an extended review, in which he assigned many reasons why the Proprietary's claim should be abrogated, but the favorable report of the Board of Trade a had marked effect in strengthening the claim of Lord Baltimore. Bennett was a diplomatist of no mean order, and he saw the time had come for compromise. He, therefore, met Lord Baltimore in a conciliatory spirit and finally secured about all for which he had contended. Whilst this compromise was being accomplished in England, a commission was issued October 25th, 1656, to Josias Fendall, as Governor of Maryland, with instructions to carry out the proclamation guaranteeing religious liberty to all. He granted "his faithful friends, Fendall 2,000 acres, Luke Barber 1,000 acres, Thomas Trueman 1,000, George Thompson 1,000, John Sandford 1,000, and Henry Coursey 1,000 acres. He further ordered that especial care be taken of the widows of Thomas Hatton, William Eltonhead and Captain Lewis.

Philip Calvert, his brother, was sent over as Secretary of the Province and one of the Governor's Council. Mr. Barber was deputised acting-governor during the absence of Governor Fendall. At that time the settlers upon the Patuxent and Severn numbered about one-half of the population of the Province.

In 1657, Captain Fuller called an Assembly to meet at the home of Colonel Richard Preston, on the Patuxent. The lower house consisted of ten members, with Colonel Richard Ewen speaker. There were present, besides the speaker, Captain Robert Sley, Captain Joseph Weeks, Mr. Robert Taylor, Captain Thomas Besson, Mr. Peter Sharp, Captain Phil Morgan, Mr. Richard Brooks and Mr. James Johnson. They confirmed the "Act of Recognition." On the 30th of November, 1657, Lord Baltimore and Richard Bennett completed their compromise. In substance it was an agreement by Lord Baltimore to overlook the disturbance of the Severn; to grant patents of land to all the Puritan settlers who could claim them, by taking an altered oath of fidelity,—whilst the law granting freedom of religion should stand as proclaimed in 1649. Bennett and Matthews signed the agreement with Lord Baltimore. Governor Fendall, who had been called to England for further instructions, returned to the province in 1658. He called his council together at St. Mary's, and sent letters to Wm. Fuller, Richard Preston and others composing the government at Providence, desiring them to give him and his secretary, Captain Thomas Cornwallis, a meeting at Leonard's Creek, in Patuxent River, upon March 18th, following, in order to carry out the agreement, already signed by Lord Baltimore and Richard Bennett, a copy of which was sent them.

On account of the stormy season, the delegates of Anne Arundel did not arrive until the 20th. They were Captain Wm. Fuller, Mr. Richard Preston, Mr. Edward Lloyd, Mr. Thomas Meeres, Mr. Philip Thomas, and Mr. Samuel Withers. The day being well spent all business was postponed until Monday 22nd. Upon reading the article of agreement, Captain Fuller and his council objected to several articles, and urged that "indemnity on both sides" should be added; this was agreed to. The oath of fidelity was amended by the Anne Arundel men to waive it for all persons then resident in the porvince, but to stand in force to all others. The Anne Arundel men further urged and secured confirmation of all past proceedings done by them in their assemblies and courts since 1652; and, lastly, insisted that none of them should be disarmed, to be left to the mercy of the Indians. Having thus secured still greater compromises than their leader in England had asked, the final agreement, as amended, was then signed by all present.

After which the Anne Arundel commissioners proceeded to give up the records.

After the lapse of six years, his Lordship's dominion was again restored, yet the settlers were still independent. Governor Fendall and his secretary had, in 1657, at a meeting on the Severn, taken up the settlement of Anne Arundel and ordered, "That Wm. Burgess, Thomas Meeres, Robert Burle, Thomas Todde, Roger Grosse, Thomas Howell, Richard Wells, Richard Ewen, John Brewer, Anthony Salway and Richard Woolman, gentlemen, should be commissioners for said county, to appear by summons of the sheriff, at the house of Edward Lloyd, to take oath of Commissioners and Justices of the Peace, and that the 23rd instant should be the first court day.—(By order of the Governor and Secretary, Mr. Nathaniel Utie, at Anne Arundel, July 12th, 1657)."

The warrant was issued by Captain John Norwood, Sheriff. Wm. Burgess, Thomas Meeres and Richard Ewen refused to take the oath of Commissioners of Justice, alleging, as an excuse, that it was not lawful to swear.

Their pleas were refused and Captain Thomas Besson, Captain Howell and Thomas Taylor were appointed in their stead.

Then was taken up the establishment of militia force. It was resolved that the forces be divided into two regiments. One for the Potomac and Patuxent Rivers, commanded by the governor himself; the other, from the coves up to the Severn, and including the Isle of Kent, to be commanded by Nathaniel Utie, assisted by Captain John Cumber, Major Richard Ewen and Captain Thomas Howell, on South River, up to the head of it.

These orders were made whilst Maryland was still under the divided government. Fuller and his council were in control of the northern section, and Governor Barber, representing Fendall, ruled St. Maries.

A writ was issued in 1657, to Captain John Norwood, to choose burgesses for an assembly to be held at St. Leonard's, in the County of Calvert. The assembly met at St. Leonard's in 1658. It was there enacted, "That the oath of fidelity shall not be pressed upon the people of the province, but instead, a promise to submit to the anthority of the Right Honorable Cecilius Lord Baltimore, and his heirs within the province, and that none should be disarmed." This was agreed to by Captain Josias Fendall and Philip Calvert, principal secretary. It was also assented to by the Upper and Lower House of Burgesses.

At the session of 1659, the House of Delegates demanded that the governor and his council should no longer sit as an Upper House. Fendall at first resisted this, but finally yielded and took his seat in the Lower House. The Upper House was then declared dissolved. Finally, Fendall resigned his commission from Lord Proprietary, into the hands of the Assembly, and accepted a new one from that body in their own name, and by their own authority.

This bold desertion was soon met by the appointing of Philip Calvert governor, of the province. Fendall was arrested, tried but respited. Thirty years of prosperity and quiet submission now succeeded the stormy revolutions just recorded. Cromwell had passed away, and Charles II. had been proclaimed king.

When Philip Calvert assumed the government in 1660, the number of inhabitants was twelve thousand. During the succeeding decade it had increased to twenty thousand.

Immigrants, direct from England, began to settle upon the Severn and South Rivers, and in some cases, to buy up the claims of the earlier settlers. Governor Calvert was authorized to use extreme measures against the leaders of the late rebellion, but he contented himself in issuing a proclamation for the arrest of Captain Fuller for sedition. Even this was not carried out, and many remained in the province.

The impetus of immigration, after 1660, was distinctly shown upon the Rent Rolls of the county. Upon Broad Neck Hundred additional surveys reached up to the Magothy. Thomas Homewood,. William Hopkins, and Richard Young, were near the Magothy.

Matthew Howard resurveyed "Howard's Inheritance," adjoining William Hopkins. Thomas Underwood located upon Ferry Creek. Thomas Turner settled as a neighbor of Edward Lloyd and Richard Young. These surveys extended north to the Patapsco, and later to the Susquehanna, Bush and Deer Creek, of Harford County.

MIDDLE NECK HUNDRED AFTER 1660.

South-side Severn settlements were increased in 1662. Matthew Howard, who had come up from Lower Norfolk, Virginia, in 1650, with his neighbor and relative, Edward Lloyd, had died before 1659, but his five sons now came. They were Captain Cornelius Howard, of "Howard's Heirship and Chance"; Samuel Howard, of "Howard's Hope"; John Howard, of "Howard's Interest"; all adjoining near Round Bay. Philip and Matthew were on North Severn. In 1664, the three sons of Edward Dorsey, the immigrant of 1650—relatives of the Howards—took up and patented their father's survey of "Hockley-in-the-Hole." They were Colonel Edward Dorsey, Joshua and Hon. John Dorsey, prominent leaders in political movements, and representatives in legislative measures.

Adjoining these, Nicholas Wyatt extended his surveys of "Wayfield," which was bought by Richard Warfield. Henry Sewell surveyed "Hope" and "Increase." General John Hammond held a large estate east of the Howards. James Warner adjoined them in "Warner's Neck." John Mackubin surveyed "Timber Neck," on Broad Creek. Henry Pierpoint's "Diamond" adjoined Nicholas Wyatt, Richard Warfield and Thomas Browne. These surveys were nine miles west of Annapolis.

SOUTH RIVER HUNDRED AFTER 1660.

Patents were issued upon beautiful South River, in 1660, for "Burgess Right," for Captain Edward Burgess; "Burgh" and "Burgess Choice," for Colonel William Burgess; "Pole Cat Hill" and "Round About Hills," for John Gaither; "Edward's Neck," for John Edwards; "Chaney's Neck," for Richard Chaney; "Baldwin's Addition," for John Baldwin; "Watkins Hope," for John Watkins; "The Landing," for Robert Proctor; "Larkins' Hills," for John Larkin; "Poplar Ridge," for Colonel Nicholas Gassaway; "Herrington," for Samuel Chew; "Todd's Range," for Thomas Todd.

CHAPTER III.

THE QUAKERS.

In 1658, when the "Non-Conformists" had settled down to accept "the engagement" instead of the "oath of fidelity," and Edward Lloyd had been elevated to the governor's council, new rebels appeared in the province. "The Governor (Fendall) took into consideration the insolent behavior of some people called Quakers, who, at court, would stand covered and refuse to sign "the engagement.' He therefore ordered, 'That they must do so, or depart from the province.' "

The coming of these Quakers had a marked effect upon the stern Virginia settlers who had preceeded them. At first their refusal to abide by the orders to which they were opposed, created much discontent, but their gentle manners soon brought friends.

Elizabeth Harris, wife of a prosperous London merchant, was among the first to brave the wilds to speak of the love of Jesus.

After her return to England, a convert named Robert Clarkson, wrote as follows: "Dear Heart: I salute thee in tender love of the Father, which moved thee towards us, and do own thee to have been outward testimony to the inward truth, on me and others, even as many as the Lord, in tender love and mercy, did give an ear to hear. And likewise, John Baldwin and Henry Carline, Thomas Cole and William Cole, have made open confession of the truth, (the latter became a Quaker preacher in 1662, and was imprisoned at Jamestown for violating the statutes). William Fuller abides unmoved. (this was the Captain of the Severn). I know not but that Wm. Durand doth the like. He frequents our meetings but seldom. We have disposed of our books, which were sent, so that all parts are furnished, and every one that desires it may have the benefit by them. At Herrring Creek, Roads River, South River, all about Severn, the Broadneck and there about, the Severn Mountains, and Kent.

"With my dear love, I salute thy husband, and rest with thee and the gathered ones in the eternal word, which abideth forever."

Thus, in 1657, before the arrival of Cole and Thurston, the planting of Quakerism had commenced and Preston, Berry and the more sober-minded citizens, listened gladly to the tenets of the society. The Non-Conformists who came from Virginia, not able in their scattered residences, to support a pastor, willingly listened to preaching of the Gospel by the new sect, developed by the agitators of the Cromwellian era.

Feeling that his stay must be brief, the feet of Fox had scarcely touched the sands of the Pautuxent before he began to preach.

He spoke at the Severn, where the members were so great that no building was large enough to hold the congregation. The next day he was at Abraham Birkheads, six or seven miles distant, and there the Speaker of the Assembly was convinced. Then, mounting his horse, he rode to Dr. Peter Sharpe's at the Cliffs of Calvert. Here was a "heavenly meeting." Many of the upper sort of people present, and the wife of one of the governor's councilors, was convinced. From thence he rode eighteen miles to James Preston's, on the Patuxent, where an Indian chief and some of his tribe came to see the strange man, who was lifting up his voice like John the Baptist, in the wilderness. His labors were incessant; neither wintry sleet nor the burning sun detained. He forded the streams, slept in woods and barns, with as much serenity as in the comfortable houses of his friends, and was truly a wonder to many.

Before he returned to England, he went up to Annapolis, attended a meeting of the Provincial Assembly, and early in 1673, sailed for his native land.

Mr. Edmondson, the Quaker preacher, when in Virginia, made this report: "Richard Bennett stopped to hear me preach. He was then known as Major General Bennett; he said he was a man of great estate, and as many of our friends were poor men, he desired to contribute with them. He asked me to his house. He was a solid, wise man, receiving the truth and died in the same, leaving two Friends his executors."

Another view of the early church in Anne Arundel, is here given. Rev. John Yoe, of the Church of England, appeared in Maryland, in 1675. He was disturbed by the movements of the Quakers, Baptists, and Roman Catholics, and other Non-Conformists. From the Patuxent, in 1676, he wrote to the Archbishop of Canterbury, the following letter:

"Most Reverend Father,—Be pleased to pardon this presumption of mine, in presenting to your serious notice these rude lines, to acquaint your grace with ye deplorable estate and condition of the Province of Maryland, for want of an established ministry.

"Here are, in this province, ten to twelve thousand souls, and but three Protestant ministers to us, yet are conformable to ye doctrine and discipline of ye Church of England. Society here is in great necessity of able and learned men, to confront the gainsayers, especially having so many professed enemies. Yet one thing cannot be obtained here, viz: consecration of churches and churchyards to ye end ye Christians might be decently buried together. Whereas, now, they bury in the several plantations where they lived."

This letter was referred to the Bishop of London, who returned it to Lord Baltimore, who replied: "That the act of 1649, confirmed in 1676, tolerated and protected every sect." And, he continued, "Four ministers of the Church of England are in possession of plantations which offered them a decent substance." The four referred to were probably Rev. Mr. Yeo, Coode, the political agitator, Matthew Hill, and a minister sent by Charles the Second.

Six clergymen came during Governor Nicholson's administration. Rev. Ethan Allen names, Rev. Duell Pead, Mr. Crawford, Mr. Moore, Mr. Lillingstone and Mr. Vanderbush.

Rev. Thomas Bray, who in 1696, had been appointed Commissary for the clergy, in company with Sir Thomas Lawrence, Secretary of Maryland, waited on Anne, Princess of Denmark, to request her acceptance of the respect shown her by naming the capital of Maryland, Annapolis.

Rev. Mr. Bray, having received a donation for libraries from the Princess, presented books to the amount of £400 to the capital. On their covers is stamped, "De Bibliothica Annapolitana." Arriving in March, 1700, Rev. Mr. Bray preached before the Assembly at Annapolis, when the Church of England was re-established.

(NEIL.)

The Quakers, as seen by the above quotations, had meeting houses in every section of Anne Arundel. At their meeting-house at West River, there is still a well-preserved graveyard. To their meetings came the Galloways, Murrays, Richardsons, Chestons, Jones, Chews, Hookers, Lawrences, Birkheads, and many others of the influential families, who later joined the Episcopal Church. It was in their meeting houses that George Fox was gladly received, when during that remarkable visit, he won over the staunch Puritans unto zealous Quakers. Governor Fendall, who had ordered them to be banished, had "to depart the province" himself, but the gentle Quakers won friends, and, like the Non-Conformists, did pretty much as they pleased, yet still held their faith and kept their hats on. In fact, the province was the resort for all kinds of rebels.

Governor Fendall was banished to Virginia, but returned and defended himself with such ability, he was acquitted. As will be seen later, he left descendants, who became leaders in the families of Maryland.

In 1662, Philip Calvert was superseded by Hon. Charles Calvert, son of the Lord Proprietary, who continued as governor until the death of his father in 1675, by which he became proprietor.

In 1680 he assumed the government in person for four years. During that time, Ex-Governor Fendall and Captain John Coode attempted to excite another rebellion. This was under the pretense of religion, but failing in it, they were arrested, tried and convicted, but escaped.

This attempt was but the precursor of the coming revolution in England, which later, was severely felt in Maryland.

From the victory of the Severn, in 1655, to the year 1683, when Annapolis was made a port of entry, there in not a single event recorded as a history of Anne Arundel. To fill this gap, I will now give the outlines of the county, some of its officers, and the biography of many who made history in that quarter of the century.

CHAPTER IV.

BOUNDARIES OF THE COUNTIES.

The original and indefinite act of 1650, setting off Anne Arundel County, "embraced all that part of the province, on the west side of the Chesapeake Bay, over against the Isle of Kent, called Providence by the people thereof."

The land grants show that the people of Providence extended from Herring Creek on the south, to the Patapsco River on the north, with the Severn as a central meeting place.

During 1650, an order was passed erecting Charles County out of the territory on the south side of the Patuxent. This order was a county grant to Hon. Robert Brooke, a special friend of Lord Baltimore, who with his family of forty persons, including his servants, had seated himself about twenty miles north of the mouth of the Patuxent. When Robert Brooke later became a leader in the independent movement of the Virginia settlers, he was deprived of his command by changing the name of Charles County to Calvert County, which had its northern limit at "a creek on the west side of the Chesapeake Bay, called Herring Bay."

After the Commissioners of Parliament had, in the ensuing October, 1654, displaced Governor Stone, an ordinance was passed declaring that "all the lands extending from Marshe's Creek down the bay, including all the lands on the south side of the bay and cliffs, with the north and south sides of the Patuxent River, shall constitute a county, to be called, as it is, "Patuxent County."

Upon the restoration of the proprietary grovernment, in 1658, all of the previous acts were annulled, and the boundaries and the names made by the Council of July 3rd, 1654, were restored. The question so rested until 1674, when the proprietary declared by proclamation, "That the north side of the Patuxent River, beginning at the north side of Lyon's Creek, shall be added to Anne Arundel County."

One hundred years later, 1777, in order to determine the eligibility of Mr. Mackall, the House of Delegates declared, "that the creek, at present called Fishing Creek, was the reputed and long received boundary between the two counties."

Nearly a half century later, 1832, an act was passed, appointing commissioners to ascertain and establish the divisional lines.

In 1823, the commissioners reported a compromise line beginning at the mouth of Muddy, or Red Lion's Creek. Anne Arundel County did not claim that its limits extended to Herring Creek, the boundary assigned by the order of 1652, but that Marsh's Creek, being the conceded boundary, the dispute was as to the true location of that creek. Calvert County claimed that Marsh's Creek, named for Thomas Marsh, the first Anne Arundel commissioner, was a creek falling into Herring Creek, near its mouth, and extending westwardly with that creek to one of the heads of Lyon's Creek, and thence with Lyon's Creek to the Patuxent. Anne Arundel County claimed that Marsh's Creek was what is now known as Fishing Creek. By the act of 1824, Fishing Creek was made the division line on the bay and the south, or middle creek, on the Patuxent. "In duration and the difficulty of arriving at a satisfactory result, the contest between Anne Arundel and Calvert was not unlike that between Lord Baltimore and the Penns.

"But the identity of Marsh's Creek, (the admitted boundary), with Fishing Creek, is clearly proved by the records in the land office. The history of the title to "Majors Choice," taken up by the Honorable Thomas Marsh, near the Cliffs of Calvert, will readily develop all the evidence upon this knotty question."—(DAVIS.)

The creation of Charles County in 1658, had no northern limit except "as far as the settlements extended."

In 1695, Prince George County was formed out of its northern territory, extending south as far as Mattawoman Creek, and a straight line drawn thence to the head of the Swanson's Creek, and with that creek to the Patuxent. The present divisional line of Charles and Prince George slightly varies to the west by an artificial line running from the Mattawoman to a given point on the Potomac, nearly opposite Mount Vernon.—(Act of 1748, Chapter 14.)

On the north and east, Prince George has always been separated from Anne Arundel and Charles by the Patuxent River.

Extending from the Patuxent to the Potomac, Prince George received its definite western limits, in 1748, by the creation of Frederick County, from which it was separated by a straight line, beginning at the lower side of the mouth of Rock Creek, and running thence north with Hyatt's plantation to the Patuxent River, at Crow's mill, west of Laurel.

This line, in 1776, upon the erection of Montgomery County out of the lower portion of Frederick, became the divisional line between Prince George and Montgomery Counties. The eastern boundary line of Frederick County, when erected, in 1748, touched the western boundaries of Prince George, Anne Arundel and Baltimore Counties.

Baltimore County was partly formed out of the northern portion of Anne Arundel, in 1659. In the proclamation of 1674, the southern bounds of Baltimore County shall be "the south side of Patapsco River, and from the highest plantations on that side of the river, due south two miles in the woods." In 1698, an act was passed defining the line "beginning at three marked trees, standing about a mile and a quarter to the southward of Bodkin Creek, on the west side of Chesapeake Bay, and near a marsh and a pond: thence west until they cross the mountains of the mouth of the Magothy River, to Richard Beard's mill: thence continuing westward with said road to William Hawkin's path, to two marked trees: thence along said road to two marked trees: thence leaving said road by a line drawn west to William Slade's path to two marked trees: thence continuing west between the draughts of the Magothy and Patapsco Rivers, until they come to a mountain of white stone rock: still continuing west to a road going to Patapsco, to Peter Bond's, to two marked trees: thence continuing west to the main road, to Patapsco Ferry, to two marked pines standing near the Ready Branch, written at large on the north side of said trees, Baltimore County; and on the south side Anne Arundel County. Then with a line drawn west northwest to Elkridge road, to two marked trees; thence continuing the same course of west northwest to Patuxent River, and so on up the said river to the extent thereof, for the bounds of Baltimore County.—

In 1725, an act was passed, limiting the southern border of Baltimore County to the Patapsco River, from its mouth to its head, but its western limits were still vague.

The head of the Patapsco was the western limit, as well as that of Anne Arundel, by the act of 1725, until the formation of Frederick County, in 1748, which enacted, "that its lines after reaching the river, should run with it to the lines of Baltimore County, and with that county to the extent of the province."

In 1750, a definite line was established between Frederick and Baltimore Counties: "Beginning at a spring called Parr's Spring, and running thence N. 35 E., to a bounded white oak, standing on the west side of a wagon road, called John Digges' road, about a mile above the place called Burnt House Woods: and running thence up said road to a bounded white oak, standing on the east side thereof, at the head of a draught of Sam's Creek: thence N. 55 E. to a Spanish oak, standing on a ridge near William Robert's, and opposite to the head of a branch called the Beaver Dam: thence N. 20 E. to the temporary line between the Provinces of Maryland and Pennsylvania, being near the head of a draught called Conawajo, at a rocky hill called Rattle Snake Hill." The western limit of Anne Andurel County was also the eastern limit of Frederick and Montgomery line, which was a straight line from the mouth of the Monocacy to Parr's Spring, where the Frederick and Baltimore County lines met. A branch from that spring to the Patapsco, limited Anne Arundel on the west. By a more recent act, 1836, creating Carroll County out of the portions of Frederick and Baltimore Counties, the western limits of Baltimore are near Woodstock, B. & O. R. R.

In 1838, Howard District, extending on the east from Laurel to Elk Ridge Landing, via the B. & O. R. R., was set off from Anne Arundel, and in 1851, became a county, though its actual settlement was begun before 1700.

Western Maryland was, from 1658 to 1776, successively included in the geographical limits of Charles, Prince George and Frederick Counties, erected in 1658, 1695 and 1748 respectfully. On July 26th, 1776, the Provincial Convention of Maryland divided Frederick County into three districts, upper, middle and lower.

The first embraced Washington, Alleghany and Garrett: second took Frederick and a part of Carroll: third embraced Montgomery County. Each by ordinance was made a separate county on Sept. 6th, 1776.

OFFICERS OF ANNE ARUNDEL COUNTY, FROM ITS ORGANIZATION UNTIL IT CHANGED TO A ROYAL PROVINCE.

1650.

JUSTICES.	DELEGATES	COMMANDER.
James Homewood,	Jas. Cox,	Edward Lloyd.
Thomas Meeres,	George Puddington.	
Thomas Marsh,		
George Puddington,		
Matthew Hawkins,		
James Merryman,		
Henry Catlin.		

1651.   No delegation sent.

1652.

PARLIAMENTARY COMMISSIONERS.

Robert Brooke,
Col. Francis Yardly,
Mr. Job Chandler,
Capt. Edmund Winder, } Administered the government.
Col. Richard Preston,
Lieut. Richard Banks,

OFFICERS OF ANNE ARUNDEL COUNTY.

1653.

JUSTICES.	DELEGATES.	COUNCILLORS.
Under { Richard Bennett, and Wm. Clayborne.	Governor Stone re-appointed Thomas Hatton, Secretary.	Robert Brooke, Capt. John Price, Job. Chandler, Col. Francis Yardly, Col. Richard Preston.

1654.

JUSTICES.	DELEGATE.	
Capt. Wm. Fuller, Rich. Preston, Wm. Durand, Edward Lloyd.	} Quorum.	Wm. Durand, Secty. of State.

Richard Preston,
Speaker, Keeper of Records.

Capt. John Smith,
Leonard Strong,
John Lawson, } Justices.
John Hatch,
Rich. Wells,
Richard Ewen,

OFFICERS OF ANNE ARUNDEL COUNTY.

1655.

Capt. Wm. Fuller's Council, as in 1654.

Council of War, after the Battle of the Severn, 1655.

JUSTICES.	DELEGATES.	COUNCILLORS.
Capt. William Fuller,	Leonard Strong,	Mr. Besson,
Wm. Burgess,	Wm. Durand,	Samson Warren,
Richard Ewen,	Roger Heamans,	Wm. Crouch.

1656.

Upon Governor Josias Fendall assuming the government, the following had him arrested:

Capt. Wm. Fuller,	Richard Wells,	Thomas Marsh,
Edward Lloyd,	Col. Rich. Ewen,	Thomas Meeres.

1657.

Governor Fendall.   Philip Calvert, Secty.

Capt. Fuller's Assembly of ten members, Richard Ewen, Speaker.

JUSTICES.	DELEGATES.	COUNCILLORS.
Wm. Burgess,	Capt. Robt. Sley,	Edward Lloyd,
Robt. Burle,	Capt. Jas. Weeks,	Capt. Wm. Fuller.
Roger Grosse,	Mr. Robt. Taylor,	
Rich. Wells.	Capt. Thos. Besson,	
John Brewer,	Mr. Peter Sharp,	
Thos. Meeres,	Capt. Phil. Morgan,	
Thos. Todde,	Mr. Richard Brooks,	
Thos. Howell,	Mr. Jas. Johnson.	
Richard Ewen,		
Anthony Salway,		
Rich. Woolman.		

1658.

Compromise of Lord Baltimore and Bennett,

Commissioners:
Gov. Fendall,
Secty. Cornwallis,
Capt. Wm. Fuller,
Rich. Preston,   } Agreed to restore records to Fendall; to issue grants for
Edward Lloyd,   lands; to guarantee indemnity for passed acts.
Thomas Meeres,
Philip Thomas,
Saml. Withers.

1660.

JUSTICES.	DELEGATES.	COUNCILLORS.
Rich. Wells,	John Brewer	Edward Lloyd.
Saml. Withers,	and	
Thos. Todd,	Saml. Chew.	
John Brewer,		
Robert Burle,		
Roger Grosse,		
Thomas Besson,		
Edmund Townhill.		
Anthony Galway,		
Francis Holland.		

JUSTICES.

Saml. Chew., Sheriff,
Capt. Wm. Burgess,
Richard Ewen,
George Puddington,
Ralph Williams,
Thos. Taylor,
Capt. John Norwood.

JUSTICES.

Capt. Wm. Burgess appoint-
Sheriff, but called to field,
succeeded by Rich. Ewen,
1664-5.

Rich. Ewen, Sheriff.

1666.
Thos. Stockett, Sheriff.

Thos. Marsh,
John Ewen,
Robert Francklyn,
John Welsh,
Saml. Chew.
George Puddington.
Robert Burle.

Thos. Stockett, Sheriff.

Wm. Burgess, ⎫
Saml. Lane,   ⎪
Robert Brooke, ⎬ Quorum.
John Homewood, ⎪
Richard Ewen, ⎭
Robt. Francklyn,
Thos. Hedge,
Richard Burton, Clerk.

Col. Wm. Burgess,   ⎫
Col. Saml. Lane,   ⎪
Major John Welsh,   ⎬ Quorum.
Robert Francklyn,   ⎪
Capt. Richard Hill, ⎭
John Homewood,
Henry Stockett,
Thos. Francis,
Wm. Jones,
Henry Lewis.

1662.
DELEGATES.
Robert Burle.

1663-1664.
DELEGATES.
Thos. Meeres,
Richard Beard,
John Homeswood,
George Puddington.

1665.
Robt. Burle,
Capt. Thos. Besson,
Richard Beard.
Thos. Taylor,
Edward Selby.

1667.
The Seal of A. A. Co. was
taken from Thos. Tay-
lor in 1667, and given
to Saml. Chew.

1668-1669.
Wm. Burgess,
Saml. Withers,

1671.
Wm. Burgess,
Thos. Taylor,
Cornelius Howard,
Robert Francklyn.

1674.

1676.
Dedimus protestatimus to Col.
Wm. Burgess and Saml. Lane.

COUNCILLORS.
Edward Lloyd.

COUNCILLORS.
Edward Lloyd.

Edward Lloyd.

Edward Lloyd.

Saml. Chew.

Saml. Chew.

Saml. Chew.

Saml. Chew.

1678-1679.

John Welsh, Sheriff,

Col. Wm. Burgess,
Jas. Rigby,

Col. Thos. Tailler,
Col. Wm. Burgess,
Capt. John Welsh,
Capt. Rich. Hill,
Thos. Francis,
} John Homewood,
Wm. Richardson.
Quorum.

1680-1682.

Capt. Nich. Gassaway,
Edward Burgess,
Cornelius Howard,
John Sollers.

Henry Ridgely.
Edward Dorsey,
Richard Beard, Jr.

Col. Wm. Burgess.

1683.

Henry Hanslap, Sheriff,
Capt, Rich. Hill, of Severn,
Edward Burgess, of Londontown,
Thomas Knighton, of Herring Creek.

Col. Wm. Burgess.

1685.

Capt. Rich. Hill,
Major Nich. Gassaway
Capt. Edward Burgess,
Major Edward Dorsey,
} Quorum.

Col. Wm. Burgess.

1687.

JUSTICES.

Mr. Henry Ridgely,
Mr. Rich. Beard,
John Sollers,
Thos. Tench,
Thos. Knighton,
John Hammond,
Nich. Greenberry,
James Ellis.

1689.

Major Nich. Gassaway,
Major Edward Dorsey,
Capt. Nich. Greenberry,
Mr. John Hammond
Mr. Thos. Tench,
} Quorum.

Mr. Edward Burgess,
Mr. Henry Ridgley,
Mr. Henry Constable,
Rich. Beard,
Thos. Knighton,
Mr. James Ellis,
Mr. John Bennett.

Mr. Thos. Tench,
Mr. John Bennett,
} Coroners.
Mr. Henry Hanslap, Sheriff,
Mr. Henry Bonner, Clerk.

1692.

Capt. John Hammond,
Mr. Wm. Holland,
} Quorum.

Mr. Saml. Young,
Major Henry Ridgely,
Henry Constable,
Capt. Nich. Gassaway,
Mr. John Worthington,
Mr. Abel Browne,
Mr. Edward Batson, Surveyor.

Mr. John Hammond,
Mr. Henry Ridgely,
Mr. James Saunders,
Mr. John Dorsey.

Col. Nich. Greenberry.
Thos. Tench.

ORDINARIES.

In 1675, there were only three authorized ordinaries for the accommodation of the public. One was at the Court House; one at Richard Hills; and one at the Red Lyon.

The expenses for meat, drink and lodging, during the Assembly of Burgesses, to be paid to the in holder of St. Maries, in 1666, were 4,586 pounds of tobacco; also necessary expenses to each member for hands and boat hire, until they arrive at their homes. In 1675, the taxable rate of 816, taxable at 165 pounds of tobacco, per poll, was 134,640 pounds.

BIOGRAPHIES OF THE FOUNDERS OF ANNE ARUNDEL CO.
RICHARD BENNETT.

Richard Bennett was the Moses from the Nansemond to the Severn. He may be termed a settler of two States.

His uncle, Edward Bennett was a wealthy London merchant, once Deputy-Governor of the English Merchants of Holland.

He was largely interested in the Virginia trade, and organized the Virginia Company, already noted. As his representative in Virginia, Richard Bennett, immediately rose to importance. In 1629 and 1631, he was in the House of Burgesses. In 1642-1649 he was a Commissioner and member of the Council.

In the latter year he secured, from the Governor of Maryland, a grant of "Towne Neck," on the Severn, for fifteen of his followers, who wished to be close together. Our land records show that he soon after disposed of this grant to his wife's kinsman, Colonel Nathaniel Utie, secretary to the governor. As Governor of Virginia, still later, his administration appears to have been acceptable, even to the loyalists.

He remained a member of the Virginia Council until his death.

(HENING.)

In 1666, he was made Major-General of Militia. He was a friend to the Quakers, and made provision for many needy families. His will was probated in 1675. The bulk of his estate descended to his grandson, Richard Bennett, 3rd, son of Richard Bennett, 2nd, by Henrietta Marie Neale, daughter of Captain James Neale, attorney for Lord Baltimore, at Amsterdam, and former representative in Spain. Captain Neale came to America in 1666, and represented Charles County in the House of Burgesses. His wife, Anna Gill, was the daughter of Benjamin Gill. Their daughter Henrietta Marie, was named for her godmother, the queen. By her marriage to Richard Bennett, Jr., they had two children, Richard Bennett and Susanna (Bennett) Lowe, ancestress of Governor Lowe and Charles Carroll, of Carrollton.

Richard Bennett, Jr., lived for a time upon the Severn. He was in the Assembly of 1666, and was a Commissioner of Kent County, in which he had an immense estate. In his early manhood he was drowned. His only son, Richard, succeeded to an estate which made him "the richest man of his majesty's dominion." He died a bachelor, leaving his property to his sister, Susannah Lowe, and to his step-father, Colonel Philemon Lloyd. His tombstone still stands at "Bennetts Point."

Ann Bennett, of Major-General Bennett, became Mrs. Theodorick Bland, of "Westover," Virginia. She died at Wharton's Creek, Maryland, as the wife of Colonel St. Legar Codd, of Virginia and of Maryland.

General Bennett and Commander Edward Lloyd were the staunch leaders in opposition to a Catholic proprietary, yet their sons both yielded to the eloquence of the good Catholic lady, Henrietta Marie Neale; whilst a descendant of Commander Robert Brooke, another rebelious subject, took for his wife, Dorothy Neale, sister of Henrietta Marie Neale. She was the progenitress of Chief Justice Roger Brooke Taney. These two Catholic mothers not only united discordant religions, but the former gave to Maryland the following distinguished sons: Governor Edward Lloyd, of 1709, and Hon. Edward Lloyd, his son; Revolutionary Edward Lloyd, and his son, Governor Edward Lloyd, of 1809, United States Senator and grandfather of Governor Henry Lloyd.

She was the grandmother of Dorothy Blake, mother of Charles Carroll, the "Barrister"; grandmother of Hon. Matthew Tilghman and of Richard Tilghman, of "The Hermitage."

She was the grandmother of Governor William Paca's wife; of Edward Dorsey's wife, and of Thomas Beale Bordley's wife. As Maid of Honor to Queen Henrietta Marie, she received a ring, which is now in possession of Mrs. Clara Tilghman Goldsborough Earle, granddaughter of Colonel Tench Tilghman, great-grandson of Anna Gill.

The descendants of this prolific mother are "Legion." They have added many brilliant pages to the history of Maryland.

THOMAS MARSH.

This first Commissioner of Anne Arundel, coming up from Virginia with William Durand, he surveyed lands, first upon Herring Creek, but later became a merchant of the Severn.

He was an active member in every movement of the early settlers. Having become prominent in the Severn contest, the proprietary government, in 1658, refused to recognize his right to lands. His tract known as "Majors Choice," became historic as a long disputed line dividing the Counties of Anne Arundel and Calvert. He assigned a hundred acres upon the Chesapeake to Edward Dorsey and Thomas Manning. The latter in his petition for a title to the land, recorded that it was taken up by Thomas Marsh, who, on account of his rebellion, was unable to secure title to the same.

Thomas Marsh assigned, also, to William Ayres, a tract upon Herring Creek.

Removing to Kent Island he was made captain of Militia. In his will of 1679, he named his wife Jane, daughter of John Clements; his son Thomas, and daughters Sarah and Mary.

Ralph Williams, of Bristol, England, residing, in 1672, upon "Towne Neck," made Thomas Marsh, senior, his residuary legatee. He was, also, that same year, a witness to the will of Robert Burle, an associate justice and legislator from the Severn.

The Foremans, of "Clover Fields" and "Rose Hill," and other representative families of Eastern Maryland, descend from this first Commissioner.

HAWKINS.

Closely allied to Bennett, Lloyd, Meeres, and others of the Nansemond settlers, several families of Hawkins were early settlers in the province. John Hawkins, through his attorney, Nicholas Wyatt, assigned unto Giles Blake one hundred acres, due him for transporting himself into the province. Henry Hawkins named "his brother Philemon Lloyd," and left his property to Edward Lloyd, Susanna Bennett and Maria Bennett.

Ralph Hawkins was on the Magothy River in 1657. He had sons, Ralph and William, to whom he left "goods out of England." His wife was Margaret Hawkins. William Hawkins wife, Elizabeth, received from Thomas Meeres "a riding horse."

Thomas Hawkins, of Poplar Island, named "Margaret Hall, daughter of Edward." His wife was Elizabeth.

Matthew Hawkins, of the Severn, was one of Edward Lloyd's first commissioners, in 1650. From his daughter Elizabeth, came State Senator George Hawkins Williams, and Mr. Elihu Riley, the historian of Annapolis.

From John Hawkins, who married Elizabeth, daughter of Nicholas Dorsey, descended Mr. James McEvoy, Dr. Frank Martin, Augustus W. Martin, Mrs. Dr. Mills, and Miss Fannie Martin, descendants of Dr. Samuel B. Martin, the "old defender," and his wife Ruth Dorsey Hawkins.

The Hawkins, of Queenstown, sent down a judge of the provincial court in 1700, and a surveyor-general of customs. Through the Fosters and Lowes, they were connected with Lord Charles Baltimore, the Lloyds, De Courseys, Marshes, Tilghmans and Chambers.

"Very interesting memorial remains," says Davis, "are now in possession of the vestry of Centreville, showing a massive piece of silver plate in excellent preservation."

HENRY HAWKINS.

An interesting case in Chancery gives us a view of some of our early fathers. The case is an inquiry to ascertain the owner of "Nathaniel Point," in Talbot County, on Wye River. Colonel Edward Lloyd called a commission of Mr. William Coursey to take depositions, and Captain John Davis gave this record:

"Mr. John Scott told me that a certain bachelor's tree, up on the road passing through 'Nathaniel Point' got its name from the sale of said point by Mr. Nathaniel Cleeve to Mr. Henry Hawkins for a case of spirits. Upon the delivery of the goods, Mr. Henry Hawkins, Mr. Nathaniel Cleeve, Wm. Jones, Henry Catlin and four others, all bachelors, under that tree consumed the whole case of spirits and at the conclusion of the feast, Mr. Cleeve before all, publicly expressed his entire satisfaction with the bargain.

Mr. Henry Hawkins held the tract, and delivered it over to his kinsman, Colonel Philemon Lloyd, whose son was the party to the Inquisition. This transfer was confirmed by three of the bachelor party.

HENRY CATLIN.

This Commissioner and neighbor of Edward Lloyd, was a Justice and Burgess of Virginia. He was also an active supporter of the Independent Church in Virginia. He came up in 1649, bringing "his wife Jane and his son," (stepson), presumably Richard Horner. He did not remain long, but, in 1661, assigned his estate to Matthew Howard, who resurveyed it as "Howards Inheritance."

JAMES MERRYMAN.

A neighbor of Henry Catlin, and a member of Lloyd's first commissioners, James Merryman, in 1662, assigned his certificate for five hundred acres to John Browne, of New England. He left no will, or other records. The Merrymans, of Hayfield, may thus descend.

John Browne held this grant and assigned it to James Rigbie, who sold to Colonel Nicholas Greenberry.

THOMAS MEERES.

Thomas Meeres was an important member of the Virginia Assembly before coming up to be one of Lloyd's council. He was high in the church. He was an active participant in the Severn contest and was upon the committee which arrested Governor Fendall. He was a Justice of Anne Arundel, in 1657, and a delegate to restore the records in 1658.

His will of 1674, shows him a man of means. His daughter, Sarah Homewood, son John, and wife Elizabeth shared each one-third of his estate. To the latter was given his "jewels, plate, bills, and bonds."

John married Sarah, daughter of Philip Thomas. One daughter, Sarah, was their only heir. She became Mrs. John Talbott. They sold "Pendenny" to Captain John Worthington. This tract was Captain Worthington's homestead, just opposite the Naval Academy. It was also the homestead of Commander Edward Lloyd, who assigned it to Thomas Meeres, who made the Quaker Society the final court of resort, in case of any dispute of his will.

The will of John Meeres left "lands bequeathed by my father, Thomas Meeres, adjoining brother-in-law John Homewood," to daughter Sarah Talbott.

He left legacies to the children of his sister-in-law, Elizabeth Coale, and referred to his brother-in-law, Samuel Thomas.

HOMEWOOD.

James, John and Thomas Homewood were all upon the Magothy. James was Commissioner under Edward Lloyd, in 1650.

John Homewood was a later Commissioner of Anne Arundel. His wife, Sarah Homewood, was a daughter of Thomas Meeres. She again became the wife of John Bennett, a Commissioner to lay out Annapolis in 1694. She was the legatee of Henry Howard, in 1683, who gave her "a seal ring with a coat of arms, and a hooked ring with the initials F. C."

John Homewood and Henry Howard were intimate friends.

Both were legatees of John Pawson, of the city of York, England, who, in 1677, also named his friend, Dr. Stockett, in his list of legatees. The Worthingtons and Homewoods were united in marriage still later.

CAPTAIN GEORGE PUDDINGTON.

Honored as one of the first Commissioners under Edward Lloyd and unanimously named as one of the first legislators of 1650, Captain George Puddington took at once a foremost place in the new county.

Of his wife, the following record from the Virginia Magazine of History, is of interest: "Colonel Obedience Robins, of "Cherrystone," born 1601, was a member, in 1632, of the first County Court of Accomac, and was a brother of Edward, merchant of Accomac. His name and associations seem to indicate that he was of Puritan affinities. His wife was the widow of Edward Waters, of Bermuda. When a girl of sixteen, Grace O'Neil arrived at the Bermudas in the ship "Diana." Becoming Mrs Waters, they removed to Elizabeth City, now Hampton, where their first son, William, was born. He became an active citizen of Northampton. Upon the death of Edward Waters, the widow became the wife of Colonel Obedience Robins. Jane, the wife of George Puddington, a member of the Maryland Assembly, from Anne Arundel County in 1650, was a sister-in-law of Colonel Obedience Robins."

Captain Puddington took up "Puddington Harbor," "Puddington Gift," and "West Puddington."

In 1667, he was an associate justice of Anne Arundel. He left no son. His will was probated by Colonel William Burgess, in 1674.

Captain Edward Burgess, named for his grandfather, Colonel Edward Robins, was Captain Puddington's residuary legatee. The sons-in-law of Captain Puddington were Ex-Sheriff Robert Francklyn; Hon. Richard Beard, the surveyor; and grandson Neal Clarke.

All named in his will as follows: "son-in-law Robert Francklyn; to each of my son Richard Beard's children; to each of my grandson Neal Clark's children; to George Burgess, William Burgess and Susanna, children of Captain William Burgess, legacies. My loving wife Jane, and Edward Burgess the rest of my estate."

PHILIP THOMAS.

With his wife Sarah Harrison and three children, Philip, Sarah and Elizabeth, Philip Thomas came from Bristol, England, in 1651. He was granted five hundred acres, "Beckley," on the west of the Chesapeake.

To this he added "Thomas Towne," "The Plains" and "Philip's Addition." On this he erected his homestead, "Lebanon," a view of which is still preserved. On his lands stands Thomas Point Lighthouse.

His neighbor was Captain Wm. Fuller, the provincial leader. With him, Edward Lloyd, Richard Preston, Samuel Withers went to St. Leonards, and delivered up the captured records. With this act he gave up political adventures and joined the Society of Friends, under George Fox. The Quaker Society was made the final court to settle his estate.

This estate was claimed by his son, Samuel Thomas, through a verbal will which Edward Talbott, his brother-in-law resisted. The question was finally decided by the Society in favor of all the heirs.

Sarah Thomas, the English born daughter, married John Meeres; Elizabeth became the third wife of William Coale, and still later the wife of Edward Talbott; Martha became Mrs. Richard Arnold.

Samuel Thomas—Mary Hutchins, of Calvert, whose mother was Elizabeth Burrage. Their daughter Sarah—Joseph Richardson; Elizabeth—Richard Snowden, son of Richard and Mary (Linthicum) Snowden; John Thomas—Elizabeth, daughter of Richard and Elizabeth (Coale) Snowden; Samuel Thomas—Mary, daughter of Richard and Elizabeth (Coale) Snowden; Ann Thomas—Edward Fell, of England.

Philip Thomas, eldest son of Samuel and Mary Thomas—first Francis Holland, leaving a son William Thomas; second, Ann, daughter of Samuel Chew and Mary his wife. Their issue were Samuel, Philip, Mary, Elizabeth—Samuel Snowden, Richard—Deborah Hughes; John Thomas resided at West River, wrote poetry and was President of the Maryland Senate. He married Sarah, third daughter of Dr. Wm. Murray—Anne: Philip, John and Sarah. Samuel, eldest son of Philip and Ann Chew Thomas, removed to Perry Point in the Susquehannah, and married his cousin Mary, daughter of Samuel and Mary Snowden Thomas; issue, Ann, Philip, Saml. Richard Snowden, John Chew and Evan William. Samuel was a minister of Friends, and married Anna, daughter of Dr. Chas. Alexander Warfield: Evan William—Martha Gray: John Chew, 4th, son of Samuel, and Mary Thomas resided at Fairland, Anne Arundel: was member of Congress, in 1799, and took part in the election of President, in which three days and thirty-five ballots were required to select Thomas Jefferson.   He married Mary, daughter of Richard and Eliza (Rutland) Snowden, of Fairland.

Having married an heiress and becoming a large slave holder, he lost his membership in the Quaker church, which he only regained by manumitting one hundred slaves.   He sold his homestead for $50,000.

The Thomas family, of Maryland, has already been fully traced in the Thomas Book.   Some descendants will be found more fully in this work, in the biographical sketches of three governors of Maryland representing different branches of Philip Thomas' descendants.

FAMILIES CONNECTED WITH GOVERNOR FENDALL.

Governor Fendall's official life has already been noted.   He closed his life as a Marylander and left a distinguished line.   His son Colonel John Fendall, of "Clifton Hall," born 1672, married Elizabeth Hanson, widow of William Marshall.

Benjamin Fendall, "of Potomack," born 1708, married Eleanor Lee, daughter of Philip Lee and Sarah (Brooke).   After her death, he married Priscilla Hawkins, widow of John and daughter of Alexander Magruder.   His daughter, Sarah Fendall, was the beautiful wife of Colonel Thomas Contee, of "Brookefield."   This estate was originally the homestead of Major Thomas Brooke, who received many thousand acres on the west side of the Patuxent.   His initials, T. B., cut on a boundary stone, gave the name to the village "T. B."

The village of Nottingham stands on a portion of his grant.

In 1660, Major Thomas Brooke was commissioned major of the Colonial forces.   His vessel brought over many settlers.   In 1673, he became a member of the General Assembly.   He married, in 1659, Eleanor Hatton, daughter of Hon. Richard Hatton, of London, whose children came with their uncle, Hon. Thomas Hatton, of the Council.   He fell in the battle of the Severn in 1655.   "Brookefield" descended to his son, Thomas, whose mother married Henry Darnell, of "The Woodyard," land commissioner under Lord Baltimore, his brother-in-law.

Mary Darnall, at fifteen, became the wife of Charles Carroll, attorney-general for Lord Baltimore.   Their son, Charles Carroll, Jr., was the father of Charles Carroll, of Carrollton.   Major Thomas Brooke and wife were Catholics.   Clement Brooke, the son, married Jane Sewall, daughter of Major Nicholas Sewall, and Susanna, daughter of Colonel William Burgess.   Elizabeth Brooke, of Clement, became the mother of Charles Carroll, of Carrollton.

Colonel Thomas Brooke, of "Brookefield," was repeatedly elected to the General Assembly, and a member of his lordship's

Council, becoming, in 1720, president of that body.   He belonged to the Church of England.   His second wife was Barbara Dent, daughter of Colonel Thomas Dent and Rebecca Wilkinson, his wife,

Sarah Brooke married Philip Lee, of "Blenheim"—Issue: Richard Lee, of "Blenheim," and Thomas Lee, father of Governor Thomas Sim Lee, whose son, John Lee, gave the name to another, and later governor of Maryland, John Lee Carroll, of "Doughoregan Manor." Governor Fendall's descendants are traced in "The Bowies and Their Kindred."

CAPTAIN THOMAS TODD.

Thomas Todd passed his youth in England.   He patented land in Elizabeth City, Virginia, in 1647.   The "Rent Rolls" of Anne Arundel show, that Thomas Todd, shipwright, surveyed a lot "on ye south side of ye Severn River."   It was a portion of the present city of Annapolis.   There was a contest in Chancery over the title to this survey.   It was decided against him, yet Lancelot Todd, of Baltimore County, in 1718, sold it to Bordley and Bladen.   Thomas Todd resided there, in 1657; he was appointed, by Governor Fendall, one of the justices of Anne Arundel.

The mansion of Charles Carroll, of Annapolis, was built upon his survey.

Thomas Todd took up lands on Fells Point, Baltimore County, and later patented land, including some seven hundred acres on the Eastern Shore.   He is supposed to have been the son of Robert Todd, of York County, Virginia, in 1642.

In 1664, Thomas Todd located at North Point.   He also held an estate, "Toddsbury," in Gloucester County. Virginia, still held by his descendants.   In 1674-5, he was a Burgess in the Assembly of Maryland, from Baltimore County.   He married Ann Gorsuch, daughter of Rev. John Gorsuch, rector of Walkham, Herfordshire, whose wife was Ann, daughter of Sir William Lovelace.   Her brother Charles Gorsuch married Ann Hawkins, as shown by the West River Quaker records.

Thomas Todd, before sailing for England, with eighty-seven hogsheads of tobacco from his plantation, wrote a letter to his son, Thomas, of "Toddsbury," Virginia, saying: "All my desire is to see you before I go, for I fear I shall never see you, as I am very weak and sick.   I want some good cider to keep me alive, which I suppose you have enough of.   We intend to set sail to-morrow, if it be a fair wind."   He died at sea.   His will was probated in Baltimore, Annapolis and Virginia.   His widow, Ann married David Jones.   Her son, James Todd, married a daughter of Mountenay, and upon their estate was started the City of Baltimore.

Thomas Todd, 3rd, who styled himself "The Younger," was the inheritor of ""North Point," and the father of Thomas Todd,

4th, and Robert Todd, to whom he left his large estate. The old homestead, that has always been owned by Thomas Todd, descended to Thomas Todd, 4th. He married Eleanor Dorsey, of "Hockley," They left a son Thomas, and four daughters, Eleanor, Elizabeth, Francis and Mary. The first three inherited "Shawan Hunting Ground," a beautiful estate adjoining Worthington Valley. Mary Todd inherited "Todds Industry," and other tracts upon the Patapsco. She married John Worthington; Elizabeth Todd—John Cromwell; Eleanor—John Ensor; Francis—George Risteau; Mrs. Eleanor Todd—2nd William Lynch. Their daughter, Deborah—Samuel Owings, Jr., of Owings Mills.

Thomas Todd, 5th, left sons, William, Dr. Christopher, Bernard, George and Thomas.

Mr. Thomas Bernard Todd, the present owner of "North Point," president of the school board of Baltimore County, descends from Bernard Todd.

Lancelot Todd, neighbor of Cornelius Howard, in his will of 1690, named "his kinsman Lancelot Todd."

The latter married Elizabeth, daughter of Mary Rockhold. Their two danghters were Ruth Dorsey, wife of Michael, and Sarah Dorsey, wife of Edward.

As Lancelot, Jr., sold the surveys taken by Captain Thomas Todd at Annapolis, he must have been the heir of James Todd, an important man in the early days of Baltimore. See case in Chancery, wherein Daniel Dulany, attorney-general for the Proprietary, enters suit against Edmund Jennings, who married the widow of Thos. Bordley, for the restoration of grant bought by Bordley and Larkins, from Lancelot Todd, representative of Thomas Todd, the surveyor. It is a very interesting review of the title to the site of Annapolis.

COLONEL WILLIAM BURGESS.

Two of the South River settlers from Virginia, were brothers-in-law and neighbors.

They were Colonel William Burgess and Richard Beard. Their wives were thus recorded in the Virginia Magazine of History: "Edward Robins, born in England 1602, came to Virginia in the bark Thomas, in 1615. He was of Northampton, now Accomac County, and built "Newport House," now Eyreville. His daughter Elizabeth married William Burgess, of Maryland. His daughter Rachel married Richard Beard."—(Standard, Vol. 3.)

After William Stone, of Northampton, became the first Protestant governor, Beard and Burgess removed to Maryland. The next record from the same source mistakes the son for the father, when it states: "Beard made the first map of Annapolis." It was Richard Beard, Jr., surveyor of Anne Arundel, who made the map. His father died in 1675, before Annapolis had been named. William Burgess began, at once, his commanding career. In 1655, he was one of the Council of War to condemn Governor Stone,—the very man he had followed to Maryland.

In 1657, he was named, first by Governor Josias Fendall, a commissioner and associate justice of the new County of Anne Arundel. Declining to take the necessary oath, on the ground it was not lawful to swear, his plea was rejected and another name was substituted. In 1660, when Governor Fendall had been banished, and Philip Calvert had succeeded him, William Burgess sent in a petition reviewing his former refusal to take the oath, and ascribing it to the influence of ill-advised friends. He announced his determination, henceforth, to devote his remaining days to the service of the proprietary. His petition was favorably received and he was set free without fine or trial.

In 1661, he was placed in command of the South River Rangers, and was ordered to send all Indian prisoners to St. Mary's for trial. In 1663, he was placed at the head of the Anne Arundel Commissioners.

In 1664, he was high sheriff of Anne Arundel. Upon receiving orders to go against the Indians, he named his successor, Major Richard Ewen, from whose family he had taken his second wife.

In 1665, Charles Calvert, son of Lord Baltimore, having succeeded his uncle Philip, honored William Burgess in the following commission:

CAPTAIN WILLIAM BURGESS,

Greeting,—Whereas, Diverse Forraing Indians have of late committed divers murthers upon our people, I have thought fitt to raise a sufficient number of men. Now know ye that I reposing especial confidence in your fidelity, courage and experience in martial affaires, have constituted, ordained and appointed you Commander-in-Chief of all forces raised in St. Maries, Kent, Charles, Calvert and Anne Arundel Counties.

Given under my hand, 34th year of his Lordship's Dom., 1665.

CHARLES CALVERT.

Then follow instructions for the campaign.

Major Thomas Brooke was ordered "to raise forty men and march to Captain William Burgess, in Anne Arundel, there to receive orders from him as Commander-in-Chief. Ordered that Captain William Burgess raise by presse, or otherwise, thirty men with arms and ammunition to proceed according to former orders."

CHARLES CALVERT.

Some Seneca Indians had killed several English settlers in Anne Arundel. The following reward was offered: "One hundred arms length of Roan Oake, for bringing in a cenego prisoner, or both of his ears, if he be slain." In 1675, Colonel William Burgess and Colonel Samuel Chew were ordered to go against the Indians on the Severn.

In 1679, it was ordered, "That Colonel Burgess supply Baltimore County with twenty men from Anne Arundel, for the defense of that county."

In 1681, Robert Proctor, from his town on the Severn, Thomas Francis, from South River and Colonel Samuel Lane, from the same section, all wrote urgent letters stating that the Indians had killed and wounded both negroes and English men "at a plantation of Major Welsh's," and "had attempted to enter the houses of Mr. Mareen Duvall and Richard Snowden."

Major Francis wrote, and Colonel Nicholas Gassaway added: "I have but nineteen men of all the Coll Troope, and cann gett noe more—men are sick, and of them half have noe ammunition, nor know where to gett it. There is such a parcell of Coll. Burges foote Company in the like condition for ammunition. The head of the River will be deserted, if we leave them, and they have no other reliefe. Wee marched in the night to the releife, Major Lane sent to our releife about thirty foote more, but we have noe orders but to Range and Defend the Plantations, which we shall doe to the best of our skill, and I suppose, if Baltimore County wants assistance that at this time it cannot be well supplyed from Anne Arundel; we have stood to our Arms all night and need enough. Just now more news of three families robbed at Seavern.

Your humble servts.,
Tho. Francis, Nich. Gassaway."

Major Samuel Lane wrote: "The county of Anne Arrundll at this time is in Greate danger. Our men marched all Monday night, the greatest part of South River had been most cutt off. Wee want Ammunition exceedingly, and have not where-with-all to furnish half our men. I hope your Ldpp. will dispatch away Coll. Burges with what Ammunition may be thought convenient. I shall take all the care that lyeth in me, but there comes daily and hourely Complaints to me that I am wholly Imployed in the Country's Service.

In haste with my humble service,

Sept. 13th, 1681.   SAMUEL LANE."

Robert Proctor wrote that Mr. Edward Dorsey had come to him very late in the night, with the news of robberies by the Indians upon the Severn.

Upon such information, followed the decisive order to Colonel William Burgess and Colonel Thomas Tailler, "to fight, kill, take, vanquish, overcome, follow and destroy them."

Colonel Taylor commanded the horse, Colonel Burgess the foot, and both were Protestants.

From that date on to 1682, Colonel Burgess was a delegate to the Lower House; from 1682 to his death in 1686, he was in the Upper House. He was upon many committees.

His epitaph is a most remarkable condensation of his eventful life. It reads:

"Here lyeth the body of Wm. Burgess,
Esq., who departed this life on ye
24th of January, 1686,
Aged 64 years: leaving his
Dear beloved wife, Ursula and eleven
children, viz.: seven sons and four daughters,
And eight grand-children.
In his life-time, a member of
His Lordship's Deputy Governors;
A Justice of ye High Provincial Court;
Colon of a regiment of Trained Bands:
And sometimes General of all ye
Military Forces of this Province.
His loving wife, Ursula, his executrix
In testimony of her true respect,
And due regard to the worthy
Deserts of her dear deceased
Husband, hath erected this monument."

The historian, Geo. L. Davis, says of Colonel Burgess:

"He was himself, through his son Charles, the ancestor of the Burgesses of Westphalia; through his daughter, Susannah, of the Sewalls of Mattapany-Sewalls, closely allied to Lord Charles Baltimore; through his granddaughter, Ursula, of the Davises of Mt. Hope, who did not arrive from Wales before 1720; and through a still later line, of the Bowies of Prince George."

Colonel Burgess left an exceedingly intelligent will of entail; naming his sons and daughters, Edward, George, William, John, Joseph, Benjamin, Charles, Elizabeth, Susannah, Anne. I give to my sonne William my message land where I now dwell, near South River, together with eighteen hundred acres adjoining, which I purchased of George Westall, and one part whereof is a Town appointed called London, provided my wife, Ursula, shall live there until my son is of age. I give unto William, all of "Betty's Choice," in Balto. Co., near Col. Geo. Wells, containing 480 acres. I give to my sonne, John Burgess, four tracts, "Morley's Lott," "Bednall's Green," "Benjamin's Choice," and "Benjamin's Addition," lying near Herring Creek, some 800 acres. I give to my sonne, Joseph, lands purchased of Richard Beard, near South River, called "West Puddington," and "Beard's Habitation," 1300 acres. I give to my sonne Benjamin, a tract, "Bessington," near the Ridge, also "Burgess Choice," near South River. I give to my sonne, Charles, a tract, purchased of Vincent Lowe, at the head of Sasafras River, of 1600 acres, and another of Vincent Lowe, on the Susquehannah, of 500 acres; provided, if any should die before attaining age, then every such tract shall descend to the eldest then living. I give all the rest of my estate, here or in England, to my dear wife, Ursula, at pleasure, and she shall have the care of the education of my children and the use of their portions. I desire that she shall be my executrix, with my friends Major Nicholas Sewall, Major Nicholas Gassaway and Captain Henry Hanslap, as supervisors, and to each of them I grant £5. WILLIAM BURGESS. (SEAL.)

His sons, Edward and George, had been provided for before his will. His daughters received £300 in money, plate and other personals.

His seal-ring of gold was willed to his daughter, Susannah, wife of Major Nicholas Sewall. She was the daughter of Colonel Burgess, by Mrs. Richard Ewen. Colonel Burgess bore arms, as the existing impression of his seal reveals, of a family of Truro, in Cornwall, but was akin to the Burgesses of Marlborough, Wilts County. (Or a fesse chequy, or, and gules, in chief, three crosses, crosslet fitchie of the last.)

Except Charles Burgess, of Westphalla, who married a daughter of Captain Henry Hanslap, the succeeding Burgess name was alone handed down by Captain Edward Burgess, the son who came up from Virginia with him. John and Joseph died early; Benjamin, under the will, claimed their estates, but finally compromised with Captain Edward. Benjamin sold his whole estate and went to England. George, after holding the office of High Sheriff, joined his wife Catherine, the widow Stockett, in deeding all their estate, and removed to Devon County, England.

Ann—Thomas Sparrow, and died the same year. Jane Sewall of Major Nicholas and Susannah Burgess—Clement Brooke, son of Major Thomas. Their daughter, Elizabeth Brooke, became the mother of Charles Carroll, of Carrollton. William Burgess, Jr., inherited the homestead; he married Ann (Watkins) Lord, daughter of John Watkins, the stepson of Commander Edward Lloyd. Burgess' will left 1,000 acres in Baltimore County to his wife's children by her former husband, Mr. Lord.

His mother became the wife of Dr. Mordecai Moore, and remained upon the homestead, near Londontown, until her death, in 1700. She was the heir of Nicholas Painter, long clerk of the Council, whose will left a large estate to her children. She was buried by the side of Colonel Burgess.

Captain Edward Burgess, was in the life-time of his father, commissioner for opening the port of Londontown; justice of the Provincial Court and "Captain of the Foote." He was the executor and heir of Captain George Puddington.

The Chew genealogy records: "Sarah, daughter of Samuel Chew, of John of Chewtown, married a Burges." She was the wife of Captain Edward Burgess, whose oldest son, Samuel, was named for Samuel Chew. Captain Burgess' will left his estate to his sons Samuel and John, having already deeded lands to his daughter, Mrs. Margaret Ware and Mrs. Elizabeth Nicholson. Mrs. Sarah Burgess, his widow, left hers to "my daughters Ann White, Sarah

Gaither and Susannah Richardson." Benjamin Gaither, her son-in-law, was made executor. Samuel Burgess (of Captain Edward), married Mrs. Elizabeth Durbin. Issue, Edward, Benjamin and Elizabeth.

John Burgess (of Captain Edward) married, first Jane Macklefresh (of David). Issue, William, Benjamin, Samuel, Sarah, Ann and Susannah.

He married second, in 1733, Matilda Sparrow. Issue, John, Joseph, Edward, West and Caleb Burgess, all revolutionary patriots, whose history belongs to Howard County.

Upon the homestead tract of the late General George Stewart, of South River, is the original site of Colonel William Burgess' home; from which, upon a commanding hill, may be seen his tombstone, quoted above. Surrounding General Stewart's home are massive oaks, which bear the imprint of ages. Upon this site, too, stood the home of Anthony Stewart, of the "Peggy Stewart," who came into possession of Colonel Burgess' home tract, which later passed into General Stewart's possession. The two families, with similar names claim no relation to each other. The road leading past the historic place and on to All Hallows Church, about three-fourths of a mile west, is the same over which General Washington passed from Annapolis to Mt. Vernon, in 1783. Along this road are yet to be seen wayside oaks, that reveal the remarkable richness of this South River section, when occupied by our early settlers.

Along this road, beautiful views of the broad South River may be enjoyed.

Between Colonel Burgess' homestead and his Londontown tract, there still stands a well-preserved old brick homestead, with massive chimneys and steep roof. It is within sight of the Alms House upon the southern bank of South River. I have not found its builder.

All of the property passed through Colonel Burgess and his son, William Burgess, Jr., to Mrs. Ursula Moore, wife of Dr. Mordecai Moore. From that family, through recorded transfers, it may be traced to the present owners. The most of it is now in the estate of General George Stewart, whose linage has been .clearly traced to Kenneth, 2nd, the first Scottish king.

Colonel Burgess' son-in-law, Major Nicholas Sewall, son of Hon. Henry Sewall, of "Mattepany," was a member of the Council from 1684 to 1689. His sons were Charles and Henry. Elizabeth Sewall, widow of the latter, married Hon. William Lee, of the Council, and became mother of Thomas Lee, father of Governor Thomas Sim Lee.

Nicholas, son of Henry and Elizabeth Sewall, married Miss Darnall, of "Poplar Hill," Prince George County.

Their descendants were: Hon. Nicholas Lewis Sewall, of "Cedar Point," member of the convention for ratification of the Constitution of United States; and Robert Darnall Sewall, of "Poplar Hill."

This was a part of the famous "Woodyard," the house of Colonel Henry Darnall of 1665, whose brother, John Darnall, held "Portland Manor," in Anne Arundel.   Colonel Henry Darnall's daughter, Eleanor, became the wife of Clement Hill.   Eleanor Brooke Darnall, of the "Woodyard," was the mother of Archbishop John Carroll and Mary Darnall, of "The Woodyard," became the wife of Charles Carroll, of Carrollton.   Robert Darnall, grandson of Colonel Henry, lost all the magnificent estate except "Poplar Hill," about eight hundred arces, which came into possession of the Sewalls, through the marriage above mentioned.—(THOMAS.)

Lady Baltimore, wife of Charles Lord Baltimore, and widow of Hon. Henry Sewall, was the danghter of Vincent Lowe and Anne Cavendish, of London, and a sister of Colonel Vincent Lowe, of Maryland.

Her daughter, Jane Sewall, became the wife of Hon. Philip Calvert, and her daughter Elizabeth, married second Colonel Wm. Digges, member of the Maryland Council, son of Governor Edward Digges, of Virginia.   Colonel Digges was in command at St. Mary's, when compelled to surrender to Captain John Coode's revolutionary forces in 1689.   He later removed to "Warburton Manor," nearly opposite to Mt. Vernon.

It was in the garrison of Mattapany, a large brick mansion, the property of Lady Baltimore, descending to her son, Colonel Nicholas Sewall, where Governor Calvert had erected a fort, that his forces retired when attacked by Coode; and it was there that the formal articles of surrender were prepared.

The house and property of the proprietary were confjscated, but came back to the possession of the Sewalls in 1722, by a grant from the second Charles Lord Baltimore, to Nicholas Sewall, son of the original proprietor, and so remained until the present century.

There are on record, at Annapolis, the wills of two residents of Wilts County, England, viz: Anthony Goddard, of Suringden, of Wilts, England, in 1663, left "to William Burgess, of Anne Arundel, his entire estate, in trust for Hester Burgess, of Bristol, England. Joseph Burgess, of Wilts, in 1672, named his brother, William and others.   Our records show that Colonel Burgess, of Anne Arundel County, settled the estate.

EDWARD DORSEY.

In the Land Office of Annapolis, may be seen the following warrant, which explains itself:

"Warrant MDCL, granted to Edward Dorsey, of Anne Arundel Co., for 200 acres of land, which he assigns as followeth; as also 200 acres more, part of a warrant for 400 acres, granted John Norwood and the said Dorsey, dated XXIII of Feb., MDCLI.   Know all men by these presents that I, Edward Dorsey, of the County of Anne Arundel, boatwright, have granted, bargained and sold, for a valuable consideration, already received, all my right, title, interest of and in a warrant for 200 acres, bearing date 1650, and also 200 acres more, being half of a warrant of 400 acres—the one

half belonging to Captain Norwood, bearing date, 1651, both of
which assigned to George Yate.—EDWARD DORSEY, Sealed."
Signed in the presence of Cornelius Howard, John Howard, Oct.
22nd, MDCLXVII, (1667).

That same year the same Edward Dorsey assigned to Cornelius
Howard, his right for land for transporting seven persons into the
province. Edward Dorsey and Thomas Manning held a certificate
from Thomas Marsh, for 600 acres adjoining Captain Norwood.
"Norwood's Fancy," held by Captain Norwood, was near Round
Bay. "Dorsey," held by Edward Dorsey, gave the name to "Dorsey's Creek," upon which was located Thomas Gates, whose will of
1659, reads: "I give to Michael Bellott and John Holloway my plantation. I desire that they give to Edward Dorsey's children free outlet to the woods and spring as formally I have given them." The
following transfer, of 1668, further locates the above testator: "George
Yate, 1668, assigned to Colonel Edward Dorsey, sixty acres called
"Dorsey," on the south side of the Severn, on Dorsey's Creek, running to a cove called Freeman's, then up said cove to Captain John
Norwood's, then bounding on a line of a place formally held by
Thomas Gates."

Colonel Edward Dorsey, son and heir of Edward Dorsey, the
immigrant, held this tract of "Dorsey" during life. It was sold by
his widow, Margaret, the wife of John Israel, in 1706, to Wm. Bladen,
of Annapolis. The following record is taken from "Our Early
Settlers."—A list of our early arrivels up to 1680.

"Robert Bullen demands lands for bringing over a number of
passengers, amongst whom was Edward Dorsey, in 1661."

The same record adds, "Aug. 25th, 1664, patented to him, John
and Joshua Dorsey, a plantation called "Hockley-in-the-Hole," four
hundred acres."

In 1683, this land was resurveyed for John Dorsey, and found
to contain 843 acres. 400 acres first surveyed heing old rents
remaining new, whole now in the possession of Caleb Dorsey.
Such is the record of "Hockley" upon our Rent Rolls, at
Annapolis.

Among the restored records, collected by a commission, Hon.
Wm. Holland, president, Samuel Young, Captain Richard Jones and
Mr. John Brice, appointed after the fire of 1704, to renew the land
records then destroyed, is the following :

"Came 1707, Mr. Caleb Dorsey, of Hockley, and petitioned the
honorable members to have the following recorded:

"To all Christian people to whom this writing shall come, be
heard, read, or seen, I, Edward Dorsey, of the County of Anne
Arundel, son and heir of the late Edward Dorsey, gentleman, deceased, for the consideration of 24,000 pounds of good merchant-
able tobacco, transfer my right in a tract of land called "Hockley-
in-the-Hole," granted to Edward, Joshua and John Dorsey, in 1664,
to my brother, John Dorsey, and I further covenant to guarantee
his right to said land against any demand that may descend from

my said father, Edward Dorsey, for or by reason of any right due to him in his life time, or by reason of any survey by him made, or warrant returned, or for any other reason of any other matter." After his signature, fully attested, follows a deed from Joshua Dorsey, for his right in said tract for a consideration of 8,000 pounds of tobacco, to his brother, John Dorsey. After which, also, John Dorsey petitioned for a resurvey and increased it to 842 acres. The date of Edward Dorsey's transfer was 1681. He states that his father, who was living in 1667, was then dead.

Edward Dorsey, the last mentioned, in 1679 and 1685, was recorded one of the justices of Anne Arundel. His name was written both Darcy and Dorsey.

From 1680 to 1705, Major Dorsey was in every movement looking to the development of the colony. From 1694 to 1696 he was Judge of the High Court of Chancery, during which time he was commissioned to hold the Great Seal. In 1694, he was a member of the House of Burgesses for Anne Arundel, and from 1697 to his death, in 1705, was a member from Baltimore County (now Howard). He was one of the subscribers and treasurer of the fund for building St. Anne's church, and a free school for the province also received his aid. He signed the protestant address from Baltimore County to the King's most gracious Majestie, upon the succession of King William III—an appeal in behalf of Charles Lord Baron of Baltimore, whose proprietary government had been wrested from the family through the influence of Captain John Coode. Though a Protestant, he was found in support of a government which left religious faith untouched.

Mrs. Potter Palmer, of Chicago, a descendant, reviewing the record, writes: "Edward Dorsey and others were joined in the protestant effort to have Lord Baltimore's government taken from the hands of the Catholics, and made a Crown Colony under a Protestant governor. They took part in all the movements to that end, but having been personal friends of Lord Baltimore, and lovers of justice, after the Protestant government was established, they joined in a petition to the king to restore Lord Baltimore's lands to him. The king acted favorably on this petition and did so restore these lands, which were enjoyed, with all their private rights, rents and revenues, by the Baltimores during all the time the government was vested in the Crown and the Protestants in power.

"Edward Dorsey would not have been given position and honors by the royal government had he been against it. He must have been one of the most influential Protestants in the colony, for the new capital was taken to his land in Annapolis, and not to that of William Burgess on the South River, or to that of Nicholas Greenberry, opposite on Town Neck. He seems to have been the presiding genius on all committees to build the town."

Major Edward Dorsey married, first, Sarah, daughter of Nicholas Wyatt, the pioneer surveyor of the Severn, who had come up from Virginia with his wife, Damaris, and her daughter, Mary, afterward the wife of Major John Welsh. She was the half-sister of Sarah (Wyatt) Dorsey. Upon the death of Nicholas Wyatt, in 1673, he left a will made in 1671, in which Mrs. Wyatt was made executrix. Upon her subsequent marriage to Thomas Bland, the attorney, there was a contest in chancery, in which Major Edward Dorsey, as the representative of his wife, the heir, contended for the administration of the estate, on the ground of a subsequent revocation of the will of 1671. From that case in chancery, a view of Nicholas Wyatt's neighbors is given.

Captain Cornelius Howard wrote the will, and testified that the testator did not appear to be in condition at that time, to remember what he owned. He stated that Richard Warfield and Edward Dorsey knew more than he did of the revocation. Thomas Bland asked for a " Commission to Samuel Chew to call before him Captain Cornelius Howard, Robert Gudgeon, Nicholas Shepherd, Richard and Ellen Warfield, John Watkins, Mary Evans, Sarah Cooper, Benjamin Stringer, Guy Meeke, Johanna Sewell, John and Mary Welsh and Maurice Baker; and that they be cross-examined concerning the revocation, or confirmation of the said deceased." The case, after an extended discussion by both leading lawyers, in which Major Dorsey contended that "the heir, not the administrator can alone make good the warranty," was decided in favor of Major Dorsey, who administered.

As Major of the Horse, he joined Captain Edward Burgess, in asking for additional arms and ammunition for defense.

In 1694, Major Dorsey was upon the committee with Major John Hammond, Hon. John Dorsey, Captain Philip Howard, Major Nicholas Greenberry and John Bennett, to lay out town lots and a town common for "the town of Proctor," or Annapolis. In 1705, he sold a row of houses upon Bloomsbury Square, Annapolis, which had been entailed to his children, but which, for want of tenants, had greatly depreciated.

At the time of his death, he was living on "Major's Choice," now Howard County. The second wife was Margaret Larkin, daughter of John Larkin. He left five minors by her. She afterwards became Mrs. John Israel, and as executrix, sold "Dorsey" and houses in Annapolis, lately owned by Colonel Edward Dorsey, her late husband."

Colonel Dorsey's will, of 1705, recorded in Baltimore City and in Annapolis, reads: "To my son Lacon, my tract "Hockley," on the Patapsco Falls. To sons Charles, Lacon, Francis and Edward, my lands on the north side of Patapsco River. (These were deeded to him by John and Thomas Larkin, 1702). To my beloved wife, Margaret, my personal estate. To my daughter, Ann, a lot of negroes. To Joshua, "Barnes Folly." To Samuel, "Major's Choice." To Nicholas, "Long Reach," at Elk Ridge. To Benjamin, "Long Reach." To son John, all the remaining part of "Long Reach" and a lot of silver spoons, to be delivered at the age of sixteen. All the remaining portion of my estate to my wife and executrix.—EDWARD DORSEY. (Seal.)"

Colonel Edward Dorsey's heirs will be found in Howard County records.

Samuel exchanged with his brother, Joshua, his interest in "Major's Choice," and held the lands of his mother, upon "Wyatt's Hill," on the Severn. His wife was Jane Dorsey. Their daughter, Patience—Samuel Howard, of Philip, in 1740.

After the death of Colonel Dorsey, Samuel contested the sale of Bloomsbury Square, on the ground that it was entailed property, and though he was of age at the time of sale, he was not consulted by his father. The title remained in the purchaser.

JOSHUA DORSEY, OF "HOCKLEY."

There is but little information obtainable of this middle patentee of Hockley. After the deed, in 1681, of his interest in Hockley to his brother, John, he located upon "Taunton," a tract taken up by Lawrence Richardson and left by him to his sons, one of whom, Lawrence, Jr., conveyed his interest to Joshua Dorsey. The will of Lawrence Richardson, in 1666, names his daughter, Sarah. She later became the wife of Joshua Dorsey, and after his death, the wife of Thomas Blackwell, who held another tract, "Burnt Wood," taken up by Lawrence Richardson. It was assigned by Richardson's heirs to Wm. Gudgeon, who conveyed it to Thomas Blackwell, and by him it was conveyed to John Dorsey, only son of Joshua. These same tracts were conveyed to Amos Garrett by John Dorsey, heir-at-law of Joshua, in which he recited the above transfers, to him from his father, Joshua Dorsey, and his father-in-law, Thomas Blackwell. Joshua Dorsey's will, of 1687-8, granted one-third of his estate to his widow, Sarah Dorsey, and made his brothers, Edward and John, guardians for the education of his son, John Dorsey, to whom he left his estate. His will further reads:

"To my loving cousin, John Howard, a grey gelding; to cousin Samuel Howard, two hogsheads of tobacco. I bequeath to my cousin, Sarah Dorsey, twenty shillings, to buy her a ring."

John and Comfort Dorsey sold the above tracts to Amos Garrett. Comfort Dorsey was the daughter of Thomas and Rachel Stimpson. The latter was the widow of Neale Clarke, and the daughter of Richard and Rachel Beard, of South River. Mrs. Stimpson became later, Mrs. Rachel Killburne, and still later, Mrs. Rachel Freeborne. John and Comfort Dorsey had issue—John Hammond Dorsey, Vincent, Captain Joshua, Greenberry, Sarah and Venetia Dorsey. John Hammond, of Cecil County, left his estate, "Success," to John Hammond Dorsey, Vincent Dorsey, Sarah and Venetia, children of John and Comfort Dorsey, of Joshua. Mrs. Comfort Dorsey, in her will, named her legatees, "Vincent and John Hammond Dorsey." To her sons, Joshua and Greenberry, she left one shilling each. "To John, of Greenberry, a memorial, and to Comfort, of Greenberry, gold ear rings."

Vincent Dorsey married Sarah Day. His will names, "John, of Greenberry; also Greenberry and Elizabeth, of John; and Vincent Cromwell."

John Hammond Dorsey, of "Success," married Francis Watkins, of John. Issue, John Hammond Dorsey, Jr.—Anne Maxwell, whose daughter, Mary Hammond Dorsey—John Hammond Cromwell, son of Thomas Cromwell, of Huntingdon, England, whose wife was Venetia Woolguist, of Wales; yet husband and wife were cousins. James Maxwell Dorsey, in 1789, married Martha McComas and removed to Ohio. Issue, Dr. G. Volney Dorsey, of Ohio. Sarah Dorsey—Alexander Cromwell, in 1735.

John Hammond Cromwell and his brother, Vincent, after the death of their father, came to Cecil and claimed relationship with the Cromwells, of Anne Arundel. Vincent Cromwell removed to Kentucky. The house of John Hammond Cromwell still stands. Its family cemetery is surrounded with a box hedge six feet high. The following recent death in that homestead gives an interesting history of the family. It is quoted from the Baltimore American.

"Elkton, Md., October 20th, 1902.—Mr. Henry B. Nickle, who was buried last week, at Oxford, Pa., near Cecil County line, was a descendant of Oliver Cromwell. "Success Farm" was the name of his homestead. It lies between Susquehanna River and Octararo Creek, and is a part of Lord Baltimore's Susquehanna Manor, in Cecil County.

"Henry B. Nickle was a great-grandson of John Hammond Cromwell, who inherited the farm from his mother, Venetia Cromwell (nee Dorsey), who inherited it from her mother, Mary Dorsey (nee Hammond), who inherited it from her father, John Hammond. Soon after the close of the Revolutionary War, John Hammond Cromwell, eldest son of Venetia and Woolguist Cromwell, and his niece, Mary Hammond Dorsey, settled on Success Farm.

"The old mansion stands as originally built by Lord Baltimore, from whom it was purchased by Lady Lightfoot, and given to her son, John Hammond. Across the lane, in front of the house, is the family burying ground, with a shaft in the centre of which are the names of those buried there: John Hammond Cromwell, 1745-1819; Mary Hammond Dorsey Cromwell, wife of John Hammond Cromwell, died 1795; Oliver Cromwell, 1775-1792; Eliza Cromwell, 1789-1796; Elizabeth Cromwell, 1786-1787; ; Mary Cromwell, 1792-1793; Rebecca Cromwell Wilson, 1708-1806; Benedict Cromwell, 1780-1806; Lewis Harlen, 1760-1825; Matilda Cromwell, wife of Lewis Harlen, 1774-1825; Frances Dorsey, died 1820, sister of John W. Cromwell; J. Cromwell Reynolds, M. D., late a surgeon in the army of the United States, born February 6, 1810, died February 20, 1849.

"John Hammond Cromwell, by will, devised money to be divided among his children to be used in the purchase of mourning brooches, each to contain some of his hair. The brooches were made in a design of onyx, inlaid with silver, in the centre of which was an oval of braided hair under glass. Mr. Cromwell was wealthy, entertained largely, and was prominent in politics. He had large peach orchards, and manufactured peach brandy. In a grove west of his mansion may be seen the ruins of the old still-house.

"Among the Nickle heirlooms is John Hammond Cromwell's silver sugar tongs. Another is an old fashioned sampler embroidered by Rebecca Cromwell, August 16, 1796."

Greenberry Dorsey, of John and Comfort—Mary Belt, daughter of John and Lucy Lawrence, daughter of Benjamin and Elizabeth Talbott. Issue, John Dorsey and Thomas Edward Dorsey.

Greenberry Dorsey, as heir-at-law of Colonel John Dorsey, who held "Dorsey's Plains," on the Gunpowder, deeded the same to his son, Thomas Edward Dorsey, of Harford County. John Dorsey, of this family—Cassandra Carnan. Their son, Elisha, of "Dorsey's Plains,"—Mary Slade, whose son, Nicholas Slade Dorsey—Maria Hance, of Baltimore, descendant daughter of the Hances, of Calvert, connected with the Dukes, Irelands, Clares and Calverts, of that county.

They were the parents of Rev. Owen Dorsey, late of the Interior Department, who collected considerable data of the family.

Captain Joshua Dorsey, of John and Comfort—Flora Fitzimmons, and resided in St. Margarets Parish, on the Severn. Their children are all recorded in that parish. His widow, in 1784, named her six absent sons, Frederick, a mariner, Peregrine, Greenberry, Joshua, John and James, granting them a nominal rememberance, if they be living. To her son Nicholas and her daughters, Providence Lane and Rebecca Dorsey, she left her estate, "Mascalls Rest."

I have seen a saucer that belonged to Providence Lane. Upon it is a sea gull on a rock, surrounded by ten stars. It was inherited by Mrs. Reuben M. Dorsey, daughter of the Prussian Minister, I. P. Krafft, who married Eliza Brice, daughter of Providence Lane.

Judge Reuben M. Dorsey, wishing to depart from the old Dorsey custom of marrying cousins, sought the hand of his wife; but when he began to study her genealogical record, found that she, too, came from one of the three Dorsey brothers, who took up Hockley, in 1664. The sons of Judge Dorsey are Dr. Reuben M. Dorsey, of Baltimore; the late Charles Krafft Dorsey, attorney-at-law; Dr. Caleb Dorsey, of Baltimore; Philip Hammond, Nicholas and Frank Dorsey, of Howard. Phillip Hammond Dorsey married Miss Duvall, of Anne Arundel County. He holds the homestead.

HON. JOHN DORSEY, OF "HOCKLEY."

Coming into possession of "Hockley," in 1683, Hon. John Dorsey married Plesance Ely, who later took up a tract of land on Elk Ridge, which she named "The Isle of Ely." In 1694, Hon. John Dorsey, was a commissioner for the development of Annapolis. He was upon many important committees during his service in the Lower House of the Assembly. In 1711, he was advanced to the

Upper House, and there remained until his death, in 1714. During his life-time he was a surveyor of a vast estate of valuable lands. He left an exceedingly intelligent will of entail, which gives a summary of his large estate. It reads: "My wife, Plesance, is to have one-third of my estate, and also the choice of my estate on South River, or my now dwelling place on Elk Ridge. To my grandson, John Dorsey, son of my son, Edward Dorsey, deceased, my Patuxent plantation and lands thereunto adjoining, called "Dorsey's Search," lying in Baltimore County. If no issue, to go to the three youngest grandchildren of my daughter, Deborah.

"I give to my grandson, Edward Dorsey, son of my son, Edward Dorsey, deceased, 'Dorsey's Adventure' and 'Whitaker's Purchase' adjoining it. If he leave no issue, then to John, of Edward, and if he leave none, then, as above, to Deborah's youngest three children. To my grandsons, Charles and William Ridgely, of Deborah, my tract called 'White Wine and Claret,' south side of the middle branch of the Patuxent. If they leave no issue, to go to Martha, Elinor and Edward Clagett.

"I give to my two grandsons, Samuel and Richard, of Caleb, my son, my plantation on South River, called 'South River Quarter,' it being the remainder of a tract given to my son, Caleb. In case of no issue, the same to go to granddaughters, Achsah and Sophia, of Caleb.

"To grandson, Basil, of Caleb, my plantation on Elk Ridge, called 'Troy.' If no issue, to my grandsons, John and Caleb, of Caleb. My son, Caleb, to be my administrator.—JOHN DORSEY. (Seal)."

Mrs. Plesance Dorsey became Mrs Robert Wainwright. Her tract, "The Isle of Ely," was sold by her grandson, "Patuxent John Dorsey," to Basil Dorsey, of Caleb, whose homestead, "Troy Hill," was the former residence of Hon. John Dorsey. It is now the Pfeiffer property, in Howard.

CALEB DORSEY, OF "HOCKLEY."

Caleb was born at "Hockley," in 1686. In 1704, he married and came into possession of the whole estate. His wife was Elinor Warfield, youngest daughter of Richard and Elinor (Browne) Warfield, They lived in the old mansion house, which stood only a few feet from the railroad, just west of "Best Gate."

On the east, looking toward Annapolis, was the Carroll estate. On the north was General John Hammond's, in the valley of which, long after the last relics of his homestead had disappeared, was found a memorial tablet, which now rests in the grounds of St. Annes. To the northwest of old Hockley, reaching back to Round Bay, were the three Howard brothers,—Samuel, Cornelius and John Howard—running with Hockley branch. On the southwest was "Todd's Gap," which opened up the way to Lancelot Todd's. Upon a hill to the south of the mansion, is the old Dorsey burial ground, now succeeded by a later one in the beautiful gardens of new Hockley, upon the southern border of the estate.   Upon the site of the old coachhouse, the plowshare turned up a silver plate, which was evidently used upon some family carriage. It represents a bended arm in armor, holding a sheaf of wheat. (This is claimed to be Eden's arms).

Caleb Dorsey increased his father's estates upon the Severn, and took up an extensive body of land in what is now Howard County. It extended from Elk Ridge Landing back to the old brick Church, upon which he placed his three sons, John, Basil and Caleb of Belmont. Still later, the three sons of Thomas Beale Dorsey, of Caleb, surveyed a still more valuable estate west of Ellicotts City. In 1732, Caleb Dorsey deeded to his son, Richard, the attorney, the homestead. After its destruction by fire Richard built upon the present site, upon the southern border. Caleb Dorsey's will, of 1742, gives us a view of the extensive farming systems of that period. "To my sons, Basil, John and Caleb, whom I have sufficiently provided for, I give £5 each. To Richard, Edward and Thomas Beale, I give twenty head of cattle, and twenty head of sheep, each.

"To Thomas Beale, the two tracts of land I bought of Thomas Higgins, after the death of my wife."

A large part of his estate had been deeded to his children through his trustee, John Beale.

His widow survived him ten years, and in her will, of 1752 named her son Edward, daughter Sophia Gough, grandson Henry Woodward, goddaughter Mary Todd, goddaughter Elinor Dorsey, of John. She made her sons, Edward and John Dorsey, her executors.

Achsah Dorsey, her oldest daughter, married Amos Woodward, nephew of Amos Garrett, first Mayor of Annapolis.

Henry Woodward was their only son. Their daughters were, Mary, Elizabeth, Eleanor and Achsah Fotterall.

Henry Woodward married Mary Young, daughter of Colonel Richard Young, of Calvert County, and Rebecca, his wife. Their issue were, Rebecca—Philip Rogers; Eleanor—Samuel Dorsey; Mary—first, Mr. Govane, second, Mr. Owings; Harriet—first, Colonel Edmund Brice, whose son , James Edmund Brice, was consul to St. Domingo; second, Colonel Murray.

Achsah Woodward, of Henry, died young.

The early death of Henry broke the male line of Amos Woodward. Mrs. Mary (Young) Woodward married, second, John Hessilius, the artist, whose portrait of her is now owned by Dr. Wm. G. Ridout. Her home was "Belfield," upon the Severn. She was a lady of strong Christian character, interested in the religious movements of the early days of Methodism. She was a member of the Church of England. "Primrose" was her later home.

Sophia Dorsey, of Caleb, of "Hockley," married Thomas Gough, of England. Their son, Harry Dorsey Gough, inherited a fortune from England, "and built 'Perry Hall.'" This has thus been described by a Methodist minister: "For the first I saw Perry Hall, the seat of Harry Dorsey Gough, when we got in sight of the house, and it could be seen far off. I felt some strange sensations. Perry Hall was the largest dwelling house I had ever seen, and all the arrangements, within and without, were tasteful and elegant; yet simplicity and utility seemed to be stamped on the whole. The garden, containing four acres of ground, orchards and everything else were delightful indeed, and looked to me like an earthly paradise. But what pleased me better than anything else, was a neat chapel attached to the house, with a small cupola and bell that could be heard all over the farm. In this chapel morning and evening prayers were offered, when the manager and servants from the farm house and servant's quarters, together with the inhabitants of the great mansion house, repaired to the chapel, sometimes numbering fifty persons at prayers. The whole family, including children, numbered about one hundred; all seemed to know their duty and did it. Mr. and Mrs. Gough, (who was Miss Carnan), were converted under Mr. Asbury, and became members of the first Methodist class organized in Baltimore; and Mr. Gough sometimes preached, though the sect was often times persecuted. At a camp-meeting near the Belair road, Mr. Gough rode up on horse back, and his family in a coach drawn by four splendid white horses. Never before had I seen people in a coach of four to hear a back-woods preacher, in a log cabin. Our house was too small, and we got up a subscription for a larger one. When Mr. Gough heard of it he went to them and said, "Take what you have and build a school-house for your children, and I will get you a meeting-house." General Ridgely, of "Hampton," Mrs. Gough's brother, gave them an acre of ground for a meeting-house and a burial ground. Mr. Gough advanced the money and paid all expenses. He named it "Camp-Meeting Chapel."

After Mr. Gough's death, Mrs. Gough took up the cross and led the worship of God in her family. She was a woman of uncommon fortitude and courage. The very day of the battle of North Point, I preached to a few old men and some females, among whom was Mrs. Gough. The report of the guns was very plainly heard while I was preaching, and the bombs were heard at "Perry Hall," twelve miles from Baltimore, nearly all night. Mrs. Gough determined to send away a part of her family, but to stay herself and plead her own cause. It was in the mouth of everyone, 'the prayers of the good people of Baltimore saved the city.'

"Mrs. Carroll, daughter of Mrs. Gough, was an accomplished lady, and what is still better an humble Christian. Her end was most triumphant. Bishop Asbury's journal notes the following: ' 'Perry Hall' was always hospitably open to visitors.'

"Harry Dorsey Gough's funeral sermon was preached; there might be two thousand people to hear. My subject was pretty much a portraiture of Mr. Gough's religious character. His hospitable home was burned down many years ago, with the portraits paneled in its dining room. The present mansion was built by Mr. James Carroll; the property has passed out of the family, but a member has a picture of the original building. The portraits of Mr. Gough have only recently been destroyed by fire. The approach to 'Perry Hall' is the Belair road."

The only daughter and child of Mr. Gough was Sophia, who married James Mackubin, son of Nicholas and Mary Clare Carroll, sister of "The Barrister." At the latter's request, to perpetuate his name and fortune, Mr. James Mackubin took the name of James Carroll. His heirs were Harry Dorsey Gough Carroll—Eliza Ridgely, daughter of Governor Charles C. Ridgely, of "Hampton." Prudence Gough Carroll—John Ridgely, son of Governor Ridgely. Charles Ridgely Carroll—Rebecca Anna Pue. Issue, Charles Arthur Carroll—Sally Heath White. Their heirs were the late Charles Ridgely Carroll, Harry Dorsey Gough Carroll, and Sally Heath White Carroll, all of New Brighton, Staten Island.

Rebecca, daughter of Charles Ridgely Carroll, married Hon. Carroll Spence; Sophia—George B. Milligan; Susan—Thomas Poultney; Mary—Robert Denison. Their daughter is the wife of Colonel Henry Mactier Warfield, of the Fifth Maryland Regiment.

When we were subjects of King George III, Mr. Harry Dorsey Gough built a block of houses on Baltimore Street, extending on the south side from Light Street to Grant Street. In these houses were Grant's Fountain Inn, the Post-Office under Miss Goddard; the American office, and Colonel Wm. Hammond's, the merchant. Several of these were lately condemned. The Carrollton Hotel stood upon the site of the old Fountain Inn, where Washington made his headquarters. The disastrous fire of February, 1904, destroyed this whole block. Upon the same site to-day, a new order of beautiful architecture has been located.

RICHARD DORSEY, OF "HOCKLEY."

Richard Dorsey, the attorney, came into possession of the homestead in 1732. He built upon the present site. His wife was Elizabeth Nicholson, widow of William Nicholson, and daughter of John and Elizabeth (Norwood) Beale.

John Beale was the son of Thomas Beale, of St. Mary's. He was Caleb Dorsey's trustee. He bought from Andrew Norwood, "Norwood's Intact" and "Proctor's Chance," in the city of Annapolis. His coat of arms may be seen upon his original will, in 1734. Mrs. Elizabeth Beale, that same year, deeded to her daughter, Elizabeth, then wife of Richard Dorsey, of "Hockley," her father's estate; a portion of which had been deeded to Beale Nicholson, only son of William, both then deceased. A portrait of Beale Nicholson is one of the heirlooms of "Hockley."

Mrs. Elizabeth Dorsey was a sister of Mrs. Anne Rutland, wife of Thomas, who in her will, of 1773, named her nieces, Ann Beale, Eliza Harrison and Mary Dorsey, children of my sister, Elizabeth

Dorsey. Mary Dorsey, of Richard and Elizabeth, married John Weems; Elinor—Chancellor John Hall; Ann—John Beale; Elizabeth became Mrs. Harrison. Caleb Dorsey, only son of Richard, inherited Hockley. He married Mary Rutland, of Thomas, the Annapolis importer, who built "Rutland Row," in Annapolis.

Caleb and Mary Dorsey had Richard, of "Hockley," who married Anne Warfield, daughter of Captain Philemon Warfield, thus uniting again descendants of the two neighboring houses of Dorsey and Warfield. Their issue were, Caleb—Elizabeth Hall Dorsey, whose dancing slippers are still at "Hockley." Issue, Colonel Edward Dorsey, who was with Colonel Harry Gilmonr's dashing trooper's; Bartus Dorsey, of Baltimore; Richard Dorsey, and Mary Elizabeth, who married the late Magruder Warfield, of Baltimore.

Edward Dorsey, of Richard and Anne—Elizabeth Worthington; Mary, of Richard and Anne—Hon. John Stevens Sellman, of the "Nineteen Van Buren Electors," who, by entering the Senate Chamber, when others refused, helped to bring on the compromise during the administration of Governor Veazey."

Anne, of Richard and Anne, inherited "Hockley"—Essex Ridley Dorsey, of Vachel and Elizabeth Dorsey, grandson of Vachel and Ruth Dorsey, and great-grandson of John and Honor (Elder) Dorsey. Vachel Dorsey, Jr., and Charles Carroll, of Carrollton, were surveyors of "Vacant Land." Essex Ridley Dorsey's mother, Elizabeth Dorsey, was the daughter of Joshua and Elizabeth (Hall) Dorsey, and granddaughter of Henry and Elizabeth (Worthington) Dorsey.

"Hockley," taken up by two brothers, Major Edward and Hon. John, is thus held by the combined descendants of those brothers, viz.: Vachel Charles, who holds the old "Hockley" estate, upon which he has built a modern house; Miss Anne Elizabeth, who presides at "Hockley," Evalina, Andrew Jackson and Richard Dorsey, of "Hockley." Evalina—Richard Dorsey Sellman, son of Hon. John Stevens Sellman. Issue, Mary Laura, Anne Elizabeth Dorsey, Eleanor and Gertrude Sellman. Mrs. Sellman died, January 1st, 1900. Her first three daughters are of the household of "Hockley." Miss Gertrude Sellman resides in Baltimore.

The original patent for "Hockley," under the seal of Lord Charles Baltimore, perfectly legible and well-preserved, is an heirloom of "Hockley." A silouette of Mr. Essex Ridley Dorsey hangs upon the walls of "Hockley," in the charming gardens of which, among the flowers and shrubs, he now sleeps beside his wife and her ancestors.

Samuel and Joshua Dorsey, of Caleb and Elinor, both died bachelors, and left their estates to their brothers and sisters.

Edward Dorsey, of Caleb and Elinor, was an attorney and resided in Annapolis. He took up an extensive estate in Frederick County, and became a member of the Council from that county. He was engaged in many important legal cases in the Court of the Chancery. Governor Sharp, in his correspondence with Lord Baltimore, noted the fact that the then existing Council was composed of relatives of Mr. Edward Dorsey, all of whom were opposed to the proprietary. As Frederick Calvert was then at the head, it was only an honor to be in opposition. Edward Dorsey was in partnership with his brother, Caleb, of Belmont, in smelting iron ore. After his early death, and the death of all his heirs, Ely Dorsey, husband of Edwards' sister, Deborah, entered a suit in chancery for the recovery of a large share of the property of the firm, then held by Caleb of Belmont. After a long and exhaustive trial, the case was compromised.

Edward Dorsey loaned money on many tracts in Howard and Frederick Counties, and made extensive transfers in real estate. He was his mother's executor. He was a brother-in-law of Governor Paca. He was a member of the Tuesday Club, of Annapolis, in its palmy days, and was one of its eloquent debaters. His wife was Henrietta Marie Chew, daughter of Samuel and Henrietta Maria Lloyd, of Colonel Philemon and Henrietta Marie (Neale) Bennett, In early manhood, whilst on a trip to Boston for his health, he died at New Port, in 1760.

His widow followed him in 1762. Their two daughters, Eleanor and Henrietta Marie Dorsey, both died before reaching womanhood, leaving their estate of £30,000 to their Dorsey relatives.

The Annapolis Gazette, in reviewing the eminent service of Captain Edward Dorsey, gave him the title of "Eminent Councilor."

Eleanor Dorsey (of Caleb and Eleanor), married Thomas Todd, of "Todd's Neck," Baltimore County, whose genealogy has already been traced. Their only son was Thomas Todd, the fifth, who left four sons, Thomas, Bernard, Dr. Christopher and Robert Todd. The daughters of Thomas and Eleanor Todd were Elizabeth, Eleanor, Francis and Mary, already noted elsewhere.

Mrs. Todd married again, William Lynch, and resided near Pikesville. Their daughter, Deborah Lynch, married Samuel Owings, founder of Owings Mill, son of Samuel and Urith (Randall) Owings. From this marriage descends Mr. Thos. B. Cockey, of Pikesville, and Richard Cromwell, of Baltimore.

(The remaining heirs of Caleb and Eleanor will be found in Howard County.)

THE HOWARDS, OF THE SEVERN.

An early certificate in the Land Office at Annapolis reads: "Laid out, July 3rd, 1650, for Matthew Howard, on the Severn, southside, near a creek called Marsh's, beginning at a hollow, called "Howard's Hollow," and binding on said creek, a tract containing 350 acres; also another tract running with Howard's swamp, containing 350 acres more." These surveys of Lloyd were not patented.

This record indicates clearly, that Matthew Howard came up with Edward Lloyd, in 1650. In support of this, the records of

Lower Norfolk County, Virginia, give us the following history of the Howards, of Virginia.

"There were three Howards, or Haywards, among the English members of the Virginia Companies," records Alexander Brown, in his "First Republic." "They were Master John, Rev. John, and Sir John Howard, Knight. They contributed, in all, £112 and 12s.

Master John, the historian, was born in Suffolk, in 1560; was D. C. L. of Cambridge; pleader in ecclesiastical courts; was knighted 1619, and an M. P. in 1621; married Jane Pascal; died in London 1627. His "Life of Edward VI." was published after his death.

Rev. John Howard, was reported in Stiths History of Virginia, as "John Howard, Clerk."

He subscribed £37. He was the author of "Strong Helper," in 1614.

Sir John Howard subscribed £75. He was the second son of Sir Rowland, by his second wife, Catherine Smythe. He was knighted at Windsor, July 23rd, 1609; was High Sheriff of Kent in 1642.

In 1622, a John Howard, who had come with Edward Bennett's first company, in 1621, was killed by the Indian massacre of 1622. His plantation formed the border line of the Isle of Wight, Virginia. From some of these Howards, members of the Virginia Company, descended Matthew Howard, a close friend, relative and neighbor of Edward and Cornelius Lloyd, in Virginia, and with the former, came to Maryland.

Matthew Howard was in Virginia, in 1635, as shown by a court record, in which he had a suit with Mr. Evans. In 1645, he was the executor of the will of Richard Hall, a merchant of Virginia, who, in 1610, was one of the "Grocers Court," of England, which contributed £100 toward the plantation in Virginia.

Colonel Cornelius Lloyd was a witness to Richard Hall's will, in 1645. The testator's property was left to Ann, Elizabeth, John, Samuel, Matthew and Cornelius Howard, children of Matthew and Ann Howard.

Philip Howard, the youngest son of Matthew and Ann, was evidently not born in 1645, for his name was not included in the list of legatees. But, in 1659, Commander Edward Lloyd surveyed for him, after the death of Matthew, the Severn tract of "Howard-stone," for "Philip Howard, Orphant."

In 1662, the sons of Matthew Howard, came up to the Severn, and seated themselves near their father's surveys. John, Samuel and Cornelius Howard, all transported a number of settlers, and received grants for the same upon the Severn. They located adjoining each other, near Round Bay.

In 1661, Henry Catlin, one of Edward Lloyd's commissioners, also, of the Nansemond Church, assigned his survey to Matthew Howard, Jr., who resurveyed the same, with "Hopkins Plantation" added, into "Howard's Inheritance."

In 1662, the five brothers, John, Samuel, Matthew, Cornelius and Philip, had nine hundred acres granted them as brothers.

It was upon one of these many hills of Severn, in the neighborhood of Round Bay, that John Howard slew the lion.

John Howard, heir-at-law of Matthew and namesake of his grandfather, John, was a progressive surveyor of lands. He located at Round Bay. In 1663, with Charles Stephens, he took up "The Woodyard" and "Charles Hills," on the south side of the Severn. Upon the death of Charles Stephens, John Howard married Susannah Stephens, the widow. She was the heir of Captain John Norwood. The only issue of John and Susannah Howard was Captain John Howard, Jr. John Howard, Sr., extended his surveys to Baltimore County, and took up "Timber Neck," upon the mouth of the Whetstone. It later became a part of Baltimore City. He also took up lands in Harford County. John Howard's second wife was Elinor, widow of John Maccubin, by whom there was no issue. She was of the Carroll family. Her daughter, Sarah Maccubin, became the wife of William Griffith, the immigrant. John Howard's will, of 1696, left his extensive estate to his son, John Howard, Jr., and to his wife's grandson, Orlando Griffith.

Captain John Howard, Jr., increased his father's estate by yearly surveys. About 1690, he married Mary, daughter of Richard and Elinor (Browne) Warfield, his neighbor on Round Bay. Their issue were Benjamin, Absolute and Rachel Howard, all minors at the death of his wife. Captain Howard married again, Katherine, widow of Henry Ridgely, and daughter of Colonel Nicholas Greenberry. Their only issue was one daughter, Katherine Howard. Mrs. Howard died before her husband, leaving five minors by her former husband, Henry Ridgely.

Captain John Howard soon followed her, and left, in 1704, the following will:

"I give unto my son, Benjamin Howard, my dwelling plantation, whereon I now do live, and all the land adjoining it, during his natural life, and to the lawful heirs of his body, and for want of such heirs, to go to the next of blood in the name.

"I give to my son Benjamin, 'Howard's Cove,' lying at Round Bay; also, a plantation on the Patapsco, bought of James Greeniffe, and another parcel, lying near the head of Bush River, and upon the branches of Deer Creek, containing four hundred acres, called 'Howard's Harbor,' and, also, a half part of 'Howard's Chance.'

"I give to my son, Absolute Howard, two tracts on Patapsco, called 'Yates Inheritance,' and "Howard's Point," also 'Howards Cattle Range,' south side of Patapsco on Mill Branch; also a tract on 'Bush River.' I give to my two daughters, Rachel Howard and Katherine Howard, all that parcel of land called "Howards Timber Neck,' lying at the mouth of Whetstone, to be equally divided between them, during their natural life, and to their lawful heirs, and, for want of such heirs, to my son Benjamin and his heirs.

I desire that the orphans of Mr. Henry Ridgely have their portion paid, according to their father's will, and I give to my son, Charles Ridgely, 'Howard Luck,' lying at Huntington, A. A. Co. I give to

Mr. Henry Ridgely's five children, twenty pounds apiece, to be paid them at the day of marriage, or at the age of twenty-one.

"I make and ordain my loving brothers, Mr. Richard Warfield and Mr. Alexander Warfield ,to be my full, whole and only executors of this my last will and testament. And my loving brothers, Mr. Charles Greenberry and John Hammond, I make and ordain overseers of this my will, and I give each of them thirty shillings to buy them a ring to wear for my sake. I desire my son Benjamin shall have my silver-headed cane, that has come in this year; and my son Absolute, shall have my silver tobacco box, that has my name on it; and my son-in-law (stepson), Henry Ridgely, shall have the other silver tobacco box, that has his father's name; and that Joshua Dorsey shall have my silver-hilted sword, that is at John Greeniffe's house, which his father Dorsey gave me. If you find three gold rings, given by me, I desire you to let Anne Ridgely have her first choice, and Betty and Rachel have the other ones. I desire to be buried by my father, on his left hand, and have the graveyard pailed.

"I desire you to send for a ring, equal in value to the others, for my daughter, Katherine Howard.

"I do advise that you take care that all the lands I have surveyed this year, have patents issued in the names of the orphans, I desire that you will give honorable satisfaction to my friend, Mr. Edward Rumney, for any trouble I may be when I draw my last breath, and that you will give his wife a ring at that period.

"I give to Mrs. Eleanor Howard, twenty shillings, to buy her a ring."   JOHN HOWARD. (SEAL.)

Witnesses: Joseph Hill, Cornelius Howard, Zachariah Taylor, Zachariah Maccubin, Benjamin Warfield, John Warfield, William Maccubin.

The above will was supplemented by seven codicils, as after thoughts, during this critical period, with both wives dead and nine young children to dispose of.

SAMUEL HOWARD.

There is still one living neighbor of the Severn, who remembers seeing, when a boy, the terraced grounds which surrounded the old stone house of Samuel Howard, and he read from the tombstone in the graveyard, the name of "Patience Howard, daughter of Samuel Howard." She was the daughter of the later Samuel Howard.

Samuel Howard married Catherine, daughter of James and Elizabeth Warner, daughter of William Harris, of South River. The will of James.Warner, names "his son Samuel Howard, to whom he left his cloth suit, and to his grandson Philip Howard, another suit of 'stuffe.' "

Peter Porter, the second, in his will names "his father Samuel Howard," and made him heir and executor. His wife was Sarah

Porter, daughter of Samuel Howard.   Samuel Howard's will, of 1703, throws considerable light on his family.   He named his wife, Catherine; his son Philip; his grandsons John and Samuel Maccubin, and his granddaughter, Elizabeth Maccubin, to whom he left £20 each.   To "cousin" John Howard, "cousin" John Hammond, "cousin's Sarah Brice, Hannah Hammond, Cornelius and Joseph Howard, and "cousin" Elizabeth Norwood, he left twenty shillings each. It is well known, all these "cousins" were his nephews and nieces. John Howard was the only son of John Howard, brother of the testator; John Hammond was the son of Major John Hammond, and Mary Howard his wife, sister of the testator.   Sarah Brice was the daughter of Matthew Howard, brother of the testator.   Hannah Hammond was the daughter of Philip Howard, another brother. Cornelius and Joseph Howard were the sons of his brother Cornelius, and Elizabeth Norwood was the wife of Andrew Norwood, and daughter of Cornelius Howard.   Samuel Howard made his nephews, John Hammond and John Howard, overseers of his will, with his son Philip, executor.   This will establishes, beyond question, that the above five Howards were brothers.   As executor of his father, Philip Howard had a case in Chancery, leading out of the will of his grandfather, James Warner, who left "Warner's Neck" to his daughter, Joanna Sewell, with the provision that it would descend to, and remain always in possession of·her heirs.   It was sold by her son, James Sewell, to Samuel Howard.   This sale was contested by other Sewell heirs, but the Rent Rolls show the same tract "in possession of Henry Pinkney, by his marriage to the widow of Philip Howard."   The latter died two years after his father and "Henry Pinkney, Cornelius Howard and Joseph Howard were made guardians of Samuel, James, Priscilla and Rachel Howard, children of Philip Howard."   Samuel, in 1744, married Patience Dorsey.   Annie Howard, of the city of Annapolis, in 1744, named her children Samuel, Harvey, Annie, Philip, Charles, Benjamin and Thomas Howard.

Samuel Howard married Miss Higginbottom.

CAPTAIN CORNELIUS HOWARD.

Named for Colonel Cornelius Lloyd, this Severn settler was made Ensign in command of the Severn.   From 1671 to 1675 he represented Anne Arundel County in the Legislative Assembly.   His colleagues were Robert Francklyn and Colonel Wm. Burgess.   This official position enabled him to increase his surveys and take up surveys for his neighbors.   He was frequently called upon to write the will and become a witness of the same for his neighbors.   He was sole executor and legatee of Wm. Carpenter, in 1676.   Captain John Sisson, in 1663, named Cornelius Howard, "my brother" and executor.   Mrs. Elizabeth Howard, wife of Cornelius, was "aunt" of Mary Todd, daughter of Lancelot.

Captain Cornelius, of 1680, left the homestead to his wife and son Joseph.   Captain Cornelius Howard, Jr., the boatwright, heired

adjoining lands.   The daughters were Sarah, Mary, the spinster, and
Elizabeth, wife of Andrew Norwood, whose daughter married John
Beale.

JOSEPH HOWARD, OF CAPTAIN CORNELIUS.

The homestead, near the old Indian trail, and a later survey of
"Howards Inheritance," became Joseph's estate in Anne Arundel.
He was twice married: first to Anne Burroughs, widow of Joseph
Burroughs, who held land on South River; second to Margery Keith.
Joseph Howard took up, for his sons, the following tracts in Howard
County, in the neighborgood of Clarksville.   In 1722, he and others
took up a tract of 2,590 acres, called "Discovery."   This was fol-
lowed by 500 acres known as "Howards Passage," in 1728.   And
"Joseph's Hazard," of 100 acres, in 1727.   His will of 1736, records:
"I give to my son, Henry Howard, "Kil-Kenny" and "Howards
Hazard" adjoining, out of a tract of "Howards Passage," and 300
acres of "The Second Discovery."   I give to son Ephriam, 500 acres
of "Discovery."   (This was later deeded by Ephriam to his brother
Henry).   I give to my son Joseph, 200 acres called "Discovery,"
adjoining Ephriam.   I give to my son Cornelius the remainder of
said "Discovery," and 400 acres of "Howard's Passage."   I give
to Joseph the plantation on which I now live, known as "Howards
Inheritance," 380 acres, and it is my desire that my friend, Dr.
Richard Hill, will instruct in the knowledge of phisick, and be his
guardian.   I give to my grandson, Joseph Higgins, 100 acres of "The
Second Discovery."   To daughter Sarah, was left money; to daughter
Ruth Duvall, and daughter Hannah Jacob, twenty shillings each.
I desire my friends, Colonel Henry Ridgely, Joshua Dorsey, and John
Dorsey, of Edward, to be overseers to look after the interests of my
sons."   JOSEPH HOWARD.

Witnesses: John Howard, John Burgess, William Phelps.

Margery Howard, his widow, in 1739, gave to her sons, Cornelius, Ephriam, Joseph Howard, and daughter Sarah, a number
of negroes.

In 1737-8, Ephriam Howard deeded his portion of "Discovery"
to his brother Henry.   This tract was on the east and south of Carrolls Manor.   500 arces of the original body of 2,590 acres, were
patented to John Beale; 1090 acres, to Joseph Howard; 200 acres,
to Abel Browne; 800 acres, to Thomas Bordley.   The tract known
as "Second Discovery" began at a line of "Altogether," which was
on the western border of Carroll's Manor, and extended west and
north toward Glenelg and West Friendship.   It was surveyed for
John Beale, Vachel Denton, Priscilla Geist and Joseph Howard, and
patented to Vachel Denton and Joseph Howard, who held 910 acres.
Denton sold his interest to William Worthington.   Joseph Howard,
Jr., was the only one who remained in Anne Arundel County.   His
will, of 1783, granted to his wife one-half of the dwelling place,
"Howards' Inheritance," a part of "Rich Neck" and "Chaney's

Hazard." After her death it was to go to Joseph Howard, Jr., and Margery, wife of Major Henry Hall; to son Benjamin the other half of the above lands. "It is my will that Benjamin give up his claim to his part of his grandmother's, Margaret Gaither's estate, willed to him by her, and he is to receive no part of my personal estate, but that it be divided equally between my granddaughter, Margaret Howard, daughter of my son Joseph, and my grandson Henry, son of my daughter Margery, wife of Henry Hall. To grandson Thomas Rutland, son of my daughter Mary, one shilling. To my son Joseph, all my tract lying at South River, known as "Howard's Angle." If Benjamin will not make over his grandmother's part, then Joseph is to have Benjamin's part." Richard Burgess, Charles Stewart, Jr., and Samuel Burgess, witnesses.

Mrs. Joseph Howard was Margaret Williams, daughter of Mrs. Margaret Gaither, widow of Edward. She inherited "Folkland." Joseph Howard, Jr., gave to his daughters the old dwelling house, whereon, as tenant, lived Richard Rawlins. After them, it was to go to Joseph Howard his son, his wife, Martha Howard, and brother Benjamin, executors. She was Martha Hall, daughter of Rev. Henry Hall, of St. James Parish. She later married Nicholas Hall. Benjamin Howard, brother of the above testator, left his estate of 500 acres to Joseph, of Joseph, and a part of the dwelling and residence to his nieces, Elizabeth, Eleanor, Martha, Margery and Kitty, and to his nephew, John Washington Hall; sister Martha Howard, widow of brother Joseph, executrix.

JOSEPH HOWARD, OF "HOWARD'S GROVE."

In 1836, the above testator left his "Mansion House" to his wife Catherine, with power to control it as he was accustomed to do, and to live in the same style; to command servants, horses and teams at her will; sons Thomas and Joseph, to assist her in its management; daughters Elizabeth, Margaret and son Allen, all to hold their interests in common. The property to be held together until the marriage of all his daughters, and then to be divided. He desired that all of his children should be baptised, and paid a high tribute to his wife. Robert Welsh, of Benjamin, Thomas G. Waters and John Thomas were witnesses. A codicil, modifying some of the provisions, was witnessed by Richard Duckett, Martha Howard and Thomas Duckett.

The above testator has been recorded in "The Bowies and Their Kindred," as descending from Matthew Howard, of Matthew, as seen by the following quotations, "Matthew Howard, of Matthew, of 1650, through his son Joseph Howard, who married Martha Hall, daughter of Rev. Henry Hall, of the Episcopal ministry, of England, left Joseph Howard, Jr., born 1786, who married Elizabeth Susannah Bowie, daughter of Captain Fielder Bowie. Issue: Dr. Joseph Howard, of 1811, married Eleanor, daughter of William Digges Clagett and Sarah Young; second Thomas Contee Bowie Howard, born 1812, married Louisa, daughter of John Selby Spence, of Worcester Co., United States Senator. Issue: Margaret Louisa Howard, married Nicholas T. Watkins, of Howard Co.; Thomas Contee Bowie Howard, Jr., married Sally Stevens, of Cambridge, and lived near Annapolis; third Margaret Howard, married Dr. Thomas S. Duckett. Issue: Marion and Ella Duvall; Allen Bowie Howard, of Joseph, Jr., married Anna Maria Spence, sister of his brother's wife and lived at "Mulberry Grove," Anne Arundel. Issue: John Spence Howard, married Mary E. Hodges. Issue: Mary, John Spence, Jr., Margaret, Ellen Howard, Sophia and James Hodges Howard; Allan Bowie Howard married Rose Alexander, of Philadelphia; Sarah Maria Howard." Captain Thos. Howard, the popular commander of the Oyster Navy, under both Governors Smith and Warfield, descends from this branch of Howards.

CAPTAIN PHILIP HOWARD.

"Our Early Settlers" notes the arrival of Philip Howard, in 1669, and his demand for fifty acres for transporting himself. In 1659, a grant was made to Philip Howard, orphan," under the title of "Howard's Stone." This was on the north side of the Severn, adjoining Edward Lloyd. Philip Howard bought lands also from Cornelius Howard, on the south side of the Severn. He bought, also, from Robert Proctor. He was one of Her Majesty's Justices in 1694, and during that same year, was a commissioner in laying off the town of Annapolis. He married Ruth Baldwin, daughter of John Baldwin, and Elizabeth, his wife. She was a sister of John Baldwin, who married Hester (Larkin) Nicholson, and also a sister of Mrs. Thomas Cruchley, of Annapolis. She was the aunt of Anne Baldwin, wife of Judge Samuel Chase and Hester, wife of Judge Jeremiah Townley Chase.

Captain Philip and Ruth Howard had one daughter, Hannah, who married her cousin, Charles Hammond. In his will, of 1701, Captain Howard named his grandsons, Charles and Philip Hammond, sons of his daughter, Hannah. Mrs. Ruth Howard was made executrix. The Rent Rolls record: "Ruth Howard, relict of Captain Philip Howard, enters a tract of land called 'Green Spring,' purchased by said Howard from Robert Proctor. She also claims 'Maiden,' and 'Howard and Porters Range,'—conveyed from Cornelius Howard to said Philip; also a tract called 'The Marsh.' She further claims that Cornelius Howard, Sr., left a portion of 'Howard and Porter's Range' to Mary Howard, spinster, and that she conveyed it to Cornelius Howard, Jr., who conveyed it to her husband, Philip Howard." All of these claims stand as demanded.

From Hannah Howard, only daughter of Philip and Ruth (Baldwin) Howard, descended a long line of Hammonds, the largest land holders in both Howard and Anne Arundel Counties.

MATTHEW HOWARD.

Matthew Howard, Jr., was in the province as early as his brothers, in 1662. Yet the following record from "Our Early Settlers" refers to him: "May 7th, 1667, Matthew Howard demanded land for transporting Sarah Darcy, his wife, John Pine, Thomas Gleve, Thomas Madloe, Wm. Cooke, Joseph Windoes, Sarah Driven, Elizabeth Warrenton, Samuel Doyle, Joane Garnish. Warrant, then issued in the name of Matthew Howard, for five hundred acres of land due him for transportation of said persons."

Matthew Howard surveyed and bought extensively upon the neck of the Severn and Magothy Rivers. He was an associate justice of the county, and upon the committee of the port of entry. Two sons and one daughter were his heirs. John held "Howard's First Choice," which he and his wife Susannah, transferred to Lancelot Todd, in 1698. He resided upon the Magothy. St. Margaret's Parish shows the births of his sons, Matthew, John and Abner. He died in 1702, when his widow, the same year, married William Crouch, who held "Poplar Plains," suryeved in 1683, by Matthew Howard, Sr., for Matthew Howard, Jr., the minor. The two sons of John and Susannah Howard, were progressive surveyors in the upper districts of Baltimore and Anne Arundel Counties. They made the following record in Annapolis: "Matthew Howard and John Howard, of Baltimore County, planters, eldest sons of John Howard and grandsons of Matthew Howard, both of Anne Arundel, and Ruth Howard, wife of said John Howard, grant to John Brice, "Hopkins Plantation," northwest of the Severn; said land assigned to Matthew Howard, in 1663."

John Howard, also, sold "Left Out," a tract near Dayton, Howard County, to John Gaither. Ruth Howard, his wife, was the widow, first of Edward Dorsey, and second of Greeniffe. Her will of 1747, named her sons, and executors John and Edward Dorsey; her grandson, John Greeniffe Howard, and her granddaughter Elizabeth Hammond. She was then residing near her sons, or with them, at Columbia, Howard County.

Sarah Howard, only daughter of Matthew and Sarah Darcey, inherited a large portion of her father's Severn estate; finally, by her two marriages to Captain John Worthington and Captain John Brice, she held all of the estate; dying in 1735, in the old Worthington homestead, just opposite the Naval Academy. Matthew Howard, her brother, held by the will of his father, in 1692, "Hopkins Plantation," "Poplar Plains" and "The Adventure," on the Patuxent. He sold, in 1728, "Poplar Plains" to Anne Price, and left no other records at Annapolis. Matthew Howard, of Frederick County, sold lands to Edward Dorsey, the attorney of Annapolis. There was, also, a Matthew Howard, of Kent County, "who left a considerable estate to his heirs." He named in his will, several tracts in Anne Arundel. I have not followed these testators.

HENRY HOWARD, THE BACHELOR.

Henry Howard, of Anne Arundel, appeared as a witness for John Homewood, in a case brought by the latter against Sheriff John Welsh. Henry Howard held lands on the Gunpowder River, but he is recorded as a resident of Anne Arundel. In his will of 1683, he left to "John Howard his wearing apparel," and to "John Howard and to Matthew Howard, of Anne Arundel, each a silver seal ring." To John Bennett and Sarah, his wife, "a seal ring with the coat of arms," and a hooked ring with the initials F. C." (The above Sarah wife of John Bennett, was the widow of John Homewood, and the daughter of Thomas Meeres, the Quaker, of Edward Lloyd's commissioners, in 1650.) He also left "to Sarah Dasey, wife of Joseph Dasey, two hundred acres of land upon the Gunpowder." His personal estate was granted to Edward Skidmore, Elizabeth Skidmore and Michael Skidmore. To Theophilus Hackett, his administrator, he left a pair of silk stockings and sixteen hundred pounds of tobacco. Richard Howard was a witness. Edward Skidmore, gentleman, of Cecil, left a remembrance to his friend, Henry Howard, and made the above Skidmores legatees.

This testator was evidently a connection of the five Howard brothers, and may have been the traditional "Sir Henry Howard," to whom descendants of a later namesake refer.

CAPTAIN CORNELIUS HOWARD, JR.

As a mariner he held but a small estate in realty. He was of the vestry of St. Anne's church, upon its organization, in 1696, with Thomas Bland, Richard Warfield, Jacob Harness and William Brown. His wife was Mary Hammond. The will of her mother, Mary (Heath) Hammond, in 1721, named her grandson, John Howard, granddaughter, Sarah Howard; grandson, Thomas Howard; granddaughter, Eleanor Howard; grandson, Cornelius Howard.

Mrs. Cornelius Howard died in 1714, and her husband in 1716. His will reads: "My son Charles, is already provided for. To my son John Howard, my lands on the Choptank. To my son Thomas Howard, my lands on the Patapsco. To Cornelius, the homestead."

His son Charles died in 1717. His will reads: "I give to my brother Thomas one-half of a tract conveyed to me by Richard Freeborne, called "Freeborne's Progress," in Baltimore County. To brother Thomas I give my part after my brother, Cornelius Howard, has had his moiety mentioned in a deed of a gift to my said brother."

"This gift to my brother Thomas, is to be void unless he gives a tract left by his father on the Patapsco, to such person my wife, Mary Howard, shall sell the said tract of fifty acres to. I authorize my wife Mary, to sell my lands on the Patapsco, called "Roger's Increase," and the money thus raised, to be paid over to my brother Thomas, as a part which I gave him by deed of gift, not signed.

"To my wife Mary and son Benjamin, all my personal estate, and appoint her my executrix." Witnesses, Jno. Beale, Jno. Cunningham and James Howard.

Thomas Howard surveyed "Hazard" in 1724, adjoining lands laid out for Samuel Dorsey. In 1731, he sold the same to Mr. Wright, who sold to William Cumming. The will of Thomas Howard, in 1771, left all his estate to his wife Anne, and made her executrix. Cornelius Howard, of Captain Cornelius, Jr., lived upon the homestead in Anne Arundel. His wife was Elizabeth, and their son, Cornelius Howard, was born in 1728. A Thomas Howard of this line and his wife, Priscilla Selby, were granted "Freeborn's Progress" by Robert and Sarah Ridgely, of Elkridge, which they sold to Mr. Peele, in 1728. In the deed of transfer, Robert Ridgely stated it came to his wife by inheritance.

Still later, a Thomas Howard married Ruth Dorsey, daughter of Elias and Mary Lawrence, daughter of Benjamin Lawrence, of "Delaware Hundred."

COLONEL HENRY RIDGELY.

From the manuscript of Judge Nicholas Ridgely, of Delaware, now in possession of Mrs. Henry Ridgely, of Dover, and from the records of Annapolis, I find the Ridgelys, of Annapolis, and of Delaware, descended from the "Hon. Henry Ridgely, of Devonshire, England, who settled in Maryland, in 1659, upon a royal grant of 6,000 acres. He became a Colonel of Militia, member of the Assembly of the Governmental Council, Justice of the Peace, and Vestryman of the Parish Church of St. Ann's."

The above is taken from the Ridgely manuscript of a grandson, and confirms the record made by Mr. Creagar, who indexed "Our Early Settlers." He assumed that the following record was intended for the above Colonel Henry Ridgely: "Henry Ridley demands lands for transporting himself, which is entered in Burles book, and Elizabeth Howard, his wife, and John Hall, Stephen Gill, Richard Ravens and Jane his servants, in the year 1659."

The next entry is 1661, when "James Wardner (Warner) and Henry Ridgely were granted a certificate for 600 acres, called 'Wardridge,' on the north side of South River, joining a tract, 'Broome,' formally Richard Beard's, adjoining Neale Clarke's."

In 1665, James Warner assigned his right to Henry Ridgely. This transfer was one of the burnt records of 1704. It was restored by Colonel Charles Greenberry, in the interest of his sister's children.

Judge Nicholas Ridgely's bible-record throws more light on Colonel Henry Ridgely's wife; it reads thus, "Nicholas Ridgely, son of Henry, (who was the son of Colonel Henry and Sarah, his wife), and Catherine, his wife, (who was the daughter of Colonel Nicholas Greenberry and Ann, his wife), all of Anne Arundel County, in the Province of Maryland), the said Nicholas was born the 12th day of February, A. D., 1694, and was married to Sarah Worthington, (the daughter of Captain John and Sarah, his wife, of Anne Arundel County, aforesaid), the 26th day of December, 1711."

This record shows that if Colonel Henry Ridgely's wife was Elizabeth Howard, she was not the mother of Colonel Ridgely's son Henry. His mother evidently belonged to the house of James Warner and Elizabeth Harris, his wife. In 1679, Henry Ridgely, Sr., was commissioned associate Justice of Anne Arundel; in 1689, he was appointed "Captain of the Foote"; in 1692, he was a member of the Lower House; in 1694, he was promoted Major, and in the same year was advanced to Colonel in the Militia. In 1685, Colonel Henry surveyed "Ridgely's Forrest." It covered all the land surrounding Annapolis Junction and Savage Factory. In 1699, he granted to his son Henry, 220 acres of "Broome" and 200 acres of "Wardridge." Upon this combined plantation, Henry Ridgely, Jr., having removed from his Annapolis homestead, died in early manhood, thirty years of age, in 1699. There in the reserved graveyard stood, for years, the well preserved tablet to his memory. In 1702, Colonel Henry sold Charles Carroll "the house and lot in Annapolis, lately in the tenture of my son, adjoining the lots of Charles and Rachel Kilburne." In 1696, Colonel Henry Ridgely married Mary (Stanton) Duvall, widow of Mareen Duvall, the Huguenot, and with her administered on Duvall's estate. He then removed across the river to Prince George's County, where he became a merchant. His will, written in 1705, with codicils, was probated in 1710. It reads: "I give to my wife Mary, my home, plantation, 'Cotton'; 'Mary's Delight' and 'Larkin's Folly,' which I bought of Thomas Larkin, to an unborn child. To son Charles Ridgely, all that plantation called 'Hogg Neck,' and 300 acres of 'Ridgely's Lot,' lying at 'Huntington, A. A.', excepting lands sold to Thomas Reynolds and Neale Clarke, near Wm. Griffiths. I give also, to son Charles, 300 acres of 'Wardridge,' adjoining 'Hogg Neck.' My wearing apparel to my brother, William, and my son, Charles. 'Larkin Forrest,' if there be no heir, to be divided between Henry Ridgely and Nicholas Ridgely, sons of his deceased son, Henry, and Henry, son of his son, Charles Ridgely. The remaining part of 'Wardridge,' to go to grandson, Henry Ridgely, son of Henry, deceased, after Charles had 300 acres out of it. If 'Mary's Delight' is not possessed by an heir, it is to be divided between John Brewer, Joseph Brewer, Thomas Odall and Henry Odall, sons of Thomas Odall, (elsewhere written Odell). I give to my daughter, Sarah Odall, wife of Thomas, a negroe girl; to all my grandchildren, £10; to my god-daughter, Martha Duvall, £51, and a cow and calf. To St. Barnabas Church, Queen Parish, Prince George, £20. Grandsons, Henry and Nicholas Ridgely, to be under the care of Thomas Odall and Charles Greenberry, until of age. The remaining part, whether here or in England, to go to my wife and executrix." Witnesses were Louis Duvall and Thomas Reynolds.

The will of John Brewer mentions his wife, Sarah, his sons, John and Joseph, and his father, Henry Ridgely, whom he made his executor, with his wife Sarah.

"Wardridge," or "Waldridge," and "Broome" the inheritance of Henry Ridgely, the second, lay southwest of "Hockley," on the road leading to the head of South River. In its old graveyard, which had been reserved, stood the following tablet:

"Here lyeth the body of Mr. Henry
Ridgely, who was born the 3rd of
Oct., 1669, and departed this life on
ye 19th day of March, 1700."

Having been fractured by the encroachment of a neighboring settler, the "Peggy Stewart Chapter of the Colonial Dames," ordered its removal to the grounds of St. Ann's Church, Annapolis. His widow, Katherine (Greenberry) Ridgely, his executrix, later married Captain John Howard, who named in his will, 1704, "the five orphans of Henry Ridgely," and requested his executors to grant them their portions, as expressed in the will of their father. They were: Henry Ridgely, the third, later, known as Colonel Henry Ridgely, of Howard County; Judge Nicholas Ridgely, of Delaware; Charles Ridgely, who inherited "Howard Luck" from Captain John Howard, and died soon after; Ann Ridgely, wife of Joshua Dorsey, and Elizabeth, wife of Thomas Worthington; Nicholas Ridgely, of Henry and Katherine, married Sarah Worthington; lived, after marriage, on "Wyatt's Ridge." Upon a portion of this stands "Belvoir," in sight of Round Bay. He also inherited a portion of "Ridgely's Forrest," near Guilford, Howard County. Upon removing first to Cecil County, he sold the former tract to his brother-in-law, John Worthington, Jr., and his wife's inheritance on the Severn, to her mother, Mrs. Sarah Brice. The heirs of Nicholas and Sarah, all named in his bible record, were, Sarah, Rebecca, Rachel, Ruth and Ann. His wife died in 1721. His daughter, Rebecca, was married "Where I lived in Cecil Co., Md., on Wed., October, 1731, to Benjamin Warfield, son of Mr. John Warfield, of Anne Arundel, Md. by the Rev. Richard Sewell, Rector of Shrewsberry Parrish, Kent Co., Md."

The will of Mrs. Brice, in 1725, named her granddaughter, Rebecca Ridgely, to whom she left, "one quart silver tankard, one dozen silver spoons, and £50, in money." Similar legacies were given to her sisters. In 1727, Mr. Nicholas Ridgely's wife was Ann French Gordon, daughter of Robert French, and widow of James Gordon. She bore him one daughter, Mary, who, became Mrs, Patrick Martain. In 1727, Nicholas and Ann Ridgely' of Cecil County, sold to John Brown, his inheritance "Ridgely's Forrest,' which was re-surveyed into "Browne's Purchase." His daughter Rachel, became the wife of John Vining, Speaker of Delaware Assembly, who owned a large estate in New Jersey. On one of his visits there, he was taken sick, died, and was buried at St. John's Church, Salem. Under the aisle, a stone with an inscription, marks the sepulcher. Mrs. Rachel Vining died in 1753, and was buried under the pew of her father, Judge Ridgely, in Christ Church, Dover.

In 1741, Governor George Thomas, commissioned Nicholas Ridgely as follows: "Reposing a special trust in your loyalty and courage, I have nominated you to be Captain of the Militia Foote, in the upper part of the county of Kent. You are, therefore, to take said Company into your charge, as Captain, and duly exercise both the officers and soldiers in arms, and for so doing, this is your commission. Given under my hand and seal as arms, at the town of New Castle, on the Delaware, 3rd Feb., 1741.

GEORGE THOMAS."

Governor Warfield, a descendant, has the original commission in his possession.

In 1745, Judge Ridgely became the guardian of Caesar Rodney, who later became the most distinguished patriot of the state. To his training, also, was due the successful careers of his son, Dr. Charles Ridgely, and of the brilliant John Vining, his wife's grandson,

Quoting again from the Ridgely manuscript: "Nicholas Ridgely second son of Henry Ridgely, was born at 'Wardridge,' in 1694. He was thirty-eight years of age when he moved to 'Eden Hill,' a handsome plantation near Dover. Mr. Ridgely at once took his place among the leading citizens of his adopted state, filling, with honor, the offices of Kent County, Clerk of the Peace, Justice of the Peace, Prothonatory, Register in Chancery, Judge of the Supreme Court of New Castle, Kent and Sussex Counties; enjoying the honor until his death, in 1755. In 1735, as foreman of the Grand Jury he signed a petition to King George II, against granting a charter to Lord Baltimore, in abrogation of the rights of the Penn family, in the three lower counties."

In 1743, his daughters, Sarah and Rachel, granted a power of attorney, attested by Nicholas Ridgely and Rebecca Warfield, to their uncle, Henry Ridgely, to receive legacies from their grandmother's estate. They were then located, "in Kent Co., on the Delaware, in Territories of Pennsylvania." Judge Ridgely's third wife was Mary Middleton Vining, widow of Captain Benjamin Vining, a lady who held a large estate. Her son, Judge John Vining, married Phoebe Wyncoop. Their son, John, was "the Patrick Henry of Delaware," of brilliant wit, lawyer, member of the first Continental Congress, and "the pet of Delaware." His sister, the beautiful Mary Vining, the admiration of General LaFayette, became the bethrothed wife of General Anthony Wayne, who died before the wedding day. Judge Ridgely's daughter, Elizabeth, became the second wife of Col. Thomas Dorsey, of Elk Ridge.

Dr. Charles Ridgely, of Judge Nicholas and Mary, was born in 1738. He became an eminent physician, residing at "Eden Hill," but later in the house upon "The Green," purchased by Judge Ridgely, in Dover. His son, Nicholas, by his first wife, Mary Wyncoop, was the first chancellor of Delaware, universally respected as an able jurist, a courteous gentleman of the old school, in dress and demeanor, holding to provincial customs.

Dr. Charles Ridgely's second wife, Ann Moore, bore him five children. Henry Moore Ridgely, his oldest son, succeeded to the homestead, in 1735; he was admitted to the bar, in 1802; was in Congress, in 1811; Secretary of State, 1817, and again in 1820 He there collected the scattered archives of the State. Repeatedly elected to the Legislature, he framed the most important laws of the State. In 1827, he was sent to the United States Senate, where he advocated a high protective tariff. He died in the old house on "The Green," upon his eighty-second birthday, 1847. He left five children. His oldest son, Henry (V.) Ridgely, in 1889, was in serene old age, an honored resident of Dover, and "Eden Hill." His brother, Henry Ridgely, was the father of Henry Ridgely (V), a prominent lawyer, of Dover. He married Matilda Lloyd, a descendant of the distinguished Maryland family, a notice of whom will be found in the list of governors. They occupy the family homestead, the exterior of which is severely plain. The interior is captivating. The floral designs of the low ceilings, are the work of a Dover artist. The delicate tints of the drawing room walls, and the artistic hangings of the guest chamber, contrast harmoniously with the dark panelings of the wide hall, which is also the library, in which is a chair known as William Penn's. In the garden, where the box bushes have grown in a century or more, into great trees and hedges, on the top of which one may walk fearlessly, as upon a wall, Judge Nicholas Ridgely and his family liked to take tea, all summer long. A rear view of the Ridgely house reveals a cluster of ivy."—MARION HARLAND.

Henry Ridgely, of Henry and Katherine, of "Wardridge," on coming to manhood, in 1711, sold his homestead to his brother-in-law, Thomas Worthington, and removed to his grand-father's extensive survey, at Huntington. His biography will be found in the history of Howard County.

Sarah Ridgely, only daughter of Colonel Henry, first became the wife of John Brewer, and after his death, she married Thomas Odell. A sketch of the Brewer family will be found elsewhere.

WILLIAM RIDGELY, OF SOUTH RIVER.

William Ridgely came to this province of Maryland, in 1672. Colonel Henry's will shows him to be his brother. His first survey, in 1697, was "Ridgely's Beginning," northside of South River. In 1690, he bought, of James Finley, a portion of "Abbington," at the head of South River, and made it his homestead.

William and Elizabeth Ridgely, his wife, sold in 1710, "Ridgely's Beginning," to Amos Garrett, the Annapolis merchant. Only one son, William Ridgely, Jr., was named by them. Upon his marriage to Jane Westall, daughter of George Westall, of South River, in 1702, William Ridgely, Sr., and Elizabeth, his wife, deeded to William Ridgely, Jr., and Jane, his wife, their homestead tract, "Abington." During that same year, another deed for a portion of the home tract was made by William Ridgely, Sr., and Elizabeth, his wife, and William Ridgely, Jr., and Jane, his wife, to Mrs. Mary Ridgely, late widow of Colonel Henry.

William Ridgely, Sr., died in 1716, as shown by his testamentary record, intestate, William Ridgely, Jr., also died intestate. His widow, Jane (Westall) Ridgely, left a will in 1748.

Upon a twelve hundred acre tract of her father's estate, Colonel Wm. Burgess located the once flourishing town of London. In his will of 1686, he named this tract as once the property of "Mr. George Westall, upon a portion of which is a town laid out, called Londontown."

Mrs. Jane (Westall) Ridgely named her heirs, William, Westall, Sarah, John, Martha Maccubbin and Alice Woodward.

John Ridgely was made executor, and heired the homestead, "Abington." He married Elizabeth Mayo, of South River, and bought of "Edward Gaither, of 'Edward,' the whole of 'Gaithers Collection.' "

Westall Ridgely inherited "Ridgely's Chance," in Frederick County, and in his will of 1772, named his heirs, Sarah, William, Jane, Deverella, Isaac, Jacob, Alice, Martha, Richard and Jemima.

William Ridgely, the third, in 1726, married Mary Orrick, daughter of James and Priscilla (Ruley) Orrick. By the will of Anthony Ruley, of South River, 1710, his daughter, Priscilla Orrick, came into possession of "Beetenson's Adventure," on South River. This tract was taken up by Edward Beetenson and Lydia Watkins, his wife. By the will of James Orrick, his daughter Mary Orrick inherited one-third of his estate. Her mother, inheriting one-third, became the wife of Abraham Woodward, son of William Woodward, of London. William Woodward (of Abraham), married Alice Ridgely, daughter of William and Jane (Westall) Ridgely. William Woodward, Jr.,—Jane, daughter of William and Mary (Orrick) Ridgely. Their son Henry, born 1770, married Eleanor, widow of Philip Turner, and daughter of Colonel Thomas Williams by his wife, Rachel Duckett. Their daughter, Jane Maria, became the wife of Judge William Henry Baldwin, of Anne Arundel, and the mother of a distinguished family of merchants.

William and Mary (Orrick) Ridgely, had issue William, Nicholas, John, Henry, Greenberry, Priscilla Griffith, Jane Woodward, Mary Pumphrey, Sophia Pumphrey and Ann Rigby. William Ridgely's will, of 1768, probated in 1780, granted to sons John, Henry and Greenberry, four tracts of land, "Ridgely's Chance," "Spanish Oak," "Good Luck" and "Piney Grove." One-third of his estate was left to his wife Mary.

Greenberry Ridgely, youngest son of William and Mary (Orrick) Ridgely, born 1745, married Rachel Ryan, daughter of John Ryan, who held an estate on Elk Ridge. She joined him in deeding his estate upon South River, and with him removed to Elk Ridge, where Rev. Greenberry Ridgely took charge of a Methodist Church. About 1800, he moved to Baltimore and became a merchant. His sons were Lloyd, Lot, Noah, Silas, Greenberry, Isaac, James and Nicholas, born 1800. This last son removed to Springfield, Illinois, where he acquired a large estate. His son and successor, Mr. Charles Ridgely, of the Springfield ironworks, and president of a bank, married Miss Barret, daughter of James Winston Barret, son of Captain William and Dorothy (Winston) Barret. Their son Hon. James Barret Ridgely, is now Comptroller of the Currency.

Greenberry Ridgely, Jr., in 1814, married Harriet Talbott, descendant of Richard and Elizabeth (Ewen) Talbott, daughter of Maj. Richard Ewen. Harriet Talbott's father was Benjamin Talbott. whose wife was Sarah Willmot—son of Edward Talbott and Temperance Merryman, his wife, son of Edward Talbott and Mary Waters, his wife, son of Edward Talbott and Elizabeth (Thomas) Coale, his wife, son of Richard Talbott, the immigrant.

Greenberry and Harriet Ridgely had issue: Charles W. Ridgely, of Lutherville; James H. Ridgely, the "Odd Fellow," grandfather of Mrs. Frank Brown; Dr. Benjamin Rush Ridgely, of Warren, Baltimore County, now over three-quarters of a century old, yet a vigorous writer and able genealogist.

Alice Ridgely, of William and Jane (Westall) Ridgely, will be found in the Woodward sketch; so will Jane Ridgely, of Mrs. Mary (Orrick) Ridgely.

RICHARD WARFIELD, FIRST VESTRYMAN OF ST. ANN'S CHURCH.

A Warfield record, one hundred years old, states that "Richard Warfield settled near Annapolis, in 1639." There was no settlement there until 1649, and Richard Warfield was not one of those settlers. He came among them, however, in 1662, and located west of Crownsville, Anne Arundel, "in the woods." His estate. reached back to the beautiful sheet of water,—Round Bay, of the Severn. Our Rent Rolls show that he held, during his life, "Wayfield," "Warfield's Right," "Hope," "Increase," "Warfield's Plains," "Warfield's Forest," "Warfield's Addition," "Brandy," "and "Warfield's Range."

In 1670, he married Elinor, heiress of Captain John Browne, of London, who, with his brother, Captain Peregrine Browne, ran two of the best equipped merchant transports between London and Annapolis.

Richard Warfield's wife inherited "Hope" and "Increase." two adjoining tracts, the history of which is as follows:

They were taken up by Henry Sewell; transferred by him to John Minter; willed by him to his daughter, Elizabeth, wife of Henry Winchester. These two joined in deeding them, in 1673, to Captain John Browne, mariner, of London. No further transfers are to be found, but in 1705, Richard Warfield appeared before the commission, to restore the burnt record of 1704, and requested a record of the above history.

In 1675, Richard and Elinor Warfield were summoned as witnesses to the chancery contest over the will of their immediate neighbor, Nicholas Wyatt. In 1689, Richard Warfield signed, as a military officer, the address to King William. In 1696, Richard Warfield's name was returned as one of the Vestry of St. Ann's Church. This was before the first building was completed. Dying at an advanced age, in 1703-04, he left an intelligent will, in which he named his heirs, John, Richard, Alexander, Benjamin, (Mary, late wife of Captain John Howard), Rachel, then wife of George Yates; Elinor, the prospective bride of Caleb Dorsey, of "Hockley."

In his old age, he began the first westward movement of the early settlements to the unexplored frontier of Howard. His sons and executors, in 1704, resurveyed "Warfield's Range," and increased it to fifteen hundred acres. John, his oldest son, lived upon "Warfield's Plains," the homestead of which still stands just opposite Baldwin Memorial Church, half-way between Waterbury and Indian Landing. "Warfield's Plains" extended up to Millersville, and "Warfield's Forest" was near Indian Landing. In 1696, John married Ruth Gaither, oldest daughter of John Gaither, of South River. Their sons were Richard, John, Benjamin, Alexander, Edward and Philip, all of whom located upon the frontier out-posts, in Howard. John Warfield's daughters were Ruth, wife of Richard Davis; Mary, wife of Augustine Marriott and Elinor who died a maiden. John Warfield, like his father, passed his life in developing his estate, but died in early manhood, 1718, before completing his surveys and transfers. His son, Richard, as heir-at-law, deeded his estate to his brothers. Returning to the homestead, he married Marion Caldwell, and had issue, John, Seth, Richard and Luke Warfield. The first two were located upon "Warfield's Range." Richard and Luke remained upon the Severn.

Richard Warfield, by his second marriage to Sarah Gambrill, of Augustine, had Joseph and Rachel who became the wife of Philip Turner. Their son, Richard Warfield Turner, heired the homestead from Joseph Warfield, his uncle, who died a bachelor.

Richard Warfield, Jr. was a vestryman of St. Ann's Church, in 1751. His estate was "Warfield's Forest." By his wife, Hamutel Marriott, he had Richard, Luke, Silvanus and John, none of whom left any descendants of their name. The homestead was willed to Joshua Gambrill.

Ruth Warfield, of John and Ruth, married Richard Davis, from whom descended Captain Richard Davis, Caleb, Thomas, Ruth and Elizabeth, wife of John Marriott.

Mary Warfield, of John and Ruth, married Augustine Marriott. Their son John married Nancy Warfield, of Alexander, and Dinah (Davidge) Warfield: Achsah Marriott—John Hall, of "White Hall," whose daughter, Sarah Hall, became Mrs. Francis Rawlings, and second wife of Captain Harry Baldwin.

Mary Marriott married John Sewell whose descendants are noted in the Sewells.

Sarah Marriott, youngest daughter of Augustine, married William Yealdhall, leaving no heirs. Their estate was left to Thomas Furlong.

RICHARD WARFIELD, THE SECOND.

By the will of Richard Warfield, Sr., his son Richard, after the marriage of his sister, Elinor, came to the homestead.

In 1723, he was one of the first organizers of the public school system of the county. He was for many years "one of his lordship's justices." He was also, in the Vestry of St. Ann's, from 1710 to 1729. He married, about 1700, Ruth, daughter of Thomas Cruchley, an attorney of Annapolis. Her mother was Margaret Baldwin, daughter of John and Elizabeth Baldwin. Richard and Ruth had one son, Alexander Warfield. Their daughter, Ruth, became Mrs. Jos. Hall. Rachel became Mrs. Robert Davidge, and Lydia became the wife of Dr. Samuel Stringer, and of Colonel Charles Ridgely, of Hampton. "Warfield's Contrivance," in Howard County, adjoining tract to "Warfield's Range," was heired by these daughters. Richard Warfield out-lived all his brothers and sisters, dying at an advanced age, in 1755. The Maryland Gazette, of that year, thus records his death: "Sunday last, died of Pleurisy, at his plantation, about nine miles from Town, on the Patapsco road, Mr. Richard Warfield, in the 79th year of his age, who formally was one of the Representatives in many Assemblies of the County, and for many years, one of our Magistrates. A gentleman of an upright and unblemished character."

Alexander Warfield, his only son, inherited the homestead and became a member of the vestry of St. Ann's. He had located, during his father's life-time, upon "Warfield's Contrivance" and "Wincopin Neck," during which time he extended his surveys along the Frederick turnpike from Cooksville to Lisbon. He married Dinah Davidge, and had twelve children. They were Dr. Joshua Warfield, of Simpsonville; Azel Warfield, near Snell's Bridge; Basil Warfield, the surveyor, removed to the Eastern Shore; Davidge Warfield adjoined his brother Azel; Rezin Warfield, of "Warfield's Contrivance." Captain Philemon Warfield inherited the homestead in Anne Arundel, and Colonel Charles Warfield, went to Sams Creek, now Carroll County.

Alexander Warfield's daughters were Mrs. Sophia Simpson, Mrs. Dinah Woodward, Mrs. Sarah Price and Mrs. Ann Marriott, afterwards Mrs. Richard Coale.

These sons settled elsewhere. Captain Philemon alone remained in Anne Arundel. He was in command of the Severn Militia Company, which conveyed the Tories to Queen Anne County. He married Assantha Waters, and had two daughters, Mary and Ann

Warfield. Mary became the wife of her cousin Lancelot Warfield, of "Brandy." Ann married Richard Dorsey, of "Hockley." The old Warfield homestead was divided between them, and, in 1845, then known as "The Black-Horse Tavern," was sold to Mr. Gott.

During the construction of the Elk Ridge and Annapolis railroad at that time, the old building was used for the engineer corps. It was later destroyed by fire, and now only an out building marks the spot, at Gott's station. It was a long building, sixty feet in length, forty feet wide, with dormer windows.

Many descendants of Richard Warfield, will be found in the history of Howard County.

ALEXANDER WARFIELD, OF "BRANDY."

One mile south of Millersville, is the only remaining survey of Richard Warfield, stil held by a descendant. It was granted to his third son, Alexander, the surveyor.

Alexander was upon the committee for extending Annapolis. He was, also, one of the executors of his brothers-in-law, Captain John Howard and Amos Peirpoint. The latter made him sole heir of his estate. From Amos Peirpoint's will it is shown that Sarah, wife of Alexander Warfield, was a daughter of Francis Peirpoint and Elizabeth, his wife, who held an estate upon South River. Alexander Warfield's children were all baptised at "All Hallows." He surveyed a thirteen hundred acre tract near Savage, known as "Venison Park," in 1720.

His will, of 1740, granted "Benjamin's Discovery" to his son, Samuel, and also, "Warfield's Addition." "Venison Park" was divided between his sons, Alexander and Absolute. The homestead, "Brandy," was left to his youngest son, Richard. His three daughters inherited slaves and money. They were Rachel, Elizabeth and Catherine.

Samuel, of Alexander, married Sarah Welsh, daughter of Captain John, by his first wife, Thomasin Hopkins, of Gerard. Issue, John, Samuel, Gerard, Vachel, Richard and Welsh Warfield. All except Samuel and Gerard remained in Anne Arundel County. Samuel removed to Pennsylvania. Gerard married Susanna Ryan, of John, who inherited "Duvall's Delight." They lived in Augusta County, Virginia.

John, of Samuel, married Mary Chaney, in 1761. Issue, Samuel—Susannah Donaldson; Richard—first Nancy Benson, second Elizabeth Lucas; Benjamin—Rebecca Spurier; John—Miss Mewshaw; Nancy—Edward Smith; Betsy—Charles Carroll; Nelly—William Westley; Polly—Thomas Forsythe; Rachel—David Clarke.

Richard, of Samuel, married a daughter of Thomas Welsh, and resided near Annapolis Junction. His children all removed to the west. Mr. John Hollister Warfield, of Salem, Oregon, who married a daughter of Wm. J. Brent, of Virginia, is one of their decendants.

He holds lands in the Red River Valley.   Another decendant was Rev. James Welsh Warfield who married Hannah McCoy, a cousin of Jas. G. Blaine.

Vachel, of Samuel, resided at Portland, Anne Arundel County. His wife was Eleanor Griffith, daughter of Charles and Ann Davidge. Their issue were Charles Griffith Warfield, Vachel, Jr., William, Allen and Henrietta. The latter became Mrs. Joshua Marriott. Charles Griffith and Allen, her brothers, were bachelors. Vachel, Jr.—Achsah Marriott. Issue, George Warfield, of Jessups, a prominent man in both political and church circles, during the war of States. His issue are: Achsah, Joseph, Mordecai, John, George, Jr., Evamina and Fannie Warfield.

Mr. Joseph Warfield is in charge of the courthouse in Annapolis, and George T., Jr., is a prominent lawyer of Baltimore.

William, of Vachel, removed to Baltimore City, and became a real estate broker. He married Sarah Ann Merryman. Issue, Oliver Charles Warfield—Adah Gartrell; Wm. Vachel, bachelor, and Adah Warfield. The firm is now known as Wm. Warfield & Sons, on St. Paul Street.

Richard, of Alexander, inherited " Brandy." His wife was Sarah Gaither, daughter of John and Agnes (Rogers) Gaither. " Brandy" was left to their two sons, Lancelot and Richard, Jr. The former bought out his brother, who removed to Frederick County.

Lancelot became an officer in the militia, and was upon the committee of the present courthouse of Annapolis. He married, first Mary, sister of Major Robosson. Issue, Charles, Lemuel, Lancelot.

Charles, of Lancelot,—Miss Sewell; dying he left an infant, George Warfield. The widow, removing to Baltimore, became the wife of Rev. Mr. Gambrall, grandfather of Dean Gambrall.

George Warfield, of Charles,—Ellen Schekels. Issue, William, Elizabeth, Sarah, Margaret, Achsah S., Richard, Joseph, Washington, Ellen, Maria and George. The last was president of the Chester River Steamboat Co.; director of the Fidelity & Deposit Co.; sheriff of Baltimore, and now a member of the City Council. He married Ellen Fryer. His father was in the war of 1812, and his brother, Richard, was in the Civil War, after which he removed to Florida, and married Ellen Williard. His older brother, William—Sarah Brushwood, of Virginia. The daughters of Mr. George Warfield, Sr., became Mrs. Wm. H. Sheets, Mrs. E. C. Chickering, Mrs. Matthias Hammond, of Nebraska.

Lemuel Warfield was a shipping merchant, of Baltimore; lost three ships laden with flour for the West Indian ports; became a British subject, and died a bachelor, 1820, at St. Bartholomew.

Lancelot Warfield, Jr., inherited the entire estate of his father, whose will required him to pay $1,000 each, to his half brothers, Captain Allen and John Warfield, sons of Rachel Marriott, second wife. Captain Allen commanded the militia at the reception of LaFayette, in 1825.

Lancelot Warfield, the second, married Mary Warfield, daughter of Captain Philemon—thus inheriting the homestead of Richard Warfield, the immigrant. Issue, Philemon, Lancelot, third, and Ann Maria, wife of Thomas Owings, of Richard and Ruth (Warfield) Owings.

To Philemon was granted, "Hammond's Inclosure," "Hammond's Connection," and "Friendship," lying upon the Millersville and Annapolis road. He married Ann Wright, and left Mary Ann Turner, Camilla Howell, later Mrs. Young and afterwards Mrs. Hartwick, of Minneapolis, whose daughter married Earl M. Goldsborough, son of S. Brice Goldsborough.

Captain Lemuel Warfield, of Philemon, was upon the staff of General O. M. Mitchell, U. S. Army; married Miss Miller, of Triadelphia; died of yellow fever at Beaufort, S. C., 1862. She removed West and died recently, leaving a son, Lemuel Warfield, of Kansas City; Mrs. George T. Webb, Mrs. Eben D. Marr, and Mrs. Chas. G. Gaither, of Kansas City.

Lancelot Warfield, third, held "Brandy"; sold the old homestead of Richard Warfield, to Mr. Gott; married Elizabeth Sarah Hodges, (of Thomas). Issue, Lancelot, Charles, Elizabeth, Sarah— Dr. William Edwin Hodges.

Lancelot, fourth, came into possession of "Brandy," in 1882; married Margaret E. Beard, descendant of Major Richard, the surveyor of South River. Issue, Lancelot, fifth, died in infancy; Dr. Clarence Warfield, formerly of Galveston, now, after a tour of the globe, residing in San Antonia, Texas; John Warfield, of Australia, and the late Victor Warfield, who died in New Mexico, and lies buried beside his father at "Brandy." In a well-preserved garden graveyard, of this homestead, are the remains of Richard, of Alexander, four Lancelot Warfields, and other members of their lines.

The recent death of the last owner, and the absence of his sons, may soon result in the sale of "Brandy." Mrs. Warfield resides in Baltimore.

Richard Warfield, of Richard and Sarah Gaither, lived at "Brandy" during the life of his first wife, Nancy Gassaway of Thomas. Their only daughter, Sarah, became the wife of Amos Warfield, of "Warfield's Range." Removing to Frederick County, Richard Warfield married again, Anna Delashmutt, daughter of Elias and Betsy (Nelson) Delashmutt, daughter of John Nelson, and sister of Dr. Arthur Nelson. Issue, Lindsey Warfield and Elizabeth Warfield.

Lindsey Warfield entered the war of 1812, and was stationed in the Genessee Valley. He was engaged in the battle of Lundy's Lane. Pleased with the country of that valley, he returned after the war, and settled there. He married Elizabeth L'amoreaux. Issue, Richard Nelson Warfield, of Rochester, Delashmutt Warfield, Andrew Walker, Charles Henry, Myron Franklin, Rowena, Hester, Jane and Sarah Warfield, all of Rushville, New York.

Richard Nelson Warfield married Rachel Elone Hill, daughter of Whitney Hill, who was one of "The Minute Men, of Lexington." Issue, General Richard Henry Warfield, of San Francisco, Cal.; Emma Elizabeth Warfield, wife of Colonel Samuel B. Williams, City Treasurer, of Rochester; and Luella A. Warfield, wife of W. A. Gracy, of Geneva, New York. A few years before his death, Mr. Richard Nelson Warfield visited Maryland in search of information of his family, and by correspondence through many states, accumulated much data, all showing that Anne Arundel was the family starting point.

His son, Brigadier-General Richard Henry Warfield, is thus mentioned: "General Warfield is of the Warfields of Maryland, who still hold lands granted by the Crown of England. His grandfather figured gallantly in the battle of Lundy's Lane, while his great-grandfather, on the distaff side, Whitney Hill, was one of the Men of Lexington. General Warfield was studying at the University of Rochester, when the Civil War broke out. In 1862, he joined the Fiftieth N. Y. Engineers, rising to first lieutenant. In 1876, he went to Healdsburg, California, as cashier of the Farmers' and Mechanics' Bank. He is now in charge of two of the leading hotels of California. In 1894, he was made Brigadier-General, commanding the Second Brigade of the National Guards of California. When the national encampment of the Grand Army of the Republic was held, in Washington, in 1892, he was elected Senior Vice Commander-in-Chief, an honor seldom conferred upon a comrade in any other city than the one in which the comrade lives. He is a member of the "Sons of the American Revolution," of the "Loyal Legion," a "Shriner," a "Knight Templar," and 32nd Degree of the A. & A. Rite.

"General Warfield has two sons, George H. and Richard Emerson Warfield. The first is cashier of the Farmers' and Mechanics' Bank, of Healdsburg, California; the second was a student in Stanford University.

General Warfield has been twice married. His present wife was Lula Emerson, eldest daughter of Colonel William Emerson, who was Colonel of the 151st New York Volunteers, and, for a time, in command of one of the Brigades of the Third Division of the Sixth Army Corps.

"At the outbreak of the Spanish War, in 1898, General Warfield personally mobilized his Brigade of the National Guard as United States Volunteers of California; and the First Californian, of his brigade, was the first twelve-company regiment of the United States Volunteers mustered out, in the United States service from any state. General Warfield was later in charge of the whole Militia of California, but after promotion resigned."

The farm of four hundred acres, of Lindsey Warfield, in Yates County, New York, is still held by Walter Walker Warfield and his wife, Sarah. Myron Franklyn Warfield, youngest son of Lindsey, born 1836, married Francis Helena Green, October 25th, 1866.

Issue, Charles Henry Warfield, born 1867, Carrie Isabelle Warfield, Anna Delashmutt, Richard Nelson, Frederick Parkman, Augustus Bennett, born July 24th, 1878.

Charles Henry Warfield was principal of Little Falls High School, New York. On June 28th, 1900, he married Janet Cook Jessup, to whom was born, May 1st, 1901, Janet MacDonald Warfield. Mr. C. H. Warfield in now a resident of New York City. Frederick Parkman Warfield is of Duell, Megrath and Warfield, Patent lawyers, of New York.

Carrie Warfield married Charles H. Barton, and has a daughter, Francis Green Barton. Augustus Bennett Warfield is now First Lieutenant, Artillery Corps of U. S. A.

Dr. Andrew Walker Warfield married Delight Weir. Charles Henry Warfield was a druggist of Rushville. Hester Jane Warfield married Alvin Chamberlain. Rowena Warfield married Dr. Jas. A. Bennett.

BENJAMIN WARFIELD, OF "LUGG OX."

The youngest son of Richard and Elinor (Browne) Warfield, was Benjamin, who joined his brother, Richard, in surveying "Wincopin Neck," in the forks of Savage and Middle River, immediately at Savage Factory. This was willed to his daughter, Elizabeth Ridgely, by both himself and his brother Richard.

Benjamin Warfield's inheritance in "Warfield's Range" was never occupied by him. He surveyed "Benjamin's Discovery," in Anne Arundel. He married Elizabeth Duvall, daughter of Captain John and Elizabeth (Jones) Duvall. Her marriage dower was a tract of 780 acres, known as "Lugg-Ox," in the forks of the Patuxent. This adjoined his own survey. One son, Joshua, and a daughter, Elizabeth, were their issue. Benjamin Warfield died in early manhood, in 1717, leaving his children minors. His widow married John Gaither, the second, who administered.

Joshua, of Benjamin, held the homestead. By his wife, Ruth Davis, of Thomas, he had Benjamin, Joshua, Henry, Thomas, Caleb, Mary, Elizabeth and Elinor. "Lugg-Ox" was divided among these heirs. Benjamin removed to Frederick County. Joshua left no records. Henry was an attorney, and died a bachelor. Thomas and Caleb remained upon the homestead and left heirs. Thomas was executor. He was an officer in the militia. He married, first, Elizabeth Holliday, and second, Elizabeth Marriott, and had issue, Mary, Lydia Ellender, wife of Captain Francis Bealmear; William, merchant of Annapolis; Dr. Anderson, legislator; Thomas Wheeler. Singleton—William Warfield and David Ridgely were merchants of Annapolis, and loaned money on real estate. At the time of his death, William Warfield held most of "Lugg Ox." His wife was Mary Tyler Worthington, granddaughter of Hon. Brice Thomas Beale Worthington. Issue, Thomas Henry Warfield and Elizabeth Holliday Warfield, legatees of Mrs. Mary Tyler Warfield; Thomas

Henry married Mary Worthington. Thomas Wheeler Warfield sold his interest in "Lugg Ox" to William; his wife was Sarah White. Dr. Anderson Warfield, the bachelor, was a ready writer, independent politician, legislator, and closed his career as a physician, of Baltimore, leaving his house and practice on Eutaw Street, to Dr. Bealmear, stepson of his sister. Caleb Warfield, of Joshua, sold his interest in "Lugg Ox" to Dr. Anderson Warfield, and resided upon his wife's interest in the Sappington estate. His daughters, Elizabeth and Elinor, died maidens. Thomas Warfield, of Caleb, married Margery Browne, daughter of Philemon Browne and Margery Gaither, sister of Colonel Edward Gaither, Jr. Their issue were, Thomas Warfield, of "Good Hope," and Caleb Warfield, who removed to Kentucky.

Thomas Warfield, of "Good Hope,"—Margaret Foster—issue, Abel Davis Warfield, of Alexandria, Virginia.—Sarah Ann Adams issue, Geo. Thos. Warfield, of 17th Virginia Infantry, killed in defence of Richmond, 1862. Edgar Warfield, druggist, of Alexandria, Virginia and commander of Lee's Legion of Confederate soldiers—Catherine Virginia Batcheller—issue, Edgar Warfield, Jr.,—Abbia Virginia Belles—issue, Edgar Ashley, George Elmon—Nellie J. Soudson. Wm. Ryland—Alice Down; Marion Roberts—Thomas F. Burroughs; Andrew Adgate Warfield—Jane Elizabeth Pattie; Ada Francis Warfield—B. P. Kurtz; Susan Alice—Walter Gahan; Frank Warfield—Cora May Smith, Richmond, Virginia. Harry Lee Warfield—Lizzie Allen. Caleb Warfield, of Thomas and Margery Brown, removed to Kentucky,—first, Nancy Livingstone; second, Nancy Ray; third, Anne Steel. Issue by second, Thomas Brown, John, Louisa, James, George; issue by third, William Warfield.

Thomas Brown Warfield—first, Sabra Ann Steele—issue, Sabra Steele Warfield; second, Margaret Rebecca Campbell—issue, Charles, Thomas, Myra Alice, Clara Maria, Nancy Margaret, and William Campbell Warfield, who married Dora Rawlings. Issue, Edwin, Herbert, Theodora Margaret. William Campbell Warfield is Superintendent of Public Schools, and State Secretary of the Reading Circle, Mt. Stering, Kentucky.

MAJOR JOHN WELSH, HIGH SHERIFF, OF A. A. CO.

In 1667, Major Welsh was a Commissioner of Anne Arundel County. In 1675, as the husband of Mrs. Anne Grosse, widow of Hon. Roger Grosse, he was executor of the large Grosse estate, and summoned John Grosse, Richard Snowden and his wife, Elizabeth, lately Elizabeth Grosse, Roger Grosse, Jr., Wm. Grosse and Francis Grosse, in settlement of the estate.

Mrs. Elizabeth (Grosse) Welsh was the mother of Silvester and John Welsh, Jr. The latter was known later as Major and Colonel John. She died before 1675, when Major Welsh married Mary, stepdaughter of Nicholas Wyatt, and half-sister of Sarah (Wyatt) Dorsey, wife of Colonel Edward.

In 1679, Major Welsh was one of "The Quorum," and was High Sheriff in 1678 and 1679. In the former year, he was defendant against John Homewood in a suit against his deputy. In 1683, Major Welsh was a commissioner for building the courthouse, and in the same year, a commissioner for the advancement of trade in Anne Arundel. In short, Major Welsh was continuously in the public service. His will, of 1686, left his South River lands, "Arnold's Grey," to Sylvester and John, because they came through his Grosse wife. Benjamin Welsh was installed in the South River homestead. The four daughters, Mary, Elizabeth, Sarah and Damaris Welsh, were joint heirs of his lands upon the Gunpowder. "Unto my wife, Mary, 'Preston's Enlargement,' near River Dam, Herring Creek. I give to my brother, Henry Welsh, my tobacco box, silver headed cane, broadcloth suit and one thousand acres of land." This brother I could not find in our records. Though named an executor, the estate was settled by son, Sylvester, and his widow, Mary, then wife of James Ellis.

Sylvester's wife was Elinor. They had issue, Sylvester, Jr., Elinor and Lucia.

Captain, or Colonel John, married, first, Thomasin Hopkins, daughter of Gerard and Thomasin Hopkins, of South River. Their daughter, Sarah, became Mrs. Samuel Warfield. Colonel John's second wife was Rachel, without doubt, daughter of John and Ann (Greenberry) Hammond. By her were Ann, wife of Nathan Hammond, son of Major Charles and Hannah Howard. (2.) Rachel; (3.) Captain John, who married Hannah Hammond, daughter of John and Ann (Dorsey) Hammond; (4.) Thomas; (5.) Benjamin; (6.) Elizabeth; (7.) Henry O'Neale; (8.) Comfort.

The above testator was a large shipping iron merchant. His partner was his cousin, Richard Snowden, son of Richard and Elizabeth (Grosse) Snowden, a half-sister of Colonel John Welsh. They bought and sold lands also as partners. His will of 1733-34, reads: "I give to my son, John Welsh, my lands, 'Arnold's Grey' and 'Neglect.' To my sons, Thomas and Benjamin, I give 'Welsh's Discovery.' I give to William Davis, 'William's Delight.'" Lands and money were left to wife, Rachel, and daughters, Rachel and Comfort. The married daughters also named were Sarah, wife of Samuel Warfield, and Sophia Hall. "To my brother, Robert, my wearing apparel, my watch, and my gold ring. My cousin, Richard Snowden, my brother, Robert, and my wife, Rachel, to administer."

Benjamin Welsh, his brother, married Elizabeth Nicholson. The daughters of Major John Welsh were: Mary, wife of Josias Toogood; Sarah—John Giles; Elizabeth—Daniel Richardson; Damaris—Thos. Stockett. A thousand acre tract in Baltimore County, known as "Three Sisters," was sold by these sisters.

Robert, the youngest child of Major John Welsh, born after the death of the Major, married Katherine Lewis. Issue, James, Lewis, Robert, Jemima Edwards, Elizabeth Tongue, Grace Elliot, Katherine Stewart, John, and Benjamin, inheritor of "Preston's Enlargement."

John Welsh, the third—known also as Captain—inherited the homestead, but married in Howard County, Hannah, daughter of John and Ann Dorsey Hammond, whose residence was adjoining the "Old Brick Church." John Welsh took up an immense tract in Northern Howard, and on it placed his sons, John, Philip, Henry and Samuel.

These sons married kindred wives. The fourth John Welsh, married both a Hammond and a Dorsey—Lucretia, daughter of Colonel Nicholas, and Sarah (Griffith) Dorsey. Philip Welsh—Elizabeth Davis, daughter of Caleb and Lucretia Griffith. Samuel Welsh —Rachel Griffith, daughter of Henry and Elizabeth Dorsey—all daughters of sisters and a brother, heirs of Orlando Griffith and his wife, Katherine Howard.

The grounds upon which St. Ann's Church stands, and the Peggy Stewart house, in Annapolis, were held by Major John and his heirs.

Dr. Welch and his brother, Robert, of Annapolis, who thus write their names, are descendants of the High Sheriff and Member of "The Quorum."

THE STOCKETT BROTHERS.

My record of this family is the work of a descendant of Annapolis, whose daughter kindly presented a copy.

Our Rent Rolls show surveys made near the Susquehanna River, in Harford, in the name of Stockett. In 1658, four brothers, Thomas, Lewis, Henry and Francis, came to the province and obtained grants under the Calverts.

The family was of the Church of England, loyal to King Charles. After the crushing defeat of the royal cause at Worcester, in 1651, these worthies gathered up all they could from the wreck of their property and came to Maryland.

Captain Thomas Stockett, of "Bourne," had in his family, George Alsop, who wrote the tract on Maryland, known as "Alsops Character of Maryland." Dr. Francis Stockett, was appointed Clerk for the Court of Baltimore, in 1658, but, resigning it, was in the Assembly of Delegates at St. Maries in, 1658-59.

Captain Thomas Stockett was in the Assembly, 1661-66.

Captain Thomas and Henry Stockett were also Judges of the County Courts until 1668, in which year Captain Thomas Stockett was appointed High Sheriff of Anne Arundel, to which he had removed. A commission was issued to Lewis Stockett, of Baltimore County, from 1636 to 1667, as Colonel and Commander-in-Chief of all the forces of Baltimore County, on the Susquehanna and Bay, as well as Kent Island.

In 1668, all three brothers removed to Anne Arundel, and located on "Stockett's Run," near Birdsville. Captain Thomas Stockett held "Obligation," 664 acres; Henry Stockett held "Bridge Hill," 664 acres; Dr. Francis Stockett held "Dodon," 664 acres. They there lived and died.

Among their old family papers, was a description of the coat of arms, and one engraving on the silver tankards, "or, a lion rampant, Sa, on a chief of the last, tower tripple toured, or between two bezants; Crest on a stump of a tree, couped and eradicated or a line sejant, Sa."

Another interesting paper was that of Joseph Tilly, the register or clerk of All Hallows Parish, in Anne Arundel County, in which the Stocketts were located.

"About or in ye year of ye Lord 1667 or 8, I became acquainted with four gents ye were brothers, and then dwellers here in Maryland. The elder of them went by the name Colonel Lewis Stockett: ye second by the name of Captain Thomas Stockett; ye third was Doctor Francis Stockett, and ye fourth brother was Mr. Henry Stockett.

"These men were but newly seated or seating in Anne Arundel County, and they had much business with Lord Baltimore, then ppetr of ye Province.

"My house standing convenient, they were often entertained there.

"They told me they were Kentish men, or men of Kent, and yet they were concerned for King Charles, ye First: were out of favor with ye following government, they mortgaged a good estate to follow King Charles, the Second, in his exile, and at their return, they had not money to redeem their mortgage, which was ye cause of their coming hither.—(Signed.)   JOSEPH TILLY."

Captain Thomas Stockett married Mary Wells, daughter of Richard Wells, of Herring Creek, who was prominent in the Puritan colony of Virginia. He was one of the Commissioners appointed to represent the parliament in 1654, with Captain Wm. Fuller, and others, and we find him in the Council of 1658, after the Calverts had regained the province. He was, also, a Justice of the Peace, owning a considerable estate.

Captain Thomas and Mary (Wells) Stockett left one son, Thomas Stockett. After Captain Stockett's death, in 1671, his widow married George Yate, the surveyor, and had issue, George Yates, John Yates and Ann Yates—sometimes written Yeates. She survived her second husband, whose will, of 1691, left his seal and silver marked with his coat of arms to his son George. The latter married Rachel Warfield, of Richard. Mrs. Yate's will, of 1699, left her daughter Frances, wife of Marius (Mareen) Duvall, her silver seal in a lozenge shield; and to her son, Thomas Stocket, "a black walnut box which hath his father's coat of arms engraved in ye bottom thereof."

Thomas Stockett married Mary Sprigg, daughter of Thomas, of West River, who owned, also, a large tract in Prince George. Upon portions of this were located the descendants of Colonel John Francis Mercer and the Stewart family, connected with, and descended from, the Sprigg family. Thomas Stockett, Jr., surveyed many disputed tracts of land—leaving by his first wife, Thomas and Eleanor. The latter married Richard Williams. His second wife was Damaris Welsh, (or Welch), daughter of Major John and Mary Welsh, of South River, and of Annapolis. Issue, Benjamin, Lewis, Mrs. Elizabeth Beale, Mrs. Beard, Mrs. Brewer, Mrs Mayo, Mrs. Rollins, or Larkin.

Thomas Stockett, the third, built the brick dwelling near Birdville, in 1743, and planted choice selections of fruit brought by him from England. He made an attractive home. He married Elizabeth, daughter of Joseph and Mary Noble, of Piscataway, Prince George County. Issue, Thomas, Mary Elizabeth and Thomas Noble Stockett. Mary Elizabeth—Samuel Harwood, son of Captain Richard, and Ann Watkins Harwood. They removed to Montgomery County, Maryland. Their daughter, Mary Stockett, married Alexander Warfield, son of John Worthington Warfield, of the Big Seneca, from whom descends Captain Noble Creager, of the United States Army, and his sister, Miss Virginia Creager, of Baltimore.

Thomas Noble Stockett, born 1747, married Mary Harwood, daughter of Captain Richard Harwood and Ann Watkins. Mary Harwood was the only daughter.

Dr. Thomas Noble Stockett took an active part in the war of the Revolution, and was a member of the Sons of Freedom.

He was appointed by commission, a copy of which is now in possession of his descendants in Annapolis, as surgeon—assistant to Colonel Thomas Ewing's Battalion of Militia, for the Flying Camp. He soon after was commissioned Surgeon, and joined the army under General Smallwood, of the Maryland Line, then in the North. The Valley Forge hardships so impared his health that he had to return home, and was employed afterwards in the recruiting service. He was large, robust, florid complexion, over six feet in height. The issue of Dr. Thomas Noble, and Mary (Harwood) Stockett were: Mary—Wm. Alexander, merchant of Annapolis; Richard Galen Stockett, M. D., of Stockwood, Howard County—Margaret Hall, daughter of Major Henry Hall and Margery Howard, of Joseph.

Thomas Mifflin Stockett was second in command of a ship, and was killed, in 1799, in an engagement with a French privateer. Joseph Noble Stockett—first, Ann Caroline Battee, and left no issue. Second, Ann Sellman, daughter of General Jonathan Sellman, whose handsome portrait now hangs in the Stockett house in Annapolis. Her mother was Ann Elizabeth Harwood, daughter of Colonel Richard and Margaret (Hall) Harwood. Their only issue was the late Francis H. Stockett, of Annapolis, whose record of the Stockett family was published in 1892, from which I quote.

The third wife of Joseph Noble Stockett was Sophia Watkins, daughter of Major Joseph Watkins and Ann Gray. Their issue were, John Shaaff Stockett—Georgetta Stockett; Thos. Richard—Jemima Edmunds, of England. Dr. Charles William—Maria L. Duvall, only child of Dr. Howard M. Duvall; Mary Sophia—first Dr. Richard Harwood Cowman, Surgeon in the United States Navy; second, John Thomas Stockett, only son of George Lee Stockett, son of Dr.

Richard Galen Stockett, of Howard County, who was a celebrated civil service engineer and Past Master of the Masons.   Ann Stockett, of Dr. Thomas Noble—Rhoderick Warfield, of "Warfield's Range," Howard County, and with him removed to Kentucky, where they raised a large family.   Eleanor, daughter of Dr. Thomas Noble Stockett—Turenne Watkins, son of Colonel Gassaway Watkins and Ruth Dorsey, and with him removed to Kentucky.

Mr. Joseph Noble Stockett, who inherited the old Stockett homestead, was an ardent member of the ancient South River Club, as his ancestors had been, and would there spend the entire day.

HARWOOD FAMILY.

One of the earliest surveys of 1651 upon Rhode River was "Harwood," in the name of Robert Harwood.   This tract was later in litigation, but Abell Browne, the Justice and High Sheriff of Anne Arundel, held it and willed it to his son, Robert Browne.   Whilst I have not found the fact, the inference is good that said Robert was named for Robert Harwood, the original surveyor.

The most remarkable courtship on record was that of a Robert Harwood, a relative of Dr. Peter Sharpe, the Quaker of Calvert. In his will, of 1672, Dr Sharpe left a personal memorial to "Robert and Elizabeth Harwood, their children and friends in the ministry."

The succeeding Harwood family seems to have come from both Robert and a certain Thomas Harwood D. D., of "Streatley," Rector of Littlelor, in Middlesex.   He founded a school for the poor, and was succeeded by several successive rectors.   One of the earliest deeds is that of Thomas Harwood, of Streatley, Berks County, England, to his son, Richard Harwood, for "Hookers Purchase," at the head of Muddy Creek, Anne Arundel County, Maryland.

The above Richard lived upon it, and by his wife, Mary, had Thomas Harwood, born 1698, who married Sarah Belt; Richard Harwood—Anne Watkins.

Thomas and Sarah Belt were the parents of Captain Thomas Harwood, of Prince George County, under General Smallwood.   His wife was Rachel Sprigg, of Osborne, of Prince George County.   Issue, Thomas, ancestor of James Kemp Harwood, of Baltimore.   (2.) Osborne Sprigg—Elizabeth Ann Harwood, daughter of Colonel Richard and Margaret Hall, his wife.   (3.)   Margaret—Wm. Hall; (4.)   Rachel—Major Harry Hall, from whom comes Dr. Julius Hall, of Baltimore.   (5.)   Lucy—John Battie; second, Colonel Richard Harwood.

Richard Harwood, second son of Richard and Mary, the settlers, married Anne Watkins, born 1737, and had nine sons and two daughters, twins.   Their first son was Colonel Richard Harwood, of "South River Battalion" (militia).   His wife was Margaret Hall, daughter of Major Henry, and granddaughter of Rev. Henry, of St. James.

Thomas Harwood, fourth son of Richard and Anne, was the first Treasurer of the Western Shore of Maryland, under the Council of Safety, about 1776, and continued in that office until his death, when he was succeeded by his brother, Benjamin. From Treasurer Thomas, came Richard—Miss Callahan, whose son, William—Hester Ann Lockerman. Their descendants hold the Harwood House, of Annapolis.

John, fifth son of Richard and Ann Watkins—Mary Hall, daughter of Major Henry Hall.

Samuel, sixth son of Richard and Ann—Elizabeth, daughter of Thos. Stockett and Elizabeth Noble, his wife. They removed to Montgomery County. Their daughter became the wife of Alexander Warfield, of the Seneca.

From Nicholas, seventh son of Richard and Ann Watkins, through his daughter, Sarah Duvall, is descended Dr. Marius Duvall, United States Navy, From Mary, second daughter, wife of Wm. S. Green, came Eliza—James Henly Iglehart. Matilda, wife of John Nicholas Watkins and Nicholas—his cousin, Mary Augusta Harwood.

Benjamin Harwood, the Treasurer, was unmarried. The minature and trinkets found in the treasury some years ago, belonged to him.

The issue of Colonel Richard and Margaret Hall, his wife, were, Anne Elizabeth—Major Jonathan Sellman; (2.) Elizabeth Anne —Osborn Sprigg Harwood; (3.) Richard Hall Harwood, Judge of the Circuit Court of Anne Arundel—Annie Green. Issue, (1.) Eliza —George Wells, of Annapolis; (2.) Mary Augusta—Nicholas Green, her cousin; (3.) Matilda—David McCulloh Brogden; (4.) Rebecca —N. L. Coulter.

(4.) Henry Hall, of Richard and Margaret—Elizabeth, daughter of Colonel Edward Lloyd, of "Wye," in 1805. Issue, (1.) Betty Francis Scott Key; (2.) Mary—Dr. William Ghiselin; (3.) Josephine —Edward G. Tilton, United States Navy.

(5.) Joseph, of Richard and Margaret—Anne Chapman, and second, Mitilda Sparrow. Issue, (3.) Ann Matilda—Charles Hoops; (4.) James—Ann Mackall; (5.) Chapman—Elizabeth Claude; (7.) Margaret—Dr. William Watkins, of Howard. Their son, Harwood Watkins, editor of the Ellicott City Times, and a popular young lawyer, died unmarried in early manhood.

(6.) Thomas was a lawyer of Baltimore, and died unmarried.

(7.) Mary—Thos. Noble Harwood, her cousin.

(8.) Henrietta—Thos. Cowman. Issue, (1.) Thomas—Matilda Battie; (2.) Richard—Harriet Green, later wife of Thomas Hall, whose daughter, Henrietta—William Hall, of Annapolis.

(9.) Benjamin, born 1783—Henrietta Maria Battie. Issue, (1.) Lucinda Margaret—Dr. John Henry Sellman, her first cousin; (3.) Ann Caroline—Benjamin Harrison, of Baltimore; (4.) Henrietta Eliza—George Johnson, son of Chancellor John Johnson. The second wife of Benjamin Harwood was Margaret Hall, of William, third, his cousin. Issue, (1.) Benjamin, of Mississippi; (4.) Mary Dryden—Thos Kent; (10.) Priscilla—John B. Weems, who had, (1.) Ann Bell; (2.) Mary Dorsey.

Osborne Sprigg Harwood, son of Thos. and Rachel Sprigg, his wife,—Elizabeth Anne, daughter of Colonel Richard Harwood and Margaret, his wife. Their second daughter, Margaret,—Wm. John Hall, her first cousin, and had issue, Mary Priscilla. Fourth daughter —Francis Henry Stockett, of Annapolis; fifth, Harriet Kent,— Philip G. Schurar, of Annapolis; sixth, William Sprigg—Elizabeth Sellman, daughter of Thos. Welsh and Elizabeth Sellman, his wife.

Third, Rachel Ann, third daughter of Osborne and Sprigg— James Iglehart; issue, Anne Sellman—Jas. J. Waddell. Second, Harwood—A. Owen Kent. Third, James—Sallie Waddell; killed at Battle of Gettysburg, 1863. Fourth, Wm. Thomas—Catherine Spottswood Berkeley. Fifth, Thos. Richard Sprigg, youngest of Osborne Sprigg and Elizabeth—Elizabeth Ann, daughter of Wm. P. Mills, of Baltimore.

The deed from Thomas Harwood, of Streatley, to his son, Richard, closes as follows: " And from and immediately after his decease, to the use of Thomas Harwood, son of said Richard Harwood, and his heirs."

Richard, of this last Thomas, left his dwelling, "Hooker's Purchase," to his niece, Lucy Battie, and to his sister-in-law, Rachel Harwood, during life. "Anthony's Purchase," being the dwelling of his late brother, Thomas Harwood, and after his death, to my nephew, Osborne Sprigg Harwood.

Thomas Harwood, of Richard, the settler, left " Brazen Harpe Hall " to his son, Benjamin; and Benjamin left it to his two children. It was afterward divided and part of it is called "Harwood Hall," and is now owned by Mr. Beale D. Mullikin, a descendant of Benjamin Harwood. The old Harwood burying ground is on that part of the estate, but there is hardly a trace of it left. "Harwood Hall" is about ten miles from Marlboro, Prince George County. Sarah (Belt) Harwood, widow of Thos. Harwood, did not " chuse " to accept, and wrote to " certifi" that she preferred her third part.

Major Sprigg Harwood was one of "the glorious nineteen electors." In 1886, when seventy-eight years of age, he gave his view of that memorable fight for constitutional reform, said he: "We had a caucus in Baltimore, and agreed to assemble in Annapolis, and to send an address to the twenty-one Whigs already qualified in the Senate chamber, waiting for three more to make a quorum. But they would hold no communication with us until we qualified. I consulted my people here for instructions. They said, 'Go; the principle is right and we will stand by you'—for the people generally thought the country was gone. John S. Sellman wrote to us to meet at Annapolis; and, after some delay, three of the nineteen concluded to go into the College. The Whigs, in return, gave us what we were demanding—the election of the Governor by the people. We were satisfied."

Major Sprigg Harwood was one of the county delegates to the Congressional Convention, in favor of the dissolution of the Union, and recognizing the Southern Confederacy. In 1864, he was a delegate to the State Convention called by the people. He was also, long Clerk of the Court for Anne Arundel.

THE HALL FAMILY.

All Hallows and St. James parish records give many items of interest concerning both Halls and Harwoods. Rev. Henry Hall, the first to come over, was a priest of the Church of England. He was sent by Henry Lord Bishop, of London, with letters to Hon. Francis Nicholson, then Governor of the Province, who inducted Rev. Henry Hall as First Rector of St. James. This office was held till his death, in 1722. A stained glass window to his memory is still in St. James Church. In 1701, Rev. Henry Hall married Mary Duvall, of Mareen, the Huguenot. They had five sons and three daughters.

From John are descended the families of Thos. J. Hall and William Hall, of St. James.

From Major Henry, the oldest son, who married Martha Howard, of Joseph, grandson of Captain Cornelius, were Henry, born 1727, and John, born 1729. This last was Barrister John Hall, a very distinguished lawyer, who refused an admiralty, but was a member of the Council of Safety, and of the Continental Congress. He married Eleanor Dorsey, of "Hockley," but left no descendants. He was buried on the farm called "The Vineyard," some seven miles from Annapolis. A portrait of him is now in possession of Miss Nellie Ridont, whose grandmother was a sister of his wife.

Henry Hall, the older brother of Barrister John Hall, was also known as Major Henry. His wife was Elizabeth Watkins. Their oldest son was Major Harry Hall, who married Margery Howard, of Joseph and Martha, of "All Hallows." Issue four children, elsewhere given. By his second wife, Rachel Harwood, he had five children. viz.: Mary Anne—Councilor Thos. W. Hall, son of Edward Hall. Their only son, Julius Hall, moved to Calvert County and there practised medicine for a number of years. His wife was Jane, daughter of Governor Joseph Kent, of Maryland. His son Julius— Elizabeth Claude Stockett, daughter of Francis Henry Stockett and Mary Priscilla, his wife.

The issue of Major Henry Hall, by his second wife, Elizabeth, Lansdale, were: First. Edward—Martha Duckett. Issue, Eleanor W. Priscilla, Henrietta, Richard, Captain John, and Thomas.

Second. Isaac, from whom descended the family of the late Harry Hall, of West River, the father of Edward, Dr. Estep Hall and Augustus Hall.

Third. Margaret—Colonel Richard Harwood.

Fourth. William, known as William, third. He married Margaret Harwood, daughter of Captain Thomas, of St. James Parish. Their son, Thomas—Henrietta, widow of Thos. Cowan. Their daughter, Henrietta—Wm. Henry Hall, of Annapolis. The second wife of Thomas, above, was Mary Watkins, who had John Thomas —Harriet Barker, of Baltimore.

Second. Richard, of William, third, left descendants in Prince George County., viz.: Richard—Miss Perkins. Issue, the late John Hall, Treasurer of Prince George; Turner, Summerfield Hall. The daughters were Mrs. Marine, of Baltimore, Mrs. Beale, Mrs. McDonald, Miss Mollie Hall, of Beltsville. Their homestead was the handsome estate of Colonel Herbert.

Third. Margaret, of William, third—Benjamin Harwood, of Colonel Richard.

Fourth. Rachel—Solomon Sparrow. Fifth. Harry—Anne Geston. Sixth. Mary Dryden—Alfred Sellman. Seven. Elizabeth Watkins, whose daughter Eleanor—Richard Sellman. Rachel Sprigg —Dr. Blake Hall. Eight. Wm. John—Margaret Hall Harwood, of Osborne Sprigg Harwood.

THE RIDOUT FAMILY.

John Ridout, secretary of Governor Sharpe, left a distinguished family. He married Mary, daughter of Governor Samuel Ogle, and his wife, Ann Tasker. Both were buried at "White Hall."

Obituary notices of them are among the records of St. Margaret's, written by their son, Horatio Ridout, Register of that parish for a number of years. Horatio Ridout married Rachel Goldsborough, of Cambridge. She bore him one son, John Ridout, whose issue by a second wife were, Eliza N., Rachel S., Ann Ogle, Horatio and Samuel Ridout.

Horatio, of John, married again, Ann Weems. Issue, Mary— Jacob Winchester; Horatio—Jemima Duvall, of Richard; Rev. Samuel Ridout—Hester Ann Chase, daughter of Thomas; Weems Ridout—first, Elizabeth Duvall, second, Elizabeth Beeman; Orlando Ridout—Margaret Atlee; Elinor Ridout, Francis Hollingsworth Ridout died single; Anna Rebecca—Captain Thos. K. Messick; James Maccubin Ridout and Miliora Ogle died single.

The descendants of Horatio and Jemima Duvall are, Horatio Sharpe—Ellen J. Rogers; Zachariah Duvall Ridout—Ellen Messick; Francis Hollingsworth—Eliza Shepherd; Weems Ridout, the courteous merchant of Annapolis—Edith Marden; Grafton Duvall—Sallie Dashiell; Charles—Carrie Conner.

Samuel Ridout, of John, of Horatio, was the friend and father-in-law of Rev. Walter Dulany Addison. From him descends Dr. Wm. G. Ridout, of Annapoils, who possesses a handsome portrait of Mrs. Mary (Young, Woodward) Hesselius.

One of her descendants, upon seeing for the first time, the above portrait of Mrs. Hesselius, asked, Dr. Ridout, "What queen is that?" The reply was, "You are not far from right in calling her a queen, for she had all the graces of a queen, and to her own family, she was a queen of hearts."

There stands, to-day, a magnificent colonial residence upon a hill overlooking the tragic battlefield of the Severn. It was built by John Ridout and is still held by his descendants, of Annapolis.

Dr. Ridout, Jr., and Mrs. Ligon, of Howard, are of his household.

THE BEALE FAMILY.

A Scottish family, with a ringing bell as its coat of arms, was early represented in our province.

The leader was a famous officer, Colonel Ninian Beale, born in Fifeshire, or near Edinburgh, about 1625. Having fought, in 1650, against Cromwell at Dunbar, he was captured and transported to Calvert County, Maryland.

This same immigrant was called the "Covenanter," whose zeal caused him in some way, to be mixed up with the killing of a Bishop Montgomery, in an effort to keep Episcopacy out of Scotland.

He came, in 1655, and located in Calvert County. Intelligent, and of a strong character, he at once became a leader in the contests of that period.

He was with Colonel Coursey and Colonel William Stephens, "When they sent Captain Beale before them to find Captain Brandt." Information being delivered into his lordship's hands by Captain Ninian Beale, it was ordered to be entered in the Council book; and by his lordship's special command, power be given to Captain Ninian Beale, of Calvert County, to press man and horse anytime, upon urgent occasion, to give his lordship intelligence." Ordered, also, at the same time, "that six men in arms, under Captain Ninian Beale, be commanded out to continue ranging between the head of the Patuxent, up to the Susquehanna, forth for discovery of the Indian enemy." Captain Beale, in 1689, signed the Declaration of Remonstrance, in which it was declared, that "All rumors of an Indian invasion, supported by Catholics, were found to be false."

For Captain Beale's services he was granted an estate that extended over several counties. He surveyed near the National Capitol, and upon one of his surveys, a number of Presbyterian families were induced to settle. One of his tracts was the "Rock of Dumbarton." Georgetown stands upon this survey. There was another one at Bennings, and still another at Collington, Prince George County. Here was located Ninian Beale, Jr., the testator of 1710, who named only two children, Mary and Samuel. His sister, Jane, daughter of Colonel Ninian and Ruth Moore, married Colonel Archibald Edmondson, whose daughter, Ruth Edmondson, married Rev. John Orme, who married Elizabeth Johns, whose daughter, Charlotte Orme, became Mrs. Daniel Douglass. Colonel Ninian died, 1717, age ninety-three years.

Colonel George Beale, youngest son of Colonel Ninian, born at Upper Marlborough, in 1695, removed to Georgetown, and there died, 1780. He built a large house upon N Street, and many believe that he gave name to Georgetown. It was upon his property.

Thomas Beale, of Colonel George, by a second marriage to the widow Beale, had twin daughters, who became the wives of George C. Washington and Major Peter, and mothers of Lewis Washington and Colonel Peter.

"The Cedars," of Bennings, for Colonel Ninian Beale, was the homestead of another Ninian Beale, whose family Bible reads as follows: "Rachel born 1711; Ninian, 1713; Charles, 1715; Elinor, 1717; Joshua, 1719." He held "The Cedars;" married Sarah Greenfield, and had Captain George Beale, whose wife was Ann Truman Greenfield. Their daughter, Ann Truman Beale, married Fielder Magruder; Susan—Samuel Sheriff, and became the mother of George Beale Sheriff, the last heir of "The Cedars."

Another Ninian Beale is found at Georgetown. He signs, in a bold hand, "Ninian Beale, of Ninian." He is thought to be the Ninian, of Ninian, who was born at Bennings, in 1713. His issue were Charles, Ruth, Margaret, Mary, Rachel, Elinor and Susannah. Ruth became the wife of Captain Charles Gassaway; Margaret—Benjamin Edwards; Mary—Dr. Watkins, and left Gassaway and Thomas Watkins, of Brookeville; Rachel—Hardidge Lane, of Virginia, and was the mother of Mrs. Coleman and Mrs. Vansweringen, of Virginia; Elinor—Zachariah Offutt, of Montgomery County, Susannah—Alexander Catlett, father of Grandison Catlett; Charles Beale—a daughter of Lord Fairfax.

In 1719, two brothers, William and Charles Beale, took up 1,200 acres in Montgomery County, known as "The Brothers." In 1720, they surveyed "Beale's Manor."

A still later Ninian Beale, of Georgetown, had a son Robert, who had a son James, who had a son Zephaniah, ensign in Captain Edward Burgess Company of Montgomery Militia. He married Keesiah White, widow of Wm. Pritchett, of "Eleanor Green," near Rockville. Their son Rezin Beale, took part in the suppression of the Indians, in 1790. The father was Major and the son became General Rezin Beale, of Wooster, Ohio. He married Rebecca, daughter of Lieutenant Johnson, and had Nancy Campbell Beale, wife of Cyrus Spink, of Wooster. Their daughter Rebecca Beale Spink—John Wilson McMillan, son of Martin McMillan and Nancy Clark. Their daughter is Miss Kate Louise McMillan, of Wooster, Ohio.

Another Ninian Beale married Elizabeth Gordon, and had George, who married Ann Magruder. Brooke Beale was the seventeenth son of his father.

Another Beale family was in Annapolis. Hannah Beale became the wife of Thomas Randall, and the mother of Urith (Randall) Owings.

John Beale, whose coat of arms upon his will at Annapolis, does not show a "ringing bell," was a distinguished attorney, connected by marriage, with Howards and Dorseys and Norwoods. His name was handed down in many allied families. His wife was Elizabeth, daughter of Andrew Norwood, by Elizabeth, daughter of Captain Cornelius Howard. Their daughter, Elizabeth Beale, became Mrs. Wm. Nicholson, the mother of Beale Nicholson, and the wife of Richard Dorsey, of "Hockley." A daughter of this marriage became the wife of another John Beale.

The following data was sent to me by Mrs. Dorsey of the Congressional Library, Washington.

Tombstones of the Beale family, formerly in the Presbyterian Cemetery, at Georgetown, but transferred to "Oakhill" at the same place.

"Here lieth Colonel George Beale, who departed this life at Georgetown, March 15, 1780; aged eighty-five years.

"Here lieth the body of Elizabeth, the wife of Colonel George Beale, who departed this life October the 2nd, 1748; age forty-nine years."

"Sacred to the memory of George Beale. He was born in Georgetown, February 25th, 1729. He died October 15th, 1807, in the seventy-ninth year of his age. He lived respected, and died lamented."

Will of George Beale probated at Rockville, the 17th of March, 1780. He married Elizabeth, daughter of Colonel Thomas Brooke and his second wife, Barbara Dent. Their children were, Mary Beale, under ten in 1750, when Barbara Dent Beale, her grandmother, made a deed of a negro girl to her; she died young. Esther died young. Thomas died young. George, born 1729. Leevin died in Martinique; Patrick, Rebecca, Lucy Magruder; Thomas died young; Mary died young.

Will of Colonel George Beale:

"In the name of God, Amen. To son Thomas Beale, 'Conjuror's Dissappointment;' also a part of 'Dumbarton,' to be divided by the main road, that part that lies south to belong to grandson, George Beale. To daughter, Elizabeth Evans, negro man to serve four years, and to be free made 15th March, 1780." Witnessed by W. Smith, Richard Cheney, Abraham Boyd.

Thomas Beale bought "Conjuror's Dissappointment" and "Rock of Dumbarton." Married Anne Deme. His will made, 14th October, 1814; probated, October 7th, 1819. She died, 1827. Their children were Elizabeth, married as first wife, G. C. Washington, and Harriet Ann, married Peter. Another daughter of Colonel George Beale married Evans. On January 18th, 1720, George Beale received a grant of 1,380 acres, known as "Rock of Dumbarton." Liber, J. L., No. A. pp. 55, Maryland Land Records.

Will of George Beale, second son of Colonel George Beale. To wife, Elizabeth, all real and personal property I received with her. Two negroes; cochehee with two horses; $100 for mourning me and right of dower in estate. To son George Beale, £100, and to his children, negroes named in the bill of sale recorded in Montgomery County, after his death. Also to children of George Beale, Patrick and Anna Beale, three negroes apiece. To son George, equal share of personal property. To son Levin Beale, land he now lives on during his life and that of his present wife, remainder between his two children John and Anna Beale, to them three negroes apiece. To grandson, Thomas, son of Ninian Beale, the same. Son Hezekiah and Captain Thomas B. Beale, executors. To son Hezekiah,

the rest of the £100. To Rev. Stephen Balch, two negroes and
their increase for his children. To Levin P. W. Balch, $150. To
Captain John Rose, negroes, etc. Will made the 11th of June, 1802;
probated, the 20th of October, 1807. Washington, J. H. p. 137.

His son, George Beale, was born 1748, died 1807. Captain
Thomas Brooke, born September 20th, 1770, died September, 1820.
Will made, November 23rd, 1808; probated, October 14th, 1820.

Anna married Captain John Rose. Elizabeth married Rev.
Stephen Balch.

I do not know the maiden name of Elizabeth, his wife, though
I have tried to discover it.

MAREEN DUVALL, THE HUGUENOT.

No more striking figure in colonial history is found than the
personal achievements of this fleeing immigrant from Nantes, about
1650.

He came as one of the one hundred and fifty adventurers, brought
over by Colonel William Burgess. He settled near Colonel Burgess,
in Anne Arundel County, on the south side of South River and
became one of the most successful merchants and planters of that
favored section.

When political influences were most active during the revolution of 1689, Mareen Duvall was among the leaders who sustained
the Lord Proprietary. His name is found in Colonel Greenberry's
letter to Governor Copley, as one of the Jacobin party, whose
mysterious meetings he could not solve.

The land records of Anne Arundel and Prince George Counties
show that this Huguenot planter and merchant held a vast estate,
and left his widow and third wife so attractive as to become the
third wife of Colonel Henry Ridgely, and later the wife of Rev. Mr.
Henderson, the commissary of the Chuch of England. Together
they built old Trinity, or Forest Chapel, near Collington, in Prince
George County.

The will of Mareen Duvall is an intelligent one. It was probated, in 1694; about the time of the removal of the Capitol from
St. Mary's to Annapolis.

It is not known who were his first wives. One of them was
closely allied to the celebrated John Larkin, a neighbor and enduring friend of Mareen Duvall. Five of his twelve children were
married during the lifetime of the Huguenot. "Mareen, the Elder,"
also called by his mother-in-law, "Marius," married Frances Stockett,
daughter of Thomas. He was the ancestor of John P. Duvall, a
member of the Virginia Legislature.

Captain John Duvall, who held another large estate, married
Elizabeth Jones, daughter of William Jones, Sr. of Anne Arundel
County. She added considerably to his estate. Their daughter,
Elizabeth, became the wife of Benjamin Warfield, the youngest son of

Richard, the immigrant.   Her wedding gift was 780 acres of "Lugg Ox," in the forks of the Patuxent.   Her sister, Comfort, became Mrs. William Griffith, of Frederick County.

Eleanor Duvall, of Mareen, became Mrs. John Roberts, of Virginia.   Samuel Duvall married Elizabeth Clarke, in 1687; Susannah became Mrs. Robert Tyler, and was the ancestress of General Bradley T. Johnson; Lewis Duvall married Martha Ridgely, only daughter of Hon. Robert Ridgely, of St. Inigoes, in 1699.

"Mareen the Elder," and "Mareen the Younger" are both named by the Huguenot testator of 1694.   The latter seemed to be his favorite.   He married Elizabeth Jacob, daughter of Captain John Jacob.   His sister Catherine, married William Orrick, in 1700. And his sister, Mary, in 1701, became the wife of Rev. Henry Hall, the English Rector of St. James Parish.

The Huguenot names his daughter, Elizabeth Roberts, and daughter Johanna, who became, in 1703, Mrs. Richard Poole.   Benjamin Duvall, of the Huguenot, married Sophia Griffith, in 1713, daughter of William and Sarah (Maccubbin) Griffith.   These were the ancestors of Judge Gabriel Duvall, of the Supreme Court of the United States.   Benjamin and Sophia's issue were, Susanna—Samuel Tyler; Sophia—Thos. Butt; Benjamin—Susanna Tyler. Issue, Gabriel, (Judge of the United States Supreme Court), who was twice married, first to Miss Bryce, daughter of Captain Robert, of Annapolis; second to Miss Jane Gibbon, of Philadelphia.

Edward Duvall and Isaac Duvall, brothers of Judge Gabriel, were lieutenants in the Revolutionary War, and remained bachelors. Isaac Duvall, of Benjamin and Jemima Taylor, married Miss Harding, of Montgomery County, and removed to West Virginia about 1812.   He owned an extensive glass factory at Charlestown, afterwards Wellsburg, on the Ohio.   He left three sons, among whom was General Isaac Harding Duvall, and four daughters.   From Julia A. descends Mrs. Anne O. Jackson, of Parkersburg, W. Va. and her sister Mrs. List, of Wheeling.   From William, brother of Isaac, by his wife, Harriet Doodridge, comes Mrs. Kate Rector Thibaut, of Washington, D. C.

Mareen Duvall, "The Younger," by Elizabeth Jacob, had Mareen in 1702,—Ruth Howard; Susannah—first, Mr. Fowler, and second, Mark Brown.   Elizabeth—Dr. Wm. Denune; Samuel— Elizabeth Mullikin; Benjamin—Miss Wells; John—Miss Fowler; Jacob—Miss Bourne, of Calvert.   Samuel and Elizabeth (Mullikin) Duvall, daughter of James Mullikin, son of the immigrant, had James—Sarah Duvall, of Mareen and Ruth (Howard) Duvall, and Samuel, in 1740,—Mary Higgins.   From Barton Duvall, of Samuel and Mary, who married Hannah Isaac, daughter of Richard and Ann (Williams) Isaac, came Richard Isaacs Duvall, Dr. Philip Barton Duvall and Dr. Joseph Isaac Duvall.

Richard Isaac Duvall—first, Sarah Ann Duvall, of Tobias, and had James M. Duvall, of Baltimore, Philip Barton Duvall, who read medicine with Dr. Samuel Chew, of Baltimore, and graduated, in 1860, at the University of Maryland, and went south in 1861, and joined the Confederate State's Army and was killed at the battle of Chancellorsville, Va. Samuel F. Duvall, of the Confederate Army, several times wounded; Daniel C. Duvall, and Sallie, and several other children who died in infancy. Richard Isaac Duvall—second, Rachel M. Waring, of Francis and Elizabeth (Turner) Waring, and had Richard Mareen and Marius Turner Duvall, twins, born 1856. Richard M. Duvall, a member of the Baltimore Bar, married, 1895, Julia Anna Webster Goldsborough, daughter of Dr. John Schley and Julia Anna Webster (Strider) Goldsborough, of Frederick, Md.

Samuel and Elizabeth (Mullikin) Duvall had a son, Isaac, who was twice married. One of his sons was Basil Mullikin Duvall, who married Delilah Duvall, of Philemon, of Montgomery, and had issue, Agrippa, of Kentucky,—Miss Smith, of Kentucky; Mary A.—Thos. J. Betts, of Baltimore; Miss Margery Duvall; Van Buren Duvall, of Texas; Augusta—Dr. Thos. C. Bussey, of Baltimore County; Kate—George Ellicott, of the family who founded Ellicott City.

The homestead of Mr. Basil Mullikin Duvall, now held by Mrs. Ellicott, is immediately upon the Cattail, of the Patuxent, in upper Howard County.

The last wife and widow of the Huguenot was Miss Mary Stanton. Before 1700, she became the wife of Col. Henry Ridgely, the immigrant, and with him, closed the administration of the estate of the Huguenot. The younger Mareen objected to his guardian, Col. Ridgely, but the courts did not sustain him. After the death of Col. Ridgely, in 1710, Mrs. Mary Ridgely bought a tract of land from Wm. Ridgely, Sr. and Jr., brother and nephew of her late husband. Mrs. Mary Ridgely next appears as the wife of Rev. Jacob Henderson, the English rector sent over to visit the churches of the province. Mr. and Mrs. Henderson left an enduring monument to their memory by the erection, in 1735, of Holy Trinity Chapel. Having endowed the same, they left it as a memorial to the public, and by act of the General Assembly, it was converted into a "Chapel of Ease." There is a marble slab in the vestibule, stating the fact of its erection at the cost of Mr. and Mrs. Henderson. There are also a number of memorial windows erected in it to the Duvalls, Mullikins, Bowies and others.

The will of Mrs. Henderson, at Upper Marlborough, shows that she had a brother in Philadelphia, and that her maiden name was Mary Stanton. She was an intelligent and attractive lady. It is not certain that she left any children by any of her three husbands.

RICHARD BEARD.

Richard Beard, of South River, came up from Virginia with his brother-in-law, Colonel William Burgess. His wife Rachel, was a sister of Mrs. Elizabeth Burgess, both daughters of Edward Robins, of Virginia. He took up "Beard's Habitation," on Beards Creek, and built Beards Mill. He represented Anne Arundel in the Assemblies of 1662 and 1663. In his will of 1675, he named his sons Richard, (the deputy-surveyor, who made a map of Annapolis), and John Beard. Daughters Ruth, Rebecca (Nicholson), and daughter Rachel Clark, and her son, Neal Clark, who married Jane, daughter of Captain George Puddington. Mrs. Rachel Clark next married Thomas Stimpson, and by him had two daughters, Rachel and Comfort. The former became Mrs. Colonel Charles Greenberry; the latter, wife of John Dorsey, only son of Joshua.

Mrs. Stimpson next appeared as Mrs. Rachel Killburne. In 1701, she deeded to her daughters, Rachel Greenberry and Comfort Stimpson, furniture, lots in Annapolis, large silver porring, small silver tankard, large silver "cordiall" cup, silver punch cups, and silver spoons. To her son-in-law, Wm. Killburne, and her daughter-in-law, Elizabeth, his wife, she gave several memorials. To Charles Carroll she gave twenty shillings for a ring. To her granddaughter, Rachel Clark, a silver bodkin and a gold ring. A memorial was also given to Henry Davis, Sr.

During that same year, 1701, she became Mrs. Rachel Freeborne. Her daughter, Comfort, was now named Comfort Dorsey. She gave to Anna Hammond, daughter of Charles and Rachel, his wife (Mrs. Greenberry), a negro girl. In 1716, Mrs. Freeborne sold to Charles Carroll a house and lot adjoining Henry Ridgely. She deeded "Turkey Quarter" to her son Neale Clark.

Thomas Freeborne took up "Freeborne's Progress," in Howard County. It was later held by Robert Ridgely, of Elk Ridge, through his wife, Sarah. This tract passed through several transfers, finally deeded by Mrs. Margaret Cumming to Rachel Hammond.

Richard Beard named, as executors, his sons, Richard and John and his "brother-in-law, Colonel Wm. Burgess." Both of his sons left large families in Anne Arundel, from one of whom descended Mrs. Lancelot Warfield, of "Brandy."

JOHN GAITHER, OF SOUTH RIVER.

The name of John Gaither was sixth on the list of the corporation of James City.—(HOLTEN.)

"Came in the Assurance, 1635, Jo. Gater and Joan Gater, aged 36 and 23 years, and John Gater, 15 years."—(HOLTEN's List of Va.)

On a neck of land, on the eastern branch of Elizabeth River, the Virginia records, already quoted, show John Gater (Gaither) seated upon five hundred acres for the transportation of ten persons. He was, also, a contributor to the support of the Non-Conformist Church.

In 1662, the following record was made in Maryland: "Then came John Gaither and demanded the renewment of a warrant for 450 acres—renewed." In 1663, John Gaither and Robert Proctor surveyed "Abington," at the head of South River. It adjoined "Freeman's Fancy," "Freeman's Stone" and "Freeman's Landing."

These three settlers were sons-in-law of Joseph Morley, whose will, of 1674, made Robert Proctor and John Gaither his executors, and legatees of his whole estate.

They sold "Morley's Lot" and "Morley's Grove" to Colonel William Burgess. Robert Proctor and Elizabeth, his wife, late widow of John Freeman, and daughter of Joseph Morley, sold Freeman's lands to Captain George Puddington, which were later bought by John Gaither from Captain Edward Burgess, executor of Captain Puddington.

Captain John Browne, mariner, of London, sold, in 1690, to James Finley, three hundred acres out of "Abington;" said land laid out for John Dearing. And during that same year, Captain John Browne sold to John Gaither, lands that had been laid off for Mr. Chapman out of "Freeman's Fancy." Captain Browne, also, sold to John Gaither, lands in Abington, recently held by Robert Proctor. At the time of his death, in 1705, John Gaither held all of Freeman's lands and all of Abington, except that held by William Ridgely and Elizabeth, his wife.

His widow, Ruth (Morley) Gaither, married again, Francis Hardesty. Dying intestate, a commission consisting of John Howard, John Hammond and John Duvall, divided the estate.

His heirs were, John Gaither, Jr., born 1677; Ruth, born 1679 —John Warfield (of Richard and Elinor Browne Warfield); Benjamin, born 1681; Rachel, born 1687—Samuel White; Mary, born 1692; Rebecca, born 1695; Susan, born 1697.

John Gaither contributed liberally to the defense of the settlers against Indian invasions.

John Gaither, Jr., as heir-at-law, deeded to his brother Benjamin, and to Edward Gaither, portions of his father's estate.

The issue of John and Jane (Buck) Gaither were, Benjamin, Alexander, Richard, David, Amos, Joshua and Rezin, all inheriting "Abington."

By a second marriage, to Elizabeth, widow of Benjamin Warfield, he had John, Edward and Samuel Gaither. These inherited and located upon "Left Out," near Dayton, Howard County.

From these descended Mr. Samuel Gaither, the Commissioner of Howard.

Benjamin Gaither will be noted in Howard County.

Edward Gaither, (of John) in 1715, resurveyed his father's estate into "Gaither's Collections." This adjoined Richard Snowden's South River estate. Edward Gaither married Mrs. Margaret Williams, whose two heirs were Joseph and Margaret Williams. Their inheritance was "Folkland," "The Plains" and "Plumbton," adjoining.

The will of Edward Gaither, in 1740, named his daughter, Rachel Jacob; son, Moses, inherited the surplusage of "Freeman's Fancy," "Freeman's Stone," "Landing," "Gaither's Range," and "Round About Hills"—some three hundred acres. "To my daughter-in-law (stepdaughter), Margaret Williams, 'Folkland,'

'The Plains' and 'Plumbton,' adjoining; a part of which was bequeathed to my son-in-law (stepson), Joseph Williams." His children named were, daughter Sarah, Edward, Jane, Leah, Dinah and Moses, to whom he left his personal property. Wife, Margaret, executrix. In her will, of 1762, she confirmed the title to her daughter, Margaret Howard, wife of Joseph, and named her daughters heirs.

Edward Gaither, of Edward, married Sarah Howard, and came into possession of "Gaither's Collection," and offered the whole tract for sale, in the Maryland Gazette, in 1752. It was bought by John Ridgely and others. He left no will, but, in 1787, his son, Edward Gaither, Jr., who was a Colonel in the Revolution, and field officer of the militia, a resident of Howard County, and a witness to the will of Charles Carroll, left the following record: "To my friend Colonel Rezin Hammond, I leave my Granby Dun horse, my saddle, bridle, sword and gold mourning ring. To my friend, David Stewart, a gold mourning ring and silver spoons. All my estate to my mother, Sarah Gaither, and brothers, Henry, Ephraim, John and Elijah Gaither, and sister Margery. To brother Elijah, my lands 'Day's Discovery,' 'Gaither's Adventure' and part of 'Rebecca's Lot,' bought of John Ellicott, and part of 'Mt. Etna,' bought of Dr. Ephraim Howard. He and Colonel Rezin Hammond my executors. Witnesses, Stephen West, Jr., Samuel Norwood and John Rallings."

In 1798, James Gaither named his wife, Patience, who was to hold his estate, which later descended to Dorsey Jacob, Jr., John Hall and others, and Elizabeth Stansbury Gaither.

Margery Gaither, sister of Colonel Edward Gaither, married Philemon Browne. Their daughter, Margery Browne married, Thomas Warfield, of Caleb, and removed to Kentucky.

Nancy Gaither, of "Venison Park," near Savage, in 1817, named her nephew, Basil Simpson, her sister, Sarah Middleton, brother, Basil Simpson, son, Ephraim Simpson Gaither and nephew, Ephraim Gaither, of William.

CHEW.

John Chew, of "Chewtown," Somersetshire, England, came to Virginia in the "Sea Flower," in 1622, and was gladly received there by members of his family, who had preceded him, in 1618, in the ship "Charitie." He settled at James City, built a house for his wife, Sarah, and was a member of the House of Burgesses. He is there recorded as a prosperous merchant.

He removed to Maryland with his neighbors, in 1649, and received a grant for five hundred acres, paid for in Virginia tobacco. With him came his wife, Sarah, and two sons, Samuel and Joseph. Descendants of the latter, through a daughter of John Larkin, are still residents of Virginia.

Samuel Chew laid out "Herrington," on Herring Creek. In 1650, a grant was issued to him as "his Lordship's well-beloved Samuel Chew, Esq." In 1669, he was sworn in as one of the justices of the chancery and provincial courts. His name appears in both Houses of the Assembly until his death, in 1676. In 1675, he was Colonel Samuel Chew, and was ordered, with Colonel William Burgess, to go against the Indians at the head of the Severn. His will, of 1676, bequeathed the Town of Herrington, negroes, able-bodied Englishmen, and hogsheads of tobacco, to his heirs, and made his wife, Ann (Ayres) Chew, his executrix. She was the Quakeress daughter of William Ayres, thus recorded in Virginia: "William Ayres received two hundred and fifty acres on the main creek of Nansemond River, in 1635, for transportating five persons." Perhaps this patentee was related to Thomas Ayres, associated with Edward Bennett in a plantation in this county." Lower Norfolk, "records a power of attorney from Samuel Chew, of Herringtown, and Anne, his wife, sole daughter and heiress of William Ayres, of Nansemond County."

Colonel Samuel and Ann Chew had a large family. Their daughter, Sarah, is recorded in the Chew records, as the wife of "a Burges." She married Captain Edward Burgess, oldest son of Colonel William. Samuel Chew, Jr., was located on "Poplar Ridge." From him descended Colonel Samuel Chew, of "Upper Bennett," a member of the "Federation of Freemen," and Colonel of Militia. He married, first, Miss Weems, and second, Priscilla Clagett, daughter of Rev. Samuel Clagett. She was a sister of Bishop Clagett.

Colonel John Hamilton Chew, married his cousin Priscilla, daughter of Bishop Claggett. Dr. Samuel Chew, of Baltimore, and Rev. John Chew, of the Protestant Episcopal Church, were his heirs. Captain Samuel Chew, of Herring Bay, and Colonel Philemon Lloyd Chew were sons of Samuel Chew and Henrietta Maria Lloyd, his wife, whose three daughters were, Henrietta Maria, wife of Captain Edward Dorsey, of the "Tuesday Club;" Mary, wife of Governor William Paca; Margaret, wife of John Beale Bordley. These three daughters resided in Annapolis.

The homestead of John Beale Bordley is now held by the Randall family. Retiring to Joppa, on the Gunpowder, and still later to "Bordley Island," John Beale Bordley ordered champagne by the cask, and Madeira by the pipe. It was an ideal home of an age when spinning wheels and looms were going incessantly; when brickyards, windmills and rope walks were in operation; when a brewery converted the hops which Governor Sharpe had imported.

Colonel Philemon Lloyd Chew married Henrietta Maria, daughter of Edward Tilghman.

Major Richard Chew, of Calvert, married Margaret Mackall, daughter of General James John Mackall. Their son married Anne Bowie, sister of Governor Robert Bowie.

Benjamin Chew, fifth son of Samuel and Anne Ayres, married Elizabeth Benson. Their son was Dr. Samuel Chew, of "Maidstone," near Annapolis, who married, first, Mary Galloway, of Samuel, of "Tulip Hill," and had Benjamin Chew, of "Cleveden;" Elizabeth, wife of Colonel Edward Tilghman, and Anne, wife of Samuel Galloway.

Dr. Samuel Chew married, secondly, Mary, daughter of Aquilla Paca, and widow of Richard Galloway. Their son was Judge Samuel Chew, who married Anna Maria Frisby, and died at Chestertown without issue. He was of the Supreme Court of Delaware.

Dr. Samuel Chew, of "Maidstone," removed to Dover, and became Judge of the three lower counties, now Delaware. He was called the fighting Quaker, and was immortalized as follows:

"Immortal Chew first set our Quakers right;
He made it plain they might resist and fight;
And the gravest Dons agreed to what he said,
And freely gave their cast for the King's aid,
For war successful, and for peace and trade."

For sustaining the law passed by the Assembly of the three lower counties, as a militia law, he was expelled from the Quaker Society. In commenting upon it, he wrote: "Their bills of excommunication are as full fraught with fire and brimstone and other church artillery, as those even of the Church of Rome."

The offense of Judge Chew was his decision that "self-defense was not only lawful, but obligatory upon God's citizens."

His son, Benjamin Chew, born 1722, rose rapidly in law and became eminent. He was Speaker of the House of Delegates in Dover, and was a neighbor of Judge Nicholas Ridgely.

In 1755, he was Attorney-General of Pennsylvania. In 1756, he was Recorder of Philadelphia. In 1774, he was Chief Justice of the Supreme Court of Pennsylvania. His definition of high treason has become historical. Said he, "Opposition, by force of arms, to the lawful authority of the King is high treason; but, in the moment, when the King, or his Ministers, shall exceed the constitutional authority vested in them by the constitution, submission to their mandates becomes treason." His object was reform rather than revolution.

His homestead, "Cliveden," on the old Germantown Road, became still more celebrated. In it had gathered the British forces, who sent out a fire of musketry upon the American forces. The delay caused by trying to drive the British from their stronghold, occasioned the loss of the battle of Germantown.

Judge Chew's four daughters were celebrated for their beauty. "Peggy" was the special admiration of Major Andre, a favorite guest at "Cliveden." Upon her his poetic pen recorded many complimentary verses, still extant. When Colonel John Eager Howard, the hero of the Revolution, had won "Peggy Chew" as his wife, she remarked to some distinguished French officers, who were guests at Belvidere, "That major Andre was a most witty and cultivated gentleman." Her patriotic husband added: "He was a ——— spy, sir, nothing but a ——— spy."

"The old homestead, with its rough walls of stone, its entrance guarded by marble lions, is now blinded and defaced by age. In its halls hang portraits older than the house."—(MARION HARLAND.)

Harriet Chew, of "Cliveden," presided at "Homewood," of
Charles Carroll, only son of the signer.   Juliana became Mrs. Philip
Nicklin and Sophia was Mrs. Henry Phillips.

From Benjamin Chew, the younger, through Katherine Banning,
came Benjamin, who married a daughter of Chief Justice Tilghman.
Eliza—James Murray Mason, father of Catherine, wife of John T.
B. Dorsey.

Henry Banning Chew married Harriet Ridgely, of Hampton.
Their descendants reside near Towson.

PRESTON, AT PATUXENT.

Colonel Richard Preston, of the Patuxent, was a leading settler
from Virginia.   He arrived in Virginia, about 1642, and held a high
position for one of his faith.   Surrounding him, in Nansemond
County, were many others of the same faith, opposed to the established church, and with him removed to Maryland, in 1649.   Richard
Preston arrived with his wife and children, numbering seven in all,
and entered land for seventy-three persons.   Upon his demand,
Governor William Stone issued the following order: "These are to
authorize Mr. Richard Preston, commander of the north side of
Patuxent River, for one month next ensuing, with the advice of
his Lordship's Surveyor General, to grant warranty to the said
Surveyor for the laying out of any convenient quantities of land,
upon said river, on the north side thereof, not formerly taken up by
any adventurers that shall make their just title appear.   Provided
that he, the said Mr. Preston, do testify such titles, particularly
unto the Secretary's office before the return of the certificate of
Surveyor.   Given at St. Leonard's, 15 July, 1651.—WM STONE."

Five hundred acres were surveyed for him in 1650.   It was
named "Preston."   Upon this he erected a house which still stands,
and is the oldest house in Maryland.   It is built of brick.   It is
two stories high, with three dormer windows front and two back.
The lower room, where the assembly met, has been divided by a
plaster partition.   The inner walls are panelled.   A porch, with
the house roof extending over it, is in the rear.   The house stands
on the neck between the Patuxent and St. Leonard's Creek.

Captain Wm. Fuller took up land adjoining it, and Governor
William Stone held lands not far below, on the south side of the
Patuxent.

In 1652, Richard Preston was commanded, by authority of
Parliament, to levy and raise one able bodied man out of every
seven of the inhabitants of the Patuxent, from the mouth of said
river as far as Herring Creek, with victuals, arms and ammunition,
to meet at Mattapania, and be thence transported for the service
under Captain William Fuller.

Colonel Preston's petition, signed by sixty of his neighbors, in
1652, to Richard Bennett and William Claiborne, Commissioners of
Parliament, was a stirring appeal for their rights.   It was followed

by another of similar tenor in 1653. Bennett and Claiborne replied that these petitioners should secure their rights, advising them to stand fast.

Then followed the struggle of the Severn.

John Hammond, in his pamphlet "Hammond vs. Heamans," records that he alone seized the records at Richard Preston's house. Yet, in 1655, "attachment was granted Richard Preston on the estate of Captain William Stone, to be liable to satisfy unto Richard Preston the summe of twenty-nine pounds for gunnes and ammunition, taken from the house of said Preston by Josias Fendall, one of Captain Stone's officers and complices, in the last rebellion."

Richard Preston's name stands either at the head or next to Captain Fuller's in all official acts of that period; and during the absence of Wm. Durand, Secretary, the records were ordered to be kept at his house. It is interesting to note the peculiar transition in the early religious faith of these Virginia leaders. We find them making stringent laws against Quakers, yet some of the most aggressive leaders soon joined the Quakers. Captain Wm. Fuller, Wm. Durand, Richard Preston, Wm. Berry, Thomas Meers, Philip Thomas, Peter Sharp, changed their faith; and even Richard Bennett succumbed before his death. Richard Preston's will left several tracts of Eastern Shore lands to his daughters; but most of his Patuxent estate to his son James, if he be living, or will come into the province, to be held by him until his grandson, Samuel Preston, shall attain to the age of twenty-one years. To his kinsmen, Ralph Dorsey, John and James Dorsey, he willed a portion of personality and real estate, in Calvert.

Samuel Preston later removed to Philadelphia, and left a long line of descendants.

Mr. Dixon, who came into possession of this historic homestead, has taken a pride in preserving the old building, which, though now delapidated through age, stands alone as the one relic of a revolution, one hundred years before our Revolution for Independence.— (ALLEN in Colonial Homesteads.)

DAVIS.

Seventy-five Davises are recorded among our "Early Settlers," during the decade of 1660-1670.

Sir Thomas Davis was of the London Company, to settle Virginia, and he came over in "The Margaret," to James City, in 1619. During that same year he was in the Assembly of Virginia from "Martin's Brandon."

In 1637, Thomas Davis was granted a plantation of three hundred acres for transporting six settlers. In 1642, his plantation was upon the east side of the Elizabeth River, in Nansemond County, from which most of our Virginia pilgrims came up to Maryland in 1650. Upon Herring Creek, in the very midst of these settlers, I find a Thomas Davis. But in the absence of any testamentary records, or Rent Roll records, in his name, previous to 1700, I am inclined to believe that Thomas Davis, Sr., wife Mary Pierpoint, whose will was made in 1743, but not probated until 1749, may be called the settler

The will of Thomas Davis, Sr., shows that he had accumulated a good estate. He names his dear wife, Mary, to whom is given all his personal estate. "To grandson, Caleb Davis, son of Richard, I give the lands where his mother, Ruth Davis, now lives, called 'Duvall's Delight,' two hundred acres. To son Thomas, 'Laswell's Hopewell.' To son John, 'Davistone' and 'Whats Left, 'adjoining. To son Samuel, lands in Prince George. To son Robert, "Ranters Ridge.' To son Francis, 'Pearl' out of 'Diamond' and 'Davis Addition' from 'Grimestone.' Wife Mary, John and Francis, executors. Personal estate, after death of wife, to go equally to five sons and five daughters."

Richard Davis was then dead, and Thomas Davis, Jr., followed soon after. Both wills probated in 1749.

Thomas Davis, Jr.,—Elizabeth, daughter of Benjamin Gaither. He names his sons, Ephraim and Amos; daughters, Mary and Sarah. To them was left a part of "Snowden's Second Addition." "To daughter, Betsy Davis, I give 'Benjamin's Lot.' " This was the mother's part of Benjamin Gaither's estate, and in her will as Mrs. Elizabeth Brown, she names her son, Amos, and her daughters, Mary Norwood and Sarah, wife of Edward Burgess, and daughter, Betsy Davis. Ephraim Davis, of Thomas and Elizabeth (Gaither) Davis, inherited the homestead at Greenwood. His wife, Elizabeth, was from the house of Cornelius Howard, of Simpsonville, and as his widow became the wife of Wm. Gaither.

Thomas Davis, the son, inherited the homestead. He was in command of a company, and was at the front in the Whiskey Rebellion in Pennsylvania. He was, also, President of the Board of Trustees of Brookeville Academy, and was succeeded by his son, Allen Bowie Davis, of "Greenwood."

Taking the name of his distinguished grandfather, General Allen Bowie, Mr. Davis has made a reputation which goes beyond the borders of his state.

As an agriculturist, he advanced to the highest success. As an educator, he was always at the front. President of the Board of the Academy, of the Public School Board and President of the Board of the Agricultural College, he struggled hard to locate that institution near his own home, where the natural soil was far better suited for a "Model Farm." Mr. Davis wrote a very good little text book upon agriculture to be used in the public schools as an entrance to the College of Argiculture.

His first wife was Comfort Dorsey, daughter of Chief Justice Thomas Beale Dorsey. The mother of his children was Miss Hester Wilkens, of Baltimore. His only son, William, died in Montana, where he had married a daughter of Bishop Whipple. His sister, Hester, died unmarried. Misses Rebecca and Mary Dorsey Davis, having retired from the beautiful old homestead, now reside in Baltimore. Many relics of the homestead were donated by them to the Rockville Historical Society.

Robert Davis, of Thomas and Mary, was seated upon "Ranters' Ridge," near Woodstock. His wife was Ruth Gaither, daughter of John and Elizabeth. Their issue are found in the following transfer of 1772, viz: "John Davis, oldest son of Nicholas, son of Robert, Sr., and Ely Davis; Robert Davis, Thomas Davis and Ichabod Davis, sons and devisees of Robert Davis, Sr., deed 'Ranter's Ridge' to Rezin Hammond." Another transfer in the name of Ruth Randall, still later Ruth Nelson, widow of Robert Davis, and widow of Nathan Randall, joined Caleb Davis, the legatee of both Nathan and herself, in deeding a portion of "Good Fellowship" to Mr. Knight. Still later Caleb, of Baltimore, deeded his interest in "Good Fellowship" to several Baltimore agents. He was the father of Hon. Henry G. Davis.

Richard Davis, of Robert, was the celebrated defender of Baltimore, in 1814. His descendants still hold portions of the large estate of Robert Davis. They are William and Richard Davis and their descendants.

Richard Davis, of Thomas and Mary, was located near Highland, Howard. He married Ruth, daughter of John Warfield and Ruth Gaither. They had sons, Richard, Thomas—Mary Sappington; Caleb—Lurcetia Griffith, of Orlando. His inheritance was "Duvall's Delight," on Patuxent. His daughter, Elizabeth—Philip Welsh. This Caleb was not, as has been stated, the father of our Democratic candidate for Vice-President. His brother, Thomas, lived upon the Sappington estate near "Warfield's Range" and "Laurel." This estate has only recently passed from the Davis name.

Sarah Davis, of Thomas,—Colonel Henry Griffith, whose son heired, through Mrs. Mary Davis and Dr. Francis Brown Sappington, a tract near Laurel.

John Davis, of Thomas and Mary,—Anne Worthington; Francis Davis, of Thomas and Mary,—Anne Hammond, daughter of John and Anne (Dorsey) Hammond, and had Thomas Davis, who settled in Carroll County. He was in the Revolution. His sons were, Henry, George and Dr. Frank Davis. The first two have many descendants in Baltimore. Mr. Harvey Davis, of Howard, is a grandson of Revolutionary Thomas Davis. Zachariah Davis, brother of Thomas, was located near Mt. Airy, in Carroll. His son, William Davis, was the father of Eldred Griffith Davis, the popular collector of taxes in Washington, D. C.

Mary Davis, of Thomas and Mary,—John Riggs, of "Riggs' Hills." Ruth Davis, of Thomas and Mary,—Joshua Warfield, of "Lugg Ox," whose mother, Elizabeth (Duvall) Warfield, married second John Gaither, whose daughter, Ruth—Robert Davis, of Woodstock.

In addition to this line of Thomas Davis, of Anne Arundel, there were several William Davis's—father and son. The latter held an estate of Captain John Welsh. There was also a Henry Davis, and from him likely descended Professor Davis, of St. John's College, the father of Hon. Henry Winter Davis.

JOHN RANDALL, SENIOR.

This founder of a distinguished line of sons of Maryland, was born in what is now Richmond County, Virginia, then a part of Westmoreland Co., in 1750. He was the youngest son of Thomas Randall, who came from England in the early part of that century; settled in Westmoreland County, married Jane Davis, a daughter of a Virginia planter; became a large land holder and a member of the Court of Justices in the Northern Neck of Virginia. John put himself under the tutelage of Mr. Buckley, of Fredericksburg, an architect and builder, who designed and constructed many of the most celebrated colonial residences and public buildings in Virginia and Maryland. He came to Annapolis in 1770, where he designed and constructed several of the most admired specimens of colonial architecture, among the rest, what is now known as the Lockerman or Harwood House, on Maryland Avenue, Annapolis. He was an earnest upholder of the rights of the colonies in the years preceding the Revolution, but earnestly protested against the repudiation of debts due to the inhabitants of Great Britian, as by published signed protests of that day appear. At the outbreak of the Revolution he was a merchant in Annapolis and was appointed, under a commission from the Governor and Council and afterwards by a resolution of the Continental Congress, as Commissary in the Army. He served during the Revolution as an officer of the Maryland Line and many of his letters are in the Archives of Maryland. Returning to Annapolis after the war, he established himself there as a merchant. President Washington appointed him Collector of the Port of Annapolis and he held that position, or that of Navy Agent, until his death in 1826, He married Deborah Knapp, of Annapolis, who survived him with eleven children and died at Annapolis in 1852, ninety years of age.

DANIEL RANDALL.

Daniel Randall, son of John Randall, the elder, was in active service during the War of 1812, as a volunteer, and thereafter was commissioned as Paymaster in the Regular Army. He served as such during the Indian Wars and the Mexican War under General Scott and was at the time of his death in 1851, Assistant Paymaster General and in charge of the Pay-Department of the Army.

He was highly esteemed and Fort Randall, then on the frontier, was named after him, as evidence of his universal popularity.

HENRY K. RANDALL.

Henry K. Randall, another son of John Randall, the elder, was in the militia during the War of 1812; was then appointed an officer in the Custom House in the City of Baltimore; was an Agent of the Government in closing up the affairs of the Choctaw Nation in Georgia and for many years afterwards was Chief Clerk of Revolutionary Pensions in the Treasury Department. He married Emily, daughter of Thomas Munroe of Washington, D. C. and died in 1877, survived by her and two daughters, Mrs. William B. Webb and Mrs. Henry Elliott. He was a large real estate holder in Washington and did much to advance the prosperity of that city.

HON. ALEXANDER RANDALL.

Honorable Alexander Randall of Annapolis, son of John Randall, the elder, was born at Annapolis in January 1803; educated at St. John's College, from which he obtained his B. A. and M. A. degrees; practiced law for over fifty years in Annapolis, for over twenty years in partnership with his nephew, Alexander B. Hagner, afterwards Justice of the Supreme Bench of the District of Columbia. He was appointed Auditor of the Court of Chancery by Chancellor Bland. In 1841 he was a member of the Congress of the United States, but declined a re-nomination; was elected by the Whig Party. His colleague from the double district, as then constituted, was Honorable John P. Kennedy. He prepared, as member of the Committee on the District of Columbia, a Code of Laws of Maryland, since the separation of the District, which were deemed important to be adopted by Congress for the District, and they were added to the District Code.

He was a member of the Constitutional Convention of 1851 of Maryland and in 1864 was elected Attorney General of Maryland. In 1877 he retired from the practice of law and became the President of the Farmers National Bank of Annapolis, of which he had been a Director and the Attorney from early life. He died November 20th 1881 at his residence, in Annapolis, leaving twelve children surviving him. He married Catharine, daughter of Honorable William Wirt, Attorney General of the United States, who died survived by five children;—his second wife was Elizabeth, daughter of the Rev. John G. Blanchard, Assistant Rector of St. Paul's Church, Baltimore City, who survived him with seven children.

During many years Mr. Alexander Randall was a Vestryman of St Anne's Church, Annapolis and a member of the Board of Visitors and Governors of St. John's College. He was a delegate to the Diocesan Conventions of his church for many years, and several times a deputy from Maryland to its General Conventions. He founded and managed for many years, as president, the Annapolis Water Company, and its Gas Company; and was one of the active promoters and directors in its first railroad company (the

Annapolis & Elk-Ridge), and telegraph company. He led a most active and useful life—as a lawyer, as a citizen and as a Christian —and left a large family of carefully educated and trained children, who represent his influence for good, both in Maryland and in other states.

BURTON RANDALL, M. D.

Burton Randall, M. D., youngest son of John Randall, Sr., was graduated as a physician at the University of Pennsylvania, and was appointed assistant surgeon in the United States Army. He had a long and active service through the Creek, Seminole and other Indian wars; through the Mexican War and on the frontiers. During the Civil War he had charge of various important hospitals and army posts. He married Virginia Taylor, a niece of General Zachary Taylor, who survived him with two children. When he retired, in 1869, he held the brevet rank of lieutenant-colonel in the army, and settled at Annapolis, where his family still resides.

JOHN RANDALL, JUNIOR.

John Randall, Jr., eldest son of John Randall and Deborah (Knapp) Randall, lived and died in Annapolis, leaving no descendants. He was a farmer and also a partner with his father in the merchantile firm of Randall & Son, at Annapolis. He married Eliza Hodges, of Anne Arundel County, and died in 1861.

HON. THOMAS RANDALL.

Hon. Thomas Randall was the second son of John Randall, the elder. After graduating from St. John's College, Annapolis, he studied law in the office of Chancellor Johnson, the elder; was an officer of the regular army during the War of 1812, severely wounded in one of the battles near Niagara, captured by the British and carried to Quebec; made a remarkable escape from prison during the depth of winter, but was recaptured and exchanged after the war; was Captain of Artillery, in 1820, but resigned and practiced law in Washington, D. C.; was appointed by President Monroe, a Special Agent of the United States in the West Indies, to endeavor to stop the depredations of pirates in that part of the world; was appointed, in 1826, Judge of the Supreme Court of the Territory of Florida, where he settled and practiced law, with his nephew, Thomas Hagner, in Tallahassee; was appointed Adjutant General under Governor Call, during the Seminole War. He married Laura, eldest daughter of the Hon. William Wirt, and left surviving him, in 1877, three daughters and numerous descendants.

RICHARD RANDALL, M. D.

Richard Randall, M. D., son of John Randall, the elder, was a graduate of the Medical Department of the University of Pennsylvania; settled in Washington, D. C., where he had a large practice.

He was one of the founders and the president of the African Colonization Society, and finally went out to Liberia as Governor. He died there of African fever, a martyr to the cause of African Colonization.

HON. ALEXANDER BURTON HAGNER.

Hon. Alexander Burton Hagner, born July 13th, 1826, in Washington, was son of Peter Hagner, for many years a First Auditor of the Treasury, and Francis Hagner, who was a daughter of John Randall, the elder, of Annapolis, Maryland. Mr. Hagner graduated at Princeton University, in 1845, read law and practiced law in Annapolis, with his uncle, Hon. Alexander Randall. He was one of the leaders of the Maryland Bar and engaged in many important cases, civil and criminal, in the lower courts and in the Court of Appeals. Also, in many important Naval Court Martials, among others he was of counsel for the defence in the celebrated prosecutions of Mrs. Warton for poisoning General Ketchum and Eugene VanNess. He served as special judge in a number of cases in Maryland, under the single judge system, which prevailed prior to the adoption of the Constitution of 1867, where the regular judge was disqualified from sitting. He was elected to the House of Delegates of Maryland, in 1854, and was Chairman of the Committee of Ways and Means; was a candidate for Congress, in 1857, and again in 1874, but was defeated. In 1860, he was a Presidential Elector on the Bell and Everett ticket. In 1879, he was appointed an Associate Justice of the Supreme Bench of the District of Columbia, and held that position until his resignation of it in 1903. During his long service on the Bench, he presided in many important trials and wrote many elaborate and important opinions. Among the chief of these is the opinion in what was known as "The Potomac Flats Case," involving the government ownership of the extensive flats opposite the City of Washington. Judge Hagner wrote that opinion, which was adopted by the Supreme Court of the United States, and which is one of the most important cases in its results upon the District welfare, and one of the most learned and able opinions to be found in our law reports. He married Louisa, daughter of Randolph Harrison, of Virginia, and they live in the City of Washington, D. C.

HON. JOHN WIRT RANDALL.

Hon. John Wirt Randall, son of Hon. Alexander and Catherine (Wirt) Randall, born at Annapolis, Maryland, March 6th, 1845; educated at St. John's College, Burlington College, New Jersey, and Yale University; read law in his father's office, who was then Attorney General of Maryland; admitted to the Bar in 1868. He was soon after appointed Register in Bankruptcy for the Fifth Congressional District of Maryland, by Hon. Salmon P. Chase, Chief Justice of the United States, who had been a student in the office of William Wirt (Mr. Randall's grand-father) whilst Mr. Wirt was Attorney General of the United States. Mr. Randall served three terms as Councilor of the City of Annapolis; revised and codified its Ordinances and By-laws; served one term (1884) in the House of Delegates, and four terms (1888, 1890, 1896 and 1898) in the Senate of Maryland. During the last named session he was President of the Senate, and was a capable and dignified presiding officer. He remodelled the financial systems of the City of Annapolis and of Anne Arundel County, by abolishing the old Collectors of Taxes and creating and regulating the Treasurer System; remodelled the Public School System of the City of Annapolis, and provided by-laws and a bonded debt for the erection of the present fine public school buildings of Annapolis, and their management; was the author, in 1884, and introducer of the Joint Resolutions of the General Assembly establishing "Arbor Day" in Maryland, and, in 1898, of the highly approved Road Laws of Anne Arundel County, and of many other valuable general and local statutes. On the retirement of his father from the law-firm of Randall & Hagner, he succeeded him as a member of that firm; and after the retirement of the Hon. Alexander B. Hagner from the firm, by reason of his elevation to the Supreme Bench of the District of Columbia, he associated with him his brother, Daniel R. Randall, recently State's Attorney for Anne Arundel County—constituting the law-firm of Randall & Randall. Mr. Randall has been, since 1879, a director of the Farmers National Bank of Annapolis, and since 1881, its president. He has been, since 1874, a Vestryman and the treasurer of St. Anne's Protestant Episcopal Church, and a member of the Board of Visitors and Governors of St. John's College, since 1881.

He has represented his parish for many years, in its Diocesan Conventions, and, in 1901 and 1904, was chosen by that Convention one of its Lay Deputies to the General Triennial Conventions of that church.

He has been president of the Maryland Bankers Association and of the Maryland Civil Service Reform Association, as well as of various industrial companies, organized to promote the prosperity of his native city.

He is fond of historical studies and has contributed a number of papers and addresses on such subjects. In 1895, at the request of the "Baltimore Sun," he wrote for that paper, a series of articles upon what was then known as "The Eastern Shore Law," considered historically and legally being the law, then prevailing, which required that one of the two United States Senators from Maryland should always be a resident of the Eastern Shore. In 1899, he was selected by the City of Annapolis, to deliver an address, as its representative, on the occasion of the 250th anniversary of the settlement of Annapolis, and the passage of the Religious Toleration Act, and delivered in the hall of the House of Delegates, an address, which was published by the city in pamphlet form, and much admired for its scholarly and historical ability. The same year he delivered, before the Maryland Bankers Convention, on invitation, an address on "Colonial Currencies," showing the peculiarities of the tobacco, wampum and fur, or peltry currencies of the early colonies, which was considered as a masterly treatment of the subject, and was published by the Convention. Some of Mr. John Wirt Randall's other published addresses have been, "Divorce, and the Marriage of Divorced Persons," a defense of the existing canons of the Protestant Episcopal Church on the subject. "The Centennial of Maryland's First Banking Institutions," delivered before the Convention of the Maryland Bankers Convention, in 1904. "Some of the Wonders of Astronomy;" "Christian Manliness;" "Lovers of the Beautiful, How They May Show Their Faith by Their Works," an address delivered before the Philokalian Society at St. John's College, etc.

He married Hannah Parker Parrott, daughter of P. P. Parrott, of Arden, Orange County, New York, in 1879. They have four children, three daughters and a son. Their eldest daughter was married, in 1902, to Wm. Bladen Lowndes, son of Ex-Governor Lloyd Lowndes. Mr. Randall owns and occupies his father's old homestead, one of the most beautiful and interesting of the old historic houses in Annapolis, with ample grounds about it, facing upon the State House Circle.

AMOS GARRETT, FIRST MAYOR OF ANNAPOLIS.

When Annapolis had arisen, in 1708, to the dignity of a city. Amos Garrett, its wealthy merchant, was its mayor. He was one of the largest land holders in the county, and though a bachelor, he seemed to buy lands simply to accommodate those who needed money. These tracts were all later resurveyed under the title, "Providence."

There is no better evidence of the Christian character of this English merchant than that exhibited in his will, which I herein condense, It was made in 1714. "I, Amos Garrett, merchant, desire, if I dye in Maryland, to be interred after the third day of decease. That there be in the house now occupied by Mr. Howell, on my plantation, preached a funeral sermon, and that the gentleman remind all present to employ their time in doing good. That my executor purchase a marble tombstone. I desire that my dear mother, two sisters, brother-in-law, any of my nieces or nephews, to see it performed. That at my funeral, there be not given such plenty of liquors as is usual, but that many people coming from far thereto, may have wine and cakes. And, if it cannot be gotten ready at my funeral, as soon after my decease as possible there be bought by my executor, at the best hand, one thousand pair of men's and women's deerskin gloves, and ye same time be delivered out to the poorest of my customers, husband and wife, widower or widow, batchelor or old maid, each one pair, and an account be kept to whom delivered.

"My funeral cost for wine and cake and gloves I would not have exceed two hundred pounds. I used to buy good thick deerskin gloves for two shillings and six pence a pair. As to the cost of my tombstone, I am not for a fine one.   I leave that to the discretion of those concerned.   I desire, also, the following books to be sent for, to be delivered to every person that has a pair of gloves, and can read, or that promises to take all opportunity of getting some person to read to him or her.   Any one having such books shall not sell them but they shall descend to the next of kin.   The party to have his name wrote or stamped on the book.

"List of books: 200 Bibles, with testaments and common prayer book; 100 of Dr. Jeremy Taylor's Holy Living and Dying.; 100 of ditto Golden Grove and Guide; 100 Dr. Wm. Sherlock on Death; 100 of Dr. John Goodman's Penitent Pardoned; 100 of Thomas Doolittle's on Lord's Suffering; 80 of Dr. Wm. Bates Sermons; 100 of Thomas Wordworth's Remains; 100 of Matthew Meade's Good of Early Obedience; 20 of John Bonn's Guide to Eternity, making in all 1,000 books.

"I give out of my personal estate, to the children of my sister, Mary Woodard, £600; to sister, Elizabeth Ginn, £600; To loving mother, £1,000; to my brother-in-law, Henry Woodard, £300.

"To Henry Faces and Elizabeth, his wife, daughter of Seth Garrett, £100 and one lot in Annapolis, where a free school is kept. To Thomas Faces, a lot in Annapolis, adjoining John Baldwin.   To James Garrett, of Seth of London, lots in Annapolis, formerly Chas. Killburnes.   To niece Elizabeth Woodward, daughter of Henry, £300 and six tracts of land; to niece Mary Woodward, of Henry, £300 and six tracts of land; to nephew, William Woodward, £400 and six tracts of land and two lots in Annapolis; to Hannah Woodward, of Henry, £300 and six tracts of land; to Amos Woodward, of Henry, £500 and six tracts and two lots, in Annapolis; to nephew Garrett Woodward, of Henry, £500 and six or eight tracts; to mother, Sarah Garrett, thirteen tracts and four lots, in Annapolis, during life, to descend to sister Elizabeth Ginn; to the Church of St. Anne's, for the use of its minister, a house bought of Samuel Dorsey, and fourteen tracts of land; to my mother, £100 for mourning rings and such memorials.

"In witness whereof to every side of this my will set my hand and seal, it containing sheets of paper fairly writ.—AMOS GARRETT."

On March 29th, 1728, was exhibited the administration bond of Amos Garrett, in common form by Amos Woodward, his administrator, with Samuel Relee, William Chapman, Caleb Dorsey, Richard Warfield, Richard Hill and John Beale, his sureties, in sixty thousand pounds sterling, dated 28th, March, 1728, which bond is ordered to be filed.   At the same time, was exhibited by said Amos Woodward, a will of said Amos Garrett, Esq., made in the year, 1714, but not evidenced or executed, which at the request of said Amos Woodward, is ordered to be recorded at the expense of the estate.

The tablet seen on Mr. Garrett's tombstone, in St. Anne's churchyard, is identical with the words of his will.   It is upon a slab of white marble, with a griffin rampant surrounded by fleur di lis, with the following inscription: "Here lieth interred the body of Mr. Amos Garrett, of the City of Annapolis, in Anne Arundel County, in the Province of Maryland, merchant, son of Mr. James and Mrs. Sarah Garrett, late of St. Olive Street, Southwark, then in the Kingdom of England, now a part of Great Brittian, who departed this life on March 8th, 1727. Aetatis 56."

WOODWARDS.

William Woodward, of London, sent three sons to Maryland. They were Henry Woodward, William Woodward and Abraham Woodward.

Henry Woodward located upon the Patuxent, and married Mary Garrett, sister of Amos Garrett, the wealthy merchant of Annapolis, first mayor of the city. They had issue, William Woodward, known as the Goldsmith; Mary—Mr. Holmes, of England; Elizabeth—Benjamin Baron, of Maryland; Sarah—C. Calhon, of England. Amos Woodward, of Henry, married Achsah Dorsey, of Caleb and Elinor (Warfield) Dorsey. Issue, Mary, Elinor, Elizabeth; Henry Woodward, only son of Amos, married Mary Young, daughter of Colonel Richard Young and Rebecca Holsworth, his wife, of Calvert County. Issue, Rebecca—Philip Rogers; Eleanor— Samuel Dorsey; Mary—first, Mr. Govane, second, Samuel Owings; Harriet—first, Colonel Edmund Brice, second, Colonel Alexander Murray; Achsah died young.

Mary (Young) Woodward—second John Hessilius Artist.

William Woodward, of William, of London, left three children, Elizabeth, Hannah and William.,

Abraham Woodward, (of William of London)—first, Eilzabeth Firlor, second, Mrs. Priscilla Orrick, widow of James Orrick. Issue, William, Rebecca, Martha, Abraham, Thomas, Mary—Wm. Tarris, Priscilla, Henry, Elizabeth and Eleanor.

William — Alice Ridgely, daughter of William and Jane (Westall)Ridgely. Issue, Jane—NelsonWaters; Henry—Mary White; Abraham, killed in the Revolution; William, Jr.—Jane Ridgely, daughter of William and Mary Orrick. Issue, William—Mary Jacobs and went west; Henry, born 1770; Alice—Stephen Watkins; Ann—William Ridgely, of Allegheny; Sarah—Mr. Connand went to Tennessee.

Henry Woodward, born 1770—Eleanor Turner (widow), daughter of Colonel Thomas Williams and Rachel Duckett, his wife. Issue, Jane Maria—Judge William Henry Baldwin; William— Virginia Burneston; Henry Williams Woodward—first, Sarah Gambrill, second, Mary E. Webb; Rignal Duckett—second, M. J. Hall; Rachel Ann, Eleanor, and Martha Ridgely—James Rawlings.

Henry Williams Woodward and Sarah Gambrill, of Augustine, had issue, Juliet—Professor Phil. Moore Leakin. Issue, Mrs. Robert Welsh, of Baltimore; Phil. Moore Leakin, of New York, and a brother in Baltimore.

Henry Williams Woodward—second, Mary Edge Webb. Issue, William Woodward, born December 31st, 1835, died March 20th, 1889, and James T. Woodward, president of the Hanover Bank, New York. (Elsewhere recorded.)

William Woodward was a cotton merchant, and one of the founders of the Cotton Exchange. In 1864, he removed from Baltimore to New York, where he died. He was a member of the Union, Manhattan, Yacht Club, Lewannaka, Tuxedo, South Side Fishing Club, Racket, and, also, member of the Baltimore and Washington clubs. He married, September 27th, 1865, Sarah Abigail, daughter of Samuel and Mary (Peckham) Rodman, of Rhode Island. Issue Mary Edge, Julia Rodman, Edith and William Woodward, graduate of Harvard, class of '98, and of the Harvard Law School, of 1901. His clubs are Institute Porcellain, Institute Zees.

Jas. T. Woodward, of New York, holds the homestead, "Edgewood," just north of Gambrill's Station. It was his birthplace. Mr. James T. Woodward went to New York soon after the war, and became connected with the importing house of Ross, Campbell & Co. His good business judgment and habit of observing closely the conditions of trade throughout the general field, gave value to his opinions on commercial matters. In the early seventies he became a director in the Hanover Bank. His acquaintance among the important men of the financial district was broadening, his experience was ripening.

In 1877, the large interest of the well-known bankers J. & I. Stewart, in the Hanover Bank, was bought by Mr. Woodward and his late brother, William Woodward, Jr. He was elected to the presidency of the bank, and retired from the importing firm in which he had become a partner.

Mr. Woodward has been president of the Hanover Bank since that time. When he assumed the presidency the deposits of the bank were $6,000,000; they are now $45,000,000. There could be no more striking evidence of the wisdom of his management.

The fact that he has brought his bank to be one of the three leading banks of the City of New York, is ample proof that he has won and enjoys the confidence of the business community. But Mr. Woodward has a broader sphere of influence than that. His attentive observation of the money market, now a fixed habit, has made him a man to be consulted in the financial district. In the preliminary discussions of large investments, in investigations that precede bond sales by the United States Treasury, and in the determination of financial policies, Mr. Woodward's views are influential and always incline to the side of safety and prudence.

He has a characteristically positive way of expressing his opinions, which is often observed in men whose conclusions are the fruit of ripe thought, and may, therefore, be given with confidence. At a meeting of the Clearing House Association, held on October 4th, last, Mr. Woodward, although he had not sought the place, was elected president of the Association; an office, at once, of both dignity and responsibility. The Clearing House is the vigilant guardian of the financial interests of the commercial community, and a tower of observation over all banks; guarantor to the business public that no bank can go far into imprudence without detection.

Like a wise man, Mr. Woodward looks also to the pleasant things of life, as the means for banishing cares.

Though a model of punctuality, when duty calls, yet when the season and weather are propitious, he comes to visit his plantations in Anne Arundel, near Gambrill's Station, and in Prince George, at Collington, to hunt across country, maintaining the old favorite pastime of his colonial ancestors. He delights to have his social companions of New York join him, at his bachelor quarters, during the hunting season. Amiable, agreeable and entertaining, his friends are lasting and loyal.

He is a member of numerous clubs, among them being the Union, the Knickerbocker, the Metropolitan, the Tuxedo, and the Riding Club.

Mr. Woodward is also taking interest in developing the usefulness of St. John's College. Woodward Hall has been erected to his name. He has also succeeded in paying off the debt upon St. John's. After the inauguration of Governor Warfield, Mr. Woodward brought a tally-ho party from New York, to call upon him at the government house.

SKETCH OF THE LIFE OF THE LATE RIGNAL T. WOODWARD, OF ABINGTON FARM, MILLERSVILLE, ANNE ARUNDEL COUNTY, MD.

Rignal T. Woodward was born at Abington Farm, Anne Arundel County, Maryland, his father's place. His father was the Hon. Rignal Duckett Woodward, the third son of Henry Woodward, of Anne Arundel County, and his wife, Eleanor Williams, of Prince George County. His mother was a Miss Elizabeth Hardisty, whose mother was Miss Hodges. The Hon. Rignal Duckett Woodward was a planter, one time sheriff of the county, and for a number of years, presiding justice of the Orphans Court. He died in 1888.

Rignal T. Woodward was educated at the Academy at Millersville. His father wanted him to go to college, but he preferred to go into business. When he was seventeen years old he entered the office of his uncle Mr. William Woodward, a commission merchant, doing business in the city of Baltimore under the firm name of William Woodward & Co. Later the firm name was changed to Woodward, Baldwin & Co. In 1863, the firm opened an office in New York City, and he was sent there. In October, 1863, he was admitted into the firm as a partner. On January 26th, 1864, he married Mary H. Raborg, the eldest daughter of Dr. Christopher H. Raborg, of Baltimore. By her he had eight children, namely:

Mary Raborg, born December 19th, 1864, died August 10th, 1865; Rignal Duckett, December 28th, 1865; Christopher Raborg born January 24th, 1867, died August 16th, 1868; William Baird, born April 4th, 1868, died August 18th, 1868; Christopher H. R., born May 31st, 1869; Mary Raborg, born December 16th, 1870; Charles Woodward, born June 2nd, 1872; Elijah, born July 14th, 1874.

Mr. Woodward continued to reside in New York City until May, 1898, when he moved to Morristown, New Jersey. His wife, Mary H. (Raborg) Woodward, died March 5th, 1900. On the death of his father, Mr. Woodward became the owner of Abington Farm. On February 5th, 1902, he married Julia Winchester Bowling, daughter of Chief Justice Benjamin Winchester, of Louisiana. The death of Mr. Woodward was recently announced in the Baltimore Sun. The interment was in his native county.

William Woodward, (of Henry, of William, of London,) and Jane, his wife, had William Garrett Woodward and Maria G. Woodward, who became Mrs. Edmiston, of London. A letter from the former to the latter, giving a good view of the trying days in which he lived, and containing some genealogical information, is still preserved by his descendants.

William Garrett Woodward married Dinah Warfield, daughter of Alexander and Dinah Davidge. They had two daughters.

Maria Graham became the second wife of Captain Henry Baldwin; Elizabeth Woodward became the second wife of Alexander Warfield, of Sam's Creek.

William Woodward, late head of Woodward, & Baldwin & Co., of Baltimore, leading dry-goods merchants, descendant of Henry and Eleanor (Williams) Woodward, removed to Baltimore, and entered the house of Mullikin & Co. He later formed the partnership of Jones & Woodward, which was merged into Woodward, Baldwin & Co. Mr. Woodward was an organizer of the first temperance society of Maryland. He was a director in numerous institutions. His wife was Virginia Barnetson, of Baltimore. Six daughters and three sons are their heirs.

Mr. Woodward was ranked as a christian philanthropist, and an .enterprising man of business, worthy to succeed the great merchant, Amos Garrett, of Annapolis.

Thomas Woodward, son of Abraham, of William, lived at Woodwardville, in Anne Arundel, upon the Patuxent. He married Mrs. Margaret Ijams, nee Margaret Waters. Issue, Abraham, Nicholas R., Priscilla. Nicholas R. Woodward married Margaret Mullikin, and left Sophia Hall—Richard Anderson; Eliza Ann, Catherine M. —Jacob Strider. By a second wife, Sarah Gambrill, Nicholas R. Woodward had John Randolph—Caroline V. Gardner; Abraham .—Annie Anderson; Emily R. Nicholas; Daniel Dodge—Jennie nderson.

Mr. William Nicholas Woodward, son of John Randolph Woodward, is now Deputy Clerk of Anne Arundel. He married Jennie G. Ashwell, of New Jersey. His sisters are, Mrs. Laura M. Moore, of West Virginia, and Annie V. Woodward.

Mr. Woodward was born at Woodwardville. He has a place south of Gambrill's Station, and also holds the old Dorsey property near Savage. He resides in Annapolis, and has recently purchased a property upon Murray Hill.

THE PINKNEY FAMILY.

In the house just opposite the Chase mansion, afterward owned by the Lockerman and Harwood families, was born William Pinkney, the fifth Bishop of Maryland. His paternal grandfather, Jonathan Pinkney settled in Annapolis before the Revolution. He was a sturdy Englishman, but "He adhered with a mistaken, but honest firmness, to the cause of the mother country, and suffered severely the consequences of his conscientiousness." All of his property was confiscated.

The five children of Jonathan Pinkney by his two wives, both sisters, were Margaret, Nancy, Jonathan, William and Ninian.

Jonathan, Jr., was cashier of the Farmers Bank of Maryland. He left a large family. William became the great lawyer and statesman, whose history is given below. The third son, Ninian, was the father of Bishop Pinkney, of Maryland. He was twice married; his first wife was a sister of Mr. Louis Gassaway, but left no heirs; the second was Mrs. Amelia Grason Hobbs, a widow with three children. She was the daughter of Richard Grason, of Talbot County, and sister of the governor. The children by Mr. Pinkney were Amelia, William and Ninian.

The father held the important position of "Clerk of the Council" for thirty years. Mrs. Pinkney's vivid remembrances of both wars are extant, and are reproduced in Rev. Orlando Hutton's life of Bishop Pinkney.

After removing from their home on Maryland Avenue, the family lived, until the death of Mrs. Pinkney, in a frame cottage, under the shadow of the Naval Academy, and close to the then governor's palace. In 1853, the site was sold to the government, but Mrs. Pinkney was allowed to remain during life.

William Pinkney, second son of the English settler, was a student of King William's School. It is related that Judge Samuel Chase, towards the close of the American war, stepping one day into a debating society, was astonished at the eloquence of a young drug clerk. Seeking him out, the Judge urged him to study law. The young clerk made known his necessities, whereupon Judge Chase offered him his library, which was accepted. The young man was William Pinkney. Admitted to the bar in 1786, he afterwards became "the wonder of his age."

In 1788, William Pinkney was a delegate to the convention which ratified the Constitiution of the United States. He was later a member of the House, Senate and Council. In 1796, was commissioner under the Jay treaty. In 1805, was Attorney-General of Maryland. In 1806, was minister to England. In 1811, was Attorney-General of the United States.

At the battle of Bladensburg, in 1812, he commanded a volunteer company, and was wounded. He handed down to his distinguished relative, Bishop William Pinkney, of Bladensburg, a statement giving the cause of that disastrous defeat as a want of both powder and preparation. Mr. Pinkney was in Congress in 1815, and a minister to Russia in 1816. Upon his return, he was given an ovation in his native city. In 1819, he was elected United States Senator, which he held until his death in 1822.

The latest Pinkney homestead, in Annapolis, stood facing the State House. The site is now occupied by the new State building for the Court of Appeals and State Library, but the Pinkney building was removed intact, to a site opposite College Green. It is still held by his descendants.

HON. REVERDY JOHNSON.

Honorable Reverdy Johnson was born at Annapolis, 21st of May, 1796, in the house, the beautiful park of which, extends to State House Circle, now the property of Hon. J. Wirt Randall.

Mr. Johnson was educated at St. John's College, and at seventeen years of age, began the study of law. He was the son of Hon. John Johnson, Judge of the Court of Appeals and Attorney-General of Maryland, who married Deborah Ghiselen, daughter of Reverdy Ghiselen, long commissioner of the Land Office at Annapolis.

Reverdy Johnson commenced his career at Marlborough. His first attempt was a failure. He became discouraged and thought of giving it up; but upon the advice of Judge Edmund Key, of that judicial circuit, determined to continue. He was appointed State's Attorney for Prince George, in 1817. Two years later removed to Baltimore, where he made the reputation of a profound student of law. With Mr. Thomas Harris, he reported the decisions of the Maryland Court of Appeals (seven volumnes).

In 1821, he was elected a State Senator and re-elected in 1825. In 1845, was chosen United States Senator; resigning, in 1849, to accept the office of Attorney-General under President Taylor. He was a member of the Peace Commission, in 1861; was elected United States Senator again in 1862. In 1868, General Grant appointed him minister to England, where he negotiated the treaty for the settlement of the Alabama claims. This treaty was rejected and he was recalled in 1869. Though a Unionist, he voted, in 1866, against the impeachment of President Johnson.

Reverdy Johnson married Mary Mackall Bowie, daughter of Governor Robert Bowie. Her portrait, painted by Sully, whilst at the Court of St. James, is now in the Peabody Institute. She was the financial manager of the household that he might be free for public duties. In 1869, they celebrated their golden wedding. She died in 1873, and he in 1876, whilst a guest at the governor's mansion in Annapolis, within a stone's throw of his birthplace, and in sight of his Alma Mater.

SAPPINGTON FAMILY.

The records of All Hallows show two brothers, Thomas and John Sappington, near South River. They had clearly come down the bay from the homestead of Nathaniel Sappington, of Cecil County, whose home was near the Sassafras River.

The will of Thomas Rutland, of South River, probated 1731, names his son, Thomas ; daughter, Elizabeth Stuart; grandson, Thomas Sappington, and granddaughter, Jeane, child of daughter Ann Wayman, wife of Leonard Wayman.

The records of All Hallows show the marriage of Thomas Sappington to Mary Rutland, and the birth of their son, Thomas Sappington, legatee of Thomas Rutland. John Sappington, of All Hallows, located his son, John Sappington, Jr., upon the estate known as "Sappington," upon which still stands the quaint little college at Sappington Station, of the Annapolis & Elk Ridge railroad. The present house is claimed to have been built by Caleb Sappington, of John, Jr. It is an interesting relic of earlier days.

The Sappington family will be continued in Howard County records.

RUTLAND FAMILY.

Thomas Rutland, the settler, married a daughter of Thomas Linthicum. Three succeeding Thomas Rutlands follow. The daughters of the first were, Mrs. Elizabeth Stuart, Mrs. Ann Wayman and Mrs. Mary Sappington. Thomas Rutland's will, of 1783, names his descendants.

The second Thomas Rutland married Ann Beale daughter of John and Elizabeth Norwood, daughter of Andrew by his wife, Elizabeth Howard, of Captain Cornelius. The will of Mrs. Thomas Rutland, in 1773, names her aunt, Hannah Norwood.

She gave a pair of sleeve buttons to Mary Snowden, daughter of Eliza (Rutland) Snowden, but left the bulk of her estate to the daughters of her sister, Elizabeth (Nicholson) Dorsey. Those nieces were Ann Beale, Eliza Harrison and Mary Dorsey. The will of Joseph Howard shows his daughter married another Thomas Rutland. There was a row of houses in Annapolis, built by Thomas Rutland, the large importing merchant of Annapolis.

RANDALL.

Early among the land holders of North Severn, was Christopher Randall, who held "Randall's Range," "Randall's Fancy" and "Randall's Purchase." He died in 1684, when an inventory of his

estate returned by Matthew Howard, shows his wife was Joan.
Richard Owings, a brother-in-law of Thomas Randall, son of Christopher, was a debtor, and Christopher, Jr., Thomas Randall and one
sister were the heirs. All these removed to Baltimore County.
Closely connected with this Randall family were the English
merchants, Thomas and Anthony Bale, written in the chancery
records as both Bale and Beal. The will of Urath Bale, who names
her aunt, Hannah Randall, is on record at Annapolis. Hannah
Bale became the wife of Thomas Randall, who died in 1722. Her
will, of 1727, names her son, Christopher, and her daughter, Urath
(Urith), later wife of Samuel Owings, of Owings Mills.
Mrs. Hannah Randall also named her daughter-in-law, Catherine,
wife of Christopher, her son, and leaves a ring to her brother-in-law,
Christopher Randall, whose wife was Ann. The latter left a will,
in Baltimore, naming his sons, Roger, Aquilla and John. The latter
heired the Anne Arundel estate. The daughters were Johanna, Ruth
and Rachel.
Christopher and Thomas united, in 1710, in selling "Randall's
Range" to John Harwood.
Both branches of this family live in the neighborhood of Ran-
dallstown and Owings Mill. The estate of Samuel Owings occupied a pretty large slice of Baltimore County, and all through the
West are descendants who still bear the name of Urith, handed
down from "Urath Bale."
Captain John Randall, of Anne Arundel, held "a flat," in 1731,
from which a man fell and was drowned.—(St. Paul Records.)
Richard Randall, of Anne Arundel, owned "Tower Hill." His
heirs were Margaret, Elizabeth and John Randall. They sold this
tract in 1792. Richard Randall's sisters were, Elizabeth—Ben-
jamin Atwell, in 1799; Lorena—Frederick Goatee, in 1800; Atridge
—John Smith, 1807; Ruth—Joseph Norman, 1792; Anna—George
Kirby, 1798.
Another Anne Arundel branch of the family was Catherine Ran-
dall, whose will, of 1729, names "her son Robert Welsh," and her
grandsons, James Lewis and Robert Welsh, and gave them "Town
Hill" and "Diligent Search."
The present Randall family, of Annapolis, comes from a
Virginia settler, who came up much later than Christopher Randall.
This branch will elsewhere be given.

JOHN GILL.

John Gill was born in Annapolis, August 15th, 1841. His
father was Richard W. Gill, son of John Gill, of Alexandria, Virginia,
and his mother was Miss Ann E. Deale, daughter of Captain James
Deale, of Anne Arundel County.
In an autobiography of his early life General Gill writes:
"My father died when I was about ten years old. My mother
was left with four children—two girls and two boys. Fortunately,
my father had left an estate sufficient to provide comfortably for

all of us, and my mother, a woman of most excellent sense and judgment, made the best possible disposition of her income, with the view of educating her children.

"My father's death left a scar that time could never efface. One of his associates at the bar, in announcing his death to a full bench of the Court of Appeals of Maryland, said: 'I will not attempt to eulogize the dead, but I cannot refrain from saying that I have never known one who more deservedly and universally possessed the esteem of all who knew him.'

"For several years after my father's death we were all kept at home. My mother secured a most excellent governess, a Miss Boyce, who proved most satisfactory, and was liked so much that she soon became part of our household.

"At the age of about fifteen, I was sent to the preparatory school of St. John's College. In 1856, my mother and sisters concluded that it was best for me to go to a boarding school, and the Lawrenceville High School, near Princeton, New Jersey, was selected.

"I shall never cease being grateful to my mother for sending me to this school. At the head of it was a very distinguished educator, Dr. Samuel Hamill, well known throughout the country, and the best man I ever knew to train boys in the way they should go. I was graduated at Lawrenceville in the fall of 1859, and from there went to the University of Virginia.

"At the outbreak of the Civil War, I enlisted as a private soldier in the Confederate Army."

General Gill came to Baltimore after the war, and went into the grain business, establishing the firm of Gill & Fisher. This firm is still in existence, and Mr. Charles D. Fisher, the original partner of General Gill, is still a member. General Gill, however, retired from the firm about twenty years ago, to become president of the Mercantile Trust and Deposit Company on its organization. He is fond of relating his early experience in the grain trade, which was before the establishment of the present perfect system of elevators and inspections. He said his firm employed its own inspectors and weighers, and he would frequently meet incoming vessels, with cargoes of southern wheat and corn, some distance down the harbor, and have all terms of its purchase and its inspection settled by the time it reached the steamship which was to take it aboard. He prides himself on the fact that, in 1879 and in 1880, his firm sent out about five hundred cargoes of grain to foreign ports.

General Gill married a daughter of Mr. W. W. Spence, and has five children, all daughters. He is still hale and hearty, and in full possession of all his faculties, mental and physical. Few in his employ have the same capacity for work as General Gill; and his tireless energy in the many intricate financial problems with which he has had to deal, has frequently caused astonishment to his associates and fellow workers.

JOHN MARRIOTT.

Following close upon the Howards and Porters of the Severn, we find John Marriott, in 1681, living upon Peter Porter's plantation, at Indian Landing. At that time the Indians had made an attack upon his household, and Mrs. Marriott had been compelled to seek her neighbors' protection. She was Sarah Acton, of the Annapolis family.

In his will, of 1718, John Marriott names a large family, viz.: "To son Joseph, my tract, 'Cordwell,' where he lives. To son Emanuel, 'Hereford' and dwelling. To son John, the remaining part of 'Hereford' and one hundred acres of 'Brookslys Point.' To two sons, Augustine and Silvanus, the remainder of 'Brookslys,' and, also, four hundred and forty acres out of 'Shepherd's Forest,' on the Patuxent. I give to John Riggs, fifty acres of 'Shepherd's Forest.' (The English wills show a close connection between Marriott and Riggs). I give to Henry Sewell the sum of forty shillings, and to Wm. Stevens a like amount. To daughter, Ann Gambrill, I give £5. To daughter, Sarah Marriott, I give £30. The balance to my five sons, Joseph, Emanuel, John, Augustine and Silvanus."

Joseph and Augustine were executors. Peter Porter, Wm. Stevens and Edward Benson were witnesses.

John Sewell's wife, Mary Marriott, was a descendant of John Marriott, who was a large land-holder on the Severn River about 1667. John Marriott's wife, Sarah Acton, was a daughter of Richard Acton, who settled on the Severn River, in 1651, at "Acton's Hill," now called "Murray's Hill," Annapolis. He came with that celebrated colony from Sewell's Point, Virginia.

A similarity of Christian names again occurs at this time, in England and Maryland, and shows close connections, mentioned so prominently by Sir Bernard Burke, in his Peerage, Landed Gentry and Armory and Heraldry, running back previous to the arrival of William the Conqueror. The Marriotts are also mentioned by Burke as having arrived in England with William the Conqueror—three brothers, viz.: Rudolphus, Guillermus and Augustine Marriott. Burke also states that there was an Augustine Marriott living in London, 1689.

John Marriott, the pioneer in Maryland, named in his will, 1716-18, his children—Sarah Yieldhall, Mary Sewell, Achsah Hall and John Marriott. Sarah Marriott was the wife of Wm. Yieldhall; Mary Marriott, the wife of John Sewell; John Marriott married Nancy Warfield, daughter of Alexander Warfield, and Achsah Marriott married John Hall, of Whitehall, and their daughter, Sarah Hall, married, first, Francis Rawlings, secondly, Captain Henry Baldwin.

Sallie Baldwin, daughter of Henry and Sarah (Rawlings-Hall) Baldwin, married Denton Hammond. Issue, Elizabeth, Camilla and Matthias Hammond. Camilla—Dr. Herbert and had a son, General James Rawlings Herbert, whose daughter, Camilla, married Wm. Pinkney Whyte, Jr. Elizabeth—Richard Cromwell; Matthias

Eliza Brown; John Marriott, who died 1798,—Elizabeth Davis, daughter of Richard Davis and Ruth Warfield, his wife, the daughter of John and Ruth (Gaither) Warfield.

John Marriott, in his will, 1798, mentions wife Elizabeth. Issue, John, Richard, Ruth, Rachel and Elizabeth Marriott. Richard— Sarah Hammond, daughter of John Hammond, and their son, General Wm. Hammond Marriott—Jane McKim; his brother, Richard Marriott, married a granddaughter of Anthony Stewart, of Peggy Stewart fame.

In 1756, Mr. Emanuel Marriott, the son of Mr. Joseph Marriott, was taxed as a bachelor for the support of the church of St. Anne's, on a schedule of £100.

The will of Augustine Marriott, who held the homestead at Indian Landing, and married Mary Warfield, of John and Ruth Gaither, in 1729, reads as follows: "My wife, Mary, if she does not marry, to hold the whole estate during life. My son, John, to hold 'Shepherd's Forest.' "

His three daughters named were Sarah, wife of Wm. Yieldhall; Mary, wife of John Sewall; Achsah, wife of John Hall, and her three danghters. John Marriott, Joseph Warfield and Joshua Gambrill were witnesses.

John Marriott, the son, married Elizabeth Davis, daughter of Richard and Ruth (Warfield) Davis. In his will, of 1798, he named his sons, Richard, John, Rachel, Ruth, and Elizabeth; wife, Elizabeth; lands, "Lancaster Plains."

THE COLE FAMILY.

Edith Cole, wife of John Mallonee, was the daughter of Dennis Garrett Cole and Rachel, his wife, of Baltimore County, November 8th, 1748. Their children were Thomas, James, William and Leonard Mallonee.

Dennis Garrett Cole was the son of John and Hannah (Garrett) Cole; and Hannah Garrett was the daughter of Dennis and Barbara Garrett. Thomas Stone and Dennis Garrett purchased "Long Island Point" in 1683, and in 1691, Thomas Stone gave his moiety in this land to the children of Dennis Garrett, deceased, and stated it was for his love and affection.

"Long Island Point" was to the east and adjoining "Cole Harbor," settled by Thomas Cole in 1668, and the latter was covered by the following lines: Beginning at Harford Run on the east, where it flows into the Patapsco River, thence west one mile, binding on the water front to about Sharp Street; thence north about half a mile to Saratoga Street, then east to Harford Run; thence to the place of the beginning, containing 550 acres. John Cole sold Richard Owings, in 1702, 809 acres, "Cole's Choice," in the same section. All of these tracts were described as on the north side of the northwest branch of the Patapsco River, and now covered by Baltimore City from Sharp Street to the east.

The Cole families, of Old England, appear to have had the same Christian names as the early settlers in Maryland and Virginia, viz.: John, Thomas, William, Skipwith, et al. Cole—Stake Lyne—John Thomas and William. There was a fine monument erected to the Cole family at Petersham, in 1624. John Cole, tenth in line from William Cole, County Devon, 1243. Cole—Marazon—Francis Sewell Cole, esquire, nineteenth in direct descent from Edward, third, and the family long in County Devon. Cole—Woodniem—John Cole, 1614, father of William Cole, officer in Cromwell's Army. James Garrett, Esquire, County Carlow, married Mary, daughter of Colonel Blake, same family as Sir William Garrett, Lord Mayor London, 1555.

Sir Bernard Burke, in his "Armory and Heraldry," gives the Sewell family in England three coats of arms; the Cole family, twenty-two; Stone, thirty; Garrett, three; Kirby, fourteen; Randall, fifteen; Warner, nineteen; Acton, twenty-seven. These names are all shown in the above as Sewall connections.

RAWLINGS.

Much has been written lately concerning this family. As none of the writers seem to have gone to the wills for information, I will reproduce them and leave interested descendants to fit them.

It has been stated that Henry Rawlings, father of Anthony, the public man, was the immigrant. There seem to have been others. The archives are full of Anthony Rawlings, and the chancery records add more light. His will of 1652, names sons, John and Anthony, who inherited adjoining lands up on the Patuxent. He names his oldest daughter, Anne, and youngest daughter, Margaret. His wife was Jane Rawlings.

In 1676, Elizabeth Rawlings, widow of Nicholas, made an oral will in which she desired Elizabeth Mackey to take care of her child, and to collect from her debtors what was due.

In 1696, Richard Rawlings named his two sons, Richard and John; his daughters were Mary and Elizabeth, and wife Jane.

In 1717, John Rawlings, of Dorchester, named his brother, Anthony, and his nephew, John of Anthony, also his nephew, John King, and his son-in-law, Mark Fisher. His wife was Elizabeth.

Daniel Rawlings, of Charles County, in 1726, held a large estate both there and in Calvert. He left his "home plantation, on St. Leonard's Creek," to my youngest son, Daniel. I confirm unto my son-in-law, John Clare and Elizabeth, his wife, part of 'Elton Head Manor,' called 'Rawlings' Choice,' now occupied by John Clare and his wife, Elizabeth. To daughter, Anne Rawlings, the north part of 'Rawlings' Choice' and five hundred acres of the same tract to son Isaac Rawlings. To daughter Mary Halloway, negroes. Son Isaac and son-in-law John Clare executors. (Seal)."   —DAN RAWLINGS.

John Parran, Wm. Day, and Alexander Parran were witnesses.

Daniel Rawlings, of Calvert County, in 1748, named sons, Daniel and John, and daughters, Nancy and Margaret. He held tract "Rawlings' Choice" "left me by my father." He bought, also, his brother Isaac's lands.

Of this family upon "Rawlings' Manor," one brother, Isaac, still later, was in Mississippi when that was only a territory. In one of his letters, which I have seen, he wrote that "his brother, Captain Thomas Rawlings, was then at the front with General Jackson in his Indian campaign at Pensacola." After the war, Captain Thomas returned to Calvert, and, at forty years of age, married his cousin, Mary Dalrymple, whose mother was Christiana Clare, of John. She was then a girl of fifteen years. Together they lived upon "Rawlings' Choice" and had one son who died in early manhood. This girl of fifteen years, later married another cousin, her first lover, Dr. S. J. Cook, and became the mother of Mrs. J. D. Warfield.

Anthony Rawlings, Jr., of Dorchester, in 1728, left a colt to his father, and named his sister Mary, and cousins, Mary and Charles Daughety. To his brother, John, he left his clothes and silver shoe buckles. Sister Margaret Hail was made legatee of all his personal property and his executrix

Aaron Rawlings, of Anne Arundel County, in 1741, named his wife, Susannah, and sons, Jonathan, Aaron, William and Stephen. The last two inherited "Darnall's Groves," in Prince George County. "My lands in Baltimore County, called 'Brown's Adventure,' to sons and daughter Ann. Aaron to hold the homestead.

This testator's wife was Susannah Beard, the daughter of Stephen. Her will closes the Rawlings previous to the Revolution. In 1762, she named her sons, Aaron, Moses, Richard, daughter Mary, and four married daughters, Ann, Susannah, Rachel and Elizabeth. Her son, Aaron, and son-in-law, Gassaway Watkins, executors.

The further records of this family have been already published.

THE SEWELLS OF VIRGINIA.

Henry Sewell came to Virginia from England previous to 1632. He gave his name to "Sewell's Point" at the entrance to Elizabeth River, opposite to Fortress Monroe. His wife was Alice Willoughby, daughter of Thomas Willoughby, who came to Virginia in 1610, and was Justice of Elizabeth City, 1628; Burgess, 1629-32, and Councilor, 1644-50. At the court holden May 31st, 1640, Henry Sewell and Captain Sibley were authorized to build a church at Mr. Sewell's Point. August 2nd, 1640, Captain Thomas Willoughby, Esquire, Captain John Sibley, Mr. Henry Sewell, Mr. Edward Windham and Mr. William Julian, are to pay for themselves and others; the church minister, Mr. Thomas Harrison.

Peter Porter's name appears in 1641. He, in 1650, settled in Maryland, at the head of Severn River, "Peter Porter's Ridge."

In 1641, the orders of the Court directed that this parish church should be built at Mr. Henry Sewell's Point at the cost and charge of the inhabitants, and chapel of ease at Elizabeth River.

Henry Sewell had two children, Anne and Henry. Anne was born 1634, and married Lemuel Mason, son of Francis Mason. Henry Sewell, the younger, was born 1639. Henry Sewell, the elder, was elected to the House of Burgesses from Elizabeth City, in 1632, and from Lower Norfolk County in 1639. He died, 1644, and at a Court holden same year in Lower Norfolk County, at the house of Ensign Thomas Lambert, February 20th, "The Court doth think fit and orders it, Mr. Matthew Phillips, the administrator of Mr. Henry Sewell ,deceased, shall within ten days satisfy and pay to Mr. Thomas Harrison, clerk, one thousand pounds of tobacco, and satisfaction in consideration for the burial and preaching of the funeral sermon of Mr. and Mrs. Sewell, deceased, and for breaking ground in the chancel of the church for the burial of Mr. and Mrs. Sewell.

Mr. James Warner was elected, in 1649, Church Warden a Sewell's Point, and, in 1651, settled on the Severn River, Maryland.

At a Court, holden February 25th, 1649, the opinion is concerning the estate of Henry Sewell, with the consent of John Holmes, overseer, with Lemuel Mason and Anne, daughter of Henry Sewell, witnesses, agreed the estate of Mr. Matthew Phillips, late deceased, be responsible for the estate of Henry Sewell, and Mrs. Ann Phillips administratrix of said Matthew Phillips, responsibility to be left to the decision of four disinterested persons. Henry Sewell, the younger then ten years old, to be sent abroad by orders of the Court for seven years, in charge of his kinsman, Mr. Thomas Lee. A deposition taken in 1662, shows Henry Sewell, the younger, to have been born, 1639, and a deposition taken in 1672, shows Henry Sewell, the younger, deceased sine prole.

The custom in England at this time, of giving the same christian name to two or more sons was not uncommon, for instance, Henry the elder, Henry the younger, and Henry the middle. The Maryland settler was evidently of this family.

There were quite a number of people in the vicinity of Sewell's Point about 1650, who came up to Maryland and settled on or near the Severn River. Among them, Edward Lloyd, Cornelius Lloyd, Matthew Howard, Thomas Todd, William Crouch, James Horner, Nicholas Wyatt, Thomas Howell, Thomas Gott, William Galloway, Peter Porter, James Warner, Richard Acton and others.

The following is an account sales, in 1638, for Henry Sewell, Sewell's Point, Virginia, from his factor in London, England, of tobacco sent over in the ships, America and Alexandria, and for one-half of a cargo in a shallop with sassafras roots, sold in England, and showed the cash receipts to have been £650, 19s. and 6d.

MUSTER ROLLS—REVOLUTIONARY WAR SEWELLS.

John Sewell, June 3rd, 1778, served during the war.

James Sewell, second battalion, Colonel William's regiment, October, 1780.

John Sewell, fourth battalion, July 27th, 1776.

Joseph Sewell, 1776, Captain Goldsborough Company.

John Sewell served until 1781.

John Sewell, 5th Regiment, 1776.

John Sewell enlisted in Captain Goldsborough Company, 1776.

Charles Sewell, July 2nd, 1776.

Daniel Sewell, enlisted July 4th, 1776.

William Sewell, 1776, discharged 1779.

Clement Sewell, May 4th, 1777, promoted Maryland Line, September 14th, 1777.

William Sewell re-enlisted, June 4th, 1778; Maryland Line April 4th, 1779.

John Sewell, June 8th, 1778; corporal 1779; sergeant 1780.

William Sewell, March 11th, 1776, 4th Infantry.

Hon. Grover Cleveland, ex-president of the United States, is a descendant of the Sewell family

Margaret Borodale married Rev. Jonathan Mitchell. Their daughter, Margaret — Major Stephen Sewell. Their daughter, Susannah—Rev. Aaron Porter. Their daughter, Susannah—Aaron Cleveland, whose son was William Cleveland, who had a son, Rev. Richard Falley Cleveland, who was the father of Grover Cleveland —eighth in direct line from Rev. Jonathan Mitchell, and seventh from Stephen Sewell.

THE SEWELLS OF THE SEVERN.

"Sewell's Point," upon which the Independent Churchmen had built their conventicle in 1638, and upon which the coming James-town exhibition will be held, sent to the Severn, along with many others, a descendant of Henry Sewell, the prominent pillar of that church.

Henry Sewell of the Severn, made surveys with the Howards in 1662. He settled near James Warner, another member of the Virginia church, and later, married his daughter, Johanna.

From a case in chancery, the following history is established. By James Warner's will, his daughter, Johanna, heired "Warner's Neck." It was "not to be disposed of by none from them, but his said daughter and her heirs forever." It was, in the face of that will, later sold by James Sewell, son of Henry and Johanna to Samuel Howard. Henry Sewell, Jr., contested this sale on the plea of entail. The Provincial Court passed upon it, but, after the death of all the original parties, it was carried to the Court of Chancery, which reversed the decision of the Provincial Court.

The Rent Rolls show that it was handed down by Philip Howard to his widow, and by her next husband, Henry Pinkney, was

held in the Howard estate. The will of James Warner names
Samuel Howard and Henry Sewell, "sons." To the first he left a
"broad cloth suit;" to the latter, a suit of "stuffe."
Henry Sewell, Jr., remained upon the homestead. He took up
"Sewell's Fancy," and bought a part of "Duvall's Delight" upon
the Patuxent, from Charles Carroll. In his will, of 1726, he named
Mary, his wife, and Samuel, Mary, Henry, Joseph, Philip and John
Sewell. Having bought, of Richard and Adam Shipley, their
father's purchase of "Howard and Porter's Range," this tract was
left to his sons. "Hereford," the Marriott tract ,was also in possession of Henry Sewell, the testator of 1726. This may have come
through his wife, Mary, a Marriott. This tract was closed out by
the heirs to their brother John Sewell.

John married Hannah Carroll, daughter of Daniel Carroll, at
St. Anne's, Annapolis, May 30th, 1721. Hannah and Daniel Carroll, of Daniel, were baptized at St. Anne's March 2nd, 1713. Daniel
Carroll married Elizabeth Purdy, at "All Hallows," 1730. John
and Hannah (Carroll) Sewell had John, born 1725, and Henry, 1723,
and were baptized at "All Hallows," July 4th, 1726.

John, of John and Hannah Sewell, married Mary Marriott,
daughter of Augustine and Mary (Warfield) Marriott, 1729. Issue,
John, born 1761, Achsah, 1768, Augustine, Sarah and Mary Sewell.

John Sewell, son of John and Mary (Marriott) Sewell, married
Lydia Baldwin, in 1804, daughter of James and Sallie (Rawlings)
Baldwin. Issue, John, Sarah, Matilda, Eliza and Mary Sewell.

John Sewell, of John and Lydia Sewell, married Juliet Gambrill,
daughter of Augustine and Maria (Woodward-Baldwin) Gambrill.
Issue, Augusta—Rev. W. L. Welch; John died single; Charles—
Elizabeth Whitney. Issue, Burnett S. Sewell and Juliet Gambrill Sewell.

Juliet Sewell, daughter of John and Juliet (Gambrill) Sewell,
married Summerfield Baldwin. Issue, Charles, Summerfield, Juliet,
Dorothy and Willard Baldwin.

Matilda Sewell married George Savage. Issue, George, John,
Lydia and Rev. Riley W. Savage. Sarah Sewell married Benjamin Clark. Mary and Eliza Sewell died single.

Mary Sewell, daughter of John and Mary (Marriott) Sewell,
married Patrick Orme, of Montgomery County, and left two children
—Mary—a Mr. Newlin, and Rebecca—Dr. Perry, of Washington,
D. C. Mr. Orme married a second time, and left three daughters.
One married Richard Sewell, another Mr. Bailey, and the third, Mr.
Landstreet, all of Baltimore City.

Augustine Sewell, of John and Mary (Marriott) Sewell, married
Mary Pitts, 1784, daughter of Thomas Pitts, of William. Issue,
John Marriott Sewell, a prominent merchant of Baltimore; Mary
—Francis Baldwin, of James of Edward. Issue, John, James F.,
Thomas Pitts, Mary Pitts, Susan and Sallie Baldwin.

Juliet Sewell—Thomas Worthington, and left a son, Thomas Worthington. Juliet (Sewell) Worthington married a second time, Augustine Sappington. Issue, Nicholas and Mary Sappington. Augustine Sewell, Jr., died single. George Sewell died, age sixteen. Charles Pitts Sewell died, age six years. Eleanor Sewell, daughter of Augustine and his second wife, Anne, married James Gaskins. Issue, Emily Stewart, Edward and Thomas Gaskins.

Sarah Sewell, daughter of John and Mary (Marriott) Sewell, married Thomas Pitts, in 1782, of Thomas of William, and brother of Mary Pitts, who married Augustine Sewell. Issue, Achsah and Thomas Pitts.

The Sewells and their allied families were among the very earliest settlers in Maryland, and held land where both Annapolis and Baltimore are now located.

The old Sewell homestead near Indian Landing at the head of the Severn River, Anne Arundel County, has been in the possession of the family since 1673, and is still owned by the descendants of the Sewells. It was surveyed for John Marriott, in 1673, and in his will, dated 1718, he left it to his sons, John, Silvanus and Augustine Marriott. Sarah, the daughter of Augustine and Mary (Warfield) Marriott, held it until 1773, when it was transferred to John Sewell and his wife, Mary Marriott, a daughter of Augustine Marriott, and sister of Sarah Marriott. In 1791, John Sewell transferred it to his son, John Sewell, and it has been in the family ever since.

The first church built in this section was known as the Cross Roads, now Baldwin's Memorial; and the members of the Protestant Episcopal and Methodist Episcopal Churches worshipped together. The first trustees were John Sewell, Matthias Hammond and Augustine Gambrill.

(This matter was given to the author before its publication in the Sunday "Sun," and by request, is republished.)

Extract from a letter written mnny years ago by one of the Sewell family.

"Our great-grandfather, John Sewell, married Miss Mary Marriott, who was born on the old Marriott estate near the Indian Landing at the head of the Severn River. John Sewell, who died 1805, and his wife, Mary Marriott, who died 1800, lived to a good old age on the old Sewell homestead, situated on the Annapolis and Baltimore road, about eleven miles distance from Annapolis, and adjoining the Marriott estate.

"A sister, Sarah, married William Yieldhall. They had no children, and left all their possessions to Thomas Furlong, whom they had reared and educated under peculiar circumstances. And this deed of kindness was never forgotten by our family, so characteristic of the Sewells and their love of hospitality.

"Achsah Sewell, daughter of John and Mary (Marriott) Sewell, married Leonard Mallonee, at that time a class leader in the Methodist Church; and, to give you some idea of the ways of Methodism at that period, I will relate a little incident. Major Philip Hammond and uncle Leonard were fast friends, both members of the church, but had previously been fond of dancing—passionately so; and on the occasion of the marriage of one of Major Hammond's family, our uncle-in-law, Leonard Mallonee, being a guest at the wedding, their old passion for dancing overcame them, and they both indulged in that pleasing dissipation, and they were both turned out of church.

"The entire community had worshipped at our great-grandfather's house—John Sewell—before there was any church in that vicinity. Bishops Asbury and George, Reverends Henry Smith, Alfred Griffith, Samuel Rozzell and Joshua Wells preached from the same desk—an heirloom still remaining at the same old homestead of the Sewell family. After our great-grandfather's death, the house was kept open for preaching; the desk still occupying the same old place.

"The piety and zeal of our great-grandparents won for them the title of "The Two Christians" throughout the neighborhood.

"This old homestead is also sacred to the memory as being the place where the first camp-meeting was held on Severn Circuit, called the Baltimore and Severn Camp-meeting, presenting quite a novelty for those times, as the grove was illuminated by lamps brought from the oldest Methodist Church in Baltimore. The first church on the Severn, called Cross Roads, adjoined this tract."

Sewell tombstones, at the old Sewell homestead in Anne Arundel County, at the head of the Severn River, near the old Cross Roads Church and Indian Landing:

John Sewell died 1805, born 1725. Wife, Mary (Marriott) Sewell died 1800. Son, John Sewell, born 1761, died 1817. Wife, Lydia Sewell, born 1781, died 1850. Son, John Sewell, born 1813, died 1844. Wife, Juliet W. Sewell, born 1814, died 1845. Son, John Sewell, born 1838, died 1850, single. Eliza Sewell, born 1815, died June 6th, 1873.

Seven generations sleep in Anne Arundel County, in consecutive line, viz.: Henry, Henry, John, John, John, John, and John Sewell.

COUNCIL PROCEEDINGS.

SEPTEMBER, 1681, ARCHIVES OF MARYLAND.

SIR:—Mr. Edward Dorsey came here last night very late, and brought news that the Indians had robbed John Marriott—beaten him and his wife, and turned them out of doors. I design, to-day being 2nd September, to go up and take ten or twelve men. If you please to give me any further orders, be pleased to direct to Towne, to him who is, Sir, your most humble servant,

ROBERT PROCTOR.

September 2nd, 1681. To Captain Thomas Francis, at Road River. Deliver with speed.

September 2nd, 1681, Anne Arundel County.

Rt. Honble.—The occasion of my present presumption is to inform your Lordship of a robbery committed by the Sinnequain —Seneca—Indians (as is supposed), on the first day of this instant, at the house of John Marriott at the head of Anne Arundel River, upon the Ridge formerly Peter Porter's. The enclosed was sent to me and the same day being our election day, I had an opportunity to speak with the said John Marriott, which for substance gave me the following narrative, viz.: That nine Indians came to his house, September 1st, inst. in the morning and pressed hard for entrance into his house, which he resisted, taking his gun in hand and standing upon his guard, willing his wife to take the children and make escape to the nearest plantation, which was hindered by more Indians, till then indescerned, but still appearing more and more, to the quantity of one hundred or thereabouts. They then pressed so sore upon him that into the house they would go; no threat or sign of anger would deter them. Out of which, they have carried all that he hath in this world, and killed his hogs, which he says he had thirty in his pen, which troubled his cornfield, some of which they have taken away, others they killed for pastime and let lye, that of numbers he finds only three or four alive. His cattle he knows not what they have killed, for they have all forsaken the plantation. His tobacco, which was hanging in the houses, they have thrown down and spoiled. All of which, tendeth to his great loss, and putting the neighboring plantations in great feare, so that there are many of them together for their future safety.

In humble manner, I have truly, though briefly, acquainted your Lordship with the robbery. I humbly crave your pardon for what is remiss, and subscribe myself, your faithful and obedient servant.   Thomas Ffrancis.

Near the old Sewell homestead, at the head of the Severn River, Anne Arundel County, Maryland, which has been in the family for about two hundred years, a tragic event transpired, and has often been spoken of in bygone days by the Sewells.

One of the early settlers in this neighborhood, started out to hunt, and took his little dog with him. After he had been out some time he heard the Indian war-whoop over the hills, and, in his effort to retrace his steps, he found he could not escape the Indians. He, therefore, took his little dog and climbed up into the hollow of a large tree. As the Indians were passing, the dog barked and the hiding place was discovered, and he was pulled down by the Indians and tied to a stake. And the Indians piled pine light wood around him and having set fire to it, proceeded to have a war dance, and he was burned alive.

Later on, when corn-husking and cider-pressing time came, the same Indians came to assist, and the white settlers put in the cider a copious supply of rum, of which the Indians drank freely, and then went into the barn to sleep off the effect.

It was now the white people had their revenge, as they barricaded the door and set fire to the barn, and the same Indians who burned the white man were consumed.

PITTS FAMILY.

William Pitts came from England to visit friends in Baltimore and, while here, went out in Baltimore County and stopped at a then fashionable hotel, and at night dreamed of a beautiful French lady, and in his dream became greatly enamored. And lo, the very next morning at breakfast there sat, directly opposite to him at the table, the veritable French lady of his dream. He was introduced and subsequently they were married, and instead of returning to England, settled in Baltimore County.

There were two sons by this romantic marriage, William and Thomas Pitts. The former remained in Baltimore County and the latter went to Anne Arundel County and married Susannah Lusby, and had eight children—Thomas, Charles, John, Elizabeth, Susan, Ann, Henrietta and Mary Pitts. Thomas—Sarah Sewell, 1782; Mary—Augustine Sewell; Ann—Mordecai Stewart, of South River; Elizabeth—Charles McElfresh; Susan died single. The Pitts family moved to Frederick County.

John Pitts, of Thomas—Elizabeth Hall, daughter of Nicholas Hall, of New Market, and had six children—Nicholas, John Lusby, Anna Maria, Thomas, William and Charles H. Pitts, the gifted lawyer of Baltimore—Elizabeth Reynolds. Issue, T. Glenn, Edward, Charles and Martha Pitts.

MALLONEE FAMILY.

Achsah Sewell, daughter of John and Mary (Marriott) Sewell, married Leonard Mallonee, of John. She was born in 1768, married in 1791, died in 1859, in her 91st year. Leonard Mallonee was born 1763, died 1854, in his 92nd year. Issue, John, Brice, William, Denton, Achsah, Mary Edith and Anne Sewell Mallonee.

John Mallonee married Rachel Lyon, a niece of Moses Sheppard, the founder of Moses Sheppard Asylum. The children of John and Rachel (Lyon) Mallonee were William, John, Rachel, Leonard, James and Benjamin Mallonee.

Brice Mallonee married Louisa Fairall, 1824. Issue, John Stephen, William, Alexander, Brice, Martin Van Buren, Achsah, Edith, Maryland and Virginia Mallonee.

William Mallonee married Thomazine Keirll, daughter of John W. Keirll, a prominent merchant of Baltimore, previous to 1840. The latter was lost on the steamer Lexington, which was burned on Long Island Sound at night, in 1840. The children of William and Thomazine Mallonee were, John, Leonard, William, Matthew, Mark and Achsah Mallonee. William Mallonee was a prominent dry-goods merchant in Baltimore, previous to 1840, and located on the corner of Baltimore and Hanover Streets.

Denton Mallonee, son of Leonard and Achash (Sewell) Mallonee —in 1821, Ann Kirby, daughter of George and Anna (Randall) Kirby. Issue, George, Leonard and Achsah Ann Mallonee. George Leonard—Amanda E. Carter, daughter of John W. and Elizabeth, Carter, of Baltimore. Issue, George Carter, John Denton and Anne E. Mallonee. Achsah Ann—Frederick Custis Hyde. Issue, Anna M. Eleanor and George M. Hyde. The last named married Elizabeth Wallace, of Westchester, New York, and had a child, Elise Wallace Hyde.

Mary, daughter of Leonard and Achsah (Sewell) Mallonee— George Bradford, of Howard County. Issue, William Charles, John, Luther, Ann, Melvina and Achsah Bradford. The latter became Mrs. Edwin Owings, of Lisbon.

Achsah Mallonee, daughter of Leonard and Achsah (Sewell) Mallonee—Alfred Fairall. Issue, Thomas, William, John, Horace, Alfred, Achsah, Henrietta, Alexina and Elizabeth Fairall. Anne Sewell Mallonee, daughter of Leonard and Achsah (Sewell) Mallonee —William Kirby, 1833.

MUSTER ROLL OF KIRBYS, IN THE WAR OF THE REVOLUTION.

Richard Kirby, in Flying Camp, July 27th, 1776.
Anthony Kirby, 1781.
John Kirky, 1781.
Nathaniel, 1783.
Joseph, of Annapolis, 1781.
John Kirby, 1776.
David Dirby.
John Kirby, blown from a barge.

KIRBY FAMILY.

Walter Kirby was early in Kent Island, and the Rent Rolls show he patented lands in 1667. In 1679, he was honored by the Lord Proprietary to take charge of important Chancery proceedings. Walter Kirby, in his will dated 1702, mentions his wife, Elizabeth, and children, William, James, Matthew, Benjamin, Mary and Rebecca Kirby.

William, son of Walter, in his will, 1717, named his wife, Ann, and children, Walter, James, Sarah and Mary Kirby. Benjamin, of Walter, in his will of 1721, mentioned, wife, Elizabeth. Walter Kirby, of William, died in 1755; his wife was Sarah Kirby. William Kirby, of Walter, died in 1768, wife, Rachel; children, Walter, Elizabeth and Ann Kirby. Benjamin Kirby, son of Matthew of Walter, died in 1774, on Kent Island. Issue, Joshua, died 1794; Benjamin, died 1783; Nicholas, died 1800; Littlelar, died 1810; Elizabeth—Edmond Custis, 1796, died 1807; Margery—Jonathan Harrison, 1786; Rebecca—Dr. Jacob Ringgold, 1787; Sarah and

William Kirby. The above named children of Benjamin Kirby went to Baltimore previous to 1783. William Kirby was in business in Baltimore, at the corner of Calvert and Water Streets, from 1796 to 1800.

William Kirby bought "Pratt's Choice," West River, in 1802, from Thomas Tillard, and in his will, dated 1818, named his wife, Mary, and children, William, Francis, Benjamin, Solomon, Joseph, George, Jane, Anne, Sarah and Charlotte Kirby.

George Kirby married Anna Randall at St. Anne's, Annapolis, October 25th, 1798. She was a descendant of Christopher Randall, who settled on the Severn River previous to 1679. Died 1847.

William Kirby, of George—Anne Sewell Mallonee, 1833, died 1872. Issue, Leonard, born 1834, died 1891; Isabella, born 1836, died 1877; Norval, Ann, William and George A. Kirby. Norval Ann Kirby—Philip Hammond, 1862. Issue, Anne—Woodland C. Phillips; Cora—Ralph Gilbert Lee; William—Anna Barbara Benson; Norval Adele—Charles Leonard Owens; Maud—William Henry Cole; Philip and Zoe Kirby Hammond, unmarried. Isabella Kirby died 1877—Arthur Hammond, 1865. Issue, Luther Kirby Hammond.

Philip and Arthur Hammond were lineal descendants of General John Hammond, who died, 1707. Upon the estate of Major Philip Hammond, now owned by Mr. George Kirby, are the following monuments:

"This monument, erected in memory of a great and good man, Philip Hammond, Esquire, who died May 10th, 1760, in the 64th year of his age."

"This monument covers the remains of Mrs. Rachel Hammond, daughter of John Brice, Esquire, and relict of Philip Hammond, Esquire; born April 13th, 1711; died, Tuesday, April 11th, 1786."

"Here lies the body of Mrs. Rachel Hopkins, daughter of Philip Hammond, Esquire, deceased, born May 2nd, 1740; died September 11th, 1773."

"This monument covers the remains of Denton Hammond, son of Philip Hammond, Esquire, born March 10th, 1745; died March 2nd, 1784."

"This monument covers the remains of Philip Hammond, son of Philip Hammond, Esquire, born April 2nd, 1739; died 1783."

"Here lies the body of Mr. Matthias Hammond, son of Philip Hammond, Esquire, born May 24th, 1740; died March 11th, 1786."

"Erected in memory of Colonel Rezin Hammond, son of Philip and Rachel (Brice) Hammond, his wife; died September 1st, 1809, in his 65th year."

"Sacred to the memory of Dr. Matthias Hammond, son of Philip and Elizabeth (Wright) Hammond, who died, 1819, in his 35th year."

"Sacred to the memory of Elizabeth Mewburn, daughter of Phillip Hammond, Esquire, who died 1819, age 22 years."

William M. Kirby—Virginia Downing Parrish, of Missouri. Issue, William Clyde, Guy Donnell, Leila Virginia and Anne Louis Kirby.

George A. Kirby—Mary Ella Hodges, daughter of James and Josephine A. Hodges. Issue, Bessie Sewell, Mary Hanson and William George Kirby. Bessie Sewell Kirby—George R. A. Hiss, in 1900, and he died in 1904. Issue, George R. A. Hiss, born 1903. Mr. Hiss, was a lineal descendant of Colonel William Burgess, who was appointed by Lord Baltimore in 1665, to command the militia of the province, and acted as governor during Lord Baltimore's absence.

ACTON.

Richard Acton was at Annapolis in 1657. Daniel Dulany, in one of his pleadings in a contest over the early surveys of Annapolis, said that Thos. Todd probably assigned his Annapolis survey to Acton, whilst Thomas Hall's lands going to Christopher, the son, who left it to his mother, Elizabeth, and both dying without issue, the land was escheated. Todd's Harbor, in the hands of Robert Lusby, also reverted back by escheat. This indeed took place pretty generally in Annapolis. The Lord Proprietary reserved lands in the city, but Thomas Bordley and Thomas Larkin, combining with Lancelot Todd, pretending to be heir-at-law of said Thomas Todd, deprived the Lord Proprietor of it.

Upon the south limits of Annapolis to-day, is "Murray's Hill," named for the distinguished family who has held it for many years. Its present owner is the former paymaster of the navy, Murray of the West River branch. This tract, upon which stands a very old colonial homestead, was formerly known as "Acton" and it adjoins, if not a part of the Carroll estate, which was the survey of Thomas Todd

John Acton was a son of Richard Acton; and Sarah, the daughter of Richard—John Marriott, the pioneer settler of "Porter's Hill." Philip Hammond, the rich merchant, built the present mansion upon the Acton tract, now Murray's Hill.

CAPTAIN JOHN WORTHINGTON.

There are many traditions but few records of this family. "All who bear the name of Worthington in this country," says Mr. W. Worthington Fowler, in his notes on the Worthington family, "derived their origin from two sources: First, from an immigrant who settled in Maryland. Second, from Nicholas Worthington, who came to New England in 1650, and was the only immigrant of that name in New England at that time."

"There is on record, in the archives of Pennsylvania, a coroner's inquest upon the body of a Worthington immigrant, who died in passage to that province, which shows he belonged to the Worthingtons of Manchester, England." Mr. Fowler adds.

"About twenty miles northeast of Liverpool, in the Hundred of Leyland, is the town of Worthington, established, "says Burke, "in high repute from the time of the Plantagenets." The old hall where the family resided for seven hundred years, was pulled down long ago. The present representative of the family is Edward Worthington, of "The Bryn," County Chester, 1868.

The family is connected by marriage with Norris, Orrell, Radcliffe, Lawrence, Ashton, Byron, Leven, Anderson and Standish, ancestors of Stout Myles Standish, "the Captain of the Puritan Band."

The coat-of-arms, given by Burke, is that of the main stem of Lancashire Worthingtons, viz.: "Argent, three pitch forks (or tridents), sable, crest, a goat passant, argent, holding in his mouth an oak branch."

Our records at Annapolis show that Captain John Worthington was here as early as 1675, and in 1686 bought "Greenberry Forest" from Colonel Nicholas Greenberry. He married, soon after, Sarah, daughter of Matthew Howard, his neighbor upon the Severn. In 1692, Captain Worthington was appointed associate justice of Anne Arundel; and, in 1699, was a member of the Legislative Assembly, during which year his will was written. It reads: "I give and bequeath to my dear and loving wife, Sarah Worthington, the whole use and profit and comfort of this my now dwelling plantation, and all my personal estate, she paying the legacies hereinafter specified, and being by me ordered to give all the children what learning the country will afford at her personal cost. And if, in case my said wife shall marry again, then the children to be for themselves at the age of sixteen, but if she continue a widow, then all my sons to live with her to be her assistance and comfort till the age of twenty-one years. And after the decease of my wife, Sarah, then the personal estate to be divided equally amongst my children.

"Then I give to my son, John Worthington, the plantation I now live on and all the land adjoining, being four hundred acres, lying on the Severn River.

"Then I give to my son, Thomas Worthington, my plantation called "Greenberry Forrest,' being four hundred acres, more or less, and 'Lowe's Addition,' being a tract of three hundred and fifty acres, all lying near Magothy River.

"Then I give my son, William Worthington, the plantation called 'Howard's Inheritance,' containing one hundred and thirty acres; also a parcel of woodland ground, part of Mr. William Hopkin's plantation, as doth appear by the last will of Mr. Matthew Howard, deceased, and two hundred acres, lying where Mr. Richard Beard's mill stands; and two hundred and seventy acres near the fish pond in 'Bodkin's Creek,' of the Patapsco River.

"Then I give to my daughter, Sarah Worthington, two young working negroes, or fifty pounds sterling, at the age of sixteen, or the day of marriage."

Charles Worthington, born after the above will was written, was similarly provided.   In addition to the above tracts, the Worthington heirs held "Howard's Pasture," "Pendenny and Expectations" and "Howardstown," formerly surveyed for Philip Howard. Upon a tombstone on the farm of the late R. Tilghman Brice, just opposite the Naval Academy at Annapolis, may be read the following inscription:

"Here lieth interred, the body of
Captain John Worthington,
Who departed this life
April 9th, 1701. Aged 51 years."

The tombstone, an immense slab of greyish marble color, is in excellent preservation, and the inscription perfectly legible.   It, also, bears on top a most beautiful and remarkable insignia.   The interpretation of the crest is, "To him who lies beneath this stone, time (represented by the hour-glass) has taken to itself wings (wings, between which stands the hour-glass).   His mortal remains must here lie (mortality represented by death's head), until summoned by the trumpet of the arch-angle (trumpets crossed behind death's head) to wear the victor's crown (laurel wreath)."   The slab covers a well-preserved walled grave, which is only a few yards north of the homestead, the form and material of which is still preserved.

About 1688, Captain John Worthington married Sarah Howard. Issue, John, born 1689; Thomas, 1691; William, 1694; Sarah, 1696; Charles, 1701.

John, 1713—Helen, daughter of Thomas and Mary Heath Hammond.   Issue, William, Charles, Vachel, Anne—Thomas Beale Dorsey, Elizabeth—Nicholas Dorsey, John, Samuel and Thomas Worthington.

John Worthington, Jr., in his will, styled himself merchant, gave to daughter, Ann Dorsey, the homestead, "Wyatt's Harbor" and "Wyatt's Hills."   To son, John, "Worthington's Fancy" and "Worthington's Beginning" and part of "Duvall's Delight," "Food Plenty" and other tracts bought of Orlando Griffith, some 2,620 acres; also "Whiskey Ridge," at Liberty, Frederick County.   To son, Charles, "Hunting Ground," "Ridgely's Range," "Broken Ground," "Howard and Porters Fancy" and "Abington," adjoining, some 950 acres.   To Samuel, 1,000 acres, "Welsh's Cradle," in Baltimore County.   To son Thomas, three tracts on the Patapsco, some 1,680 acres.   To Elizabeth Dorsey, "Todd's Risque" and "Andover."   To granddaughter, Helen Lynch, £60.   To grandsons, John and William, sons of William, deceased, "Whiskey Ridge" on the Linganore, 700 acres.

William, 1734—Hannah Cromwell.   Issue, William, John— Mary Todd.   Her will, of 1776, announced herself as the widow of John Worthington, and named her daughters, Elinor, Ann, Elizabeth, Hannah and Margaret.   She made her brother, Wm. Linch,

and Wm. Wilkinson executors. Elinor Griffith was a witness.
Hannah Worthington, her daughter, 1798, named her sisters, Ann
Craddock, Margaret Lamar, and niece, Elizabeth Mary Tolley.
    John Worthington, of John and Helen, married Susannah
Hood, sister of Zachariah, the stamp agent. Issue, Thomas, Nicholas,
William, James, Ann, Sarah and Elizabeth—Caleb Dorsey. Thos.
Worthington named Margaret, daughter of my late brother William;
niece, Sarah Wilson; nephew, Abraham Worthington
    Samuel Worthington, of John and Helen, 1759—Mary Tolley,
daughter of Walter Tolley, of Joppa. Issue, John, Tolley, Comfort,
wife of John Worthington Dorsey, Ann Hawley, Martha Love,
Thomas Tolley, James Tolley, Edward, Samuel, Jr., Walter and
Vachel Worthington, all inheriting from $3,000 to $8,000 each.
By his second marriage to Martha Garrettson, he willed her "Bat-
sons' Forest," "Welsh's Cradle," negroes, plate, furniture. Named
his daughters, Charlotte Merryman, Sarah Dorsey, Catherine Larsh,
Susannah Worthington, Eleanor Worthington, Martha and Elizabeth Worthington. Sons, Nicholas and Garrett Worthington. To
John Tolley Worthington he left the family graveyard, to be handed
down by him, whom he made executor with son Charles.
    By codicil be revoked the legacies of real estate to his daughters,
and left it to his sons, John Tolley, Walter and Charles Worthington.
His son Garrett was given a large estate under the condition of his
paying certain legacies to his daughters, Susannah, Eleanor and
Martha. Son Nicholas was also required to aid in their support.
    John Tolley Worthington, executor of Samuel and Mary,
married Mary Worthington, daughter of Hon. Brice Thomas Beale.
Issue, Brice, Ann Ridgely and Mary—John T. H. Worthington.
The will of John Tolley Worthington left to his "grandson, John
Tolley Wortihngton, son of my daughter Mary, 'Cottage, or Welcome
Here,' all of 'Welsh's Cradle' and 'Murray's Plains,' purchased of
Garrett G. Worthington, and most of my real estate. To grand-
daughter, Polly Worthington Johns, daughter of my daughter,
Nancy Ridgely Johns, all lands not divised to grandson, John
Tolley. To granddaughter, Ann Maria Worthington, lands in
Baltimore City. To grandson, Richard Johns, lands in Baltimore
City. Named son-in-law, John T. H. Worthington. He named,
also, as residuary legatees, his grandchildren, Comfort, Samuel,
Polly Worthington, John Tolley and Sarah Weems Johns.
    He referred to the helplessness of his wife and urged his grand-
son to give her all necessary attention. To him, also, was committed
the care of the family graveyard.
    Walter, of Samuel and Mary—Sarah Hood. Issue, Mary—
Charles Worthington Dorsey, Martha, Elizabeth, Comfort, Hannah,
John Tolley Hood, Samuel and Charles. Samuel Worthington, Jr.,
the bachelor, named his sister, Ann Hawley; brother, Vachel;
nieces, Mary Tolley and Comfort Worthington, daughters of brother
Walter, and nephew John Tolley Hood Worthington (children of
Walter and Sarah Hood, daughter of John Hood, Jr., by Hannah

Barnes). Nephew Samuel Worthington, son of brother Edward, inherited "my ciphered china and tea caddy," or, if he preferred, one hundred dollars instead, the said china to go to niece Ann Ridgely Worthington, daughter of brother John Tolley Worthington. "All the remainder of my estate to my brother, John Tolley.

WORTHINGTONS OF SAMUEL AND MARY TOLLEY.

Thomas Tolley Worthington was born in Maryland, 17th December, 1771, (a twin of James Tolley Worthington infra.). and died at his home in Mason County, Kentucky, near Bryant's Station, 30th July, 1843. On 6th June, 1799, he married, first, Lydia Whipps, who died 15th December, 1803. The issue of this marriage were, (1) Rachel, born 24th April, 1800; died 7th December, 1837. (2) Walter Tolley, born 17th May, 1802 died 5th May, 1828.

On 1st November, 1804, he married his sister-in-law, Avery Whipps. The issue of this marriage were, (1) Lydia, born 4th August, 1805; (2) Samuel, born 25th January, 1807; died 3rd October, 1862. (3) Comfort Ann, born 8th May, 1808; died 29th May, 1830. (4) Edward, born 1st April, 1809; died 28th September, 1829, unmarried. (5) John Tolley, born 6th March, 1811; died 20th May, 1836. (6) Mary Ann, born 2nd September, 1812; died 12th April, 1881. (7) Vachel, born 7th May, 1814; died 5th May, 1856, unmarried. (8) Thomas Tolley, born 25th November, 1815; died 28th September, 1856, unmarried. (9) Charles, born 5th July, 1817; died 1st September 1838, unmarried. (10) Garrett, born 15th June, 1819; died 12th October, 1857. (11) Madison, born 10th April, 1821; died 12th June, 1897. (12) Martha, born 25th February, 1823, living. (13) Nicholas Brice, born 25th May, 1825; died 27th September, 1862. (14) Henry, born 1st September, 1826; died 18th October, 1895.

Rachel married Thomas Mannen, of Mason County, Kentucky. Walter Tolley married Elizabeth Slack, of Mason County, Kentucky. Lydia married James G. Pepper, of Mason County, Kentucky. Samuel married, first, Elizabeth Robinson; second, Malusia Robinson (sisters), of Tuckahoe County, Kentucky; third, Sarah Runyan, of Mason County. Comfort Ann married John Robinson, of Tuckahoe County. John Tolley married Rachel Donovan, of Mason County. Mary Ann married, first, George Barker; second, Evan Pickerell, both of Bracken County. Garrett married Laura Adams, of Fleming County. Madison married, first, Lizzie Bledsoe; second, Tillie Holton. Martha married William T. Craig, of Bracken County. Nicholas Brice married, first, Jane Craig; second, Maria Goward, both of Mason County. Henry married Maria Slack, of Mason County.

James Tolley Worthington, twin of Thomas Tolley, was born in Maryland, 17th December, 1771, and died at his home in Mercer County, Kentucky, near Harrodsburg, 28th September, 1829. In the early spring, 1801, he married Margaret P. Stade. The issue of this marriage were: (1) Vachel, born 2nd February, 1802; died 7th July, 1877. (2) Mary Tolley, born January, 1804; died February, 1878. (3) John Tolley, born 1808-9. (4) Comfort, born 28th August, 1812; died 28th August, 1890. (5) William, born 1814-15; died in early youth. (6) Margaret Elizabeth, born 23rd February, 1817; died 19th June, 1862. (7) Charles Thomas, born 3rd April, 1819; died 14th December, 1876. (8) Ellen Catherine, born 1st March, 1821; died 27th January, 1872. (9) Edward Strade, born 29th October, 1824; died 30th April, 1874. (10) Augusta, born 1827; died in infancy.

Vachel married, first, 25th May, 1825, Mary Ann Burnet, of Cincinnati, Ohio, born 29th June, 1802; died 25th October, 1834, and had issue, (1) Rebecca Burnet, (2) James Tolley, (3) Jacob Burner, (4) Rebecca Burnet, (5) Jacob Burnet, all dying in infancy but James Tolley, still living. On 6th January, 1839, he married, second, Julia Wiggins, of Cincinnati, Ohio. born 18th October, 1816; died 7th September, 1877, and had issue, (1) Edward, (2) Samuel, (3) Julia, (4) William.

James Tolley married Anne Mary Postlethwaite, of Lexington, Kentucky. No issue. Edward, unmarried, Samuel died, 6th December, 1848.

Julia married William Pope Anderson, of Cincinnati, Ohio. Issue, Vachel Worthington, Larz. Worthington, Catherine Longworth, Julia Wiggins, died 21st January, 1876; William Pope, Laura Wiggins, died 4th August, 1891; Ida Longworth, died 24th October, 1897; Francis Baldwin, William Pope Anderson, her husband, died 20th November, 1897. William married Susan Carpenter. Issue, Julia, Helen, Louise Skinner, Elizabeth Carpenter.

Mary Tolley married, first, Madison Worthington, son of her uncle, Edward Worthington, and had issue, Margaret Stade, died, 1886, and Caroline, died in youth. She married, secondly, Dr. George Venable, of Hopkinsville, Kentucky, and had issue, George Worthington, and James Edward. Margaret married Frederic Augusta de Seebach-Juny, and had issue, George Ousley, Frederic Augustus, Madison, Edward de Seebach. George Worthington Venable married Louisa Blair and had issue, Mary Tolley, died 1880; Julia Augusta, died 1896; Susanna Worthington; Agnes Louise, died 1884.

John Tolley married Susan Hoard, of Mercer County, Kentucky, and had issue, Margaret Strade, Maude, Mary Tolley. Comfort married Buckner Miller, of Jefferson County, Kentucky, and had issue, James Tolley, Margaret Stade, Charlie, Henry, Anna, Julia Worthington. William died in youth.

Margaret Elizabeth married, 27th September, 1834, George Mason Long, and had issue, Margaret Mason and Francis Martin. Margaret Mason married Smith Gordon, and had issue, Margaret Elizabeth, Francis Zacharie, Archie Calvert. Frances Martin married John Thomas Janney, of Baltimore, Maryland, and had issue, Anna Mason, Margaret Marshall, Alice Moore, Ethel Hyams, Thomas, George Mason Long.

Charles Thomas married Joanna Theresa Gill, and had issue, Erasmus Tolley, Anna Elizabeth, James Tolley, Vachel, Hood, Joanna Theresa, Charles Thomas, Union, Vachel (2), Mary Tolley.

Ellen Catherine married, first, James Bruce Johnstones, and had issue, Margaret Anna, Edward Worthington, Charles Worthington, Julia James, Ellen Bell, Mary Tolley, of whom Charles Worthington only is surviving. She married, secondly, William Edward Keyes, of Louisville, Kentucky. No issue.

Edward Stade married Anna Eliza Powell. No issue.

Edward Worthington was born in Maryland, 18th June, 1773, and died in Hopkinsville, Kentucky, 1846. In 1899 he married Eliza G. Madison, of Point Pleasant, Virginia. The issue of this marriage were, (1) Samuel Madison, (2) John Tolley, (3) Edward, (4) James Tolley, (5) Rowland Madison, (6) Mary Ann Lewis, (7) Eliza Martha Augusta, (8) Lucy Lewis, (9) Margaret Jane Catherine. Samuel Madison married his cousin, Mary Tolley Worthington, of James Tolley, supra.

John Tolley married, first, Ann Hoard Slaughter, of Mercer County, Kentucky. Issue, William Hoard. He married, secondly, his cousin Elizabeth Ann Worthington, of Maryland. Issue, Walter Edward, Sarah Martha Ann, Eliza Madison, John Tolley Hood. He married, thirdly, Jane Alida Holland, of Whitestone, New York. Issue. James Edward, Rowland Madison, Lewis Gilmore.

Edward, unmarried. James Tolley, unmarried. Rowland Madison, married Ann Maria Wells, of Rushville, Illinois. Issue, Eliza Madison, Edward, Mary Lewis, James Wells, Anna Maria, Lucy Jane, Sarah Grier.

Mary Ann Lewis, unmarried. Eliza Martha Augusta married Judge English, of Sacramento City, California, and had one daughter.

Lucy Lewis, unmarried. Margaret Jane Catherine married Dr. Charles Shackelford, of Hopkinsville, Kentucky. Issue, Lucy, Elizabeth Madison, Edward Worthington.

Charles, of Samuel and Mary,—Susan Johns. Issue, Mary Tolley, Samuel, Richard, John, Sallie, Henry, Benjamin, Rosetta, Edward.

Ann Worthington, of John and Helen,—Thomas, Beale Dorsey, youngest son of Caleb and Elinor (Warfield) Dorsey, of Hockley. Issue, Caleb, John Worthington Dorsey, Thomas Beale Dorsey, Jr., and Sarah Meriweather.

Elizabeth Worthington, of John and Helen,—Nicholas Dorsey, of Joshua and Anne Ridgely. (See Dorsey.)

Thomas Worthington, of John and Helen, 1761,—Elizabeth Hammond. Issue, John Worthington, 1785,—Anne Dorsey, of Nicholas and Elizabeth, of Annapolis Junction. Issue, Nicholas, Lloyd, John, Noah, Thomas, Reuben, Elizabeth, Ann, Comfort and Henrietta. Nicholas was the large landholder; Lloyd went to

Missouri; Reuben was drowned; Noah and Thomas were bachelors. John—Miss Cockey. Issue, Nicholas—Miss O'dell, granddaughter of General Towson,—Issue, John—Miss Parshall, of Pennsylvania, whose daughter is Mrs. Matilda Pomeroy of Toledo, Ohio.

Judge Dye Worthington, of Howard, long judge of the Orphans Court, married Henrietta Ridgely, of Dr. Charles C. Ridgely, of Clarkesville. Otis Worthington, his brother,—first, Miss Walters, and, second, Nellie Dorsey, of Amos. Thomas Worthington—second, Marcella Owings, of Joshua. Issue, Mary, Noah, Thomas Dye, Rezin Hammond—first, Rachel Shipley, of Robert; second, Mary Shipley. Issue Thomas Chew Worthington, whose large estate was near Woodstock.

John Tolley Worthington—Mary Govane, daughter of James Hood, of Hood's Mill, whose wife was Sarah Howard, daughter of Benjamin Howard and Mary Govane. Issue, Mary Govane Hood, whose inheritance was later sold by her husband and herself to Samuel Bentz, and by him named "The Stock Farm." It bordered on "Dexterity" at Hood's Mill; took in "Sally's Chance," her mother's tract. It was deeded by John Tolley Worthington, and Mary Govane, his wife, to Samuel Bentz, in 1858.

The following notice of his estate is taken from the Baltimore Sun: "John Tolley Worthington, son of John Tolley Worthington, who died in 1860, holds an estate which covers most of Worthington Valley. His mother was Mary Govane Hood. Mr. Worthington inherited the 'Shawan' Hunting Ground, about 1,000 acres, near Cockeysville. His father's estate called 'Mont Morency,' was left to him, Mrs. Sallie Conrad and L. W. Cipriani, his nephew."

The following quotation from a Washington paper refers to him: "There are many persons living in Baltimore to whom the name, Bodisco, will recall another brilliant marriage; that of the beautiful daughter of Mr. and Mrs. John Tolley Worthington. Some years before the war, Miss Mary Worthington went abroad with the Count and Countess Bodisco. She was presented at the French Court, which was then the most brilliant in Europe. On this occasion she wore a superb pink watered silk gown, the front of which was trimmed with rosettes in which glistened diamonds. She married Leonette Cipriani, an Italian general of noble birth. One year later, the daughter returned to her home and there died. Her only son inherited her interest in Worthington Valley.

James Worthington, of John,—Elizabeth Griffith, of Colonel Henry, Jr. Issue, John Hammond Worthington, Nicholas Griffith, Sarah, Susan, Thomas, William, Mary H., Upton and Elizabeth Worthington.

John Hammond — Ann Hammond Dorsey, of Joshua and Henrietta Hammond. Issue, Joshua Dorsey Worthington, Nicholas, John T. Worthington.

Nicholas Worthington, of John H. and Ann,—first, Sarah E. Anderson. Issue, Laura—Lloyd E. Dorsey. Second, Henrietta A. Dorsey.

Charles Worthington, of James and Elizabeth,—Ann Brashear. Upton Worthington, of James and Elizabeth—Catherine Dorsey, of Joshua and Henrietta. Nicholas Griffith Worthington, of James and Elizabeth,—in Kentucky, Eliza White.

Thomas Worthington, second son of Captain John—Elizabeth Ridgely, daughter of Henry and Katherine (Greenberry) Ridgely. Issue, Ann, born 1713; Sarah, 1715; Elizabeth, 1717; Katherine, 1720; Rachel Ridgely, 1722; Thomasine, 1724; Brice Thomas Beale, 1727; Ariana, 1729; Thomas, 1731; Nicholas, 1734.

Thomas and Elizabeth Worthington bought "Broome" and "Wardridge" of Henry Ridgely, third, and resided there. It bordered upon "Hockley", and upon it are both the Ridgely and Worthington graveyards.

From that old homestead went forth to Elk Ridge, the following daughters, whose history belongs to Howard County: Sarah Worthington—Basil Dorsey, born at Hockley; Elizabeth—Henry Dorsey, of Joshua and Ann Ridgely; Katherine—Major Nicholas Gassaway, of Colonel Nicholas, of South River; Rachel Ridgely Worthington—Cornelius Howard, of Joseph, her neighbor; Thomasin—Alexander Warfield, of John; Ariana—Nicholas Watkins, Jr. All inherited portions of "Worthington Range," at Clarksville, and "Partnership," between Highland and Fulton.

The sons of Thomas and Elizabeth Ridgely Worthington remained in Anne Arundel. Thomas Worthington died in 1753, when the following obituary notice was written upon his life; his wife, Elizabeth, died 1734: "Last Monday morning, died at his plantation, about five miles from town, in the 63rd year, or grand climatical year, of his age, Mr. Thomas Worthington, who, for many years past, and to the time of his death, was one of the representatives for this county in the Lower House of the Assembly. He served his country with a steady and disinterested fidelity; was strictly honest in principle and practice, and, therefore, had the esteem of all that knew him. He was a good father and sincere friend; was frugal and industrious, and was possessed of many qualities which constituted the character of a good and sincere Christian."—(Maryland Gazette, 1753.)

Hon. Brice Thomas Beale Worthington, his son, was a member of the colonial legislature preceding the Revolution, and was upon the active list in the defense of the province. He married Ann Ridgely, daughter of Colonel Henry and Elizabeth (Warfield) Ridgely. Their daughter Mary — John Tolley Worthington, of Samuel and Mary Tolley, of Joppa. Issue, Brice, Mary and Ann.

Mary Tyler Worthington, granddaughter of Hon. Thomas Beale, became the wife of William Warfield, the Annapolis merchant, great-grandson of Benjamin Warfield, of "Lugg Ox."

Major Nicholas Worthington, next son of Thomas and Elizabeth, married Catherine Griffith, daughter of Captain Charles and Catherine (Baldwin) Griffith. Their homestead was "Summer Hill." It stood west of Hockley, and south of the Annapolis and Elk Ridge railroad, until destroyed by fire. Major Worthington was a representative in the General Assembly at Annapolis, and commanded the militia of his section. His oldest son, Thomas Worthington, was located near "The Rising Sun," a celebrated wayside resort. He married Margaret Mullikin. Charles—Elizabeth Booth; Nicholas—Elizabeth Rutland; Catherine—Colonel Baker Johnson; Brice John Worthington—Ann Fitzhugh.

John Griffith Worthington, his twin brother, was a representative in the Legislature, and died a bachelor. Achsah—Dr. Richard Goldsborough; Sarah—Dr. William Goldsborough. These daughters of "Summer Hill" have left long lines of distinguished men and women, in Frederick and upon the Eastern Shore.

Thomas and Margaret (Mullikin) Worthington's descendants were Thomas and Dr. Charles Griffith Worthington, the history of whom belongs to Howard County.

"BELVOIR."

Upon a commanding ridge overlooking an extensive landscape, and in full view of Round Bay, stands the best preserved colonial home near Annapolis. It is "Belvoir," built upon "Wyatt's Ridge." It is a long brick building with wide hallway and well-proportioned rooms. It was built by John Ross, when Register of the Land Office. It became next the property of Colonel Maynadier.

Hon. Brice John Worthington, son of Colonel Nicholas, of "Summer Hill," to extend his estate from Eagle Nest Bay to South River, a distance of seven miles, purchased "Belvoir" at a cost of $25,000, and, it is claimed, made $13,000 on tobacco in one year. He married Anna Lee Fitzhugh, niece of Colonel Maynadier of "Old Windsor," Baltimore County, whom he met on one of his fox-hunting runs with the Colonel.

In a large field, nearly a fourth of a mile from the dwelling, surrounded by an iron railing, rest the remains of Mrs. Maynadier and those of Mrs. Ann Arnold Key, grandmother of Maryland's poet. The latter grave has the protective stamp of the Colonial Dames of Maryland; and upon the old tombstone one may read: "In memory of Mrs. Ann Arnold Key, who departed this life January 5th, 1811, in the 84th year of her age."

She was the daughter of John Ross, who held land in several counties, viz.: "Ross Range," in Frederick County; "Carpenter's Point," Talbot County, and later, the builder of "Belvoir." upon Nicholas Wyatt's survey of "Wyatt's Ridge."

Mrs. Key's sister, Elizabeth Ross, married Dr. Upton Scott, a wealthy citizen of Annapolis, whose homestead has been made the seat of the hero, "Richard Carvil."

Ann Arnold Ross married Francis Key, son of Philip Key, of St. Mary's. Upon the burning of her house at Carpenter's Point, her sight was destroyed by fire and smoke while rescuing two servants from the flames. She then crossed the bay and took up her

residence with her daughter, Elizabeth Ross Key, wife of Colonel
Henry Maynadier, of "Belvoir," where she ended her days. Mrs.
Key had, also, two sons, John Ross and Philip Barton Key. The
former was an active patriot of the Revolution; the latter a Tory,
whose property was confiscated. This same property came to him
through the generosity of his brother, heir-at-law of the estate, who
shared with his brother; and, after the war, again shared his estate
with his Tory brother.

General John Ross Key married Anne Rhoche Charlton, whose
son was Francis Scott Key, author of the "Star Spangled Banner."
His sister, Anne, became the wife of Chief Justice Roger Brooke
Taney.

Francis Scott Key married Mary Tayloe Lloyd: their son,
Philip Barton Key, met a tragic death—killed by General Daniel
E. Sickles. His brother, Samuel P. Key, fell in a duel at Bladensburg. His daughter, wife of Senator George H. Pendleton, also met
a tragic death, in falling from her carriage. He, himself, died
suddenly in Baltimore, in 1843, and now lies in Mt. Olivet Cemetery,
Frederick, under a handsome monument erected over him in 1898.
His wife rests beside him." The above quotation is from an
excellent contribution to the Ellicott City Times.

The unprotected tomb, thus described, has only recently been
guarded by the Society of Colonial Dames, which is rescuing many
more graves from desecration.

Hon. Brice John Worthington was fourth in line in distinguished
service in legislative halls, at Annapolis. He was an ardent Federalist. When Alexander Contee Hanson, General Lingan, "Light-
Horse" Harry Lee, Dr. Peregrine Warfield, Majors Ephraim and
William Gaither, and other defenders of Hanson's Press, had been
mobbed in Baltimore, Hon. Mr. Worthington rode in his carriage
to bring them to his home at "Belvoir." When Samuel Chase had
been impeached in Washington, he rode there and remained with
him during his trial.

Upon the arrival of United States Senator Henry Moore Ridgely
at Washington, he asked General Samuel Smith if "his cousin,
Brice John Worthington, still lived." The General answered, "Yes
and his heart is as big as this capitol." This big-hearted Federalist
and friend in need, though his county had been democratic, still
kept a seat in the halls of legislation, where three of his direct
ancestors had sat before him—all from the neighborhood of "Eagle
Nest Bay."

His issue were Catherine—Dr. Wm. Gautt; Elizabeth—
Edward Rutland; George Fitzhugh—Elizabeth Harwood; Nicholas
Brice—Sophia K. Muse; Hester Ann—Dr. Richard McCubbin;
Brice John—Matilda Pue; Caroline—William Holliday; Mary and
Charles F. Worthington.

"Belvoir" is now held by a Catholic society, but its history
belongs to the brightest and most palmy days of the province.

William Worthington, of Captain John, 1717,—Sarah Homewood. He was a justice in 1719. He bought, or held, a tract of
Thomas Homewood near the Magothy River in Anne Arundel County.
Wornell Worthington was the only son of William, who left descendants. He married Anna Hammond. The "William Worthington,"
recorded in "The Bowies and Their Kin," "born, 1748," was his
son. I quote from the above: "Reared by his grandfather, he
inherited a large estate upon the Magothy, opposite 'Three Sisters,'
and called his home 'Mount Ida.' "

In 1773, his land was named "Worthington's Courting."

He married Jane.Contee, daughter of Colonel Thomas Contee
and Sarah Fendall. He was polished, affable and generous; but
his property, some 1,200 acres, was sacrificed to pay his friends'
debts. He went to Nottingham. His wife inherited "Brookefield"
and its graveyard. It is now known as "The Valley," and is held
by his granddaughter, Mrs. Thomas F. Bowie, Jr. It was willed to
Walter Worthington, the eldest son.

General Thomas Contee Worthington, of William, born 1782,
died at Frederick, 1847. He was a member of the Governor's
Council, and was in Congress, in 1830. He was an officer in the
State Militia, and in the war of 1812, in which he was commissioned
Brigadier-General of 9th Brigade of Maryland Troops. He never
married.

Judge Wm. G. D. Worthington, of William,—Eliza Jordan.
He was minister to South America; trod the sunburnt pampas, and
climbed the snow clad peaks of the Andes; was sent to Greece, and
advocated its independence. He was Judge of the Court in Baltimore. Alexander Contee Worthington and his son, of Baltimore,
are descendants.

Walter Brooke Cox Worthington, youngest son,—Mrs. Priscilla
Oden, daughter of Governor Robert Bowie. His daughter Elizabeth Margaret—Thomas F. Bowie, Jr., and inherits "The Valley."
He was wealthy and kind. His son William—a daughter of General
Thomas F. Bowie, United States Congressman and political leader
in Prince George. His son, Hal. Bowie, my classmate at Dickinson College, a splendid soldier during the War of 1861, was one of
its victims.

Charles Worthington, of Captain John,—Sarah Chew. Issue,
Elizabeth, Charles and John. He removed to Baltimore County.

Sarah Worthington, of Captain John,—Nicholas Ridgely, of
Henry and Katherine Greenberry. Her descendants are in both
Maryland and Delaware.

CAPT. JOHN BRICE.

From a copy held by Nicholas Brice, of Philadelphia, made
from Judge Nicholas Brice's record, the following is taken, by
permission of Mrs. Edith Marden Ridout, of the Severn:

"Captain John Brice came from Hamershire, England. He is
recorded as gentleman, merchant, planter, member of the House

of Burgesses, Justice of the Peace, and Captain of the Severn Hundred. He married Sarah, widow of Captain John Worthington. His crest and coat of arms, a lion's head, are still extant.

"Captain Brice was guardian for the Worthington heirs and extended the estate. One son and two daughters were the issue of his marriage to Mrs. Worthington. Ann—Vachel Denton: Rachel —Philip Hammond, the Annapolis merchant. John Brice, Jr., Judge of the Provincial Court—Sarah Frisby, daughter of James and Ariana (Vanderheyden) Frisby."

Mrs. Ariana Frisby was three times married. Her last husband was Edmund Jenings, secretary of the province, by whom she had a son, Edmund Jenings, Jr. John and Sarah Frisby Brice left Ariana—Dr. David Ross; Sarah—Richard Henderson, of Bladensburg. John, the bachelor official of Annapolis; Colonel James Brice—Juliana Jenings, whose wedding gift was the magnificent colonial homestead on Prince George Street, Annapolis.

Colonel James Brice left a note book with maps of the battles of the Revolution, in which he was engaged. His daughter, Juliana Jenings Brice became the wife of Judge John Stephen, of St. Mary's County, son of Rev. Stephen of St. Mary's, whose church still stands.

Judge Stephen removed to Bladensburg. He had eight sons, only one of whom, Nicholas Carroll Stephen, had issue. Benjamin D. Stephen, John Stephen and Mrs. Juliana Jenings Dieudonne, all of Bladensburg, are his heirs. From these I have seen the Brice records.

Mr. James Frisby Brice, son of Colonel James Brice, left the following record of the families of Edmund and Thomas Jenings, the two distinguished officials of the province. He records: "Thomas Jenings, my grandfather, was born in England. The place and time of his birth are not known to us; nor do we know the christian names of his father and mother. The former died when he was quite young. He was a cousin to the Duchess of Marlborough, whose name was Sarah Jenings. He came to this country when nineteen years of age. My brother, Thomas J. Brice, found in the Executive Chamber a record of his commission as Attorney-General of the State, about the year 1773.

"He studied law in England with Mr. James Best, and at his request, named a son and daughter for Mr. and Mrs. Best, who left them legacies. Elizabeth Jenings was a celebrated beauty. She became Mrs. Hodges of Baltimore. We are related to the family of Edmund Jenings, Secretary of the Province, through his marriage to my great-grandmother, Ariana, mother of Sarah Frisby.

"Edmund Jenings and wife went to London, where she died. He returned and died in 1757. Their son, Edmund Jenings, remained in England, and wrote to his half sister, Sarah (Frisby) Brice, for information of the family."

Mr. Thomas J. Brice, brother of the above recorder, held the Brice mansion until his death, which was caused by a blow given him whilst asleep, presumably by a servant to secure a legacy.

The historic house descended to Nicholas Carroll Stephen, the attorney of Bladensburg, who sold it to Ex-Mayor Martin, its present owner. It is by all odds, the most elegant home in Annapolis.

Edmund Brice, of John and Sarah,—Harriet Woodward. Their son, James Edmund Brice was consul to St. Domingo. His mother, later, became the wife of Dr. William Murray, of West River.

Margaretta Augusta, of John and Sarah, became the wife of Major Andrew Leitch, of General Washington's staff. Their daughters were Mrs. John Addison, Mrs. Dr. Thomas Scharff, of Georgetown, whose daughter, Jane, married Rev. John Johns, rector of Christ Church.

Elizabeth, of John and Sarah,—first, Lloyd Dulaney, who fell in duel with Rev. Mr. Allen, in Hyde Park; second, Major Walter Dulaney, of the British Army. They resided at Annapolis. Their daughter Mary, married Henry Rogers; Sally Grafton Dulaney— Oliver Donaldson.

The wives of General James Lingan, who was killed in the Baltimore mob of 1812, and of Patrick Sim, were daughters of Sarah Brice and Richard Henderson, of Bladensburg.

John Brice, the third, married Mary Clare Carroll MacCubbin. Their sons were John, Nicholas, Henry and Edmund.

John, the fourth,—Sarah Lane, and had issue, Mary Clare— Christian Keener; Providence Dorsey—Darius Clagett; Eliza— I. P. Kraffth, Prussian Consul. Their daughter, Mary E., became the wife, and (now deceased.) widow of Judge Reuben M. Dorsey, of Howard County.

Judge Nicholas Brice—Anna Maria Margaret Tilghman. Their son, John Henry Brice—Sophia Howard; Charles Carroll Brice— Susan Selby. Issue, Anna Maria Brice—Jesse Marden. Their daughter, Edith, is now Mrs. Weems Ridout, of St. Margaret's Parish.

Richard Tilghman Brice, of Charles Carroll, held the historic homestead overlooking the beautiful Severn, a picture of which he kindly offered me.

JOHN BALDWIN, OF SOUTH RIVER:

This Virginia descendant of John Baldwyn, the hero of 1622, became a Quaker convert of the South River settlement. His will of 1684, named his wife, Elizabeth; daughter, Margaret, wife of Thomas Cruchley, the Annapolis attorney; his danghter Lydia, widow of Thomas Watkins and mother of Thomas Watkins, Jr.; his daughter, Ruth, wife of Captain Philip Howard; his son, John heir and executor. The testator also names his grand children, viz.: Hannah Howard, Lydia Cruchley (sister of Ruth Warfield), and Thomas Watkins, Jr.

John Baldwin, the son, married Hester, widow of Nicholas Nicholson and daughter of John Baldwin. Their sons were Thomas and John. Catherine, wife of Captain Charles Griffith, was the only daughter. From Thomas and Agnes Baldwin came Anne, wife of Judge Samuel Chase, signer of the Declaration of Independence, and Hester, wife of Judge Townley Chase.

John Baldwin, the third, removed to Cecil County. He was the progenitor of the McLane and Milligan families of Delaware; represented in Maryland by Hon. Louis McLane, once president of the Baltimore and Ohio Railroad, father of. Governor Robert McLane, ambassador to France under President Cleveland. The late Mayor Robert McLane, a nephew, by his courageous work, succeeding the disastrous fire of 1904, has helped to restore a more beautiful city.

There is a will at Annapolis, which shows that John Baldwin, the Quaker, must have had another son not named in his will, viz.: James Baldwin, the testator of 1727. He names his sons John, James, Thomas, Tyler; and daughters Susanna and Mary Baldwin. "To son James, the homestead of my father, John Baldwin, by his last will and testament." Thomas Baldwin was a witness.

The will of Robert Tyler sheds further light on this family. It reads: "My tract, 'Borough,' to go afterwards to grandson, John Baldwin; to grandson, Tyler Baldwin; to grandson, Thomas Baldwin; to grandson, James Baldwin—sons of Mary Baldwin."

The Baldwin family of Anne Arundel, suppose that their progenitor, Edward Baldwin, descended from one of the sons of James Baldwin, the testator of 1727. I am aware that he is put down in the Baldwin book as an independent member, not further traced.

Edward Baldwin settled in Anne Arundel, on a tract, "Brogdens" His wife was Miss Meeks. Issue, James, Henry, Deborah and Lydia. The oldest son, James, bore the name of the testator of 1727; this indicates a connection.

Mr. Edward Baldwin and his wife, both died young, leaving minors. These were well brought up by a Mr. Wilson, of Annapolis, Mr. Guildhall and Mr. Woodward. James inherited the homestead; Henry was seated at "Rising Sun," adjoining his brother.

Coming to manhood at the beginning of the Revolution, Henry raised a company of militia, and later served in the field. Captain Henry married, first, Sarah Hall, widow of James Rawlings. Their daughter, Sarah, became Mrs. Denton Hammond. Issue, Colonel Matthias; Elizabeth — Richard Cromwell; Camilla — Dr. Fairfax Herbert, of Howard. Their sons were the noted Confederate General James Rawlings Herbert, and his brothers John and Edward.

Captain Henry Baldwin—second, Maria Woodward, daughter of Wm. Garrett Woodward, by Dinah Warfield, his wife. Their only son was Judge William Henry Baldwin, who married Jane Maria Woodward, of Lieutenant Henry Woodward. Eliza, his sister, married Thomas Worthington. Their two children were Dr. Wm. Henry Worthington and Achsah Dorsey. Judge Wm. Henry Baldwin, of Annapolis, left sons and daughters of distinction: Maria Eleanor—Hon. Benjamin Gantt; Martha E.—Rev. N. J. B. Morgan;

Wm. Henry Baldwin, Jr., Richard, Christopher Columbus, Summerfield, Rev. Charles Winterfield, presiding elder of the Methodist Church, graduate of Yale,—first, Annie E. Hopkins; second, Annie M. Thomas.

Christopher Columbus Baldwin married Miss Roman, of Hagerstown.

The late Richard Baldwin, former Register of Wills in Anne Arundel County, lived at Waterbury, upon Howard's and Porter's Range. His wife was Sophia Furlong. Their oldest daughter, Jane, now Mrs. Cotton, has completed indexes of wills and testamentary proceedings in Anne Arundel. Her brothers and sisters are Wm. Henry, H. Furlong, Richard, Christopher Columbus, Fannie, Louisa and Washington.

Summerfield Baldwin — Fannie Cugle. Issue, William and Summerfield Baldwin. He married, second, Miss Juliet Sewell.

Rignal Baldwin, attorney-at-law, Baltimore,—Rosa Hall, of Washington, D. C. Issue, Rignal, Morgan H., Springfield, Henry Wilson and Charles Severn Baldwin. Mr. Rignal Baldwin graduated from Dickinson College, but died in his prime.

William Henry Baldwin, Jr., at fourteen years, was employed by Jones & Woodward, later William Woodward & Co., and still later, in 1844, when Mr. Baldwin became a partner, it took the name still held, Woodward, Baldwin & Co. The death of Mr. Woodward, in 1896, left Mr. Baldwin senior member. He founded the Maryland Savings Bank, and was its first president. He was of the board of Eutaw Savings Bank, Maryland Trust Co., Merchants National Bank and The American Fire Insurance Co.; president of the Mercantile Library; member of Merchants and Manufacturers Association; and, lastly, the owner of Savage Factory.

In 1859, he married Mary P. Rodman, daughter of Samuel, of Rhode Island. Their son, Frank Gambrill Baldwin, is of the same firm. Carroll Baldwin represents the New York branch. The daughters are Misses Maria Woodward and Sallie Rodman Baldwin.

Mr. Baldwin was a vestryman of Grace Church. He died October, 1902, and was interred at Baldwin's Memorial Church, near Waterbury.

James Baldwin, oldest son of Edward, through his son Edward, had granddaughters, Eilzabeth—Joseph Tate; Lydia—John Sewell.

Francis Baldwin, of James,—first, Sarah Duvall, of Ephriam, and second, Mary Sewell, of Augustine. He died at "Boyd's Chance," an inheritance from his father, James. His heirs were, Mary Pitts, Sarah, Susan, John and Thomas Pitts Baldwin.

PITTS:

Thomas Pitts, of William, settled at "Pitts' Orchard," Anne Arundel, and married Susannah Lusby. Issue, Thomas, Charles, John, Elizabeth, Susan, Henrietta, Ann and Mary Pitts. Thomas Pitts, Jr.,—Sarah Sewell, of John. Issue, Thomas and Achash.

Mary—Augustine Sewell; Elizabeth—Charles McElfresh, of Frederick County; Ann—Mordecai Stewart, of South River. Third daughter, Eleanor,—Philip McElfresh. Rev. Thomas Pitts, of Thomas,—Elizabeth Hall, of Nicholas, of New Market. Their sons were Nicholas, John Lusby, Thomas, William and Charles H. Pitts, the gifted lawyer of Baltimore. He married Miss Reynolds, and had Charles, Edward, Glen and Martha Pitts, who became Mrs. John Nicholson.

CAPTAIN JOHN NORWOOD.

After leaving the Glebe Land of Elizabeth River Church, Captain John Norwood located upon the Severn, by the side of the Dorseys and Howards. He became the first Sheriff of the new settlement of Providence.

The following records show that he was a man of influence among the Virginia settlers: "John Norwood demands six hundred acres for transporting self, wife and two children, John and Andrew, and two servants, John Hays and Elizabeth Hills, in 1650."

In 1657, another record reads: "John Norwood demands lands for transporting three other servants, Thomas Hill, 1654, and George Barrett and Elizabeth, in 1657. Ivane Barrington, John Heild, Franc Evans, Amy Severie, Mary Webb, Demetrius Cartrite, Mary Browne and Edward Pyres were transported by him in 1661. He assigned these rights to Richard Cheary. He demands land, also, for transporting John Horrington into the province in 1662, and assigned the same to Susanna Howard, for the use of her son, Charles Stephens, son of Charles Stephens, deceased."

In 1661, a commission was issued to Captain John Norwood, of the Severn, to command all the forces from the head of the river to the south side of the Patapsco.

Captain Norwood and Edward Dorsey, gentleman, took up lands together on the Severn in 1650.

The archives contain the following record of Captain John Norwood as sheriff of Providence: "Mr. John Norwood, sheriff of Providence, hath petitioned this Court, that, whereas, Wm. Evans, Thomas Trueman, Captain William Stone, Mr. Job Chandler, Edward Packer, George Thompson, Robert Clarke, Henry Williams and John Casey owe him for charges and fees due to him from said persons when they were prisoners upon the last rebellion of Captain William Stone (as the said sheriff hath deposed in Court), it is ordered, that, if said persons shall not satisfy the several sums to said John Norwood, the sheriff of those counties shall seize by distress," etc.

Andrew Norwood, of Captain John, was one of the commissioners for laying out the town of Annapolis. He married Elizabeth, daughter of Captain Cornelius Howard. Their daughter, Elizabeth, married John Beale, the attorney.

From this marriage came Ann, wife of Thomas Rutland, and Elizabeth Nicholson, wife of Richard Dorsey, of "Hockley."

COLONEL NICHOLAS GREENBERRY, KEEPER OF THE GREAT SEAL.

This name has been handed down in nearly every family of Anne Arundel.

Nicholas Greenberry, his wife Anne, their two children, Charles and Katherine, and three servants, arrived in the ship "Constant Friendship," in 1674. In 1680, he acquired, by purchase from Colonel William Fuller, son of Captain William Fuller, a tract of land called "Fuller"; later known as "White Hall." This he resurveyed as "Greenberry Forest."

Five years later, he sold a portion of this tract to Captain John Worthington; and, in 1685, bought the tract of two hundred and fifty acres known as "Towne Neck." This became later, "Greenberry Point." The history of its transfers has already been given in the early settlement of Anne Arundel. Upon this tract Colonel Greenberry died.

Colonel Greenberry was one of the commissioners, in 1683, to lay out "towns at Towne Land at Proctor's—att South River on Colonel Burgess' Land and att Herring Creek on the Towne Land."

He rose to prominence during the transfer of the proprietary government to King William and Queen Mary. In 1690, he was a staunch follower of Captain John Coode, and signed the address to King William. Took the desposition of John Hammond concerning the alleged treasonable words of Richard Hill, in reference to the Prince of Orange.

During that year, John Coode was made commander-in-chief of his majesty's forces in the province, with Major Nicholas Greenberry, and Colonel Nicholas Gassaway as two of his lieutenants. They were a prominent part of the committee of twenty, who held political sway in Anne Arundel. In 1691, Major Greenberry was one of the seventeen citizens who signed 'articles of impeachment against my Lord Baltimore. That same year he was appointed one of the Judges of the Provincial Court. As a member of the Governor's Council under Sir Lionel Copley, he attended all of its meetings with great punctuality.

In 1692, as one of the military commanders, Colonel Nicholas Greenberry was authorized to erect three forts against invading Indians; being especially in charge of the one in Anne Arundel. He was further authorized to press all smiths in cleansing and fixing the public arms. Colonel Ninian Beale, of Calvert, then in charge of all the provincial forces, was ordered to offer Colonel Nicholas Greenberry all necessary assistance in erecting the several forts.

On the death of Sir Lionel Copley, in 1693, Colonel Greenberry, as president of the Council, became Acting-Governor of the Province, until superseded by Sir Edward Andros.

Colonel Greenberry's letter to Sir Lionel Copley, captain general and governor of Maryland, strikes thus at the opposition in the province: "Sir,—I have been creditably informed lately of a great cabal in our county, held by the Grand Leaders of the Jacobite Party, viz.: Colonel Coursey, Major Sayer, Colonel Darnall, Major Dorsey, Richard Smith, Samuel Chew and John Hanson. Their rendezvous was at Darnall's, Chew's, Dorsey's and one Mareen Duval's, but the occasion of their meeting is not to be known."

Signed. NICHOLAS GREENBERRY.

Severn River, July 25th, 1692.

During that same year, he addressed a letter, signed by the members of the Council, reflecting on the loyalty of Governor Francis Nicholson. Charges of misconduct in office were also brought by him and other members of the Council, against Sir Thomas Lawrence, Thomas Bland and Colonel Jowles.

Colonel Greenberry died 1697, aged seventy years. His widow, Ann, died 1698. Both were buried at "Greenberry Point Farm," on the north side of the Severn River, opposite Annapolis.

His tombstone bears this inscription: "Here lieth interred, the body of Colonel Nicholas Greenberry, Esq., who departed this life the 17th day of December, 1697. Aetatis suae seventy."

The will of Colonel Greenberry, stamped with a remarkable seal, left his dwelling plantation to his beloved wife, Ann; after her death to son Charles; in case of his death without issue, to go to his three daughters, Catherine, Ann and Elizabeth, forever. "I give to son Charles, my plantation ' White Hall.' The remainder of my personal estate here and in the Kingdom of England, after my wife's third part thereof is deducted therefrom, to be divided by equal portions to son Charles and daughters, with this proviso: as to my daughter, Ann, in case her husband, John Hammond, be not seized in fee simple of the plantation on which he now dwells, or any other, then in that case, my portion to her shall remain in my executors' hands till the death of said John Hammond, as a reserve for her support in widowhood. If she die before her husband, then my bequest to her children. Wife Ann and son Charles executrix and executor. March 5th, 1697-8. NICH. GREENBERRY. (Seale.) "

The colonel's home tract was later held by Mr. Palmer, the recent Register of Wills of Anne Arundel County. It is now owned by Mr. Charles E. Remsen.

Colonel Greenberry's letters show him to have been a man of marked intelligence. As president of the Council, and Chancellor, he was Keeper of the Great Seal, and Judge of the High Court of Chancery.

His only son, Colonel Charles Greenberry, bore many of the busy characteristics of his father. He was the life and support of St. Margarets Church, to which he left his estate, "White Hall," after the death of his wife, Rachel Stimpson.

Colonel Charles Greenberry went before the special Court for restoring the records which had been destroyed in 1704, and entered all the transfers of his family connections, including those of his brother-in-law, Henry Ridgely. From deeds transferred to his wife, we learn that she was the daughter of Thomas Stimpson, by Rachel Clark, daughter of Richard Beard, of South River. Her history is fully recorded in the sketch of Richard Beard.

Colonel Charles Greenberry had one daughter, Ruth, who became Mrs. Williams. A silver dram cup and other memorials were given her by Mrs. Rachel Killburne.

Colonel Charles Greenberry died in 1713. His widow married, in 1715, Colonel Charles Hammond, son of Charles and Hannah (Howard) Hammond. Colonel Charles Greenberry, in his will, left his estate, "White Hall," to his wife; to descend, at her death, to the vestry of Westminster Parish, for the maintenance of a minister.

He named his sister, Katherine Ridgely's children, Henry, Nicholas, Ann and Elizabeth Ridgely; his sister, Elizabeth Goldsborough, and his sister, Anne Hammond.

His brother-in-law, John Hammond, Jr., was made an executor with his wife.

BROWNE, OF ANNE ARUNDEL.

Upon an original will, at Annapolis is the stamp of a Stork. Burke traces the LeBrune name, which is fiftieth on the Battle Abbey Roll to Sir Stephen, oldest son of Hugh, one of the Lords of Wales. His wife was Eva, sister of Griffith, Prince of Wales. His descendants were Sir John of Essex, and Thomas Browne, of London, from whom descended Thomas Browne, heir, and John Browne, second son, of London.

Their crest, says Burke, is a Stork. This John Browne, of London, is upon our records in the following letter:
To Philip Calvert,
    Hon. Sir:

These are to certify, that whereas, George Goldsmith hath promised me to procure me a parcell of land if I could get a warrant, these, therefore, are to desire that you will be pleased to grant me a warrant upon the rights hereunder written. I shall remain, your ever loving friend to command.

JOHN BROWNE.

January ye 16th, 1659.

For bringing into the province John Browne, James Browne. John Browne (and two others.) "Warrant issued to lay out 500 acres of land for John Browne upon the rights entered as above. Return the last day of August, next. Signed by the
Governour."

In 1673, "John Browne, mariner, of London," bought two tracts "Hope" and "Increase," near Round Bay. These tracts, showing the history of their purchase are to be seen in our Record Office, in the name of Richard Warfield and at his request, were so recorded among the restored records after the burning of the State House. As no transfers attended the record, the inference is clear they came into Warfield's possession through his wife, Elinor Browne, the heiress of Captain John Browne, of London. Captain Browne was closely allied to Robert Proctor, who held the Port of Annapolis, known then as "Proctor's Landing." In 1690, Captain Browne sold Proctor's interest in Abington and Freeman's Lands, to John Gaither, a brother-in-law of Proctor. Captain Browne and Peregrine Browne, his brother were earnest advocates of the Proprietary during the Revolution, which placed King William in control of Maryland in 1690–91. Their vessels were anchored in the harbor of Plymouth, when Captain John Coode, the leader of the King's adherents in Maryland, came on board with a packet of letters for his allies in Maryland.

Colonel Coursey, Captain Hynson, Mr. Lillington, Mr. Lingan and Richard Warfield, all loyal subjects of the Proprietary, were on board of these vessels, bound for the Province. Captain Coode gave his packet to Benjamin Ricand for delivery. During the passage the packet disappeared and upon an investigation, in which there were many depositions, no light was thrown on the subject, but Coode was successful in his rebellion. When Coode had caused the dismissal of Captain Richard Hill from the Council because the latter had urged the people of Anne Arundel not to send delegates to Coode's Assembly, telling them that their property came to them through the grant of the Proprietary and they had better not risk it by rushing to the support of the King, who might not be able to hold the Province. Captain John Browne wrote in defence of Captain Hill the following:

"Captain Richard Hill is a Scotchman, bold in speech, who spoke what others only dared to think. On returning to our vessels we came across him in the woods. He seemed much cast down. I trust his past usefulness in this Province will be taken into consideration and hope you will be able to restore him to his former position,
Your friend,
JNO. BROWNE and others.

The friends of the King were equally as severe on Captain James Frisby, "a brother of Captain Peregrine Browne and his brother, John Browne, refusing to admit him to his appointed seat in the Council of 1692, on the ground that all three were enemies to the King.

From their records, Captain Browne seems to have made his residence while in Maryland with Richard Warfield and with him was summoned as a witness in the Chancery case of Dorsey vs. Bland.

Captain John Browne was closely allied to Thomas Browne, an adjoining neighbor of Richard Warfield.

Thomas Browne was the son of Thomas Browne, Sr., who took up lands in 1650, adjoining Edward Lloyd. John Browne, his brother, also took up adjoining lands to Edward Lloyd, both coming up with the Virginia settlers of 1650. John Browne was in the Severn contest of 1655. They both died about 1673. In 1674, Thomas Browne, Jr., heir-at-law sold his father's plantation to his father-in-law, William Hopkins.

Thomas Browne married Katherine Harris, aunt to Katherine Howard, wife of Samuel. Their issue were, Thomas, John, Valentine and Joshua.

In 1692, Thomas Browne was appointed a "Patuxent Range" from Mr. Snowden's plantation to the limits of the Patuxent. He thus saw the many beautiful tracts along that river and surveyed about thirty. His "Brown's Chance" and Captain Dorsey's "Friendship" at Clarksville, "Brown's Forest" at Columbia, "Brown's Adventure," 1,000 acres and "Ranter's Ridge," near Woodstock are magnificent bodies of land. When Doughoregan Manor was surveyed in 1701, Thomas Browne's plantation, adjoining it was the only habitation. In 1713, he mortgaged all these tracts to Amos Garrett, the Annapolis merchant and banker, and died in 1715, before redemption, leaving his equity to his sons.

His homestead, upon which stood "the large house of Thomas Browne,'' was on the Severn. It was known as "Clink" and descended to John Browne, his executor. "Brown's Forest" went to Valentine; "Ranter's Ridge" to Joshua. Both succeeded in redeeming them.

John Brown recovered a large part of the Severn estate and in 1728, surveyed "Brown's Purchase," near Guilford.

"Clink," after the death of his wife, Rebecca (Yieldhall) Brown, descended to son John, who also inherited "Providence" adjoining "Norwood's Fancy," running with the late Richard Warfield's to Round Bay. A large amount of stock, six negroes, a man's saddle with green seat and housing, guns, pistols, sword, furniture, a nine-hogshead flat, a twelve-hogshead flat and a yawl were also given to son John.

"To my daughter Katherine, I give 'Grimes' Hill,' now a part of 'Providence,' adjoining Edward Hall. Household goods, a trooper's saddle, four negroes were given also. To my daughter, Margaret, I give 200 acres of 'Brown's Purchase,' lying on the south side of Ridgely's branch, four negroes, stock of all kinds, a woman's saddle. To my daughter, Ruth Brown, 200 acres of 'Brown's Purchase,' stock, furniture, negroes and saddle. To daughter Ann Brown, 200 acres of 'Brown's Purchase,' negroes, stock, furniture and saddle.

Signed JOHN BROWN.''

His signature dropped the final e, though his father always added it. His witnesses were Absolute Warfield, John Hall, Benjamin Yieldhall. His wife was Rebecca Yieldhall.

Margaret Brown (of John) married her cousin, a son of Valentine Brown and in her will of 1774, named her son Amos Brown to whom she gave "My part of 'Brown's Purchase,' north side of Ridgely's Branch. To son Valentine, over and above what I shall hereafter give him, six negroes and money."

Elizabeth Brown, widow of Valentine, refers in her will to "her grandson, Amos Brown."

"Brown's Purchase" adjoins the old homestead of Nicholas Greenberry Ridgely, between Savage and Guilford. Sarah Ridgely (of Nicholas Greenberry) married Nicholas Griffith, whose daughter Sarah married Amos Brown, father of Colonel Ridgely Brown, Confederate State's Army.

"John Brown (of John)" held the homestead of the Severn and in his will of 1773, recorded: "To my son John, I give the homestead and 'Brown's Purchase.' To Basil I give 'Providence.' To Benjamin and Philemon, the remaining part of 'Providence' and 'Salmon's Hills'— wife Elizabeth Brown, executrix." She was Elizabeth Yieldhall, granddaughter of Elizabeth (Sisson) Brown.

In 1774, she became the wife of Vachel Worthington, reserving by marriage contract, her own property for William Yieldhall.

Vachel Worthington became the guardian of John Brown's sons with Captain Philemon Warfield (of Alexander) their surety.

Valentine Brown (of Thomas) heir of "Brown's Forest," evidently received his name from Valentine Browne, one of the auditors of Her Majesty's Exchequer, previously a Commissioner in Ireland and Scotland for Edward VI and Mary I. His arms were granted him in 1561. The funeral entry of Sir Thomas Browne, Knight of Hospitall, records him the third son of Sir Valentine Browne, Knight of Crofts, by Thomascine, his second wife, sister of Sir Nicholas Bacon, Lord Keeper of England.

Valentine Brown (of Thomas) took possession of his estate upon "Brown's Forest," near Columbia. He left no will, but his namesake and relative, Valentine Brown of 1713, left his estate in the Province to a merchant and goldsmith, of Dublin.

Elizabeth Brown, widow of Valentine (of Thomas) named her sons Valentine and John. Her daughters were Sarah, Sidney and Elizabeth Pierpoint. She named her grandson Amos Brown and made her daughter Sidney her executrix.

Sidney Brown was a witness to the will of Mrs. Ely Dorsey, her neighbor. Her will of 1783, named her nephew, Valentine, son of Thomas, nephew William, son of brother John and niece Sidney Brown.

"Brown's Forest" descended to John (of Valentine) who left it to his wife in 1805. It adjoined Rezin Hammond on[the Patuxent in Howard County. It descended to Valentine and Joshua and still later, was sold to Nicholas Worthington (of John). William, E isha and Charles Brown received lands near Fulton, where they still have many descendants.

Joshua Brown (of Thomas) located upon the lower part of "Ranter's Ridge." The upper part was bought by John Dorsey, of Edward, and given to his son Nathan.

Here later lived Governor George Howard. Joshua Brown married a daughter of Christopher Randall and from lands of his estate surveyed "Brown's Addition." In 1757, he and Roger Randall sold "Good Fellowship" to Benjamin Browne.

In his will of 1774, Joshua Brown left "Ranter's Ridge" to his son John Browne. "To Joshua Browne, Jr., was given 'Whole Gammon' and 'Half Pone.' His daughter Hannah, became Mrs. Hipsley. She inherited her brother Joshua's estate, including 'Brown's Loss' and 'Dorsey's Gain.'"

ABELL BROWNE.

This name is not on the list of our early settlers, yet he came from Dumfries, Scotland. He was Sheriff of Anne Arundel during the exciting revolutions preceding the transfer of the Province to King William.

Finding it impossible to make collections of the levies for county expenses and not wishing to resort to harsh measures, he used his own means to meet necessary expenses. The Archives contain his petition for an extension of official tenure in order that he might recover his outlays.

The Commissioners made an arrangement with his successor for the relief of the petitioner.

Abell Browne in 1692, was one of the Associate Justices of Anne Arundel. He married first, a daughter of Samuel Phillips, of Calvert County, a sister of Mary, wife of Michael Taney, who with Abell Browne, was an executor of their brother-in-law, Ambrose Landerson, of Calvert.

Samuel Browne, son of Abell, appeared later in a petition concerning his father's claim to "Harwood," a tract upon Rhode River. In that petition, Robert Browne appears as another son of Abell Browne. He was issue, of the second wife, the heir of "Harwood," which by Abell Browne's will of 1702, was left to son Robert as also "Abell's Lot" on Bush River.

The testator further added: "Should Robert die without heirs, the above property is to go to "my nephews, Samuel and James Browne, sons of my brother James, of Bermuda." This nephew Samuel is claimed by the Browne family to be the Naval officer of 1692, commander of the Phenix from South River to London. There is no other record of Samuel Browne, first son of Abell, by his Phillips wife, but as Samuel Phillips was a commander of a vessel and left his property to his nephew Samuel Browne, the inference seems to point to the latter as the commander. One of these was on Bush River.

Accepting, however, the family record, Mr. Samuel Browne seems to have located in Baltimore County, on Bush River as early as 1689, where with Major Edward Dorsey he signed a petition to King William, in favor of restoring the Province to Lord Baltimore. From his son Samuel likely descended Benjamin Browne, of "Good Fellowship," near Woodstock, the family homestead still.

The earliest will in Baltimore County is that of Samuel Browne, of 1713. He named his sons Samuel, James and Absolom.

The above testator was evidently related closely to James Brown, the nephew of Abel, and was no doubt the other nephew.

Robert Browne, of Abell, sold "Harwood," and bought of Mr. Chapman, a tract on the Patuxent, taken up by Mr. Wright, and named "Wrighton." By his wife, Mary, daughter of Thomas Tindale, who granted her "Dinah's Beaver Dam," on Herring Creek, he had the following heirs named in his will of 1728: Abell, John, Robert, Joseph and Benjamin. This last son had a daughter, Elizabeth Browne, who married Jacob Carr. They joined, in 1772, in deeding their interest in "Wrighton" to John Browne, of Robert, who bought out the remaining heirs.

Abell Browne, the eldest son of Robert, settled in the neighborhood of Sykesville. He upset, by a case in chancery, the sale of "Harwood" by his father, and sold his interest in the same, in 1786, to Vachel Dorsey, of Vachel. His wife, Susannah Browne, joined him. Samuel Browne, of Abell, by Elizabeth, his first wife, was one of the "Minute Men" of Governor Thomas Johnson. Five of his relatives were killed in the Revolution.

The issue of Abell and Susannah Browne were Elias, Moses, Ruth, wife of Thomas Cockey, and Rebecca, wife of George Frazer Warfield. Elias Brown—Ann Cockey, and had Thomas Cockey Browne, Stephen Cockey Browne, who was a lieutenant on the Canadian frontier in the War of 1812, and died from consumption by exposure; Elias Brown, Jr., the congressman, and William Browne were the four sons.

Elias Browne, Sr., died a young man, in 1800. His brother, Moses Browne—Mary Snowden. Issue, Frank—Lucinda Edmondston, and had Moses, of Missouri.

Susanna, of Moses, was the wife of Elias Browne, the Congressman; Ellen Browne was the wife of Edward Dorsey, brother of Chief Justice Thomas Beale Dorsey. Their daughter, Comfort, married Gilchrist Porter, member of Congress from Missouri; and their daughter, Mary—James A. Broadhead, United States Senator and Minister to Switzerland. Ann Browne, of Moses, married Colonel Steele, of Kentucky. Their daughter, Florence, is now the widow of Senator Vance, of North Carolina. Mary Ann Browne, of Moses, —Westley Bennett, whose daughter, Susan Ann—Stephen Thomas, Cockey Browne, father of Ex-Governor Frank Browne. Rebecca Browne, of Moses,—Dr. Benjamin Edmondston, brother of Frank Browne's wife. Theresa Browne, of Moses,—Larkin Lawrence. All of these, viz.: Edward Dorsey, Frank Browne, Colonel Steele, Dr. Edmondston, and a number of other relatives, went west in 1831.

They formed a great caravan of wagons, with their children, negroes and cattle. Some went to Kentucky, some to Illinois, and others to Missouri, then the far West.

Thomas Cockey Browne, of Elias and Ann Cockey,—Susan Snowden, sister of Mrs. Moses Browne. Their issue were Lewis H. Browne, Stephen T. C. Browne and Prudence Patterson.

William Browne was the father of Mr. Benjamin Browne, of Washington, to whom I am indebted for information.

Mr. Chas. T. Cockey, of Pikesville, descends from Ruth Browne, of Abell, wife of Thomas Cockey.

Rebecca Browne, of Abell, became the wife of George Frazer Warfield, son of Azel and Susannah (Magruder) Warfield, half-brother of Dr. Chas. Alexander Warfield. His Frazer name came from the Scottish Clan of Frazer, descendants of McGregor.

Lord Lovat was chief of that clan when George Frazer Warfield was named. The latter became a merchant of Baltimore, and built "Groveland" at Sykesville. Their issue were Dr. George Warfield, Lewis, William, Henry, Rebecca, Susanna, Ann Elizabeth.

Rebecca—Richard Holmes, a Virginia gentleman of large wealth, who removed to Maryland, and settled near Norbeck. Their son, George Holmes, bequeathed $5,000 to Hannah Moore Academy. Ella Holmes—Jno. R. D. Thomas, of the Baltimore Bar.

Susanna Warfield was an authoress and accomplished musician. She composed the ode used in the inauguration of President William Henry Harrison. Her homestead, "Groveland", descended to her brother, Lieutenant William Henry Warfield, a graduate of West Point, a devout Christian, who devised it, after the death of his sister, to the Episcopal Church. It is now known as Warfield College.

Ann Elizabeth Warfield bcame Mrs. John Wade, residing for many years at the St. James Hotel; dying without issue in her eighty sixth year.

Dr. George Warfield removed south for his health. He married Sarah Brooke Bentley, daughter of Caleb. Their son, the late Lewis M. Warfield, of Savannah, married Phebe D. Wayne, grandniece of Judge James Wayne ,of the Supreme Court of United States, and daughter of Thomas Smyth Wayne. Issue, Louis M. Warfield, Jr., graduate of Johns Hopkins University, and Edith Wayne Warfield, of Savannah.

Other descendants of Samuel Brown, the naval officer, will be found in the history of Howard County.

COL. NICHOLAS GASSAWAY.

Nicholas Gassaway came to South River in 1650. He came with Richard Owens and his wife, Mary, who settled in the same neighborhood.Nicholas Gassaway assigned the lands due him unto Thomas Bradley, stating therein that he came in 1650.

In 1663, a tract of land called "Poplar Ridge," on the north side of South River, was laid out for him. It adjoined Captain Thomas Besson, whose daughter, Hester, as shown in Captain Besson's will, became the wife of Nicholas Gassaway. John Besson, her brother, had "lands adjoining son Nicholas Gassaway." In 1677, Mr. Gassaway took up "Charles His Purchase," on the Gunpowder, and "Gassaway's Ridge" in 1679; "Gassaway's Addition" in 1688. In 1678, he was Captain of the Provincial Militia; in 1681, was Major. The archives give his letter concerning the insolency of the Indians. In 1684, with others, he was a commissioner to establish ports of entry; was Justice in 1684. In 1687, he joined Major Edward Dorsey and Captain Edward Burgess in a letter refuting the pretended invasion of the Indians. In 1691, he was assistant Commander of the Rangers, and, at the same time, one of "The Quorum." He was also a lieutenant under Colonel John Coode.

Colonel Gassaway came into possession of "Edward's Neck," taken up by John Edwards. In transferring that tract to Mr. Anthony Ruley, he recorded, "That it came to him by inheritance." His will of 1691 reads: "First. I give to son Nicholas, my dwelling and lands in "Love's Neck," and seven negroes; to son John, three hundred acres in the Gunpowder, and after his sister Hester Groce's (Grosse) decease, the land she lives on and fifty pounds and furniture. To son Thomas, lands upon South River and nine negroes. To sons Nicholas and Thomas, seven hundred and eighty acres on Gunpowder, in two tracts, to be divided equally between them. To my danghter, Hester Groce, ten pounds sterling. I give to my daughter, Ann Watkins, two negroes; to my daughter, Jane Gassaway, £200 sterling; to my daughter, Margaret Gassaway, £200 sterling, and a negro each. (This daughter married Thomas Larkin, of John.) I give to my grandchildren, John Watkins and Elizabeth Groce, the sum of ten pounds sterling, per year, to be paid out of 'fund left me by my uncle, John Collingwood, of London, merchant, and in possession of my cousin, Samuel Beaver.' My son, Thomas, to be under the tuition of his brother and sister, John and Ann Watkins, until he come of age. My sons, Nicholas Gassaway, John Watkins and his wife, and my son, Thomas Gassaway, to be executors."

This will was proved at a Court held at Captain Nicholas Gassaway's, on the 27th of January, 1691. This act shows his importance in the province.

Captain Nicholas Gassaway, Jr., was a merchant of South River. He sold, in 1698, lot No. 28 in Londontown, to Thomas Ball, of Devon, England, merchant. His wife, Anne Gassaway, survived him, and became Mrs. Samuel Chambers, who continued the business at Londontown. At "Gresham," on South River neck, the home of Captain Nicholas Gassaway, was placed a stone which reads: "Here lyeth interred, the body of Nicholas Gassaway, son of Colonel Nicholas Gassaway, who departed this life the 10th day of March, anno dom., 1699, and in the 81st year of his age."

"Gresham" later became the property of Commodore Mayo, and is now owned by Mrs. Thomas Gaither, of Baltimore. The stone, with her permission, has been removed by Mr. Louis Dorsey Gassaway, to the grounds of St. Anne's Church, Annapolis.

John Gassaway, next son of Colonel Nicholas, in 1698, married Elizabeth Lawrence, daughter of Benjamin and Elizabeth Lawrence, the Quakers. Their son and executor was Nicholas Gassaway. Captain John Gassaway was buried in All Hallows, 1697.

His widow, Elizabeth Gassaway, married John Rigby, and was buried in the Quaker burial ground, one mile west of Galesville, on West River, in 1700. Nicholas Gassaway, the son, will be noticed in Howard.

Captain Thomas Gassaway, youngest son of Colonel Nicholas, married Susannah Hanslap, daughter of Major Henry Hanslap. His will, of 1739, names his heirs: "I give to my wife, Susannah, my plantation for life; after her decease, to son Henry: to son John, all remaining lands adjacent to him: to Thomas, 500 acres where he now lives in Baltimore County: to Nicholas, 280 acres on the Gunpowder: to daughter Elizabeth Howard, 250 acres in Baltimore County called "James' Forrest': to my grandson, John Beale Howard, one lot in Annapolis: to Gassaway Watkins, 100 acres on which he now lives. Wife and son, John, executors."

John Gassaway, executor of the estate, married Sarah Cotter. Their heirs were named in his will, and, also, in the records of "All Hallows."

From notes in possession of the Boyle family, the following references to Captain John Gassaway are given:

"Annapolis, June 17th, 1763.—Last Thursday, died at his plantation near South River, after a long and tedious indisposition, in the 55th year of his age. Captain John Gassaway, a gentleman who was for a number of years in the Commission of the Peace; three years sheriff and eight years one of the representatives for this county; in all which public trusts he gained applause. He was exemplary in his several relations of husband, parent, master, friend and neighbor, and has left behind him the character of an honest and upright man."

His daughter, Ann, married Gassaway Rawlings. Their daughter, Ann,—Samuel Maccubbin, in 1788. Eliza Gassaway Rawlings became Mrs. Sanders and Mrs. Richard Alexander Contee. Eliza Gassaway Contee—Dennis Magruder.

By Captain John Gassaway's will, of 1762, the home plantation was to be held by wife Sarah, and then by Nicholas, heir-at-law. Nicholas heired, also, the plantation of his uncle, William Cotter, on Rhode River, and two other tracts purchased of Thomas Rutland and James Cadles. To him, also, "I give my silver spurs. To my daughter, Ann Chapman, a lot of negroes. To son, Thomas a lot of negroes and my silver hilted sword. To my granddaughter, Sarah Johns, negroes and my stone studs set in gold, also a lot of stock. To my beloved wife, my silver watch." He directs his executors to sell several tracts of land, and appoints his wife and Thomas executrix and executor.

Nicholas Gassaway, heir-at-law, made no objection. Mrs. Sarah Gassaway renounced the administration and asked for her third part of the estate.

The will of Captain Thomas Gassaway, the executor of Captain John, shows a liberal guardian of the poor. "To my wife, Mary, my dwelling plantation during life. To brother Nicholas, my gold seal and silver-hilted sword, and all my lands purchased of Charles Stewart. To my cousin, Thomas, son of Henry; to cousin Henry, son of uncle Nicholas; to cousins Susannah and Elizabeth Howard; to my uncle, Henry, all the money he is owing me; to Rebecca Welsh, widow; to John Jacobs, my teacher; Elizabeth Purdy, a widow; Sarah Burgess, widow; Ann Stewart, widow, all twenty pounds," with as many more legacies to the needy. His personal estate was left to his nephews and nieces. His wife, Mary, executrix, in 1773. Through his deed, of 1768, the grounds of the Parish Church of "All Hallows," were granted to Rev. David Love, rector; Henry Hall, Richard Williams, Jr., Wm. Ijams, Richard Watkins, Lewis Lee, Richard Beard, Jr., vestrymen, and Plummer Ijams and Richard Burgess, church wardens.

Nicholas Gassaway, of Captain John of South River, in 1791, named his son, John, to whom he gave all his real estate, provided he did not marry before twenty-one years old. His daughters were likewise required to remain single until twenty-one years. To John, "I give my clock, watch, gold seal, my silver spurs, one silver strainer and one silver tankard." To his daughters, Mary and Sarah Cotter Gassaway, he also left silver memorials, and all bonds, notes and open accounts, equally. "Doctor Robert Pottenger, my relative, to be my executor."

Dr. John Gassaway, son of the above testator, in 1800, made the following will, which was probated, 1812: "Intending shortly to go to Europe, I desire to record my will. I wish to be buried in my graveyard on my place called 'Cotter's Desire to Wm. Gassaway,' in Prince George County. I wish a sermon by some respectable devine of the Protestant religion. I give all my personal and real estate, except what I give to my daughter Caroline, (daughter of Eliza Newman:) First, one-half of my real and personal estate to my sister Mary Gassaway, during life; the other half, with above exception, to my sister Sarah Cotter, while during life. I give to my daughter Caroline, the sum of fifteen pounds per annum, until fifteen, and ten pounds until twenty. Whenever she marries, I give her thirty pounds, to be paid by my two sisters, or their heirs.

Henry Gassaway, oldest son of Major Thomas and Susannah (Hanslap) Gassaway, was the founder of the Annapolis branch.

He took up "Wrighton," and sold it to Horatio Sharpe; he sold his interest in the homestead to his brother, John, Horatio Sharpe and Joseph Dick, and removed to Annapolis.

His first wife was Rebecca Chapman Gassaway. Their son, Thomas, born 1747, was the legatee of his cousin Thomas. Thomas Gassaway, of Henry, was Deputy Sheriff and Register of Wills at Annapolis prior to 1790, when his widow, Elizabeth Brice Gassaway, made a deposition concerning the Rutland estate. He was succeeded by his half-brother, General John Gassaway, an officer in charge at Annapoils during the War of 1812.

Louis C. Gassaway, of Thomas, was an attorney, and trustee in numerous transfers and estates. In 1811, John, Henry and Louis C.

Gassaway were voters in Annapolis, when electors for Senators were chosen. In 1818, John and Louis Gassaway voted for Representatives in Congress, and for two delegates to the General Assembly. The marriage register at Annapolis shows the following records: "1787, Henry Gassaway and Margaret Selman; 1788, John Gassaway and Mary Quynn; 1791, John Gassaway and Elizabeth Price; 1807, Henry Gassaway and Levinia Killman."

General John Gassaway left an only daughter, Louisa, who left her house and lot in Annapolis to "her dear friend, Miss Whittington." Louis C. Gassaway—Rebecca Hendry. Issue, Louis Gardner, Charles, John, Augustus, Thomas R., Sophia and Amelia Gassaway, Rebecca, Hester, Wm. Hendry and Mary Elizabeth.

Louis Gardner Gassaway—Ellen Brewer. Issue, Rebecca—Wm. Bryan; Hester—Nicholas B. Worthington. Issue, Ann—I. H. Hopkins; Mary Eliza and William Hendry—Emily Clayton. Augustus Gassaway—Emily Whittington. Issue, Renna—Mr.Caulk.

Louis Gardner Gassaway, Jr., only child—Marion B. Dorsey, daughter of Michael, of Howard County. They had only two children, Louis Dorsey Gassaway and Ellen Brewer, wife of Lieutenant Ronald Earle Fisher, United States Cavalry, who has only recently returned from the Philippines.

Louis Dorsey Gassaway is assistant cashier of the Farmers National Bank, of Annapolis, and recorder of the ancient South River Club. He married Miss Mary Brooke Iglehart, daughter of Wm. T. Iglehart, of Annapoils, whose mother was a descendant of the first Thomas Harwood, of South River. Through her, Mrs. Gassaway is connected with descendants of Rev. Henry Hall, the first rector of St. James Parish (1698): descended, also, from Colonel Ninian Beale, of Calvert County (1676): from Colonel Joseph Belt, of Prince George. Her mother was Katherine Spottswood Berkeley, of Virginia.

The head of the Berkeley family in England, is the Earl of Berkeley, of Berkeley Castle, Gloucestershire. One of the Maryland family was entertained there, and taken into the dungeon where Edward, the Second, was murdered, and where his bed still stands.

Mrs. Iglehart and Mrs. Gassaway are thus descended from Governor Spottswood, of 1710; from King Carter; from the first Nelson, father of the governor; from Robert Brooke, of the Virginia branch of Brookes.

WILLIAM RICHARDSON, OF WEST RIVER,
ANNE ARUNDEL COUNTY.

A friend of William Penn, he came to Virginia in the "Paul," of London, in 1634. He removed to Maryland in 1666, and became a member of the Lower House of the Assembly from 1676 to 1683. He was frequently the bearer of messages to the Upper House with instructions from Parliament.

During his service, he was upon the Committee of Security and Defense of the Province, and of the Committee upon Laws for the Province. With Henry Ridgely, Edward Darcy, Nicholas Gassaway and others, he was, in 1683, also, upon a committee to erect a building for the Courts and Assembly, and for keeping the records of the Secretary's office in this Province.

On December 19th, 1682, William Penn met Lord Baltimore at West River, and after an interview upon their divisional line, Penn set out, the Lord Baltimore accompanying him several miles, to the house of William Richardson, and from thence two miles further to a religious meeting of his friends, the Quakers, at the house of Thomas Hooper.

William Richardson married Elizabeth Talbot, widow of Richard, and daughter of Matthias Scarborough. She brought to him "Talbott's Ridge" adjoining "His Lordship's Manor," surveyed in 1662.

Among the early land grants at Annapolis, are those in the name of George Richardson, for transporting himself in 1661; and Lawrence Richardson, about the same time. The latter was upon the Severn. His will, of 1666, named his daughter, Sarah Richardson, and sons, John and Lawrence Richardson.

Sarah Richardson became the wife of Joshua Dorsey, of "Hockley," who sold his interest to his brother, Hon. John, and removed to the estate of his wife. This descended to their only son, John Dorsey, by whom it was sold, his wife, Comfort Stimpson,' assenting, to Amos Garrett.

John Richardson came from London and took up a series of grants aggregating 13,000 acres.

Thomas Richardson took up some 5,000 acres. He is believed to have been the proprietor of Thomas and Anthony Richardson, of White Haven, in 1722-41.

Wills of six William Richardsons are on record at Annapolis, running from 1698 to 1775. William Richardson held, in 1677, one thousand acres in Anne Arundel. All of this family were men of means and education, holding important positions in the province.

They had issue, William, born 1668; Daniel, 1670; Sophia Elizabeth, died young, and Joseph, born 1678, married Sarah Thomas. There were, also, two twin daughters, Sophia and Elizabeth, born 1680. William Richardson, Sr., died 1697, and his will is probated at Annapolis.

William Richardson, Jr., married Margaret Smith. Daniel Richardson married Elizabeth Welsh, daughter of Major John Welsh by his second wife, Mary, step-daughter of Nicholas Wyatt. They had issue, John, Lauranah, Daniel—all dying young. The remaining heirs were, William, Elizabeth—Wm. Harrison, and Sophia—Charles Dickinson, of Talbott County, 1725. Daniel Richardson married, second, Ruth (Ball) Leeds, widow of John Leeds, of Talbot County. Issue, Daniel and Benjamin.

William Richardson, of Daniel and Elizabeth Welsh, resided in Talbot County, and married Ann Webb, daughter of Peter Webb, of Anne Arundel County. Issue, Peter and William, who was Colonel of the Flying Camp, in the Revolution. He married Elizabeth Green: was Treasurer of the Eastern Shore, and lived to be ninety-two years old, with many great-grandchildren.

William Richardson, of William and Elizabeth Talbot, had by Margaret Smith, five sons —Joseph, Daniel, Richard, Nathan and Thomas; and two daughters—Sarah Hill and Sopha Galloway.

Sarah Hill was the mother of Henry Hill and Margaret Hill, both mentioned in the will of William Richardson. Sarah Richardson, wife of Henry Hill, was grandmother of Priscilla Dorsey, of Belmont, and of Mary Gillis. In connection with these, the will of Sarah Hill, mother-in-law of Joseph Hill, named her daughter, "Elizabeth, now wife of Thomas Sprigg, two kinswomen. Sarah Hopkins and Elizabeth Bankston, daughters of my cousin, Cassandra Giles. My sister, Margaret Richardson, my wearing apparel. To my five cousins (nephews and niece), sons of my sister, Margaret Richardson, Sarah Hill, Joseph Richardson, Daniel Richardson, Richard Richardson and Nathan Richardson, all of my plate. Sarah Hill to have my silver skillet and porringer that cover it as her part. To my cousin (niece), Sophia Galloway, daughter of my aforesaid sister Margaret, another memorial. To Richard Sprigg, son of Thomas Sprigg, my spice box. To Henry Hill, son of Dr. Richard Hill, a colored man. Son-in-law, Joseph Hill, executor."

Witnesses, Mary Gillis, John Gillis, John Davidge.

The will of Joseph Hill, in 1761, named his daughter, Mary Wilkinson, a spinster, to whom he gave "Folly Point." "To granddaughter, Henny Margaret Hill, 'Horn Neck,' 'Piney Point,' 'Yeate's Come by Chance,' 'Yeate Addition' and 'Hill's Forest,' in Baltimore County. If without heirs, to go to cousin (nephew), Henry Hill. To my sister, Mary Gillis, Priscilla Dorsey and sister Milcah, cousin, Joseph Richardson, all personal property. To cousin Nathan Richardson, two hundred acres of 'Hill's Forest,' in Baltimore County. To cousin, Joseph Richardson, three hundred acres of "Hill's Forest.' To brother Richard Hill,, personal estate. To Elizabeth Hill, land in Anne Arundel County. To brother-in-law, Joseph Richardson, £10 for the Quakers. To Sophia Galloway, personal estate. To John Ruley, 'Edward's Neck' and 'Ruley's Search.' Thomas Sprigg and Robert Pleasant, personal estate and executors of my will."

Daniel and Joseph Richardson, brothers of William, Jr., also remained in Anne Arundel County, and owned parts of "Hickory Hill," about 1707.

Joseph Richardson, Jr., bought "Moneys True Dealing," of John Edmondson, in Dorchester.

He married Dorothy Eccleston, daughter of General John Eccleston, of Dorchester County.

In 1789, Joseph Richardson married Elizabeth Noel, of Dorchester. He was Justice of the County Court, in 1775, and one of the commissioners to settle disputed boundaries of Dorchester, by Frederick Calvert.

The arms of the Richardsons are those of the Richardsons of "Rich Hill." Crest a dexter arm, erect, coupled below the elbow, holding a dagger in the hand. Motto: "Pro Deo et Rege."

JOHN MACCUBIN.

John Maccubin, of the Lowlands of Scotland, known in the Highlands as McAlpines, claiming descent from Kennith II, who, having united the Scots and Picts into one government, became the first King of Scotland, came to the Severn with the Howards, and married Susan, daughter of Samuel Howard. He took up "Timber Rock," and left by his first wife, John, Samuel and Elizabeth Maccubin, all named by Samuel Howard in 1703.

John Maccubin married again, Elinor, and died in 1686, leaving a will in which he named his wife, Elinor, executrix, and sons, Samuel, William, Zachariah and Moses inheritors of his tract, "Wardrope." His son, John, to inherit the homestead, "Bramton," after the death or marriage of his widow. She became the second wife of John Howard, without issue.

Zachariah Maccubin, her son, married Susannah Nicholson, daughter of Nicholas and Hester Larkin. The former was the son of Sir John Nicholson, of Scotland, and the latter, (said to be the first child born in Anne Arundel), was the daughter of John Larkin, from whose family, also, came the wives of Colonel Edward Dorsey, Judge Samuel Chase and Judge Townley Chase.

The issue of Zachariah and Susannah Maccubin were Nicholas and James Maccubin (with others). Nicholas—Mary Clare Carroll, only daughter of Dr. Charles Carroll and Dorothy Blake. The former was the immigrant son of Charles Carroll and Clare Dun, of the old Irish houses of Ely O'Carroll and Lord Clare. The latter was the daughter of Henry Blake and Henrietta Marie Lloyd, daughter of Colonel Philemon and Henrietta Marie Lloyd. An interesting view of these two families may be found in a chancery case of Carroll vs. Blake.

Mary Clare (Carroll) Maccubin, was the sole heiress of her father's and brother's immense estate, which included "The Plains," west of Annapolis; nearly all of the southeastern portion of Annapolis; "Mt. Clare" and "The Caves," near Baltimore. To her sons, who assumed the name of Carroll, it was willed by Charles Carroll, the Barrister, her brother. Her son, Nicholas Carroll, married Ann Jenings, daughter of Thomas Jenings, Attorney-General of Maryland.

Nicholas and Ann Jenings Carroll held their homestead upon the site of the present public school, in Annapolis. Their son, John Henry Carroll, inherited "The Caves." He married Matilda

Hollinsworth, of Horatio and Emily Ridgely, daughter of Judge Henry and Matilda (Chase) Ridgely. Their son is General John Carroll, of "The Caves."

James Carroll, son of Nicholas Maccubin and Mary Clare Carroll, has been elsewhere recorded in the families of Henry Dorsey Gough and General Charles Ridgely, of Hampton.

Mrs. Elinor Maccubin, widow of John, was, as I believe, of the family of Dr. Charles Carroll, and James Carroll, of "All Hallows" Parish; both of whom were witnesses to her will, in 1711. Her daughter, Sarah Maccubin, became the wife of William Griffith, and the mother of Orlando and Captain Charles Griffith, of Anne Arundel.

Charles Carroll, barrister, son of Dr. Charles and Dorothy (Blake) Carroll, was born 1723. He was educated at Eton and Cambridge and studying law in Middle Temple, returned to Annapolis in 1746. He was an elegant, able, fluent speaker, and a terse writer. Many State papers were the porduct of his pen. He wrote the "Declaration of Rights"; was on the Committee of Correspondence; president of the Maryland Convention; in the Council of Safety; member of the Convention which asked Governor Eden to vacate; he helped to form the government; he was elected to Congress, but declined the office of Chief Judge of the General Court of Maryland; a member of the Maryland Senate.

He married Margaret Tilghman, daughter of Matthew. They left no children.

He died at Mt. Clare, near Baltimore. His tomb is in St. Anne's grounds, at Annapolis.

His estate went to his sister's sons, the Maccubin boys, who changed their name to Carroll at the command of the barrister, to perpetuate his distinguished name.

HAMMOND.

John Hammond, author of "Leah and Rachel," was in Maryland during the Severn Contest, in 1655. From him several quotations have already been made.

The next immigrant in Anne Arundel County, was John Hammond, of the Severn. His estate joined the Howards, and he was a brother-in-law of them, having married Mary Howard, and not Mary Dorsey, as the will of Samuel Howard shows.

In 1689 he was a member of the Provincial Court of Anne Arundel, and one of "The Quorum." In 1692, he was elected a delegate to the Lower House, with Colonel Henry Ridgely and Hon. John Dorsey. Still later he was appointed by the royal administration, with whom he was in favor, Judge of the High Court of Admiralty.

A concise history of his career is recorded in the annals of St. Anne's Church, as an obituary notice. He was one of the vestry at the time of his death, and was an ardent member of the Church of England. He gave, in 1695, a deed for a church site upon "Severn

Heights" to his friends, members of Westminster Parish. The only consideration was, "the love he bore his neighbors." He acquired a large estate in both the City of Annapolis, and upon the Severn. He was a witness and executor of his brother-in-law, Captain Cornelius Howard, and was considered a leading man in the county.

It has frequently been written that his English progenitors were men of eminence in both medicine and politics.

St. Anne's records upon his death, in 1707, read: "Hon. John Hammond, Esq., Major-General of the Western Shore of Maryland, one of her majesty's most honorable Council and Judge of the High Court of Admiralty in the Province of Maryland, was buried the 29th of November, 1707."

In St. Anne's grounds his tombstone now rests. Long after all vestiges of his old homestead upon the Severn had disappeared, this memorial was found and removed to the church grounds of his devotion. St. Anne's Church has, also, a well-preserved Bible, purchased by the vestry from a legacy of £10 left by him to the church.

General Hammond's will reads: "I leave my home plantation to my wife, Mary. My eldest son, Thomas, my plantation called 'Mt. Airy Neck.' To son, John, the plantation where he lives, a part of 'Swan Neck'; to son, William, the other part. Son Charles Flushing, 'Deer Creek Point,' 'Rich Neck' and 'Hammond's Forest.' To my first three sons, my houses and lots in Annapolis. My four sons to be my executors."

General Hammond was one of the commissioners, in 1694, to lay out lots and organize the town of Annapolis. All of these commissioners saw the coming capital; each took up several lots in the town.

Thomas Hammond was a neighbor of his uncle, Captain, Cornelius Howard. He married Mary Heath, daughter of Thomas, whose will distinctly shows that her daughter, Mary Hammond, was the wife of Cornelius Howard, Jr., Helen, her other daughter, became the wife of the second John Worthington, the rich merchant. She bore him a long and distinguished line of sons and daughters.

John Hammond, Jr., was the executor of his uncle, Samuel Howard, under the title of "cousin"—clearly shown to mean "nephew. "He married Ann Greenberry, youngest daughter of Colonel Nicholas. She bore him two daughters, Comfort and Rachel, and two sons, Thomas John and Nicholas.

Colonel William Hammond left his inheritance on "Swan's Neck" and became the Baltimore merchant. His store was one of Henry Dorsey Gough's row, near Light Street, on Baltimore. He had a distillery at Elk Ridge and a forge mill at "Hockley," near the Relay. He was a member of the vestry of St. Paul's Church, Baltimore. His wife was Elizabeth Ravin. Their daughter, Mary Hammond, married Colonel John Dorsey, another Baltimore merchant, and member of St. Paul's vestry.

Colonel William Hammond died at forty, and lies buried at "Hammond's Ferry." Mordecai and William Hammond were sons. Charles Hammond, next son of General John, took up his residence near Gambrill's Station. It was evidently the same site, if not the present house, of Major Philip Hammond, now owned by Mr. George A. Kirby.

Charles Hammond married his first cousin, Hannah Howard, daughter of Philip and Ruth Baldwin. They left a long and wealthy line, viz.: Colonel Charles, the treasurer; Philip, the big merchant; Nathaniel, the planter; Rezin, bachelor; John, the big planter of Elk Ridge; and two daughters, Hamutel and Ruth Hammond. His will, of 1713, was witnessed by his neighbors, John, Richard, Alexander and Ruth Warfield, all of the neighborhood of Millersville.

Colonel Charles Hammond was State Treasurer. Having married Mrs. Rachel (Stimpson) Greenberry, widow of Colonel Charles, they resided at "White Hall."

His will, of 1772, named his daughter Mrs. Ann Govane; his granddaughter, Ann Marriott; grandsons, Thomas and James Homewood Marriott; William, Ann and Hamutel Bishop, children of his granddaughter Rebecca Bishop; grandson, Charles Homewood. All were legatees of "Meritor's Fancy," a tract that came through his wife.

"Madam Rachel Hammond, the worthy consort of Colonel Charles Hammond," records the Maryland Gazette, "died last Saturday night, February 25th, 1769."

Colonel Charles Hammond's death was, also, recorded thus: "On Sunday night, September 3rd, 1772, died Hon. Charles Hammond, Esq., president of the Council and treasurer of the Western Shore."

After the death of Mrs. Hammond, "White Hall" passed to the vestry of St. Margaret's Church. By an act secured by Governor Sharpe it was later sold to him. Among the Ridout papers are letters between Governor Sharpe and Colonel Charles Hammond, negotiating for a portion of his daughter's estate adjoining.

Philip Hammond, of Charles and Hannah Howard, inherited the Annapolis portion of his father's estate. He was a leading import merchant, having his warerooms in "Newtown," a recent addition to the Port of Annapolis. He was, also, prominent in legislative and church affairs. His wife was Rachel Brice, daughter of Captain John Brice, of Annapolis.

His will, of 1753, probated in 1760, names his heirs. "To son, Charles, all the cargo of goods in store in this country at Newtown. He is to manage the estate, not only the goods now here, but such as are to come. My brother, John, to be employed to assist him. My daughter, Ann Hammond, is to be paid £1000. All the rest of my estate to be divided among my six sons, Charles, John, Philip, Denton, Rezin and Matthias."

The last four were bachelors. Charles was known as Colonel Charles, of Curtis Creek. He does not appear to have succeeded in settling up the estate. He resigned, and at the time of his death, was recorded as "Colonel Charles Hammond, of Curtis Creek." He married Rebecca Wright and left sons, Rezin, Charles, Philip, John; and one daughter, Hannah. His estate extended from Curtis Creek to Elk Ridge. He died in 1772..

John Hammond, of Philip, the merchant, married Henrietta Dorsey, of Henry Hall Dorsey. His will, of 1784, named his son, William, to whom he left "Champion Forest," extending from the Severn to Elk Ridge, and "Hammond's Search," and "Support." "To Doctor Pue, my attending physician, my tract at Henry Dorsey's mine bank, called 'Prospect.' " Named his three daughters, Henrietta, Sarah and Mary Hammond, to whom he left a long list of tracts,which, in case of failure in heirs, were to go to Dr. Thomas Wright Hammond. "To my daughter, Elizabeth Ann Hammond, my South River Quarter composed of ' Abington' and Hereford.' "

To his son, William, he left, also, all of his interest in the uncollected claims of the late Philip Hammond. To his housekeeper, Miss Anne Walker, for her kind attention and education of his children, he gave several tracts and several negroes to wait on her.

To son, Thomas Hammond, a large list of tracts at the head of the Severn. Finally, tired of naming them, he stopped with the hope of being spared to finish his lengthy will of six or eight pages, but he died before finishing it. His amanuensis, Mr. Thomas Pitts, completed it from a schedule left for him by the testator. It provided for his daughter, Henrietta, a long list of tracts. To daughter, Sarah Hammond, another long list, and to daughter, Mary, a still longer one, including all of his lands in Annapolis.

The four bachelor sons of Philip and Rachel (Brice) Hammond, handed their estates down successively to their remaining brothers. By the side of their father and mother their tombs may yet be seen at the early homestead, near Gambrill's Station, Annapolis & Elk Ridge Railroad.

The father is recorded "a just and good man."

Denton Hammond died in 1782, leaving twenty-eight different tracts of land, many negroes, and much stock to his brothers and to the children of his late sister, Mrs. Anne Hopkins. Philip Hammond, Jr., died in 1783, leaving twenty-seven tracts to his brothers and nephews. Matthais and Colonel Rezin were the Revolutionary patriots in conventions and the Council of Safety. The former died in 1789, leaving his estate to his surviving brother, Colonel Rezin Hammond, whose English brick house stood north of Millersville.

Colonel Rezin, in 1809, left several tracts to William Hammond Marriott, and his nephew, Philip Hammond Hopkins. "To Denton Hammond, son of my nephew Philip, 2,348 acres of 'Hammond's Inheritance,' 1,877 acres of 'Hammond's Enlargement,' a part of

'Brown's Addition' and 300 acres of 'Hammond's Ridge.' To Matthias Hammond, son of my nephew Philip, 636 acres of 'Finland,' 1,680 acres of 'Hammond's Inclosure,' 1,200 acres of 'Hammond's Plains,' 773 acres of 'Piney Plains' and parts of 'Hickory Ridge' and 'Marsh's Forest.' "

After setting free a number of his most faithful servants, with land and houses for their use, Colonel Rezin gives all his remaining hosts of negroes, stock, farming utensils, crops and money to these two heirs; making them his executors.

The above "nephew Phillip" was the son of Colonel Charles, of Curtis Creek, better known as Major Philip, inheritor of the old Hammond homestead; parts of which are still as well-preserved as when built by him. Five fields of a portion of that home still bear their original names. One known as "Deer Park" fed the celebrated herd of deer which adorned Major Hammond's Park.

Major Philip Hammond married Elizabeth Wright. His ten thousand acres were divided into one thousand acre tracts among his sons. His will, of 1822, granted to his wife, Elizabeth, " 'Hammond's Connexion,' adjoining Rezin Hammond's lands; to descend to son Thomas, and, if no issue, to George Washington. Son Philip, to hold the 'Sixth Connexion'; Rezin to hold 'Warfield's Forest,' 'Owen's Range' and 'Hammond's Connexion'; John to hold 'Hammond's Green Spring'; Henry 'Snow Hill'; Matilda 'Hammond's Fifth Connexion'; Harriet, a mortgage of $10,000."

Dr. Thomas Hammond, of Major Philip, was a member of the legislature at the time of his death, in 1856. His wives were Margaret Boone and Mary Ann Wesley, and his heirs were Philip T. A., William Edger, Charles, Arthur, Silas Wright, Mary Ann and Arabella.

Philip and Arthur married sisters of Mr. Geo. A. Kirby, present owner of the Hammond Manor House.

The other sons of Major Philip were John—Harriet Dorsey; Charles — Achash Evans; Henry, died single; Denton — Sarah Baldwin; Philip—Julia Ann Hammond Rezin; —Ann Mewburn; Matthias — Eliza Brown; Elizabeth — Dr. Mewburn; Harriet — Henry Pue; Matilda—Rev. Richard Brown; Mary Ann—John W. Dorsey, father of the late Judge Reuben Dorsey, of Howard.

Denton Hammond, in 1805, married Sarah Hall Baldwin, daughter of Lieutenant Henry Baldwin by his wife, Sarah Hall Rawlings. Their daughters were Mrs. Richard Cromwell and Camilla, wife of Dr. Thomas Snowden Herbert, and mother of General James R. Herbert, C. S. A., ex-commander of the Fifth Regiment of Maryland Militia, and ex-police Commissioner.

Matthias Hammond, in 1810, married Eliza Brown. Their sons were Denton and Matthias, who inherited all, but were to pay their sister, Caroline Brown Hammond, $5,000. Rezin Hammond, brother of the testator, was executor. Philip Hammond, Sr., and Philip Hammond, Jr., were witnesses.

Matthias Hammond, of Matthias, in 1846, a resident of Anne Arundel, left all of his lands, bank accounts, to his wife, Margaret D. Hammond, son Henry and daughter Elizabeth.

NATHAN HAMMOND.

This son of Charles and Hannah Hammond started with "Hammond's Forest," and became very rich in lands and negroes.

His wife was Captain John Welsh's daughter, Ann, who bore him seven sons and six daughters. Philip, their son, married Barbara Wright, and in 1799, named his heirs Nathan, Philip, Lloyd Thomas, George, Walter Charles, Ariana Mackelfresh and Mary Ann Hammond.

Dr. Lloyd Thomas Hammond held an estate near the Pine Orchard, in Howard. His neighbor was Colonel Matthias Hammond, with one thousand acres in one body. Dr. Lloyd T. Hammond, in 1806, was one of the building committee of the Old Brick Church. He married a daughter of Thomas Beale Meriweather. Issue, Reuben T. Hammond, Judge Edward Hammond and Mrs. Dr. Wm. Magruder.

Rezin Hammond, of Nathan, left all of his lands on the Patapsco to Rezin, his son, wife and daughter, both named Rebecca. Rezin Hammond, Jr., named his sister, Rebecca Gist, and his brother Matthias Hammond, to whom he left his estate in Delaware Bottom, near Abel Browne. Matthias willed his to brother, Nathan.

Captain Thomas Hammond, of the Revolution, made the following will on the eve of his departure: "As I am ordered in a day or two, to join General Washington's army, and if it should please our Supreme Judge that I should not return, I make the following will:

"To my son, Thomas Hughes Hammond, my dwelling and lots on Howard's Hill, in Baltimore, whereon is a small wooden house. If he die without issue, it is to go to my brother Andrew. My lot of ground purchased of Henry Gough, and part of my lot on Howard's Hill to be sold."

William Hammond, of William, began his will thus: "Glory be to God on high, peace and love among men." His lands at Liberty, devised to him by his uncle, Hon. Upton Sheredine, had been sold to General Richard Coale. His sons were Larkin and William Hammond.

William Hammond, a famous attorney and writer of Annapolis, built, in 1770, one of the historic houses of Annapolis, now known as the Harwood House, on Maryland Avenue, nearly opposite the "Chase Mansion." The foundation walls are five feet thick. Its parlor has a carved wainscot surrounding it. Its mantel piece, window, door frames, shutters and doors are carved in arabesque, the handsomest specimen in Maryland.

Mr. Hammond built it for an intended bride, and had even visited Philadelphia in search of furniture, when the engagement was broken and Mr. Hammond remained a bachelor.

In 1811, the house and grounds extending from King George Street to Prince George Street, were purchased by Chief Justice Chase for his oldest daughter, Francis Townley, wife of Richard Lockerman. She designed and laid off its garden and planted its box walk. It descended to Mrs. William Harwood, granddaughter of Judge Jeremiah Townley Chase, and is still held by descendants.

DULANY.

The Dulany records of Maryland, Virginia and Kentucky, make mention of two Delany brothers and three sisters, from Cork, Ireland, landing near the town of Bellhaven, now Alexandria, about 1700. The eldest brother, William, moved to Culpepper, Virginia, and returned to Wye in Queen Annes, Md., and there died.

The Maryland record mentions William and Daniel Delany, brothers, sons of Thomas and Sarah Delany, from Queen County, Ireland, who, in 1700, changed the spelling to Dulany, after their arrival.

In support of these traditions, we find the will of Thomas Delany on record in Baltimore, dated 1738. It names Wm. Delany, to whom was left "Wright's Forest," and Daniel Delany, to whom one shilling was given. There were two more sons, Thomas and Dennis.

In the biography of Daniel Dulany, of Annapolis, we find him at the time of the above will of Thomas, quite a prominent man in the province; for he was then commissioner. Still later, by the influence of Colonel Plater, into whose family he is said to have married, Daniel Dulany rose to Attorney-General and judge of admiralty; ending as commissary general, agent and receiver, in addition to being in the Provincial Councils of Governor Bladen, Ogle and Sharpe. He was for several years the leader of the country party in the Lower House.

His second wife was Rebecca Smith, daughter of Colonel Walter Smith. In the grounds of St. Anne's, at Annapolis, his elevated tomb, erected to his wife before 1753, pays a marked tribute to her memory. He died in 1753, and his official title is added to the marble slab of the same tomb.

The issue by her was Hon. Daniel (the younger), Walter and Rebecca—Jas. Paul Heath; Rachel—first, William Knight, second, Rev. Henry Addison; Dennis, clerk of Kent County; Mary—first, Dr. Hamilton, of Annapoils, second, William Murdock; and Lloyd Dulany.

Walter Dulany succeeded him as commissary-general. He married Mary Grafton, daughter of Richard. His letters to her, and her letters to him during the critical period of the Revolution, have been preserved as interesting bits of history in the work of Miss Murray, of West River, in her biography of Rev. Walter Dulany Addison, entitled, "One Hundred Years Ago."

The family ,as a whole, belonged to the Tories of the Revolution, and as such lost their vast estate by confiscation. The sisters, Rebecca, Mary, Kitty and Peggy Dulany were later allowed four hundred acres by Congress.

These ladies have become corner stones of very important family buildings in Maryland history.

Rebecca Dulany became the wife of Thomas Addison, Jr., of "Oxon Hill." Much has been written of his coach and four, with liveried outriders; of his handsome English coach horses, and of the truly magnificent display of this planter.

The oldest son of this marriage was Rev. Walter Dulany Addison, the friend of Washington and founder of the first church in Washington City, to which flocked the aristocratic parishioners in their stylish outfits. He also built Addison Chapel.

Miss Murray has given us an interesting sight into the Dulany homestead, which then stood at the water's edge of the Naval Academy.

The letters of Miss Rebecca Dulany to her three sisters, tell of a boat excursion to "Rousby Hall"; of her dinner at Colonel Fitzhughs; of her ride in Colonel Taylor's vessel, to Colonel Platers; of the garden walks and guitar concerts; of the handsome entertainment at Mrs. Platers; of a dinner next day at Colonel Barnes, to which she went in Colonel Platers' chariot and four, where there were a great number of gentlemen whose names she would not reveal.

The son of the above writer, tells also, of his experience upon arriving at Annapolis, from his school in England. He was invited to an evening party at the Dulany homestead. Soon after dinner he took a ride in his English costume of yellow buckskin, blue coat, red cassimere vest and fine top-boots. Returning, he presented himself at the door, but was met by his grandmother (Mrs. Mary Grafton Dulany), in highly offended dignity. "What do you mean, Walter, by such an exhibition? Go immediately to your room and return in a befitting dress."

He next appeared in silk stockings, embroidered vest, etc.; and, to his amazement, was ushered into an apartment splendidly adorned, filled with elegantly dressed ladies and gentlemen. The scene equalled anything he had seen in London. This view of Annapolis was just at the close of the Revolution, when the French officers who had aided us were lions in society.

The daughters of Mr. Walter Dulany and Mary Grafton, were Rebecca Addison Hanson, Mrs. Mary Fitzhugh, Mrs. Kitty Belt, Mrs. Peggy Montgomery.

HON. DANIEL DULANY. (THE YOUNGER).

Both father and son were leading men in political affairs, but the son eclipsed the father. Yet the father decided most of the

Chancery records I have reviewed. The son was educated at Eton and Clare Hall in Cambridge. He entered the Temple and returning was admitted to the bar in 1727.

He became a member of the Council, and Secretary of the Province. His celebrated essay against the Stamp Act made him renowned, but the position he took in the debate with Charles Carroll, of Carrollton, classed him among the enemies to American Independence.

His wife was Rebecca Tasker, daughter of Hon. Benjamin and Ann (Bladen) Tasker.

Their three children were Daniel, Barrister of Lincoln's Inn, London; Colonel Benjamin Tasker Dulany, aid to General Washington. He married Eliza French, whose daughter Eliza French Dulany became the wife of Admiral French Forrest, of the Confederate Navy.

Ann Dulany (of Hon. Daniel) married M. De la Serre, whose daughter Rebecca, was married at the residence of Marquis of Wellesley, to Sir Richard Hunter, physician to the Queen.

McMahon, the historian, pays Hon. Daniel Dulany the following tribute:

"For many years before the downfall of the Proprietary Government, he stood confessedly without a rival in the Colony, as a lawyer, a scholar, and an orator, and we may safely regard the assertion, that in the high and varied accomplishments which constitute these, he has had amongst the sons of Maryland but one equal and no superior. The legal arguments of Mr. Dulany that yet remain, bear the impress of abilities too commanding, and of learning too profound to admit of question. For many years before the Revolution, he was regarded as an oracle of the law. It was the constant practice of the Courts of the Province to submit to his opinion every question of difficulty which came before them and so infallible were his opinions considered, that he who hoped to reverse them was regarded as 'hoping against hope.'

"Nor was his professional reputation limited to the colony. I have been creditably informed that he was occasionally consulted from England upon questions of magnitude, and that, in the Southern counties of Virginia, adjacent to Maryland, it was not unfrequent to withdraw questions from their Courts and even from the Chancellor of England, to submit them to his award. Thus, unrivalled in professional learning, according to the representations of his contemporaries, he added to it all the power of the orator, the accomplishments of the scholar, the graces of the person, the suavity of the gentleman.

"Mr. Pinkney, himself, the wonder of his age, who saw but the setting splendor of Mr. Dulany's talents, is reputed to have said of him, that even amongst such men as Fox, Pitt and Sheridan, he had not found his superior.

"Whatever were his errors during the Revolution, I have never heard them ascribed, either to opposition to the rights of

America, or to a servile submission to the views of the Ministry, and I have been creditably informed, that he adhered, throughout life, to the principles advanced by him in opposition to the Stamp Act. The conjecture may be hazarded that had he not been thrown into collision with the leaders of the Revolution, by the proclamation controversy and thus involved in the discussion with them, which excited high resentment on both sides, and kept him at a distance from them until the Revolution began, he would, most probably, have been found by their side, in support of the measures which led to it. Mr. Dulany was Secretary of the Province when he conducted the famous controversy with Charles Carroll, of Carrollton. He was also a member of the Upper House, under the Proprietary Government.

"He wrote under the name of "Antilon" in opposition to 'First Citizen.' Full copies of that discussion are still extant in the Maryland Gazette of our Maryland State Library. The political differences which it engendered survived the close of the Revolution. Mr. Dulany held no public office after it, and the brilliancy of his talents displayed alone in the forum of Provincial Courts, did not shed its effulgence in National Councils, and his fame, reflected from the humble pedestal of State history, has not depicted to the Nation the phenominal proportions of his intellect. Mr. Dulany died in Baltimore, March 19th, 1797, aged seventy-five years and was buried in St. Paul's Cemetery, corner of Lombard and Fremont Streets."—(Riley).

The Dulany mansion in Annapolis stood in the present Naval Academy grounds, and for a number of years was occupied by the Superintendent.

Lloyd Dulany's old homestead is now the public school building. The famous bowl which was brought over in the Peggy Stewart belonged to him. A few evenings after its arrival, Mr. Dulany gave an entertainment in which he explained how the bowl was saved when the vessel was burnt. Charles Carroll, of Carrollton, in reply to Mr. Dulany's explanation, remarked, "we will accept your explanation provided, this bowl always furnishes this same kind of tea."

Daniel Dulany (of Walter) married Mary Chew, widow of Governor Paca. Their son Lloyd was killed by Rev. Bennett Allen, former Rector of St. Anne's. Walter Dulany was a brother.

To get a definite idea of the all-prevailing influence of the Dulany name in legal quarters, study, as I have done, the Chancery records, wherein their opinions were the power behind the throne.

JUDGE SAMUEL CHASE.

Samuel Chase known in history as "The Torch of the Revolution," was born in Somerset County, in 1741. His father was the Rev. Thomas Chase of the Church of England, half of whose salary was cut off by an Act supported by his son.

Samuel Chase studied law in Annapolis. He joined the "Sons
of Liberty." When Zachariah Hood's property was destroyed in
revenge for his attempting to distribute stamps in the Colony,
Chase was an active participant. Hood's friends who were prominent and distinguished families, resented Chase's conduct, saying,
"Chase was a busy-body, restless incendiary, a ring-leader of mobs,
a foul-mouthed and inflaming son of discord and faction—a pro-
moter of the lawless excesses of the multitude." To these charges
Chase replied in a vehement address, in which he admitted his
agency, but justified his conduct. Fierce, vehement, fearless, he
bore a tinge of harshness which was redeemed by noble and generous
qualities—but the adherents of the Maryland Court looked upon
him, then, as a dangerous fanatic. He was a delegate to the
Continental Congress in 1774, and continued until 1778. He was a
signer of the Declaration of Independence. In 1783, was sent to
England to collect a bank claim; recovered $650,000 of it. In 1778,
was made Judge of the newly established Criminal Court in Baltimore. Colonel John Eager Howard induced him to remove to Baltimore and granted him a whole square, now in the centre of the city.

He was a member of the State Convention that adopted the
Federal Constitution; he thought it not democratic enough. In
1791, he became Chief Justice of the General Court of Maryland.

In 1794, on the occasion of a riot, he had arrested two of the
rioters. They refused to give bail and the Sheriff was afraid of a
rescue, if he took them to jail. "Call out a posse comitatus, then"
said the Judge—"Sir, no one will serve." 'Summon me, then 'I will
be posse comitatus. I will take them to jail." Instead of presenting
the rioters, the grand jury indicted the Judge for holding a place in
two Courts at the same time.

In 1796, President Washington appointed Judge Chase an
associate Justice of the Supreme Court.

In 1804, he was impeached for misdemeanor. He was defended
by Luther Martin, Attorney-General of Maryland, who in that
defence was thus pictured. "Rolicking, witty, audacious Attorney-
General, drunken, generous, slovenly, grand — shouting with a
school boy's fun at the idea of tearing John Randolph's indictment
to pieces and teaching Virginia Democrats some law." His address
was never exceeded in "powerful and brilliant eloquence," in the
forensic oratory of the country."

It defeated the impeachment, for the two-third majority could
not be secured.

Judge Chase's temper was better fitted for the bar than the
bench, yet his courage and ardor were needed where he held sway.

Judge Chase married first, Ann Baldwin, by whom he had two
sons and two daughters. His second wife was Hannah Kitty Giles,
of Kentbury, England. He died June 19th, 1811.

JUDGE JEREMIAH TOWNLEY CHASE.

Judge Jeremiah Townley Chase, was born in Baltimore, in 1748, and removed to Annapolis in 1779. He was Mayor of Annapolis in 1783, and there delivered an address of welcome to General Washington upon his resignation of this commission. Judge Chase also welcomed LaFayette to Annapolis, in 1825. He was upon the Committee of Safety for Baltimore and was a private in the first military company.

In 1775, he was elected a member of the convention from Baltimore County to frame a Constitution and was a member of the body which framed the declaration for Maryland. He served in Governor Thomas Johnson's council; was a member of Congress in 1783; in 1789, was Chief Judge of the Third District and Chief Judge of the Court of Appeals, from which he resigned in 1824. He was firm, dignified, impartial, kind, temperate, and a sincere Christian. He married Hester Baldwin, name-sake and descendant of Hester Larkin, daughter of John Larkin, of South River. As the widow of Nicholas Nicholson she married John Baldwin, Jr. She died in 1749, aged one hundred years and is supposed to be one of the first persons born in Anne Arundel County.

She left a long line of distinguished descendents, one of whom, Hester Ann Chase Ridout, daughter of Thomas Chase (of Judge Townley) presented the Chase mansion to the Episcopal Church. Judge Chase died in 1828, and was buried in the City Cemetery.

THE REVOLUTION OF 1688.

There were several contributing causes in Maryland which helped to swell the Revolution of 1688 in England. The Proprietary rule of the Province had suffered greatly from the fact that during its whole existence, with the exception of the few years between 1675 and 1684, and the one short period of 1732, all the proprietors and their secretaries resided in England. The Province was held by representatives not always faithful, not even always discreet, but always in conflict through their varying responsibilities. They were the Governor, Secretary, Commissary-General, two Judges of the Land Office, and an Attorney-General, aided by many more minor appointees.

Cecilius, son of the first Lord Baltimore, was a trained administrator, discreet, politic, able, deeply interested in the project for which, it is estimated, he must have spent some £40,000 sterling with but little received in return. His representative Governor, Leonard Calvert, was likewise an able and well-disposed administrator, but Charles Calvert, son of Cecilius, a busy man of strong personality, succeeding in 1675, was not the able diplomat that his father had been. Succeeding his uncle, Philip, as Governor, there was at once jealousy and dissension.

It is true he suppressed the Fendall rebellion, but he was not able to suppress the men engaged in it.

Lacking the gentleness, sympathy and persuasive appeal of his father, he was charged with being cold, stern and self-interested.

He married the widow of his secretary, Henry Sewall, and gave her children and other members of his family some of the most important offices in the Province. He restricted the suffrage and endeavored to keep the leaders of the opposition out of the House of Delegates by not summoning them, when elected. When the house was obstinate he did not hesitate to use personal influence to secure reluctant assent.

Only a few years subsequent to a fall of more than fifty per cent. in the price of tobacco, the rent of all lands after 1670, was doubled, and further, while a large per cent. of the people were Protestants, the government was under the control of Catholics. Added to this, he left the province in 1684 to his minor son and a board of deputy governors, at the head of which was his cousin, the notorious George Talbott, to be followed later by William Joseph, a quaint fanatic, to succeed him, whose ideas of "divine right" were not well received, but in reality brought on a rebellion in the lower House of the Assembly (Mereness). A crisis was now at hand, not only in the province, but in the mother country—it ended in the revolution of 1688, which drove King James from the throne and placed William and Mary in control

Enemies of the Proprietary now began a contest for control under the false cry that Catholics were plotting with Indians to murder Protestants. Col. Henry Darnall, Colonel Pye and Mr. Boarman were charged with conspiring with the Seneca Indians for that purpose, and it was only by the prompt action of Colonel Darnall in hurrying from place to place, convincing the people of the falsity of the rumor, that an uprising was quelled in its early stage. Certain Protestants, viz.: Henry Hawkins, Captain Edward Burgess, Colonel Nicholas Gassaway, Captain Richard Hill and Major Edward Dorsey, addressed a letter to Colonel Digges, of Lord Baltimore's council, to know if there was any truth in the rumor. Colonel Digges replied by a total denial of the charge, assuring the writers that Colonel Jowles, Colonel Darnall and Major Ninian Beale would scour the woods to see if any Indians could be found. His reply satisfied the writers who then joined in letters to the people and to the Council announcing their belief in the falsity of the charges, and they were rewarded by military appointments, viz.: Mr. Edward Dorsey, Major of Horse; Mr. Nicholas Gassaway, Major of the Foote; Mr. Nicholas Greenberry, Captain of the Foote, in the room of Captain Richard Hill; Mr. Edward Burgess, Captain of the Foote; Mr. Henry Hanslap, Captain of the Foote; Mr. Henry Ridgely, Captain of the Foote. Captain John Coode was the leading spirit in this revolutionary movement against the lord proprietary. He had been suppressed by Charles Calvert during an earlier attempt at rebellion, but his spirit was still undaunted. He and Captain Josias Fendall had been tried for revolt. Coode had married a daughter of Thomas Gerrard, who had been a Councillor under Fendall. He was first a Catholic and then a Protestant, and although once a clergyman, he was considered vain, unprincipled, caring nothing for Protestantism, but using it only as a pretext in his revenge against the lord proprietor. With such a man as leader, was organized, in 1689, a Protestant Association to put William and Mary in control of the province. The records were seized by Colonel Coode, head of the militia. The officers of the Proprietor could only collect a force of eighty men, who surrendered without a shot.

This association met with but little approval by the Protestants of Anne Arundel County, who even refused to send delegates to a convention at St. Mary's. Captain Richard Hill, of Anne Arundel, urged the inhabitants to think well before renouncing the proprietors who had given them their property, to rush to a government which might not be able to hold it. For that effort he was denounced by Captain Coode and driven from power. In his defence, Captain John Browne, of Anne Arundel, wrote: "Captain Hill is a Scotchman, bold in speech, who spoke what others only dared to think." But the Association was successful; Coode was put in command of the King's forces, assisted by Colonel Nicholas Greenberry. The new monarchs were proclaimed, an assembly was called and all the offices filled with Protestants. Each of the counties, except Anne Arundel, sent an address to the King in support of the movement, beseeching him to take the government into his own hands, but counter addresses, denouncing Coode and his followers, were also sent. The signatures to the former, however, numbered twice as many as the latter.

Charges, strong and forceful, were brought against the government of the Proprietor. The King approved the measures of the Association, but the opinion of Lord Chief Justice Holt in 1690 was, "I think the King may constitute a governor whose authority will be legal, though he must be responsible to the Lord Baltimore for the profits."

The royal government, however, was established in 1692 and continued for nearly a quarter of a century in control of the province.

Sir Lionel Copley was appointed Governor. He summoned a General Assembly which met May 10, 1692, O. S., at St. Mary's. The first act was to acknowledge William and Mary, and the next to establish the Episcopal Church as the State church of Maryland. Every county was divided into parishes and taxes were levied upon the people, without distinction, for the support of the ministers, the repair of the old and the building of new churches. In 1704 an act was passed "to prevent the growth of popery," by which it was made a penal offence for a priest of the Catholic Church to say mass or to perform any of their sacred functions, or for any Catholic to teach a school. This was subsequently modified in allowing Catholic priests their functions in private houses. This led to the custom of building chapels connected with the dwellings of Catholic families; nor were Catholics alone so deprived. All dissenters were alike treated, even the gentle Quakers. In 1702 the English toleration act for "Dissenters" was extended to Maryland, and in 1706 relief was granted to the "Quakers" or "Friends."

The Assembly next attempted to deprive the Proprietary of his rights in the province. He was still entitled to all of the unsettled lands, with the right of making grants for them, to the quit rents and certain duties, not connected with the government, viz.: port duties of two shillings per hundred on all tobacco exported from the colony. The Assembly disputed his claim, but Lord Baltimore having appealed to the King, the latter, by royal letter, authorized him to collect his revenues in the province. The Assembly finally yielded up to the Proprietary his port and tonnage duties and entered into a compromise in issuing land patents. The Assembly now turned its attention to the location of the State Capital.

St. Mary's was the home of the Catholic element of the province and it was now too remote for a convenient meeting place. Both of these reasons were made effective. All prayers for retaining the government upon its historic ground were laughed at and rejected. The capital was removed to "the town land at Proctors," which was henceforth to be called Annapolis, and so, in a few years, old St. Mary's, "in the very State to which it gave birth, in the land which it redeemed from the wilderness, now stands a solitary spot dedicated to God and a fit memento of perishable man" (McMahon). Its successor, rising upon its ruins, grew into an attractive centre of wealth. A portion of St. Mary's population followed the government to the new capitol. The very first record of this new seat shows that progress had been made for a coming city.

There is one venerable building on State House Hill which must have been built as the Court House for the Port of Entry in 1683. It is the time-honored Treasury building. When it was repaired during the administration of Treasurer Spencer Jones, a special search was made to get its date of erection, but nothing could then be found. The present efficient Chief Clerk of the Land Office, Mr. George Schaeffer, had a picture of it from a New York journal showing the members of the Assembly in continental dress standing about it under the shade trees surrounding it. Mr. David Ridgely, in his excellent "Annals of Annapolis," published in 1841, tells us that the Lower House met in the larger room and the Upper House in the smaller one, but when that meeting took place was left to conjecture.

The first Assembly, by the records, met in Major Dorsey's house, which a living historian, Mr. Elihu S. Riley, thinks was probably the house No. 83 Prince George Street, now Mrs. Marchand's.

The first State House was built in 1697, when the Assembly met there until its destruction by fire in 1704, after which Major Dorsey's house was again occupied until the completion of the second State House in 1706. We have a record of the Armory which stood north of it; of King William's School, which stood south of it, but no mention of the Treasury building. Even when the third State House was projected in 1772 and its corner stone was laid by Governor Eden, the clap of thunder from a clear sky was noted, but still no mention of this quaint little building, which must have then taken the place of the second State House for a season until the completion of the third.

Judging from the want of record after 1694, the inference is clear that our historic little Treasury building was built after the organization of Anne Arundel Town as a port of entry in 1683, and at the time of Governor Nicholson, was the house in which he called his Council together for the organization of the capital

GOVERNOR NICHOLSON.

In 1694 Governor Nicholson met in Council at the Court House in Anne Arundel Town and issued an order for the removal of the records from the city of St. Mary's to Anne Arundel Town, to be conveyed in good, strong bags, to be secured with cordage and hides, and well packed, with guards to attend them night and day, and to be delivered to the Sheriff of Anne Arundel County, at Anne Arundel Town. This removal took place in the winter of 1694-5.

The first Assembly was held in a house of Major Edward Dorsey on 28th February 1694, O. S., and in 1695, the town became Annapolis, with a resident naval officer and a public ferry across the Severn.

A contract was made with Casper Herman, a burgess from Cecil, for building the parish church, school house and State house, all from brick made near Annapolis.

The foundation of the first State House was laid April 30, 1696. In June, 1697, the building was so well advanced as to be set apart for public use. The officers in charge were Governor Nicholson, Hon. Sir Thomas Lawrence, Baronet, Secretary; Hon. Henry Jowles, Chancellor; Hon. Kenelm Cheseldyne, Commissary-General. Struck by lightning in 1699 and entirely consumed by fire in 1704, the first State House had but a brief existence. This gave Governor Seymour occasion to say, "I never saw any public building left solely to Providence but in Maryland."

Major Dorsey's house was again rented for the Assembly Hall until a new State House could be built.

Governor Nicholson was a man of integrity, liberal in views, firm in purpose.

When John Coode, the apostate clergyman, had been elected a burgess, Governor Nicholson was determined that he should not sit, because no clergyman had ever sat in the Assembly. The House stood on its privileges, but Nicholson would not swear him, and having won the cause, Coode retired to swear vengeance on the Governor. In the face of it the burgesses thus addressed the Governor, "We have not the least doubt of our rights or liberties being infringed by our gracious Sovereign or our noble and worthy Governor, and we do sincerely acknowledge that his Excellency governs by the fairest measures and freest administration of the laws we are capable of understanding, and therefore, have not the least apprehension of his invading our rights or privileges."

A Commission, consisting of Major John Hammond, Major Edward Dorsey, Mr. John Bennett, Hon. John Dorsey, Mr. Andrew Norwood, Captain Philip Howard, Mr. James Saunders and Colonel Nicholas Greenberry laid out the town. Four of these were property holders on the North Severn side and four were residents of Middle Neck. They were authorized to buy, or condemn, all that parcel of land within the present Grave Yard Creek and Spa Creek, to be fenced in and called the Town Common, or Pasture; Governor Nicholson's lot was within this enclosure, which ran along East Street to State House Circle. His house was of curious and ancient design. It stood on the corner of Hyde and Cornhill Streets and was for many years occupied by Mrs. Richard Ridgely (Riley).

During Governor Nicholson's administration in 1695, a public post, extending from the Potomac, through Annapolis to Philadelphia was organized. The post-man was required to traverse it eight times a year, to carry all public messages, to deliver letters and packages, for which service he received £50 a year. This was succeeded, in 1710, by a general post throughout the colonies.

A picture is extant of a house, No. 83 Prince George Street, Annapolis, which tradition decides is a part of the house owned by Major Edward Dorsey, which became the first Governor's mansion, being later occupied by Governor Nicholson. The house is well preserved and is of solid architecture. It was formerly the residence of Judge A. B. Hagner and is now owned by Mrs. Francis T. Marchand. An addition was made some years ago on the right wing.

Annapolis lately retained three more Governor's mansions.

In 1696 the Assembly of Annapolis appointed His Excellency, Sir Francis Nicholson, Sir Thomas Lawrence, Hon. Nicholas Greenberry, Hon. Thomas Tench, Major Hammond, Major Edward Dorsey, Mr. James Saunders and Captain Richard Hill a Commission "for keeping good rules and orders," making them a body corporate for the new capital. Mr. Richard Beard, surveyor, made a map of the place. This body was authorized to erect a market house and hold a fair yearly; a new State House was ordered to be built, and if any one would build it a "Bridewell" was proposed. This was not built, but a handsome pair of gates was ordered to be placed at the "coming in of the town" and two triangular houses built for rangers.

"To have the way from the gate to go directly to the top of the hill without the towne, to be ditched on each side and set with 'quick setts,' or some such thing.

"That part of the land which lye on ye creeke by Major Dorsey's house, whereby His Excellency at present lives, be sett aside for public buildings, and if in case the same happen to come within any of ye said Major's lotts—we propose that land be given him elsewhere for it."

A forty-foot water front for warehouses was reserved, and a committee was appointed to consider the erection of a church. Major Edward Dorsey, of that committee, reported a fund already in "banck" amounting to £458. The carpenter's estimate was £250; brick maker, £90; bricklayer, having all stuff upon the place, £220. The entire charge would amount to £1,200. The Assembly imposed a three-pence tax on tobacco to be continued until May 12, 1698, to be applied to building a church at Annapolis. The Assembly employed Mr. Gaddes, sent by the Bishop of London, to read prayers in some vacant parish, for which 10,000 pounds of tobacco were appropriated in remuneration. The next act was the founding of "King William School." The valuable library presented by the King was increased by Governor Nicholson, who used a portion of the public revenue in the purchase of necessary books. Many of the volumes presented by the King to Annapolis are now in the library of St. John's College.

Following these was the erection of a jail on the corner of a lot belonging to the Episcopal parsonage. When completed, Annapolis was made the chief seat of justice, where all writs were made returnable.

In 1700 a general visitation of the provincial clergy was held on May 23rd. Anne Arundel was represented by Rev. Henry Hall, of St. James Parish; Rev. Joseph Colback, of All Hallows, and Rev. Edward Topp, of St. Anne's.

This convocation inaugurated the first missions of the province. Rev. Ethan Allen's History of St. Anne's Parish has given considerable light upon early Annapolis, but the loss of the first twelve pages of the parish records leaves the completion of the church to conjecture. Referring to the early Puritans at Annapolis, he adds, "It is not known that there were any other than Puritans among the residents in 1657. There were the Lloyds, the Maccubins, the Ridgelys, the Griffiths, the Greenberrys, the Worthingtons and others, nearly all of Welsh descent. Their place of worship was "Town Neck." In 1683, he further adds, "And that there was, thus early, Church of England families in the neighborhood, is unquestionable. Such we take to have been the Warfields, the Gassaways, the Norwoods, the Blands, the Howards, the Dorseys, and the Hammonds."

The Assembly Act of 1692, organizing thirty parishes in the Province, required returns from existing churches. In 1696 Rev. Mr. Coney, rector of St. Anne's, reported 374 contributors and named the following vestry: Thomas Bland, Richard Warfield, Laurence Draper, Jacob Harness, William Brown and Cornelius Howard. In 1704, its second vestry, reported by Rev. Mr. Topp, its second rector, and by Rev. James Wootten, its third, were Colonel John Hammond, Mr. William Bladen, Mr. William Taylord, Mr. Amos Garrett, Mr. John Truman and Mr. Samuel Norwood. The entries upon the parish records of that date show the church then finished. The site, the most attractive and interesting in the city of Annapolis, was selected by Governor Nicholson and was bought of Benjamin and Henry Welsh, for £130. The church was built in the shape of a T. The principal entrance was from the east. One lot of the selected ground was designed for the rector, one for the sexton and the third for the vestry clerk.   Within, and outside of the present circle was the cemetery, now removed to Cemetery Creek.   A few remaining memorials may yet be read in the sacred enclosure.

The second State House was finished in 1706.   It stood upon the site of the present stately building.   It was in form an oblong square, entered by a hall; a cupola surmounted it.   On the north side of it stood an armory which was also the ballroom.   On the south side of the State House was King William School.

To restore the land records destroyed by the fire of 1704, a special commission was organized to hear and determine claims for land grants.   Colonel William Holland was Chief Commissioner. The report of that Commission now forms a part of the land records of Annapolis.

GOVERNOR BLACKISTON.

Governor Blackiston, who succeeded Governor Nicholson, on account of his health, did not long remain, and Hon, Thomas Tench, President of the Council, acted as Governor until 1703, when Governor John Seymour was appointed.

GOVERNOR SEYMOUR.

Finding the Assembly averse to granting a charter to the embryo city, the Governor, in 1708, granted one in his own name.   This act created much resentment among the landed officials.   They were ready to admit such power was given by the charter to the Proprietary, but in no manner could a royal Governor claim it.   The two delegates elected under the charter were expelled from the Assembly. The Governor tried to conciliate the opponents, but failing, finally dissolved them.   The new Assembly was of the same sentiment.   Its first act was to demand the Governor's authority from the Queen to erect a city.   A compromise was finally effected, with certain restrictions.   A writer from Maryland, who saw the young capital then, recorded: "There are several places for towns, but hitherto they are only titular ones, except Annapolis, where the Governor resides. Colonel Nicholson has done his endeavors to make a town of that place.   There are about forty dwelling houses in it, seven or eight of which can afford good lodging and accommodations for strangers. There are also a State House and a free school built of brick, which make a great show among a parcel of wooden houses; and a foundation of a church is laid, the only brick church in Maryland.   They have two market-days in a week, and had Governor Nicholson continued there a few months longer, he had brought it to perfection."

But Annapolis on Proctor's Landing was no recent production of Governor Nicholson.   As early as 1681, Robert Proctor, writing to Captain Thomas Francis, of Rhode River, asked a reply to be made to him at "town."   Major Edward Dorsey was then living at Proctor's Landing and had more than one house in that town when the Assembly rented his house.   In 1705, just before his death, he sold to Charles Carroll "a row of houses on Bloombury Square" which he had designed for his children, but on account of a lack of "tenants they were going to decay." These are evidences that Annapolis, when incorporated the capital, had a claim to its present name of "ancient city." Nor was Annapolis the only town then existing. It had its neighbor, Westminster Towne, near the Magothy, as will be seen in a notice of Westminster Parish, which was named for the town and had its rival down on South River, known as London Town.

In visiting the site of this once prosperous enterprise on the beautiful South River, I asked an officer of the steamer that has for many years made almost daily trips up and down that river, if he could point out London Town. The astonished officer replied, "I never heard of it," and yet, in 1683, this town was made a port of entry.

Upon a sloping plateau between two creeks, just at the present Almshouse, rose a town which was intended to rival its namesake. It only failed because of the death of its projector, Colonel William Burgess, in 1686.. It was his gift to the county, and his son, Captain Edward Burgess, was a Commissioner. When the Lord Proprietary determined, in 1683, "to locate the Court House on South River as soon as a suitable building should be erected," Colonel Burgess secured a Commission, all of whom were large land-holders in that section. A meeting of that Commission was held at "The Ridge" (John Larkin's house where the Assembly met), just west of South River. After that meeting, which reported progress, the Archives are silent, but the following deed shows that a Court House was erected and John Larkin then held it. In 1699 John Larkin sold to John Baldwin "two lots in London Town with all houses, outhouses and other improvements, excepting the twenty-five-foot house wherein the court was formerly held, as also as much ground besides, between the said house and the water, as shall be sufficient to erect and build a twenty-foot house upon."

When the magnificent, stately old building, now used as the Almshouse was built, may never be known, but its appearance and its large rooms point rather to public, than private purposes. It is upon the town site of London Town, described in Colonel Burgess' will of 1686. An official of Anne Arundel, now seventy-five years of age, tells me it was an old building when he was a boy. Near it stood a store. There are several houses upon the same plateau which show kindred age. The probabilities are, that our present Treasury Building in Annapolis and the present Almshouse of South River were both built as Court Houses when Proctor's Landing and "Colonel Burgess' land on South River" were made into ports of entry, in 1683.

London Town had its shipping wharf and its streets named in honor of the most important land-holders. Its commission, all of whom held lots, were Colonel Thomas Taylor, Colonel William Burgess, Major John Welsh, Thomas Francis, Richard Hill, Nicholas Gassaway, Henry Constable, Edward Dorsey, John Sollers, Henry Ridgely, Richard Beard and Edward Burgess.

Thomas Gassaway in 1718, sold Lot No. 28 in London Town to Thomas Ball, a merchant of London. It adjoined a lot granted to

Colonel Thomas Taylor. Honorable George Plater and Elizabeth, his wife, deeded Lot 29 to Thomas Gassaway, son of John, in 1749; John Burgess and Jane, his wife, sold a lot to Stephen West before 1733. Alexander Warfield and Francis Pierpoint, his brother-in-law, sold a lot to William Maccubbin, in 1719, which lot had been taken up by Francis Pierpoint, the elder.

Colonel Henry Ridgely held lots in London Town, which he sold before his death, in 1710. Many other transfers of lots may be seen in our Record Office.

London Town was a port of entry at the same time as Annapolis. Surrounding it was the richest agricultural section of the country. The largest land-holders were there located. Near by was All Hallows Church and the South River Club, both still in existence and both bearing abundant evidence of their dignified age and eminent respectability.

South River had a rector, Rev. Duell Pead, who baptized at Proctor in 1682 and preached to the assembly at the Ridge, in 1683, as recorded in "Old Brick Churches." He later became the rector of All Hallows. This church dates from 1722. Its church-yard has the following monuments to the titled men who dwelt therein.

A tablet with his coat of arms announces the death of Samuel Peale, of London Town, in 1733. A Latin inscription in 1766, records the virtues of Margaret, wife of James Dick, merchant of London Town. The oldest inscription is that of Major Thomas Francis, of Rhode River, a pioneer ranger of that section. Colonel Burgess' memorial tablet follows and will be elsewhere found. Dating back to 1733, the Anne Arundel Society have found inscriptions to the following: Greenberry, Gassaway, Ridgely, Worthington, Newman, Homewood, Howard, Peele of Weshire, Dick, Allein, Craggs, Norwood, Rawlings, Norris, Davidson, Maccubbin, Hammond, Graham, Curten, Key, Robinson, Robosson, Brewer and Carroll.

Family records so collected are Sellman, Stockett, Harwood, Griffith, Worthington, Davis, Riggs, Frisby, Dorsey, Warfield, Humphrey.

All Hallows Church is entered by the south door and opens into a vestry room at the west end which was once surmounted by a belfry with a bell bearing date 1727. The floor of the aisle is tiled and lies lower than that of the pews. The windows are double with segmental arch.

In 1727, the Bishop of London sent for the rector, Rev. Joseph Colbatch to come to England for consecration. The civil authorities procured a writ of *ne excat*, which prevented his leaving the Province and Maryland had no bishop until the consecration of Bishop Claggett.

St. James Parish, at Herring Creek, had a church that needed repairs, in 1695, as shown by the following record:

"At a meeting of the vestry, April 1, 1695, it was ordered that the Sheriff pay to Morgan Jones eight hundred pounds of tobacco for covering the old church and finishing the inside according to agreement." At another meeting the same month, an order was made to build a new church "forty feet by twenty-four and twelve feet high." This was not carried out until 1717, when the vestry ordered and paid for, in 1718, twenty thousand brick made on the glebe—acquired, in 1707, from James and Elizabeth Rigby.

The vestry of St. James had a long contest over a tract of land containing 715 acres. It was willed by Nicholas Terret to St. James Church. Upon it was a town Pig Point. It was known as Wrighton and had been transferred by several deeds to Robert Browne, of Abel and was later held by his heirs. The vestry resolved to sell its interest in the tract to purchase a glebe elsewhere. Pig Point lots were to be reserved. This new town was located on the Patuxent. Our modern maps have, somehow, lost sight of it, but the present post-office of Bristol is near or upon the original site.

THE SOUTH RIVER CLUB HOUSE.

The South River Club House, near All Hallows Church, still stands and has taken on new life. Its founders are no longer known, but there is a record of a deed, dated 1740, executed between John Gassaway, on the one part and Robert Saunders, a trustee on the other, confirming a previous transaction between the "Society" or company, called the South River Club and John Gassaway's father, acknowledging the receipt by the latter of eight pounds current money for the half acre of land and club house standing on it. A new club house was built in 1742 and from that date a list of members has been preserved. The following recent account of a fourth of July dinner will here be of interest. It is taken from the Baltimore Sun, and is the work of Mr. L. Dorsey Gassaway, Recorder of the Club:

"At the historic old South River Club, in the beautiful First District of Anne Arundel County, where the hillsides show Nature's beauty and giant oaks thrust their green tops high in the sky, there was served yesterday as delightful a Fourth-of-July dinner to as congenial a company as ever sat down together."

The club house, where the dinner was given, is a little, old frame building, white-washed within and without. No carpet adorned the floor and the walls were not ornamented with paper; yet there it has stood for, not years but, centuries. Long before the War of the Revolution, before even the city of Baltimore was in its infancy; in the days when there was a desperate hazard in being a Marylander, the ancestors of the diners of yesterday gathered at this little building and founded the South River Club. Records show that it was in existence with a long list of members in 1742, and there is a tradition, that its organization occurred prior to 1700. Through all the years that followed it flourished, with occasional breaks, due to wars and factional strife, but the early settlers of Southern Maryland continued to meet and be good fellows. The same *esprit de corps* that existed then exists now, and every present member of the club is

firmly convinced that it is the oldest social organization in the world,
and certainly antedates anything of the kind in this country.

That it shall never die and the spirit that has maintained it so
long never lessen is their determination. When they themselves are
gone the keeping alive of the South River Club will be transmitted
as a sacred heritage to their sons and grandsons. .

The present membership is limited to twenty-five, all of whom
are lineal descendants of former members, and four times a year they
meet at the little frame house to dine, to renew old friendships and
talk over old days. Generation after generation has done this since
the founding of the club, and it is the purpose of the members to have
future generations follow in their footsteps.

Yesterday the host was Mr. T. Stockett Sellman, the youngest
member of the club, who, however, was preceded by a numerous
array of ancestors. Some of the twenty-five came to Annapolis the
night before the Fourth, others came down on morning trains and
others still came from various sections of the country, but the hour
of noon found them assembled beneath the great branches of the
magnificent oak that stands near the house.

Horses were unharnessed and fed and the guests were refreshed
with brimming glasses of the far-famed South River punch. There
were in the crowd that gathered about the table inside the humble
little cabin, merchants, bankers, brokers, members of the Stock
Exchange, lawyers and farmers, many of them men of means and
mark, but all imbued with an intense pride in the South River Club.

The dinner was delightfully served, the *piece de resistance* being
a fine young, well-roasted pig, which was skillfully carved by Mr.
Harry Brogden, a member who dates his election from 1872.

Judge Alexander Hagner, chairman of the club, presided over
the feast, and a feature of the dinner was the presentation to the club
of a handsome silver loving cup. It was filled with the famous punch
and passed around the board, the members standing as they drank.

Mr. John Wirt Randall accepted the gift in behalf of the club,
saying that it was symbolical of the love and affection that existed
among the members and would serve, as it passed from hand to hand,
to strengthen the bond between them. He spoke of the former days
of the club and of the fact that its earliest rule—not to discuss
politics or religion at its meetings—had never been broken.

Mr. Brogden spoke of the pleasure and pride in the club taken
by its members and of their appreciation of the gift. Mr. Samuel
Brooke and Mr. Daniel R. Randall also spoke in a similar vein.

Judge Hagner, in response, declared it to be an honor to him
that the cup had been accepted. He recalled the historic time when
members of the club drank the health of his Royal Highness the
Duke of Cumberland in that very room because of his victory over
the Scotch rebels. He made an impressive plea for the continuance
of the spirit that had kept the club alive all these years. His remarks
were enthusiastically applauded.

The speech-making was concluded by Mr. John M. Nelson, who told of his admiration for the club and of the fact that the first money he had ever earned had been in that county by driving a reaper for Mr. Iglehart when he was a lad.

The health of Judge Hagner as chairman, of Mr. Sellman as host and of future reunions were drunk. The loving cup passed some several times and good fellowship reigned supreme.

After the feast a business meeting was held. Judge Hagner was re-elected chairman, and the following resolution, offered by Mr. Daniel R. Randall, was adopted:

"Resolved, That the South River Club accept with profound respect and thanks the gift of a loving cup from its honored chairman, Judge Alexander B. Hagner; and further

"Resolved, That in accepting this beautiful gift the club fully realizes and appreciates the spirit of amity and fellowship which has always actuated this member in his relations with the club and prompted this gift and will ever keep alive that loving spirit so long as this club exists."

The members present were: Judge Alexander B. Hagner, Harry H. Brogden, John Wirt Randall, Blanchard Randall, Daniel R. Randall, T. Stockett Sellman, Thomas S. Duckett, Samuel Brooke, Louis Dorsey Gassaway, Beale D. Worthington, Nevett Steele, Dr. D. Murray Cheston, Benjamin Watkins, John T. Parrott and Thomas S. Iglehart, Jr.

The invited guests were: John M. Nelson, Ramsay Hodges, Jr., O. Bowie Duckett, R. S. Worthington and William L. Amos.

The other members not present at the dinner were: Frank H. Stockett, George H. Stewart, Dr. James D. Iglehart, Paul Iglehart, Richard B. Sellman, James Middleton Munroe, Franklin Weems, Richard W. Iglehart, George R. Gaither, Jr., and William Meade Holladay.

The officers of the club are: Judge A. B. Hagner, chairman; Frank H. Stockett, treasurer; L. Dorsey Gassaway, recorder.

The following list of the former members of the club from the year 1742 has been compiled by Mr. Gassaway, the recorder. In the lists are names of men whose descendants are scattered all over the State and who have had much to do with shaping affairs in Maryland. The list follows: Prior to 1742, Robert Saunders, Thomas Stockett, James Murat, John Gassaway, Samuel Jacobs, Benjamin Stockett, John Howard, Samuel Burgess, Samuel Day, Robert Harding, Thomas Sparrow, Rev. William Brogden, Captain Joseph Cowman, John Watkins, William Chapman, Turner Wootton, James Dick, Samuel Chambers, Dr. Samuel Preston Moore, William Chapman, Jr., Captain Anthony Beck, James Nicholson, John Brewer, Captain Christopher Grendall, Zachariah Maccubbin, James Hall, Darby Lux, Henry Gassaway, Jonathan Sellman, Charles Steward and Richard Moore.

John Dixon, 1742; Thomas Cator, 1744; Joseph Brewer, 1744; John Ijams, 1744; William Reynolds, 1746; Stephen West, Jr., 1751; John Watkins, 1752; John White, 1755; Rev. Archibald Spencer, 1755; Henry Woodward, 1755; Thomas Gassaway, 1755; John Dare, 1755; Joseph Cowman, 1755; Samuel Chapman, 1756; William Strachan, 1756; Richard Burgess, 1757; Joseph Brewer, 1757; Lewis Stockett, 1761; Samuel Watkins, 1762; Thomas Gassaway, 1762; Andrew Wilkie, 1762; Colonel Richard Harwood, Jr., 1762; Thomas Stockett, 1763; Captain Thomas Harwood, 1764; Stephen Watkins, 1764; Dr. Thomas Noble Stockett, 1765; Dr. James Thompson, 1765; Rezin Hammond, 1770; Thomas Harwood, Jr., 1770; Richard Watkins, 1770; Captain Thomas Watkins, 1770; Dr. Thomas Gantt, 1772; Henry Jones, 1775; William Harwood, 1775; William Saunders, 1775; Dr. William Murray, 1776; John L. Brogden, 1778; William Sellman, Robert John Smith, 1780; Edward Sefton, 1784; Nicholas Watkins, 1784; Ferdinando Battee, 1784; Charles Stewart, 1784; Benjamin Howard, 1784; Dr. Robert Welsh, 1784; Rev. Mason Locke Weems, 1785; John Weems, 1785; Solomon Sparrow, 1786; Major Jonathan Sellman, 1786; Mr. Samuel Maccubbin, 1788; Richard Harwood, 1792; David Stewart, 1792; Benjamin Watkins, 1792; Samuel Watkins, 1795; Joseph Watkins, 1795; Dr. Robert Welsh, 1798; John Bard, 1798; Caleb Stewart, 1798; Thomas Purdy, 1798; William Stewart, 1798; James Macculloch, 1798; Benjamin Welsh, 1798; Edward Lee, 1798; Solomon Sparrow, Jr., 1798; Major Thomas Harwood, 1798; William Brogden, 1798; Joseph Cowman, 1798; Robert Welsh, 1803; Osborn S. Harwood, 1805; William Elliott, 1805; Richard Stewart, 1805; James Noble Stockett, 1806; John Gassaway, 1806; William Sanders, 1807; Ferdinando Battee, 1807; John B. Weems, 1810; Joseph Harwood, 1814; John Watkins, 1814; Samuel Harrison, 1814; John S. Stockett, 1818; Thomas Snowden, 1825; Richard Sellman, 1825; Dr. William Brogden, 1825; John Stevens Sellman, 1826; John Mercer, 1826; Virgil Moxcey, 1826; Thomas Snowden, 1835; O. S. Harwood, 1835; Richard C. Hardesty, 1835; John T. Hodges, 1835; Ramsey, Waters, 1835; Colonel Robert W. Kent, 1835; Dr. Benjamin Watkins, 1835; Thomas Welsh, 1835; James. H. Harwood, 1835; Alfred Sellman, 1835; James Harper, 1835; W. H. Woodfield, 1835; Edward Clagett, 1836; David McC. Brogden, 1836; Joseph E. Cowman, 1836; Dr. Richard Harwood, 1837; James B. Smith, 1837; Thomas Hodges, 1837; John Mercer, 1838; Captain Isaac Mayo, 1842; Thomas S. Iglehart, 1842; Charles C. Stewart, 1844; George Gale, 1844; William O'Hara, 1844; John H. Sellman, 1848; R. S. Mercer, 1848; John C. Rogers, 1849; Franklin Deale, 1849; James Kent, 1849; George D. Clayton, 1850; Dr. William N. Pendell, 1850; Colonel G. W. Hughes, 1851; Thomas S. Mercer, 1851; Henry Latrobe, 1851; Hamilton Hall, 1852; Charles S. Contee, 1852; N. H. Shipley, 1852; W. R. S. Gittings, 1853; Frank H. Stockett, 1856; Dr. Howard M. Duvall, 1859; Nicholas H. Green, 1859; William D. Stewart, 1864; William Mayo, 1872; James Boyle, 1872.

THE DESERTED RUINS OF MARLEY CHAPEL.

"In some pine woods, near Marley, nine miles from Baltimore," says Mrs. Helen Stewart Ridgely, "are faithful relics of the past— the ruins of an Episcopal chapel."

The ceiling of Marley Chapel is a segmented arch from which much of the plaster has fallen. It is supported by wooden cornices, and the brickwork over the doors and windows follows the same curve. Between the windows at the east end a stretch of cleaner plaster indicates that some of the church furniture once stood there. The bare ground enclosed in this ruin indicates that either a brick or tile pavement covered the aisle and that the pews were raised above the pavement and probably floored with boards. There remain only a few beams of all the woodwork.

GOVERNOR EDWARD LLOYD.

During the time between the death of Governor Seymour and the appointment of his successor, Edward Lloyd, President of the Council, became acting Governor. He was the son of Colonel Philemon Lloyd, whose wife was Mrs. Henrietta Maria (Neale) Bennett, daughter of Captain James Neale, a former representative at the Court of Spain. Governor Edward Lloyd inherited from his grandfather, Commander Lloyd, in 1695, the celebrated homestead, "Wye House," ever since owned by an Edward Lloyd. His wife was the beautiful Quakeress, Sarah Covington. From them came Edward Lloyd, the legislator of 1739 and husband of Ann Rousby. Their daughter, Elizabeth, married General Sam Ringgold; Henrietta Maria became Mrs. Nicholson, and Richard Bennett Lloyd, their brother, married the charming Joanna Leigh, of the Isle of Wight; his brother, Edward Lloyd, was the hero of the Revolution, rival of Thomas Sim Lee for Governor, the husband of Elizabeth Tayloe and the father of Governor Edward Lloyd of 1809—exactly one hundred years later than his ancestor, the royal Governor of 1709.

McMahon pays this tribute to Governor Edward Lloyd's administration of 1709: "It is as conspicuous in our statute book, even at this day, as the blessed parliament in that of England. A body of permanent laws was then adopted, which for their comprehensiveness and arrangement, are almost entitled to the name of a code. They formed the substratum of the statute law of the Province, even down to the Revolution."

Secretary Calvert, in his correspondence with Governor Lloyd, touched upon bills of exchange, abuse of his lordship's manors, rent rolls, town lands, the King's temporary line, advancement in the value of his lordship's lands, arrearages of rent, the Ohio territory and French encroachments.

Governor Lloyd was succeeded by Governor John Hart, the appointee of Leonard Calvert, endorsed by George the First.

GOVERNOR JOHN HART.

After the King had held the Province from 1689 to 1715, the fourth lord proprietor, Charles, the sixteen-year-old son of Benedict Leonard, was restored as a Protestant. He was represented by Governor John Hart, who had been appointed by the Crown in 1714 and endorsed by both King and Proprietor in 1715. Hart was an enthusiast, but failed to make his enthusiasm useful. He tried to improve the tobacco trade; recommended the growth of hemp; called attention to the need of better roads; urged the building of a government house; but he became involved in a contest with the leading Catholics. He quarreled with Charles Carroll, who, after the restoration, had been commissioned "chief agent, escheator, naval officer and receiver-general of all our rents, arrears of rents, fines, forfeitures, tobaccos, or monies for land warrants; of all ferries, waifs, strays and decedents; of all duties arising from or growing due upon exportation of tobacco aforesaid, tonnage of ships, and all other monies, tobaccos, or other effects," and also authorizing him "to sell or dispose of lands, tenements, or hereditaments to us now escheated or forfeited." Governor Hart, the new Protestant governor, when he learned that the new Protestant Proprietor had permitted a strong Catholic to retain so much power, was furious. The Assembly stood by the Governor, holding that no private employee of the Proprietor should receive the fines imposed by the Assembly. A petition was sent to the Proprietor asking the restoration of the Governor to his full powers. Mr. Carroll fixed the salary of the Governor and even advised him not to assent to some bills awaiting his signature. Mr. Carroll held his agency, but was not continued Register of the Land Office. Governor Hart was also involved, as Chancellor, by taking the part of the people against His Majesty's Surveyor-General of Customs. He had warm supporters among Protestants, but before his recall in 1720, was broken in health.

THE CALVERT GOVERNORS.

Charles Calvert, his successor, was a cousin of the Lord Proprietor. During his administration the bad condition of the tobacco interest led the Lower House to begin the contest over "officers' fees."

His successor, Benedict Leonard Calvert, brother of the Proprietor, became a still weaker supporter of the proprietary interests. His hostility to the clergy was now the controversy. He was an open enemy of two such leaders as Dulany and Bordley. He stood boldly on his ancestry, but died on his way to England.

From these preccedings it is seen that the question of land grants was a cause of dissatisfaction thus early in the history of the county —and it may be of interest to give here an able review of this question from the recent historian, Mereeness, upon Provincial Maryland.

The first conditions of plantation had been declared before the colonists had left England. The size and rent of the grant frequently varied, but each person, so entitled, was required to record his right in the Secretary's office. Following this came the demand for land, a warrant of survey, directed to the Surveyor-General, who gave his certificate, which was embodied in a patent passed by the Governor under the seal of the Proprietor. Still later this simple arrangement was complicated by requiring proofs of right, sales of right, petitions, caveats and resurveys.

About 1670, the·Proprietor and his son, Charles, then Governor, began to increase their revenues. A clerk and register, out of the office of the Secretary, was put in charge especially to prove rights, issue land warrants and draw up grants; this was followed, later, by a council of four, consisting of members of State, which was empowered to hear and determine all matters relating to land. This held until 1689, when the Land Office was closed, only to be opened in 1694. Then Henry Darnall, the Proprietor's cousin and Receiver-General, was put in charge of the Land Office, dying in 1712. Charles Carroll, Solicitor and Register in the Land Office, became Darnall's successor, for which he was most liberally rewarded by magnificent manors.

During the royal administration represented by Governor Hart, a dispute arose concerning the two Proprietors. interests. The Governor and his Council undertook to grant numerous petitions for resurveys and to decide disputes. Secretary Sir Thomas Lawrence claimed the custody of all papers giving evidence of land titles, and also the right to issue warrants, refusing the Proprietor's agent the right to search the records without the usual fee. This was compromised by leaving the records in the Secretary's office but granting the Proprietor's agent to use them to correct his rent-rolls, the Secretary claiming one-half of the fees for land warrants. This led the Proprietor to increase the purchase money from 240 to 480 pounds of tobacco per 100 acres. The Assembly now came into the contest with a demand to publish the changed conditions of plantation and laws were passed requiring surveyors to qualify according to law. Upon the restoration of the Proprietary in 1715, a new Commission was issued to Charles Carroll, still further increasing his power, which brought on the contest with Governor Hart, ending in a reduction of the fees of the agent, until 1733. The rent rolls, after Carroll's death, fell into confusion. Governor Ogle was now in office and the Land Office gave him much trouble, which continued to grow worse.

In 1760, Mr. Lloyd, in charge of the Land Office, was required to build a house for the Receiver-General to contain all land records. Upon the completion of the building in 1766, a Board of Revenue, consisting of public officers, was authorized to audit all accounts of the Land Office and make a report to the Proprietor. This Board of Revenue was comprised of the Governor and leading officers. The Lower House charged that its members were growing independently rich. The Lower House even urged that the Proprietor had no right to dispose of vacant lands different from former proclamations, nor to settle the fees paid for services performed in the Land Office, claiming the office as a public repository of the first evidence of every man's title to his real estate; they asserted that the records had been made at the expense of the people and were, therefore, considered as public records. If the land-holders have no right to have copies, except at the will of his lordship, or on terms his lordship may be pleased to allow them, they are but tenants at will of the Proprietor. The controversy remaining unsettled, was absorbed in the coming struggle with England. Governor Eden conceded that the Land Office was public so far as the custody of the records, but the question of public or private control remained to be solved.

The continual cultivation of tobacco in the early period of the Province did not encourage industrial development and few towns grew up. The tobacco trade was with England direct, and in return English goods were returned.

Located at first upon navigable waters, planters held their social intercourse through the bay and its tributaries, and roads were not made until the back country became settled. Abundance of food was furnished in the bay, and the backwoods gave wild turkeys, deer and other choice meats. With the lavish gifts of nature for their support and the money returns from their tobacco crops, but little incentive for progress existed.

As early as 1663, Governor Charles Calvert had begun to sow wheat, oats, peas and barley, and even flax and hemp. Tobacco planters were required to grow at least two acres of corn; a bounty for raising flax and hemp was offered.

In 1715 Governor Hart addressed both Houses of the Assembly upon the necessity for devoting spacious tracts of fertile lands not adapted to tobacco, to the growth of hemp, but none of these suggestions seemed to bring the Province up to industrial development until 1710, when the fertile soils of Howard and Frederick Counties were devoted to the production of wheat.

Liberal inducements had been offered by Charles Calvert to Palatine settlers. Two hundred acres of back lands were offered to every family, requiring no payment of quit rent for three years, and then only four shillings per hundred acres.

In 1735 Daniel Dulany induced about one hundred families to settle on his lands in Frederick County. In 1749 another large body arrived and were offered homes upon any terms agreeable. At the beginning of the Revolution, Frederick County had a population of nearly 50,000, about one-seventh of the whole Province. The influence of their sturdy subduing of forests, converting them into wheat fields,was extended even to the eastern shore, and in 1770 the Bordley wheat field of 300 acres on Wye Island became an object lesson to wealthy planters.

At last mines opened up. Manufactures of iron implements followed. In 1749 there were eight furnaces for making pig iron and nine forges for bar iron.

Public roads began in 1739, followed by an act of Assembly for clearing, marking and improving roads. The Assembly also loaned money to Howard and Anne Arundel to open, straighten and improve the same. The result was that before entering statehood, wagons, drawn by eight horses, had taken the place of post-horses upon rolling roads.

Fifty vessels were owned in 1749 by inhabitants of the Province, transporting then about 28,000 hogsheads of tobacco, in addition to £16,000 sterling exports of wheat, corn, pig iron, lumber and furs. Twelve years later the tobacco exports had decreased, while exports of other products amounted to £90,000.

In 1762 Philadelphia offered a better market for Maryland products than could be found in Maryland owing to the scattered ports of delivery in the Province.

The need of money now became imperative. Paper currency came and with it a law for inspection of tobacco, added to the development of the western counties; the Province at last began to be more independent of the mother country. (Mereness.)

Now there were many evidences of advancement in the Province.

ANNAPOLIS IN 1718.

In 1718, "New Town," upon Powder Hill, was added to Annapolis. It was ten acres, secured by a Commission of Colonel William Holland, Colonel Thomas Addison, Captain Daniel Mariartiee and Mr. Alexander Warfield for the encouragement of trade in the city. The lots were given to builders who did not hold other lots in Annapolis. Philip Hammond, the merchant, had his warehouse in "New Town."

The lotholders of Annapolis, at that time, were Dr. Charles Carroll, Samuel Young, Thomas Bladen, Patrick Ogleby, Robert Thomas, Amos Garrett, the merchant and ex-mayor, Benjamin Tasker, James Carroll and Philip Lloyd.

In 1820 Benjamin Tasker laid out his "Prospect to Annapolis" on the north side of the Severn.

St. Anne's Church was now so crowded a gallery had to be added in 1723. During that year, too, an act for encouraging learning was passed and Rev. Joseph Colebatch, Colonel Samuel Young, William Locke, Captain Daniel Mariartiee, Mr. Charles Hammond, Mr. Richard Warfield and John Beale were commissioned to procure land, build and visit schools for Anne Arundel.

In 1727 several parishioners of St. Anne's, headed by Rev. Alexander Frazier were authorized to build a chapel in the upper part of the parish. The site selected was near Indian Landing; its patrons were Vachel Denton, Thomas Worthington, John Beale and Philip Hammond.

William Parks was authorized to print, in 1727, a compilation of the laws of the Province, and in 1728, Henry Ridgely, Mordecai Hammond and John Welsh were empowered to lay out land for a custom house.

GOVERNOR SAMUEL OGLE.

In 1732 Lord Baltimore appointed Samuel Ogle, son of Samuel Ogle, of Northumberland, England, as his representative in Annapolis. The Legislature gave £3,000 for a Governor's residence, but it was not used by Governor Ogle, then a bachelor. The Governor soon engaged in the controversy concerning the dividing line of Maryland and Pennsylvania. Lord Baltimore, despairing of receiving his rights, had decided to accept a compromise. Disturbances had for several years been created by the German settlers on the disputed territory. Captain Thomas Cresap formed an association to drive out the Germans. In this contest one man was killed; Cresap was wounded and was taken prisoner. Governor Ogle sent Edmund Jennings and Daniel Dulany to Philadelphia to demand Cresap's release: they failed. Reprisals were ordered; four Germans were arrested and taken to Baltimore. Cresap's exclamation, when he saw Philadelphia, was, "Why this is the finest city in the Province of Maryland."

Penn sent a committee to Governor Ogle to treat, but the Governor's demands were not accepted. Riots upon the contested border increased and Governor Ogle addressed the King, who replied by enjoining both Governors to keep the peace, to allow no settlers in the disputed territory until his wishes were made known. Affairs were in such a serious condition that Lord Baltimore came over to the Province and assumed charge for one year.

Governor Ogle had found the Province excited over English statutes. He possessed many essential qualities for a successful governor. He won over Daniel Dulany, one of the strongest opposers, but he could not silence the opposition. He settled the controversy over English statutes by appointing four of the ablest members of the Lower House, but the act of Assembly which supported the government, having been allowed to expire, the House expelled those four members who had been appointed to office.

New leaders rose in the House to oppose "officers' fees," and to quiet the Province, the Lord Proprietor determined on a new Governor.

GOVERNOR SIR THOMAS BLADEN.

In 1742, Sir Charles Calvert appointed his brother-in-law his representative. Both had married daughters of Sir Theodore Jansen, Baronet of Surry.

In 1742, £1,000 more were added to the fund for a Governor's mansion and Governor Bladen was empowered to buy four lots and to erect thereon a residence for himself and future Governors. In 1744, he bought four acres, from Stephen Bordley and built the stately hall now the central building of St. Johns College, an architect from Scotland planned it, but before completing this magnificent banquetting hall, the Legislature and Governor disagreed upon its designs and refused further aid. It so stood for a number of years a decaying monument of splendor and was dubbed "Bladen's Folly." In 1784, it was granted, with its grounds, to St. Johns College.

Governor Bladen made the treaty with Thomas Penn. "The Six Nations" had also given trouble by claiming land along the Susquehanna and Potomac. The Governor was disposed to a peaceful settlement by buying their lands. The Assembly agreed, but disputed his authority in appointing Commissioners. To his appointments the Assembly added the names of Dr. Robert Key and Charles Carroll, and drew up instructions for their action. This gave offense to Governor Bladen. The Indians pressed an answer, but the Assembly would not yield and the Governor appointed his commission alone. It met and adjusted the controversy, by paying £100 currency for the Indian claim. By that treaty, the Nanticokes left the Eastern Shore and paddled their canoes up the Susquehanna River and settled in the Wyoming Valley.

The members of the Assembly from Anne Arundel and Annapolis City in 1745, were Major Henry Hall, Dr. Charles Carroll, Mr. Philip Hammond, Mr. Thomas Worthington, Captain Robert Gordon and Dr. Charles Stewart, of Annapolis. This Assembly refused to aid the Governor in sending troops to Canada. It occasioned considerable discussion, but the independent descendants of the old settlers of the previous century held their ground in able remonstrance. This led Governor Bladen to ask a recall and Samuel Ogle was again named as his successor, in 1747.

The Maryland Gazette, the earliest newspaper of the Province, made its re-appearance, in 1745, under Josias Green, and henceforth its pages furnish a reliable history of the county.

GOVERNOR OGLE'S SECOND TERM.

On March 12, 1747, the new Governor brought over his bride in the ship Neptune, from Liverpool and on the 9th of June, Governor Bladen, the only royal Governor born in the Provinces, sailed for England. His father was Hon. William Bladen, Clerk of the Council and first public printer, who held an estate of 2,000 acres in St. Mary's. His daughter Ann, married Hon. Benjamin Tasker, whose daughter Ann, became the wife of Governor Samuel Ogle.

In December, Governor Ogle called the Assembly to raise funds for the support of the Maryland troops in Canada. The Assembly refused and was dissolved. Governor Ogle's report upon the condition of trade, population and expenses of the Province was a comprehensive exhibit, which he sent to the Board of Trade, of London.

The Act of the Assembly for the inspection of tobacco and the limitation of officer's fees, passed shortly after his restoration to office increased the general good feeling toward him. During his administration the land grants extended to Howard District of Anne Arundel. He built the house which stands on the corner of King

George and College Avenue.   During his second term of service, the
prosperity of the Province was well-marked.   Upon his death in
1752, the Maryland Gazette paid this tribute:
"His great constancy and firmness in a painful illness were suitable to a life exercised in every laudable pursuit.   His long residence
among us made him thoroughly acquainted with our Constitution
and interests and his benevolent disposition induced him to promote
the public good.   He was a pattern of sobriety and regularity; a
sincere lover of truth and justice.   That his administration was mild
and just, his enemies, if such a man had any, dare not deny.   In
private life he was an amiable companion and in his friendship warm
and sincere."

THE GROWTH OF A CENTURY.

We have reached the Centennial year of the settlement, of Anne
Arundel, and in that review the words of Rev. Ethan Allen are of
interest. Says he: "The Puritans as such, were then no longer heard
of; their places of worship were desolate and their grave-yards,
where are they?"

At Proctor's Landing a city had grown up; it was the seat of
government for the Province.   The State House, the church, the
school houses and magnificent dwellings, some of which still remain,
had taken the place of the log-hut of the emigrant and the wigwam
of the Indian.   Luxury, fashion and commerce, with their attendant
dissipations and extravagances, had taken the place of the severe
and stern simplicity of the early settlers.

A hundred years had given the match-lock of the Marylander
for the quiver of the Indian; the pinnace for the canoe; the printing
press for pictorial chronicles; skilled tillage for the unthrifty hunt;
African slavery for savage liberty; the race course for the wrestling
match; the school for the war-dance; substantial edifices for the
wigwam; the grand ritual of a mighty church for the artless appeal
to the Great Spirit; the busy throb of an important capital for the
still-hunt of the savage.

Annapolis had now been the capital for half a century.   Opulent
men had built costly, elegant houses as their city dwellings and had
large plantations, or manors, where they dwelt when overlooking
their tobacco crops.   Lumbering equipages, drawn by superb horses
were their traveling outfits in the country.   "In town, sedan chairs,
borne by lacquies in livery were often seen.   They sat on carved
chairs, at quaint tables, amid piles of ancestral silverware and drank
punch out of vast, costly bowls from Japan, or supped Madeira, half a
century old."

The legal lights of Annapolis were Jennings, Chalmer, Rogers,
Stone, Paca, Johnson, Dulany.   The clergy were men of culture, who
could write Latin notes to their companions; they enjoyed their
imported Madeira; were hearty livers and enjoyed the renowned
crabs, terrapins and canvass-back ducks, for which the city was
famous.   With races every fall and spring, theatre in winter, a card

party each evening, assemblies every fortnight, dinners three or four times a week, at which wit, learning and stately manners were exhibited, all softened by love of good fellowship, it is not surprising that a foreigner should declare: "There is not a town in England, of the same size as Annapolis, which can boast of a greater number of fashionable and handsome women."

The style in winter is to enjoy the capital, but in milder seasons, to travel among the great estates and manors until the principal families in Calvert, St. Marys, Charles, Prince George and Arundel and even across the bay, had been visited.

They were bold riders, expert in hounds and horse flesh, and the daily fox-chase was as much a duty as it was to go to church with proper equipage and style on Sunday.

Between the old colonial mansions of the Northern and Southern colonies a striking contrast seems to exist. In Maryland and Virginia there are brick buildings of remarkable solidity and considerable architectural pretensions. In solidity they shame the mock shallowness of our modern pretension. A noble hospitality is expressed in the great mansions of this time. The central building lodged the family and guests; the two wings, connected by corridors, served for kitchen, offices and servants quarters. In the less-imposing homes of the people, the "hipped-roof" was almost universal, now revived by our Mansard. The cosy comfort, the burnished brass knockers, the low ceilings, the Queen Anne garden with box edging, all speak to us lovingly of ancestral days worthy of being reseen and reviewed.

Our modern clubs are only imitations of the South River and the Tuesday Club, of Annapolis. The former has been separately noted elsewhere. The latter was an assembly of wits, who satirized every one and did it successfully. The most distinguished and influential men of the ancient capital, graduates of British Universities, wits of first order were its members. The meetings were held at the houses of its patrons. Offensive topics were laughed out of discussion. Hon. Edward Dorsey, known as "the honest lawyer" was at one time speaker. "He was charged with negligence in office in not displaying his talents in oratory to the club. Speaker Dorsey rising with that gravity and action, which is his peculiar talent on all such occasions, discoursed in a nervous and elegant style, which is natural to that gentleman on all occasions." Notes of this club's discussions have been preserved in the Archives of the Maryland Historical Society.

Other pastimes of that period, were the races. On 30th of May, 1745, "a race was held at John Conners, about seven miles south of London Town, near West River. A purse of £10 for the best horse, open to all, except "Old Ranter" and "Limber Sides," three heats over two miles."

In 1746, the gentlemen of the "Ancient South River Club," to express their loyalty to his Majesty on the success of the inimitable Duke of Cumberland's obtaining a complete victory over the Pretender, appointed a grand entertainment to be given at their club house, on Thursday next. The birthday of George II was observed here, October 29, 1746, "by firing cannon and drinking loyal healths."

In 1752, the "Beggars Farce" was at the new Theatre by permission of President Tasker. A lottery under Benjamin Tasker, Jr., George Stewart and Walter Dulany was organized for purchasing a town clock.

A French writer of this period who saw the capital city, thus records it. "In that very inconsiderable town standing at the mouth of the Severn, where it falls into the bay, at least three-fourths of the buildings may be styled elegant and grand. Female luxury exceeds anything known in the Province of France. A French hairdresser is a man of importance among them, and it is said, that a certain dame here, hires one of the craft for a thousand crowns a year. The State House is a very beautiful building, I think the most so, of any I have seen in America."

GOVERNOR TASKER.

Upon the death of Governor Ogle, the office devolved upon his father-in-law, Hon. Benjamin Tasker, by virtue of his Presidency of the Council, which position he had held since 1744. We get a glimpse of him in his correspondence with Lord Baltimore as President of the Council, in which he declared: "The Assembly is now at a conclusion, but as to the real services, they have done, they might as well have stayed at home. They have prepared an address, offering your Lordship two-sixth pence per hogshead on all tobacco to be exported, but have not agreed to make good any number of hogsheads, but the surest way would be to let the country farmers make good such a sum as can be agreed upon and leave them to find a way to raise it."

Letters upon encroachments upon the Potomac; under the grant of Lord Fairfax; upon leases, copper ore, patents of land, Spanish gold, remittances and rents make up the scope of Colonel Tasker's voluminous correspondence.

Lord Baltimore, in reply, lamented the death of Governor Ogle, but congratulated himself in having so able a representative to take his place; acknowledged the rights of the President of the Council to assume the government upon the death of the Governor.

As President of the Council, Colonel Tasker made a digest of the Provincial laws and even after Governor Sharpe had arrived Colonel Tasker was placed in charge of the private correspondence and affairs of the Proprietary.

His son, Benjamin Tasker, Jr., was appointed by Governor Sharpe, Commissioner to secure the assistance of "The Six Nations." This commission resulted in the Confederacy of 1752—a union of colonial interests for defense about a quarter of a century before the Declaration of Independence.

Both of these distinguished men lie buried at St. Anne's.

GOVERNOR HORATIO SHARPE.

On August 11, 1753, Horatio Sharpe, Esquire, Governor of the Province, arrived in the ship Molly, from London. He was a member of an able English family. His brother in England secured for him, soon after his arrival, an important military appointment as commander of the Colonial Forces. Governor Sharpe entered upon a momentous period. The French and Indian war was at hand; the House of Delegates insisted on taxing the Lord Proprietor's estates and denying his right to ordinary licenses. The Stamp Act following the war, was another grevious complaint. It was altogether a trying ordeal for the Governor, who had to be impartial toward the Crown, the Lord Proprietor and the people, as well as to protect the Province from a common enemy. But he was equal to the occasion.

Meeting General Braddock at Frederick, he there built Fort Frederick. Braddock's advance and defeat created a panic in the Province. Many fled to Baltimore, where women and children were embarked on vessels to be sent to Virginia.

Ordering out the militia and calling for volunteers, Governor Sharpe, assisted by Captain Henry Ridgely and Captain Alexander Beall with two companies of thirty men each, went to the front. The people of Annapolis began to fortify the town. Ninety-five Marylanders, joined by South Carolinians, under the cover of bushes and trees, kept at bay a fierce Indian attack at Fort Duquesne. The English were defeated, but the Marylanders covered their retreat, losing twenty-four out of ninety-five men engaged. The Indians could not withstand our provincials. Governor Sharpe, in sympathy with the joy that filled the colony over the bravery of our Maryland forces, appointed a public thanksgiving, and the Assembly appropriated a fund for the defenders.

It is a peculiar incident in the history of the State, that the dying interest of the last unpopular Proprietor should be so ably and efficiently sustained by two such popular governors as Sharpe and Eden.

The clergy tendered Governor Sharpe their grateful acknowledgements "for his amiable virtues, both in public and private character." The Lower House acknowledged "it is our opinion that his own inclination led him very much toward that desirable object"— the good of the Province. Kent County, St. Mary's and Frederick County all sent him addresses complimentary and approving. Governor Sharpe's able correspondence covers three volumes of the Maryland Archives. He was a bachelor, yet he built a homestead that still bears testimony to the magnificence of our colonial architecture. In 1763, by Legislative act, Governor Sharpe purchased from the vestry of St. Margaret's Parish, the "White Hall" estate, which had been left to the church by Colonel Charles Greenberry. In 1764 the vestry, headed by William West, gave a power-of-attorney to John Merriken to convey to Horatio Sharpe their tract known as "White Hall." This tract had descended to Colonel

Charles Greenberry from Colonel Nicholas Greenberry, who had secured it from Colonel William Fuller, of Virginia, the son of its first surveyor, Captain William Fuller, hero of the Severn. Governor Sharpe resided in "White Hall" mansion. When he retired from the office of Governor, his secretary, John Ridout, of England, held it and by the will of Governor Sharpe, through his trustees, Benjamin Ogle. and Dr. Upton Scott, it was transferred by deed to John Ridout. Governor Sharpe's full-length portrait is upon its walls, and the bed on which he rested is still among its relics. "White Hall" has passed to Mrs. Story, wife of Captain Story, U. S. A.

GOVERNOR ROBERT EDEN.

Governor Robert Eden was the last Proprietary Governor. He came in 1769. It was in the lovely month of June. The guns of the battery gave him welcome. He was a gentleman "easy of access, courteous to all, and fascinating by his accomplishments." Mr. William Eddis, to whom we are indebted for much of our most interesting bits of gossip, came in 1769 to take the position of English Collector of Customs. His pen records are still extant and valuable. Of Governor Eden he wrote, "The Governor is returned to a land of trouble. To stem the popular torrent will require all his faculties. Hitherto his conduct has secured to him a well-merited popularity —and I can assert that he conducts himself in his arduous depart- ment with an invariable attention to the interests of his royal master, and the essential welfare of the Province over which he has the honor to preside." That this sentiment was shared by the Assembly of Maryland was clearly manifest when it refused to subject Governor Eden to the indignity of arrest as demanded by General Charles Lee, the Englishman, then in charge of the American Army. In face of the clamors of the Whig Club of Baltimore, the latter felt he could trust the Convention of Maryland which had solemnly pledged his safe departure.

The foundation stone of the present State House was laid by Governor Eden in 1772. On his striking the stone with a mallet there was a clap of thunder, although a cloud could not be seen. This building is the third upon the same site. The appropriation was £7,500 sterling. Its building committee were Daniel Dulany, Thomas Johnson, John Hall, William Paca, Charles Carroll, Barrister, Lance- lot Jacques and Charles Wallace. In 1773 it was covered with a copper roof, which during the gale of 1775 was blown off. The dome, so much admired by all critics, was added after the Revolution.

Governor Eden bought of Edmund Jennings the historic man- sion, long the Governor's mansion of our State Governors. He added its wings.

Mr. David Ridgely, the State Librarian and author of "Annals of Annapolis" in 1841, thus describes Governor Eden's mansion: "This edifice has a handsome court and garden extending,with the exception of an intervening lot, to the water's edge. From the portico, looking to the garden, a fine prospect regales the vision. The building consists of two stories and presents an extensive front; there are on the lower floor, a large room on each side of the hall as you enter and several smaller ones; the saloon, on the same floor, is nearly the length of the house. On each side of the edifice are commodious kitchens, carriage house and stables, with spacious lots. Towards the water, the building rises in the middle in a turreted shape. It stands detached from other structures, and is altogether a delightful and suitable mansion for the Chief Magistrate of our State." At the outbreak of the Revolution Governor Eden's property was confiscated. This mansion was held for our Governors until 1866, when it was sold to the Naval Academy and became the Library Hall. It was intended for the residence of the Superintendent, but was condemned and torn down in 1901. The same act of 1866 located our present Gubernatorial mansion on its quintangular lot, fronting on State House Circle. Upon this lot stood the residence of Mr. Absalom Ridgely and his son, Dr. John Ridgely, surgeon of U. S. Ship Philadelphia, captured in the harbor of Tripoli in 1804. It was built by the grandfather of General George H. Stuart.

In social circles Governor Eden was a favorite. When the controversy concerning "officer's fees" was at its height during his administration the hostility was directed more against the members of the Upper House than against the Governor. The two great debaters and writers upon that controversy were Daniel Dulany and Charles Carroll, of "Carrollton," under assumed names of "Antillon" and "First Citizen." Full copies of that discussion are now on record at the State Library, Annapolis. In it Charles Carroll, then unknown, just returned from his studies in Europe, took the popular side and received the public thanks of the Lower House of the Assembly. He contended that the government of Maryland had for years been held by one family, viz: Tasker, Ogle, Bladen and Dulany. The latter's father-in-law, Benjamin Tasker, had been President of the Council for a number of years. Dulany, the writer, was a brother-in-law of Benjamin Tasker, Jr., who was also of the Council and at the same time Secretary of the Province. The office of Commissary-General and Secretary were almost hereditary in the Dulany family. Colonel Tasker, Sr., was Commissary-General between the two Dulany's, father and son, and at the time of the discussion in 1773, Walter Dulany held the place while his cousin was Secretary. Mrs. Daniel Dulany's mother, wife of Benjamin Tasker, was a Bladen, and Governor Robert Eden, last in line, while he married Lord Baltimore's daughter, had also connected himself with the Bladens, as this lady was a niece of Governor Bladen's wife.

The "Independent Whigs" in a letter to "The First Citizen," declared, "We thank you for the sentiments which you have spoken with honest freedom. We had long waited for a man of abilities to step forth and tell our dozing ministers the evils they have brought upon the community. While we admire your intrepidity in the attack, permit us to applaud that calm and sturdy temper which so precisely marks and distinguishes your excellent performance.   Go on, sir, and assert the rights of your country; every friend of liberty will be a friend to you.   Malice may rage and raw heads and bloody bones may clatter and rattle, but the honest heart, bold in the cause of freedom feels no alarm."

Carroll's exposure of the "Proclamation" was seen in the next election in Annapolis, when a tumultuous crowd with sound of muffled drums, bore the proclamation in a coffin, and with a grave-digger, marched to its burial; a committee was appointed to thank "The First Citizen."

COUNCIL OF SAFETY.

Two governments were now in Annapolis—Governor Eden and the Council of Safety.—Fearing the action of the Assembly, Eden continued by prorogation, to keep down the voice of the people, but the people of Anne Arundel sent out an invitation for committees from the several counties to meet at Annapolis for forming non-importation associations, a full meeting was the result.   It was resolved not to import any of the dutiable goods; to exclude a list of merchandise summing up a hundred articles; while this agreement was being signed came the news that only tea would be taxed, but the committees appointed at Annapolis unanimously resolved to stand by their former declaration.   Closely following came the Congress of all delegates.

When the Council of Safety took charge of the State of Maryland Governor Eden was notified that the time for his departure had arrived, and after its members had taken an affectionate leave of their late Supreme Magistrate, he was conducted to a barge with every mark of respect due his elevated station he had so worthily filled.   He reached the vessel amid the booming of cannon.   In 1783 ex-Governor Eden returned to America to secure the restitution of his property.   There was some criticism of his action, but after an interview with Governor Paca, matters were adjusted.   He died soon after his arrival in a house now owned by the Sisters of Notre Dame on Shipwright Street.   This house was the homestead of Dr. Upton Scott, a rich citizen of Annapolis.   It now attracts more visitors than any other in Annapolis by having been made the imaginary home of "Richard Carvel," of Revolutionary days.   The house commands a beautiful view of the creek into which entered the St. Mary forces, and also the opposite neck upon which was gained the Battle of the Severn.   Just east of it stands the Carroll mansion, upon "Carroll Green"," all now in the grounds of the Catholic orders of the city.

"Governor Eden was buried," says Mr. Ridgely in his Annals of Annapolis, "under the pulpit of the Episcopal church on the north side of the Severn, within two or three miles of the city."

"This church was some years since burned down" Mr. Riley adds.   "I have tried by diligent inquiry to locate this church.   The nearest approach to the truth is found in the fact that on the farm of Mrs. Winchester, near the track of the Annapolis and Baltimore Short Line Railroad, is an ancient graveyard, the site of an Episcopal church that was burned down about a hundred years ago. There is a grave in the cemetery marked by a çross of bricks, and the tradition is that an English lord lies buried here. It would not take many repetitions of oral history to change an English governor to an English lord."

Mrs. Helen Stuart Ridgely in her "Old Brick Churches," locates the early Church of Westminster Parish on "Severn Heights." My own researches show a deed from John Hammond, whose estate was on the Severn, for 200 square feet upon "Deep Creeke," for building a church for Westminster Parish in 1695. The only consideration was "the love he bore his neighbors." In 1707-8 the parish of Westminster obtained a deed for "two acres on the south side of the Magothy River, adjoining a town called Westminster Towne." The tract was "Luck," granted to Mary Garner, mother of Edward Gibbs, to whom it descended and by whom it. was sold, to Charles Greenberry, principal vestryman and his brothers, John Peasly, Philip Jones, Thomas Cockey, John Ingram and Richard Torrell." Its communion silver dates from 1713, the year of Colonel Charles Greenberry's death. His will left a liberal provision for maintaining a minister. His estate "White Hall," was left to his widow, to descend to Westminster Parish. This was still later the estate of Governor Sharpe, who granted it to his secretary, John Ridout, of England, whose burial notice reads, "Be it remembered that John Ridout, Esquire, a native of Dorset, England, departed this life 7th October 1797, and was buried at 'White Hall,' the ceremony being solemnized by the Rev. Ralph Higginbotham, of St. Anne's Parish." Another record reads, "Rachel Ridout, wife of Horatio Ridout and daughter of Robert Goldsborough, of Cambridge, Maryland, departed this life 17th of June, 1811, and was buried at 'White Hall,' in this Parish, the funeral ceremony being solemnized by the Rev. Robert Welsh, of the Methodist Society, Entered by Horatio Ridout, Register."

"Mary Ridout, daughter of Governor Samuel Ogle, and wife of John Ridout, died at 'White Hall,' August, 1808." Ann Ogle, wife of Governor Samuel, was buried at "White Hall" in 1817.

We get a view of some church officials in 1706 from the records of St. Anne's Church.

On Easter Monday, April 19, 1756, at the parish church, there were present Dr. Richard Tootell, Mr. Thomas Beale Dorsey, Mr. Robert Swan, Mr. James Maccubin and Mr. William Roberts, of the vestry, and sundry parishioners, who went through the usual vestry election and selected Mr. Lancelot Jaques and Mr. Richard Mackubin church wardens to fill the expired terms of Messrs. Thornton and Woodward. Mr. Alexander Warfield, son of Richard, and Dr. George Stewart were made vestrymen in the place of Dr. Tootell and Mr. Dorsey. At that meeting of the vestry the following list of bachelors was returned to the vestry, to be taxed for the support of the church:

Those possessing £100 and less than £300, were Mr. Rezin Gaither, at Mrs. Elizabeth Gaithers, at the head of the Severn; Mr. Emanuel Marriott, at his father's, Mr. Joseph Marriott; Mr. Caleb Davis, at Mr. Philip Hammond's. Those possessing over £300 were Mr. Zachariah Hood; Charles Carroll, barrister; Mr. William Gaither, at the head of the Severn; Mr. Charles Hammond, son of Philip. The Register also added that His Excellency Horatio Sharpe and Rev. John MacPherson were bachelors, but he did not count them.

After qualifying according to law the vestry proceeded to nominate and recommend the following persons for Inspectors of tobacco for the ensuing year, viz: Mr. Moses Mackubin and Mr. Richard Mackubin for the port of Annapolis, Mr. Augustine Gambrill, Mr, Joseph Sewell, Mr. Richard Warfield, Jr., and Mr. John Hall for Indian Landing. It was then ordered that the tobacco in the hands of the Sheriff, belonging to the vestry, be sold at public vendue, on Wednesday next and that the Register set up notices for the same. The tobacco sold at sixteen-ninth pence per hundred.

Mr. Alexander Warfield was ordered, in 1758, to have a window cut in the chapel at the expense of the vestry and to see that the stones in the aisles were relaid.

At the outbreak of the Revolution, St. Anne's Church had become quite dilapidated, but it still held a communion plate of solid silver, made by Francis Garthorne, engraved with the arms of William III. This is still a cherished memorial in the present magnificent building, which is the third upon its historic site. It also has two Bibles, the gifts of General John Hammond, its vestryman of 1704 and Mrs. Henrietta Maria Dorsey, wife of Captain Edward. Its stone font is the work of Rinehart. Its burial ground is now occupied by the city streets, but in its capacious circle, now enclosed by an iron railing, we may still read some records of historic interest. "Here lieth Rebecca, wife of Daniel Dulany, fourth daughter of Colonel Walter Smith;" "Margaret Carroll, relict of Charles Carroll, (barrister) of Annapolis and daughter of Matthew Tilghman—born 1742, died 1817." "Henry Ridgely, died 1700;" General John Hammond, 1707; Nicholas Gassaway, 1711. Upon a slab of white marble with a griffin rampant, surrounded by fleur de-lis, the following inscription is preserved:

"Here lieth interred the body of Mr. Amos Garrett, of the city of Annapolis, in Anne Arundel County, in the Province of Maryland, merchant, son of Mr. James and Mrs. Sarah Garrett, late of St. Olive Street, Southwork, then in the Kingdom of England, now a part of Great Britain, who departed this life on March 8, 1727, Aetatis 56."

The bell given by Queen Anne was destroyed in the fire of 1858. The present building dates from the same year. Its north grounds have elevated memorials, also, to William Bladen, who died 1718, aged forty-eight; to Benjamin Tasker, Jr., late Secretary of Maryland, who died 1760, in his thirty-ninth year and to Hon. Benjamin Tasker, Sr., President of the Council, who died 1768, aged seventy-eight.

St. James Parish, Herring Creek, noted further on "Old Brick Churches," discarded its brick church of 1718 and rebuilt one in 1760, which is still standing. It is nearly square, with a hip-roof, like that on the present All Hallows, which dates from 1722, but while the latter is open inside to the roof, St. James has a vaulted ceiling spanning and slanting off at the ends to harmonize with the conformation outside. There are two aisles and three sections of square pews with doors. The windows with their deep embrasures are rounded at the top and in most of them the small panes are preserved. There are two stained glass windows in the chancel and the corners near it are boxed off into vestry-room and choir, which necessary contrivances mar the effect of the otherwise perfect interior; they, moreover, hide the tablets containing the Lord's Prayer and the Creed, which, with the Ten Commandments covering the space between the chancel windows, were probably procured with the legacy of £10 given in 1723, by the wife of William Locke, Esq., "toward adorning the Altar of St. James with Creed, Lord's Prayer and Ten Commandments."

William Locke also gave money for a silver basin or baptismal font, which is now one of the four pieces, of which the church plate consists. It bears the date of 1732, and also the donor, with the word "Armigeri" after it.

The alms basin was the gift of the rector, Rev. Henry Hall, who died in 1723. The other pieces look as if they might be of earlier date. The records also show that whipping posts and stocks were then in order.

Rev. Henry Hall lies in St. James church-yard, under a horizontal slab mounted on a brick foundation. Another slab, flat to the ground, is in honor of Hon. Seth Biggs, Esq., who died 1708, aged fifty-five years.

KING WILLIAM'S SCHOOL, NOW ST. JOHN'S COLLEGE.

The first dates from 1696; the second from 1785. The trustees of the first were Governor Francis Nicholson, Hon. Sir Thomas Lawrence, Colonel George Robothan, Colonel Charles Hutchins, Colonel John Addison, Rev. Divine, Mr. Peregrine Coney, Mr. John Hewitt, Mr. Robert Smith, Kenelym Cheseldyne, Henry Coursey, Edward Dorsey, Thomas Ennals, Thomas Tasker, Francis Jenkins, William Dent, Thomas Smith, Edward Boothy, John Thompson and John Bigger, gentlemen.

It stood upon a lot given by Governor Nicholson, on the south side of the State House, the spot of the DeKalb Statue. It gave the name to School Street. It was completed in 1701. The earliest rector was Rev. Edward Butler, rector of St. Anne's and master of the free school in Annapolis. Its records are meager, but William Pinkney was educated there.

In 1785, the property of King William's School was conveyed to St. John's College. Among the list was a number of "quaint and curious volumes of forgotten lore," which still remain in the library of St. John's. Governor Eden, early after his arrival, strongly recommended an institution of learning which would preclude the necessity for crossing the ocean to obtain an education. Governor Bladen's unfinished residence was selected as its site. The war intervened, but at its close the Legislature passed a wise and public-spirited act of incorporation, granting, if located in Annapolis, four acres purchased by Governor Bladen, from Stephen Bordley, for his public residence. The sum of £1,750 annually and forever was granted as a donation. A committee of the Board of Visitors, viz: James Brice, Charles Wallace, Richard Sprigg, Thomas Hyde and Thomas Harwood, announced in 1789, the appointment of John McDowell, A.M., Professor of Mathematics. His name to-day, is perpetuated in McDowell Hall. In 1806, the Legislature repealed its charter in the face of an eloquent appeal from William Pinkney, in which he said: "The day which witnessed the degradation of St. John's College would prove the darkest day Maryland has known."

In 1832, the sum of £3,000 was given, providing the Board would accept it in full satisfaction for any claim it might have against the State. Thus, has the college lived for a century, during which time it has presented a long array of Maryland's most honored sons, who started out from its halls. Its present able President, Dr. Fell is holding it to its purpose with success.

ANTE-REVOLUTIONARY MOVEMENTS.

We have now reached the close of our Provincial era. Busy preparations for an independent nation are at hand. The causes which led to the Revolution are known to every school boy, but the part that Maryland took in that Revolution has never had its just recognition.

In Bancroft's voluminous history, of eight large volumes, not more than a half-dozen pages are given to a notice of Maryland's share in the great work. Even this slight notice is in detached paragraphs of deprecatory allusions to the influence of "its profligate Lord Proprietary," in shaping the conservatism of the State. Though Maryland, through Thomas Johnson, had nominated George Washington as Commander-in-Chief, it is there recorded as the wish of the East. Chase, whose wisdom was felt in every convention, only received a passing word of commemoration. Maryland, it is true, penetrated the disguise of patriotism which enveloped our English General, Charles Lee and became indignant, when such a man had tried to depose her respected Governor Eden, but her conservatism stood not in the way, after it was seen, that the cause of defense could be made one of independence. When that hour had dawned, her spirit of devotion became manifest. Like others, Maryland had hoped for the recovery of American rights through the blockade of trade, but now in a convention of fifty-five members from sixteen counties, it "resolved unanimously to resist to the utmost of their power, taxation by Parliament, or the enforcement of the penal acts against Massachusetts." Charles Carroll, disfranchised, was placed on her committee of correspondence. Chase, strong, downright brave and persevering, vehement even to a fault, won the confidence of the people. Her delegates to that Convention in April, 1775, had been instructed to proceed "even to the last extremity, if indispensably necessary for the safety and preservation of their liberties and privileges."

On 26th of July, following, the Convention at Annapolis resolved fully to sustain Massachusetts and to meet force by force. It saw "no alternative, but base submission or manly resistance and it approved by arms its opposition to British troops." It directed the enrollment of forty companies of minute men; authorized one quarter of a million of currency to be raised; extended its franchise; and recognizing the Continental Congress it managed the affairs of the State through a "Council of Safety" and subordinate Executive Committees in every county of the State.

At a meeting of the voters of Anne Arundel County, in 1774, it was resolved, "That Thomas Dorsey, John Hood, Jr., John Dorsey, Philip Dorsey, John Burgess, Thomas Sappington, Ephraim Howard, Caleb Dorsey, Richard Stringer, Reuben Meriweather, Dr. Charles A. Warfield, Edward Gaither, Jr., Greenberry Gaither, Elijah Robosson, Thomas Mayo, James Kelso, Benjamin Howard, Ely Dorsey, Sr., Mark Brown Sappington, Brice T. B. Worthington, Charles Carroll, barrister; John Hall, William Paca, Thomas Johnson, Jr., Matthias Hammond, Charles Wallace, Richard Tootell, Thomas Harwood, Jr., John Davidson, John Brice, John Weems, Samuel Chew, Thomas Sprigg, Gerard Hopkins, Jr., Thomas Hall, Thomas Harwood, West River; Stephen Steward, Thomas Watkins, Thomas Belt, the third, Richard Green and Stephen Watkins be a committee to represent and act for this county and city, to carry into execution the association agreed on by the American Continental Congress."

On 26th of July, 1775, at Annapolis, a temporary form of government was established, which endured until the Constitution of 1851 was adopted. In this action Maryland moved solely by its own volition. Charles Carroll, of Carrollton and Charles Carroll, barrister, were members of the Committee of Safety, from Annapolis City.

The new Government of Maryland, which succeeded the exciting Administration of Governor Eden, showed a gloomy prospect in its early hours of the Revolutionary struggle.

The Council of Safety in its address to the Maryland Delegates recorded, "Our people are very backward in carrying the New Government into execution. Anne Arundel County has named no electors to the Senate—nor any committee of observation—none of the Judges attended and very few people. The city of Annapolis has not named any Elector and we expect news of the same kind from other places." But when once awakened to the necessity of defence, the people of Anne Arundel faltered not, as will be seen in the records that follow. Ordered, "That the Treasurer of the Western Shore pay to Dr. Charles Alexander Warfield, £400 to enable him to carry on a crude Nitre manufactory."

At a meeting of Delegates appointed by the several counties of Annapolis, on 26th of July, 1775, were Samuel Chase, Thomas Johnson, John Hall, Dr. Ephraim Howard, Charles Carroll, barrister; Charles Carroll, of Carrollton; Thomas Dorsey, Thomas Tillard and John Dorsey. Upon an adjournment to Thursday, July 27th, there were present, William Paca and Rezin Hammond, for Anne Arundel.

At a meeting of the inhabitants of Anne Arundel, on January 1775, the following were appointed upon the committee of observation, with full power to rule the county. They were Brice T. B. Worthington, John Hall, Matthias Hammond, Philemon Warfield, Nicholas Worthington, Thomas Jennings, Thomas Dorsey, John Hood, Jr., John Dorsey, Philip Dorsey, Ephraim Howard, Caleb Dorsey, Jr., Richard Stringer, Reuben Meriweather, Charles Warfield, Edward Gaither, Jr., Greenberry Ridgely, Ely Dorsey, John Burgess, Michael Pue, Edward Norwood, James Howard, Henry Ridgely, William Hammond, Thomas Hobbs, John Dorsey, son of Michael; Brice Howard, Edward Dorsey, son of John; Amos Davis, Elisha Warfield, John Dorsey, son of Severn John; Samuel Dorsey, son of Caleb; Joshua Griffith, Vachel Howard, Charles Hammond, son of John; Thomas Mayo.

On Friday, July 28th, Brice Thomas Beale Worthington was present for Anne Arundel and on Saturday, 29th, Matthias Hammond represented Anne Arundel.

"Resolved by the "Association of Freemen," on July 26, 1775, That four companies of Minute Men be raised in Anne Arundel, of sixty-eight men besides officers."

Thus was the ball set in motion for that year.

1776.

On January 20th it was resolved that registers of the Commissaires and Land Office and Clerks of the Provincial Court of Anne Arundel immediately furnish the Council of Safety with lists of record books in their respective offices and prepare for removal of the records and papers to such place as shall be directed by said Council."

Mr. John Brice delivered the Court and land record books and and judgment books.

"Resolved, That Charles Carroll, of "Carrollton," Thomas Dorsey and John Weems collect all the gold and silver that can be gotten in Anne Arundel in exchange for continental money for the use of Congress."

In 1776 commissions were issued by the Council of Safety to Thomas Tillard, First Major, and to Joseph Galloway, Second Major of the South River Battalion of Militia; Pollard Edmondson, Third Lieutenant in Fourth Independent Company; to Henry Hanslap, Captain; John Worthington (of Brice), First Lieutenant; Nicholas

Worthington, Second Lieutenant, and Gilbert Guldhall, Ensign of the Severn Militia.

"Ordered, That the records be removed to Rezin Gaither's house and there committed to the care of the clerks of Mr. John Brice."

The Council then sent a notice to Congress that gold and silver cannot be procured from the people without cash in Continental money.

Commissions issued to Joseph Maccubin, First Lieutenant, and Joshua Cromwell, Second Lieutenant, and Benjamin Wright, Ensign in Anne Arundel Militia. To Joseph Burgess, First Lieutenant; John Norwood, Second Lieutenant, and Thomas Cornelius Howard, Ensign in Captain Brice Howard's Company of Militia in Anne Arundel County. To Richard Weems, Captain; Gideon Dare, First Lieutenant; Joseph Allingham, Second Lieutenant, and Benjamin Harrison, Ensign of a company of militia in Anne Arundel.

The Council then corresponded with Mr. Samuel Dorsey, of Belmont, upon the subject of furnishing tents for the militia. Mr. Stephen Steward, of Anne Arundel, was requested to purchase the necessary militia stores of Annapolis Hospital according to the memorandum furnished by Dr. Tootell.

Colonel Thomas Dorsey, as one of the field officers of the Elk Ridge Battalion, recommended Levin Lawrence as First Lieutenant, Thomas Todd, Second Lieutenant, under Captain Thomas Watkins, Jr., of Colonel Weems' Battalion, agreeable to a resolve of the Convention.

John Weems, Richard Harwood, Jr., and Joseph Galloway, Field Officers, recommended Thomas Watkins as Captain and John I. Ijams as Ensign in one of the companies to be raised in Anne Arundel.

John Hall, Delegate of Anne Arundel, refused the office of Judge of Admiralty.

Samuel Barber, Adjutant of the Severn Battalion, was paid £20 for four months' service.

Commission issued to Thomas Mayo, Second Lieutenant in Captain John Boone's Company of Militia—Anne Arundel.

"Resolved, That the record books be removed from Annapolis on Wednesday next, if fair, to Mr. William Brown's house in London Town, and thence to Upper Marlborough, and that two gentlemen of the Committee of Observation be requested to attend the records.

Commission issued to Thomas Watkins, Captain; Thomas Noble Stockett, First Lieutenant; Samuel Watkins, Second Lieutenant; and William Harwood, Ensign of Company of militia of South River. To Abraham Simmons, Captain; Thomas Tongue, First Lieutenant; Thomas Morton, Second Lieutenant, and Abell Hill, Ensign of South River Company of Militia. To James Tootell, Captain; Philemon Warfield, First Lieutenant; Lancelot Warfield, Second Lieutenant, and Thomas Warfield, Ensign, of Company of Militia of the Severn. To George Watts, Captain; David Kerr, First Lieutenant; Joseph Maccubin, Second Lieutenant; Joshua Cromwell, Ensign, of Com-

pany of Militia of Anne Arundel.   To Vachel Gaither, Captain;
Absalom Anderson, First Lieutenant; Stephen Bosford, Second Lieutenant, and Thomas Fowler Bosford, Ensign, of Company belonging
to the Severn Battalion of Militia.

Ordered, That Colonel John Hall, of Anne Arundel, be requested
to detach a company of militia to guard the coast from Thomas Point
to Horn Point.

Ordered, That all citizens between Annapolis and St. Mary's
County be requested to give aid in getting the cannon and ammunition to St. George's Island in this county.

Commission issued to John Bullen, Captain; Benjamin Harwood,
First Lieutenant of Independent Company of Militia in Anne Arundel
County.   Anne Arundel Militia, Elk Ridge Battalion: Thomas Dor-
sey, Colonel; Mr. John Dorsey, Lieutenant Colonel; Dr. C. A. War-
field, First Major; Mr. Edward Gaither, Jr., Second Major; Benjamin
Howard, Quartermaster.   Severn Battalion: John Hall, Colonel;
Rezin Hammond, Lieutenant Colonel; Nicholas Worthington, First
Major; Elijah Robosson, Second Major; Worthington Hammond,
Quartermaster.   South River: John Weems, Colonel; Richard Har-
wood, Jr., Lieutenant Colonel; John Thomas, First Major; Thomas
Tillard, Second Major; Ed. Tillard, Quartermaster.

Passing over the busy preparations of the "Council of Safety,"
now at the helm, I will enter now upon the birth of our statehood
through the administration of our governors, all of whom helped to
make the history of Anne Arundel County.   To these will be added
the biographies of those families who have been makers of the history
of both counties.

GOVERNOR THOMAS JOHNSON.

Thomas Johnson, first Governor of Maryland, was born in Calvert
County, Maryland, on November 4, 1732.   He was the son of Thomas
and Dorcas (Sedgwick) Johnson, and grandson of Thomas Johnson,
of Yarmouth, who came in 1660.   He was a descendant of Sir Thomas
Johnson, of Great Yarmouth.   The family had been members of
Parliament since 1585.   Dorcas (Sedgwick) Johnson was the daughter
of Joshua, whose granddaughter married John Quincey Adams.

Removing to Frederick County, their son Thomas was there
educated.   At an early age he was sent to Annapolis and was
employed in the office of the Provincial Court.   There he studied law,
with Mr. Bordley, rising at once to distinction.   He was a member
of the First Continental Congress and upon every important committee.   His speech against the Stamp Act, full of patriotism, carried
conviction.   Upon his motion, George Washington was made Commander-in-Chief of the American forces in the United Colonies.   He
served until the 9th of November, 1776 upon the Committee of the
Constitution; he was appointed by Congress Brigadier-General of
the Frederick Militia, which was with Washington in the Jerseys,
and whilst in the field was elected Governor, 13th of February, 1777,

to succeed the Council of Safety. He was inaugurated 21st March, 1777, at the State House, Annapolis, as the first Republican Governor of Maryland. A great concourse of patriotic Marylanders witnessed the ceremony; three volleys were fired by the soldiers, with a salute of thirteen guns, followed by a sumptuous dinner and a ball at night.

Governor Johnson's first proclamation, calling out the militia, was in these words: "To defend our liberties requires our exertions; our wives, our children and our country implore our assistance. Motives amply sufficient to arm every one who can be called a man." The interior counties answered promptly. The Maryland Line was then engaged at Staten Island. Busy times had now dawned, and ₍Governor Johnson had almost dictatorial authority. The severe winter at Valley Forge had exhausted both magazines and supplies, and to keep up the necessary aid for the Quartermaster required the utmost energy of the Governor, yet by the middle of June the Maryland Line had its complement.

During his second term the contest between the House of Burgesses, which demanded higher pay and the Senate, which was too aristocratic to grant it, grew almost as exciting as the war in the field. Though Charles Carroll, of "Carrollton," made a forcible speech in opposition to granting the additional increase, the House was victorious. During that term, also, the first naturalization laws were passed. At the close of his second term, the limit of his eligibility, Governor Johnson was succeeded by Governor Thomas Sim Lee, in 1779. The General Assembly, upon his retirement, transmitted to him the following address:

"The prudence, assiduity, firmness and integrity with which you have discharged in times most critical, the duties of your late important station, have a just claim to our warm acknowledgement and sincere thanks."

He retired to Fredericktown but was soon returned to the House of Delegates; was appointed Chief Judge of the General Court and afterwards Associate Judge of the Supreme Court of United States.

He resigned it 1793, because of ill-health and for the same cause declined a position in Washington's Cabinet, but did accept the office of Commissioner of Washington City, in which he laid out the plans and fixed the site of the Capitol, President's house and other buildings.

He retired to "Rose Hill," near Frederick, the country-seat of his son-in-law, Colonel John Grahame, in October, 1819. His wife, whom he had married in 1766, was Ann Jennings, only daughter of Thomas Jennings, of Annapolis, who died early, leaving five children. His daughter, Ann Jennings Johnson, became Mrs. John Grahame, with whom he spent the last days of his life.

In 1800, Governor Johnson performed his last public act at Frederick, in the delivery of an eulogy upon Washington. He was of middle stature, slender in person, with keen, penetrating eyes and an intelligent countenance. He had a warm, generous heart, and was a kind husband and father. He died October 26, 1819, at "Rose

Hill," eighty-seven years of age, and, before an immense conclave of citizens, was buried in the Episcopal burial ground of Frederick overlooking a beautiful valley. "Between the hills of Linganore and Catoctin, he sleeps long and well."

When John Adams was asked why so many Southern men held leading positions, he replied, "If it had not been for such men as Richard Henry Lee, Thomas Jefferson, Samuel Chase and Thomas Johnson, there never would have been any revolution."

Governor Johnson's portrait, taken when young, hangs in the State House at Annapolis. The late Mrs. Ross, his granddaughter, by will, has made the Maryland Historical Society guardian of all his public papers and mementoes, until the home of his adoption shall prepare a suitable place for their safe keeping.

Colonel Baker Johnson, son of Governor Thomas Johnson, was a member of the Convention of Maryland, which met in Annapolis 21st June, 1776. He commanded a battalion at Paoli, near Philadelphia. His wife was Catharine Worthington, daughter of Colonel Nicholas and Catharine (Griffith) Worthington, of "Summer Hill," Anne Arundel. Their daughter, Catharine Worthington Johnson, married William Ross, an eminent lawyer of Frederick.

Charles Worthington Johnson, son of Colonel Baker Johnson, married Elinor Murdock Tyler, of Frederick. Their son is General Bradley Tyler Johnson, late of Virginia. Mrs. Colonel Dennis, of Frederick, is a granddaughter.

GOVERNOR THOMAS SIM LEE.

Thomas Sim Lee, second and seventh Governor of Maryland, born in Maryland, 1743, descended from Colonel Richard Lee, the progenitor of Virginia, through his grandson, Philip Lee, who came to Maryland. Thomas Sim Lee was the son of Thomas and Christian (Sim) Lee, daughter of Dr. Patrick Sim and Mary Brooke, greatgranddaughter of Robert Brooke, the commander.

Thomas Sim Lee was educated in Europe. In 1777, October 27, he was married to Miss Mary Digges. In November 8, 1779, he was elected Governor to succeed Thomas Johnson. His opponent was Revolutionary Edward Lloyd.

Governor Lee's proclamation upon the urgent necessity of supplying flour and forage for the army enjoined all justices, sheriffs and their deputy constables, to exert themselves in procuring provisions. The effect of the proclamation was instantaneously successful and provisions were sent to the needy army. The Legislature also passed an act calling into service 1,400 men to serve three years, or during the war, at the end of which term recruits were to receive fifty acres of land, whilst the county Courts were authorized to draw upon their county treasurers for the maintenance of the needy families of these recruits. Colonel Williams wrote from the South concerning our Maryland troops in these words:

"Absolutely without pay, almost destitute of clothing, often with only half ration and never a whole one, not a soldier was heard to murmur."

Colonel Otho Holland Williams was then placed at the head of the brigade of the Maryland Line, and from it four companies of picked men were made into a light infantry battalion under Lieutenant-Colonel John Eager Howard. The Maryland troops now arrived and filled the gap made by the withdrawal of Colonel Howard's battalion.

When the State was thus embarrassed to meet the demands of the army, the Legislature, under Governor Lee, set an example by subscribing each according to his means, a magnificent sum, which had its effect in corresponding subscriptions throughout the State. Governor Lee's uncle, Joseph Sim, contributed 500 hogsheads of tobacco. The prompt and generous response of the planters of Maryland, many of whom were equally as liberal, saved the army.

A Congressional Committee having been appointed in June, 1780, to urge the Governors of each State to call out an additional quota of troops and supplies, General Washington accompanied their appeal by a letter asking for immediate attention. Maryland's quota was four regiments of 2,205, to he located at the head of the Elk River. Governor Lee immediately laid it before the Assembly. The reply of that Assembly deserves to be written in letters of gold.

"We propose to exert our utmost endeavors to raise 2,000 regulars, to serve during the war. It will be necessary to draw from our battalions under Baron de Kalb a number of officers to command, form and discipline these new recruits."

General Washington, having accepted this proposal, the Assembly issued this stirring appeal:

"Rise into action with that ardor which led you, destitute of money, of allies, of arms and soldiers, to encounter one of the most powerful nations of Europe, single and unsupported, raw and undisciplined, you baffled for three successive years the repeated attacks—now, when strengthened by a mighty alliance, shall we droop and desert the field to which honor, the strongest ties, the dearest interests of humanity unite us? We have hitherto done our duty; the General has acknowledged our exertions, and we entreat you by all that is dear to freemen not to forfeit the reputation you have so justly acquired.

"Our army is weak, and reinforced it must be. Let us, like the Romans of old, draw new resources and an increase of courage even to brave defeats, and manifest to the world that we are the most to be dreaded when most depressed."

To this eloquent appeal, Maryland made a noble response. Recruits, provisions and supplies of all kinds, were offered and at the required time her quota of 2,065 gallant men had been added to the Continental Army. To the South all eyes were now directed, for Gates, whose laurels had been won in the North, was now about to cast the darkest shadows of gloom upon his campaign in the South.

In the following August came the announcement which General Washington transmitted in September to Governor Lee. "Sir, In consequence of the disagreeable intelligence of the defeat of the army under Major General Gates, which I have just received, I think it expedient to countermand the march of the troops who were ordered from Maryland to join the main army. I am, therefore, to request your Excellency to give directions for the regiment enlisted to serve during the war, as well as for all recruits, as soon as they can possibly be collected and organized, to march immediately to the southward, and put themselves under the orders of the commanding officer in that department. And I can not entertain a doubt that your Excellency and the State will use every exertion to give activity and dispatch to the march of the troops with all measures necessary for the protection of the Southern States."

Governor Lee sent in answer to this demand, seven hundred rank and file to the Southern Army.

Nor did the patriotic efforts end with her public men. Mrs. Mary Lee, wife of the Governor, as the representative of the voluntary efforts of the patriotic women of Maryland, wrote to Washington for advice as to the most acceptable mode of expending the contributions of these organizations.

The following reply shows his appreciation:

HEAD QUARTERS, 11th October, 1780

Madam:

"I am honored with your letter of the 27th of September, and cannot forbear taking the earliest moment to express the high sense I entertain of the patriotic exertions of the women of Maryland in favor of the army. In answer to your inquiry respecting the disposal of the gratuity, I must take the liberty to observe that it appears to me the money which has been, or may be collected, can not be expended in so eligible and beneficial a manner as in the purchase of shirts and black stocks for the use of the troops in the Southern Army. The polite offer you are pleased to make of your further assistance in the execution of this liberal design, and the generous disposition of the ladies, insures me of its success and cannot fail to entitle both yourself and them the warmest gratitude of those who are the object of it."

General Greene having now, October 5, 1780, superceded General Gates, on his way South, stopped at Annapolis and with a letter of introduction from General Washington to Governor Lee, waited upon him and was entertained at his house. Having urged both the Governor and the Legislature to assist him in recruiting the army, and trusting them to furnish "all the assistance in their power," leaving General Gist to take charge of Maryland and Delaware recruits, General Greene pushed on South.

In 1780, the House again brought forth "An Act to seize, confiscate and appropriate all British property within the State," followed by an appeal and an indictment against the British Government in its mode of carrying on the war. Charles Carroll, of "Carrollton" and Joseph Sim, the uncle of Governor Lee, were both opposed to confiscation, deeming it inexpedient, yet so great was the necessity of the occasion, the Senate yielded and passed it. Thus, with an increase of ten million of dollars to carry on the war; with its Governor exerting every nerve to keep up the quota of the State, Maryland stood in the foreground of the perilous period, claiming one-half of the army then in General Greene's service in the South. Discouragement sat supreme mistress over National and State prospects, yet in the midst of this gloom, two heroic figures rose above the trials. Greene at the front and Lee, at Annapolis, with Otho Williams and John Eager Howard in the command of the Maryland Line. Upon these four men, sustained and soothed by the unfaltering patriotism of the Maryland Assembly, rest to-day most of the glory of that masterly campaign, of the South, begun in gloom, carried on by retreats, unfaltering in every trial, but ending at last in a well-earned, glorious fruition.

General Greene in his official report of Eutaw Springs, said: "The Marylanders under Colonel Williams, were led on to a brisk charge, with trailed arms, through a heavy cannonade and a shower of musket balls. Nothing could excell the gallantry and firmness of both officers and soldiers upon this occasion. I cannot help acknowledging my obligations to Colonel Williams for his great activity on this and many other occasions, in forming the army, and for his uncommon intrepidity in leading on the Maryland troops to the charge, which exceeded anything I ever saw."

In 1781, the people of Dorchester County, through their committee, Robert Goldsborough and Gustavus Scott, having addressed Governor Lee for assistance in arms and ammunition necessary for their militia, to meet the ever present demands for protection from maraudings. Governor Lee laid the subject before the Legislature, and they passed "an Act to collect arms."

In February, 1781, Governor Lee received from General Washington information of the movement of Lafayette's corps through Maryland and requesting his assistance in furnishing the necessary provisions, forage, wagons and vessels.

Governor Lee, upon Lafayette's arrival at the head of the Elk, wrote to him. "We have ordered all the vessels at Baltimore and this port to be impressed and sent to the head of the Elk to transport the detachment under your command, and have directed six hundred barrels of bread to be forwarded to them. The State will most cheerfully make every exertion to give force and efficacy to the present important expedition by every measure in our power."

In another letter to Lafayette, the Governor added, "We have prepared a dispatch boat to convey your letter to the Commanding Officer, near Portsmouth, which will be sent off as soon as the winds will permit; and have given directions to the Master to throw it overboard if he should be in danger of being taken."

The Governor and Council also dispatched a messenger down the bay to give information of the arrival of the French fleet and beacon signals were raised for the shores.   A chain of riders were to go through the State as special messengers.

The pressing needs of the State were now to be seen in Governor Lee's letter to the citizens of Baltimore, who had come to his assistance in supplying the wants of Lafayette's corps. "We very much applaud the zeal and activity of the gentlemen of Baltimore, and think their readiness to assist the executive at a time when they were destitute of the means of providing those things which were immediately necessary for the detachment under the command of the Marquis de Lafayette, justly entitle them to the thanks of the public."   "We cannot but approve of the proceedings of those gentlemen and assure you we will adopt any expedient to prevent any individual of that body from suffering or being in the least embarassed by his engagements for the State.   We think it reasonable the State should pay the value of money advanced with interest thereon, and will give an order on the collectors of Baltimore for their reimbursement."

Governor Lee, also wrote to Governor Jefferson, of Virginia, asking him to assist in sending the necessary transports to the head of the Elk.   Lafayette in his letter to Washington, acknowledged Maryland's help as follows: "The State of Maryland have made me every offer in their power; Mr. McHenry has been very active in accelerating the measures of his State."

As a result, pretty much all of the necessary equipments and nearly one hundred transports for Lafayette's corps, had come out of Maryland, through her Governor and citizens.

The successful arrival of Lafayette's fleet in the harbor of Annapolis, was on the 13th of March, and on the 15th, Governor Lee announced to Governor Jefferson—"The arrival of our express, with Your Excellency's letter of the 12th, this moment received, gives me an opportunity of informing you, that all the transports with the troops from Elk got safe into Harbor, on Tuesday morning, March 13th."   The next morning at daylight, two ships, apparently British, of the rate of eighteen and twenty-eight guns, came to an anchor opposite the mouth of our River Severn.   We judged that you would be anxious for the safety of the troops, but they are fortunately safe and the armed vessels, which conveyed them down are prepared for defence.

The French fleet's failure in arriving at Portsmouth led Lafayette back to the Elk and the threatening attempts in the Chesapeake became now the paramount concern of Governor Lee and his council. Baltimore took advantage of the Legislature's "Act to embody a number of select militia and for immediately putting the State in a proper posture of defence."   The Western Shore was authorized to select 1,200 men and the Eastern Shore 800 militia—subject to the call of the Governor—all in addition to the Act "to procure recruits," amounting to 1,000 men for the war, which was supplemented by another "for the defence of the bay," which enabled the Governor to purchase a galley, and have one built, equipped and manned.   He was also empowered to fit out barges to the number of eight. In April, Governor Lee wrote to Lafayette upon the threatening attitude of six of the enemy's ships upon the Potomac, in having destroyed private property and now proceeding to Alexandria, with a view of destroying it. "The Military stores and provisions at this place and Baltimore town, must be a capital object, and as we have the strongest reasons to think, as soon as they have perpetrated their designs in Potomac, if not before, they will visit this city and Baltimore. Under these circumstances, we beg leave to submit to your consideration the propriety of detaining your detachment in this State and marching such part as you may deem necessary, to our assistance in Baltimore town and in this city."

Two days after, General Lafayette replied: "However inadequate I am to the defence of Annapolis, Baltimore and Alexandria at once, I will hasten to the point that will be nearest to those three places, I request your Excellency to furnish me speedy, minute and frequent intelligence." "It will be necessary that a collection of wagons and horses be made at Baltimore, and I beg your Excellency will please order a quantity of live cattle and flour be also collected at that place; I hope Sir, that precautions will be taken for the safety of the stores now at or near Indian Landing."

Arriving at Baltimore a few days after, Lafayette borrowed from its citizens, upon his own personal credit, for it was better than that of Congress, the sum of ten thousand dollars for supplying his army. Congress, however, in May following, in appreciation of this generous act, Resolved, "That the Marquis de Lafayette be assured that Congress will take the proper measures to discharge the engagements he entered into with the merchants." In the old Assembly room, of Baltimore, when the most distinguished ladies and gentlemen of that city had honored him with a ball, he again brought patriotism to the test in that memorable reply to the lady, who asked the cause of his sadness, "I cannot enjoy the gayety of the scene while so many of my poor soldiers are in want of clothes." As the noble women of Baltimore lately met a similar call, so did the words of a patriotic lady that historic night kindle the fire which ceased not to burn until its necessity no longer existed. "We will supply them," was the response and all history knows how well she kept her promise. The ragged and wearied troops left Elk Ridge Landing with new outfits and new hopes, but Marylanders were yet once more to be called to the rescue.

Lafayette finding Cornwallis making an attempt to get in his rear, felt he could not risk an engagement and so retreated toward Maryland. Again the watchful eyes of Governor Lee were on the outlook. Exhausted, but still patriotic, he addressed Congress thus: "The extraordinary exertions made by this State on every occasion in complying with the demands of Congress, the Marquis detachment, the Southern Army, our militia and other expenditures have altogether exhausted our treasury and stores of arms and clothing, so that it is not in our power to furnish the troops with clothing and arms, nor properly equip our militia to repel the enemy. Under these distressing circumstances, we request you to make known our wants to Congress in the most earnest manner and endeavor to obtain the proportion of all clothing, arms, etc., that Congress now or may hereafter have for this State."

On the following day, the Governor and Council sent out this circular letter to the counties.

"From the intelligence we have received of the rapid movements of the enemy in Virginia, we have reason to apprehend an invasion of this State; and it will be necessary that every precaution be taken preparative for our defence. We, therefore, request you to order the militia in your county to hold themselves in perfect readiness to march at a moment's warning to such places as may be necessary, and to have all the arms in your county proper for defence, immediately repaired and put in best condition, cartridges made and everything ready to take the field." In answer to this urgent appeal, Baltimore was put on the defence: Smallwood and Gist collected the militia, which came pouring in from all the counties. Rushing these troops of horse and unequipped militia to the front, Lafayette with Wayne's corps now turned upon the enemy marching toward Richmond. Cornwallis began that retreat which was finally to end in surrender.

In August, General Lafayette wrote to Governor Lee what his apprehensions were, and Governor Lee in a letter to General Andrew Buchanan in charge of the militia of Baltimore County, thus expressed them:

"From information just received from Marquis and Dr. McHenry, we are no longer in doubt of the designs of the enemy. They are certainly destined for Baltimore Town or the head of the Bay. Now must the State of Maryland exert herself. We confide in your skill and activity. We have directed the Lieutenant of Frederick County to order his troops of horse and all their select militia to your assistance, and have enclosed commission for troops. The Marquis with his army is moving this way. The Lieutenant of Harford has directions to order the militia of that county to be in readiness to march when ordered." At the same time, Governor Lee sent his information to the President of Congress, in which he added that, "We have taken every possible precaution to prevent the stores and provisions and valuable property belonging to the Continent and State falling into their hands." However, both General Lafayette and Governor Lee were mistaken as to the destination of Cornwallis. A destination to end in gloom—and Governor Lee at once wrote to Colonel Samuel Smith at Baltimore, who discharged the militia. As a fitting compliment and full appreciation of the executive watchfulness of Governor Lee, let me quote the words of General Washington to the Governor in reply to an earlier letter of June 29th.

"I have the honor to acknowledge the receipt of your Excellency's favor. It is with great satisfaction I observe the proceedings of the general assembly of 'your State, which you have been pleased to communicate to me, the exertions of that Legislature have hitherto been laudable and I am exceedingly glad to see the same spirit still prevailing. For my own part, I have not a doubt but that if the States were to exert themselves with that spirit and vigor which might reasonalby be expected at this favorable period, they might not only drive from the Continent the remains of the British, but obtain to themselves their independence, an event which you will be assured I most evidently wish." Now began the the culmination of vital movements in Maryland, which aided by the arrival of French support was to bring out of trials the glory of results.

General Washington from afar off was mapping out the final scene of tragedy, knowing that upon General Lafayette in Virginia and Governor Lee in Maryland, all his plans would be carried out and thus revealed his movements and thus were they carried out by the Governor of Maryland, in his circular letter to the Commissaries of the counties.

"A detachment of the main army with the French troops to the number of 7,000 men, will be at the head of the Elk, in eight days, on their way to Virginia to act against Lord Cornwallis. General Washington has written us very pressingly for an immediate and large supply of fresh provisions, we therefore direct you to procure by purchase, beef cattle, preferring those parts of your country which are most exposed to the ravages of the enemy; and in case the owners will not consent to sell them upon the terms prescribed by the Act for procuring an immediate supply of clothing and fresh provisions, you will seize them agreeably to the Act, to procure a supply of salt meat, passed June, 1780." Five thousand seven hundred cattle were enumerated as the contributions from the different counties, and minute directions for the storing of salt provisions were made by the Governor together with specified places for money contributions. In addition, warrants were issued to the quarter masters empowering them to impress all vessels capable of transporting troops or stores.

Nor did Governor Lee stop there, but in a letter to General Washington, August 30th, thus assures him of his support: "We are honored by your Excellency's letter of the 27th, and we receive with the greatest satisfaction the intelligence of the approach of the fleet of our generous ally. You may rely, Sir, on every exertion that is possible for us to make, to accelerate the movements of the army on an expedition, the success of which must hasten the establishment of the independence of America and relieve us of the calamities of war. Orders have been issued to impress every vessel belonging to the State and forwarding them without delay to the head of the Elk, but we are sorry to inform your Excellency that since the enemy has had possession of the bay, our number of sea vessels and craft has been so reduced by captures that we are apprehensive what remains will not transport so considerable a detachment. We have directed the State officers to procure immediately 5,000 cattle and a large quantity of flour. There is very little salt provisions in the State; what can be obtained, we trust will be collected." Then follows the information as to the place of deposit.

To Robert Morris, Governor Lee wrote: "Everything that is within our power and within the exhausted abilities of this State, shall be done cheerfully and immediately to promote and render effectual the expedition which his Excellency, General Washington, has formed against the enemy in Virginia, in which we are fully sensible, the care and safety of this State in particular is deeply interested."

These were stirring days in Maryland. The arrival of Washington in Baltimore and the arrival of the French fleet in the Chesapeake brought rays of hope and abounding patriotism. Governor Lee's pen was almost incessantly at work urging the State officers to their duty. Writes he again in a circular letter: "There never has been a time which required of the State more than the present. The fate of Lord Cornwallis and his army will, in a measure depend upon them. Relying on your patriotism, zeal and activity, we trust you will do everything in your power to procure the cattle here before ordered. Not a moment is to be lost; and to enable you to act with more facility and to ease the inhabitants, we have sent you: To Somerset, £1,700; Worcester, £1,700; Dorchester, £1,100; Talbot, £950; Caroline, £350; Queen Anne's, £950; Kent, £800; Cecil, £950; Harford, £800; Baltimore, £1,100; Anne Arundel, £500; Prince George, £500; Charles, St. Mary's and Calvert, £500; Montgomery, £800; Frederick, £1,100; Washington, £800."

Washington, having sent an urgent message to Governor Lee to hurry on the troops with all despatch, Governor Lee, on September 9th replied, "Your Excellency's address of the 15th is this moment presented to us. We are truly happy to be informed that the Count DeGrasse is returned to his station and that our vessels may pass down the bay without hazard. We feel your Excellency's distress from an apprehension that your operations may cease or be impeded for want of provisions, and the more so because we can't instantly furnish you. In consequence of your requisition we directed our commissaries to collect all the public flour and deposit it at convenient places on navigable water, all the vessels of the State being impressed and now employed in transporting the troops to the point of destination, puts it out of our power to forward the flour on that service. The number of beeves we agreed to furnish your Excellency may depend upon."

The next day Governor Lee wrote to Colonel Moses Rawlings, of Frederick County, conveying the urgent necessity for haste in collecting the stores and forwarding the same to Georgetown.

Thus in sight almost of the final and victorious end of a struggle in which Governor Lee was the great war horse of the Revolution, the closing acts of administration were recorded. Having served his allotted time, William Paca, at the next Assembly, was called to the Governor's chair. The House and Senate, upon Governor Lee's retirement, thus addressed him:

"Your close attention to the public welfare, and your firm, unshaken conduct in times of greatest danger, are proofs that the confidence of your country has not been misplaced. Accept this public testimony of our appreciation and our sincerest thanks for the zeal, activity and firmness with which you have so faithfully discharged the duties of your station."

Governor Lee, in response said: "I feel myself happy in having executed the powers intrusted to me to the satisfaction of my country."

During the closing days of his term, Governor Lee entertained with special ceremony, the French officers visiting Annapolis, and for this the Assembly again addressed, in complimentary terms. Governor Lee's munificent entertainments were a heavy drain upon his income, and at his wife's suggestion, he declined another election.

"Lady Lee" was the name of his vessel launched at Annapolis.

Thomas Sim Lee was a delegate to the Continental Congress in 1783-4, and a member of the Convention which ratified the Constitution. In 1792 he was again called to the Governor's chair to fill the unexpired term of Governor George Plater, who retired from ill-health. This embraced the exciting whiskey insurrection in 1794, during which he organized the militia and sent Maryland's quota to the scene. He spent his declining years at "Needwood," Frederick County, afterward the home of Mr. John Lee, his oldest son, and grandfather of Ex-Governor John Lee Carroll. It is still the homestead of the Lee family, represented by Mr. Thomas Sim Lee, who married a daughter of Mr. Columbus O'Donnell.

In 1812 Hon. Outerbridge Horsey, United States Senator from Delaware, married Eliza, daughter of Thomas Sim Lee; Mrs. Governeour was also a granddaughter.

Governor Lee died at "Needwood," November 9, 1819, in the seventy-fifth year, in the same year and nearly the same month as that of his predecessor, Governor Johnson.

GOVERNOR WILLIAM PACA.

William Paca, signer of Declaration and third Governor of Maryland, was born October 31, 1740, at "Wye Hall," Harford County, Maryland. He was the second son of John Paca; Bachelor of Arts from a college in Philadelphia in 1758 he was admitted to Middle Temple, London, after which he studied law with Stephen Bordley. He was admitted to the bar in 1764. Early in life he was sent to the Legislature, was a delegate to the Continental Congress in 1774-1778, was appointed upon the Committee of Correspondence in 1774, was in the Council of Safety in 1775. On August 2, 1776, he affixed his signature to the Declaration of Independence; on August 17, 1776 was elected on the Committee "to prepare a declaration and charter of rights and a form of government for Maryland." Upon the organization of the State he was elected to its first Senate.

In March, 1778, he was appointed Chief Judge of the General Court of Maryland and held it until 1781; subsequently he was Chief Judge of the Court of Appeals and Admiralty. In November, 1782, he was elected the third Governor of Maryland to succeed Thomas Sim Lee.

During Governor Paca's early administration General Greene received from the General Assembly a flattering address upon his masterly retreats which had proven to be victories, to be crowned, still later, by the modest message from the Commander-in Chief, sent by a Marylander, announcing the end of the struggle. It read:

"I have the honor to inform Congress that a reduction of the British army under Lord Cornwallis, is most happily effected."

This message was placed in the hands of Colonel Tilghman, who immediately started out for Philadelphia. At midnight the clatter of his horse's hoofs was the only sound that woke the silence as he rode rapidly to the house of the President of Congress with the announcement "Cornwallis is taken." It was caught up by the watchmen, who cried, " One o'clock, and Cornwallis is taken." The inhabitants, pouring into the streets, sent shout after shout into the air. The old bellman was aroused from his slumbers, and again the same old bell proclaimed "Liberty throughout the land to all the inhabitants thereof."

On April 12, 1783, Robert R. Livingston wrote to Governor Paca asking his support to the stipulations of the treaty of peace.

On 22nd of April Governor Paca issued his proclamation declaring a cessation of arms by sea and land, enjoining obedience to the treaty. On 25th of November he addressed the sheriffs to read the treaty in public places. At Annapolis, when the sheriff had assembled the people and had read the treaty, thirteen cannon were fired and a public dinner was given, at which Governor Paca presided. Thirteen patriotic toasts were offered, each attended by the discharge of thirteen cannon. At night the State House was illuminated and a ball given to the ladies.

On May 6, 1783, Governor Paca placed before the General Assembly the preliminary Articles of Peace, congratulating the Assembly on the return of peace and paying a high tribute to the army.

The old Maryland Line, five hundred strong, now returned in rags. Brigadier-General Gist was in command.

General Greene wrote to Governor Paca repeating the high compliment to The Maryland Line. General Greene's diary recorded, "Left 26th, dined with the Governor, who is a very polite character and a great friend of the army. We drank several toasts which were accompanied by the discharge of thirteen cannon." He also addressed a letter to Governor Paca thanking him for the support of the Maryland troops.

In May, 1783, Congress left Princeton and in December assembled at Annapolis by the invitation of the Governor and General Assembly, the Governor giving up his house to the President of

Congress.   His house stood on the northeast side of Prince George near East Street, and was afterward held by Chancellor Bland.   Its garden, springhouse, expanse of trees, octagonal two-story summer-house, representing "My Lady's Bower," with artificial brook, revealed the happy life of that era.

On the 19th of December, General Washington arrived at Annapolis.   A public reception and a welcome by Governor Paca followed.   On 23rd December, 1783, General Washington laid down his commission in the old Senate Chamber before Governor Paca and his Council, the Assembly and general public, and on the 14th of January, 1784, Governor Paca proclaimed to the people the treaty of Peace as ratified by Congress.

Then was organized the order of the "Cincinnati," with Governor Paca as a delegate.

Ex-Governor Eden having now returned and having made effort to issue patents to parties who had taken out lands before his forced exile, Governor Paca asked for an explanation and matters were satisfactorily explained.

In 1781, Governor Paca, at the request of the Assembly, employed Mr. Francis Deakins to survey lots of fifty acres for the Maryland soldiers, west of Fort Cumberland.

Governor Paca was the special friend of Washington College and secured its charter rights.

At the expiration of his term he was succeeded by Governor William Smallwood, the war governor.

In 1774 Governor Paca was elected Vice-President of the Society of the "Cincinnati" and a member of the Maryland Convention that ratified the Constitution of the United States.

In December, 1789, he was appointed, by Washington, Judge of the United States Court of the District of Maryland and served until his death in 1799.   His wife was Mary Chew, daughter of Samuel and Henrietta Maria (Lloyd) Chew.

One of Governor Paca's daughters married Consul Roubelle, who, with Napoleon, ruled France.   Their son bore such a striking likeness to the accepted ideals of our Saviour he was often called on by artists to sit for such studies.

Governor Paca's son, John, built the magnificent Paca homestead.   He married Juliana Tilghman, now represented in the Razin family of Kent County.

A striking portrait of Governor Paca hangs in the State House at Annapolis.   He died at his birth-place, a pure and zealous patriot with a character that was spotless.

His widow became Mrs. Daniel Dulany, whose son Lloyd was slain in a duel with Rev. Bennett Allen, in a London park.

GOVERNOR WILLIAM SMALLWOOD.

Governor William Smallwood, fourth Governor of Maryland, was born in Kent County, Maryland, 1732.   He was the son of Bayne Smallwood, a merchant and large planter, who was presiding officer

in the Court of Common Pleas and a member of the House of
Burgesses. His mother was Priscilla Heaberd, of Virginia, a lady
of family and fortune.

At an early age he was sent to England to be educated. He
completed his education at Eton.

On April 24, 1775, Colonel Smallwood, with a command of 1,444
men, left Annapolis for Boston. Smallwood's command was
incorporated with Lord Stirling's brigade and was in the Battle of
Long Island.

The following tribute to our Marylanders who were with Stirling
at Long Island, is taken from the Century Magazine:

"Sullivan's division was in wild rout and Stirling's left had been
doubled back upon his centre, when he resolved upon a ghastly
sacrifice to save the flying, floundering columns. Changing front
and calling forward the remnant of the Maryland regiment—less than
four hundred lads, tenderly nurtured, who now, for the first time,
knew the rapture of battle—he hurled them against the iron wall
that Cornwallis had drawn about the Cortelyou house. Loud and
clear rang the shout of Mordecai Gist, "Close up! Close up!" They
drove the British advance back upon the Cortelyou house till
Cornwallis flung grape and cannister into their very faces. Every
page of sober history has its tribute of proud love for those heroic
lads, whose fate wrung from Washington his undying exclamation of
anguish—"Great God! what brave boys I must this day lose!"

Thus our Maryland boys covered themselves with glory by
repeated charges upon an overwhelming force. They practically
destroyed themselves to save the Continental Army. They made
five bayonet charges against Cornwallis' brigade. Upon the sixth
charge the brigade recoiled and gave way in confusion. The
Marylanders were outnumbered two to one.

Assaulted by Hessians, and a British brigade in the rear, Lord
Stirling, with a portion, surrendered, but three companies cut their
way through the British ranks, swam the creek and in that charge
the 400 lost 256 officers and men. They were engaged from sunrise
August 27, 1776, till the last gun was fired and maintained the battle
unaided against the brigades of the enemy. Four days later they
were at Fort Putnam, within two hundred and fifty yards of the
enemy's line.

Colonel Smallwood's regiment, in the following month, at
Washington's request after others had deserted him, covered
Washington's withdrawal into lines below Fort Washington. They
attacked the enemy, drove them from their position and were in full
pursuit when recalled.

Smallwood was engaged at White Plains. He met the
Hessians under Rawle, under the fire of fifteen British cannon;
Smallwood was wounded, and with a loss of 100 men, fell back in
good order.

The Maryland Line was at Trenton and Princeton. Washington's
record of them was, "Smallwood's troops had been reduced to a mere

handful of men, but they took part in the engagement with their usual gallantry and won great renown."

The next campaign Maryland added 4,000 more to the army—one-tenth of the whole army—and the Line was in October increased by 2,000 more.

In August, 1777, they were at Staten Island, with the first brigade under Smallwood. They took 141 British prisoners. The Line was at Brandywine, on the right wing. At Germantown they advanced with such resolution that British Light Infantry were driven from the field and their encampment taken. They there received the highest encomiums, and the gallant defence of Fort Mifflin closed the year.

That winter Smallwood's men, of 1,400 in number, were stationed at Wilmington and there captured a British vessel.

In 1778, 2,902 more men were added to the army, whilst Count Pulaski raised an independent corps in Maryland.

Smallwood was at Monmouth. The British were driven back with a loss of 300 men killed outright. When Sir Henry Clinton left the field for New York, in 1779, Smallwood, with The Maryland Line, met the British at Scotch Plains and again drove them back.

In 1780 the Line marched south; Smallwood returned to Maryland and in ten days secured 700 non-commissioned officers and privates. He was retained in the army as second in command.

For his action at Camden he received the thanks of Congress and a promotion to Major-General. On account of a conflict of authority and a personal dislike for Baron Steuben, General Smallwood remained in Maryland.

In 1785, he was elected to Congress and in November of that year, was made Governor to succeed William Paca. During Governor Smallwood's administration, King Wiillam's School at Annapolis was consolidated with St. John's College with £32,100 by private subscription and an annual endowment of £1,750 sterling current money.

The first movement for the improvement of the Potomac River was begun by General Washington, in 1784, which ended in an enactment, in 1785, the first internal improvement which after repeated trials, ended in 1820, in the formation of the Canal.

The first steamboat upon the Potomac, the conception of James Burney, was run from Shepardstown to Harpers Ferry, during Governor Smallwood's term, in 1786. During his term were adopted the methods of paying the National debt created by the war.

The first navigation of the Chesapeake and Potomac led up to the discussions which became the germs which brought forth a new Constitution, upon the failures of the Federal compact; and in 1786, at Annapolis, a Convention of five States made the move for a Convention to revise the Federal Constitution. Maryland had declined to be represented unless all the States agreed to send delegates. The result of the Annapolis Convention was the united action of

Maryland and Virginia in urging the Philadelphia Convention, which gave us our new Constitution.

Governor Smallwood was succeeded in 1788, by Governor John Eager Howard, his associate in revolutionary fame. Retiring to his home, now in Charles County, he lived only four years, dying in 1792, February 14th, at "Mattawoman," a celebrated colonial homestead, built of English brick and is still standing lamenting the seeming indifference of a busy age to the fate of dead heroes.

McSherry has said, "But the memory of Smallwood seems nearly forgotten, and on his paternal estate now in the hands of strangers, he sleeps in a lonely grave, by the waters of the Potomac, almost in sight of the tomb of his great leader at Mt. Vernon, near him in death as he adhered to him in life. Faithful, modest, brave, and patient in life, he sleeps in death unhonored, without a tombstone on the spot, or an enclosure to protect his last resting place from desecration."

The Sons of the Revolution, since the above was written, have erected a fitting memorial to the memory of the Maryland hero, in the form of a granite tablet recording his deeds of valor. It stands within a few yards of his old homestead, overlooking a vast stretch of country. Governor Smallwood never married.

His only sister married Colonel William Grayson, of Virginia. There were several sons and one daughter Mrs. Carter, of Kentucky, whose sons were William Grayson and Alfred G. Carter. Alfred Grayson married Miss Breckinridge, of Kentucky, aunt of Vice-President John C. Breckinridge and left a son, Colonel John Breckinridge Grayson, head of the Commissary in the Mexican War.

In 1827, it was found that Colonel William Grayson, eldest son of William Grayson was entitled by entail to the whole estate of General Smallwood, no transfer having taken place; Colonel Grayson was at the head of the column, when Washington upbraided General Charles Lee and he heard and related these words of Lee to Washington. "Sir, these troops are not able to meet British Grenadiers"—and Washington's reply, "Sir, they are able and they shall do it"—immediately giving the order to counter-march the column.

GOVERNOR JOHN EAGER HOWARD.

Governor John Eager Howard, soldier and fifth Governor of Maryland, was born in Baltimore County, June 4, 1752. He was the son of Cornelius and Ruth (Eager) Howard, daughter of John and Jemina (Murray) Eager. His grandfather was Joshua Howard, of Manchester, England, who was an officer in the army of the Duke of York during the Monmouth Rebellion. Coming to Maryland about 1685, he married Joanna O'Carroll, of Ireland, and took up a tract of land near Pikesville, Baltimore County.

At the time of the Revolution the Howard family were large land-holders and wealthy. John Eager Howard was educated by private tutors. Coming to manhood at the beginning of the Revolution, he was offered a commission as Colonel, but thinking he was too inexperienced, declined it, accepting a Captaincy upon the condition of being able to raise thirty men. He enlisted that number in two days and marched at once to the front. His company was made a part of the "Flying Camp" and was with General Hugh Mercer at White Plains, October 28, 1776. Commissioned Major in the fourth Maryland Regiment, he was at Germantown and Monmouth.

In 1780, Georgia and South Carolina being in the hands of the British, Maryland's First Brigade under Major General de Kalb, marched south with an additional regiment raised in the State.

At Camden, Gist's Maryland Brigade stood firm as a rock and William's Regiment, with Howard at its head, broke upon the enemy and severed his front, driving the opposing corps before them.

In 1781, 400 of the Maryland Line, under Lieutenant Colonel Howard fought with General Morgan at the Cowpens. The British were under Tarlton. The latter assailed the Marylanders, but they never faltered. Tarlton ordered his reserves: this endangered Howard's right. Morgan ordered Howard to change front and take a new position. Howard had not gained that position, when Tarlton mistaking it for a retreat, rushed forward. Suddenly facing about, Howard poured into the enemy a deadly fire. Their ranks recoiled. Howard ordered his men to give them the bayonet. It was a terrible, but decisive charge; the day was won. The whole British Infantry were either captured or killed. Tarlton narrowly escaped, after a personal encounter with Colonel Washington. Morgan rode up to Howard and said—"Colonel you have done well, for you are successful—had you failed I would have shot you." Colonel Howard replied, "Had I failed, there would have been no need of shooting me." At that moment he held in his hands the swords of seven British officers. For this gallant charge, Congress presented Colonel Howard with a gold medal.

In September, 1781, Howard's regiment was at Eutaw Springs. He was received by the Buffs and Irish Corps of Raudon's army. Here the fiercest struggle of the war took place. Neither would yield, but crossing bayonets their ranks mingled together. Opposing files sank down, each pierced with the bayonet of his antagonist. They were found grappled in death and transfixed together on the field. The officers fought hand to hand. The British line had given way and the Buffs, unable to maintain the conflict, broke and fled. General Greene rode up and complimented the Marylanders in the midst of the action. Three hundred British prisoners were taken in the pursuit. Howard's men were reduced to thirty and he was the only commissioned officer left. Green said that success was due to the free use of the bayonets of the Maryland troops in their charge in the face of a murderous fire of artillery and musketry. Each corps engaged received the thanks of Congress. Marylanders were engaged from this time on to the surrender.

The State had furnished 15,229 men in addition to those enlisted in the independent companies. The State companies, the marines and naval forces amounting to 5,407 militia, brought the total up to 20,636.

McSherry records—"Entering the war two strong battalions, they were soon reduced to a single company. Again swelled to seven regiments, they were thinned to one and before the campaign had well passed, they were once more promptly recruited to four full battalions of more than 2,000 men. Two of their officers, Williams and Howard were considered the best of their grade. Entitled to a Major-General and two brigadiers they submitted to be led by strangers.

Amos Cummings, himself a New Yorker, said:—"The old guard occupied no higher station in the French Army than that held by the Maryland Line in the Continental Army. As Napoleon and Ney relied upon the old guard, so did Washington and Greene rely upon the Maryland Line, when the independence of American colonies was at stake."

Colonel Howard upon his final charge, at Eutaw Springs, was wounded; he was brought home to the house of his attending physician, Dr. Thomas Cradock, cf Pikesville. Colonel Howard was then seeking the hand of Miss Peggy Chew, then much admired by several English officers. Fearing delay might endanger his cause, Dr. Cradock carried on the correspondence and was successful.

At a ball given in Baltimore in honor of General Washington, who led Nellie Gittings in the minuet, Dr. Cradock walked next with Betty Moale. She later became the Doctor's neighbor and named his home "The Pill Box." (Annals of St. Thomas Church). General Washington attended the wedding of Colonel Howard to Peggy Chew.

Colonel Howard, in 1787, was a member of the Continental Congress, when war was imminent with France. President Washington tendered him the offices of Major General and Secretary of State, both of which he declined with friendly courtesy. In 1789 he was elected Governor.

The Assembly of Maryland having voted to cede to Congress a district ten miles square for the seat of Government, the Legislature of 1789, voted $72,000 to assist Virginia's offer of $120,000 to build the Capital and authorized the sale of her public lands to meet the outlay.

In 1790, the Assembly passed an Act for the better administration of Justice. Charles Carroll, of "Carrollton" and John Henry, our United States Senators, wrote to Governor Howard asking him to appoint men of high character, who might be better able to present the State, claim in the ablest manner before Congress. With Charles Carroll, of "Carrollton," Governor Howard drafted the Militia law of the State.

In 1790, President Washington arrived in Annapolis and with the Governor, attended a meeting of the trustees of St. John's College. He was entertained by the Governor and honored by a ball.

At the expiration of his eligibility, Governor Howard was succeeded by George Plater. In 1795, Governor Howard was elected by the Maryland Senate and in 1796, was sent to the United States Senate, vice Mr. Potts and was re-elected for the full term, which extended to 1803. Retiring to his beautiful home at "Belvedere," wherein both General Washington and General LaFayette had been entertained, Colonel Howard spent his remaining days in quiet comfort.

"Belvedere" stood at the head of Calvert Street. Its history covers an interesting epoch of colonial days. Colonel Howard gave to the city of Baltimore the site upon which Washington's Monument stands, yet it is only at this late day, our patriotic citizens have at last determined to honor him with a like memorial.

During the war of 1812, Governor Howard raised a company of veterans for home defense; when the news reached him that the Capitol had been burned and capitulation was being considered, he said:—"I have as much property at stake as most persons and I have four sons in the field, but sooner would I see my sons weltering in their blood and my home reduced to ashes, than so far disgrace my country." He lived to see the dawn of Peace and the "era of good feeling." His second son, George Howard, was later made Governor, during the era of good feeling. Having taken cold, the old hero soon followed his fascinating wife, dying in 1827. His funeral was attended by President Adams and his Cabinet.

Governor Howard's sons were General Benjamin Chew Howard, prominent in the late history of Maryland and in 1860, a candidate upon the Peace Party platform for Governor. He married Jane Grant Gilmor; John E. Howard, the eldest son, married Annabella Read; George Howard, his second son, and Governor, married Prudence Gough Ridgely; William Howard married Rebecca Key; James married Sophia Gough Ridgely, and second, Catharine Murdock Ross; Charles married Elizabeth Key. The daughters were Mrs. John McHenry and Mrs. William George Reed.

GOVERNOR GEORGE PLATER.

Governor George Plater, sixth Governor of Maryland, was born at "Sotterly," near Leonardtown, St. Mary's County, November 8, 1735.

His home is well described in Thomas' Colonial Maryland—as a handsome model of antique architecture, built in the form of the letter "Z," one story and a half, with steep gambrall roof, surmounted by a cupola and penetrated by triangular capped dormer windows, a frame building with brick foundations, brick gables, brick porches and flagstone colonade. Handsomely paneled wood from ceiling to floor finished the parlor, hall, library and dining-rooms. Shell carvings forming the ceilings of the parlor alcoves were unique and handsome. Walnut window frames, doors of mahogany, swung on solid brass strap hinges, offer an exhibit of colonial interior decorations unexcelled in Maryland. Its stairway was of mahogany, with grooved rail and balustrade and newel post of filigree work. This magnificent homestead was built for Hon. George Plater, father of the Governor, about 1730. He was Naval Officer and Collector of the Patuxent District and his little square office with cone-shaped roof still stands in the yard by the side of his wine cellar and smoking-room. This celebrated homestead, taking its name from the Plater homestead named in Sucklings Annals, of Suffolk, England, was originally a part of "Fenwick Manor." It contained 2,000 acres and was purchased by Hon. James Bowles, who married Rebecca, daughter of Colonel Thomas Addison and Elizabeth Tasker, daughter of the Treasurer, Thomas Tasker.

In 1729, the Maryland Gazette announced the marriage of the widow Bowles to Colonel George Plater. The Sotterly homestead was built after that marriage. The issue of Colonel Plater and Mrs. Bowles were Governor George Plater, Ann, Elizabeth and Rebecca, who became Mrs. Colonel John Tayloe, of Mt. Airy, Virginia. She handed down a coterie of distinguished wives, including Mrs. Francis Lightfoot Lee, wife of "the signer;" Mrs. Colonel William Augustine Washington and Mrs. Colonel Edward Lloyd, of Maryland, mother of Governor Lloyd. She was also the mother of John Tayloe, who married a daughter of Governor Benjamin Ogle.

Colonel Plater's second wife was Mrs. Elizabeth Carpenter. Colonel Plater's coach and four and his sailing boats have elsewhere been noted. He indulged also in the popular races, of 1750, as shown by an announcement in the Maryland Gazette of that date, "September 20, 1750, a race was run on the race course between Governor Ogle's bay gelding and Colonel Plater's grey stallion, which was won by the former."

Five years later, that same paper announced:" Saturday last, died at his seat in St. Mary's County, aged upwards of sixty, the Hon. George Plater, Esq., who was for many years one of his Lordship's Council of State, Naval Officer of the Patuxent and lately appointed Secretary of the Province; a gentleman eminent for every social virtue which could render him truly valuable; he was as Horace says, "ad unquem factus homo." As his life was a pleasure, so was his death a grief to every one who knew him.

George Plater, his only son, and heir of "Sotterly," was educated at William and Mary's College. In 1760, he visited England, where he was introduced by letters from Governor Horatio Sharpe. He made an agreeable impression on Lord Baltimore, who desired the Governor to associate him in the affairs of the Province. After studying law, George Plater took active interest in the discussions preceding the Revolution. He was a member of the Convention which requested Governor Eden to retire. In 1776, he was one of the Council of Safety; was in the Convention of 1776 and upon the Committee to prepare a Declaration and Charter of Rights and a form of Government for Maryland. From 1778 to 1781, he was in Congress and in 1788 was President of the Maryland Convention that ratified the Constitution of the United States. In 1791, he was elected Governor to succeed Governor Howard.

The location and aid to the National Capital were the chief events in his administration. Virginia had voted a loan of $120,000 to be devoted to the necessary buildings upon the territory, which had been ceded by the two States and the Legislature of Maryland voted to contribute $72,000, payable in three yearly installments. To meet these payments the public lands of Maryland were authorized to be sold.

The Indian campaign of 1791 in which General St. Clair and Colonel Henry Lee, of Virginia, were in command, was a disastrous defeat and Maryland was compelled to raise additional recruits, under Colonel Otho H. Williams, in 1792.

Governor Plater's wife was Ann Rousby, the only child of Colonel John Rousby, of "Rousby Hall," in Calvert, another once famous and popular resort.

Mrs. Plater possessed rare beauty and stately elegance. Her rich patrimony, added to her busband's large estate, enabled them to entertain in a manner suitable to their distinguished position. They left two daughters, Ann and Rebecca, accomplished and beautiful, and three sons, George, John Rousby and Thomas Plater. Ann Plater—Philip Barton Key, the jurist and statesman; Rebecca —General Uriah Forrest, of the Maryland Line; George Plater inherited "Sotterly" and handed it down to his son, George, who lost it; Judge John Rousby Plater, second son, through his son, John, was the progenitor of Charlotte Plater, widow of General E. Law Rogers, once heir to Druid Hill Park. Mrs. Rogers has a handsome portrait of the Governor; Thomas Plater, third son, inherited "Rousby Hall," and sold it; his daughter, Ann Plater, another noted beauty, became the wife of Major George Peter, of Montgomery County, in command at the Battle of Bladensburg. Their descendants in line are the heirs of the late Hon. George Peter, of Rockville, and Senator William B. Peter, of Howard.

These three sons of Governor Plater were also prominent in affairs. George was a Colonel in the Maryland Line. Thomas was a member of Congress from 1801 to 1805, and Judge John Rousby Plater was Presidential Elector in 1797, and also a member of the Maryland Legislature, acting as Associate Judge of the First District at the time of his death.

Governor George Plater died at Annapolis February 10, 1792. His remains, "attended by the Council and State officials, were taken the next day, by way of South River, to "Sotterly," where he is buried in what is now an open field and without even a simple slab to mark the last resting place of a son of Maryland, whose statesmanship and zeal so closely are interwoven with her government and whose life, from dawn of early manhood to the grave, was conspicuous for disinterested devotion and distinguished service to the State and to the nation. Oh, Spirit of Liberty! where sleeps your thunder?"

(Thomas.)

GOVERNOR JOHN HOSKINS STONE.

Governor John Hoskins Stone, eighth Governor of Maryland (1794-97), was born in Charles County, Maryland, in 1745. He was the son of David Stone, who married Elizabeth Jenifer, daughter of Dr. Daniel Jenifer. He was descended from Governor William Stone and was the younger brother of Thomas Stone, signer of the Declaration of Independence. He was educated at private schools and studied law.

In November, 1774, he was one of the committee from Charles County, Maryland, to carry out the resolutions of Congress, and was one of the Committee of Correspondence for the County. He was one of the Association of Freemen of Maryland in 1775.

On January 14, 1776, was elected Captain of the first company of Colonel William Smallwood's First Maryland Regiment, and in December following was appointed Colonel. He fought with distinction at Long Island, White Plains, Princeton and Germantown, where he was wounded and was compelled to retire, resigning in 1779. He was in the Executive Council of Maryland and member of the "Cincinnati Society." His commission is still in possession of the heirs of his grandson, Nathaniel Pope Causin.

Governor Stone held the chair from 1794 to 1797. He was the first Governor to send a written message to the Assembly, and suggested as a modification of the mode of electing the President a division of the State into ten districts. His brother, Michael Jenifer Stone, was in Congress 1789-91 and Judge of the Circuit Court of Charles County.

Governor Stone, in 1795, wrote to President Washington a letter which was accompanied by the resolves of the Maryland Assembly in denunciation of the calumnies that had been heaped upon the President.

The President replied in an appreciative letter.

Governor Stone asked a modification of the mode of electing the President and Vice-President.

President Washington applied to Governor Stone for an additional appropriation of $150,000 from the Maryland Assembly to complete the national Capitol. Maryland had already given $72,000 and Virginia $120,000. The Assembly loaned $10,000 in 1797, and in 1799, $50,000 more. In 1800 the building was reported ready for use.

Governor Stone married Miss Conden, a Scotch lady. His daughter, Eliza Stone, married Dr. Nathaniel Pope Causin, of Port Tobacco, Maryland. His son, Nathaniel Pope Causin, married Eliza Mactier Warfield, daughter of Daniel and Nancy Mactier Warfield, of Baltimore. They were the grandparents of Messrs. S. Davies Warfield, Colonel Henry Mactier Warfield and Dr. Mactier Warfield, of Baltimore, and of Richard Emory Warfield, of Philadelphia.

Governor Stone died at his residence in Annapolis, October 5, 1804.

GOVERNOR JOHN HENRY.

Governor John Henry, first Senator and ninth Governor of Maryland, was born at "Weston," Somerset County, Maryland, November, 1750. His paternal grandfather was Rev. John Henry, a Presbyterian minister, who came from Ireland in 1700 and settled first near Rehoboth, upon Pocomoke River, Somerset County, Maryland; he married Mary Jenkins, widow of Colonel Francis Jenkins, who brought to him the immense estate of her late husband. She was the daughter of Sir Robert King, an Irish baronet, and was known as "Madam Hampton," having married for the third time, Rev. John Hampton, another Presbyterian minister. Her two sons by Rev. John Henry became eminent. They were Francis Jenkins and Colonel John Henry, who married Dorothy Rider, daughter of Colonel John Rider, son of John Rider, of England, who had married the only child of Colonel Charles Hutchins, an early settler of Somerset and lived at "Weston," afterward the home of John Henry. Mr. Hutchins' daughter, whilst at school in England, married, and died on her return home. Their son, Colonel John Rider, was born in England and married Anne Hicks. Their daughter, Dorothy, became the mother of Governor John Henry, who was prepared for College at West Nottingham Academy, Cecil; went to Princeton and graduated in 1769; studied law in the Temple, England; was a member of the "Robin Hood Club," and in their discussions, defended the colonists. He left England in 1775, a thoroughly educated, popular and attractive young man; was elected to the Legislature. In 1777 was sent to the Continental Congress, remaining until the adoption of the Constitution. He opposed Jay's treaty with Spain, wherein our right to navigate the Mississippi was to be surrendered for the small benefit to the Eastern States. In 1783 he received two votes for President. In 1787 he was upon the committee to prepare an ordinance for the Northwest Territory. With Charles Carroll, of "Carrollton," he was elected one of the first United States Senators. He voted to locate the Capitol on the Potomac. Resigning the senatorship, he was elected Governor of Maryland, which office he soon resigned, from ill-health.

In 1780, the English having plundered the town of Vienna and burnt a new brig, called at Colonel John Henry's and destroyed his house and furniture. The Colonel, being alone, except his servants, retired to a neighbor's whither he removed his plate and valuable papers. They took away a slave.

Governor Henry married in 1787, Margaret, daughter of John and Elizabeth Goldsborough Campbell, of Caroline County. One of Mrs. Campbell's sisters was the grandmother of Governor Philip Francis Thomas.

Governor Henry died in 1798, leaving two sons, John Campbell Henry and Francis Jenkins Henry. The former married Mary Nevett Steele, sister of J. Nevett Steele, the Baltimore attorney.

The character of Governor Henry has been thus depicted by the memoirs of Mrs. Winder Townsend:

" His manners were easy, engaging, and in person was graceful and elegant."

He directed the education of his nephew, William Henry Winder afterward commander of the American forces at Bladensburg in 1814. There is no portrait of him because of the fire which destroyed the homestead of " Weston" in which were many of his papers.   Mrs. Townsend, however, holds the original letter of Thomas Jefferson to Governor Henry upon the authenticity of Logan's speech.

Governor Henry's granddaughter " Kitty," daughter of John Campbell Henry, married Daniel Lloyd, youngest son of Governor and Senator Edward Lloyd, and became the mother of Governor Henry Lloyd, who succeeded Governor Robert McLane.

GOVERNOR HENRY'S ADDRESS TO THE LEGISLATURE.

" We are taught to rely upon the militia for our general defense; it is especially important now to place them upon the most respectable footing.   All men are now satisfied of the propriety of putting the country in a complete state of defense; and in case of war it would be unbecoming the wisdom of the Legislature to trust the peace and safety of the country to this present weak and defective system, menaced as we are by a brave, intelligent and enterprising nation, this subject is all important."

Colonel John Rider was the maternal grandfather of Governor John Henry and was the only son of John Rider (of Edward and Dorothy the only daughter of Colonel Charles Hutchins).   (See her beautiful picture in a recent publication of Governor John Henry's Letters and Papers, by his great-grandson.)   Colonel Hutchins was an early settler of Dorchester; was of Council commissioned to treat with Indians and was Colonel of the Militia.

GOVERNOR BENJAMIN OGLE.

Governor Benjamin Ogle, tenth Governor of Maryland, 1798-1801, was born in Annapolis, February 7, 1746, in the house of his father, corner of King George and College Avenue.   He was educated in England.

Benjamin Ogle was, by appointment, a member of the Executive Council, and in 1798 was elected by the Assembly as Governor.   He was a personal friend of President Washington, by whom he was frequently consulted.

Upon the death of President Washington in 1799, the Governor issued a proclamation that the 11th of February, 1800, be observed throughout the State " as a day of mourning, humiliation and prayer for the deceased."   His precedent is still observed under the " New Style," on 22nd February, yearly.

Governor Ogle's administration was in the midst of violent political excitement between the Federalists, represented by

President John Adams, and the Republicans, led by Thomas Jefferson. In Maryland the people were about equally divided. The election having failed in the Electoral College, it was after seven days of intense contest in the House of Representatives, decided in favor of Thomas Jefferson.

The home of Governor Benjamin Ogle was "Belair," Prince George County. In 1760 it was the homestead of Colonel Benjamin Tasker, and from there Governor Sharpe wrote to his brother William, in England, asking him to entertain Charles Carroll, Mr. Key and Mr. George Plater, members of the Lower House who were friendly to his administration. "Belair" descended, through Colonel Tasker's daughter, to Governor Ogle. It was laid out as an English manor. The large, square manor house was approached by an avenue 120 feet wide. A descendant daughter thus pictures it from her girlish memory: "'Belair' was an ideal old Colonial home, built of English brick. For me it holds many interesting memories of my childhood, when life seemed one long summer day. I wandered over the spacious rooms, whose walls were covered with paintings from old masters. Its conservatory, opening into the dining room, was filled with all kinds of plants and flowers. Around the family table gathered many friends to enjoy a wholesome hospitality. The entrance to the mansion was an avenue fully a mile long, lined with tulips and poplar trees. At the rear was a long sweep of velvety green, terraced and broken here and there by lovely beds of roses and plants. Beyond was the park, with its huge forest trees, in which deer wandered and from which they sometimes escaped, affording sport for the young huntsmen. During the exciting days of our Civil War many met there who never returned. The pictures that adorned 'Belair' are now in possession of Harry Tayloe, of Mount Airy, Virginia, great-great-grandson of Governor Benjamin Ogle."

Some of the living descendants of this old homestead, wherein Charles Carroll, of "Carrollton" and General Washington were honored guests, and around which cluster the associations of many more of distinguished men, are Benjamin Ogle, of Baltimore; Mrs. John Hodges, now ninety years old, Washington, D. C.; and Miss Rosalie Ogle, of Baltimore.

One of the daughters of "Belle Air" became Mrs. William Woodville, whose nephew, William Woodville Rockhill, was Mr. Cleveland's Assistant Secretary of State. Of the younger line of descendants are Mr. Marbury Ogle and his sister, Miss Rosalie Ogle, of Baltimore.

"Belair," to-day, is the property of Mr. James T. Woodward, President of the Hanover Bank, New York. He has restored the old homestead to its former grandeur.

The Ogle family postilion it still remembered by the older neighbors.

Governor Benjamin Ogle married, first, Rebecca Stilly, whose daughter, Elizabeth, married Michael Thomas, son of Christian Thomas, of Frederick County. David Ogle Thomas, of Michael, came into possession of "Rose Hill," the former homestead of Governor Thomas Johnson. His daughter, Mrs. Cecilius Warfield, of Baltimore, still holds it. Governor Ogle married, second, Henrietta Margaret Hill, daughter of Henry and Mary (Thomas) Hill, daughter of Philip Thomas, of West River, by Ann Chew. His son, Benjamin Ogle, married Miss Ann Maria Cooke. They had twelve children. A daughter of Governor Ogle married John Hodges, whose son perpetuates the name. Dr. Benjamin Cooke Ogle, youngest son of Benjamin and Ann Maria Cooke Ogle, was the last of the name to hold the homestead.

GOVERNOR JOHN FRANCIS MERCER.

John Francis Mercer, soldier and eleventh Governor of Maryland, 1801-3, descended from Noel and Ann (Smith) Mercer, of Chester, England. Their son Robert married Eleanor Reynolds and their son John married Grace Fenton. John, of Dublin, Ireland, son of John and Grace Fenton Mercer, went to Virginia in 1720, becoming Secretary of the Ohio Company. He was a noted Crown lawyer and published "Mercer's Abridgement of the Laws of Virginia." John Francis Mercer, his son by a second marriage with Ann Roy was born at "Marlboro," Stafford County, Virginia, May 17, 1759, and was graduated from William and Mary College, Virginia, in 1775. In 1776 he entered the Third Virginia regiment as lieutenant, and was made captain June 27, 1777. He served as aide to General Charles Lee until the battle of Monmouth, New Jersey, and his sympathy with that officer in his disgrace led him to resign. But returning to his own State, he raised and equipped, at his own expense, a troop of horse, of which he was commissioned Lieutenant-Colonel. He joined General Robert Lawson's brigade and served with it at Guilford, North Carolina, and elsewhere until its disbandment. He then attached his command to the forces of General LaFayette, with whom he remained until the surrender of Yorktown. He afterwards studied law with Thomas Jefferson. From 1782 to 1785 he was one of the Virginia delegates to the Continental Congress. He married February 3, 1785, Sophia, daughter of Richard Sprigg, of "Cedar Park," West River, Maryland, whose wife was Margaret Caile, daughter of John and Rebecca (Ennalls) Caile, of England.

Removing to his wife's estate at "Cedar Park," he became an active and prominent partisan. He was sent as a delegate from Maryland to the Convention which framed the Constitution of the United States, and was with Luther Martin in opposition to the several provisions which obliterated State rights. He finally withdrew from the Convention because he was not willing to endorse the Constitution as drafted. He was a member of the Maryland Legislature for several years and a member of Congress from Maryland (in 1792-4) in which the permanent location of the Capitol was excitedly discussed and was with the Southern members in trying to locate it upon the Potomac. In 1801 he was elected Governor of Maryland, and was re-elected in 1802.

As a friend and student of Thomas Jefferson he was influential in bringing out legislative action favorable to his Democratic administration.   Mr. Joseph Hopper Nicholson, one of the Democratic Representatives in Congress from Maryland during the exciting seven days in deciding Mr. Jefferson's election, was ill and his physicians prohibited his attendance, saying it would cause his death.   His wife agreed with her husband that his duty was to be at his post, and accompanying Mr. Nicholson, remained with him and assisted him in casting his vote for Jefferson.

In 1801 the controversy over the property qualification of voters in Maryland was the chief one, and the Democrats, being in favor of abolishing it, were victorious.   Early in the session of 1801 an amendment allowing all free white citizens of the State to vote was passed, and in 1802 the confirmatory act was passed.   Up to this time voters in Maryland must possess a freehold of fifty acres of land.

Governor Mercer was succeeded by Governor Robert Bowie in 1803.   Retiring to his estate, "Cedar Park," he was again called to the Legislature.

His son, Colonel John Mercer, married Mary Swann, and his son, Richard Sprigg Mercer, married Miss E. Coxe, both connections of Governor Thomas Swann and Lieutenant-Governor C. C. Cox, elected under the Constitution of 1864.   The latter would have succeeded Governor Swann, who was elected to the United States Senate, had he accepted.   He was the only Lieutenant-Governor of Maryland

Some of the children of Richard Sprigg Mercer were Miss Margaret Mercer, who presided at Governor Swann's house during his term in Congress, Mrs. George Peter, now Mrs. Edwin J. Farber, and Colonel Richard Mercer, of New York.

Governor Mercer's daughter, Margaret, was the author of "Studies for Bible Classes," "Ethics," and a "Series of Lectures for Young Ladies."   She became noted for her sacrifice in freeing her slaves and sending them to Liberia.   She was known as the "Hannah More of America."

Governor Mercer died August 30, 1821, at Philadelphia, Pa., whither he had gone to consult a physician as to his health.

GOVERNOR ROBERT BOWIE.

Governor Robert Bowie, the War Governor, of 1812, was the third son of Captain William Bowie, and Margaret Sprigg.   He was born at Mattaponi, 1750.   At twenty-five years of age he was upon the Committee of Correspondence for his county and commissioned Captain of a company of "Minute Men."   His father was a member of the Convention, which met in Annapolis, in June, 1775 and issued the "Declaration of the Association of Freemen."   This antedated by one year the Declaration of Independence.

When scarcely twenty years of age, young Robert Bowie married Priscilla, daughter of General James Mackall, of Calvert, who held thirty thousand acres near the Cliffs.   Captain Bowie commanded the

Second Battalion of the Flying Artillery, maintaining his men at his own expense. Ordered to join General Washington in New York, his battalion was too late for the battle of Long Island, but covered itself with honor at Harlem Heights and White Plains, where Captain Bowie was wounded in the knee. Acting as his own surgeon, he cut the limb and removed a splintered bone. With Colonel Luke Marbury, he was at the battle of Germantown. There he was wounded in the shoulder.

In 1786, he was elected to the House of Delegates. His colleagues were his brother, Major Walter, and his cousin, Captain Fielder Bowie. They continued to sit until 1790. They opposed the bill for maintaining ministers of gospel at the State's expense.

In 1794, Robert Bowie was promoted to Major. In 1796, he was an elector of Senators. Again a member of the House of Delegates in 1801–2–3, he was elected in 1803, as the first Democratic Governor of the State.

He was re-elected in 1804–5. In 1809, he was Presidential elector for Madison. In 1811, he was elected Governor for the fourth time. The war was at hand and Governor Bowie was in favor of aggressive measures. When Congress formally declared war "the Governor was so rejoiced he did not wait for his hat, but, with a few friends, proceeded to the State House, where he congratulated the leaders upon the news." He at once issued a Proclamation, directing the militia to be organized, disciplined and equipped: Calling upon the Field Officers and Captains to assemble in Baltimore, he selected a "uniform dress" and trumpet soundings for the cavalry.

Maryland's quota was six thousand men.

Governor Bowie, after the murderous attack upon the press and person of Alexander Contee Hanson, was called to investigate the riot. His report exonerating the military officers in charge and counseling moderation in the interest of the public did not serve to allay party indignation, and the Governor at the ensuing election was defeated by Levin Winder, the Federalist.

He received the entire Democratic vote and at each succeeding election still held his party's confidence, only falling short two votes in 1814.

In 1815, he opposed Charles Carnan Ridgely, of Hampton, who only received two votes over him. The same fight occurred again in 1816.

In 1817, the old War Governor was a candidate for the United States Senate. A bitter contest ensued.

The defeat at Bladensburg was charged to him because of his appointment of incompetent officers. Others charged him as "too good a hater." Yet the old chief held his admirers and would have won other honors had not death intervened, in 1818.

Then partisan rancor was stilled and all united in paying tribute to the patriotism, bravery and integrity of the deceased. There was a softer side in this old hero's life. As the guardian of many estates, his liberality and kindness endeared him to many.

He was long in the vestry of St. Paul's Church. A born leader of men, he was to his friends as true as steel. A handsome portrait of him is still extant. His remains were interred in the family grave-yard as Mattaponi, where lie his parents, and his wife, who survived him four years. Five of his children arrived at maturity, two sons and three daughters. Governor Bowie was a breeder of blooded stock and was fond of the race track, upon which many of his horses appeared.

GOVERNOR ROBERT WRIGHT.

Three times elected Governor, Robert Wright, thirteenth Governor of Maryland, (1806–09), was born at "Blakeford," in Queen Anne County, Maryland, November 20, 1752. He was the son of Judge Solomon and Mary (Tidmarsh DeCourcy) Wright, who was the son of Justice Solomon and Anna Wright, who was the son of Nathaniel Wright, the immigrant from England, in 1673, who settled in Queen Anne County.

Judge Solomon Wright was a member of the Maryland Convention of 1771-1776; member of the Assembly, 1771-3-4; member of the "Association of Freemen" and signer of the "Declaration of Freemen;" Chairman of the Committee of Correspondence for Queen Anne, in 1774–75–76; was appointed Judge of the Provincial Court, but resigned; was special Judge for the Eastern Shore during the Revolution. Upon the State's organization was appointed Judge of the first Court of Appeals and served until his death.

Robert Wright was educated at the Public Schools, studied law, was admitted to the Bar and began the practice in Chestertown, but subsequently in Queenstown, Maryland. He served as a private in Captain James Kent's Company of Queen Anne "Minute Men," against Lord Drummond's Tories of the Eastern Shore of Virginia, February, 1776. He was Captain of a Company in the Maryland Line; was at Pauoli and Brandywine; was in Colonel Richardson's Battalion. His commission was dated on "July 7, 1777," and was embodied under the late resolution of Congress.

In 1801, he was elected United States Senator. This he resigned in 1806, when elected Governor of Maryland.

During his term much excitement was caused by the Embargo Act and the Enforcement Act, which followed it. He presided at a meeting in Annapolis called to endorse his administration. It passed resolutions asking President Jefferson to recall his determination to decline another nomination.

In 1807, Governor Wright appointed Major Samuel Turburt Wright, Adjutant-General of the State Militia. He was authorized to furnish 5,863 men as Maryland's quota of 100,000 ordered to take the field at a moment's notice. The Embargo Act reduced Maryland exports from 14,000,000 in 1807 to 2,000,000, yet, for patriotic reasons, the Governor and Legislature still endorsed the administration, but the election of 1809, brought a Federalist majority in the House of Delegates, which elected Edward Lloyd his successor.

In 1810–12–14 Governor Wright was sent to Congress. He was returned in 1820 and was elected District Judge of the circuit comprising Queen Anne, Kent and Talbot Counties, in 1823. He died at "Blakeford," near Queenstown, on Sept. 7, 1826.

His wife was Sarah De Courcy. Their sons were Robert Theodore DeCourcy Wright, who was a member of the Governor's Council and married, first, Deborah Thomas and, second, Margaret Fedderman.

All of Governor Wright's sons, except the youngest, fought in the War of 1812.

William Henry DeCourcy Wright, youngest son, was born at "Blakeford," Sept. 9, 1795. The old building, a large square one, was burned during Governor Wright's first term. Mrs. William H. DeCourcy Wright was Eliza Lea Warner, of Delaware, widow of Samuel Turbutt Wright, Jr. They had issue, Clintonia, Gustavia, William H. DeCourcy, Gustavus, W. T., Carolina Louisa, Victoria Louisa and Ella Lee.

Clintonia—first, Captain William May; second, Governor Philip Francis Thomas. Victoria Louisa—Samuel Levering. Ella Lee—Captain J. Pembrooke Thom, of Virginia. Captain H. DeCourcy Wright was the founder of the coffee trade of Rio, which city became his residence for a number of years. He was under General Bolivar, in the States of Columbia, in the War of Independence.

Governor Wright was a breeder of race horses and fine cattle. The DeCourcy family, from whom his wife descended, was of the ancient Barony of Kingsall, in the days of King John.

The first home of the DeCourcy family was "My Lord's Gift," near Queenstown. It is one of the quaintest old homesteads in Maryland. It was a direct gift to Colonel Henry DeCourcy from Lord Baltimore, in recognition of the Colonel's loyalty during the Puritan ascendency in Maryland. "Cheston on the Wye" is another old DeCourcy homestead. Here were buried Governor Wright, his wife, Sarah DeCourcy, his daughter Louisa and his son, Gustavus William Tidmarsh. Governor Wright's second wife was Miss Ringgold, of Kent County.

The late Benjamin Nicholson Wright, of Annapolis, long chief clerk in the Comptroller's office and Warden of St. Anne's Church, descended from Thomas, son of Thomas, son of Colonel Thomas Wright, the immigrant. This branch was known as the Wrights of "Reeds Creek," from whom came Samuel Turbutt Wright, Captain in General Smallwood's brigade. Captain Wright's company was, during the Revolution, stationed upon Kent Island to command the entrance to Chester River. A striking portrait of Governor Wright hangs in the State House at Annapolis.

GOVERNOR EDWARD LLOYD.

Edward Lloyd, of "Wye House," was the son of Edward Lloyd IV., the Revolutionary Legislator, who failed in the election when Thomas Sim Lee was made Governor. "With Maryland and North American interests at stake, ingrained through full five generations, prior to 1776, and in deed from the earliest immigration, Edward Lloyd, of "Wye House," had an honest claim upon the confidence of his constituents. His business tact in caring for the industrial interests of the Province, promoted by regular immigration in certain English shires, gave importance to his election in 1774–76, along with Matthew Tilghman, James Lloyd Chamberlaine and Pollard Edmondson, families of ample means. He rode at times in a coach and four. He had a tract of land for a deer park and he let his friends and guests rejoice in horses and hounds. After the burning of Wye House by a predatory band of a military expedition, he rebuilt it with a town house in Annapolis, that stands still sufficiently high to overtop the neighboring ones. It gave him an outlook towards the eastern bay of the Chesapeake and the mouth of Wye River. When Governor Lee, in 1792, was in the chair, John Edmondson, son of Pollard, with Judge Joseph H. Nicholson, the Democratic leader, moved to have the property qualifications removed, Colonel Edward Lloyd, the largest land-holder of the State, gave his support and thus gained political eclat. His assessment in 1783, after his heavy loss, in 1781, in plate, jewelry, negroes, clothing and £800 in cash, by English depredations, covered 261 slaves, 799 head of sheep, 147 horses, 571 head of cattle, 579 head of hogs, 215,000 pounds of tobacco, 500 ounces of plate, 30 pounds of pork, 72 tracts of land, covering 11,884½ acres.

Though he failed to be Governor, his son, Edward Lloyd, succeeded in 1809, just a century after his distinguished ancestor of 1709. Governor Lloyd was fifth in line. He was a man of talent, of a large estate and an honest politician. He was in the Legislature, from 1800 to 1805; a member of Congress, from 1806 to 1809; Governor from 1809 to 1811. He was in Congress when the "Embargo Act" was passed and was Governor when it was repealed. The free ballot act, repealing the viva voce vote, and all property qualifications, introduced by John Hanson Thomas, was confirmed by Legislative Act, in 1809. After Governor Lloyd's term had ended, in 1811, he was returned to the Senate of Maryland, when he offered a series of resolutions, endorsing "the course of President Madison toward England and condemning the measures of Great Britain, as destructive of our interests and ought to be resisted; that the independence established by the valor of our fathers will not tamely be yielded by their sons; the same spirit which led Maryland regulars to battle still exists and awaits only our country's call." Governor Lloyd was presidential elector, in 1812, and voted for President Madison. In 1819 he was elected United States Senator, serving until 1826, when he resigned. Retiring to his large estate, he directed his agricultural interests and dispensed hospitality. He inherited, also, the town house in Annapolis. This was built by Samuel Chase, the signer, in 1770. It is probably the most stately house in the city, being three stories high, the only colonial one of that height. This is still known as the "Chase House," though it was bought by Colonel Lloyd before its completion. The dining-room is handsomely ornamented in carved wood, and the marble mantelpiece represents a scene from Shakespeare in sculpture.

Governor Lloyd conveyed this mansion to his son-in-law, Henry Hall Harwood. In 1847, it was purchased by Miss Hester Ann Chase, daughter of Judge Jeremiah Townley Chase. As the property of Mrs. Hester Ann Chase Ridout, wife of Rev. Samuel Ridout, it was willed to the Episcopal Church, as a home for the aged women.

In it is Governor Sharpe's eight day clock, a colonial bedstead with steps to get into bed, and a china set with the Chase arms.

Governor Lloyd's wife was Sally Scott Murray, daughter of Dr. James Murray. Their issue were Edward Lloyd VI.—Elizabeth Winder; James Murray, Sally Scott Lloyd—Charles Lowndes, U.S.N. Catherine—Franklin Buchanan, U. S. N.; Daniel Lloyd; Mary Ellen—William Tilghman Goldsborough, of Dorset and Mrs. Harwood.

Edward VI. was President of the Maryland State Senate and married Alicia McBlair, of Baltimore. Issue, Edward VII, Elizabeth —Charles Henry Key; Alicia—Charles Sidney Winder, U. S. A. Sally Scott Lloyd—David Churchhill Trimble, father of Dr. Isaac Ridgeway Trimble, of Baltimore.

Edward VII., also President of the Maryland Senate, married Mary Lloyd Howard. He still holds Wye House, which has a library of 1,000 volumes. The crest of the family is a demi-lion quadrant, or.

GOVERNOR LEVIN WINDER.

Governor Levin Winder, sixteenth Governor of Maryland (1812 —1815) was born in Somerset County, Maryland, September 4, 1757. He was the son and eighth child of William Winder, who married Esther Gillis, grandson of John Winder and Jane Dashiel and great-grandson of John Winder, who came from Cumberland, England, to Princess Anne, Somerset County, Maryland, and was appointed Justice of the Peace, in 1665, and Lieutenant-Colonel, in 1697.

Levin Winder was a brother of William Winder, who married the daughter of Governor John Henry—father and mother of General William Henry Winder, of the War of 1812.

Levin Winder began the study of law, but abandoned it upon the outbreak of the Revolution and entered the army. He was appointed by the Convention of Maryland on January 14, 1776, First Lieutenant of the Fifth Company, Captain Nathaniel Ramsey commanding, in Colonel William Smallwood's Battalion. He was afterward, April 17, 1777, made Major of the Fourth Regiment of the Maryland Line, and, at the close of the war, was Lieutenant-Colonel. At the conclusion of hostilities he engaged in agricultural pursuits in Southern Maryland, near Princess Anne. He was several times elected to the Legislature of Maryland, serving as Speaker of the House of Delegates. He was Governor of Maryland from 1812–1815. Governor Winder's election was due to the intense disgust which had grown out of the barbarous attempt of the Baltimore mob to suppress the freedom of the press.

The "Federal Republican," under the editor, Charles Contee Hanson, had ably opposed the War of 1812. The Federal Party was a unit in its support of his opposition, and many of Hanson's friends had determined to stand by him in his determination to issue his paper. The War Party, in Baltimore, determined that the paper should be suppressed. The result was a conflict, in which the mob attacked the building and some were killed. Hanson's party surrendered to the authorities; were taken to the gaol for protection, when the mob there entered and murdered General Lingan, an honored Revolutionary soldier, wounded General Henry Lee, who had led Lee's Legion to victory in the Revolution—wounded Captain Richard Crabb, Dr. Peregrine Warfield, William and Ephraim Gaither and many other Federalists, who had risked their lives in defense of the press.

Intense and bitter partisan feeling followed this contest and rendered President Madison's administration very unpopular with the Federal Party.

Petitions poured in upon Governor Bowie to break up these lawless proceedings and to investigate the conduct of the officers who had permitted this outbreak. The Governor's reply calling upon all, "when our country is engaged in an open and declared war with one of the most powerful nations of Europe, to cultivate a spirit of harmony," failed to allay the excitement, but resulted in a Federal victory, which put Governor Winder in his chair for three successive terms. As soon as the enemy had appeared in the bay Governor Winder addressed the Secretary of War upon the defenseless condition of Annapolis, but receiving no reply, wrote again. The Secretary replied that one battalion would be ordered to Annapolis, but not arriving, the Governor called out the militia for the defense of the towns, and at the same time set to work equipping and sending forward Maryland's quota to the general defense of the frontier, called out a portion of the militia of the State to garrison the forts of Annapolis and Baltimore. These were paid by the State. Whilst protecting these forts the army of invasion was not neglected, for within six weeks after the declaration of war Captain Nathan Towson, with an artillery company, joined Colonel Winfield Scott in the North. A number of companies tendered their services to the President, but could not be accepted, unless the State would pay for their services. In Baltimore a regiment was sent forward under Colonel William H. Winder, nephew of the Governor, with ample funds from private subscriptions.

On the arrival of the enemy in the bay Governor Winder addressed a letter to the Secretary of War, stating the helpless condition of Annapolis. One drafted battalion of militia was promised but never came to its defence. The records of Easton being in danger, the Governor urged, but received no assistance. This refusal, when Virginia was protected and her militia paid by the Government, brought the Federalists to exclaim! "Virginia has but to ask and she receives; but Maryland, for her political disobedience, is denied." The Governor called an extra session of the Legislature and laid before it his whole correspondence with the Government.

In his message the Governor claimed the right to demand protection of the general Government. The committee upon the Governor's message reported to the Assembly as follows: "That the State of Maryland is entitled to a fair distribution of the National means for its protection, and that the refusal of the Executive to assume the liquidation of the claims arising from the employment of the militia of this State, in the same manner that they have liqui- dated those of Virginia, is partial, unjust and contrary to the spirit of our Constitution." The report of the committee was adopted and the sum of one hundred thousand dollars was appropriated, to be applied by the Governor to defray the expenses of the militia already called out.

At this time a large number of citizens of the different counties of the State, unable to bear the burdens of war, abandoned their homes and moved to new settlements in the West. At the next Gubernatorial contest, owing to a very close vote in one of the counties, which gave the Federalists majority, seventeen members refused to vote, but Governor Winder was re-elected.

In his next message, Governor Winder declared. "If the expenses of a war waged by the National authorities are to be borne by the States, it is not difficult to foresee that the State treasury will soon be exhausted and the annihilation of the State Government must soon follow."

After recommending an amendment to the militia law "to compel the services of those who on any sudden emergency are unwilling to assist in defence of the country," and the organization of volunteer corps of mounted infantry, be submitted to the Legisla- ture "the propriety of adopting a system of general education."

The last Act of the Assembly of 1813 was the endorsement of the war by the Senate and the condemnation of the administration by the House.

General William Henry Winder who had in June, 1814, been placed in command of a new division, embracing Maryland and Virginia, wrote from Marlboro: "The Governor of Maryland has issued orders for calling out the drafts under the requisition of July, and, at my suggestion, has appointed Bladensburg as the place of rendezvous," and again he writes: "The Governor is exerting himself to collect a force at Annapolis." All this force, though not under the command of General Winder, did co-operate and were on their way to Bladensburg, when the British, having driven back its defenders, pushed on to the destruction of Washington.

The blame for this defeat fell upon the President, his Secretary of War and General Winder, who was honorably acquitted, for he had done his duty, and, after a successful career as a lawyer, died an honored and lamented patriot.

In the gubernatorial election of 1814, Governor Winder received forty-eight votes and Robert Bowie twenty-three. The State was now decidedly Federal, yet the Federalists never refused their aid to the war and appropriated $450,000, with $1,000,000 more from the city of Baltimore, to carry out the defence of her citizens. Forty-two thousand six hundred and thirty-six soldiers were Maryland's quota of the War of 1812. The Governor retired to his farm, near Princess Anne.

In 1816, Governor Winder was returned to the Senate of Maryland. He was a prominent Mason and was grand-master, in 1814–15. At the time of his death in Baltimore, July 1, 1819, he was Senior Major-General of the State Militia. In person and presence, Governor Levin Winder was very firm. He was eloquent, moral, gentlemanly. Of him his opponent said: "General Winder was incapable of misstatement; that he believed his spirit could not possibly bear its own reproach of anything that was disingenuous."

The camp-chest of General Washington came into the possession of General Winder and afterward of his son, William Sydney Winder, who presented it with all necessary documents to Congress, through John Quincy Adams.

Governor Winder married Mary Sloss. Issue, Edward Stougleton William Sydney and Mary Anne Stougleton. Edward Stougleton Winder married Elizabeth Tayloe Lloyd, daughter of Revolutionary Colonel Edward Lloyd. Their daughter, Elizabeth Tayloe Winder married Charles Josias Pennington, father of Josias Pennington, of Baltimore, of the firm of Baldwin & Pennington. Charles S. Winder, son of Edward S., was the Confederate General who was killed at Cedar Mountains.

GOVERNOR CHARLES CARNAN RIDGELY.

Governor Charles Carnan Ridgely, seventeenth Governor of Maryland (1815–18), was born in Baltimore County, December 6, 1762. He was the son of John Carnan and Achsah Ridgely. In obedience to the will of his uncle, Captain Charles Ridgely, of "Hampton," he assumed the Ridgely name and was placed at the head of the entail of "Hampton." His wife was Priscilla Dorsey, daughter of "Caleb of Belmont," sister of his uncle's wife. She bore him the following heirs: Charles—Maria Campbell; Rebecca— Judge Charles Wallace Hanson; John Carnan Ridgely—first, Prudence Gough Carroll; second, Eliza Eichelberger Ridgely (of Nicholas Greenberry Ridgely and Eliza Eichelberger.) The estate descended to their son, Captain Charles Ridgely, who married Margaret Sophia Howard (of James and Sophia Gough Ridgely). She was a granddaughter of Governor John Eager Howard and lately held " Hampton." Her son, Captain John Ridgely—Helen West Stuart, the author of " Old Brick Churches."

Charles Carnan Ridgely was a Federalist and represented Baltimore County five years in the Legislature. In 1815, he was elected Governor by a majority of two votes. In December, 1816, he sent his message to the Assembly, announcing the cession of Forts Washington and McHenry to the Government; urged the necessity of collecting the State's war claim, placing it in charge of Representative Robert H. Goldsborough. Of that claim, President Madison said: " The claim of Maryland for her expenses during the war stands upon higher ground than any other State in the Union." Yet, only a portion was ever collected. The expenses of that war exhausted the State's surplus and became the nucleus of a debt, which caused many serious considerations. During Governor Ridgely's term, seven counties and two cities, with a majority of 9,000 votes, sent only thirty-two members to the Legislature, while twelve counties in the minority, sent forty-eight members. This fact was the beginning of a long and exciting conflict which finally ended in the reform measures succeeding.

In 1817, " the good feeling era " of President Monroe was inaugurated.

GOVERNOR CHARLES GOLDSBOROUGH.

Governor Charles Goldsborough, eighteenth Governor of Maryland (1818–19), was born at Hunting Creek, Dorchester County, July 15, 1765. The progenitor of the Goldsboroughs, of Maryland, was Nicholas, who settled in 1670 on Kent Island. His wife was Miss Margaret Howes, of Newberry, Berks County, England, by whom he had Robert, Nicholas and Judith Goldsborough. Mrs. Goldsborough survived and married George Robbins, of Talbot County, who held the " Peach Blow" farm, where peaches were first grown in the United States, brought from Persia by a traveling brother, who retained his residence in England.

Robert Goldsborough (of Nicholas) married Elizabeth, daughter of Colonel Nicholas Greenberry, of Greenberry Point. Their son, Charles Goldsborough, married a sister of Colonel Joseph Ennals. Robert H., a son of this marriage, became a member of the Continental Congress and a member of the Committee of Safety. His wife was Miss Yerbury, of Bassing Hall Street, London. Among his children was Charles Goldsborough, of Horn's Point, Dorchester County, a magnificent estate on the Choptank, five miles below Cambridge, a seat of refinement and hospitality until it passed from the hands of Hon. Wm. T. Goldsborough some years after the war. His only child was Sarah Yerbury, who became the second wife of Hon. Charles Goldsborough, of Shoal Creek farm, near Cambridge. He was the son of Charles and Anna Maria (Tilghman) Goldsborough and grandson of Charles Goldsborough, of 1707.

Hon. Charles Goldsborough's first wife was Elizabeth, daughter of Judge Robert and Mary Emerson (Trippe) Goldsborough, of Myrtle Grove, Talbot County, who bore him two daughters, viz: Elizabeth Greenberry married Hon. John Leeds Kerr; Anna Maria Sarah married William Henry Fitzhugh. On May 22, 1804, he married Sarah Yerbury, daughter of Charles and Williamina (Smith) Goldsborough. By her he had nine sons and five daughters. Hon. William Tilghman Goldsborough, his son, married Eleanor Lloyd, daughter of Governor Edward Lloyd; Williamina Elizabeth Cadwalader married Rev. William Henry Laird, late rector of St. John's Church, Brookeville, Md.

Hon. Charles F. Goldsborough was a graduate of St. John's College, member of the bar, married Charlotte, youngest daughter of John Campbell Henry, of Hambrooks. She was a granddaughter of Governor John Henry. In 1818, Hon. Charles Goldsborough was elected by the Federal party Governor of Maryland. During his term an attempt was made to alter the Constitution in order to give Baltimore City two additional members in the Legislature. It failed as did the attempt to relieve Jews of their political disfranchisement.

The people of Baltimore urged that the city furnished capital and loans in a few hours which could never be obtained in the counties. It contained one-half of the increase of population in the State. By its gallant defence it had regained much of its lost popularity induced by the mob, of 1812. Yet the Governor and Assembly would not listen to these arguments and defeated the city's claim. The Jews of the city were now a growing factor of the voting power and they too had their friends who thus felt aggrieved. These facts were felt in the counties, and at the next election there was a Democratic majority in the Lower House, and, on joint ballot, Mr. Goldsborough was defeated by the young Democrat, Samuel Sprigg.

Governor Goldsborough urged the repeal of the law imprisoning debtors and it was enacted.

His report upon the turnpike roads to Frederick, York and Reistertown showed considerable benefit to the State, yet they had not received much assistance from the State.

In 1819, the first lodge of Odd Fellows in the United States was instituted in Baltimore by Thomas Wildey. Yellow fever raged throughout all the cities. The Federalist majority which elected Governor Goldsborough was reduced and the two parties were about equally divided. The election of 1819, was bitterly partisan, resulting in the election of a Democrat.

Governor Goldsborough died in Dorchester County, December 13, 1834.

GOVERNOR SAMUEL SPRIGG.

Governor Samuel Sprigg, nineteenth Governor of Maryland (1819-21), was born in Prince George County. His father was Joseph Sprigg, descendant of Thomas Sprigg, who settled in Calvert and became a Commissioner for the trial of Causes and High Sheriff, in

1664. His son, Colonel Thomas Sprigg and Margaret Osborne, his wife, held "Northampton," Prince George County. A full-length portrait of him, in court costume, was long a part of the old "Northampton" homestead, which later was bought by Lord Fairfax. Mary Sprigg, daughter of Colonel Thomas, became Mrs Thomas. Stockett, Jr.

Osborne Sprigg (of Colonel Thomas) was a leader in politics. His daughter, Margaret, married Colonel William Bowie and became the mother of Governor Robert Bowie. By a second wife, daughter of Colonel Joseph Belt, came Osborne Sprigg, Jr., signer of the Declaration of Freemen. His brother, Joseph, married, first, Hannah (Lee) Bowie, and by a second wife was the father of Governor Samuel Sprigg. "Northampton" came to Governor Sprigg from his uncle, Osborne Sprigg, Jr.

Governor Sprigg married Violetta Lansdale, first cousin of Catharine (Lansdale) Bowie, wife of Robert William Bowie (of Governor Robert); these were heirs of General Isaac Lansdale, of the Revolution, a wealthy planter.

Governor Sprigg's only son was Osborne Sprigg.

Governor Sprigg was elected in 1819, during a campaign of extreme partisan excitement, in which the Democrats gained a slight majority on joint ballot. Proscription was the watchword throughout the State, and many changes were made. Governor Sprigg was aided by a new Council composed of Democrats, and the first attempt to revolutionize existing inequalities was the attempted alteration of the election of Governor, providing for an election by the people. The Federalists bitterly opposed it, declaring it would throw the whole government of the State into the power of Baltimore City, with its one-third foreign vote. It was a fight between city and county and the Senate defeated it. The City of Baltimore again attempted to gain additional representatives, but that was also defeated.

A resolution asking that Missouri be admitted without conditions was sent to the Maryland delegates in Congress.

Criticism of President Madison's conduct of the war gave the Federalists considerable power in the State, but the Democrats were victorious at the next election and re-elected Governor Sprigg in 1820 by fifty-seven votes, which was made unanimous. President Monroe again received the electoral vote of Maryland in 1820. The ensuing election of Governor in 1821 resulted in honoring Governor Sprigg for the third time. Governor Sprigg was, later, a strong supporter of the internal improvements and was a member of the Canal Board in which he presided as president.

GOVERNOR SAMUEL STEVENS.

Governor Samuel Stevens, twentieth Governor of Maryland (1823-25), was born in Talbot County and was the son of Samuel Stevens, who had taken up a considerable estate. He was educated in the public schools, and in 1804 married Eliza May, of Chester County, Pennsylvania.

Governor Stevens succeeded Governor Samuel Sprigg, receiving a Democratic majority of sixty-nine votes on joint ballot. In 1823 he reported to the Legislature the Congressional resolution proposing an amendment providing for internal improvements.

The report of the Maryland and Virginia Commission for examining the condition of the Potomac Company, endorsed the formation of a canal company, along the bed of the Potomac, with a branch canal connecting Baltimore City. This proposition ended in the Chesapeake and Ohio Canal Company, with a capital of $6,000,000.

After much discussion, in 1824, the bill enfranchising Jews was passed.

Theodoric Bland was authorized to survey another canal route connecting Baltimore City with the Susquehanna River.

Congress made an appropriation for the great national road to Cumberland.

President Monroe started on his tour through the country, followed by a visit from General LaFayette. Annapolis made extensive preparations for the reception of its distinguished visitor. He was met at the dividing line of Anne Arundel and Prince George Counties by Hon. Joseph Kent; George E. Mitchell, Representative in Congress; Samuel Sprigg, late Governor; Hon. Jeremiah Townley Chase, late Chief Justice; Theodoric Bland, Chancellor; Colonel HenryMaynadier, an officer of the Revolution; John Randall, Collector of the Port. Judge Chase delivered the address of welcome. The military escort consisted of Captain Bowie's elegant company of mounted riflemen from Nottingham, Prince George; Captain Sillman's troop of horse from South River; Captain Dorsey's company from West River; Captain Warfield's company from Millersville; Colonel Charles Sterrett Ridgely's troop of horse from Elk Ridge, and Captain Hobb's Company of Upper Howard. The entertainment at the State House is thus described by an eye witness:

"I was a schoolboy at St. John's College. The State Legislature being in session, the Governor invited General LaFayette to visit the historic seat of the Continental Congress. My father, Rev. Alfred Griffith, was at that time Chaplain of the Senate. He was the son of Captain Samuel Griffith, who had fought with General LaFayette, and knowing his father's regard for the distinguished hero, he sent for him to be present, to again meet his old companion in arms. Although but a boy of twelve years, the grand pageant still lives in my memory. General LaFayette entered the grounds from the east. Carpeted walks led from the base of the hill to the old, stately building crowning its summit. On either side of the avenue leading to the colonaded entrance stood children, principally girls, clad in white and crowned with flowers, whilst in their hands they carried bouquets and baskets of flowers. As the old hero supported on one side by his son and staff, and on the other by the Governor and State officials, advanced up the aisle, the children broke into a chorus, "Hail to the Chief," strewing his path with flowers. Fronting the doorway stood on one side the members of the House, on the other the Senators. Having reached the portico, the General was introduced to the members of both Houses. Then prominent citizens pressed forward to be presented. When the Governor named my grandfather and gave the battles of Brandywine and Germantown in which he had fought, the old men rushed into each other's arms and wept like two children. This scene made an impression on my young mind which can never be erased."— (Griffith's Genealogy.)

Governor Stevens left no son. Descendants of a daughter still reside in Cambridge, Maryland. The following is an obituary notice of him:

"On 7th instant (1860) at 'Compton,' near Trappe, his beautiful residence, died Ex-Governor Samuel Stevens, in his eighty-second year. Thus has another, and about the last, of the strong pillars which characterized the last generation, toppled and fallen."

GOVERNOR JOSEPH KENT.

Upon the expiration of Governor Stevens' term, in 1825, Hon. Joseph Kent was chosen. He was the son of Daniel Kent, of Prince George County. He studied medicine and entered into partnership with Dr. Parran, in Lower Marlborough. In 1807 Dr. Kent removed to the vicinity of Bladensburg and became Surgeon's Mate, under the State Government. He was promoted to Major Lieutenant Colonel and Colonel of Cavalry. He presided at the first public meeting in Washington for the organization of the Chesapeake and Ohio canal, and became a director. Nominated for Congress, he defeated Hon. John Francis Mercer. He was Presidential Elector in 1816, casting his vote for James Monroe. He was elected to the Tenth and re-elected to Seventeenth, Eighteenth and Nineteenth Congresses, resigning upon his election as Governor

At the meeting in Washington over which Dr. Kent presided was an attempt to connect Baltimore with Cumberland by way of the Potomac River. Subsequent surveys developed the impracticability of this enterprise.

At a meeting held in Baltimore in 1827 the idea of a railroad was first developed. Dr. Kent was on the committee which reported in favor of immediate efforts to establish a double track between Baltimore and some point on the Ohio River. He, with Charles Carroll, of "Carrollton," Charles Ridgely and others, was upon the committee to secure the charter. This was promptly granted on February 28th. On April 1st the stock was subscribed and on April 28th the company was organized by electing Philip Evan Thomas president. On July 4, 1828 the corner stone was laid by Charles Carroll, of "Carrollton," with civic honors. Governor Kent, in his message to the Assembly, urged the support of both rival enterprises. He also urged the United States to grant Maryland her portion of the public lands, to be devoted, as the Western States were doing, to the cause of education. He suggested the propriety of changing the mode of electing the President and Vice-President; urged the Legislature to dispose of its three per cent. United States stock, worth then eighty per cent., to be invested in a sinking fund.

The national Republican party was friendly to John Quincy Adams and opposed to Andrew Jackson.

Governor Kent was Vice-President of the first convention which met in Baltimore. After a bitter contest upon the platform of the Whigs he was elected United States Senator and served four years.

Dr. Kent married, first, Eleanor Lee Wallace, daughter of Dr. Michael and Eleanor (Contee) Wallace, granddaughter of Colonel Thomas and Sarah (Fendall) Contee. Mrs. Contee was a very beautiful woman with a wealth of golden hair, and Colonel Thomas Contee left a portrait which reveals a mild, handsome face, powdered hair, ruffled shirt and stock. His inheritance was "Brookefield," the home of his mother, Jane Brooke. His wife, Sarah Fendall, was the daughter of Benjamin and Eleanor Lee, who was the daughter of Philip Lee and Sarah Brooke. Benjamin Fendall was the son of Colonel John Fendall and his wife Ellen Hanson, and grandson of Governor Josias Fendall, of 1655.

Governor Kent had, by his first wife, five children, one of whom became the wife of Governor Thomas G. Pratt. One of his descendants, Joseph Gates Kent, recently died in Baltimore. Dr. Kent married after 1826 Alice Lee Contee, of Charles County, leaving no issue. He died at his family residence, "Rose Mount," November 24, 1837. He was succeeded in 1828 by Daniel Martin.

GOVERNOR DANIEL MARTIN.

Governor Daniel Martin, twenty-second (1828-29) and twenty-fourth Governor (1830-31), was a native of Talbot, son of Thomas and Hannah Martin, grandson of Tristam and Mary Oldham, descendant of Daniel and Ann Martin of 1725.

Young Martin was thoroughly educated. Distinguished ancestors encouraged him; they were Dr. Ennals Martin, the celebrated physician; James Lloyd Martin, whose ability was never surpassed; Robert Nichols Martin, son of Judge William Bond Martin, member of Congress.

Daniel Martin married in 1816 Mary Clare Mackubin, of Annapolis, a descendant of John Mackubin, of the Severn, a Scottish immigrant, connected by marriage with both Howards and Carrolls.

At the time of Governor Martin's election, the absorbing questions were the rival sources for internal improvements. In 1828 the first spade of earth was removed from the bed of the canal by President John Quincey Adams. Thirty-four sections were put under contract. The United States subscribed $1,000,000; Washington City $1,000,000, and the State of Maryland $500,000.

Governor Martin reported the completion of twelve miles of the Washington turnpike.

Governor Martin was upon the committee which secured a charter for the Baltimore and Ohio Railroad in 1827. He was an earnest and able advocate for developing educational institutions. He favored manufacturing in the penitentiary; urged the economy of having but few State officers and was in favor of holding them to a strict accountability. He said: "To preserve the simplicity of our institutions is a deep concern; to guard them as far as possible from innovation is a sacred duty."

The national contest between the Jackson and anti-Jackson parties was brought into the State election in 1829, and resulted in placing the Democratic candidate, Thomas King Carroll, by a joint ballot of seven votes, in the chair of Governor Martin. At the next election the anti-Jackson party regained their majority and re-elected Daniel Martin by a majority of forty-one. His health soon gave way, early in his second term, and upon his death, in 1831, was succeeded by Hon. George Howard, son of Governor John Eager Howard.

Governor Martin was endeared to the society in which he passed his life by his manly and independent course, his liberal sentiments and his generous hospitality. He had filled several important public stations with much credit, and died in the occupation of the office of Chief Magistrate, whose duties he had discharged with dignity and general satisfaction. His obsequies on the 13th of July, 1831, were witnessed by a numerous concourse of fellow citizens.

At a special meeting of his Council, Mr. Worthington submitted the following record for the journal: "We hereby testify our high esteem for his frank, manly and polite deportment; his liberal, social and benevolent disposition; his republican simplicity of manners; his firmness and consistency as a politician, and his ever warm and unerring devotion to what he conceived to be the public good."

"Resolved, That the armorer cause nineteen guns to be fired on Thursday morning at sunrise and nineteen at sunset, and that the State flag be half-hoisted, as funeral honors to the deceased." Similar resolutions were offered in the Lower House and Senate. Governor George Howard, his successor, in his first message, paid another eulogy to his predecessor.

GOVERNOR THOMAS KING CARROLL.

Governor Thomas King Carroll, twenty-third Governor of Maryland (1829-30), was born in St. Mary's County in 1792. He was the son of Colonel Henry James Carroll, of St. Mary's, a family connected with Mr. James Carroll, of "All Hallow's" Parish, Anne Arundel. Although Colonel Carroll was a Catholic, his children were educated in the faith of their mother, Elizabeth Barnes King, of Somerset, only daughter and sole heiress of Colonel Thomas King, of Somerset, a descendant of Sir Robert King, baronet, whose descendants built the first Presbyterian church erected in America, at Rehoboth, in 1691.

At twenty years of age, Thomas King Carroll, having graduated at Princeton with highest honors at the age of seventeen, married Juliana, daughter of Dr. Henry Stevenson, of Baltimore. He studied law with General Robert Goodloe Harper. In early life he became a mason. He advocated the colonization of the negroes and organized a company for that purpose and was its president. In 1824 he was appointed Inspector for Somerset. He was barely of age when elected to the Legislature. As a speaker he had marked powers. When chosen Governor his surprise was great.

During his administration the question of electing the President and Vice-President was under discussion, and he reported to the Legislature the committees from the several States to form a convention for changing the prevailing system.

In 1829 the Baltimore and Ohio Railroad had laid its track as far as the Relay. This was the first road in the United States, and upon it Peter Cooper put the first locomotive built from his shop in Baltimore. It was built in Mt. Clare shops, upon the property of a relative of the Governor. Mr. Cooper himself opened the throttle and started on his trip to Ellicott's Mills. The right of way for the Chesapeake and Ohio Canal was secured to the State during the same year and the work of construction was finally begun.

Governor Carroll's message of 1830 suggested an educational system; advocated the penitentiary as a reformatory, but disapproved promiscuous social intercourse; advocated the cessation of military parades, because they drew large crowds from their daily business; urged an appropriation from Congress for copying Revolutionary records, then in the archives of Great Britain; recommended the adoption of relief for Revolutionary soldiers; endorsed the movement to improve the collegiate department of the University of Maryland and expressed sympathy for the French then gallantly defending their rights.

The anti-Jackson party of 1830 recovered its usual majority in the Legislature and Governor Carroll was succeeded by his predecessor, Governor Daniel Martin.

Governor Carroll retired to his large estate in Dorchester, near Church Creek, and lived respected by all, dying at an advanced age, October 3, 1873. He was buried in the churchyard of the "Old Church," which was heavily draped, and the entire neighborhood were mourners. He left "to posterity a noble name unsullied and adorned." His children were Dr. Thomas King Carroll, Mrs. John E. Gibson, Mrs. Dr. Bowdle, Mrs. Thomas Caddock and Misses A. E. and Mary Carroll. His daughter, Anna Ella, was a campaign strategist during the civil war.

GOVERNOR GEORGE HOWARD.

Governor George Howard, twenty-fifth Governor (1831-33), was born at "Belvidere," November 21st, 1789. He was the son of Governor John Eager Howard. His mother was the eldest daughter of Chief Justice Benjamin Chew, of Pennsylvania, and, like her sisters, was noted for her beauty and fascinating manners.

Hon. George Howard was a Federalist, and upon the death of Governor Daniel Martin, in 1831, he was appointed Governor to fill the unexpired term. Early in his administration and continuing through it began the anti-Mason excitement, which placed William

Wirt, the eminent Marylander in nomination for the Presidency, in 1833. His nomination was in opposition to Henry Clay, Federalist, but "High Priest of the Masons." The Federal party had elected Daniel Martin by forty-one majority. In 1832 it gave a still greater majority of forty-nine for Governor George Howard. With both wings of the Federal party in array against Jackson, the National Republican party at the next election secured the election of James Thomas as Governor to succeed Governor Howard. The Federal party now became the Whig party. It held sway in Maryland with varying success until 1852. Its National and State issues called for a United States bank, internal improvements and a high tariff.

Governor George Howard was a presidential elector in 1837 and 1841, voting both times for William Henry Harrison. His estate "Waverly" had been taken up by Thomas Browne. It was sold to John Dorsey (of Major Edward) and by him willed to his son, Nathaniel Dorsey. From his brother it was bought by Governor John Eager Howard. It is on the old Frederick road, just south of Woodstock. During the exciting slavery agitation of 1845 Governor Howard presided at a Convention called for the protection of slave-holders. He also presided at a meeting of the people of Howard County to pass resolutions upon the death of Colonel Gassaway Watkins, in 1840. He married in 1811, Prudence Gough Ridgely, daughter of Charles Carnan Ridgely, of Hampton. She bore him eight sons and five daughters, two of whom married. Eugene Post, John Eager Howard, Charles Ridgely Howard, William Waverly Howard and George Howard were his sons.

Governor Howard died in 1846. "Waverly" has passed from the family and most of his descendants are in Baltimore or elsewhere.

GOVERNOR JAMES THOMAS.

Governor James Thomas, twenty-sixth Governor of Maryland (1833-35), was born at De-la Brooke Manor, March 11, 1785. He was the son of William Major Thomas and Catharine Boarman, daughter of Mary Brooke, through whom "De-la Brooke" passed from Roger Brooke to the Thomas family. William Thomas was the youngest son of John Thomas, of Charles County. He removed to St. Mary's; was a member of the House of Delegates; was chosen Captain and Major of the militia; was a member of the Committee of Safety. His wife was Elizabeth Reeves (of Thomas).

James Thomas was educated at Charlotte Hall, in 1804, and graduated from the University of Pennsylvania in 1807. He practiced with success; was commissioned Major of the Fourth Maryland Cavalry in 1812 and was subsequently brevetted Major-General. In 1820 he was elected a member of the Maryland Legislature and was re-elected six times. In 1833 he became Governor of Maryland. During his administration much excitement arose from the "Nat Turner" negro insurrection.

The boundary line between Maryland and Virginia was still unsettled, and this dispute caused the Governor considerable correspondence.

In his message he announced the completion of the Baltimore and Ohio Railroad as far west as Harper's Ferry. The road between Baltimore and Washington was then under construction. He urged the enrollment of the militia and asked the general government to apportion Maryland's share of vacant lands.

The disastrous fire in Cumberland, in 1834, and the "Bank Mob" in Baltimore called for executive action. Governor Thomas met these with prompt and decisive action, receiving favorable comment. The cause of the "Bank Mob" was the financial disaster following President Jackson's withdrawal of Government funds, from the National Bank. This caused the failure of the Maryland Bank, which held the savings of many poor people, leading to a bitter feeling against the bank officers and finally ending in a riot, which destroyed their houses. The Governor calling out the militia and appealing to the President for aid soon quelled the riot, but not until $200,000 worth of property had been destroyed. This the State was compelled to refund.

The Baltimore and Ohio Railroad called on the Legislature for assistance, and a loan of $2,000,000 was made during the Governor's term. The State also aided the Susquehanna or Northern Central Railroad to the amount of $1,000,000.

Governor Thomas died at "Deep Falls," St. Mary's, December 25, 1845. Descendants of Governor Thomas were Dr. Thomas, a member of the State Grange; Professor Thomas, Principal of Charlotte Hall, and Hon. William M. Merrick and Richard Merrick, of Howard County, sons of United States Senator Merrick, whose wife was a descendant of Governor Thomas.

"Deep Falls," the Thomas homestead, is situated near the village of Chaptico. The present mansion was built by Major William Thomas, in 1745. It is in appearance an English country dwelling-house, and while its builder aimed at massive simplicity, it is of graceful and pleasing design and finish. It is a large, double, two-story frame building, with brick foundations and brick gables to the upper line of the first story, where the brick-work branches into two large outside chimneys at each gable end of the house. It is sixty feet long and forty feet deep, with wide piazzas, front and back, running the whole length of the house and supported by handsome, massive pillars. The hall is a large, well-finished square room and is flanked on one side by a parlor and on the other by a dining-room, separated by folding doors. The stairway with maple newel posts and rosewood top, surmounted with an ivory knob, rosewood rail and bird's eye maple balustrade, extends around the corridors above.

The surrounding grounds, once highly ornamented with shrubbery and flowers, are gently sloping and terraced. "Deep Falls" is still held by its original family and the old grave-yard there, dedicated to family burial more than a century and a half ago, contains many successive generations. (Thomas.)

De-la-Brooke, containing two thousand acres, was erected into a manor, with the right of Court Baron and Court Leet, and Baker

Brooke, eldest son of Robert, was made lord of the manor. The house at De-la-Brooke stood about a mile from the river, on the brow of a hill. It was a commanding situation with broad plains below. It was a brick building, thirty by forty feet, one and a-half stories, with steep roof and dormer windows. The rooms were handsomely wainscotted and the parlor was also embellished with massive wooden cornice and frieze, on which were carved in relief roses and other floral designs. The house was destroyed many years ago, but a mass of moss-covered bricks and an excavation still mark the spot where for nearly two hundred years stood the first manor house on the Patuxent. (Thomas.)

Near Battle Town is the handsome Taney homestead, the seat of the distinguished family for many generations and the birthplace of the illustrious Chief Justice Roger Brooke Taney, while separated from it by Battle Creek is Brooke Place Manor, in later life the home of Governor Robert Brooke.

GOVERNOR THOMAS WARD VEAZEY.

Thomas Ward Veazey, twenty-seventh Governor of Maryland (1835–38), was born January 31, 1774, at "Veazey's Neck," Cecil County, Maryland. He was the son of Edward and Elizabeth (DeCoursey) Veazey, a descendant (of John) of "Cherry Grove," an old Norman family, "De Veazie," of the eleventh century. John settled in Kent County, prior to 1670, and received a grant of land on Elk and Bohemia Rivers, known as "Veazey's Neck," now in Cecil. His will of February 28, 1697, names his sons William, George, Robert and James. The latter married Mary Mercer, whose son, Captain Edward Veazey, of Seventh Regiment of the Maryland Line, was killed at Long Island, 1776. Colonel Thomas Ward Veazey (of Edward) was Colonel of the militia, in the war of 1812 and made a gallant defence of Frederick Town, in Cecil, against Admiral Cockburn. He was a member of the Maryland Legislature during several sessions; was a presidential elector in 1807 and in 1813, when he voted for President Madison. He married, first, Sarah Worrell, of Kent, and had one daughter, Sarah. His second wife was Mary Veazey, who bore him five children; his third was Mary, daughter of Dr. Joseph and Elizabeth (Black) Wallace, whom he married in 1812 and she bore him five children.

Colonel Veazey came to the Governor's chair in 1835, when a strong man was needed.

The most popular act of his administration was the grant of eight millions of dollars for internal improvements; $3,000,000 were given to the Canal, and $3,000,000 to Baltimore and Ohio Railroad.

This act was hailed with joy in Baltimore, resulting in a dinner to the Governor and Legislature and accompanied by bon-fires. Baltimore City subscribed in addition, $3,000,000 loan to the road.

The most exciting event in the administration of Governor Veazey was the attempt to reform the mode of electing the Senate and Governor of the State. The discussion had grown stronger with each succeeding administration since the election of Governor Ridgely, in 1818. A condensed history of that struggle, from the researches of Dr. Bernard Steiner, the Librarian of the Pratt Library, is of interest.

"The electoral college was established by the aristocratic Whigs of the Revolution and lasted through sixty years until it went down under the Democratic ideas of Jackson. Major Sprigg Harwood, who died in 1894, was the last survivor of the electoral college. This college was composed of two members from each county and one from Annapolis and one from Baltimore. This body elected fifteen Senators, each holding property valued at £1,000 current money. A quorum of the college was fixed at twenty-four. The property qualification for membership in the college was £500. By this system of election it was said, "The Senate of Maryland consisted of men of influence and ability and as such were a real and beneficial check on the hasty proceedings of a more numerous branch of popular representatives."

By a special election for electors in 1776, the electors chosen met in Annapolis, December 9th, and chose the Senate. On February 10, 1777, this body met with the House of Delegates, elected annually by the people, and thus formed the first Assembly of Maryland.

In 1806 the form of voting for electors was changed from viva voce to ballot. After 1810 there was no property qualification needed for Senators.

The Senate of 1781 were the most distinguished men of the State. They were unanimously Whigs. The Senate of 1791 and 1796 were also of the Federalist party, showing the same complexion in the electorial college. In 1801, the Republicans (Democrats) carried the Senate, holding the power, also, in 1806 and in 1811. With the election of 1816 came the first decided opposition to the prevailing system of election.

Baltimore, with more wealth and nearly the full population of eight of the smaller counties, had only one-fortieth part of the power of Legislation, while these counties had two-fifths. Several of the larger counties joined Baltimore to get a better division.

The Republicans, in 1816, elected twelve of the electoral college. The Federal returns were twenty-eight, but twenty-two of these represented only 93,265, while the other six and the twelve Republican electors represented 176,000 people. Yet a solid Federal Senate was chosen for five years. In 1821 an entire Republican Senate was chosen by an electoral college of twenty-eight Republicans and twelve Federalists. In 1826, a like Republican majority was returned, but six of the twenty-two voted with the fourteen Federalists and elected a mixed Senate of eleven Republicans and four Federalists.

In 1831 an electoral college of twenty-eight National Republicans and twelve Jackson men elected a Senate entirely composed of National Republicans. This was the last peaceful election under that system. The spirit of reform was in the air. The election of Jackson as the Democratic President swept the country.

In Maryland, Jackson and VanBuren found their supporters chiefly in Baltimore and the large counties.   In 1836 Van Buren supporters elected nineteen electors and the Whigs twenty-one.   In that election, Baltimore with a vote of 10,000 and Annapolis with a vote of 300 each sent one elector, while Frederick County with a vote of 6,000 and Charles County with a vote of 567 each sent two. Baltimore, Harford, Washington, Frederick and Baltimore City sent Van Buren electors.   Montgomery sent one of each party.

Congressman Francis Thomas, of Frederick County, finding that the majority of the electoral college represented but 85,179 white men, while the minority was chosen from counties and towns with a population of 205,922 white men, organized a revolt.   The Whigs had but twenty-one and a quorum required twenty-four.   The nineteen Van Buren men determined to refuse to·enter the college until assured by the Whig members that they would not vote for a Senator who would oppose calling a Convention of the people and also to elect eight Van Buren men as Senators, so as to give a majority of that body known to be favorable to a radical revision of the Constitution, granting equal rights and privileges.   No action having been taken in reply, the nineteen Van Buren electors met at City Hotel and offered propositions.   Mr. Thomas was in Annapolis directing the negotiations.   As no compromise was in sight the "nineteen" went to their homes, leaving the Whigs in Annapolis, waiting for help to organize.

In the meantime meetings were held.   At one in Baltimore, John V. L. McMahon, the historian, spoke eloquently in support of the Whig position and opposed "the bold proposition to overthrow the whole Government at one blow."

The Whig electors issued an address in reply to that of the Van Buren nineteen, claiming that if they had gone into the college they would have found advocates of their reforms, and thus discussions filled all channels until another election day for members of the House came, which proved to be a defeat for the Van Buren nineteen. Counties which had sent Democrats now returned Whigs.   In all there were sixty Whigs to nineteen Van Buren men.   Immediately upon this election Mr. John S. Sellman, of Anne Arundel, regarding the election as an instruction from his constituents, entered the college.   Mr. Wesley Linthicum from Anne Arundel refused to enter.

Dr. Washington Duval from Montgomery refused, not considering the election a defeat to Van Buren, but demanded a Convention.

Criticisms were loud upon the revolutionary conduct of Governor Francis Thomas.   Mr. Sellman, of Anne Arundel, attempted to bring about a compromise, saying that he would not enter the college until a quorum was secured, and such a quorum could not be obtained without a compromise of conflicting interests.

The Whigs only replied by calling his attention to their address to the people.   Thus his efforts proved futile.

The National election, a few days later, proved a complete overthrow of the Van Buren party in Maryland.

Governor Veazey now came to the front and issued his proclamation, declaring the Senate elected in 1831 shall continue to be the Senate of Maryland, and shall so continue until superseded by the election of successors, as constitutionally and lawfully provided for, and with the house elected in October last, now constitute the general assembly of this State. He assembled it to meet on November 21, assigning as his reason the failure of eighteen electors to do their duty. He further declared, that he would use all the powers in his office to break up such lawless proceedings. He concluded with a solemn declaration, "that the Constitution of the State must be preserved until altered, in the manner constitutionally provided for." Great excitement followed. Major John Contee called the people of Prince George together and offered "our services to the executive in case of necessity." Mr. Wesley Linthicum, of Anne Arundel, determined to yield. Mr. Sellman again addressed the Whigs to know if they were in favor of Constitutional reform. They answered, yes, not in a restricted, but a comprehensive sense, and would elect a Senate in favor of amendment. The Van Buren men were compelled to surrender unconditionally.

Fifteen Whig Senators were elected, the new Legislature, at the suggestion of the Governor, provided for the amendments urged by the nineteen and provided that the election of Governor should be by the people.

The electoral college was abolished. The Senate was to consist of one member from each county and the City of Baltimore, elected by popular vote for six years, one-third going out of office every two years. The executive council was abolished and a Secretary of State substituted.

When the first election under the reformed Constitution occurred, October 2, 1838, the Van Buren candidate for Governor, William Grason, "The Queen Anne Farmer," won by a very narrow margin, while the Legislature was Whig by small majorities in each house. The so-called "glorious nineteen" claimed much of the credit for these changes.

Governor Veazey was the last Governor elected by the Senate. He died in Cecil, June 30, 1842.

GOVERNOR WILLIAM GRASON.

Governor William Grason, twenty-eighth Governor (1838–1841), was born 1786, in Queen Anne County. He was a Federalist of the old school and in after years a Jackson Democrat. He served in both branches of the State Legislature. In 1836, he became the leader of his party in the contest for a new Constitution and became the first Governor under it by a very small majority of 300. The excitement of the close campaign was followed by a riot in Baltimore as the returns came in. Governor Grason was known as the "Queen Anne Farmer."

During his administration, President Louis McLane announced the completion of the Washington Branch of the Baltimore and Ohio Railroad and the advance of the main stem to Harper's Ferry.

The Chesapeake and Ohio Canal, by its report of 1839, showed progress as far as Cumberland. Three millions of dollars had already been expended, for which the company had receipted. "The State retained $500,000 to pay premium. The work had proved to be a stupendous one and the company asked for a modification of the law of 1836, in order to render certificates more available. When completed the Canal ought to pay six per cent. dividends, but with the present appropriation, the company can not keep work going more than six months."

Governor Grason sent in the first report of the President and Directors of the Eastern Shore Railroad, showing receipts $40,000 above expenses, he also sent in a report on abolishing imprisonment for debt, and the report of the Elk Ridge Railroad and its progress.

His message upon the pecuniary embarrassment of the State and his criticism of the condition of the State's internal improvements was considered the most important measure of his administration. The public debt was shown to be $14,587,689. The annual revenues were barely sufficient to pay the ordinary expenses of $250,000. We cannot expect the companies now in process of organization to pay their annual interest promptly.

In 1836 the State had authorized a loan of $8,000,000 from foreign sources. The money was plentiful and securities in demand. This has changed and it is impossible to sell our bonds. The Northern Central Railroad owes the State $200,000; the Eastern Shore road owes $100,000 more. These debts are due to the wild spirit of internal improvements. We must resort to rigid economy and increase our revenues by a moderate tax on real and personal estate. Two hundred thousand dollars in addition to our present revenue might be enough for present emergencies.

Governor Grason also urged a change in the Constitution to limit the power of the Legislature. "Ours is a Constitution for the judiciary and executive, but not for the Legislature."

His communication to President Van Buren urging the United States Government to deliver its stock in the Canal Company to the State upon its assumption of the working expenses, was an able presentation of the State's demand. Governor Grason's message led to widespread discussion. It was answered by President Louis McLane, of the Baltimore and Ohio Railroad, and the Governor issued an additional message maintaining his position, that the wholesale hypothecation of the State's bonds was disastrous to the State and must cause trouble.

In 1840, Governor Grason showed the debt had increased over one million more whilst the deficits for the year were over a half a million. His message pointed out the hopeless prospect of realizing from the Government anything like enough to pay the State's indebtedness.

He reported the Susquehanna road, Elk Ridge road and the Tidewater Canal, all finished, whilst there was nothing to be reported from the Chesapeake and Ohio Canal.

Francis Thomas, President of the Canal, later made an exhaustive report in which he showed it had already expended $7,000,000, and when completed it would amount to $9,500,000. The Legislature thereupon insituted an investigation, on the ground that its management was in the interest of the political ambition of its President.

The campaign of 1840, known as the "hard cider and log cabin campaign," resulted in the election of William Henry Harrison. His sudden death and the desertion of John Tyler ruined the Whig party, and in 1841 Francis Thomas, Democrat, was made Governor.

Governor Grason was afterward the nominee for the United States Senate, but was defeated by the Senate refusing to go into an election. He was a member of the Constitutional Convention of 1851.

His wife was a daughter of Dr. James Sullivane, of Dorchester. Their son Richard, born 1820, was educated at St. John's College and was admitted to the bar in 1841. He removed to Elkton, where he was appointed deputy attorney, then State's attorney. Removing to Towson, in 1864, he was elected Judge, but was unseated by the Legislature. Under the Constitution of 1867 he was elected Chief Judge for fifteen years.

In 1847, he married the eldest daughter of General Charles Sterrett Ridgely, of Howard County. He died of paralysis at Towson, in 1893. His father died in 1868.

GOVERNOR FRANCIS THOMAS.

Governor Francis Thomas, twenty-ninth Governor of Maryland (1841–44), was born in Frederick County, February 3, 1799. He was the son of Francis and Grace (Metcalfe) Thomas, who was the son of William Thomas, son of Hugh Thomas and Betty Edwards, of "Montevue." This progenitor descended from the family of Bishop William Thomas, of Caermarthen, who came from Wales to Pennsylvania.

Francis Thomas, seventh child of his father, entered St. John's College, Annapolis, as early as 1811, but as there were no classes from that date until 1822 was not graduated. He was admitted to the bar in 1820 and settled in Frankville, Maryland, to practice.

In 1822, 1827 and 1829 he represented his county in the Legislature, rising to Speaker the last year.

In 1831 he was sent to Congress. He became President of the Chesapeake and Ohio Canal in 1839–40. When a candidate for Governor he fought a duel with William Price. He was the second. Governor under the provision making elections triennial.

Governor Thomas in his message of 1842, made this stirring review: "The public debt, destroying public credit, has been our burden. Met by your predecessors in a public spirit, the means are yet inadequate, a decided course is needed.

"Baltimore City had borrowed by legislative act nearly $5,000,000, to pay the interest on which requires $270,000. The public debt of the State is $15,000,000. The assessment of $196,000,-000 requires a tax of seventy-one cents in Baltimore and thirty-one cents in the State.

"The general stagnation of business, depression in prices and diminution of currency all tend to urge the necessity for an extension of time for paying taxes. The expediency of using the bank stock of the State by transferring it to creditors is entitled to consideration.

"In 1830 the State had means for all its uses, but within seven years our State debt has been increased $12,000,000 for internal improvements, and now our State of 10,000 square miles and a population of 318,194 is staggering with an undertaking that would test the resources of Great Britain. Now we must either repudiate or submit to the tax-gather.

"The 'glorious 19' of Van Buren's forces accomplished good results, modifying the difficulties of a minority ruling the majority, but even now the majority of the Senate can repudiate any means for expressing the will of the two-third majority of the State. The House and Senate cannot concur in the appointment of officers controlling the works of improvement. The Governor cannot appoint.

"The power of these companies is great in its effect upon the destiny of the State. Their influence has created this debt. If the minority are to direct and the majority to pay there will always be difficulty.

"The distributive share of the proceeds of the public lands is hereby made known. Maryland gets $15,000, but the Government claims against the State amount to $20,000. So the United States retains the whole amount and lays claim to the balance. This cry that the United States would pay our State demands has been our delusion. High tariff and land sales were the delusions that we thought would enrich us. These have made our debt, and the result is a fund not sufficient to pay the interest on bonds held in trust for the Indians.

"The land bill is as fruitless as ashes. Our public debt, if paid, must be taken out of our own resources. Whoever thinks otherwise follows a phantom. Reject any idea that the National Government can be made to pay State debts.

"The Chesapeake and Ohio Canal reports are not encouraging. It ought to be completed. The people are willing to be taxed if any results of returns for outlays are visible. To do so we must amend the Charter and grant preferred stock to an amount sufficient to complete the work and to pay the debts."

Governor Thomas also opposed the payment of unnecessary salaries to Judges. He charged that $500,000 had been wasted. In his message of 1843 he announced "that our debt had been increased to over $16,000,000. Our ordinary revenues are only sufficient to pay ordinary expenses. The assessment has been reduced from $196,000,000 to $178,000,000. With interest upon the debt nearly $2,000,000 in arrears, the tax system, now imperfect, must be improved. Even the executive office has been curtailed and no power is given to it to help the State. Political ascendency has done it. The executive can only suggest. There is a feeling of discontent by taxpayers. It is unjust to make a portion pay the burden. The Legislature must see that the law is vigorously carried out. The sale of stock for internal improvements would not pay our debt. The Baltimore and Ohio Railroad has not been a burden. It has paid its interest. The general Government needs all the land sales. We must remodel our tax laws; exchange the State's stocks in public works and use its bank stock for debts. This will give relief."

His third message, in 1844, still pointed out a failure to meet the State's obligations. The Baltimore and Susquehanna Railroad was not able to pay its interest.

The repudiation talk induced by Governor Thomas' message became a campaign cry in the next election and resulted in a Whig victory. Governor Thomas G. Pratt succeeded.

When an attempt was made in 1867 to take the Naval Academy from Annapolis because of the atmosphere of disloyalty, Governor Thomas, then in Congress, joined Congressman Philips in an eloquent defence, which resulted in retaining the Academy. but when the people were trying to adopt the Constitution of 1867 he asked Congress to give Maryland a Republican form of Government, declaring, "I deny utterly here, and have denied it for thirty years, that there is a Republican form of government in Maryland."

Congress failed to follow the Governor's advice, though many petitions were sent in from the Federal men of Maryland. The Constitution of 1867 was secured, notwithstanding all opposition. Governor Thomas was fearless, active and eloquent and his influence in every sphere was remarkable. For a long time he lived the recluse life of his mountain home.

In 1850, as a Delegate to the State Convention, he exerted his influence to reduce the power of the slave-holding counties of the State.

On the outbreak of the Civil War Governor Thomas raised a volunteer regiment of 3,000 men for the Union Army, but refused to command it. In 1866 he was a Delegate to the Loyalist Convention at Philadelphia and became a strong opposer of the policy of President Johnson. In April, 1870, Governor Thomas was appointed Collector of Internal Revenue for the Cumberland District and served until March 25, 1872, when he was appointed Minister to Peru.

He resigned this position in 1875, and returned to his farm, "Montevue," near Frankville. While walking on a railroad track he was killed by a locomotive, January 22, 1876.

Governor Thomas was married to Sallie Campbell Preston, daughter of Governor James McDowell, of Virginia.

GOVERNOR THOMAS GEORGE PRATT.

Governor Thomas George Pratt, thirtieth Governor of Maryland (1844–47), was born in Georgetown, D. C., February 18, 1804. He was a descendant of Thomas Pratt, of Prince George, by his wife, Eleanor Magruder. Educated in his native town, he studied law, was admitted to the bar and began his career in Upper Marlborough, in 1823. In 1832–35 he was sent to the House of Delegates; in 1836 was a member of the electoral college and President of the last Executive Council of Maryland. In 1838 he was State Senator.

After a fierce contest on the Whig ticket, opposed to repudiation, he was elected Governor. During his administration he succeeded in restoring the public credit.

Governor Pratt began his administration by calling on the Legislature for power to enforce the laws already existing for the collection of taxes. "From the abundant harvest now at hand, now is the time to pay our debts;" proposed the renewment of revenue laws; called for a new assessment and the collection of all bank direct taxes amounting to $1,000,000; proposed an improvement of the indirect tax law, especially in executor's and administrator's accounts; advised to return to the stamp tax; urged the extension of the Baltimore and Ohio Railroad to Ohio. In his message of 1847 his resumption law had brightened prospects and reduced the debt; referred to the good office of Mr. George Peabody in enabling the State to borrow and sell in foreign markets; condemned the course of the Governor of Pennsylvania in his action against the fugitive slave law.

The Legislature of 1845 passed the biennial Assembly of the Legislature, thereby saving $30,000 yearly; referred the question of a new Constitution back to the people; reduced the salaries of Governor and Legislature and his Secretary of State; abolished the Chancery Court. In the election of 1846 the Government and Legislature were sustained by large Whig gains.

During 1846, Governor Pratt in his Proclamation, calling for two regiments of infantry for the Mexican War, said: "The sons of Maryland have always obeyed the call of patriotism and duty, and will now sustain the honor of the State."

Volunteers came from every section, but only one battalion of Maryland and District of Columbia Volunteers was at first selected, but companies of volunteers in nearly every county awaited the call and many went as independent companies. During the war Maryland supplied 2,500 men. He afterward resumed the practice of law in Annapolis.

In 1849 he was elected United States Senator to fill the unexpired term of Reverdy Johnson, resigned, and was elected for a full term in 1850. Upon the expiration of his Senatorial term he settled in Baltimore, becoming an ardent advocate for secession. For a few weeks he has confined in Fortress Monroe. In 1864 he was a

Delegate to the Chicago National Democratic Convention and to the Philadelphia Union Convention in 1866. In 1837 he was a presidential elector on the Van Buren ticket.

Governor Pratt married Adelaide, daughter of Governor Joseph Kent. He bought the Governor Ogle residence in Annapolis, corner of King George and College Avenues. He was a man of distinguished presence and an able speaker. He died in Baltimore, November 9, 1869, when the following resolutions were passed by the bar of Baltimore:

"Resolved, That we remember with gratitude and with pride the noble disregard of personal popularity to the discharge of his duty which marked the official course of our lamented brother, when, as executive of Maryland, he linked his name forever with the re-establishment of good faith of the State." He was with Clay, Webster and Calhoun in the Senate and his arguments in the Maryland reports showed his ability. His funeral services were held from St. Anne's Church, Annapolis, November 11, 1869. Governor Oden Bowie and Staff were in attendance. George Peabody, whose aid was combined with Governor Pratt in redeeming the State, died on November 4th of that year. Governor Pratt left a widow and several children.

GOVERNOR PHILIP FRANCIS THOMAS.

Philip Francis Thomas, thirty-first Governor of Maryland (1848–51), was born at Easton, September 24, 1810. He was the oldest son of Dr. Tristram and Maria (Francis) Thomas and grandson of Tristram and Elizabeth (Martin), and great-grandson of Tristram Ann (Coursey) Thomas, daughter of Christopher. His mother was the daughter of Philip and Henrietta Maria (Goldsborough) Francis, granddaughter of Tench Francis, Attorney-General of Pennsylvania, in 1744, a descendant of Philip Francis, Mayor of Plymouth, in 1644, and father of Sir Philip Francis, the reputed author of "Letters of Junius."

Philip Francis Thomas was educated at Easton Academy and Dickinson College; was admitted to the bar in 1831; was a member of the Legislature in 1838 and subsequently was in Congress in 1839–41; was elected Governor in 1848.

On January 3, 1848, he laid before the Legislature a message of great force on constitutional reforms and retrenchments; he was in favor of the resumption of the payment of State debts; urged the effective collections of taxes; favored a call for a Constitutional Convention; started a "Reform Party," which re-elected him. His next message showed marked financial improvements; removed the doubts and restored confidence by meeting all obligations; and predicted by strict adherence to his suggestions the entire debt would be extinguished in thirteen years. His closing words were, in urging a new Constitution, "unless the Legislature yields to the wishes of the people, the sanction of the Legislature will no longer be invoked." This warning resulted in a "reform bill," which passed both Houses. It called a Convention; adopted a Constitution which went into effect in 1851. By that Constitution Baltimore City gained five members and the counties lost seventeen members in the Assembly. Governor Thomas was elected Comptroller of the Treasury in 1851; resigned it in 1853, and was made Collector of the Port in Baltimore under President Pierce; was offered, but declined, the Governorship of Eutah; was appointed by President Buchanan Secretary of the Treasury, which he resigned in 1861; was again elected a member of the Legislature, during which session he was elected United States Senator, but was refused admission because of alleged disloyalty. In 1868 he was elected to Congress, where he became an able representative. He was afterward returned to the Maryland Legislature and became Chairman of Ways and Means.

Governor Thomas married, first, Sarah Maria Kerr; second, Mrs. Clintonia (Wright) May. His daughters are Mrs. Sophia Kerr Trippe, Mrs. Maria Thomas Markoe and Mrs. Nannie Bell Hemsley. Governor Thomas died in 1890. Mrs. Clintonia Thomas has outlived all of her sisters and brothers.

GOVERNOR ENOCH LOUIS LOWE.

Governor Enoch Louis Lowe, thirty-second Governor (1850-8), was born 1820. He was the son of Lieutenant Bradley S. A. Lowe, a graduate of West Point who served through the War of 1812. His mother was Adelaide Bellumeau de la Vincendine. Their residence was the "Hermitage," a fine estate of 1,000 acres, about three miles from Frederick, on the Monocacy River. There Enoch Louis Lowe was born. Lieutenant Lowe was the the son of Lloyd M. and Rebecca (Maccubbin) Lowe and grandson of Michael and Ann (Magruder) Lowe, all of Western Maryland.

Enoch Louis Lowe was educated at Frederick and from there went to a college near Dublin and then to the Roman Catholic College of Stonyhurst, Lancashire, England, where he remained until 1839. He was admitted to the bar in 1842. In 1845 he was elected to the House of Delegates, becoming an able and eloquent champion of democracy in Western Maryland. In 1850, whilst quite young, he was elected Governor. A new Constitution was about to be adopted. Governor Lowe suggested the following amendment: First, a revision of the election laws; second, a revision of the criminal code in regard to the inequality of punishment, pardons and remissions of fines; Third, a modification of the tax on civil commissions; ascertainment of the number and salaries of deputy clerks, and an entirely new system of issuing licenses.

In his message Governor Lowe recorded: "It gives me profound pleasure to announce the completion of the Baltimore and Ohio Railroad to the Ohio River. This opens up wealth for our own State. The Washington branch has paid a capitation tax of $59,826.29 and the road is highly satisfactory, but misfortune seems to attend the Chesapeake and Ohio Canal. A year ago I announced its completion, but the Spring tide has crippled it, causing a loss of $100,000, but its revenue, $250,000, will enable it to pay interest in 1854. The Susquehanna Railroad is advancing and with the exception of the canal, the internal works are helping the State, and the finances are now on the advance. From direct and indirect revenue laws and internal improvements the State will realize $1,500,000. The new assessment will probably reach $50,000,000." Upon that basis he urged a reduction in taxation. "The sinking fund has been pronounced a fallacy, but taxpayers pay no more to the sinking fund upon bonds of the State purchased for and held by the State for its use, than they would if held by public creditors. The debt is still over $15,000,000, less the sinking fund. Said my predecessor, 'It has been my duty, owing to pressing debt, to seize upon every expedient by which money could be placed in the treasury. It will, I trust, be my successor's pleasure to recommend the repeal of those taxes which have proved most oppressive to the people of the State.' Following that wish, I recommended last year a reduction of twenty per cent. on direct tax. I recommend now a reduction of forty per cent."

His message of 1854 urged that the execution of criminals should be private. The canal was then in good condition. The Baltimore and Ohio Railroad was leading to success. The Washington branch had increased its revenues and the sinking fund had reached $3,000,000. He had underestimated the increase of the new assessment when placed at $50,000,000. The gross amount of taxable bases had reached $261,243,660, an increase of $68,421,081. The reduction in taxation has given tangible relief.

In 1857 the position of minister extraordinary and plenipotentiary to China was offered him, which he declined.

He was a Democratic elector in 1860 and voted for John Cabel Breckinridge for President. He was present when Governor T. Holliday Hicks gave his assent to the burning of the bridges leading to Baltimore, in order that Northern soldiers might not be able to pass through the city. In 1861 Governor Lowe went south and remained during the war. In 1866 he removed to Brooklyn, New York, and practiced law, bearing with him letters from distinguished Southern leaders.

He married May 29, 1844, Esther Winder Polk, daughter of Colonel James and Anna Maria (Stuart) Polk, of Princess Anne, son of Judge William Polk, of the Court of Appeals, a cousin of President Polk. Mrs. Anna Maria Stuart Polk was the daughter of Dr. Alexander Stuart, of Delaware.

Governor Lowe had eleven children: Mrs. Austin Jenkins and her sister, Mrs. Jenkins, are daughters; his sons are in New York, Chicago and San Francisco.

Governor Lowe died August 27, 1892.

GOVERNOR THOMAS WATKINS LIGON.

Governor Thomas Watkins Ligon, thirty-third Governor (1853-7), was born in Prince Edward County, Virginia, 1812. He was the son of Thomas D. Ligon, whose wife was a daughter of Colonel Thomas Watkins, an officer under General Washington, in command of a troop of horse raised by his own exertions in Prince Edward County, and took an active part in the battle of Guilford, North Carolina. His ancestors on both sides were in the Revolution. His father died young, leaving Thomas Watkins and James in the care of their mother.

At an early age Thomas Watkins Ligon was sent to Hampden Sidney College, where he was graduated, and completed his education at the University of Virginia, after which he entered Yale Law School. Returning to Virginia, he was admitted to the bar and removed to Baltimore.

In 1840 he married and removed to Howard County, near Ellicott City.

In 1843 he was elected to the Legislature, after which he was sent to the Thirtieth Congress.

In 1853 he was elected Governor to succeed Governor Lowe under the Constitution of 1851 for four years. He was a Democrat and was confronted by a Whig Legislature in the height of the Know-Nothing excitement. He sent a message to the Assembly in which he took a strong stand against secret political parties, declaring, " All history warns us that a war of races or sects is the deadliest curse that can afflict a nation." In that message he asked for a committee to investigate the prevailing reports then circulating concerning the secret movements of that party. The Legislature assented to his request and a committee was ordered. The majority of that committee refused to enter into an investigation, but contented themselves in attacking the Democratic party, on which the Governor stood. The minority report sustained the Governor's charge. The State was soon convinced of the correctness of the Governor's charges in the succeeding election for the Mayor of Baltimore.

Failing to get the co-operation of Mayor Swann in correcting the abuses then prevalent, Governor Ligon issued a special message to the Legislature in which he deplored the partisan discord in the election in Baltimore.

At the next election the Democratic candidates withdrew and the judges of the elections resigned. Voters appealed to Governor Ligon for protection. He went to Baltimore and commenced a correspondence with Mayor Swann, and failing to get the Mayor's consent to co-operate, issued orders to call out the militia to protect voters; at the instigation of the citizens of Baltimore, a compromise was effected; he revoked the call, but the result of the election was so unsatisfactory and abuses were so palpable, that Governor Ligon in his next message made a vigorous attack upon the returned members. The House refused to receive his message, but the Governor's forcible arguments and earnest efforts started a reform movement in Baltimore which ended in a conservative victory.

Retiring from office he resumed farming; took interest in advancing institutions of learning and religion. He was president of the Patapsco Female Institute and member of several charitable institutions.

He died at his home, near Ellicott City, January 12, 1881, in the seventieth year of his age.

Governor Ligon married, first, Sallie Dorsey (of Charles Worthington Dorsey). Issue, Mrs. Dorsey Thompson. His second wife was Mary Tolley Dorsey, sister of his first wife. Two daughters and one son, Charles W. Dorsey Ligon, survive.

GOVERNOR THOMAS HOLLIDAY HICKS.

Thomas Holliday Hicks, thirty-fourth Governor and United States Senator of Maryland (1857-61), was born September 2, 1798, about four miles from East New Market, Dorchester County, Maryland. He was the son of Henry and Mary (Sewell) Hicks, who was a relative of General Sewell, of the American army. They were members of the Methodist Church and had eleven children.

Thomas Holliday Hicks attended school near home. In 1824 he was elected Sheriff. Purchasing a farm on the Choptank, from there he was sent to the Legislature.

In 1833 he removed to Vienna and became a merchant, running a line of boats to Baltimore.

In 1836 he was elected a member of the State Electoral College which then had the election of the State Senate, Governor and his Council. The election was a deadlock, lasting two months, and resulted in considerable disorder. Whilst at Annapolis Mr. Hicks was elected a member of the Legislature which made the Senate and Council elective.

In 1837 he was a member of the Governor's Council, and in 1838 Governor Veazey appointed him Register of Wills in Dorchester County, which he held by reappointment until 1851, when that office was made elective.

In 1857 Mr. Hicks was nominated and elected Governor by the American Party, from January, 1858, for four years. His administration covered a momentous period. His efforts to stop the movement of government troops through Maryland were not effectual. Both President Lincoln and Secretary Seward endorsed General Butler in his plan of route.

Governor Hicks visited President Lincoln to sue for sick Confederate soldiers and was in correspondence with Southern Governors with a hope of averting conflict, but when the war had begun he gave the Union cause his untiring support in encouraging enlistment and supporting the soldiers of the army. The city of Annapolis being full of soldiers, Governor Hicks called the Legislature to assemble at Frederick "to take such measures as in their wisdom they may deem fit to maintain peace." That Legislature tried to discharge the duties devolved upon it; by a vote of fifty-three to twelve the House declared against secession, yet, later, every member was arrested by military orders and thrown into prison.

At the close of his term, in 1863, he was appointed United States Senator by Governor Bradford, to fill the unexpired term of James Alfred Pierce, and his selection was ratified at the next annual elec-

tion. He had now become a thorough Republican and a member
of the Union League. Although a slave-holder, he voted for the
Constitution of 1864.

Having, in 1863, sprained a leg, erysipelas set in, which neces-
sitated amputation. In the height of his notoriety he died from
apoplexy, February, 1865.

Governor Hicks was married three times. His first wife was
Ann Thompson, of Dorchester; second, Leah Raleigh, of Dorchester;
third, Mrs. Mary Wilcox, widow of his cousin, Henry Wilcox.

B. Chaplain Hicks, of Baltimore, is the only living son. A full
length portrait of Governor Hicks hangs in the State House.

GOVERNOR AUGUSTUS WILLIAMSON BRADFORD.

Governor Augustus Williamson Bradford, thirty-fifth in line
(1861-5), was born in Belair in 1806. His parents were Samuel and
Jane (Bond) Bradford, both of English parentage. He was well
educated and became a surveyor. He studied law with Otho Scott
and was admitted to the bar in 1827. Removing to Baltimore, he
became a prominent member of the Whig party. He was an elector
for Clay in 1844, but took no part in politics until 1860.

In 1835 he married Elizabeth Kell, daughter of Judge Kell, of
Baltimore.

Governor Pratt appointed Mr. Bradford Clerk of Baltimore
County, and Governor Hicks made him a Peace Commissioner in
1861. That same year, upon the first ballot, Mr. Bradford was
nominated as the Union candidate for Governor. He was elected
by 31,000 majority and was inaugurated January, 1862.

A full history of his administration covers the history of the war.
He was willing to aid the government, but he resented any military
interference in State elections, yet he presided at a large meeting in
which the President was authorized to require the oath of allegiance,
and at that meeting a resolution was passed which General Wood
declared "would send 20,000 men to swell the army of Jefferson
Davis."

The invasion of General Lee's army in 1862 urged Governor
Bradford to issue a call for the citizens to enroll themselves in military
companies.

In 1863, on a second invasion, the Governor called for 10,000
volunteers, and armed all who volunteered; many aged men offered
themselves for home defence. Three regiments were formed in 1863.

After the battle of Gettysburg, Governor Bradford appointed a
day of thanksgiving.

On hearing a rumor that troops were to be sent to the polls in
1863, Governor Bradford wrote to the President, protesting against
it. The President's reply was not satisfactory and the Governor
issued a proclamation in opposition to the orders of General Schenck.
The latter issued orders to the papers not to publish the Governor's
proclamation. In his message to the Legislature upon Schenck's
action the Governor declared, "A part of the army was, on election

day, engaged in stifling the freedom of election in a faithful State, intimidating its sworn officers and obstructing the usual channels between them and their executive."

At the January session of the Legislature the Governór reviewed the question of negro emancipation and called a convention to meet in Annapolis in 1864. This convention abolished slavery and issued the Constitution of 1864, which disfranchised all who sympathized with the rebellion. That Constitution granted the right of soldiers in the field to vote, and agents were sent to the army to receive the vote. Knowing that this innovation would be fought out in the courts, the Governor was particularly explicit in his instructions. Sixty points of exceptions were taken to the courts and the arguments consumed two days. The Governor's opinion was an able presentation of the case. The new Constitution went into effect in November, 1864, and slavery went down by the people's vote, some time before it had disappeared elsewhere by military orders.

In 1864, upon a Confederate raid, the Governor's house was burned, in retaliation, it was claimed, for the burning of Governor Letcher's mansion in Virginia. He never received any pay for its loss.

Governor Bradford's attachment to the Union was expressed in these words: "The loyal men of Maryland have no parties to sustain, no parties to create, no parties to revive; but the Union and its preservation is their only object." He attended the convention of loyal Governors in 1862.

On the inauguration of his successor, Thomas Swann, Governor Bradford spoke thus: "This Maryland, this loyal, Union-loving, freedom-loving Maryland, this upward-bound, expanding, regenerated Maryland—this is, indeed, our Maryland." Applause and thanks were tendered him for his able administration.

In 1867 Governor Bradford was appointed by President Johnson Surveyor of the Port of Baltimore. He held it until 1869, when President Grant removed him, but offered in its stead the position of Appraiser in Baltimore. This was declined on the ground that it required mercantile training, which he did not possess.

Governor Bradford was a member of the Methodist Episcopal Church. Two of his sons, Messrs. Augustus W. Bradford and Thomas Kell Bradford, are in business in Baltimore.

GOVERNOR THOMAS SWANN.

Thomas Swann, thirty-sixth Governor of Maryland (1865-67), was born about the close of the first decade of the nineteenth century in Alexandria. His father, Thomas Swann, was a prominent lawyer of Washington, and, under President Monroe, was United States Attorney for the District of Columbia. His mother was Jane Byrd, daughter of William Byrd, Receiver-General of the Colonies.

Thomas Swann was educated at the University of Virginia and became a law student under his father. He was afterward sent by President Jackson as secretary of the United States Commission to Naples.

In 1834 Mr. Swann married Miss Sherlock, daughter of an English gentleman and granddaughter of Robert Gilmor. His daughter Louisa, married Ferdinand Latrobe, seven times Mayor of Baltimore.

Mr. Swann, upon removing to Baltimore, became a director in the Baltimore and Ohio Railroad in 1845, and two years afterward became president, succeeding Louis McLane. He remained in that office until the completion of the road to Ohio in 1853, and received the thanks of the directors for the ability of his administration. Mr. Swann next was president of the Northwestern Railroad from Baltimore to Cincinnati.

In 1856 he was elected Mayor of Baltimore and was re-elected in 1858. During his term he introduced the fire department, the police and fire-alarm telegraph, the water-works system, the street car system and Druid Hill Park.

In 1861 he took strong ground against the war. In 1863 he was elected president of the First National Bank. In 1864 was elected by the Union party Governor of Maryland, and in January, 1865, succeeded Governor Bradford. He supported President Lincoln and was with President Johnson in his measures of reconstruction. As war measures were no longer needed, Governor Swann began to remove the disfranchisements of 1864.

When the Police Commission of Baltimore refused to allow a single Democratic judge, Governor Swann removed the Board and appointed others. Judge Bond, under a bench warrant, caused the arrest of these; Judge Bartol, under the "habeas corpus," decided their appointment was legal. This decision brought on a riot in Baltimore. Governor Swann called on President for aid. General Grant was sent over to investigate; he reported against Federal interference. At the next election, without a single Democratic judge of election, the Democrats triumphed, and at the next session of the Legislature Governor Swann was elected United States Senator. Under the Constitution of 1864, Lieutenant-Governor C. C. Cox would have succeeded to the Governor's chair; he still held to the faith of the party which elected him. Governor Swann determined to decline the senatorship and hold his chair in order to aid the Democrats in securing a new Constitution. For this act he was applauded by the people, but denounced by his party. Governor Swann urged a convention for the revision of the Constitution.

Hon. Philip Francis Thomas introduced in the Legislature a bill to restore full citizenship in the State of Maryland. This secured the revised Constitution of 1867.

In his final message of 1868, Governor Swann reported "the finances of the State prosperous; the Baltimore & Ohio Railroad was making large returns; schools were doing good work; he opposed negro equality or manhood suffrage; he was not in favor of political rights for the negroes; Congress has no right 'to make a Constitution for Maryland; he objected to the suspension of the 'habeas corpus'; all of these have led to anarchy." He called attention to the completion of the new Government house for the residence of the executive.

At the expiration of his term, Governor Oden Bowie, Chairman of the Democratic Committee, in the campaign which secured the enfranchised Constitution of 1867, was elected Governor.

In 1868 Governor Swann was honored by the Democratic Party as their representative in Congress. He was repeatedly re-elected until 1876. He became Chairman of the Committee upon Foreign Relations and exerted a marked influence in Congress.

Governor Swann married, as his second wife, Josephine Ward, the belle of New York, daughter of General Aaron Ward, of Sing Sing. Her first husband was Hon. John R. Thompson, United States Senator of New Jersey. She was a popular leader of society and entertained largely in her Newport cottage. Governor Swann died near Leesburg, Virginia, July 24, 1893.

GOVERNOR ODEN BOWIE.

Oden Bowie, thirty-seventh Governor of Maryland (1867–72), was born at "Fairview," Prince George County, Maryland, November 10, 1826. He was the son of Hon. William Ducket and Eliza (Oden) Bowie, the former of Scotch and the latter of English descent, both early settlers. Colonel Bowie represented Prince George County in the House of Delegates and for six years was in the Senate of Maryland. Governor Bowie lost his mother when nine years of age and was sent to St. John's College and St. Mary's College and graduated there in 1845.

The next year he enlisted in the Mexican War in Colonel William H. Watson's Battalion of Maryland and District of Columbia Volunteers. Colonel Watson was killed at Monterey, dying in the arms of Lieutenant Bowie, who was the only officer left with Colonel Watson. He was afterward appointed Senior Captain of the Voltigeur regiment, one of the ten regular regiments of the army. This office he resigned because of illness, brought on by the climate. In 1847, at the age of twenty-one years, he was elected to the House of Delegates, returning several times. In 1860 he was elected President of the Baltimore and Potomac Railroad, in which he won national reputation for his ability. In 1864 he was a candidate for Lieutenant-Governor, but defeated by C. C. Cox. In 1867, he represented Prince George County in the Senate of Maryland and in November, 1867, was elected Governor, but in consequence of the provision of the new Constitution, which permitted Governor Swann to serve his four years' term, Governor Bowie did not take his seat until January, 1869.

Governor Bowie's message of 1870 reads: "Two years of health, peace, contentment and average prosperity have been granted us. Our debt is now $12,000,000; our bonds and stocks amount to $7,000,000; our balance due is $5,000,000, offset by bonds of internal improvement amounting to $19,000,000."

He urged that our school system be placed under a board of commissioners; he favored immigration and urged bureaus of agriculture and mechanic arts be established; he urged that support be given to the Western Maryland Railroad; that a general road system be organized—and asked that our war claims against the Government be collected. The Legislature was entirely of one political party. His message of 1872 again urged immigration as a necessity under our present system of labor.

During his term the difficulty with Virginia upon the limit of oyster beds was settled. He collected the arrearages of the Baltimore and Ohio Railroad and secured the payment of the large loans Maryland had made to the Government. He also secured a large quantity of arms from the Federal Government. Governor Bowie reported a wonderful improvement in the Chesapeake and Ohio Canal.

At a dinner given at Saratoga Governor Bowie established the celebrated "Dinner Stakes and Breakfast Stakes," which made the Maryland Jockey Club a noted organization. He bought the Pimlico race course. Introduced from his own estate the Southdown and Cotswold sheep into Druid Hill Park.

In October, 1873, Governor Bowie was elected President of the Baltimore City Passenger Railway, in which he paid off the park tax of $100,000 and advanced the value of the stock from fifteen per cent. to thirty-five per cent. As President of the Maryland Jockey Club, he brought it to its highest success.

Governor Bowie married Miss Alice Carter, daughter of Charles H. Carter, a descendant of "King Carter," of Virginia, sister of the distinguished attorney, Bernard Carter. Her mother was Rosalie Eugenie Calvert, of Riversdale. Governor Bowie died at "Fairview" and his remains were interred there. He left seven living children. Mrs. Bowie died recently and lies beside her distinguished husband.

GOVERNOR WILLIAM PINKNEY WHYTE.

Governor William Pinkney Whyte, who has just celebrated his eighty-second birthday and who has been singularly honored by all who know him, is the son of Joseph Whyte and the grandson of Dr. John Campbell Whyte, an Irish patriot, member of the United Irishmen of 1798, who refused to be reconciled to the union of his country with England and resolved to make his future home in Baltimore.

Governor Whyte's mother was Isabella Pinkney, the handsome and intelligent daughter of Hon. William Pinkney, the nation's orator and statesman. Starting life in the banking house of George Peabody, later a law student of Harvard, as early as 1847 he was sent to the Legislature of Maryland and in 1851 was a candidate for Congress. This young Democrat could not overcome the Whig majority of his district, but he became Comptroller of the Treasury in 1853. In 1857 he was once more defeated for Congress. In 1868 he became a delegate to the National Democratic Convention.

Upon the appointment of Senator Reverdy Johnson as Minister to Great Britain, Mr. Whyte succeeded to the vacancy in the United States Senate. In 1871 he was elected Governor, but resigned when elected to the Senate.

At the expiration of his Senatorial career he returned to Baltimore and became Mayor of the city in 1882, and was called, in 1888, to the office of Attorney-General of the State. He was upon the committee to select a site for the Naval Observatory and one of its delegates to the Conference of American Republics, in 1889.

Still later, called from his large legal practice, he once more yielded to the demand to serve his city as City Solicitor, under Mayor Hayes. One of the busiest of men, this octogenarian still stands erect, dignified, handsome, the idolized statesman and genial friend of all.

In 1847 Mr. Whyte married Louisa D., daughter of Mr. Levi Hollinsworth. His second wife was Mrs. Raleigh Thomas, daughter of William McDonald.

Two of Governor Whytes's speeches in the United States Senate crown him a statesman of the highest order. The first was his almost solitary stand against the fierce political clamor against President Johnson, in which he defeated the combined opposition, and his still more celebrated objection to the desertion of Samuel Tilden, by the Democrats yielding to the adoption of the Electoral Commission. In that speech he pointed out prophetically the very result which happened, viz: that eight Republicans would outvote seven Democrats.

His warning was unheeded and the elected Democrat had to make place for the defeated Republican. Governor Whyte's devotion to his religion, to his friends and to the needy make him our idol.

A biography of Mr Whyte would be a history of Maryland for that period, so closely has his life been bound up with State affairs.

The long and brilliant political career of Mr. Whyte began in 1847, when he was elected to the House of Delegates of the General Assembly of Maryland. He has always been a Democrat and has made many public speeches in behalf of the political principles in which he believes. He was the representative of the Democratic party in his first political office and also in the positions of Comptroller of the Treasury, Governor of the State, United States Senator, Mayor of Baltimore and Attorney-General.

In 1899, Mr. Whyte was chairman of the commission which drafted the present City Charter, and in 1900 he became City Solicitor. In March, 1903, he resigned as City Solicitor, and since then he has devoted himself to his private business, which requires all his time.

While City Solicitor Mr. Whyte demonstrated his capacity for work. The enormous legal business of the city passed through his hands at that time, but he gave every detail close attention and care.

While in Congress he drafted the laws under which the District of Columbia is governed.

GOVERNOR JAMES BLACK GROOME.

Governor James Black Groome, successor to Governor William Pinkney Whyte, was the son of Colonel John C. Groome, of Cecil. His grandfather Dr. John Groome was a distinguished physician and representative of Cecil in the State Legislature, when only the ablest citizens were sent. On his maternal side, his grandfather was Hon. James R. Black, of New Castle, Delaware, Judge of the Superior Court.

Colonel John C. Groome, father of the Governor, was himself a candidate for Governor when T. Holliday Hicks was elected. His son was born in Elkton, April 4, 1838. After a preparatory course for Princeton College, James Black Groome pursued his legal studies with his father. He was a member of the Reform Convention which secured the Constitution of 1867. In 1871 he was elected to the House of Delegates. After the Legislature had been in session two weeks an election was held for United States Senator; Mr. Groome received a flattering vote. In 1873 Mr. Groome was again a member of the Legislature. He was made Chairman of the Judiciary Committee and also upon Ways and Means.

Upon the election of Governor Whyte to the United States Senate Mr. Groome was made the caucus nominee on the first ballot, and, a few days later, upon joint session, was elected Governor.

His messages were able and dignified State papers. His first official act was a graceful tribute to the friend of his father, Mr. George Spencer, whom his father had promised to appoint his aid if elected.

During his term Mr. S. Teackle Wallis made a contest over the office of Attorney-General. The Governor's decision was in favor of Mr. Gwynn. The executive mansion was made a centre of true hospitality. At the end of his term the following able candidates confronted him for Senator: George R. Dennis, Ex-Governor Philip Francis Thomas, Hon. Robert McLane, Hon. Montgomery Blair, Samuel Hambleton, Judge Robinson, Frederick Stump and Joseph A. Weeks. Yet, at forty-one years of age, Governor Groome was elected.

After the first election of President Cleveland in 1886 Governor Groome was appointed Collector of the Port of Baltimore. After retiring from this office he continued to reside at No. 2 East Preston Street, Baltimore.

On February 29, 1876, Mr. Groome married Miss Alice L. Edmondson, daughter of Colonel Horace Edmondson, of Talbot County. They had one daughter, Maria.

Governor Groome died in Baltimore, October, 1893. His funeral services were held in Baltimore and his remains were taken to Elkton. His honorary pall-bearers were United States Senators T. S. Cullen and Arthur P. Gorman, Charles N. Gibson, Hon. William Pinkney Whyte, Mayor F. C. Latrobe, Judge Pere L. Wickes, Judge Albert Ritchie, Colonel I. E. Jacobs, A. T. Leftwich, I. Freeman Raisin, Frederick Shriver, Charles H. Mackall, William J. Montague, I. Boykin Lee and Edwin Warfield, now Governor of Maryland.

Governor Groome's widow married later P. F. Young, cousin of Governor Groome, now of Philadelphia. The Governor's sister

was Mrs. Maria G. Knight, wife of Hon. William M. Knight, only son
of William and Rebecca (Ringold) Knight.

Hon. William Knight was in the Legislature when his brother-
in-law was a member. He is now of the Baltimore firm of Frame &
Knight, Commission Merchants.

GOVERNOR JOHN LEE CARROLL.

Governor John Lee Carroll, of "Doughoregan Manor," the
centennial Governor of Maryland, was born at "Homewood," Balti-
more County, in 1830. He is the second son of Colonel Charles and
Mary Digges (Lee) Carroll. His father was the grandson of Charles
Carroll, of "Carrollton," and his mother was the granddaughter of
Governor Thomas Sim Lee, the able supporter of the Revolution.
"Doughoregan Manor" was inherited by Colonel Charles Carroll when
his son, John Lee Carroll, was only three years old.

At ten years John Lee Carroll began his course at Mt. St. Mary's
School. He next entered Georgetown College and afterwards St.
Mary's, in Baltimore. His law course was taken at Harvard Law
School. Entering upon practice from the office of Brown & Brown,
he was admitted to the bar in 1851. Spending a year in traveling
through Europe, he was, in 1855, nominated for the Legislature of
Maryland in opposition to the popular Know-Nothing party of that
year; after an able canvass he was defeated. In the fall of that
year he removed to New York. There he met and married Anita,
daughter of Royal Phelps, of the extensive importing house in trade
with South America.

In 1861, because of the feeble health of his father, Mr. Carroll
returned to "Doughoregan" in order to manage his father's estate.

In 1862, upon the death of his father, he became his executor.
In 1866 he purchased his brother's interest in "Doughoregan" and
has since made it his residence.

Nominated and elected to the Maryland Senate in 1867, he was
returned in 1872 and in 1874 was made President of the Senate.
His wife died that year and he returned to Europe to place his children
at school. Returning in 1875, he was nominated and elected
Governor of Maryland.

In the succeeding summer Governor Carroll and staff were
invited to represent the State at the Centennial Exposition at Philadelphia. Accompanied by Brigadier-General James R. Herbert, the
Governor and staff became the central figure of Maryland Day; when
mounted and at the head of the magnificent body of the Fifth Maryland Regiment he rode before the assembled masses to the reception
hall of the exposition. There he met with distinguished honors,
receiving flattering compliments as the illustrious descendant of an
illustrious patriot who risked fortune to secure the benefits now
enjoyed by this generation. In answer to these addresses and
compliments the Governor returned a dignified and graceful
acknowledgement.

Two years subsequent to this Governor Carroll married Miss Mary Carter Thompson, of Staunton, Virginia, daughter of the late Judge Lucas P. Thompson.

During Governor Carroll's administration, the Baltimore and Ohio Railroad, in seeking to reduce expenses, brought on a determined strike of its laborers, which culminated in a riot at Cumberland. In reply to the authorities, the Governor ordered out the Fifth and Sixth Regiments of Militia. At Camden Station the sympathizing mob in Baltimore attacked the Sixth Regiment and set fire to the station. The Governor promptly called for United States troops, but before they could arrive the police force of Baltimore, aided by the militia, had quelled the riot. For their successful fight against such great odds Governor Carroll publicly and gracefully acknowledged his thanks, complimenting them upon their splendid work. That celebrated strike gave birth to the Workingman's Party, which lived for a while and died.

Governor Carroll became an elector during the Cleveland campaign of 1882, in which he made several able and effectual speeches in his interest. He has been urged to allow his name to be used for Congressional honors, but refused. Since the death of Mrs. Carroll and the marriage of his sons and daughters he has spent considerable time in traveling.

For several years Governor Carroll has been President of the National Society of the Sons of the American Revolution.

The issue of Governor Carroll and Anita Phelps, his wife, are Mary Louisa—Comte Jean de Kergoloy; Amelia Maria—Baron Louis de la Grange; Royal Phelps—Maria Langsdon, of New York; Charles—Susanna Bancroft; Mary Helen—Herbert D. Robbins, of New York; Albert Henry and Mary Irene Carroll died unmarried. Philip Acosta Carroll, born 1879, is the only son of Governor Carroll by his last wife. He is a member of the Elk Ridge Hunt Club, of Howard County.

"Doughoregan Manor," under the care of Governor Carroll, still keeps up its stately and retired grandeur. At its chapel the neighboring members are accustomed to worship. Under it lies the remains of its builder, Charles Carroll, of "Carrollton."

Governor Carroll still takes interest in puplic affairs, and at a recent convention of his party in Howard made a forcible speech on the proposed amendment to the State Constitution.

Howard County is doubly honored in having its handsome Ex-Governor and its handsome Governor, both bidding fair to be still more useful as years roll on.

GOVERNOR WILLIAM T. HAMILTON.

Governor William T. Hamilton, successor to Governor Carroll, was born near Hagerstown September 8, 1820. He was the son of Henry Hamilton, of Boonesboro, brother of Rev. William Hamilton, of M. E. Church. His mother was Mary M. Hess.

William T. Hamilton was educated at Hagerstown Academy and Jefferson College, Pennsylvania. When six years of age his mother died and two years later, his father died. He was brought up by his maternal uncle, who was of the old Jefferson School of Democracy. Entering the law office of Hon. John Thompson Mason, in 1843, he was admitted to the bar. In 1846 he was elected to the House of Delegates. In 1847 he was defeated. In 1848 he was upon the Cass Electoral ticket and in 1849 was elected to Congress. He there voted and spoke in favor of the Clay Compromise Bill. In 1851 he was re-elected to Congress. In 1853 he received his largest majority for the same position. He supported President Pierce. Chosen Chairman of the Committee upon the District of Columbia, he voted for an appropriation to bring water to the city from Great Falls. In 1855 he again ran for Congress, but was defeated by the Know-Nothings. He then became associated with Richard H. Alvey, later Judge of the Court of Appeals. In 1861, Mr. Hamilton was urged for Governor, but declined. In 1868 he consented to be a candidate for the United States Senate, succeeding William Pinkney Whyte, who had been appointed to succeed Reverdy Johnson. Mr. Hamilton exerted considerable influence in the Senate.

In 1875, at the expiration of his term, he became a candidate for Governor. He was opposed by John Lee Carroll. After an exciting contest, during which Mr. E. B. Prettyman, a Hamilton delegate from Montgomery County, spoke all night, Hon. John Lee Carroll, of Howard County, was nominated.

In 1879 Mr. Hamilton had practically no opposition and was elected Governor by 22,000 majority, over James A. Gary. His inauguration was made a popular demonstration. Governor Hamilton's message was a vigorous attack upon many of the offices of the State. He opposed the Insurance Department and the State fishery force as signal failures. The land office had survived its usefulness. He wished to abolish it and place the records under the control of the Court of Appeals. The expenditure for public printing was too great; the Legislative expenses ought to be reduced; taxes ought to be fairly imposed and suggested one tax collector for each county.

Governor Hamilton took great interest in developing all the agricultural interests of the State. He had a large estate near Hagerstown and resided upon the beautiful heights of Hagerstown.

Governor Hamilton married Clara, daughter of Colonel Richard Jenness, of Portsmouth, New Hampshire. They had four daughters and two sons. Governor Hamilton died in Hagerstown, 1888, and was buried at Rose Hill Cemetery.

GOVERNOR ROBERT M. McLANE.

Governor Robert M. McLane, forty-first Governor (1884–85) was born in Wilmington, Delaware, 1816. He was the son of Lewis and Catharine Mary (Milligan) McLane. His father after twenty years of distinguished service as a representative in Congress, Senator, Minister to Great Britain, Secretary of the Treasury and Secretary of State, retired in 1837 and settled in Maryland as President of the Baltimore and Ohio Railroad.

Colonel Allan McLane, of Delaware, grandfather of Hon. Robert M. McLane, was an officer of distinction in the Revolution. Catharine Mary Milligan, mother of Robert M. McLane, was a woman of superior character and accomplishments, eldest daughter of Robert and Sally (Jones) Milligan, of Cecil. This family descended from, and was connected with, the Larkins, Baldwins and Chases, of Anne Arundel County.

After leaving St. Mary's College, Robert M. McLane was taken to Paris and placed in school. There he engaged the friendship of General LaFayette.

In 1831 he was appointed a cadet at West Point. After graduation Mr. McLane was in Congress in 1856 and supported the Mexican War policy.

In 1856 he was a member of the National Convention which met in Cincinnati and nominated James Buchanan for President. In 1859 President Buchanan appointed him Minister Plenipotentiary to the Republic of Mexico. There he signed the treaty between Mexico and the United States, for the protection of the lives and property of our citizens, but our difficulties at home convinced him of the uselessness of it.

In 1863 Mr. McLane was counsel for the Western Pacific Railroad, in San Francisco and New York, during which time he visited Europe often. He was a delegate to the St. Louis Convention that nominated Samuel J. Tilden. In 1879 he was elected State Senator and in 1878 was elected to Congress. There he became an able advocate for his State and took a leading part in the exciting debates. In 1884 he was elected Governor of Maryland. He held his office only one year, resigning in 1885 to accept from President Cleveland the charge as Minister to France.

Governor McLane continued to reside in Paris, returning once a year, except 1887, to look after his estate.

He died in Paris in 1888, nearly eighty-eight years of age. His body was brought over and his funeral was held from Emanuel Church. His remains were interred at Greenmount.

GOVERNOR HENRY LLOYD.

Governor Henry Lloyd, forty-second Governor of Maryland (1885–87,) was born near Cambridge, February 21, 1852. His father was Daniel Lloyd, youngest son of Governor Edward Lloyd of 1809.

Daniel Lloyd married "Kitty," daughter of John Campbell Henry, and granddaughter of Governor John Henry. Henry Lloyd was educated at Cambridge Academy and taught school whilst studying law. In 1881, he was elected State Senator from Dorchester County and was returned in 1884, when he was chosen, though the youngest member of the Senate, its President. In the following year, upon the resignation of Governor McLane, who had accepted the mission to France, by virtue of his office became Governor to fill Governor McLane's unexpired term. At the next election he was nominated and elected Governor.

Governor Lloyd is a Mason, having served as master four times and in 1885-86 was Senior Grand Warden. He is a vestryman of many years' service in Christ Protestant Episcopal Church, Cambridge, Maryland. In July, 1892, he was appointed by Governor Frank Brown to the bench as associate judge of the First Judicial Circuit of Maryland. In 1893 he was nominated and elected by the people to that office for a full term of fifteen years and is now filling the same. He is also president of the Merchants' National Bank.

In 1886 he married Mary Elizabeth Staplefort, daughter of William T. and Virginia Staplefort, descendants of old and prominent families of Dorchester County, Maryland.

GOVERNOR ELIHU JACKSON.

Governor Elihu Jackson, forty-third Governor (1888-92), was born in Somerset County, 1836. He is the son of Hugh and Sally (McBride) Jackson, grandson of John and great-grandson of Elihu Emory Jackson, Judge of the Orphans Court of Somerset.

Mr. Jackson began life as a merchant. In 1863 he removed to Salisbury and with his father and brothers, entered into his present lumber business. It was soon extended to branch offices in Baltimore and Washington. Beside large lumber interests in the State, the firm owned 80,000 acres of timber in Alabama.

Mr. Jackson was in the Legislature for several sessions, including the Senate.

In 1887 he was elected Governor to succeed Governor Henry Lloyd. During his administration the compulsory features of tobacco inspection were abolished.

An attempt was made to lease the canal to the Western Maryland Railroad. In 1889 the canal was completely wrecked by freshets and the State could do nothing for it. Private resources having failed, the Baltimore and Ohio Railroad foreclosed its mortgage.

Governor Jackson recommended a decrease in tobacco warehouses, as the production of tobacco had decreased.

In 1890 the Court decreed the sale of the canal.

Governor Jackson is president of the Bank of Salisbury and of the Seaford National Bank.

He married Nannie, daughter of Dr. William H. Rider, of Somerset. He has three sons and two daughters.

The people of his district seem loath to let the Ex-Governor retire to the enjoyment of a well-deserved peaceful life. His name was prominently before the last Legislature for the Senate of the United States. His opposing candidates were Ex-Governor John Walter Smith, Mr. Rayner and Mr. Carter. The withdrawal of Governor Jackson resulted in the election of Senator Rayner. The Governor was also in the front in the last campaign.

GOVERNOR FRANK BROWN.

Governor Frank Brown, forty-fourth in line (1892-96), is the son of Stephen Thomas Cockey Brown, of "Brown's Inheritance," Carroll County. His mother was Susan Bennett. He descends from Abel Browne, the Scottish immigrant and High Sheriff of Anne Arundel, elsewhere noted.

Beginning his business career in Baltimore, he entered the firm of R. Sinclair & Company, and was later connected with the State Warehouse. In 1875 he represented Carroll in the Legislature.

During the campaign of 1885 he became Treasurer of the State Democratic Central Committee, when the party met with marked success. As a State representative he was a director in the Baltimore and Ohio Railroad Company. He was Postmaster of Baltimore under President Cleveland. In 1881 he became President of the State Agricultural Association, in which he displayed much energy and made a success in its State Fairs.

In 1891 he was the choice of the people for Governor and was nominated and elected by 30,000 majority. At the inauguration of President Cleveland, Governor Brown and staff made a fine display, but the inclement weather caused him a serious illness.

There were three exciting events in his administration: the veto of the Legislative bill for taxing mortgages; his action in commuting the sentence of four murderers of Dr. Hill in Kent County, and the miners' strike in Allegany County. Opinions were divided upon his action in the first two, but all united in praising his prompt action in ordering the militia to the scene of conflict in Allegany. He accompanied the troops in person and soon restored order.

An unusual number of vacancies occurred during his administration in the different judicial districts of the State, all of which were filled by him.

In the succeeding campaign the Democratic candidate for Governor was defeated by Hon. Lloyd Lowndes.

At the close of his term he was elected President of the Baltimore Traction Company, in which office the business was largely increased. This position he resigned several years ago.

He married in 1879, Mrs Mary (Ridgely) Preston, widow of Horatio Preston, of Boston, and daughter of David Ridgely, of Baltimore. She died after his term of service in 1895, leaving two children, Frank Snowden and Mary Ridgely Brown.

Governor Brown bought out the interests of his cousin, Mrs. Carroll, in the Springfield estate of Mr. George Patterson. This, in addition to his father's adjoining property, put him in possession of a magnificent body of land. He was engaged in farming this estate when elected Governor. The Springfield estate had long been noted for its excellent stock, and Governor Brown not only continued that reputation, but even extended it. After the death of his wife he sold the Springfield homestead to the State as an asylum for the insane.

Upon a portion of his estate in Sykesville he has erected several houses for tenants.

He is a member of several clubs and director in various business enterprises. Of a genial temperament, he is popular in many circles. He takes considerable interest in political movements and was active in organizing a peoples' movement, which resulted in the election of Mayor Hayes. Governor Brown has devoted much time in traveling upon the Continent of Europe.

GOVERNOR LLOYD LOWNDES.

Governor Lloyd Lowndes, forty-fifth Governor (1896), the only Republican Governor since 1867, was born in Cumberland in 1845. He was the son of Lloyd and Maria Elizabeth (Moore) Lowndes. His grandfather was Commodore Charles Lowndes, of the United States Navy, and his grandmother was Elizabeth Lloyd, daughter of United States Senator and Governor Edward Lloyd. Commodore Lowndes was born at "Blenheim," upon a commanding hill of Bladensburg, a survey of Governor Bladen. This estate descended to Elizabeth Tasker, wife of Christopher Lowndes and mother of Commodore Lowndes.

Though Governor Lowndes was the first of his family name in the gubernatorial chair, he was closely connected with six preceding provincial and State Governors, viz., Samuel Ogle, Thomas Bladen, Benjamin Tasker, Benjamin Ogle, Edward Lloyd and Henry Lloyd.

Entering Washington College, Pennsylvania, and graduating from the Law School of Pennsylvania, in 1872, he was elected a Representative in Congress from a Democratic district, and, though one of the youngest members, was put upon important committees. His vote on the Civil Rights Bill defeated his next election.

In 1879 he was a delegate-at-large to the Republican National Convention at Chicago. In 1895 he was elected Governor, upon a canvass of reform.

During his administration four important enactments were put upon the statutes. The first was the establishment of the State Board of Immigration, the duty of which is to advertise the advantages of the State through reference maps, statistics from each county, all gratuitously furnished; the Superintendent is required to visit Europe and solicit a class of immigrants best suited to our requirements. The Board is also empowered to make special terms with railroads and steamship lines for reduced rates of transportation. As an aid to this bureau, a State Geological and Economic Survey was enacted. This bureau was placed under Professor Clark, of Johns Hopkins University. Its object is to examine geological formations with reference to economic products, viz., building stones, clays and ores; to examine and classify soils and show their adaptability to various crops; to examine the physical features bearing upon the occupation of the people of the State; to prepare maps illustrative of our resources, and to make special reports upon all scientific subjects looking to the development of the State.

The third enactment was the establishment of Farmers' Institutes, wherein object lessons of scientific knowledge may be exhibited to practical farmers. Men, competent to instruct, at convenient places are required to meet the farmers of the counties and answer all questions of general interest The board is a part of the work of the Agricultural College, forming an adjunct to the Experiment Station. Especial attention is directed to the study of exterminating all enemies to farm products; to teach the best modes of feeding, fattening and marketing all farm stock; to teach the best modes of fertilization of crops. Governor Lowndes was active in his support of all these measures.

The fourth enactment under his administration was the Election Law, based upon the basis of the Australian ballot.

Governor Lowndes was a formidable candidate for the United States Senate, but withdrew early in the contest in favor of Senator McComas. He received, contrary to the custom, the second nomination for Governor, but was defeated by Governor John Walter Smith.

At the beginning of the Spanish War he offered the First and Fifth Regiments of Militia to the service of the government; they were accepted and were fully equipped by the State.

During his term the Board of Public Works determined to sell the State's interest in both the Baltimore and Ohio Railroad and the Chesapeake and Ohio Canal and put the proceeds into the sinking fund of the State, which was greatly increased during his administration.

Governor and Mrs. Lowndes made Annapolis their home during his entire term. They entertained extensively and their official receptions were not only frequent but were very popular in Annapolis.

Retiring to his home in Cumberland he was engaged as president of the Cumberland National Bank, but also was extensively interested in the mining industries of the State.

Governor Lowndes died very suddenly. The tributes to his memory are a history in themselves of a noble life nobly appreciated.

GOVERNOR JOHN WALTER SMITH.

The home of Governor John Walter Smith is Snow Hill, Worcester County, on the Eastern Shore of Maryland. Here he was born, on the 5th day of February, 1845. His Christian name is the same as his father's. His mother's name was Charlotte (Whittington) Smith. His paternal ancestors were, for many generations, among the most prominent people, socially and financially, on the Eastern Shore. Through intermarriage, he is related to the Saulsburys, of Delaware, who have for so many years dominated the politics of their State. His father was a prominent merchant, and removed from Snow Hill to Baltimore, there largely engaging in mercantile pursuits, but owing to reverses brought on by a financial panic, whereby he lost large sums of money in the South, he returned to Snow Hill, where he died in 1850, leaving the subject of this sketch an orphan, with but small means available for his education and support. Governor Smith's grandfather (William Whittington) was one of the early judges of the Judicial Circuit, a part of which now constitutes the First Judicial Circuit of Maryland. He was a man of wealth, owning a large quantity of real estate in Worcester County. He was an able lawyer and learned judge.

Governor Smith has a brother living in Louisiana and a widowed sister residing at Snow Hill. His family consists of a wife and a daughter, the latter being the wife of Mr. Arthur D. Foster, a rising young lawyer of Baltimore. Mrs. Smith's maiden name was Mary Frances Richardson. She is a sister of his former partner, the late George S. Richardson, of Snow Hill. She was educated at Oakland Female Institute at Norristown, Pennsylvania. She is a woman of charming personality and of cultured tastes. Their married life has been a most happy one, marred only by the death a few years ago, of their eldest daughter, Miss Charlotte Whittington Smith, a beautiful young lady just blooming into womanhood, with a host of friends and greatly admired and beloved by all who knew her.

Governor Smith was educated at private schools and at Union Academy at Snow Hill, where he studied the classics, the usual English branches, excelling especially in mathematics. During his minority his guardian was the late Senator Ephraim K. Wilson. At the age of eighteen he left school to accept a position with the large and prosperous mercantile house of George S. Richardson and Brother with whom he was afterward taken in as a partner. That house continued to the present day and is now composed of Ex-Governor Smith, Senator John P. Moore and Mr. Marion T. Harges.

In 1887 Governor Smith assisted in organizing the First National Bank in Snow Hill and has large interests in the oyster industry in his county. He is one of the largest real estate owners of his county and has large timber interests in North Carolina. He is president of the Equitable Fire Insurance Company of Snow Hill, a corporation chartered by the Legislature of 1898 with a capital of $100,000 and doing a prosperous business. He is vice-president of the Surry Lumber Company, of Surry County, Virginia, and of the Surry, Sussex and Southampton Railroad Company.

As a result of his energy, activity and business sagacity, Governor Smith has become a man of large wealth. He was strongly urged by his political friends to accept some political office, but persistently refused until 1889, when, at the solicitation of Senator Wilson in 1889, he for the first time became a candidate for State Senator, was unanimously nominated and elected by a large majority.

In the contest of the Legislature of 1890 over the United States Senatorship he was the acknowledged leader of Senator Wilson's forces, and his efforts were crowned with victory. At that session of the State Senate Governor Smith was chairman of the important Committee on Elections, especially important at that session because of the fact that the new Australian election bill, which excited so much discussion in the General Assembly and throughout the State, was before his committee. He had many intricate questions to deal with.   The bill became a law and received his cordial support.   He was re-elected to the Senate in 1893; at the session of 1894 was made President of that body, serving as such with distinction; was re-elected to the Senate in 1897.   At the Legislative session of 1892 he was a candidate to succeed Senator Wilson, who had died in office the year before.   Though not elected, he received a large and flattering vote.

In 1896, when the Legislature was Republican, he was the caucus nominee of the Democratic party for the same position.

He introduced in the session of 1892 what is known as the "Smith Free School-Book Bill."   Through his persistent efforts it was pressed every session thereafter; it finally became a law in 1896.

Governor Smith, owing to the pressure of his business affairs, refused a unanimous tender of a candidacy for Congress by the Democratic Congressional Convention of his district when a nomination was equivalent to an election.   During his unexpired term in the State Senate, in 1898, his friends throughout the First Congressional District, which at the previous election had gone Republican, urged him again to become a candidate for Congress.   After an unanimous nomination and a hotly contested election, he was returned to Congress by a large majority.

Following a warmly contested primary election, he was made the choice of his party for Governor and was elected by more than 12,000 majority over Governor Lowndes, his Republican competitor.

The chief event of Governor John Walter Smith's administration was his successful discovery that the census of the State had been made a fraudulent one and his determination to correct it by calling an extra session of the Legislature to enable him to do it. A new census was ordered to be taken, which was accordingly done at the State's expense, but it clearly demonstrated that the Governor's information was correct, and instead of returning additional delegates to the Legislature from counties that were Republican, the increase in population was a benefit to the Democratic counties.   The other chief act of the extra session was a modification of the election law of the State requiring voters to be able to read and understand the ballots cast.   Under the law thus passed the counties heretofore classed as Republican returned Democratic representatives to the succeeding legislative body, thereby electing, by a unanimous Democratic vote, Ex-Senator Arthur Pue Gorman to the United States Senate for the fourth time.

Governor Smith was succeeded by Governor Edwin Warfield.

At the last session of the Legislature Governor Smith was a leading candidate for the Senate of United States.   He was opposed by Ex-Governor Jackson, Mr. Isadore Rayner and Mr. Bernard Carter.   After a long and exciting contest, the forces of Governor Jackson threw their votes to Mr. Rayner and elected him.

GOVERNOR. EDWIN WARFIELD, OF OAKDALE.

Born at "Oakdale," May 7, 1848, Edwin Warfield early learned the advantage of making the most of his opportunity. Entering upon his public career as Register of Wills of Howard County in 1874, he filled the office with such fidelity as to receive the unanimous nomination in 1875 for a term of six years more.

In 1881 he was elected State Senator to succeed Senator Gorman, who had gone to the United States Senate.

In 1886 Senator Warfield was chosen President of the Senate. At the close of his term, as a testimonial of his acceptable record of impartiality, a gold watch was tendered him.

Senator Warfield went from the Senate to accept the position of Surveyor of the Port of Baltimore, under President Cleveland, which position he filled most acceptably until 1890.

The future Governor owned and edited the "Ellicott City Times" from 1882 to 1886. He was the prime mover in the establishment of the Patapsco National Bank, of Ellicott City, being a member of its directorate until 1890. In 1887 he purchased the "Maryland Law Record," changing its name to the "Daily Record." This paper is now the leading journal of legal and real estate news in the State. It is edited and managed by John Warfield, his brother.

Governor Warfield's most important and successful business achievement was the conception and organization of the Fidelity and Deposit Company of Maryland, the first of its kind in the South, and now the largest surety company in the world. At the commencement of business in 1890 Mr. Warfield was chosen Second Vice-President and General Manager. He was the leading spirit in the direction of the affairs of the company and soon advanced to the position of First Vice-President, and almost immediately thereto to the Presidency. From the beginning, Mr. Warfield was indefatigable in advancing the interests of the company. He had absolute confidence in its future success and devoted himself to its building up on broad, vigorous and yet conservative lines. In consequence the company, which fifteen years ago was regarded as a doubtful local venture, is now an institution of national, indeed international, importance in the financial world, continually increasing in prosperity and strength.

In 1899 Mr. Warfield was a candidate for the Democratic nomination for Governor of Maryland, and submitted his candidacy to the people of Baltimore City, at the primary election. He received a very large popular vote, but was defeated for the nomination, his successful competitor being John Walter Smith, of Worcester County. He again became a candidate in 1903 and was chosen unanimously as the Democratic candidate by the State Convention in that year, and was elected in November, 1903, by a majority of more than 13,000 votes, and inaugurated as Governor on January 13, 1904.

Governor Warfield has given most painstaking and careful attention to the duties of the office. No detail of the administrative affairs of the State has been too small to escape his notice and constructive ability, notwithstanding the fact that at the same time he continues to be the active directing executive of the Fidelity and Deposit Company of Maryland and of its sister institution, in which he also was the prime mover in founding, The Fidelity Trust Company. No other man who has ever filled the executive chair at Annapolis has been more conscientious in doing what he believed to be his duty. He is consistently endeavoring to enforce all that is cleanest and best in public affairs. His aim has been to maintain and honor the best traditions of the State, and upon every occasion he is delighted to tell the glorious story of his native Maryland. He has stood for a clean, economical administration, and his Message to the Legislature upon its assembling in January, 1906, made him stronger than ever in the affections of the people, who believe absolutely in his sincerity and honesty of purpose. In this Message he rebuked in the strongest terms political corruption, lobbying and "graft" of every kind. The clean methods he has inaugurated, the adoption of which in many cases he has compelled, will have far-reaching and lasting results.

Governor Warfield has stood like a rock for what he believes to be right. Notwithstanding the fact that his party organization unanimously endorsed an amendment to the State Constitution, introduced to limit the suffrage of the negro, and disregarding the fact that he himself heartily favored the elimination of the ignorant, shiftless negro vote, in his opinion the manner in which it was framed and presented had within it such dangerous possibilities of corruption and fraud that he declared he would veto the measure if presented to him as Governor for his signature. In order to avoid this the Legislature, after its adoption by both Houses of the General Assembly, ignored the usual custom and sent the bill direct to the Court. When this measure came up for adoption or rejection by the people of the State, Governor Warfield's attitude was still understood by the people, but so many misrepresentations of the Governor's position were made by designing politicians that his Excellency found it necessary to come out with a newspaper interview giving in strongest and clearest possible language his reasons for the belief that the measure was inimicable to the liberties of the people generally. The Governor's consistent position and this interview, published on the eve of the election, were undoubtedly the immediate causes of the ignominious defeat of the amendment by the people by a majority of more than 35,000 votes.

In his inaugural address Governor Warfield declared that he would under no circumstances use the power and patronage of the great office of Governor of Maryland to advance his own political fortunes, or the political fortunes of any other man, or set of men. He has been steadfast in his adherence to this declaration, notwithstanding the fact that within sixty days after his inauguration the tempting offer of election to the United States Senate was held before him as a temptation, provided he would use his patronage to that end, but the Governor stood steadfast to his declaration of two years ago.

When urged during the organization of the Legislature to indicate his choice for president and speaker, the Governor replied: "I am not making officers for the Legislature. I am only interested in the selection of such as will best serve the State."

The Press throughout the State was almost unanimous in sustaining the Governor's practical suggestions and criticisms in his last message to the Legislature. The Governor is justly proud of the work of restoring the old Senate Chamber.

By the aid of the advisory commission appointed by him, we may again view the scene described by Phillips, the Englishman, when he said of Washington: "But his last glorious act crowns his career and banishes all hesitation; who, like Washington, after having emancipated a hemisphere, resigned its crown and preferred the retirement of domestic life to the adoration of a land he might almost be said to have created?" When we look upon that restored chamber we may recall, too, the august presence of the idolized old hero, who gave youth and fortune to the cause of our Independence. LaFayette, the friend of Washington, turned the tide toward Yorktown and freedom.

Fifty years later little girls, upon carpeted walks, strewed flowers before his triumphal entrance into the Senate Chamber wherein the great commander had laid down his sceptre. Henceforth it will be the work of patriotic women, descendants of those little girls, to strew love and admiration down the corridors of all coming ages.

Governor Warfield has well said: "This room, hallowed by so many sacred memories and historic associations, will, I am sure, become the mecca of every patriotic person in the State of Maryland, and will, each year, become more priceless in historic associations.

"It will, in connection with the two adjoining rooms, be kept for historic memorials."

As an evidence of the Governor's pride in his native State, I will quote his speech upon Maryland Day at the St. Louis Exposition. Said he:

"Mr. President, Ladies and Gentlemen:

"The three greatest epochs in American history have been commemorated by expositions. In 1876 the end of the first century of our independence was celebrated at Philadelphia in a manner that profoundly impressed our poeple and demonstrated that the United States possessed the spirit and the resources that were fast making her the greatest Government on the globe.

"In 1892, following the suggestion first made by the Baltimore "Sun," the four hundredth anniversary of the discovery of the Western Hemisphere by Columbus was signalized by the World's Fair at Chicago. That Fair brought the whole world together in a grand display of its progress to commemorate that historic event. The growth of the North American Continent during those four centuries was exhibited there in a marvelous and instructive way.

GREATEST FAIR OF ALL.

"This Louisiana Purchase Exposition, the greatest of them all, emphasizes what has been accomplished during the hundred years that have elapsed since the acquisition of this vast Western domain by Thomas Jefferson in 1803.

"You, Mr. President Francis, and your associates are entitled to the applause and gratitude of our people for this wonderful Exposition of the magic growth and material development of our country, and especially of what the Louisiana territory has added in wealth to the United States.

"Your conception and execution of the plans for this Fair have resulted in a consummation unequaled in the annals of such enterprises. It is acknowledged to be the best exhibition of the world's development that has ever been assembled. All honor and glory to you, sir, and your associates!

MARYLAND'S TRIBUTE.

"Maryland, one of the States which favored the Treaty with France ceding Louisiana, has commanded me to lay her tribute at your feet and join with you to-day in praise of the statesmen whose wisdom and prompt action secured this splendid domain for our common country—Jefferson, Monroe and Livingston.

"I am pleased to note that our Commissioners, headed by General Baughman, have co-operated with you in your work, and that our State is so creditably represented here under their direction.

"It is not my purpose to dwell upon the advantages to the people of such Expositions. The lessons taught by those of the past have satisfied us that the results flowing from such exhibitions of our material growth, and of our wealth and resources, are of untold benefit.

"On your opening day I sent you greetings from our people and promised that in due course of time Maryland would be with you to add her voice in praise of the statesmanship which gave us this Western territory, that has added so much to our national greatness and glory. For that purpose we, her sons and daughters, are here to-day.

A DAY OF DAYS TO MARYLAND.

"We have come on this Twelfth of September, because it is one of the proudest and most sacred days in Maryland annals. It is the anniversary of the battle of North Point, the battle that turned the tide against the triumphant British Army, saved Baltimore from destruction, and virtually ended the War of 1812. It is known and celebrated by us as 'Old Defenders' Day,' and has for ninety years been annually observed in honor of the valor of our citizen soldiers.

"The British Army, under command of General Ross, having captured and sacked Washington City and laid the Capitol in ashes, sailed up the Chesapeake Bay with their combined military and naval forces for the purpose of destroying Baltimore.

ROSS KILLED; BRITISH REPULSED.

"Their general, Ross, was killed by sharpshooters, and our citizen soldiers met the British and repulsed and defeated them.

"Following up the attack, the British vessels, on the next day, made an attempt to take the city of Baltimore by bombardment from the ships. All night long there was fierce and constant cannonading, to which the defenders in Fort McHenry and from other temporary forts along the waterside replied with spirit.

WHERE KEY COMPOSED NATIONAL ANTHEM.

"It was during this bombardment that Francis Scott Key, a son of Maryland, who was detained on the flagship of Admiral Cochrane, where he had gone under a flag of truce to procure the release of a friend, composed 'The Star-Spangled Banner,' the national anthem of our country.

"All during the dark hours of that night he waited and watched with anxiety the outcome of the battle. At one time his heart sank in him, as it seemed that Fort McHenry had been silenced.

"We can appreciate his anxiety because he realized that, if such were the case, the fate of Baltimore would be the fate of the Nation's Capital. With eagerness he watched the dawn of day, that he might see whether the flag was still flying. It was during these trying moments that he wrote the immortal verses which have been so touchingly declaimed here to-day by one of our fair and gifted daughters.

SUCCESS OF THE SONG IMMEDIATE.

"The lines were written in pencil on the back of an envelope whilst leaning on the top of a barrel on the deck of the British ship. He carried them with him to the city when he was released, had them adapted to a tune already existing, and they were sung to the public for the first time in the city of Baltimore. The success of this song, written under such stress of patriotism, was great. 'The Star-Spangled Banner' has taken its place as our beloved national anthem.

"A noted Maryland orator, referring to this historical incident, said:

"'The Stars and Stripes themselves had streamed at the front of two wars before the kindling genius of a Maryland man, exercised in the white heat of battle, translated the dumb symbol of national sentiment into a living voice, and made it the sublime and harmonious interpreter of a nation's progress and power.'

MARYLAND'S SERVICE TO THE NATION.

"The people of the United States owe to the State of Maryland a great debt for the part she played in establishing our independence and the formation of the Union.

"It was her bold, determined and unswerving stand against the ratification of the Articles of Confederation that resulted in the cession to the United States of what was then known as the North-west territory.

"Many of the original colonies which had received charters from the Crown believed that there were no set boundaries at the West, and that their grants extended to the 'Western waters.' New York, Massachusetts, Connecticut and Virginia were foremost in making such claims. Virginia, whose charter antedated all others, had the best title to the lands in dispute. Hence, she was the most tenacious in her claims.

"The other States naturally felt that, as these larger States grew and waxed powerful, they might tyrannize over their smaller neighbors.

THIS STATE AROSE TO THE OCCASION.

"Of all these protesting States, it was Maryland alone that rose to the occasion and suggested an idea, which at first seemed startling, but which became a fixed fact, from which mighty and unforseen consequences afterward flowed.

"The Articles of Confederation were about to be presented to the respective States for ratification when the question naturally arose as to how the conflicting claims to these Western lands should be settled.

"A Marylander, Daniel Carroll, offered in Congress a resolution that

"The United States, in Congress assembled, should have the sole and exclusive right and power to ascertain and fix the Western boundary of such States as claimed to the Mississippi, and lay out the land so ascertained into separate and independent States from time to time as the number and circumstances of the people may require.

"To carry out this motion it was necessary for the States claiming this Western territory to surrender their claims into the hands of the United States, and thus create a domain which should be owned by the Confederation in common.

BOLD STEP, BUT SUCCESSFUL.

"This was a bold step taken by Maryland, and was considered to smack somewhat of centralization of power. Maryland was the only State that voted for it. She stood firm, pursued her purpose resolutely, and was rewarded with complete success.

"New York, Virginia, Connecticut and Massachusetts finally ceded their title to these lands, and Maryland ratified the Confederation, having first secured as the common property of the United States all of the immense territory which has since been parceled out and established by Congress into the free and fertile States of Ohio, Indiana, Illinois, Michigan and Wisconsin.

"Thus, the Confederation was perfected, the Union preserved, and this great territory was saved for the benefit of the whole united people.

LAID CORNER-STONE OF UNION.

"Maryland, by taking the stand she did and leading the way in this fight, laid the corner-stone of our Federal Union.

"The rising tide of immigration poured into this Western country, creating a sturdy and determined citizenship there, so that, when Spain claimed the exclusive right to navigate the Mississippi River and decided to abrogate the privilege that had been enjoyed by these settlers to deposit their products at the mouth of the Mississippi River for exportation, the cry of hot protest came from these fearless pioneers of the West notifying the politicians of the New World that these freemen of the frontiers of the nation would not tolerate the abridgment of their rights and would insist upon the free navigation of the Mississippi River and their right to send their products through it to the ocean.

WORK OF JEFFERSON AND MONROE.

"It was this vigorous protest of these new sons of the West, demanding prompt action by the Administration at Washington, that aroused President Jefferson and caused him to take steps looking to the acquisition of New Orleans and securing from France the right of deposit and free, uninterrupted navigation of the Mississippi River.

"He at once sent James Monroe to Paris to negotiate—not the purchase of the entire Louisiana Territory, but simply to acquire New Orleans and the Floridas east of the Mississippi River—and, failing in that, then to secure the right to our citizens to own property in New Orleans and to deposit their products for export.

"When Mr. Monroe reached Paris he found that our resident Minister, Mr. Livingston, had been in negotiation with the French Government for the purchase of New Orleans and the Floridas. He also found that Napoleon, then the First Consul, had declared his purpose of selling the whole of Louisiana to the United States, because of the fear that England would seize that territory as her first act of war. In an interview with Marbois, one of his Ministers, upon the subject, Napoleon said:

"'Irresolution and deliberation are no longer in season. I renounce Louisiana. It is not only New Orleans that I cede—it is the whole colony, without reserve. I know the price of what I abandon. I have proved the importance I attach to this province, since my first diplomatic act with Spain had the object of recovering it. I renounce it with the greatest regret; to attempt obstinately to retain it would be folly. I direct you to negotiate the affair, and have an interview this very day with Mr. Livingston.'

"I will not weary you with the details of the negotiations resulting in the purchase of the whole of Louisiana. The price paid was $15,000,000, and France ceded this immense territory to the United States on April 30, 1803.

STATES CARVED OUT OF WILDERNESS.

"What a progressive, prosperous group of States and Territories has been carved out of this land—Arkansas, Iowa, Missouri, Nebraska, North and South Dakota, parts of Kansas, Colorado, Montana, Minnesota, Wyoming and Louisiana, all of the Indian Territory and part of Oklahoma! Its area is more than seven times that of Great Britain and Ireland. It is larger than Great Britain, Germany, France, Spain, Portugal and Italy combined, and is only one-fourth less than the area of the thirteen original States.

"Two of these States, Colorado and Montana, produced in one year $89,938,708.95 in gold, silver, copper and lead—over five times the purchase price paid by the United States.

"The annual agricultural products reach a total of billions in this territory, and its present population is over 13,500,000.

THE STORY OF MARYLAND.

"We Marylanders are proud of the history of our State, and venerate the deeds of our forefathers. Therefore, I ask your indulgence whilst I briefly tell you the story of Maryland. She stands as the seventh in the original galaxy of thirteen States, because she was the seventh to adopt the Constitution forming the permanent Union. The very foundation of the colony of Maryland was of national importance, because the principal of religious toleration was introduced by the founder. From the time of the landing at St. Mary's until to-day, liberty of conscience has been the fundamental right of every person in Maryland.

TRUE HISTORY OF ACT OF TOLERATION.

"Much has been written upon the subject of the Act of Toleration of 1649. The true history may be briefly stated. Cecilius Calvert, being vested with extraordinary power over a great territory, determined to found there a free English State, where all the rights and liberties of every English freeman would be protected. To do this he divested himself and his heirs of the princely prerogatives granted to him by his charter. He caused to be drafted at home, and then adopted by the freemen of Maryland, codes of laws which transferred English institutions to Maryland. By orders, proclamations and conditions of plantation he strengthened and fortified these institutions thus transplanted. Believing that Magna Charta and the right of petition guaranteed every Englishman the right to liberty of person and security of property, he was wise enough to see and brave enough to declare that these rights were worthless without liberty of conscience.

" He, therefore, adopted and declared that to be the principle on which the foundations of Maryland should be laid. From the first, he intended to secure all those rights, privileges and franchises, not alone to Roman Catholics, nor yet alone to Englishmen, but to all Christian people of all the nations of the world.

" In doing this he was supported by the whole social influence of the Roman Catholics of England and by the power of the Society of Jesus.

SAFETY AND SHELTER FOR ALL.

"Under this institution the Puritans settled at Providence, the Quakers at West River and the Presbyterians on the Patuxent. It gave shelter to the Huguenots after the massacre of St. Bartholomew, and to Roman Catholics from the murders and burnings of San Domingo.

" Notwithstanding its repeated external overthrow by force or faction, it has always been imbedded in the life of the people. In the wars, insurrections, revolutions, rebellions and civil broils which swept the province in its earlier days, neither life, liberty nor property has ever been sacrificed in the fury of religious fanaticism. Blood has been shed in the struggles of factions, but no man has ever been put to death on account of his religion in Maryland.

STRUGGLED FOR FREEMEN'S RIGHTS.

"The growth of popular government was early manifested in Colonial Maryland. In the very first Assembly, in 1635, every freeman was entitled to a seat and voice in the proceedings. The second Assembly was held in 1637, and the freemen rejected the code of laws offered by Lord Baltimore, although liberal and just, claiming the right to originate legislation for themselves. Thus began the fight in Maryland for the rights of freemen.

" In 1739 the Assembly successfully opposed taxes being imposed without its consent, and this fight went on until 1765, when the attempt to place taxes by Parliament and the tea tax of 1767 so aroused the people that the protest was universal throughout the colony.

" Meetings were held all over the State to protest against the closing of the port of Boston, and provisions were sent to aid the almost starving people of that city, thus showing the earnest sympathy of the people of Maryland in their fight for the great principle of 'No taxation without representation.'

BURNING OF THE PEGGY STEWART.

" In all of the movements that led up to the Declaration of Independence and the Revolutionary War Maryland stood in the forefront. The first overt act of her people against the authority of the King of England was on October 19, 1774, when her fearless patriots compelled Anthony Stewart to burn his brig, the Peggy Stewart, with her cargo of tea, in the harbor of Annapolis. This was done in broad daylight, by men undisguised, whose motto was 'Liberty, or death in the pursuit of it.'

"Thomas Johnson, of Maryland, nominated George Washington in the Continental Congress to be Commander in Chief of the American Army.

"The Maryland Riflemen, under Michael Cresap, were the first organized troops to respond to the call of liberty. They fought side by side with the Puritans of Massachusetts at Concord and Lexington.

MARYLAND'S "FOUR HUNDRED."

"It was Maryland's 'Four Hundred,' under the intrepid Gist, who, after six successive bayonet charges, saved Washington's army at Long Island, in August, 1776. The greatest crisis in that battle was the superb action of these immortal Marylanders. They held the British Army of 4,000 in check until the Americans moved across to the Jersey shore. Two hundred and sixty-seven of their number were killed or wounded.

"Their bravery and heroism caused General Washington to exclaim, 'Great God! what brave men I must this day lose.'

COVERED WASHINGTON'S RETREAT.

"The 'Maryland line,' under command of Colonel Smallwood, composed Washington's rear guard in his masterly retreat through New Jersey.

"Maryland soldiers participated in every hard-fought battle of the Revolution, from Long Island to Yorktown, and were especially distinguished for bravery at Camden, Eutaw Springs, Guilford Courthouse, Hobkirk's Hill and Cowpens. They were the 'old guard' of the Continental forces, 'the bayonets of the Revolution.'

COLONEL TILGHMAN'S FAMOUS RIDE.

"It was a son of Maryland, Colonel Tench Tilghman, Washington's aide, who rode from Yorktown to Philadelphia, carrying the news of Cornwallis' surrender to the Continental Congress. He crossed the Chesapeake Bay to the Eastern Shore of Maryland in an open boat, where, procuring a horse, he started on his way, riding in the dim watches of the night. When his horse gave out he would ride up to a house and call out, 'A horse for the Congress, Cornwallis is taken!' There was a flash of light, a patter of glad feet, a welcome and a godspeed. This was repeated time and again, until, finally, thundering into Philadelphia at midnight, Independence bell was rung, Congress convened, and the watchman on his rounds proclaimed, 'Twelve o'clock; all's well and Cornwallis is taken.'

"Maryland has taken a foremost place in our wars since the Revolution, and in every movement for the advancement of liberty, the welfare of the people, and the maintenance of the peace, prestige and dignity of the Government.

HER CONTRIBUTION TO WAR OF 1812.

"She contributed more money and men for the War of 1812 than any other State. The annals of that war show that of the 240 naval officers who served on our ships, Maryland furnished forty-six, nearly one-fifth, and more than any other State; all of the New England States together sending only forty-two, and New York but seventeen. And in the number of privateers sent out to prey upon British commerce, Baltimore headed the list of cities.

"Her quota of volunteers for the Mexican War was promptly recruited. They were a brave band of soldiers, and won glory for their State. When General Taylor called for 'a little more grape, Captain Bragg,' it was Ringgold's Flying Artillery (from Maryland) that furnished the grape.

SENTIMENT DIVIDED IN 1861.

"In 1860 Maryland's electoral vote was cast for Bell and Everett, showing that a majority of her people were for the Constitution and the Union. Although a majority of her most substantial citizens sympathized with the cause of the South, she refused to secede from the Union. Her sons were divided in the contest. Those who wore the gray believed that the South was right, and, so believing, fought bravely, and endured suffering and privations for the faith that was in them and the cause they espoused. So with those who volunteered to sustain the Union. Maryland honors the valor of all of her sons, those who wore the gray as well as those who wore the blue.

"In evidence of this spirit she has erected a monument upon the battlefield of Antietam to commemorate their devotion to duty. On the tablets are inscribed the names of the commands, Union and Confederate, and the battles in which they participated.

"This monument was presented to the National Cemetery Commission by the State of Maryland in the presence of old soldiers of both armies, and was accepted by our martyred President, William McKinley, who did more than any other public man to obliterate the animosities of the war and reunite our people.

DID NOT HANG BACK IN 1898.

"Maryland's quota of volunteers for the Spanish War was quickly furnished. Her National Guard responded enthusiastically, each regiment clamoring to be sent to the front.

"Maryland took the initiative in many important matters of legislation. She passed the first law to naturalize a foreign-born citizen. She was the first State to recognize by law the possibility of steam navigation. She did this by granting to James Rumsey the exclusive right of steam navigation in the waters of the State. She was the first State, after Virginia, to embody in her form of government the famous Bill of Rights formulated by George Mason.

HISTORICAL EVENTS UPON HER SOIL.

"Many interesting historical events have taken place upon her soil. It was in the Senate Chamber, in the old Capitol now standing at Annapolis, that Washington resigned his commission as Commander in Chief of the army and returned it to Congress and retired to private life—the sublimest act of his sublime life.

"It was in that hallowed chamber that the treaty of peace with England, which ended the war, was ratified by Congress.

"It was in that same historic chamber that the initial convention was held to promote the organization of a more permanent Government. It suggested the calling of a convention to formulate a Constitution and found the Union.

CRADLE OF PRESBYTERIAN CHURCH IN AMERICA.

"Maryland was the cradle of the Presbyterian Church in America. The first regularly constituted church of that denomination in the United States was erected at Rehoboth, Somerset County, now Wicomico County, with Rev. Francis Makemie as its first minister. Maryland was the only colony where the Presbyterians could get toleration.

"It was in Maryland that the first bishop of the Episcopal Church consecrated in America, resided—Right Reverend Thomas John Claggett, Bishop of the Diocese of Maryland, who performed an important part in laying the foundations of this great and historic Church.

"It was in Maryland that the Methodist Episcopal Church of America was established, and the first house of worship built by that now powerful Christian denomination that has done so much for the upbuilding of both civilization and religion in this as well as in other countries.

OLDEST ROMAN CATHOLIC DIOCESE.

"In Maryland is the oldest Roman Catholic diocese in the United States—the Archdiocese of Baltimore.

"The first Archbishop of that Church in this country was a Marylander, and it is fitting that the name of Archbishop Carroll should be linked in State pride with that of his kinsman, Charles Carroll, of Carrollton, the signer of the Declaration of Independence.

"Maryland to-day is the head of the Roman Catholic hierarchy. Representing that Church we have in Baltimore its only Cardinal in the United States—Cardinal Gibbons, that man of simple and pure life, true Americanism and high patriotism.

"Thus, it will be seen that upon Maryland's soil was first established in the United States these four great Christian Churches, that have been such potential forces in shaping the destiny and greatness of our nation.

"Not only has Maryland been the scene of historical events, but many of the important industrial, inventive and scientific conceptions have been born within her borders.

FIRST STEAMBOAT FLOATED IN HER WATERS.

"It was in Maryland waters that the first steamboat was floated. It was invented by a Marylander, James Rumsey, twenty-five years before Fulton launched the Claremont. General Washington, who witnessed the trial on the Potomac, gave a certificate of the success of the experiment.

FIRST RAILROAD IN AMERICA.

"It was in Maryland that the first steam railroad in America was built and the first electric railway in the world was operated. It was in Maryland that the first iron plates for ship-building were made. It was in Maryland that the first telegraph line in the world was constructed, and the first water company and the first gas company were organized. It was a Marylander, Obed Hussey, who in-invented the first sickle-knife for reapers, and the first perfect and successful self-raking reaper was invented by Owen Dorsey, of Howard County, Maryland.

"The heraldic device of the Great Seal of Maryland discloses the fact that the supporters of the shield are a farmer and a fisherman. In the days of the Province these two avocations were the only ones, and to-day they form the most important factors in the prosperity of the State.

AS AN AGRICULTURAL STATE.

"The agricultural products of the State amount to $43,823,419 annually. No more favored land for agricultural purposes can be found in the United States. While corn, wheat and tobacco are the staples, yet every product of the temperate zone can be produced within her borders in the greatest abundance.

"Frederick County, the home of General Baughman, ranks as the third agricultural county in productiveness in the United States.

"Of Maryland's total area of 12,210 square miles, 2,350 are covered by the waters of the Chesapeake Bay and its tributaries, which teem with terrapin, oysters, crabs and fish in almost endless variety, while to the swamps and the marshes annually come thousands of ducks, geese and other wild fowl. The value of the annual yield from the products of these waters is over $10,000,000.

NOT BACKWARD IN MANUFACTURES.

"Maryland is also taking her place in the front rank of manufacturing States. Her output of manufactured goods last year amounted to $242,752,990. By reason of her proximity to the stores of raw material, to the great coal fields and her splendid water power, with unequaled water courses and great railroad connections, there is every inducement for the establishment of manufactories.

"The mineral resources of Maryland are extensive, and but partly developed. Iron ore is abundant and of good quality. Limestone and marble of good quality, and granite unequaled, are pro-

fusely distributed throughout the State. Her coal mines are practically inexhaustible, and yield more than $5,000,000 annually. Her
deposits of clay and kaolin furnish material for brick and pottery.

HEALTHY CLIMATE, HOSPITABLE PEOPLE.

"Her climate is salubrious and healthy. Her hills and dales are
pleasing and attractive to the eye. Her people are hospitable and
cultured. Her public schools rank with those of any State in the
Union. Her taxation—for State, county and municipal purposes—
is moderate. Her churches are numerous, and her people are moral
and law-abiding.

"In fact, Maryland can boast of a citizenship, of a culture, of
everything that promotes happiness and contentment. In the words
of her distinguished poet, Randall, the author of 'Maryland, My
Maryland,' 'There is faith in her stream; there is strength in her
hills; there is life in the old land yet.'

BALTIMORE A CITY OF FAIR WOMEN.

"I cannot close without referring to our metropolis, Baltimore,
our beautiful city, famed for her fair daughters, her monuments, her
beautiful parks, her churches, her colleges of medicine and law; her
great Johns Hopkins University, which has in a quarter of a century
won a position in the front rank of the universities of the world; of
her hospitals—unsurpassed in their equipment for ministering to
suffering humanity; of her libraries; her old Historical Society, filled
with the data that tells the brilliant story of our Commonwealth,
and, above all, of her progressive, wide-awake and up-to-date
merchants.

"Our city ranks next to St. Louis in population, but she stands
upon an equal footing with her in all of the characteristics that go to
make up an enterprising community. Baltimore sends greetings to
St. Louis and hopes that this Exposition will prove advantageous to
her, and be an inspiration that will yield fruit in the future.

PLUCK AND ENERGY AFTER THE FIRE.

"A great fire swept away the very heart of our city on the 7th
of February, 1904, destroying property valued at $75,000,000. Our
people, with a courage and grit unsurpassed, turned at once to the
task of restoration and worked with a vim, so that to-day the work
of reconstruction is so well under way that within a year a new,
substantial and beautiful city will have been built upon her ruins,
thus demonstrating that our people are of that type that knows no
failure or discouragement, and who can meet with stout hearts any
emergency.

"Without aid, but with warm sympathy from every quarter, our
merchants have rehabilitated themselves, taken care of their customers, and pushed forward Baltimore's fame.

PRIDE OF MARYLANDERS IN MARYLAND.

"These facts about Maryland justify the love that every Marylander bears for his native State. He can point with pride to her record of patriotism, to her contribution to the progressive work of the world, to her statesmen, her soldiers, her sailors. Her sons and their descendants have furnished much of the brain and brawn which have contributed to 'The Winning of the West.'

"Missouri is a large debtor to Maryland. Many of her sturdy, enterprising, wide-awake business men are of Maryland stock or natives of our State. We are proud of such sons. They reflect credit upon their Maryland ancestry."

Personally, Governor Warfield is a man of great magnetism and strength of character.

Feeling that the people were the source of all political power and advancement, he went to them, and it was only after the people had indicated their choice that the organization leaders yielded and followed after.

Perhaps the most popular speech ever made by the Governor was that spoken in Middletown Valley, before an immense concourse of admiring farmers, their wives and their children. In that happy line of thought which comes from the heart, the Governor spoke of true home life. He spoke knowingly, for it is his greatest delight to be at home directing and admiring and resting when official cares are removed and all nature offers him a home of rest.

Concerning that Middletown speech, the Baltimore "Sun," in an editorial, thus endorsed the Governor:

"In his own well-regulated and happy home life, based on order, peace, contentment, the Governor of Maryland is deservedly entitled to be rated as the first citizen of the State. As the Governor, he, in fact, occupies such relation. As the head of a family governed by such principles as he has enunciated, he is worthy of following, for he is a man of plain, orderly living, active and industrious in his personal business, solicitous for the welfare of his fellow-citizens in the education of their children and in the regulation of their home life, and is inspired by high ideals for others, as well as himself. He cannot fail to hold a firm place in the hearts and homes of his countrymen."

In 1886 Mr. Warfield married Emma, daughter of the late J. Courtney Nicodemus, a prominent merchant of Baltimore, originally of the Cumberland Valley family, who were descendants of noted Indian fighters, and who were revolutionary soldiers and patriots.

Governor and Mrs. Warfield have four children. Their only son, Edwin Warfield, Jr., is a student of St. John's College. Their daughters, Carrie and Louise, are still at school upon the Hudson. Miss Emma, the youngest, is at home and governs the Governor.

DISTINGUISHED MEN OF ANNE ARUNDEL.

Distinguished Marylanders Who Claim St. John's College as Their Alma Mater.

Daniel Clarke, Associate Judge First District; John Done, Judge of General Court, Judge of Fourth District and the Court of Appeals; Clement Dorsey, Judge of First District; Benjamin Ogle, Governor; Ninian Pinkney, Clerk of Executive Council, Class 1793. Richard Harwood, Adjutant-General; John Carlisle Herbert, Member of Congress and Speaker of House of Delegates; Alexander Contee Magruder, Judge of Court of Appeals, Reporter of the Decisions of the same Court; John Seney and John C. Weems, Members of Congress, class 1794. Robert H. Goldsborough, United States Senator; Francis Scott Key, author of "Star Spangled Banner;" John Ridgely, Surgeon United States Navy; Washington Van Bibber, Member of Congress, Class 1796. John Leeds Kerr, United States Senator; John Taylor Lomax, Judge of Court of Appeals, Virginia, Class 1797. Alexander Hammett, Consul at Naples; Thomas U. P. Charlton, Chancellor of South Carolina; William Rodgers, United States Navy; TobiasWatkins, Auditor United States Treasury and Assistant Surgeon United States Army; John Wilmot, Adjutant-General of Maryland, Class 1798. Thomas Beale Dorsey, Attorney-General of Maryland and Chief Judge of Court of Appeals; Dennis Claude, M. D., Treasurer of Maryland; George Washington Park Curtis, Class 1799. Nicholas Harwood, M. D., Surgeon United States Navy; George Mann, Lieutenant United States Navy; James Thomas, Governor of Maryland, Class 1800. James Murray, Examiner-General; Charles W. Hanson, Judge of Sixth District; Alexander Contee Hanson, Editor of "Federalist" and United States Senator; David Hoffman, Professor of Laws, University of Maryland; Charles Sterrett Ridgely, Speaker of House of Delegates, Class 1802. John Contee, Lieutenant United States Marine Corps; William Grason, Governor of Maryland; Christopher Hughes, Charge to Sweden; Thomas Williamson, Surgeon United States Navy, Class 1804. George Mackubin, Treasurer of Maryland; John Wesley Peaco, Surgeon United States Navy and Governor of Liberia; Daniel Randall, Deputy Paymaster-General United States Army; Hyde Ray, Surgeon United States Navy; John R. Shaw, Purser United States Navy; Seth Switzer, Consul to Guayquil; William T. Wooten, Secretary of State, Class 1806. Thomas Randall, Judge of District Court of Florida; John Ridout, Visitor and Governor; John Gwinn, Captain United States Navy; William Latimer, Admiral United States Navy; William H. Marriott, Collector of Port of Baltimore, Class 1810. Nicholas Brewer, Judge of Circuit Court, Anne Arundel; William Caton, Surgeon United States

Navy; Reverdy Johnson, United States Senator, Attorney-General, Minister to England; David Ridgely, State Librarian, Author of "Annals of Annapolis;" William Greenberry Ridgely, Chief Clerk in Navy Department at Washington; John Nelson Watkins, Adjutant-General of Maryland, Class 1811. Thomas S. Alexander, L. L. D., United States Navy; John Johnson, Chancellor of Maryland; Landon Mercer, Lieutenant United States Navy; John Denny, Surgeon United States Navy; Richard Randall, M. D., United States Army; Governor Francis Thomas, Member Congress; Ramsey Waters, Register in Chancery; John B. Wells, Surgeon in United States Army; George Wells, President Maryland Senate, Classes 1811 and 1821. Alexander Randall, Member of Congress and Attorney-General of Maryland, Class 1822. Nicholas Brewer (of John), Adjutant-General of Maryland; Burton Randall, Surgeon United States Army; John Henry Alexander, L. L. D.; William Harwood, State Librarian, Professor at Naval Academy; School Examiner of Anne Arundel; William Pinkney, Bishop of Protestant Episcopal Church of Maryland; William H. Tuck, Judge of Court of Appeals; John Bowie, Lieutenant United States Navy, Class 1827. John Randall Hagner, Paymaster United States Navy; Thomas Kavney, Professor of Ethics and Librarian United States Naval Academy; Ninian Pinkney, Medical Director United States Navy; Augustus Bowie, Surgeon United States Navy; Sprigg Harwood, Clerk of Circuit Court; John H. T. Magruder, State Librarian; Richard Swann, State Librarian, Class 1830. Rev. Orlando Hutton; John Green Proud, poet before the Alumni; F. W. Green, Member of Congress; Peter V. Hagner, United States Army, Class 1834. Abram Claude, Professor of Chemistry, St. John's College, Mayor of Annapolis, Class 1835. William R. Hayward, Commissioner of Land Office; Rev. Samuel Ridout, Class of 1836. William Tell Claude; Henry H. Goldsborough, President of State Convention of 1864, Comptroller, Judge of Eleventh District; William H. Thompson, Professor of St. John's; Marcus Duvall, Medical Director United States Navy; Frederick Stone, Judge of Court of Appeals; Luther Giddings, Major United States Army; Richard Grason, Judge of Court of Appeals; Llewellyn Boyle, State Librarian; John Thomas Hall, Lieutenant United States Army; James Kemp Harwood, Purser United States Navy; John Scheff Stockett, State Reporter Court of Appeals; Nicholas Brewer, State Reporter Court of Appeals; Richard M. Chase, Secretary Naval Academy; James Munroe, Mayor of Annapolis, Class 1846. James Shaw Franklin, Clerk of Court of Appeals; John Mullan, Captain United States Army; Charles S. Winder, Captain United States Army and Brigadier-General of Confederate Army; James Revell, State's Attorney; Thomas J. Nelson, Paymaster United States Army; Charles Brewer, Surgeon United States and Confederate States Armies; William Sprigg Hall, Judge of Court of Common Pleas of Minnesota; Daniel R. Magruder, Judge of Court of Appeals; John H. Sellman, Paymaster United States Navy and Collector of Revenue; Andrew G. Chapman, Member of Congress; John W. Brewer, Assistant Surgeon United States Army; William Hirsey Hopkins, Vice-President of St. John's and President of Female College of Baltimore; Samuel McCullough, Lieutenant Confederate States Army.

Some Prominent Men Who Have Gone out of Anne Arundel and Others Who Still Live There.

BRASHEARS.

The popular Representative of Anne Arundel in the Legislature of 1902, who refused to be Speaker when he might have secured that honor, comes from the Huguenot Benjamin Brasseurs, Commissioner of Calvert County, in 1660. Our Archives contain an interesting record of his naturalization. It reads:

"Cecilius Calvert—Whereas, Benjamin Brasseurs, late of Virginia, have sought leave to inhabit as a free Denizen, to purchase lands, I do hereby De Clare that said Bendjs. Brasseur, his wife and children, to be full Denizens of this our Province and that he be held, treated, reputed and esteemed as one of the faythfull people."

The Brasseurs homestead upon the Patuxent shows its antiquity in the ancient graveyard. It is known as "Brashears Purchase."

Mr. Brashears, attorney-at-law at Annapolis, married a daughter of Joshua Browne, former President of the Annapolis and Elk Ridge Railroad.

HOPKINS.

There seems to have been four distinct Hopkins families in Anne Arundel and Montgomery Counties. The first is that of William Hopkins, of "Hopkins' Plantation," Greenberry Point. He came up with the Virginians to the Severn in 1649, but left no descendants of his name.

Gerard Hopkins was here as early as 1658. His will of 1691 names his children Gerard, Anne, Thompsin and Mary. Thompsin was the first wife of Captain John Welsh, of South River. The second Gerard married Margaret Johns, and their issue were Joseph, Gerard, Philip, Samuel, Richard, William and Johns Hopkins, all born between 1706 and 1720. The founder of Johns Hopkins University was a descendant of this family.

In 1742 Matthew Hopkins, of County of Ayr, Scotland, came to Rock Creek, now Montgomery County. His widow, Mary, became Mrs. Henry Thralkeld. No issue of his name is known.

John Hopkins, said to have come from Scotland, was also located upon the Maryland side of the Potomac, about 1775. He married Eleanor Wallace, daughter of James Wallace, of Montgomery County. They left Herbert Hopkins, William, Richard, Alexander, James and John Hopkins. The affable Chief Clerk of the Comptroller's office, Mr. Harry Hopkins, comes from Talbot County.

PROFESSOR ROBINSON.

The most popular agriculturist of the North Severn section of Anne Arundel is Professor Robinson, of the Horticultural Department of the Agricultural College. He has long been a Granger and lectured throughout the State during the life of that order.

Professor Robinson's family have long been located upon the Broad Neck of the Severn. The family came from the Eastern Shore. His grandfather was a privateer in the War of 1812. Professor Robinson is a connection of Judge Robinson, of the Eastern Shore.

DR. JOSEPH MUSE WORTHINGTON.

Dr. Joseph Muse Worthington, son of Professor Nicholas Brice and Sophia Kerr (Muse) Worthington, of Annapolis, is a grandson of Brice John and Ann Fitzhugh (Lee) Worthington, and a great-grandson of Major Nicholas Worthington, First Major of the Severn Militia Battalion, commanded by Colonel John Hall. Dr. Worthington's uncle, Brice John Worthington, was a lay reader at Crownsville Church for a number of years. He married Matilda Pue, daughter of Henry, of Howard County.

Dr. Worthington has corresponded extensively in tracing the genealogy of the Worthingtons of Maryland, and is thoroughly posted on all the facts that can be secured in this country. He also found traces of a William Worthington who came to the Severn with Richard Moss, but left no records here.

Beale Worthington, of Anne Arundel, is the son of Thomas Beale and Margaret Sellman Worthington, grandson of Richard and Eleanor Watkins Sellman, and great-grandson of Jonathan and Anne Eliza Howard Sellman. He is also grandson of Dr. Beale Worthington and great-grandson of Brice Thomas Beale Worthington, member of the Maryland Convention.

RICHARD PARRAN SELLMAN.

Richard Parran Sellman, of Anne Arundel, is a son of Alfred and Ann Parran Sellman, grandson of Jonathan and Ann Elizabeth Howard Sellman.

Major Jonathan Sellman was Second Lieutenant of Captain Henry Ridgely's company. In 1777 he was commissioned Captain of First Maryland Regiment, commanded by Colonel O. Holland Williams, and he became a member of the Cincinnati.

GEORGE H. SHAFER.

George H. Shafer, late of the Land Office, Annapolis, who was thirty-eight years in its service, was the son of George and Martha Bond Van Swearingen Shafer, grandson of John and Elizabeth B. Van Swearingen, great-grandson of Charles and Susanna Stull Van Swearingen. Charles was Second Major of the Maryland Militia under Samuel Beall.

THE SWEARINGEN FAMILY.

Feudal tenants under the lords of Dillingen, Garrett Van Swearingen, a descendant of the old Bavarian family, was born in Holland, 1636, died 1712; married Barbara De Barrette, of Norman-French lineage, in 1660. By her he had Thomas, born 1665. He married Jane. Their son Van, born 1695, died 1785; married Elizabeth Walker, of Patuxent, Maryland. Their son Charles—Susannah Stull. Their son John—Elizabeth Bond, third daughter of John Van Swearingen, born 1805, died 1887, married George Shafer—issue Elizabeth Susan Shafer—Rev. John Beck.

Arms of Bond: First and fourth sable, a fesse, or. Second and third quarters, argent, on a chevron sable three bezants.

Crest: A demi-pegasus azure, winged and semi of estailes. The colors shown in the sketch.

JUDGE NICHOLAS BREWER.

Judge Nicholas Brewer, of the Second District of Maryland, came down through a line of sturdy men commencing with John Brewer, a Justice of Calvert County. "Brewerton" and "Larkinton," near London Town, were the early surveys of his son, John Brewer, son-in-law of Colonel Henry Ridgely. Dying early, Colonel Henry Ridgely became the executor for his two sons, John and Joseph and one daughter, Elizabeth, named for her grandmother, a Pierpoint. Colonel Henry Ridgely made these grandsons his heirs. John Brewer, third in line, through his wife, Dinah Battee, left four sons and four daughters.

John, the elder, married Eleanor Maccubin, in 1727; five sons and four daughters were their issue. The youngest, Rachel, became the wife of the artist, Charles Wilson Peale, father of Rembrandt Peale, of Philadelphia; Joseph, her brother, through his wife, Mary Stockett, left Joseph, with others, who married a relative, Eleanor Brewer, daughter of John and Eleanor Maccubin. Their son, Nicholas Brewer, married Fanny Davis, daughter of the Revolutionary Robert Paine Davis. Their daughter, Mary Jane Brewer, married Richard Ridgely, Judge of the Orphans Court and Register of Chancery. He was the son of Absalom Ridgely, the merchant, by Anne Robinson, and grandson of Henry Ridgely and Catharine Lusby —coming down from Charles and Eliza Ridgely (of Colonel Henry).

Of this line of Absalom Ridgely was Dr. John Ridgely of the Tripolitan war, and David Ridgely, the merchant, the State Librarian, and Ridgely, the historian, herein often quoted. Another descendant is our honored historian, Elihu S. Riley.

The obituary notice of Nicholas Brewer, father of Judge Nicholas Brewer, in 1839, written by the editor of the "Maryland Gazette," pays this tribute: "Thus, in his sixty-eighth year, closes another of the most active, firm, steady and undeviating politicians of the State or age. A man who, as an opponent, was always a man, open, undisguised, straightforward and high-minded. As a friend, no man was ever more ardent, whole-hearted and sincere. For many years he represented this city in the House of Delegates. He seldom spoke, but never failed to command attention when he did speak. He was twice an Elector of the Senate. As a next-door neighbor and most intimate friend, as an associate for the third of a century, in peace and in war, in sickness and in health, I can testify that Nicholas Brewer was a man of inflexible integrity."

Colonel Nicholas Brewer, born at Marley in 1789, known as "the mill-boy of Marley," removed to Baltimore in 1815. He was the son of Captain Nicholas and Julia Brewer. Their ancestors came to Massachusetts with the Puritans in 1644; went to Virginia with the one hundred invited northern Puritans. Four years later they were driven out of Virginia and came to South River. The pioneer was John Brewer. Captain Nicholas Brewer was with Smallwood in the Revolution. He was an extensive planter. His wife was the daughter of Colonel Psalter, of Braddock's army.

Colonel Nicholas Brewer was a member of the " Old Defenders" of Baltimore in 1840.

Hon. Nicholas Brewer, Judge of the Second District, was born 1795. Graduating at St. John's College, he studied law. His wife was Catharine Musser Mediary, a descendant of John Bauer, who lived in and took the name of the Isle of Madeira.

Judge Brewer had ten children. Of his legal record, Hon. Reverdy Johnson has said: "As an equity pleader he had few superiors. As a judge he possessed the entire confidence of the legal fraternity. His influence was great and his decisions just."

CHIEF JUSTICE ROGER BROOKE TANEY.

In front of the State House at Annapolis, upon a pedestal far below the height of his fame, sits the heroic form of a Marylander whose name is world-wide. Born only a few miles south of the Anne Arundel line, upon Battle Creek, he goes back through Roger Brooke to the first commander 'of the Patuxent, Robert Brooke, of "Brooke Place." Roger Brooke Taney belongs to the history of a stormy period. From a little leather-covered pocket book, dated 1710, written by Roger Brooke, grandson of the commander and progenitor of Roger Brooke Taney, let me quote the following: " At the close of the month of June, 1650, there landed on the Patuxent, twenty miles from its mouth, a family of forty persons, the body-guard, male and female, of Mr. Robert Brooke and his wife, Mary Mainwaring, and ten children, born in England." " Dela Brooke" was their first homestead.

In 1654 the family removed to " Brooke Place," on Battle Creek, a name given by Mr. Brooke in honor of his first wife, Mary Baker, of Battle. Her two sons, Baker and Major Thomas Brooke, of "Brookfield," accompanied the immigrants. The former became a member of the Provincial Council. The latter commanded the Provincial forces and was the founder of the present village of T. B., taken from a landmark bearing his name.

I quote again: "My father, Roger Brooke, Sr., second son of Robert Brooke, by Mary, his second wife, daughter of Roger Mainwaring, D. D., Dean of Winchester, lived at Battle Creek and lies buried in the graveyard betwixt his two wives."

Dorothy Neale, sister of Henrietta Maria (Neale, Bennett) Lloyd, was the mother of Roger Brooke, Jr., the Recorder of 1710. The latter took for his wife, Eliza Hutchins, sister of Mary, wife of Samuel Thomas (of Philip). Their son, Roger Brooke, the third, was the progenitor of the Pennsylvania Brookes, represented by General Brooke, United States Army. James Brooke, second son of Roger and Eliza Hutchins, through Deborah Snowden (of Richard), became the progenitor of a large and progressive Brooke settlement at Sandy Spring. His survey of "Brooke Grove" covered 33,000 acres, ten miles in extent. His pioneer house, built in 1728, still stands near Sandy Spring. At that date it was the first frame house of his forest home. From it, with a button pulled from his coat, Mr. James Brooke shot a panther.

Two daughters of Roger Brooke married and remained upon the Brooke estate. They were Mrs. Walter Wilson, mother of Walter Brooke Wilson; and Monica, wife of Michael Taney, High Sheriff of Calvert, and mother of Roger Brooke Taney.

Walter Brooke Wilson married Mary (Dalrymple) Rawlings, widow of Captain Thomas Rawlings, and daughter of Hon. James Duke Dalrymple, of Calvert—issue, one son, William Wilson. After the death of Mr. Wilson she married Dr. Septimus J. Cook, of Prince George, and had one daughter, Margaret, wife of Professor J. D. Warfield. Dr. Cook and his wife both descended from two daughters of John Clare, of Calvert County.

To write the life of Chief Justice Taney would only duplicate his own modest autobiography, but the words of S. Teackle Wallis, in unveiling the statue which now stands at the State House, may be of interest. Said he:

"In the Chamber where we meet to-day to do him honor he sat for years a Senator of Maryland, the peer of the distinguished men who sat around him, when no legislative body in the Union surpassed that Senate in dignity, ability or moral elevation.

"In the Chamber there, above us, at the zenith of his reputation as advocate and council and in the very ripeness of his powers, he shone, the leader of the Bar of Maryland.

"The artist has chosen to present us his illustrious subject in his robes of office as we saw him when he sat in judgment; the weight of years that bent the venerable form has not been lightened, and the lines of care, and suffering, and thought are as life traced them.

"The figure has been treated in the spirit of that noble and absolute simplicity which is the type of the highest order of greatness.

"The State of Maryland here silently and proudly presents to posterity her illustrious son. Already the waters of the torrent have nearly spent their force, and high above them, as they fall, unstained by their pollution and unshaken by their rage, stands, where it stood, in grand and reverend simplicity, the august figure of the great Chief Justice."

COMMODORE MAYO OF SOUTH RIVER.

Commodore Isaac Mayo, who distinguished himself in the Mexican War, married, in 1835, Sarah Battaile Fitzhugh Bland, daughter of Chancellor Theodoric Bland, Consul to Brazil by his wife, Sarah Glen, widow of Mayor Jacob Davies, of Baltimore. The mother of Chancellor Bland was Sarah Henrietta Thornton, daughter of Admiral Thornton, of the British Navy.

Commodore Mayo's only daughter, Sarah Battaile Mayo, is the wife of Thomas Henry Gaither, of Baltimore, only surviving son of the late George R. Gaither. They have one son, Thomas Henry Gaither, Jr., and one daughter, Georgiana Mayo, wife of Lawrence Bailliere. They are residing in the historic "Peggy Stewart" house in Annapolis.

Commodore Mayo descended from Joshua Mayo, of South River, who, in 1707, married Hannah Learson. One son, Joseph, and four daughters, were all baptized at "All Hallows." Joseph, through his wife, Sarah Mayo, left Thomas and Joseph Mayo, Jr.; Mrs. Sarah Waters was a daughter.

Joseph Mayo, the second, through his wife, Henrietta, had Henry, John, Isaac, Edward and James Mayo. Isaac Mayo and Captain John Mayo and wife, were parishioners of "All Hallows" in 1845 when Isaac Mayo took the oath to "demean himself in the office of vestryman thereof according to the best of my skill and judgment and without Favor affection or Partiality."

Commodore Mayo held a historic tract, once the home estate of Captain Nicholas Gassaway, upon the Neck of South River, now known as "Mayo's Neck." This estate is now held by his daughter, Mrs. Thomas Gaither.

The daughters of the early Mayos of South River, married into the families of Jonathan Waters, John Ridgely, John Wilmott and Francis Linthicum.

HENRY WINTER DAVIS, THE WAR CONGRESSMAN.

Hon. Henry Winter Davis, the war Congressman, was the son of Rev. Henry Lym Davis, Rector of St. Anne's Church and at the same time President of St. John's College. Young Davis was born in Annapolis in 1817. His mother was Jane Winter Davis, a lady of intellectual attainments and elegance of person. Her sister was Henry Winter Davis' first teacher.

Graduating from Kenyon College, Ohio, in 1837 and taking a law course in the University of Virginia, Mr. Davis began practice in Alexandria, Virginia. There he married Constance Gardiner, of Virginia. He came to Baltimore in 1850, and soon became a leader of the new Know-Nothing party. Upon the outbreak of the war he represented the Union party, becoming its Congressional delegate.

His chaste, fervid diction always attracted attention. His eloquence and power as an orator soon brought him to the front. Always, when speaking, in full dress, with kid gloves, handsome in person, dignified in manner, he became the shining light of his party. Although dealing in controversial subjects, his addresses showed considerable literary ability.

He married in Baltimore, for the second time, Nancy, daughter of John B. Morris.

He died at the close of the war, in the full vigor of his manhood and fame, December 30, 1865.

C. IRVING DITTY.

C. Irving Ditty, born at West River in 1838, was the son of George T. Ditty, of Virginia, and Harriet, daughter of Benjamin Winterson. His only sister became Mrs. Jacob W. Bird. His father was a descendant of Sir Jeremiah Jacob, one of Lord Baltimore's immigrants.

C. Irving Ditty entered Dickinson College in 1854 and graduated in 1857. He entered the Confederate service with Colonel Ridgely Brown, and rose to Captain, and when the war was ended at Appomattox, his company refused to surrender, but cut through the ranks, and when attacked checked the charge. This was the last firing of of the war.

Mr. Ditty married Sophia, daughter of Henry Swartze, sister of Captain Swartze, of the same Confederate army. Irvington, a suburb of Baltimore, takes its name from Mr. Ditty. He entered into the reform movement of 1875, which ended in his joining the Republican party. He was sent to Louisiana to review the Presidential count of that State and reported that both parties were about equally guilty, but the evidences were in favor of Hayes.

Mr. Ditty died in Baltimore in early manhood.

Dr. MARIUS DUVALL.

Dr. Marius Duvall, Medical Director United States Navy, was born in Annapolis in 1818. He is the son of Lewis and Sarah (Harwood) Duvall, and was the youngest of eleven children. His grandmother was Miss Callahan, from the North of Ireland. His father represented Annapolis in the State Legislature for ten years. His name is among the students of St. John's College.

Dr. Duvall married a sister of Professor Lockwood. After filling many important stations, he was transferred to the Naval Hospital at Annapolis.

HON. MICHAEL BANNON.

Hon. Michael Bannon, was born in the County Tyrone, Ireland, in 1827. His grandfather was an officer in the Rebel Army of 1798.

At eighteen years of age young Bannon set out for America. His own account of his struggle is interesting. Reaching Baltimore, in 1847, with a capital of ten cents, he expended it for his first night's lodging. Having been well taught, he soon secured a position with a relative to teach his children. With his savings he branched out into other side speculations and succeeded in securing a college education. After graduation he succeeded his friend who had helped him. After teaching for a season he removed to Anne Arundel County and there continued teaching near his home at Jessups. Then studying law, he opened an office in Baltimore. In this last venture he succeeded in building up a large business in real estate exchanges. He built the Bannon Building.

Becoming next a political leader, he became State Senator and Clerk of the County Court. After accumulating an estate of $100,000 he traveled extensively. His wife was Eveline Clark, of Anne Arundel, who bore him eight children. Mr. James Bannon, of Anne Arundel, his son, succeeds as a political leader.

DEACON ABBOTT.

Deacon William M. Abbott, of the "Evening Capital," Annapolis, in addition to being a zealous member of the Democratic Editorial Association, is an elder in the Presbyterian Church and a graduate of the composing-room of the Baltimore "Sun." He was a compositor "on the wait" in the "Sun" office on the night Abraham Lincoln was assassinated, and after midnight "set up" the news of that lamentable event in our national history. Deacon Abbott was born in Trappe, Talbot County, Maryland, May 31, 1839, and was partly educated there and partly in a private school in Baltimore City. He has never held any public office. He was long in the employ of the late George Colton, and on May 12, 1884, started the "Evening Capital," which he has published daily, Sundays excepted, ever since. When he began this work his editorial desk was a dry goods box and he counted out the papers on a barrel head. Mr. Abbott has recently bought the "Chronicle" of Annapolis, and has removed the "Evening Capital" to the "Chronicle" office.

RILEY, THE HISTORIAN.

One of the most industrious members of the association, especially on historical lines, is Mr. Elihu S. Riley, former editor of the Annapolis "Record." Living at the seat of the State Government, where the public archives are kept and historical memories cluster thickly about, Mr. Riley is thoroughly informed upon the legislation and other matters pertaining to government. He was born in Annapolis, May 2, 1845, and educated in the public schools. He is an attorney-at-law as well as an editor. He was City Counselor of Annapolis from 1892 to 1895. He is widely known for various writings on Maryland historical subjects. With Mr. Conway W. Sams, Mr. Riley compiled a history of Bench and Bar of Maryland. He has lately published a history of the Maryland Assembly.

Captain Hugh Riley, his son, of the Annapolis Militia, has once represented the county in the Legislature. He is now counsel for the City government.

A MASTER OF ARTS.

Another editor of Annapolis who was an active member of the Democratic Editors' Association was also a lawyer and the School Examiner of Anne Arundel, and a very efficient school man at that. He was Mr. F. Eugene Wathen, of the "Maryland Republican." He was born in Leonardtown, St. Mary's County, June 29, 1860. He graduated from St. John's College in 1880 and received his degree of master of arts in 1889. He was president of the Board of Supervisors of Elections for Anne Arundel County from 1892 to 1894 and resigned to become School Examiner in January, 1895.

During the Republican reign Mr. Wathen had hard work to keep at the head of the public schools of his county, but by pluck and skill and ability, the master of arts did it.

W. MEADE HOLLIDAY.

Another Annapolis editor who is a member of the Democratic Editors' Association is Mr. W. Meade Holladay, publisher of the "Anne Arundel Advertiser." He is a bright political writer; never held any public office and never a candidate until his recent appointment of Supervisor of Elections by Governor Warfield in the place of Mr. Revel, resigned.

He was born in Spottsylvania County, Virginia, March 24, 1869, and was educated in the public schools of Fredericksburg, Virginia. He came to Maryland in 1888 and has ever since resided in Annapolis, where the associations are congenial.

INTERESTING DOCUMENTS.

After the repairs to the Courthouse, some five or six years ago, many valuable old papers and records belonging to the Circuit Court and County were put into the cellar of the Courthouse without order and, in many cases, without care whatever. The County Commissioners appointed Major William H. Gassaway, late of Annapolis, to rearrange and preserve the most valuable of these documents. In his work Major Gassaway found many curious bits of local history, amongst them returns of the currency and silver belonging to the citizens of Anne Arundel County. That for 1780 shows that of the R's, Mr. Absalom Ridgely, an Annapolis merchant, had the most currency in hand, that sum being £2,156 12s. 6d. Returns of the Elk Ridge tobacco warehouses of colonial period have come to light, and, amongst other curiosities, the venire of the juries of 1775. Habitues of the Courthouse have been busy picking out ancestors in this old list that is replete with the Anne Arundel names of to-day. The venire is: Abraham Woodward, Thomas Wilson, Stephen Gambrill, Joseph Meeke, Richard Sappington, Gilbert Yealdhall, Samuel Warfield, Thomas Warfield (son of Joshua), Amos Gaither, Richard Beard, Henry Hall, John Burgess, Edward Lee, Robert Paine Davis, Robert Welch, Richard Watkins, Samuel Watkins, Thomas Noble Stockett, Charles Hammond (son of John),

Charles Dorsey (son of Henry), Rezin Mobberly, Nicholas Aldridge, Joshua Marriott, John Barnes (son of Adam), Vachel Warfield (son of Samuel), John Dorsey (son of Michael), John Dorsey (son of Severn John), Thomas Cornelius Howard, James Walker, William Ridgely, Jr., William Fennell, John Rolls, Ezekiel Steuart, Zachariah Gray, Joshua Cromwell, John Scrivener, Thomas Miles, Benjamin Brashears, William Evans, James Cooley, Gabriel Lane, Wilkinson Brashears, Thomas Lane.

MR. JAMES MUNROE.

Upon the highest point of West street, Annapolis, lives the genial attorney, Mr. James Munroe. He has been requested to give me a history of his family, but has, perhaps, forgotten it. In the absence of it, his present life is a history in itself. Broad and liberal in his political views, correct and somewhat exacting in his legal work, Mr. Munroe exerts a living influence in the community of an interesting old city.

At present he is a member of the Board of Visitors for the Agricultural College. He holds no other official position, but his legal practice is large and he is by all men held in the highest esteem.

His present home is the beautiful one of the late Judge Tuck.

MR. ROBERT MOSS.

Coming down from one of the first settlers of Anne Arundel, located on the North Severn Neck, Mr. Moss is exerting considerable influence in Anne Arundel. He was graduated from the Agricultural College; was a member of the Senate of Maryland. He has been, for several sessions, the reading clerk of the Senate and also an attorney for the City government of Annapolis. He is now a member of the Board of Visitors of St. John's College. He is liberal in his views and endorses progressive movements in public institutions.

OWENS.

This family was represented by Richard Owens, who was seated in the southern section of the county, when Edward Lloyd, in 1649, was given a grant near him. Mr. James Owens, the popular attorney of Annapolis, and Dr. Owens, Registrar of the Maryland Agricultural College, are descendants. My sketch of this family was left with Mr. James Owens for revision, but it has not yet reached me. Mr. Owens is not only an interesting talker, but a forcible political writer and speaker who has made himself felt in several recent campaigns. May he continue to guide us.

DR. GEORGE WELLS.

As a successful physician and popular leader in political affairs of the County of Anne Arundel, Dr. Wells has long been at the head of the progressive men of the State. He comes from eminent ancestry. His father was Hon. George Wells, former President of the Farmers'

Bank of Annapolis, President of the Senate and the chief head of the Annapolis and Elk Ridge Railroad in its earlier struggle for existence. Hon. George Wells was a warden of St. Anne's Church when the furnace which caused its destruction was put into it. He remonstrated against and declined to aid in rebuilding the present edifice, but after it had been completed, with its belfry in which there was no bell, a thousand-dollar bell was soon at hand, the gift of the good-hearted warden, who kept his vow, yet showed his generous spirit. (Riley.)

As President of the Annapolis and Elk Ridge Railroad he made it a success. In 1863 the road paid the State $14,286.72, nearly five per cent. on the investment. Upon his retirement, Mr. Joshua Brown, the builder and superintendent of the road, succeeded to the presidency.

At a special meeting, in 1865, Hon. George Wells was elected State Senator. He was twice married, first, to a sister of Hon. John Stephens Sellman, of the "Nineteen Electors." The mother of Dr. George Wells was Eliza Harwood, cousin of Major Harwood.

Dr. Wells is third in line of his family in Maryland. His grandfather, George Wells, came direct from England. In 1833 he was one of the first trustees of the Methodist Episcopal Church which stood near the present record office on State House Hill. His associates of that Board were Absalom Ridgely, Joseph Evans and John Miller. In 1834 Mr. George Wells and Nicholas Brewer were delegates to the State Legislature.

Dr. George Wells, the present popular Clerk of the Court, was in 1869 chosen upon the issue of the Fifteenth Amendment a Democratic Alderman for Annapolis. He was elected to the House of Delegates in 1872 and to the Senate of Maryland in 1880-82. He was chairman of the committee upon the appropriation for the Agricultural College in 1880, in which he made a favorable report of the institution, securing its continued appropriation. In 1887 Dr. Wells was unanimously elected Treasurer of the County. He came into the office of Clerk in 1896 and has held it ever since.

Courteous and prompt in all official duties, he is a popular leader in the Democratic party, an able speaker, and almost idolized by those who know him best.

Dr. Wells holds one of the old historic dwellings of Annapolis, in the southern section of the city, just opposite the old homestead of the first editor of the "Maryland Gazette." He was a delegate to the convention that nominated Grover Cleveland in 1884, and was a member of the State Convention which sent delegates to the St. Louis Convention which nominated Bryan and was again present at the nomination of Judge Parker.

Dr. Wells is still a bachelor. Dr. John D. Wells, United States Army, was an uncle.

DR. WIRT ADAM DUVALL.

Dr. Wirt Adam Duvall, of Baltimore, was born in Anne Arundel County, 1863. He is the son of Judge Grafton and Mary Rebecca (Sullivan) Duvall, descendants of the Huguenot Mareen Duvall and of the English Sullivans. Of the former we had Judge Gabriel Duvall, of the Supreme Bench of United States, and of the latter, revolutionary soldiers of renown. Judge Grafton Duvall sat as Chief Judge of the Orphans Court for a number of years. He likes to spell his name with two "l's" and says he claims no relation to those who drop one of them, but all, alike, come from Mareen Duvall, the Huguenot merchant, who owned an immense estate, including "Great Marsh," and handed down a large and distinguished family of large landholders, prominent in official positions.

Dr. Wirt A. Duvall completed his general education at St. John's College in 1885 and was graduated from the Medical Department of the Maryland University in 1888. He is Demonstrator of Anatomy in the University and a member of its associations.

He married a daughter of Captain William Mitchell, of Baltimore, and has several children.

DR. JAMES DAVIDSON IGLEHART.

Dr. James Davidson Iglehart, of Anne Arundel, born 1850, now a resident of Baltimore, is the son of the late John Wilson Iglehart and Matlida Davidson, his wife. The Igleharts came from Germany and located near Marlborough, Prince George County, in 1740. James Davidson came to Pennsylvania from England in 1775 and enlisted in the Pennsylvania regiment of the patriot army, was transferred to the Maryland Line under General Smallwood and served throughout the war, becoming, also, in 1812, one of the "Old Defenders" of the Battle at North Point. He settled at Davidsonville, Anne Arundel County, dying in 1841. John Wilson Iglehart was born 1814, and at twenty-one years was appointed magistrate, serving also as County Commissioner and Judge of the Orphans Court. He owned an extensive plantation in Anne Arundel, dying in 1881. His son, James Davidson Iglehart, took his B. A. degree at St. John's College in 1872. He studied medicine under Dr. William P. Bird, of Anne Arundel, and was graduated from the University of Pennsylvaina in 1875. He was appointed by John W. Garrett as one of the surgical staff of the Baltimore and Ohio Railroad. He was an organizer of the Baltimore and Ohio Relief Department and is a member of the Board of Managers of the House of Refuge, member of the Sons of the American Revolution and of the Historical Society of Maryland.

He married Monterey, daughter of Colonel William Watson, who commanded the Baltimore Blues in the Mexican war and was killed at the battle of Monterey. Husband and wife are prominent in colonial orders. He is a member of Colonial Wars and War of 1812.

A GLANCE AT ANNE ARUNDEL COUNTY OLD AND NEW.

From "One Hundred Years Ago" I quote a charming review of a century ago:

"Judging the people of Annapolis by their houses, they were of refined and cultivated tastes. Externally without architectural pretension, but within beautifully proportioned rooms, with doors of solid mahogany and sometimes with handles of silver, with many elegant mantel-pieces and stairways—these evidences may still be seen. The dining-rooms, the largest of all, usually open into gardens, beautiful and well kept. After dinner a stroll under the shade of trees or a view of the river till tea served under the trees, was the summer order of the day.

"There still remain in some of the old families pieces of silver of very elegant design. In Dr. Ridout's family I have seen an exquisite piece which was used as an ornament for the centre of the table; also old Dresden china worthy to have graced the collection of Queen Mary at Hampton Court. In the matter of coaches the love of display cropped out and seems to have been unrestrained. The coaches were imported from England, with the horses and liveries. I have heard that some of the panels on which the escutcheons were emblazoned are still preserved as relics of a gorgeous past. Dr. Ridout once told me that his father remembered when six coaches-and-six were kept in the town, and it was not the style for grandees to appear with less than four.

"With the surrounding country abounding in game and the waters of the Chesapeake with oysters, ducks and terrapin, it was not difficult to maintain a bountiful hospitality. The lovely Severn River, the high banks of which remind one of a miniature Hudson, widens a few miles from town into a beautiful sheet of water called Round Bay, where lovely scenery, as well as abundance of fish invited the angler to indulge his favorite pastime. On the other side of the town the "Spa" winds past fine old mansions with terraced gardens, among them "Carrollton," the seat of Charles Carroll, and in front of the city the Severn loses itself in the blue waters of the Chesapeake.

"Everything, therefore, combined to make boating and sailing attractive. The gentlemen kept their sailboats as the ladies did their coaches, and many pleasant excursions were made to the country-seats of friends on the Eastern Shore and in St. Mary's."

At the beginning of this new century we are either tearing down or else trying to preserve the priceless relics of historic Annapolis. At the same time both the city and the State are rivaling each other in remodeling streets and buildings. Even the United States Government has at last recognized the charming advantages of this ancient city of the Severn. With three such combined influences centering at our State Capital, with a delightful climate, a most charming location, midway between two great cities, the future of Annapolis can even now be pictured.

Where Colonel Edward Dorsey, in 1705, sold a row of houses on "Bloomsbury Square," because "for want or tenants they were going to decay," the Government has erected a handsome new postoffice facing historic St. Anne's, three times erected on its original site. St. Anne's graveyard, which frightened tenants from "Bloomsbury Square," now rears its silent white columns upon Cemetery Creek, and Bloomsbury Square, facing St. Anne's Circle, is destined to become still more attractive.

For a century or more the Pinkney House, sacred in memory and solid in masonry, stood facing State House Circle and opposite the Governor's Mansion. Yielding up its site to the State, it moved in stately dignity down College Avenue and took its stand facing St. John's College, and now bids fair to shed its lustre through another century. In its place now looms up a new Court of Appeals temple, a new State Library, a new Land Office, a new Comptroller's Office. Even our venerable State House, ashamed of the modern additions that almost obliterated its grandeur, has been relieved of all these blemishes; new legislative and gubernatorial halls and committee rooms, after its original designs, have been added. Its old Senate Chamber has been restored as it was when Washington therein laid down his commission as Commander-in-Chief and bade good-bye to the Continental Congress therein assembled, passing to South River and thence to Mount Vernon. King William School long since gave up its site on the south of the State House; the Armory, on the north, no longer bristles with muskets—a gallant fighting foreigner stands upon the site of the former and now let us have the handsome form of our fighting Revolutionary Governor, Thomas Sim Lee, on the latter, for without him and his Maryland soldiers there might have been no Revolution.

Whilst all these changes have taken place on State House Circle, there is one little building, with its iron chest and its doors that defy robbers, still standing as a reminder of the organizers of the County-seat and State-seat. Let it stand.

For half a century the Government has held the Severn shore of the city. One by one old landmarks in that section have disappeared. A century ago the commodious Dulany house, built by Daniel Dulany in 1735, stood with its garden extending to the water's edge. The tragic history of this brilliant family would fill a volume. Near it stood the mansion of Governor Eden, who, with Daniel Dulany, almost alone championed the cause of the proprietary until the booming cannon announced the beginning of the people's government. From this latter mansion our State Governors held sway until it, too, was absorbed by the Naval Academy, to give way, in turn, to modern advancement. Old Fort Severn is no more. Upon these sites marble palaces of a great naval school have been erected. Until recently five Governors' mansions stood in Annapolis. Some declare the sixth, and the earliest, still stands upon Prince George Street. The first home of Governor Nicholson was upon the town common, as was also Major Edward Dorsey's. Prince George Street is upon that common, but our records do not further locate them, nor are there any records to locate Seymour and the first Edward Lloyd, of 1709.

Governor Hart occupied a house then standing upon "Proctor's Choice" and "Norwoods," somewhere in the Naval grounds.

Governor Bladen's attempt at building "Bladen's Folly" gave McDowell's Hall to St. John's College, and preceded Governor Samuel Ogle's success in building his still well-preserved homestead on College Avenue. The next in line, in 1763, was "White Hall," seven miles out on Whitehall Creek, by Governor Sharpe, upon the estate of the two Colonel Greenberrys. Governor Sharpe's full-length portrait still looks down upon its spacious dining-room. This was followed by Governor Eden's addition of wings to Mr. Bordley's Severn River house. Governors Johnson and Thomas Sim Lee followed Governor Eden in the charming home that had been confiscated, but William Paca built his own home upon Prince George Street, the charming gardens of which have been so often described. This is now Hotel Carvel, with its driveway.

The Chase House seems to have been the combined product of Judge Samuel Chase and Governor Edward Lloyd, of 1809, who held it then; he added an additional story.

Last in line is the present gubernatorial mansion between State House Circle and St. Anne's Circle. This was built under Governor Swann and has lately been enlarged by Governor Smith and its grounds improved by Governor Warfield.

The English settlers of 1660 followed their home river, the beautiful Severn. From Greenberry Point to Round Bay, or "Eagle Nest Bay," and the Isle of St. Helena in the center of Little Round Bay, is a distance of nine miles. The shores, sloping from the uplands to the river, are varied by decided eminences attaining 155 feet elevation. Forty such little mountains can be seen in sailing up the river. The river scenery of the Severn has been compared to the Hudson, and, excepting always the grand gorge of the Highlands, the comparison can be maintained.

The sail to Indian Landing, where three islands stand out boldly in the river, was once the attraction of the English settlers. From "Mount Misery," at the northern side of Round Bay, at a height of 155 feet, the view commands the bay, three miles in width, and looking east, takes in the headlands, slopes of the Magothy and the Chesapeake beyond. At this point, during the war, was a signal station. It is an eligible site for a summer hotel and suburban park— and Round Bay may yet be utilized by the Government when the contemplated enlargement of the Naval Academy shall have been completed.

Around these hills, named after the pioneer surveyors, settled a neighborly English colony. (Scharff.)

CEMETERY CREEK RECORDS.

In the beautiful but neglected grounds of Cemetery Creek, where rest the unknown dead of Annapolis' early history, there are many still to give us some idea of the lives and characters of our distinguished families. Every conceivable memorial and tribute may there be found. I copied some of them as follows:

"Nester Ann, dau. of the late Hon. J. T. and Hester Chase—born 1791—died 1875."

"Thomas Chase"—(letters almost obliterated).

"Mary, consort of Richard M. Chase, died 1836."

"Mrs. Hester Chase" (inscription obscure).

"Theodorick Bland, Chancellor of Md., died 1846 in 70th year."

"Alexander Randall, 1852." In this lot are many handsome memorials that could not be read from closed gates.

"Col. Daniel Randall, of John and Deborah, Paymaster-General—born 1790—died 1851."

"Richard Lockerman Harwood—a Confederate soldier of Maryland Cavalry, only son of Mrs. Hester Ann Harwood."

"Ninian Pinkney, Medical Director of U. S. A.—born 1811—died 1877."

"Mary Sherwood, wife of Ninian Pinkney."

"Mary Amelia Pinkney, daughter of Ninian and Amelia."

"George Mackubin, son of Edward and Mary C. Hammond—died 1852."

"Ann Carroll Brice—died 1858—74 years."

"Elizabeth Brice—died 1889—80 years."

"Father—Jas. Munroe, Sept. 1827—Sept. 1896."

"Harry S. Munroe—born 1839—died 1863."

"John, son of Grafton and Mary Munroe—born 1839—died 1878."

"Ann, daughter of Grafton and Mary Munroe—died 1890, aged 64 years."

"Davidson Hall, son of Frank and Mary Munroe—1900—1903."

"In memoriam of Nicholas Brewer—born 1795—died 1864."

"Arthur Tillard Brewer—1873—1897."

"Kate Brewer Sutherland, wife of Charles Sutherland, U. S. Army."

"Thomas S. Beall—born 1816—died 1890."

"Barbara M. Beall, wife of Thomas S. Beall—born 1820—died 1891."

"William Iglehart, son of James and Eliza Iglehart—1848—1896"

"William Iglehart, son of James and Eliza Iglehart—1848—1896."

"Emily Green, daughter of William Saunders Green."

"Eliza, daughter of William S. Green and Widow of James H. Iglehart—1812—1838."

"Mary Harwood—1815—1891."

A flat slab to "James Murray—1786—1866 and Catharine, his wife—1780—1870."

"Catharine, wife of James D. Murray and daughter of William A. and Catharine Spencer—born 1835—died 1859."

"In memory or Eliza Maynadier—born 1786—died 1852."

"Colonel Henry Maynadier....died 1849—91 years."

"Hannah Maynadier Murray, wife of Charles Calvert Stewart—1826—1894."

"Beneath this stone are deposited the remains of Mary Owings, widow of Samuel Owings, of Stephen, of Baltimore County, who departed this life 1835—76 years."

"Elizabeth Maynadier, wife of Colonel H. Maynadier."

"Charlotte, wife of James Murray—1791—1845."

"Henry M. Murray—1824—1870."

"Harriet, second daughter of Rev. Daniel Maynadier and Mary, his wife—1825."

"Margaret, third daughter of Rev. Daniel Maynadier and Mary his wife—1825."

"Helen, daughter of Charles Calvert Stewart—1856—1882."

"Sally, daughter of Charles Calvert Stewart—1821—1863."

"Charles Calvert Stewart 1819—1863."

"Dr. Upton Scott—died 1814—92 years. Native of Antrim, Ireland, and for 60 years a distinguished and respected inhabitant of this city."

"In memory of Mrs. Elizabeth Scott, beloved and respected by all who knew her—died 1819—80 years."

"Mrs. Ann Ogle Steele, wife of John N. Steele—1839—40 years." (A long and handsome tribute to her memory.)

"Mrs. Mary Steele, only daughter of the late John Rider Nevitt and Sarah Thomas, and relict of James Steele."

"Mrs. Anne Upshur, second daughter of James Steele and relict of Arthur Upshur, of Virginia—1791—1835."

"Billings Steele, son of Hy. M. and Maria Steele—1845—1897."

"Mary Nevitt, daughter of C. H. and C. R. Steele—1841—1870."

"Charles H. Steele, M. D.—1812—1889."

"Rispah, wife of Francis Welch—1799—1862."

"Sarah Steele, youngest daughter of James Steele."

"Isabella Elizabeth Steele, fourth daughter of James Steele, of Annapolis—1825."   (A beautiful tribute to her memory.)   A monument by its side stands also over "James Steele."

"Elizabeth, consort of Charles Calvert Stewart and daughter of Hy. M. and Maria Steele—died 1857, aged 25."

"Ellen Key Steele."

"Henry M. Steele."

"Maria Lloyd Key, daughter of Hy. Maynadier Steele—1805—1897."

"Charles H., son of C. H. and C. R. Steele."

"Charlotte, wife of Charles H. Steele, of West River—1884—68 years."

"Robert Henry Goldsborough, sixth son of Charles Goldsborough, Governor of Md. and Sarah G. Goldsborough—1814—1819."

"Richard Moale Chase, son of Richard Moale and Mary Marriott Chase—1827—1901."

"Thomas Baldwin Chase, late Surgeon of U. S. A., son of Richard M. Chase—1830—1894."

"Henry Murray, Counsellor at Law, died 1824, aged 35."

"Dr. James Murray, of Annapolis—1819."

"Mrs. Sarah E. Murray, wife of Dr. James—1837."

ADVANTAGES OF ANNE ARUNDEL.

Bordered on her entire eastern front by the Chesapeake bay, into which flow the Elk, Sassafras, Chester, Third Haven, Choptank, Nanticoke, Wicomico and Pocomoke, on the east, with the Bush, Gunpowder, Patapsco, Magothy, Severn, South Rhode, West, Patuxent and Potomac Rivers on the west, she has eighteen outstretched arms inviting abundant resources and opportunities.

What cannot be grown in her soil may be found in her neighboring waters. Says Professor William K. Brooks, of Johns Hopkins University:

"The Chesapeake bay is a great river valley, not as large as the Nile or Ganges, but of enough consequence to support in comfort and prosperity a population as great as that of many famous States. It receives the drainage of a vast area of fertile land stretching over the meadows and hillsides of nearly one-third of New York and nearly all of Pennsylvania, Maryland and Virginia.

"More than forty million acres of this great tract of fertile soil send its rich deposits into the bay, in the green waters of which it sinks as fine black sediment, known as oyster mud. This is just as valuable to men and just as fit to nourish plants as mud which settles every year on the wheat fields and rice fields of Egypt."

This alluvium sustains an endless variety of microscopic plants and animals on which the Chesapeake oyster fattens and multiplies, becoming, in flavor, unrivalled. Since the beginning of the oyster packing trade in 1834 up to 1891, an estimate places the output of the bay and its tributaries, in packing and shipment, at 400,000,000 bushels, and when legislative enactments shall have succeeded in regulating that output, the same sources of supply will continue a boundless wealth of comfort and prosperity to many thousands of our people.

The Chesapeake also modifies the climate of Anne Arundel, enabling out-door labor comfortable for three-quarters of the year. The cheap transit of the bay offers special inducements to the growth of manufacturing towns along the borders of its tributaries.

The soil of Anne Arundel is rich in variety and mineral deposits, including porcelain clays and glass sand. Fruits, vegetables and tobacco growing are about equally divided. Chief Howard, of the Bureau of Statistics, reports: "Lands can be purchased by immigrant settlers in tracts of from one acre to 1,000 acres." Many portions of Anne Arundel are identical in soil with the famous small-fruit growing county of Cumberland, New Jersey, in which is situated

Vineland. The climate of Anne Arundel is more favorable than that
of Cumberland County, New Jersey, and offers special inducements
to fruit growers, for the location is such that there is a choice of
excellent city markets.

With a few exceptions, nearly all of the old manor estates have
been subdivided, necessarily, by the present labor system, which puts
most of the estates under tenants. Excellent oyster-shell roads are
yearly connecting the more remote sections with market centers.
In the southern sections of the county, corn and tobacco are the
chief crops, aided by fruits. Here tenants lease the estates at a
rental of one-half of the products. Remote from railroads, their
markets are reached through the various lines of steamers that touch
at available river harbors. Here, daily, upon the arrival of the boat
may be seen the congregations of ox-teams employed in hauling the
hogsheads of tobacco or the more inviting boxes of peaches.

The assembled conveyances at the two wharves of West River,
on the boat's arrival, have much the appearance of a small-sized
camp-meeting. Summer sojourners in the many boarding cottages
--along these rivers come in their rowboats to see the crowd of excur-
sionists, as well as to learn lessons of patience and of agriculture in
loading and unloading of all manner of freight. The combination
passenger and freight steamers of the bay grow greater in population
yearly. A whole day's ride upon the bay may be enjoyed, and in
that ride many interesting points herein recorded may be seen and
appreciated.

Old Anne Arundel, the "Providence" of the sturdy settlers, is
yet to make history and rival her ancient prestige.

HOWARD COUNTY.

With a history that covers two centuries, Howard County has had no historian to record it. With a river unrivalled in tragedy and unexcelled in picturesque sublimity, no artist has immortalized it. With every evidence of a pioneer race who roamed as hunters upon its waters and through its forests, no Washington Irving has snatched up one of its rude types to dress him in his native garb, or make him "King of that enchanted realm where comedy and pathos dwell; where laughter touches tears and sadness blossoms into mirth." Bordered by the rocky profiles of the Patapsco on the north and by the rich levels of the Patuxent on the south, this gem, set in a frame of rushing, tragic waters, with a lustre as brilliant as the patriotic career of the Revolutionary hero for whom it was named, now adorns the glittering diadem of Queen Henrietta Marie's crown.

There are many living who can remember when this western section of the Mother County was erected into Howard District, but there are none to tell the struggles of our pioneer settlers.

The Patuxent was known as early as the St. Mary's. The Patapsco was ranged as early as the Severn. Up these rivers and along the blind paths, blazed by Indian hunters, came the lowland settlers to the Ridge of Elks, to build their cabins by the side of the Indian wigwams.

When Thomas Browne, the Patuxent Ranger, was commissioned "to range from Mr. Snowden's plantation to the farthest limits of the Patuxent," we find him before 1699 up as high as Clarksville.

When Charles Carroll, of Annapolis, the friend of Lord Proprietary, received his 10,000 acre grant of "Doohoregan," it extended "from the Patuxent by a blind path to Thomas Browne's plantation and to four Indian cabins and thence to some oaks."

Carroll's grant came from the Proprietary himself, but Browne's grant was through the friendship of Captain John Dorsey, of the Council. The evidence of this is shown in the name of the survey. "Brown's Chance" and Captain Dorsey's "Friendship," better known as "Walnut Grove," at Clarksville. There is, also, evidence that our Patuxent Ranger was a progressive farmer, for he knew the value of a limestone quarry that was upon it.

He marked the boundary lines of "Brown's Forrest," adjoining his friend, Captain Dorsey, at Oakland Mills, and after a survey of some thirty tracts he is finally found up on "Ranter's Ridge," overlooking the Patapsco, at Woodstock.

Long before that Benjamin Hood had followed it to Hollofields, where a former highway had crossed it, and there built his mill upon "Hood's Haven." Browne and Hood were close enough to each other to talk through their wireless telephone.

Richard Snowden next started out to follow Thomas Browne into his beautiful forest country. He had already backed out from his iron mills upon South River and had built his furnace upon the Patuxent, east of Laurel, the first internal improvement of Upper Anne Arundel.

He had built "Birmingham Manor House," in 1690, and had encompassed the whole town of Laurel. We next find him upon the Patuxent as high as Fulton, taking in that whole section under the title of "Snowden's Second Addition to Birmingham Manor."

Colonel Henry Ridgely, hearing of the lovely forest homes in Upper Anne Arundel and Baltimore Counties, followed Snowden on the north to Huntingtown. Here he took up that whole section as "Ridgely's Forest."

Richard Warfield rode thirty miles on horseback to plant the first stake of "Warfield's Range" upon the beautiful falls of Middle Patuxent at Savage Factory, running back two miles.

Honorable John Dorsey sent his surveyors out from "Hockley," to go beyond Richard Warfield on the north. Taking up "Troy Hill," at Waterloo, he backed up to Oakland Mills and Columbia and then stretched out from Simpsonville to Clarksville, where he again met Thomas Browne.

Colonel Edward Dorsey followed him to the same neighborhood in his "Long Reach," which joined Hon. John, at Columbia.

All of these surveys were made before 1700. A quarter of a century later, this whole area was occupied by the sons and grandsons of these pioneer surveyors.

The Ridge of Elks had become the summer resort of fashion. It was so popular, in fact,.as to cover the whole territory, from Laurel to Elk Ridge Landing, to Ellicott City, to Clarksville, and back to Laurel.

Thomas Browne's sons, Richard Snowden's sons, Colonel Ridgely's grandsons, Richard Warfield's grandsons, Hon. John Dorsey's grandsons, seven in number, and Colonel Edward Dorsey's sons, all were located upon the excellent tobacco lands of the Ridge. Even Colonel Edward and Hon. John left the attractions of the official life in Annapolis to seat themselves upon "Major's Choice" and "Troy Hill," near Waterloo.

Elk Ridge Landing, the first outlet for the settlers of Howard County, and the starting point of the dividing line from its mother county, is herein made my starting point to trace the tracts of land and families reared upon them.

ELK RIDGE LANDING.

At this northern terminus of Elk Ridge, overlooking in picturesque beauty the gorges of the Patapsco on the north, and spreading out to the east in a water-way which no longer exists, was early erected a Port of Entry to accommodate the tobacco growers of Upper Anne Arundel.

As early as 1746, it was a rival of Annapolis. In 1763 there were 1,695 hogsheads of tobacco, more than half of the crop in Anne Arundel County, inspected at Elk Ridge, and during the Revolution it was at the height of its usefulness. The great Northern and Southern Post Road ran through it. Into this highway other "rolling roads" entered.

Excellent iron-ore mines surrounded the Landing. The Ridge to the west offered magnificent sites for homes, and to this splendid business centre came the English factors, inspectors of tobacco and capitalists to develop the iron mines.

"Moore's Morning Choice" was one of its earliest surveys. It took in the commanding expanse three miles west of the landing.

It was a survey of Dr. Mordecai Moore, husband of Colonel Wm. Burgess' widow, who sold it to Caleb Dorsey of "Hockley," who transferred it to his son, Caleb. The latter saw his opportunity. Mines were opened, forges built, lands ten miles in extent were bought or surveyed; furnaces were erected and ships were sent laden with the output to the English markets.

In 1738 Caleb Dorsey built "Belmont," a house which is a history in itself. The founder of the Landing was known as the rich iron merchant of Elk Ridge, and when he made his will, it was a revelation of a progressive age and a subject worthy of study.

Previous to the Revolution it was the custom to load tobacco of the planters in small bay ports, and in the creeks and rivers in front of large plantations, but after the Revolution the English "Factors," who had been located in Bladensburg, Calvert County, St. Mary's, Annapolis and Elk Ridge Landing, returned to England, leaving a profitable business to German and American tobacco merchants, who shipped their tobacco by small boats and by wagons to Baltimore, where, to-day, the venerable State warehouses, by their size, attest the importance of this provincial crop, which still gives employment to thousands of persons.

When the Ellicott brothers landed at Elk Ridge, just previous to the Revolution, they found the surrounding homesteads attractive, adorned with gardens, fruits, graveled walks.

Henry Howard, Judge Richard Ridgely, Horatio Johnson, Nicholas Ridgely Warfield, all officials of the Port of Entry, held houses in the town.

With the receding of its water-way and the growth of Baltimore, "The Landing," as a business center, passed into history, leaving but meagre data of its once busy mart. To-day there are no relics of its taverns for the accommodation of the drivers; of its stables for the keep of their horses; of its tobacco warehouses, wherein were deposited the immense hogsheads which were rolled over those "rolling roads" from their starting point, at least twenty-five miles distant from "The Landing."

Elk Ridge Landing could have had no artists, else they would have left us pictures of the impromptu gatherings at our early Elk Ridge Landing; of the vessels; of the wharves; of the old houses

now lost to us. Fortunately for the historian, there are some landmarks remaining. Its founder built his house upon a rock and upon
a hill which the floods could not destroy.

His forge at Avalon has gone with the tide, but "Belmont"
stands, to-day, to teach us how he lived. From the pen of Dr. J.
Williamson Palmer we get an interesting picture of it. It is after
the old colonial type of the Province.

"In 1738 Caleb Dorsey built, with English brick brought over
in his own vessels, the historic house of "Belmont," home of the
Dorseys and the Hansons.

The walls of the hall and the drawing-room were paneled in oak
and the grounds in front and rear were terraced in the large old
English fashion, while boxwood in the garden, gigantic now, seems still
to babble of the sweet old times, when Caleb and Priscilla set them out.
Here, later, was the home of a man of great intellectual and moral
force, who stamped upon the chronicles of his bailiwick the mark of
his distinguished talents, his indomitable energy and his reckless
courage. Alexander Contee Hanson, son of the Chancellor of Maryland, editor of the "Federal Republican" and afterward United States
Senator; staunch Federalist and frank opponent of Madison's administration and of the War of 1812, was an undaunted champion of the
freedom of the press, in defiance of the mobs and assassins in the
State which was first of the American colonies to own a public press
and employ it as an active engine of light and liberty, while the
Puritans of New England and Virginia abhorred it as an engine of
the devil and would have none of it. In 1689 the Province of Maryland had a public press at St. Mary's, which was kept busy with the
printing of public documents, and no other colonies had one."

Caleb Dorsey's descendants still tell of the long hunts of this
master of Belmont, upon one of which he met a young lady on horseback, who kindly invited him to her father's residence for the night.
The fox-hunter was so charmed that he frequently renewed the chase
in the direction of the West River, and finally brought to Belmont
the same young lady, Miss Priscilla Hill, as his bride; she was the
daughter of Henry Hill and Mary Denwood, of West River.

It has been said, also, that "Caleb of Belmont" could ride ten
miles in a straight line on his own lands; they extended from Curtis
Creek to Ellicott's City and Clarksville pike, including the "Long
Reach" of Major Edward Dorsey.

Caleb and Priscilla Dorsey's son, Henry Hill, married Eliza
Goodwin; from these descend Judge Parkin Scott and Dr. Samuel
Chew.

Samuel Dorsey (of Caleb) ran the forge during the Revolution
and supplied guns and cannon for home defence. His wife was Margaret Sprigg. She survived him with three children, Edward Hill,
Mary and Eleanor. She made Edward Dorsey (of Caleb) their guardian.

Edward Hill Dorsey later appeared in several contests over the
estate of his father. His wife was Elinor Pue, who bore him Mary—

William H. Freeman; James—Miss Welsh. Their heirs were, James, Dr. Robert Dorsey, late of Baltimore, and Mrs. Handy, of Richmond. Her daughter is a popular leader of society. The daughters of Samuel and Margaret Dorsey were Mrs. Bailey and Mrs. Eleanor Dorsey, of Dorsey's Station.

Edward Dorsey (of Caleb) inherited "Belmont," and, with his brother Samuel, ran the two forges at Avalon and Curtis Creek. His sale of the Curtis Creek property brought on several contests in the Court of Chancery. His wife, Elizabeth Dorsey (of Colonel John and Mary Hammond) was his cousin. Their daughters were Mary—Daniel Murray; Caroline—Johnson Donaldson; Priscilla—Alexander Contee Hanson. She inherited "Belmont."

Hammond Dorsey (of Edward) built his brick homestead, still standing, in sight of Relay. His wife was Elizabeth Pickering, of Massachusetts. Descendants of Edward Dorsey still reside at Elk Ridge.

Daniel Murray, the attorney, descends from Daniel Murray and Mary Dorsey. Daniel Murray, Sr., was the son of Dr. William Murray and Sallie Maynadier, of Annapolis, whose daughter, Sally Scott, was the wife of Governor Edward Lloyd. Annie Murray became the wife of General John Mason, of Virginia.

The heirs of Daniel and Mary Dorsey were Dr. James Murray, West River; Sally Scott, wife of Dr. James Cheston; Mary—Dr. Worthington, and Colonel Edward Murray, U. S. A. and C. S. A.

The Murrays were descendants of Marquis John Murray, who came to the Barbadoes. His son, John, settled in Chestertown and married Ann Smith. Dr. William Murray (of John and Ann Smith) married Harriet Hesselius. The Murrays were connections of the Steuarts who can claim an unbroken line from Kenneth II. first King of Scotland. This Steuart family was represented by the late General George Hume Steuart, of South River, who held the homestead tract of Colonel William Burgess. General Steuart, genial and entertaining, was the son of General George H. Steuart, of the War of 1812, whose house in Annapolis stood upon the present site of the Executive Mansion.

With Colonel Elzey and Major Bradley T. Johnson, young Steuart, a graduate of West Point, formed the First Maryland Regiment in the Confederate Army, and remained at the front until the surrender. His father, also, though too old for service, gave his experience to the Southern cause. Returning, he died soon after the surrender, at his son's residence, on West River.

Other Elk Ridge descendants of Edward of Belmont were Dr. Frank Donaldson and his brother Thomas Donaldson, the dignified, thoroughly equipped lawyer and scholar of "Lawyers Hill." The records at Ellicott City show that he held a large clientage. He was known as "the honest lawyer."

John J. Donaldson, successor and son, represented Howard in the Legislature and is now practising law in Baltimore.

Alexander Contee Hanson and Priscilla, his wife, had one son, named in honor of Mr. Hanson's brother-in-law, Honorable Charles Grosvenor, member of Congress.

Charles Grosvenor Hanson, of Belmont, married Maria Worthington. Their son, Hon. Grosvenor Hanson, has been a School Commissioner of Howard County and has twice represented the county in the Maryland Legislature. He has also taken active interest in securing the bridge at Avalon. He is now a member of the Stock Commission. His brothers are Murray Hanson, Notary Public, and John Hanson, merchant, of Baltimore. Their sisters reside at Belmont.

The daughters of Caleb Dorsey, of Belmont, were Mary—Dr. Michael Pue, whose son Dr. Arthur Pue—Sarah, daughter of Thoma, Beale Dorsey, Jr., by Achsah Brown. Issue, Samuel, Williams Ventress, of Texas; Ferdinand Pue, of Highlands, and Robert, of Morgan's Station.

Milcah Dorsey, of Caleb, of Belmont—William Goodwin; Rebecca —Captain Charles Ridgely, of Hampton; Priscilla—Governor Charles Carnan Ridgely, of Hampton. Elinor inherited lands "above the forge" and died a maiden; Peggy Hill—William Buchanan. Large legacies were left to these daughters by Caleb, of Belmont, the iron merchant.

WATERLOO.

At this junction of the Northern and Southern Post Road with the Annapolis and Frederick road, stands the handsome home of Captain John R. King, now head of the Grand Army. Here was once located a famous inn, the successor of Spurrier's Tavern, which stood near there. Waterloo Inn was the central headquarters and popular resort for many years.

Nearby two distinguished brothers, Colonel Edward and Hon. John Dorsey, had seated themselves before 1700. Historic tracts were there located. They were "Troy Hill," "The Grecian Siege," "The Isle of Ely," "Major's Choice" and "Long Reach."

The first three were heired by Hon. John's grandson, Basil Dorsey, who inherited, also, 1,255 acres, known as "Caleb's Purchase." Here, still later, Colonel Thomas Dorsey (of Basil,) Field Officer of the Elk Ridge Militia, made his headquarters for rallying the Revolutionary patriots who were called to the aid of Annapolis.

Upon "Troy Hill," to-day, stands a large stone house with extensive barns and grounds. It is now the Pfeiffer property.

This estate under Basil Dorsey adjoined Caleb of "Belmont" and extended a mile or more along the Post Road, from Elk Ridge Landing to Spurrier's Tavern. Basil married Sarah, daughter of Thomas Worthington and Elizabeth Ridgely. Sarah Dorsey's inheritance was a portion of "Worthington's Range," near Clarksville. Basil Dorsey was not content to limit his surveys to the neighborhood of Waterloo. Holding this extensive estate, he invested in lands in the neighborhood of Liberty, Frederick County, upon a portion of which were seated his three daughters, Elizabeth, wife of Ephraim Howard; Elinor, wife of Hon. Upton Sheredine, and Ariana, wife of Thomas Sollers. Basil Dorsey's youngest son, Dennis, died in early manhood and Colonel Thomas Dorsey heired most of his estate.

Mrs. Sarah Dorsey named her heirs, Basil Burgess, John Burgess and Sarah Burgess, children of Captain John Burgess by her daughter Sarah. She named her niece, Elizabeth Watkins, daughter of her sister Ariana. She appointed her son, Colonel Thomas Dorsey, and her son-in-law, Captain John Burgess, executors.

They sold, in 1789, to William Gaither other Frederick County tracts, known as " Pleasant Fields," " Woods Lot," " Chillum Castle" and "Friendship." They sold to Ephraim Howard "The Resurvey on Woods Lot."

Colonel Thomas Dorsey married two Ridgely cousins, both named Elizabeth. The first was the daughter of Colonel Henry Ridgely and Elizabeth Warfield; by her he had Captain Daniel Dorsey, of "The Flying Camp," referred to in the following letter:
" To the President of the Council.

"SIR:—When the Elk Ridge Militia left this place for Annapolis, I promised to send down more on Sunday. Captain Daniel Dorsey's Company will certainly be down on that day and Captain Norwood's on the day following.

"Yr. most obedient servant,
"THOMAS DORSEY."

Captain Daniel, a mere boy, fought through the war. He was with Colonel Carvil Halls' " Flying Camp." Returning after the war, he married his cousin, Eleanor, daughter of Ely and Deborah Dorsey; later removed to New York State, where he became judge and minister. He left a large family in Upper New York, named in " Warfield's of Maryland."

Colonel Thomas Dorsey and his brother-in-law, Colonel Henry Ridgely, Jr., were rivals for the military honors of the Ridge. Their personal letters to the Council of Safety may be found in the archives. Colonel Dorsey's second wife was the daughter of Judge Nicholas Ridgely, of Delaware, by his third wife, Mrs. Mary Vining; she is thus recorded by the Judge himself. " And I have another daughter, named Elizabeth, born on Sunday, December 15th, 1745. She married, June 21st, 1761, Colonel Thomas Dorsey, of Elk Ridge, Anne Arundel County—in the Province of Maryland and left by him a large issue." (Ridgely Bible.) Their children were Dr. Archibald Dorsey, whose residence was just west of Waterloo; Theodore, Nicholas, Mary, Elizabeth, Juliet, Harriet and Matilda Dorsey.

We get a view of the speculative spirit of that period, and the disastrous effect upon the estate of Colonel Dorsey, from his will of 1790. From it, too, we see the love, confidence and splendid executive ability of his wife and widow in her management of it.

COLONEL DORSEY'S WILL.

"I request to be decently buried with only a few invited friends. The services of the Protestant Episcopal Church to be read. No mourning other than black ribbons, handkerchiefs and gloves. As it has pleased God, heretofore, to bestow on me a liberal fortune, which I have lately lost by my indiscretion and ill-judged confidence, and as the small remnant that can be saved out of the wreck of my fortune cannot be placed in the hand of any person more truly prudent and frugal than my beloved wife, who as she divides her affection among her children, will, I have no doubt, distribute equally among them anything that can be saved. I give her, after my just debts are paid, all my estate and make her sole executrix.

"I desire my wife to apply to the General Assembly respecting the debt I owe the State in paper money, called State and Continental Money, which had depreciated at the time I passed bonds to the State at the rate of three said paper dollars for one silver dollar. I wish her to hand over to the State all the property I bought of the Samuel Chase estate.

"Witnesses: Joshua Dorsey, John Henry Johnson, William Squire, D. Griffith." The Assembly passed a bill accepting Mrs. Dorsey's tender and exempted her from other liabilities.

As executrix, Mrs. Elizabeth Dorsey made the following transfers:

"Deed of 1817, from Owen Dorsey and Nicholas Dorsey to Rosalie, wife of George Calvert, for lands deeded by Elizabeth Dorsey (widow of Colonel Thomas) for 'Troy,' part of 'The Isle of Ely,' 'Grecian Siege,' part of 'Caleb's Purchase,' part of 'Brother's Addition,' near 'Herbert's Care,' (Colonel Marshall's) intersecting the lines of the lands given by Thomas Dorsey to Daniel, which Daniel deeded to Elizabeth Dorsey, for part of 'Caleb's Purchase,' running with the Post Road from Elk Ridge Landing to Spurrier's Tavern; running between the lands given to Archibald Dorsey and the lands sold by Mrs. Elizabeth Dorsey to Clemson and Bailey.

"As Owen Dorsey has paid Nicholas Dorsey the amount of the mortgage, the deed was given to Rosalie Calvert.

"Daniel Dorsey sold his tracts to Henry Ridgely, who sold to Samuel Chase, Thomas Chase and William G. Ridgely."

In 1823, Archibald Dorsey, of Harford County, sold "Grecian Siege" to Mr. Pierce. It is still held by that family.

Mrs. Elizabeth Dorsey's will left her lands, taken up recently in Kentucky, to her heirs. To son Dr. Archibald Dorsey she gave her eight-day clock; she named her son Theodore and his son Alexander, whom she appointed her attorney to settle some city claims. Her daughters were Elizabeth Berry, Mary Norwood, Harriet Berry and Matilda Dorsey. She named her son Nicholas, and sons-in-law, Benjamin and John W. Berry. She died in Baltimore County.

COLONEL EDWARD DORSEY OF "MAJOR'S CHOICE."

Before 1700 Colonel Edward Dorsey removed from Annapolis to "Major's Choice," west of Waterloo, and north of the old brick church, but continued to sit in the House of Burgesses as a delegate from Baltimore County. He was then married to Margaret Larkin, who inherited from her father, John Larkin, a large estate upon the north side of the Patapsco. Her children were Lacon (Larkin,) Charles, Francis, Edward and Ann Dorsey, who married her neighbor, John Hammond (of Charles).

Colonel Dorsey's sons by Sarah Wyatt were located near him, upon "Long Reach" and "Major's Choice." Edward Dorsey, Jr., youngest son by Margaret Larkin, a minor when his father's will was probated in 1705, inherited the Colonel's riding horse "Sparke," his best gun, largest silver tankard, his tobacco box, his seal gold ring and one sealskin trunk, marked "E. D." The other sons inherited, with Edward, their mother's lands across the Patapsco. Edward located at Dayton, and bought lands of Thomas Reynolds, known as "Thomas Lot," to which he added "Dorsey's Addition." His will named his wife Phoebe executrix, aided by Michael Dorsey. The tradition is that she was a Todd, a relative of Michael's wife, Ruth Todd. In 1769 she was Phoebe Williams, and, with her son Lacon, deeded her late husband's estate to John Worthington Warfield.

Joshua Dorsey (of Edward and Phoebe) married Rachel, whose daughter married Major George Stockton, of Shepardstown, West Virginia. They removed to Kentucky and left many descendants.

Western descendants say that Mr. Williams, who married the widow Dorsey, was the father of General Otho Holland Williams. Later records do not confirm this.

Ann Dorsey (of Colonel Edward), the widow of John Hammond, named her daughters, Hannah, wife of John Welsh, and Ann, wife of Francis Davis. Both of these left many Welsh and Davis descendants in Upper Howard. From Hannah Welsh descends Governor Warfield and the author of this history. Her sister, Hamutel Welsh, heired her portion of the homestead, "Major's Choice." She died in the stone house, now a part of Brookeville Academy. Her daughter Carolina—Captain Elisha Riggs and was the mother of Colonel John Hammond Riggs, from whom descended two distinguished physicians, Dr. Augustus and Dr. Artemas Riggs; one of Cooksville, Howard County; the other of Brookeville, Montgomery County.

JOSHUA DORSEY OF "MAJOR'S CHOICE."

Coming into possession of the homestead of Colonel Edward, and inheriting a large tract, known as "Barnes' Folly," Joshua Dorsey married, in 1711, Anne Ridgely, oldest daughter of Henry and Katherine (Greenberry) Ridgely. Joshua sat with his brother-in-law, Colonel Henry Ridgely, in pew No. 1, Christ Church. His heirs were Henry, Philemon, Joshua, Nicholas, Charles, Rachel, Anne, Elizabeth.

His will of 1747 located Henry on "Dorsey's Hills" and "Dorsey's Angles;" Philemon on "Brother's Partnership;" Joshua in "Locust Thicket;" Nicholas at "Huntington Quarter" and Charles upon the homestead "Major's Choice," which afterward went to Joshua.

Henry Dorsey, born 1712, married Elizabeth, daughter of Thomas Worthington and Elizabeth Ridgely, who inherited 389 acres of "Worthington Range." Their heirs were Joshua, Thomas, Elizabeth, Sarah, Nicholas, Ariana, Ann, Vachel, Henry and Charles Dorsey.

Joshua (of Henry)—Elizabeth, daughter of Rev. Henry Hall, of the Episcopal Church, of West River, and had Henry Hall Dorsey, Isaac, Allen, Major Thomas Hall Dorsey, Joshua, John, Elizabeth, Margaret, William Henry and Mary Goldthwait, whose daughter married Samuel Beale Owings.

Henry Hall Dorsey—Mary Wright and their daughter Harriet became the wife of John Hammond (of Philip). Issue, Dr. Thomas Wright Hammond, Charles and Margaret Mullikin; William Henry Dorsey, the oldest son of Henry Hall Dorsey, died a prisoner in England, during the Revolution.

Major Thomas Hall Dorsey, his brother—Ann (Warfield) Dorsey, widow of Richard, of "Hockley." Issue, Margaret Harrison, whose children are Anne Warfield, Thomas Dorsey, Mary, Margaret Elizabeth, William Henry Harrison, all single.

Allen Dorsey—Eleanor Dorsey (of Samuel and Margaret Sprigg). They resided at "Woodlawn," at Dorsey's Station, Washington Branch, B. & O. R. R. Issue, William, Eliza, Mary, Caroline, all maids. William Dorsey (of Allen) has a son, William H. Dorsey, now of Baltimore.

Elizabeth Dorsey (of Joshua and Elizabeth Hall)—Vachel Dorsey, Jr. (of Vachel and Ruth Dorsey). He was a partner of Charles Carroll, of Carrollton, in surveying waste lands. Upon his list of surveys, still to be seen at "Hockley," were numerous tracts in all sections of Howard and Anne Arundel.

Vachel Dorsey's son, Essex Ridley Dorsey—Ann Dorsey, the heiress of "Hockley;" Elizabeth Hall Dorsey (of Vachel)—Caleb Dorsey; Evalina Mary—Barnes Comegys; Ann Dorsey (of Vachel) remained a maiden.

Thomas Dorsey (of Henry) inherited his mother's interest in "Worthington's Range"—Mary Warfield, only daughter of Benjamin and Rebeckah (Ridgely) Warfield, of "Warfield's Range." Issue, Benedict Dorsey; Elizabeth—Joshua Warfield, of "Warfield's Range;" Rebecca—Captain Vachel Burgess; Mary Ridgely—Philemon Burgess; Benedict Dorsey—Margaret Watkins (of Nicholas and Ariana [Worthington] Watkins. Issue, Thomas, Washington and Elizabeth Dorsey. The early death of their father left them in charge of Mr. Nicholas Watkins. They were all legatees of Nicholas Ridgely Warfield, who granted them his portion of "Worthington Range." Washington Dorsey removed to Wilmington, Delaware, married

Hannah Chapman and left George Washington—Mary Ann McKee, whose daughter, Emily Dorsey—W. J. Ellison, of Wilmington. Her sisters are Anna and Bessie; her brother, George Washington Dorsey, Jr.—Lizzie Spence, of New York. Washington Dorsey, Sr., left other sons—Thomas, Robert and William Dorsey—and daughters— Lizzie and Tamer.

Elizabeth Dorsey (of Benedict)—George Ford.

Elizabeth Dorsey (of Henry)—Elisha Warfield (of Benjamin). Issue, Mary Ford, of Kentucky, who left Charles, James C. and Eliza P. Ford; James C. Ford—Mary, daughter of Justice Robert Trimble, U. S. Supreme Court. He was a distinguished Kentuckian.

Ann Dorsey (of Henry)—Davidge Warfield (of Azel).

Sarah Dorsey (of Henry)—Benjamin Dorsey (of Patuxent John). Ariana Dorsey (of Henry)—Beni Warfield (of Seth) and lived upon "Warfield's Forest."

HUNTINGTON.

Annapolis Junction.

South of Waterloo, upon the Post Road, were Huntingtown on the east and Guilford on the west. Into this section came Colonel Henry Ridgely, his nephew, Nicholas Dorsey, Orlando Griffith and John Worthington, son of the merchant, who resurveyed upon "Ridgely's Forest" the Worthington homestead, still standing upon "Worthington's Plains," known as the Bowie estate.

Out of this old Griffith house, through a daughter of Gideon White, successor to the estate by purchase, comes Colonel King (of Howard), former member of the Maryland Legislature, attorney-at-law and colonel of Eleventh United States Regiment during the Civil War.

He is upon a neighboring estate of Dr. Jonathan Waters, upon the old Warfield survey, west of the Junction.

Colonel King's grandfather, Gideon White (of Joseph), the miller and surveyor of "White's Contrivance," came down from Peregrine White, the first white child born in Massachusetts.

In this same section, just west of the Junction, was "The Fourteen-mile House," a stage coach-stand kept by Mr. Haslup, grandfather of the two popular Haslup brothers, one an ex-member of the Legislature and the other in charge of the State House. They reside close by this old stand; both have very fine estates along that road.

Huntingtown, the home of Orlando Griffith, west of the railroad and just north of Annapolis Junction, was a Griffith home of historic importance. It is now known as the "White Place."

William Griffith came to Maryland in 1675.

The history of the Griffiths, of Wales, forms an exciting review of the feudal splendor of Griffith, Prince of Wales, but that history is too voluminous for quotation here. Their descendants in Maryland, as will be seen, fought as valiantly for American independence as did their sires in Wales.

William Griffith took for his wife a daughter of another distinguished house in Scotland. She was Sarah Mackubin, daughter of John Mackubin, who came from the Lowlands, and claimed descent from the McAlpines, of the Highlands, who go back to Kenneth II., the first king of Scotland.

The issue of that marriage were Orlando, Captain Charles, William and Sophia—Benjamin Duvall, youngest son of Mareen, the Huguenot.

Orlando Griffith followed the tide of western settlers to Huntington. His homestead was later transferred to the Whites; it borders on Snowden's "Summer Hill," lately owned by Major Powell, of Annapolis Junction. Orlando Griffith married, at thirty, Katharine, only daughter of Captain John Howard by Katherine, widow of Henry Ridgely, and daughter of Colonel Nicholas Greenberry. She inherited "Howard's Luck," at · Huntington. Orlando Griffith became, in 1728, a member of the vestry of Queen Caroline Parish, occupying pew No. 8 with Captain John Howard and Nicholas Dorsey, his neighbor. "Griffith's Adventure" was his survey. It is upon a draft of the Patapsco; upon this he placed his sons Joshua, Benjamin, Orlando and Charles Greenberry Griffith.

Hon. Henry Griffith, eldest son and executor of Orlando, took up lands in both Howard and Montgomery; he was Tobacco Inspector, Commissioner in the formation of Montgomery, Register of Queen Caroline Parish, Commissioner of Peace, Member of the Colonial Assembly from Frederick County, upon the Committee of Observation for Frederick County, Member of the Convention which formed the Association of "Freemen of Maryland" and one of the Justices in the organization of Montgomery County, in 1777. He married, first, Elizabeth Dorsey (of Edward and Sarah Todd), and had issue, Sarah—Rezin Todd, Rachel—Samuel Welsh, Ruth, Amos Riggs and Colonel Henry Griffith, who was one of the Committee of Observation for Frederick County to carry out the Resolves of the Provincial Convention. He resided upon "Hammond's Great Branch," near Laurel, and married, first, Sarah Warfield (of John and Rachel [Dorsey] Warfield, of "Warfield's Range"); issue, Henry, Allen, Nicholas, Elizabeth, Henrietta Griffith; Colonel Henry—married second, Sarah Davis (of Thomas) and had Thomas Griffith, who held the old homestead, which has only recently passed from the family.

Colonel Henry Griffith's descendants by Sarah Warfield located upon "Griffith's Range," in the neighborhood of Unity and Laytonville, and they still hold their greatly improved estates.

Hon. Henry Griffith married, second, Ruth Hammond, daughter of John and Ann (Dorsey) Hammond, and became joint executor of John Hammond's estate. Their issue were Captain Samuel Griffith, John Hammond Griffith, Colonel Philemon Griffith, Lieutenant Charles Griffith, Joshua Griffith and several daughters.

From the home of Hon. Henry Griffith, who later located on the road leading from Unity to Damascus, went to, and returned from the Revolution three colonels, one captain, one lieutenant, one ensign and one "high private."

The old dilapidated roadside home of Captain Samuel Griffith, who took his first wife, Rachel, from "Warfield Range," may still be seen, deserted. Near by is the home of one of their descendants, who sent four more sons to a later war.

Captain Samuel Griffith was upon the Committee of Observation for Frederick County in 1775, and entered the army under La Fayette.

Colonel Philemon Griffith entered as lieutenant in Captain Price's Rifle Company; he was Captain of Third Company of Rifles of Colonel Rawlings regiment, at Fort Washington; was taken prisoner and was exchanged and promoted to major in 1776; the rank of colonel was conferred on him by the Governor of Maryland.

Captain Samuel Griffith and his brother, Colonel Philemon, were both in the disastrous campaign of the North. At Germantown, or Brandywine, with General La Fayette, Captain Samuel led a company of ninety men in storming a "Cheveaux de Frieze" and came out with sixteen. When La Fayette was given an ovation in Annapolis in 1825 these old heroes met, embraced and shed tears.

Captain Griffith was twice married; first, to Rachel Warfield (of John), and, second, to Ruth Berry (of Richard and Sarah Dorsey); many of his descendants are scattered in every State; one daughter, Ruth, remained to guard the old home. The writer stood within that old, unpretending roadside homestead when many of his descendants were then at the front; still later, she, too, had gone: its lights were out; its old hero, sleeping near by, had heard not the war-cry, for he and his brothers had answered their last call.

Colonel Philemon Griffith's daughter, Ruth, first—Caleb Dorsey, and resided at Glenwood, Howard County, issue, John A. Dorsey. She married, second, Charles D. Warfield, of "Bushy Park" and left Charles D. Warfield, Jr., and Sallie, wife of Dr. Evan William Warfield, of Glenwood.

Pictures of both Captain Samuel and his brother, Colonel Philemon, are to be seen at Messrs. Gustavus Warfield's and Alfred Mathews, at Glenwood; both exhibit striking features, which show the sterling characters of these old heroes we now love to honor.

Greenberry Griffith (of Orlando) inherited "Ward's Care" and "Howard's Luck;" he married Ruth Riggs, his neighbor, of "Riggs' Hills;" he was warden and vestryman of Queen Caroline Parish, and upon the Committee of Observation for Frederick County in 1775. His son, Hezekiah—Catharine Warfield (of Azel); their son, John Riggs Griffith—Sarah Tracey, whose daughter, Rebecca—William Davis, parents of Eldred Griffith Davis, Collector of Taxes, Washington, D. C., and his sisters, Mrs. Dickinson and Mrs. Clarke.

Sarah Griffith (of Orlando)—Colonel Nicholas Dorsey; Lucretia —Caleb Davis.

Joshua Griffith was Deputy Surveyor in 1759 and Tobacco Inspector at Elk Ridge Landing; by his wife, Ann Hall, their son was Dennis Griffith. He was a lieutenant in the Continental Army and surveyed the State of Maryland in 1794; he published a map of the State which is still extant.   He was also a vestryman in Queen Caroline Parish and a delegate to the Episcopal Convention; he married Elizabeth, daughter of Greenberry and Lucy (Stringer) Ridgely. Their son, Stephen, was in the United States Army.

Rachel Griffith—Henry Gassaway, son of Brice John.

Elizabeth Greenberry Griffith—Rev. Ethan Allen.

Rachel Griffith (of Joshua)—John Sprigg Belt, Captain of Fourth Company, First Regiment Maryland Line; he was a member of the Society of the Cincinnati.

Benjamin Griffith (of Orlando) was Tobacco Inspector in Queen Caroline Parish in 1762, during which time he was Church Warden. After 1772 he removed to the neighborhood of Poplar Springs, Maryland.   He married Mary Riggs, daughter of John and Mary Davis. Their daughter, Ann—Aquilla Dorsey; Mary—Richard Stringer.

Colonel Charles Greenberry Griffith, youngest son of Orlando, was Colonel of First Baltimore Flying Camp, 1776.   He married Sarah Ridgely, daughter of Colonel Henry and Elizabeth (Warfield) Ridgely.   Their daughter, Elizabeth—General Jeremiah Crabb, of Fourth Battalion in Continental Army, Brigadier-General of Militia 1794, Representative in Congress in 1795-6.

Captain Charles Griffith (of William) of South River, left a record of his family in which he recorded the births and deaths of his "dafters."   He lived on the north side of South River within six miles of Annapolis.   He outlived his two wives over thirty-eight years, dying in his seventy-eighth year and was recorded as Captain Charles Griffith.   He married, first, Mrs. Mary Mercer (nee Wolden), and had William, Charles and Mary Griffith.   He married again in 1727 Catharine Baldwin, daughter of John Baldwin and Hester (Larkin) Nicholson his wife.   The issue of his first wife were:

William Griffith—Priscilla Ridgely and lived near the head of the Severn in 1752; Charles Griffith, Jr.—Ann Davidge (of Robert and Rachel [Warfield] Davidge, and lived near Stoner's Mill, Anne Arundel County.   He inherited "Griffith's Island" on the Severn. His daughter, Eleanor Griffith—Vachel Warfield, son of Samuel, and lived at Crown Point, now Portland, Anne Arundel County; issue, Vachel, Jr.—Achsah Marriott;   William—Sarah Jane Merryman; Henrietta—Joshua Marriott.

Sarah Griffith (of Charles, Jr.—John Boone, son of Captain John.

Mary Griffith (of Captain Charles and Mary)—Joseph White, who bought of Mrs. Henry Ridgely a portion of "Wincopin Neck."

John Griffith (of Captain Charles and Catharine Baldwin)—the widow of Benjamin Williams, who later became the wife of Thomas Rutland.   John Griffith's estate was on the Severn.

Sarah Griffith (of Captain Charles and Catharine)—Azel Warfield, son of Alexander and Dinah Davidge.

Catharine Griffith—Colonel Nicholas Worthington.

William Griffith, youngest son of William and Sarah Mackubin, removed to the Catoctin Mountains and became Commissioner and

Justice of Frederick County. He married Comfort Duvall, daughter of Captain John and Elizabeth (Jones) Duvall, of Anne Arundel, and granddaughter of Mareen Duvall.

COLONEL HENRY RIDGELY.

Colonel Henry Ridgely, the surveyor, son of Henry and Katherine Greenberry and grandson of the first surveyor of "Ridgely Forest, heired his father's homestead "Waldridge" and "Broome." These tracts were transferred to his brother-in-law, Thomas Worthington, who resided there.

Colonel Henry and his uncle, Charles Ridgely, were joint owners of "Ridgely's Forest," at Huntington, and also joint owners of the South River estate. By deeds of transfer, Charles Ridgely held the South River tracts and yielded up his interest in "Ridgely's Forest" to his nephew.

Colonel Henry, in 1711, seated himself upon the ridge east of Guilford. His estate was then in Baltimore County. He became an aggressive surveyor of this new territory. He resurveyed "Ridgely's Forest" into "Harry's Lot," which extended back to Savage and Guilford. Following up the Patuxent, beyond "Snowden's Second Addition," we find him on "Hickory Ridge," at Highlands. Joining his brother-in-law, Thomas Worthington, they took up "Henry and Thomas," "Partnership," "Altogether," stretching back to Glenelg. Beyond that, Colonel Henry is again found at "Round About Hills," "Ridgely's Great Park" and "Ridgely's Great Range," thirty miles west of his starting point. In 1722, Colonel Henry married Elizabeth, only daughter of Benjamin Warfield. Her father had taken up for her a considerable tract called "Wincopin Neck," lying between the Middle and North Branches of the Patuxent at Savage; it adjoined "Warfield's Range" on the south and "Warfield's Contrivance" on the north.

In 1728, Colonel Henry Ridgely was the chief surveyor and builder of Christ Church, Queen Caroline Parish. He held pew No. 1 in the original building in 1736. His homestead is now the Pattison estate. The large graveyard of this early surveyor may still be seen there.

Upon this ridge are three Ridgely homesteads, all upon the road leading from Guilford to Savage. Beyond them, still further west, on the middle, or Savage River, there stands another building in perfect preservation, a rough-cast brick mansion, worthy of note. It is "Montpelier." Its perfect walls, large rooms, high ceiling, wide hallway, music balcony, hand-carved woodwork, speak unerringly that it was once the home of luxury. Its last Ridgely owner was the bachelor, Harry, who weighed five hundred pounds and rode in a chair-carriage especially designed for him. He was the only son of Colonel Henry Ridgely, fourth, hero of the French and Indian war. Harry Ridgely died about 1812 and lies buried under a huge tree in the rear of his mansion, which some say was built by him, but such a building was not designed for, or by, a bachelor. It was built for daughters who entertained largely. As I stood within I could almost hear from the balcony the music leading those stately daughters in the minuet. Perhaps the four distinguished daughters of the first surveyor here met their military husbands and from there went out to be mothers of a long line of descendants, not even bounded by oceans. It was certainly the home of the later Colonel Ridgely, who took his cousin, Ann Dorsey, as wife. From it Dr. Charles Alexander Warfield took his bride in 1771. From it "Polly Ridgely" went down across "Warfield's Range" to "Sappington Sweep" upon Hammonds Great Branch, where still stands her headstone to-day. From it, as late as 1806, went forth Sally Ridgely, the second wife of Jessie Tyson. From it, too, Ann Ridgely, "the heiress," went further down the Patuxent as the bride of Major Thomas Snowden, to name her more magnificent home "Montpelier" of Prince George.

The second Colonel Henry Ridgely's sons are fully named in his will of 1749. It reads:

"I Coll. Henry Ridgely, of A. A. Co., give the use of my tract called 'Harry's Lot' to my dear wife during life and one-third of the personal property.

"To Son Greenberry, 500 acres to be laid out as follows: All my part (being one-third) of 'Partnership' and all of 'Hickory Ridge' that is clear of other surveys, and if less than 500 acres, then I give him a part of 'Resurvey of Tracts' nearest to him, to be laid out at the discretion of Mr. Philemon Dorsey.

"I give to Son Henry my tracts 'Broken Land,' 'Sapling Range,' 'Coopers Lot,' bought 'of Mr. Wm. Fisher. Mr. Philemon Dorsey to assign him lands on Sapling Range."

"To Son Joshua the 'Resurvey of Tracts' and 'Round About Hills.'

"To Charles Greenberry all my part (one-half) of 'Huntington Quarter' with the lands I have added to it and 'Harry's Lot.'

"To Nicholas Greenberry my tract called 'Small Land' and part of 'Altogether,' laid out by Messrs. Nicholas Watkins and Philemon Dorsey, and also a tract to be bought of Aquilla Dorsey by Philemon Dorsey and myself. I give to Nicholas Dorsey, of Joshua, my right to the other half of 'Huntington Quarter.' And Whereas, by a resurvey made by Mr. Thomas Worthington and myself of 'Partnership,' we could not find enough land to equal the warrant, even though we took up some vacant land, now, if Mr. Thomas Worthington will pay to my executors my part of the charge and will make over to my son Greenberry ten acres included in said resurvey then I give to Mr. Worthington sixty acres which is nearest to his lands, provided he and my son Greenberry shall desire to exchange any part of 'Hickory Ridge' and 'Partnership,. I desire my son Joshua to be placed in the care of Mr. Philemon Dorsey, and to be brought up by him, and if he die without issue, his lands to go to Nicholas Greenberry.

"Test Alexander Warfield, James Macgill, John Warfield, Joseph Hall and Joshua Warfield.

Mrs. Elizabeth (Warfield) Ridgely survived her husband some twenty years, and in her will of 1769, named the same sons and daughters, transferring her estate to them. Her daughters, thus named were: Ann, wife of Hon. Brice Thomas Beale Worthington; Elizabeth, wife of Colonel Thomas Dorsey; Sarah, wife of Colonel Charles Greenberry Griffith, and Catherine, wife of Captain Philemon Dorsey. Upon her estate of "Wincopin Neck" stands, to-day, the regenerated Guilford, famous for granite.

THE DORSEYS OF ANNAPOLIS JUNCTION.

By the will of Joshua Dorsey, of "Major's Choice," he conveyed his share of "Huntington Quarter" to his son Nicholas Dorsey.

There stands, to-day, in sight of Annapolis Junction, an old hipped-roof cottage in good preservation. It was built by Nicholas Dorsey and is still held by his decendant. Near the old house and close to the Elk Ridge and Annapolis Railroad is the family burial ground, surrounded by a cluster of cedars.

Nicholas Dorsey and his wife, Elizabeth Worthington, daughter of John and Helen (Hammond) Worthington, left Nicholas Worthington, who married Rachel Warfield and removed to the Seneca River; Lloyd remained at home; Joshua—Henrietta Hammond; Mary—Amos Dorsey; Ann—John Worthington; Elizabeth—Lieutenant Joseph Warfield, of Smallwood's Battalion; Sarah—William Ball; Henrietta—Judge Owen Dorsey; Achsah—Isaac Owings and went west.

Lloyd Dorsey inherited the homestead at Annapolis Junction. By his wife, Catharine Thompson, he left Noah and five brothers and five sisters. One of those brothers, Tristram Shandy Dorsey, held "Rich Neck" and "Riggs Hills." He was a bachelor and represented his district in several sessions of the Legislature. Noah Dorsey remained on the homestead, and by his marriage to Sarah Dorsey, of Joshua and Henrietta Hammond, left one son, Lloyd Egbert Dorsey, who holds the estate. He is a member of the Vansville Farmers' Club and has built his modern house in sight of the pioneer cottage, from a window of which, Sarah Dorsey lost her white slipper in the snow upon her run-away marriage to William Ball. Mr. Dorsey, also, married his cousin, Laura, a Worthington descendant of Joshua and Henrietta Hammond Dorsey. They have one daughter, Edith. Their son, Ernest Dorsey, formerly of the staff of Johns Hopkins University, is now connected with the educational staff of the Department of Agriculture. Wilbur and Claude are brothers.

This property of Nicholas Dorsey is one of the few estates that has been held by its original owners. It has handed down a long line of descendants, including the Worthingtons of Howard, of Frederick, the Macgills of Frederick, the Dorseys and Warfields of Montgomery, the Dorseys of Texas, of Kentucky, the Balls of Maryland and Virginia, and the descendants of Rev. Peyton Brown, of Virginia. From a large collection of silhouettes of this family, now in possession of Mr. and Mrs. Dorsey, interesting views of the dress and fashions of their ancestors may be studied. Among the collection is a striking photograph of Mr. Noah Dorsey, who was accidently killed by a railroad train at Annapolis Junction.

LAUREL.

In sight of this southern terminus of Howard, upon the east, looms up "Riggs Hills," from which John Riggs sent out many daughters to be wives and mothers for several Howard County families. Looking to the south of it was "Birmingham Manor," which, with "Rutlands Purchase" covered the present site of Laurel, and extended to "Venison Park" in Howard.

Here Colonel Capron organized the first mill of Laurel, in which was sunk the fortunes of several of his Snowden kindred.

To-day a beautiful town, reaching back to the heights on both sides of the Big Patuxent, bids fair to rise to the dignity of a manufacturing centre. It commands the trade of four counties. With new water-works and an electric railway, Laurel, now boasting of its large water power, has already become a splendid flour market.

RIGGS OF ANNE ARUNDEL, FREDERICK AND MONTGOMERY COUNTIES.

The name existed early in Maryland. One Francis Riggs, of Calvert County, had 800 acres issued to him by warrant July 10, 1663, and, during the year following, acquired 2,300 acres in the province. He died in 1664 at the house of Richard Lench, on "Chickacome" River, Virginia, leaving his estate to John Edmondston and Richard Collett, equally, but proceedings in the High Provincial Court of Maryland were instituted by Joseph Riggs, of Virginia, claiming as cousin of the deceased Francis. In these proceedings it is set forth that the claimant (Joseph) was the son of Francis Riggs, of Fareham, Hampshire, England, and that his deceased cousin (Francis) was the son of John Riggs, of Southampton, England. Joseph Riggs established his claim, settled in Calvert County, dying there in 1671, leaving his wife Jane sole executrix and heiress of both realty and personalty, including "Lower Bennett."

In 1681 the name Thomas Riggs is found in a list of tobacco planters making settlement with the Provincial Government (Md. Archives, Vol. 7, p. 251).

In 1689 Ensign John Riggs brought to Lieutenant-Governor Nicholson the official announcement from England of the accession of William and Mary to the throne. An investigation of the English families of Riggs has been made and published by Mr E. Francis Riggs, of Washington, as his contribution to the recent work of J.

H. Wallace, of New York, on the Family and Descendants of Edward Riggs, of Roxbury, Massachusetts. Although the evidence does not clearly establish the exact branch from which our Maryland settler came, Mr. Riggs says: "I have always been convinced that the New England, New Jersey and Maryland clans were of the same origin and that their origin was English. In England the name is, I believe, extinct. I have been unable to find it there. I had research made in England years ago, and from wills filed in the public records it seems that the name, under various forms, Rygge, Rigge, Rigges and Riggs, appears early in the fifteenth century."

One Thomas Riggs, of Southampton, whose will was proved in 1551, was an alderman of that town (County of Hampshire); his wife was Jane Richardson. Issue, Thomas, of the Sussex Branch; John, of Scotland; William, of Lincolnshire; Miles, of Suffolk; Clement, of Middlesex.

Thomas, Jr., held the Manor of Fareham, near Southampton, and left a son Rafe (Ralph), who married Mary Blake. They had nine children.

1. Thomas of Fareham; buried at Fareham 1638.
2. Robert; married Margery Chambers, of Southampton. Will 1664.
3. Ralph; three times Mayor of the City of Winchester (Hampshire), married Mary Johnson, of Buckinghamshire. Will 1647.
4. Francis; married Katharine Knight, died before 1636.
5. William; baptized at Fareham 1593.
6. John, of Southampton; merchant, married Mary Hopgood. Will proved 1636.
7. Mary; baptized 1585, married thrice.
8. Elizabeth; baptized 1591.
9. Anne; baptized 1596, married twice.

Ralph (or Rafe) Riggs, of Winchester; third son of Rafe and Mary (Blake) Riggs, married Mary Johnson, had

1. Francis; 2. Ralph, ob. s. p.; 3. Thomas, married Constance Hook, of Hook, County of Southampton; 4. Edmund, of Winchester, will proved April 27, 1660, buried in Winchester Cathedral, married Margaret Savage of King Clere, County of Southampton; 5. Ogle, married Mercy, co-heiress of John Lock, of Hollist, County of Sussex, died 1705, aet. 69; 6. Mary; 7. Elizabeth.

Francis, fourth son of Rafe and Mary (Blake) Riggs, married Katharine Knight, and had

1. Francis; 2. Joseph; 3. Benjamin; and four daughters.
John Riggs, of Southampton; merchant and sixth son of Rafe and Mary (Blake) Riggs, married Mary Hopgood at Fareham, January 12, 1622, had:
1. John; 2. Thomas, born 1636; 3. Francis and three daughters.

In the chancel of the parish church, Fareham, are the monuments of several of the above family, with armorial bearings. The arms as given by Berry (Hampshire Pedigrees) are: Gules, a fesse vair, between three water spaniels argent, each holding in the mouth a bird, bolt or, plumed argent. Crest: A talbot passant, gules, eared or, holding in the mouth a birdbolt of the second (or), plumed argent.

Mr. E. Francis Riggs has had recent searches made in Prince Georges County and has found a Mr. James Riggs' family there as early as 1703.

No definite connection, though, has yet been established as to the parentage of his progenitor, John Riggs, of Anne Arundel County, whose name first appeared in the will of John Marriott, in 1716, as legatee to 50 acres of "Shepard's Forest."

Mr. Riggs has, also, in his library an old Baxter's Directory, which contains many valuable records of the Davis' and Riggs' births and deaths.

From this Davis heirloom, it is established that John Riggs was born in 1687 and died August 17, 1762, aged 75 years. His wife, Mary Davis, was born in 1702 and died in 1768. The Davis family were among the early Virginia settlers of Herring Creek, but at the time of John Riggs' marriage to Mary Davis, in 1721, Mr. Thomas Davis was near Millersville. The will of Jabez Pierpoint (of Henry), names Sarah, wife of Alexander Warfield, and Mary, wife of Thomas Davis, his sisters. (See Mr. Nelson, genealogist.)

In 1723 John Riggs surveyed "Riggs' Hills," just east of Laurel. In 1725 he bought of Colonel Charles and Rachel Hammond their adjoining tract, "Rich Neck." In 1751, he bought of Beale Bordley 1,000 acres of "Bordley's Choice," at Brookeville, Montgomery County. Robert Davis, his brother-in-law, surveyed this tract and divided it among the sons of John Riggs.

In 1736 John Riggs and Joseph Hall held pew No. 16 in Queen Caroline Parish. At "Riggs' Hills" a few unmarked graves may still be seen, and John Riggs and his wife are probably among them. She survived him several years and left a will in which she named her sons and daughters, leaving them her estate.

1. Thomas, born October 20, 1722, died October 25, 1797; unmarried.

2. Rachel, born June 11, 1724;; married to Edward Warfield, of John, October 6, 1741, by the Rev. Jas. Macgill, at Queen Caroline Parish; died April 16, 1794, having had twelve children.

3. John, born July 11, 1726; died 1808; unmarried.

4. James, born April 13, 1728; was "tobacco inspector" for the Parish September 6, 1736; was taxed from 1756 to 1762, 300 pounds of tobacco annually as a bachelor; married Sarah, daughter of Ephraim Howard; died August 14, 1780; left no issue.

5. Ruth, born October 20, 1730; married Greenberry Griffith, had ten children; died October 18, 1779.

6. Mary, born September 24, 1732; married Benjamin Griffith, had eight children.

7. Catharine, born February 24, 1734; married —— Hyatt; died April 8, 1802.

8. Ann, born July 29, 1738.

9. Samuel, born October 6, 1740, was also a tobacco inspector in Queen Caroline Parish September 2, 1766-7; married in 1767, Amelia, daughter of Philemon Dorsey and Catherine Ridgely; was witness to several of his neighbors' wills near Riggs Hills; on his marriage removed to "Bordley's Choice," and built the homestead which still stands upon a hill overlooking the village of Brookeville. During the Revolution he was second lieutenant in Colonel Zadock Magruder's Montgomery County Militia. A striking portrait of him is still extant, taken by an artist who saw him on the street

in Washington. He died at his farm at Brookeville, May 25, 1814, and is there buried with his wife, who was born August 23, 1749, and died August 6, 1807. They had twelve children.

10. Elisha, born October 4, 1742; married Carolina, daughter of Hamutal Welsh, granddaughter of John and Anne (Dorsey) Hammond; was prominent in the beginning of the Revolution, as seen by the following correspondence:

"July 14, 1776.

"GENTLEMEN:

"Captain Riggs waits on you with a company of militia out of my battalion. The extreme busy time has prevented my being able to send them sooner. I hope they will be relieved by the Flying Camp in a few days. If they are not, I propose to relieve them by another company out of my battalion.

"I am, gentlemen, your mo. Humble Servt.,

"THOMAS DORSEY."

"Ordered July 15, 1776, That Commissary of Stores deliver to Captain Elisha Riggs for the use of his Company, 6 muskets, 30 gun flints, 72 cartouche boxes and a quantity of ammunition sufficient for his Company.

"July 20th, 1776, Ordered, That the Treasurer of Western Shore pay to Capt. Elisha Riggs Eighty five pounds, one shilling and three pence, to discharge the pay of his Militia Company."

Colonel Edward Gaither, of Elk Ridge, wrote to the Council of Safety January 21, 1776:

"GENTLEMEN:

"Whereas the Hon. the Convention has thought Proper to appoint me a Field Officer of the Elk Ridge Battalion, I therefore aprehend the nomination of the Capt. is with Hon. the Council of Safety. I am requested by my Company to beg leave to recommend Mr. Elisha Riggs their Captain if it should be thought necessary to appoint one; he is the first Lieuft. of the Company. I can assure you Gentl. he is much the Properest Person in my opinion and from the beginning of our unhappy disputes discovered a disposition which does Honour to him as an American.

"ED. GAITHER, JR."

"Whereas, Mr. John Marriott, 1st Lieutenant of Capt. Elisha Riggs is dead, I nominate Mr. Joseph Walker. Capt. Riggs wishes the vacancy filled with all convenient speed."

Captain Elisha Riggs died June 6, 1777, left three children.

11. Achsah (or "Nackey"), married Samuel Brown, born January 27 1745-6.

12. Amon, born April 21, 1748, married Ruth Griffith (died 1830, aet. 83), December 21, 1769, was Captain of Militia in Montgomery County. "Sept. 13, 1777. The Treasurer will pay Capt. Amon Riggs 72 lbs. per acc't, passed." Amon Riggs died March 16, 1822, had nine children.*

FAMILY OF SAMUEL RIGGS (OF JOHN) AND AMELIA (DORSEY):

1. Mary, born August 14, 1768, married Henry Griffith, died January 21, 1846.

2. Henrietta, born December 22, 1769, married Daniel Gaither, died April 3, 1854.

3. Thomas, born January 12, 1773, married November 17, 1796, Mary, daughter of his uncle Elisha (of John) Riggs, was ensign in Captain Frederick Gaither's Company of Militia in 1801, died January 10, 1845, and had issue.

---

* Captain Amon Riggs sold "Riggs Hills" and "Riggs Neck" to Nicholas Dorsey.

4. Anna, born August 12, 1773, married her cousin, John H. (of Elisha), died February 18, 1796.

5. Reuben, born May 23, 1775, married Mary Thomas, died April 25, 1829, and had issue.

6. George Washington, born August 8, 1777, was a successful merchant in Georgetown, D. C., and later in Baltimore; married, first, Eliza Robinson, of Montgomery County, by whom he had four children, second; Rebecca (Smith) Norris, widow of William Norris and daughter of Job Smith, of Baltimore, and had by her also four children. Geo. W. Riggs lived and died at "Woodville," now within the city limits of Baltimore.

7. Elisha, born June 13, 1779, married Alice, daughter of James Lawrason, of Alexandria, Va., September 12, 1812 (who died April 16, 1817, aged twenty-five), leaving two sons; and, second, Mary Ann, daughter of Joseph Karrick, July 16, 1822, having by her issue. He was highly successful in mercantile pursuits in Georgetown, D. C., in Baltimore, Md., and later in New York City, where he died August 3, 1853, and was buried. George Peabody was his business partner.

8. Eleanor, born June 7, 1781, died August 9, 1804.

9. Romulus, born December 22, 1782, married Mercy Ann Lawrason (sister of Alice above mentioned) May 29, 1810, was also a merchant in Georgetown; removed to Philadelphia where he was prosperous, and well known. He died in Philadelphia October 2, 1846, and is buried there. Left issue.

10. Julia, born December 22, 1784, died September 26, 1862, unmarried.

11. Samuel, born June 14, 1786, died 1805.

12. Remus, inheritor of the homestead, born January 12, 1790, married Katharine Adams, and had issue. He died December 18, 1867.

FAMILY OF ELISHA RIGGS (OF JOHN) AND CAROLINA WELSH:

1. John Hammond, married, first, Anna Riggs (of Samuel); second, Rebecca, daughter of Henry and Rebecca (Boone) Howard, and had issue.

2. Mary, born May 23, 1776, married Thomas Riggs (of Samuel), died May 10, 1829.

3. Sarah, born 1777, died October 22, 1795, *s. p.*

FAMILY OF AMON RIGGS (OF JOHN) AND RUTH GRIFFITH:

1. John, born 1771; 2. Henry, born 1772; 3. Charles, born 1774, died 1802; 4. Amon, born 1776; 5. James, born 1779; 6. Samuel, born 1781; 7. Joshua, born 1790, died 1810, and two daughters.

FAMILY OF THOMAS (OF SAMUEL) RIGGS AND MARY RIGGS:

1. Sarah Hammond, born September 19, 1797; married Philemon Griffith, son of Colonel Philemon Griffith, of the Revolution.

2. Samuel, born August 20, 1800, in the old building now part of the Brookeville Academy, married Margaret Norris,* became a member of the firm of Riggs, Peabody & Co., of Baltimore, and after the withdrawal of Elisha Riggs the firm consisted of George Peabody, Samuel Riggs and Jeremiah Peabody, under the name of Peabody, Riggs & Co.; later—on the withdrawal of George Peabody—Riggs, Jenkins & Co., and later still, Riggs, Babcock & Co., in both Baltimore and New York. The firm was afterwards Riggs, Hitchcock & Co., of New York. A few days before the formation of a partnership with his nephew, George W. Riggs (of Elisha), and his son, Wm. T. Riggs, under a proposed name of Riggs & Co., Mr. Samuel Riggs died in New York. He is buried in Greenmount Cemetery, Baltimore. His wife died in Newport, R. I., and also lies in Greenmount. Left issue.

3. Caroline Eleanor, born June 7, 1803, married Caleb Dorsey, son of Colonel Richard Dorsey, of "Happy Retreat," died April 13, 1877, and left issue.

---

* Daughter of William Norris, of Harford County.

4. Elisha, born July 6, 1810, married Avolina Warfield (of Joshua), resided upon the Patuxent near Triadelphia, died June 16, 1883.

5. Thomas John, born May 15, 1815.

FAMILY OF REUBEN (OF SAMUEL) RIGGS AND MARY THOMAS:

1. Samuel, member of the Legislature, and other children.

FAMILY OF GEORGE WASHINGTON RIGGS (OF SAMUEL) AND FIRST WIFE, ELIZA ROBINSON:

1. Amelia, born 1805, married Edward Norris (son of William), died April 23, 1878, leaving issue.

2. Anna, born 1811, married Wm. C. Pickersgill, of Blendon Hall, Kent, England, died July 29, 1892.

3. Samuel, of Goshen, born 1808, died June 9, 1883, unmarried.

4. Eliza, born February 22, 1817, married Adolphus W. Peabody, cousin of George Peabody, died May 18, 1886, *s. p.*

FAMILY OF GEO. W. RIGGS (OF SAMUEL), AND SECOND WIFE, REBECCA NORRIS:

1. Rebecca, born August 22, 1822, married Jas. Bogle, of South Carolina, and had issue, died August 27, 1880.

2. Virginia, born July 12, 1824, married, first, Major N. S. Waldron, U. S. M. C.; second, Robert Spence, of Baltimore, died *s. p.* February 2, 1901.

3. George Smith, born February 8, 1826, married Caroline M. Field, of New York, 1853, has two children and in 1905 died in Winchester, Va.

4. Remus Dorsey, of Goshen, born June, 1828, married Sallie (of Thomas) Coward, of Baltimore, has issue. He died in 1905.

FAMILY OF ELISHA RIGGS (OF SAMUEL) AND ALICE LAWRASON:

1. George Washington, born at Georgetown, D. C., July 4, 1813, married at Madison, N. J., June 23, 1840, Janet Madeline Cecelia Shedden, daughter of Thomas Shedden, of Glasgow (Scotland). He was educated at Round Hill School, Mass., and Yale (class of 1833), partner of W. W. Corcoran in the banking firm of Corcoran & Riggs, 1840 to 1848, and head of the firm of Riggs & Co., Washington, from 1845 to the time of his death at his country-seat, Greenhill, Prince George County, August 24, 1881. Left issue. Mrs. Riggs died in London, October 14, 1871.

2. Lawrason, born November 22, 1814, in Georgetown, D. C., married February 4, 1840, Sophia Crittenden, who died in 1841 without issue; married, second, in 1843, Frances Behn Clapp, who died January 4, 1849; married, third, February 24, 1859, Mary Bright, daughter of Senator Jesse D. Bright, of Indiana, and died in Baltimore, October 13, 1888, leaving issue by his last two wives. Lawrason Riggs lived for many years in St. Louis, Mo., and was in business with his cousin, Lawrason Levering. He moved to New York in 1858 and to Baltimore in 1868.

FAMILY OF ELISHA RIGGS (OF SAMUEL) AND MARY ANN KARRICK:

1. Elisha; 2. Joseph Karrick; 3. William Henry; 4. Mary Alice.

FAMILY OF ROMULUS RIGGS (OF SAMUEL) AND MERCY ANN LAWRASON:

1. Samuel James, born September, 1811; married September 24, 1835, Medora Cheatham, of Nashville, Tenn., where he died July 4, 1847, *s. p.*

2. Amelia Dorsey, born 1813; married January 8, 1834, James P. Erskine, of Quincey, Ill., died ――.

3. Alice Ann, born 1815; married March 24, 1836, Jas. W. Bacon, M. D., of Philadelphia, where she died February 21, 1839.

4. James Lawrason, born 1817; married, first, Mary Charlotte Napier, of Tennessee; second, Matilda King, of Tennessee; third, Marietta Francis, of Springfield, Ill., by whom he left one daughter, Alice.

5. Mercy Ann, born 1819; died November 12, 1821, at Georgetown, D. C.
6. Mary Elizabeth, born 1821; married July 22, 1844, at Philadelphia, Robert Colgate, of New York.
7. Henrietta, born 1623; married November 8, 1843, Samuel G. Battle, of Mobile, Alabama, and had issue.
8. Julia Mandeville, born 1625; married May 20, 1844, Geo. H. Boker, of Philadelphia, died 1899, and had issue.
9. Illinois,   married March 20, 1847, Charles H. Graff, of Philadelphia, and had issue.

FAMILY OF REMUS RIGGS (OF SAMUAL) AND CATHARINE ADAMS:

1. John, married Ann Hutton, and had issue.
2. Thomas, bachelor, of Brookeville.
3. Remus, died at Washington, unmarried.
4. William C., married.
5. Amelia, married, first, —— MacGill; second, William E. Wood, of Baltimore; died March 9, 1902, *s. p.*

FAMILY OF SAMUEL RIGGS (OF THOMAS) AND MARGARET NORRIS:

1. William Thomas.
2. Henry Irvine, died in infancy.
3. Anna, married Maybury Harrison.
4. Thomas, married, first, Elizabeth Donnell Kemp, daughter of Judge James Kemp, by whom he had two daughters; second, Catharine Gilbert, daughter of Samuel Gilbert, of Gilbertsville, Otsego County, New York, and has by her issue.
5. Margaretta, married J. Hall Pleasants, of Baltimore, and has issue.

FAMILY OF ELISHA RIGGS (OF THOMAS) AND AVOLINA WARFIELD:

1. Mary Olivia, married Thomas Lloyd MacGill, leaving one daughter.
2. Rachel G., married Evan Aquilla Jones, of Florence, Howard County, and had Dr. Wm. Jones, late of Baltimore, Anne—Sprigg Poole of Washington, Elisha R.—Mattie Banks, Kate W—and Walter M. Black.
3. Avolina Riggs (of Elisha)—Festus Griffith.
4. Joshua Warfield, of Mosby's Cavalry, C. S. A., married Matilda, daughter of Jno. A. Dorsey, and had issue, Florence Campbell and Mattie Sheldon.
5. Catherine A. Riggs (of Elisha)—Humphrey Dorsey—issue, Stephen Boone, Sarah, Evie, Rachel, Mary, Hester, Laura and William Thomas Dorsey.

FAMILY OF GEORGE SMITH RIGGS (OF GEO. W.) AND CAROLINE M. FIELD:

1. George Field, a retired surveyor.
2. Mary, married Chas. Hunt, of New York.

FAMILY OF GEORGE WASHINGTON RIGGS (OF ELISHA) AND JANET SHEDDEN:

1. Alice Lawrason, born July 7, 1841.
2. Katharine Shedden, born December 15, 1842, married 1872, Louis de Geofroy, of the French Diplomatic Service, died in Washington, D. C., February 7, 1881, leaving two sons.
3. Cecelia Dowdall, born June 20, 1844, married October 2, 1867, Henry Howard, of Her Britannic Majesty's Diplomatic Service, son of Sir Henry Howard, G. C. B.
4. Janet Madeline, born August 16, 1845, died January 30, 1861.
5. Mary Griffith, born March 15, 1848, died August 2, 1849.
6. George Shedden, born December 25, 1849, died May 20, 1856.

7. Elisha Francis, born October 2, 1851, married February 19, 1879, Medora, daughter of James S. Thayer, of New York City, and Medora, his wife (who was widow of Samuel James Riggs, of Romulus). He was a member of the firm of Riggs & Co. from 1876 to its dissolution in 1896, and has (1902) two sons.

8. Jane Agnes, born October 28, 1853.

9. Thomas Lawrason, born April 11, 1858, became a member of the firm of Riggs & Co., September 1, 1881, died unmarried, at Washington, January 19, 1888.

FAMILY OF LAWRASON RIGGS (OF ELISHA) AND FRANCES CLAPP:

1. Benjamin Clapp, born February 16, 1844, married June 1, 1874, Rebecca Fox. He died April 18, 1883, at Saranac Lake, N. Y., leaving issue.

2. Alice Lawrason, born July 10, 1846; married December 2, 1873, Riggin Buckler, M. D., of Baltimore, and has issue.

3. George Washington, born December 22, 1848; married October 8, 1879, Catharine Cheeseman, of New York, and has issue.

FAMILY OF LAWRASON RIGGS AND MARY BRIGHT.

4. Mary Bright, born January 5, 1860, died April 7, 1862.

5. Lawrason, born October 17, 1861. Lives in Baltimore, is Brigadier-General of Maryland National Guard.

6. Bright, born March 26 and died November 11, 1863.

7. William Pickersgill, born August 11, 1864, in New York.

8. Clinton Levering, born September 13, 1866, in New York; married October 23, 1894, Mary Kennedy Cromwell; lives in Baltimore; now Adjutant-General under Governor Warfield.

9. Jesse Bright, born February 3, 1870, in Baltimore, married October 5, 1893, Charlotte Morris Symington, and has issue.

10. Alfred Randolph, born April 19, 1871, in Baltimore.

11. Francis Graham, } born November 29, 1872 in Baltimore.
12. Henry Griffith,

13. Thomas Dudley, born January 28, 1875, in Baltimore; married.

SNOWDEN.

A tradition exists that Major Richard Snowden, of Wales, who held a commission under Cromwell, was our immigrant.

In 1675 Major John Welsh, husband of Mrs. Roger Grosse, and executor of the Grosse estate, summoned the heirs to a settlement. Two of them were Richard Snowden and Elizabeth, his wife, "lately called Elizabeth Grosse." In 1679 Richard Snowden bought of George Yate a tract of iron-ore land on South River. In 1686 he was granted "Robin Hoods Forest," a tract of 10,500 acres: in 1688 he bought lands of William Parker, near West River. He was living in 1704.

Richard Snowden, Jr., was a partner with his cousin, Captain John Welsh, as iron merchants, and in 1733 was executor of Captain Welsh. He was married before 1691, to Mary, daughter of Thomas Linthicum. In 1717, Richard and Mary Snowden signed the second marriage certificate of their son Richard, whose first wife was Elizabeth Coale, daughter of William and Elizabeth (Sparrow) Coale. By her he had Elizabeth, wife of John Thomas; Mary, wife of Samuel Thomas (sons of Samuel and Mary [Hutchins] Thomas), and Deborah Snowden, the Quakeress wife of James Brooke. They removed to "Snowden's Manor" at Sandy Spring in 1728.

Richard Snowden, the third, married his second wife in 1717. She was Elizabeth Thomas, daughter of Samuel and Mary (Hutchins) Thomas and a sister of his sons-in-law, John and Samuel Thomas.

Thomas Snowden, of Richard and Eliza (Thomas) Snowden, born 1722—Mary Wright, daughter of Henry and his wife, Elizabeth Sprigg, daughter of Colonel Edward Sprigg.—Richard Snowden, of Thomas and Mary Wright, brother of Major Thomas Snowden, of Montpelier, and of Samuel and John, married Elizabeth Rutland, daughter of Thomas. She brought to his estate "Rutland's Purchase," which took in most of the land from Laurel to Annapolis Junction. His homestead was "Fairlands." His sole heiress, upon the death of her parents, resided at "Montpelier" and married John Chew Thomas, member of Congress when President Jefferson was elected over Aaron Burr.

Ann Snowden became the wife of Henry Wright Crabb, father of General Jeremiah Crabb; Margaret Snowden married John Contee.

Samuel Snowden built the large brick house, still standing deserted near Montpelier, and "Birmingham" now in ruins.

This manor-house, built in 1690, was heired by John Snowden; it stood just above the Snowden forge of the Patuxent. Its huge fireplaces, its walls of brick and shingles, its portico looking out upon a semi-circle of barns for stock and tobacco; its graveyard with its huge slabs, headstones and monuments are all well remembered by the author. This was the later centre of a family who held not only the whole area surrounding Laurel, but were heirs of an estate which commenced on South River and extended beyond Sandy Spring, a distance of fifty miles.

In sight of it, just across the river in Prince George, is still to be seen a magnificent type of our colonial manor houses. It is "Montpelier," of the Snowdens, built by Major Thomas Snowden for his bride, Ann Ridgely, who named it for her birthplace, "Montpelier," of Anne Arundel.

This house stands but a short distance southeast of Laurel, upon the Great Northern and Southern Post Road, which connected Annapolis and Washington. Upon this road coaches ran between the two cities. Amid surrounding woodland it looms up as a relic of the past to teach us how our colonial progenitors lived. Before its door the family coach was habitually drawn up for the daily morning ride.

Within a hospitable reception ever awaited weary travelers. It was the stopping place of General Washington on his trips from Mt. Vernon to Annapolis. The bed upon which he rested is still in possession of a descendant daughter, now of Sandy Spring. "Montpelier" was last held by the Misses Jenkins, of Laurel. When I saw it last its doors were closed, its halls were silent, its well-graveled walks and driveways were lined by closely cropped box-wood; its flower beds were encircled by boxwood; its hand-carved doorways and pillars, its extended wings and corniced gables, all speak of the life of ease and comfort when Major Thomas and Ann (Ridgely) Snowden held this beautiful home. In a cedar grove in the rear, unprotected and unmarked, now lie the remains of the master and mistress of "Montpelier" in Prince George County. "Montpelier" has lately passed to Mr. Pendleton, the author, who will make it his winter home.

From Thomas and Mary Wright came Major Thomas Snowden, of "Montpelier." He took his bride, Ann Ridgely, the heiress-daughter of Colonel Henry and Ann Dorsey,—issue Richard, of "Oakland," now known as "Contees." His wife, Eliza, daughter of Major Charles Alexander Warfield, was therefore his first cousin, and after her death he married her sister, Louisa Victoria Warfield (no issue).

Ann Louisa Snowden, the oldest daughter—John Contee and inherited the extensive homestead, which still stands upon an eminence at Contee station, into which Major Richard Contee afterward took his bride, Anna Bolling. They still hold it. Thomas Snowden (of Richard)—Ann Rebecca Nicholls, issue. Sarah Rebecca —Colonel Charles Marshall, of Baltimore. Caroline Eliza (of Richard) —Hon. Albert Fairfax. Issue—the late Lord John Contee Fairfax, of "Northampton," Prince George County. Emily Roseville (of Richard)—Colonel Timothy P. Andrews, U. S. A., brevetted Brigadier-General at Chapultepec. Issue, the late Colonel Richard Snowden Andrews, C. S. A., Civil Engineer of Baltimore. Richard Nicholas (of Richard)—Elizabeth Ridgely Warfield (of Dr. Gustavus of "Longwood"). Issue, Gustavus Warfield, Richard, George, Thomas, Evan Warfield, Mary, Thomas and Elizabeth Warfield Snowden—William Dorsey, grandson of Colonel Richard.

Nicholas (of Major Thomas, of "Montpelier")—Elizabeth Warfield Thomas (of Samuel and Annie Warfield Thomas, of "Roxbury."

Their residence was "Avondale," now the handsome Ober homestead, near Laurel. Ann Elizabeth—Francis M. Hall; 2nd, Charles Hill Thomas, Jr., died at Magnolia, Florida; Louisa—Colonel Horace Capron, who built the Laurel Manufacturing Mills; a monument stands over her grave at "Birmingham;" Julia Maria—Dr. Theodore Jenkins, of Baltimore. Issue, Theodore, killed at Cedar Mountain, 1862; Elizabeth Snowden, Louis, William, Francis Zavier, Mary Eliza, Ann Louisa, Arthur Jenkins; Adelaide Snowden—W. W. W. Bowie; Edward—Mary Thomas Warfield, of Longwood; Dr. DeWilton—Emma C. Capron; Henry—Mary C. Cowman; Eliza entered Georgetown Convent; Emily Roseville—Charles C. Hill— issue, Ann Elizabeth, Charles; Ann, Ida, Edward, Snowden, Emily Roseville, Edith and Albert.

From this line comes Colonel Nicholas Hill, formerly the popular proprietor of the "Carrollton Hotel and Merchants Club," of Baltimore. Nicholas—Henrietta Stabler; issue, Emily Roseville—Gerard Hopkins; Marion, Lucy, Helen, Francis, Mary. Dr. Arthur Monteith—first, Ella Snowden (of Thomas); second, Mary Vaux, of Virginia. He was a surgeon in C. S. A., and was drowned. His home, afterward the tavern at Scaggs Corner, he named "Herring Bone Hall."

Thomas Snowden (of Major Thomas and Ann) lived a bachelor at Summerville, the brick house at Annapolis Junction, a portion of his mother's inheritance.

Mary (of Major Thomas and Ann)—Colonel John Carlisle Herbert, son of William, who married a daughter of John and Sarah (Fairfax) Carlisle, of Virginia. Colonel Herbert built another magnificent homestead near Beltsville, the white walls of which may be seen from the verandah upon which this is written. Issue, Dr. Thomas Snowden Herbert, Ann Caroline—Hon. Henry Fairfax; Alfred, Professor and Lieutenant in Florida wars. Sarah—Captain Archibald Fairfax, U. S. N.; William Fairfax, Emma—Rev. W. Boynton; Mary Virginia—Captain Thomas T. Hunter, U. S. N.; Julia Eugenia; Lucinda—John Eversfield; Eliza, Edward—Mary H. Barrett. Dr. Thomas Snowden Herbert—first, Camilla Hammond (of Denton); second, Elizabeth Duer, (with no issue), issue of Camilla—John Carlisle Herbert: General James R. Herbert, C. S. A., Colonel of Fifth Regiment, Commanding General of Militia and Police Commissioner. He was at the front at the first attack upon Gettysburg and was there wounded. He married Elizabeth Coleman, daughter of Colonel Mark Alexander, of Virginia. His only son died in the late war with Cuba. General Herbert held the last tract of the immense Herbert estate, now all passed from the name. "Birmingham" descended to the youngest son.

John Snowden, of "Birmingham"—Rachel, daughter of Gerard and Mary (Hall) Hopkins. Issue, Rachel—Judge John S. Tyson; Rezin Hammond—Margaret McFadden; they handed down "Birmingham" to the late William Snowden—Adelaide Warfield, youngest daughter of Dr. Gustavus and Mary (Thomas) Warfield, of "Longwood." Issue, Julius, of New York; Louisa Victoria, Marie Antionette, Adelaide Warfield, Sophia Carroll, Eugenia; John (of Rezin Hammond)—Sarah E. Hopkins; issue, Mrs. Charles H. Stanley, of Laurel, and John Snowden Jr., former Commissioner, of Prince George's County.

SAVAGE FACTORY.

Hidden from view by surrounding hills, back from the old Washington road, yet now reaching out to it, is a little manufacturing centre, a perfect model of one-man enterprise. Its factory buildings, its neat brick houses, all recently painted, its stores and private dwellings all bear evidence that a master hand rules the town; that revelry and dissipation have no home there; that industry and thrift there meet. Upon one of its hills stands the proprietor's residence, stately, yet modest, overlooking the whole village. Off to the south looms up an attractive, commodious house of a former manager of the Savage Factory, who, seeing that war was inevitable, bought largely of southern cotton, which returned him alone some eighty thousand dollars upon his investment.

Savage Factory was chartered in 1812 by three Williams' brothers. They bought parts of several adjacent tracts, viz., "Warfield's Range," "Venison Park," "Harry's Lot," "Whites Contrivance" and "Rich Level," but there was a mill there long before that. Alexander Warfield (of John) built a mill upon "Venison Park," near the great falls in 1750. He left it to his sons, John Worthington and Brice Warfield. They failed to see the coming manufacturing opportunity and sold it to their father-in-law, Francis Simpson. Savage is now owned by the Baldwin Company, chief of which was the late William Henry Baldwin, Jr., the successful merchant of Baltimore, whose record has already been recorded in Anne Arundel.

"WARFIELD'S RANGE."

Five miles north of Laurel, extending from Savage Factory two miles west, is this historic range, surveyed more than two centuries ago. Then it was a frontier outpost, approached only by the Indian trail which led from Annapolis.

One generation later this was the center of pioneer settlers engaged in growing a most excellent grade of tobacco. Elk Ridge Landing was its shipping port. Near the Range passed the Great Northern and Southern Post Road, and along that route was the popular line of settlement.

The magnificent water-powers of the two branches of the Patuxent were soon to be utilized. Laurel, Guilford and Savage were to rival the individual mills of the pioneers, and the Baltimore and Ohio Railway was soon to take up the tobacco output which had before found its market over the rolling roads of the pioneers.

Standing, to-day, upon the many commanding points of "Warfield's Range," and looking up and down the varying valleys of the Patuxent, the wisdom of those pioneers becomes apparent, but of that sturdy host of settlers, all allied by matrimonial ties, only silent graveyards, neglected and unmarked, near the old remaining relics of their forest homes, are left to us. In their places, and upon their plantations, a new people have arisen.

Suburban homes, fine roadways, large barns and prolific grass and grain fields succeed their tobacco barns and cabin homes.

Not only have these pioneers departed, but even their descendants. The great west-bound movement, which they inaugurated, has carried them still further west, in many cases even beyond the bounds of the state.

Amid all the political upheavals of the first century of the history of the Province, Richard Warfield had great faith in agriculture as the best means to enhance the prosperity of his children.

In his will of 1703 he left 280 acres of the "Range" to his youngest son, Benjamin, and 150 acres to his daughter Rachel Yates. In 1704 his sons and executors, John, Richard, Alexander and Benjamin, resurveyed this tract and took up a large body of land adjoining it. John and Alexander took up "Venison Park" on the south and Richard and Benjamin surveyed "Wincopin Neck" and "Warfield's Contrivance" on the north. None of these brothers occupied these ranges. The real settlers were their sons.

About 1725, John Warfield's three sons, John, Benjamin and Alexander, were granted through their eldest brother, Richard, heir-at-law, adjoining tracts upon "Warfield's Range."

John settled upon what is known as the Marriott place, upon which is the old family burial-ground. Benjamin adjoined him on the north and west. Alexander adjoined him on the north and east. It was later known as the Jerome Berry place, but now in possession of Senator Gorman. One hundred and fifty acres of the "Range" were assigned to Eleanor (Warfield) Dorsey. It descended to her son, Basil Dorsey, who conveyed it to Thomas Warfield, of Alexander. It was later known as the homestead of Dr. Charles Griffith Worthington, and still later, the home of Mr. Peter Gorman. North of this tract, and embracing the site of Senator Gorman's "Fairview," is the original grant to Benjamin Warfield, youngest son of the first surveyor. It descended to his son Joshua, whose executor, Thomas Warfield, conveyed it to John Warfield, thence to Joshua Warfield, his brother, who lived in a quaint old house which still stands upon it. It descended to "Gentleman John," of Joshua, the last of his line, and after his death was sold to Mr. Bentley and to Senator Gorman. Still further north is the original grant of Rachel Yates, daughter of Richard Warfield. After her death in 1709, her husband, George Yates, sold it to John Warfield (of John). This is the most northern survey of the Range. Upon it stands the homestead of the late Dr. Thomas C. Worthington, now owned by Joshua Warfield Baxley, a descendant of the original surveyor. Richard Warfield (of John) deeded the remainder of the Range to his sons, John and Seth Warfield. John later exchanged with Edward Hall, of Frederick County. The latter sold to Basil Burgess, who sold to William Sellman. This property was the Benjamin Dorsey homestead.

Seth Warfield (of Richard) held, through his descendants, a large part of the western border of the Range, which has only recently passed from the Warfield name. The last owner was Randolph Ridgely Warfield, attorney of Baltimore. Seth's five sons surveyed "Warfield Forest," near Lisbon, Howard County. His youngest son, Amos, held the homestead and built the substantial stone house which still stands. Adjoining him on the west and south, across Hammond's Great Branch, stretches out the thirteen hundred acres of "Venison Park," upon which were located the two younger sons of John Warfield, the first. They were Edward and Philip Warfield. The latter sold his inheritance to Seth Warfield and removed to the neighborhood of Clarksville. Edward Warfield's estate descended to his son James, whose heirs all removed to Tennessee. This tract became a part of Dr. Charles Worthington's estate.

Still further south and leading to Laurel, were the two estates of Alexander and Absolute Warfield, sons of Alexander, third son of Richard Warfield. They sold their portion to Thomas Sappington, who resurveyed it into "Sappington Sweep," and all their remaining interest to Alexander Warfield (of John). Alexander (of Alexander) removed to some other State and left no records behind. Absolute Warfield was a witness to several wills as late as 1777. He did not marry.

The Rent Rolls show the peculiar authority of an heir-at-law in the early grants. Every deed of transfer in "Warfield's Range" was given by Richard Warfield (of John), the executor of the estate. Even when new surveys were added, they were conveyed through him. Just previous to his death, in 1765, he made a systematic survey of the titles of all the heirs and confirmed them. The smallest grants were to his sons, John and Seth Warfield. Benjamin Warfield (of Richard) did not settle upon his, nor did his son. Yet Richard, the executor, in his will of 1765, still further confirms the title by these words. "All my interest in 240 acres of "Warfield's Range" I grant to Joshua Warfield (of Benjamin.)'' In his deed to his brothers he records "For the love I bear to my brother, I grant him and his heirs forever all my right in a certain number of acres of Warfield's Range." As a brotherly guardian his example is worthy of being handed down to posterity.

John, Benjamin and Alexander Warfield, of "Warfield's Range," all married cousins. John's wife was Rachel Dorsey, daughter of Joshua and Anne Ridgely. John and Rachel Warfield built the quaint little house still standing on the Marriott place. Their oldest son, Dr. John Warfield settled upon the property north of "Fairview," now Mr. Bentley's. He took up, also, "Warfield's Addition," in Upper Howard, which descended to his nephew, Allen Griffith, and to Captain Benjamin Warfield, of "Cherry Grove." He died in 1775, a bachelor, and left his homestead, to his younger brother, Joshua.

Charles Warfield, his brother, settled upon "Fredericksburg." He married Catherine Dorsey, daughter of Captain John and Ann Dorsey, of "Walnut Grove." Their son Charles H. Dorsey, married Mrs. Johnson, mother of William Cost Johnson, member of Congress from Frederick County. Tilghman and Feilder were two bachelor brothers, and "Cousin Kitty Warfield" was not only a proud, intelligent maid, but a good lawyer. Their estate is now held by the heirs of the late Horatio Griffith and by Joshua N. Warfield, of Florence.

Joshua Warfield (of John and Rachel) was married twice before twenty-one years old. His first wife was Elizabeth Dorsey, of Thomas and Mary (Warfield) Dorsey, who had one son Thomas John, named for both grandfathers, who married Mrs. Sellman and removed to the neighborhood of Westminster. Joshua Warfield married, second, Mary Ann Jones, daughter of Captain Isaac, of South River. Their sons were Roderick, Warner and "Gentleman John." The latter died in 1860. His tombstone, bearing the inscription "John Warfield of Joshua," stands in the old burial-ground upon the Marriott place. By his side lie his maiden sisters, who preceded him. Roderick

Warfield married Miss Stockett and removed to Kentucky, leaving a large family recorded in the "Warfield's of Maryland." Warner Warfield removed to "Bagdad," near Sykesville. He married his cousin, Catherine Warfield (of Beale,) and left Marcellus, William Henry and Manelia Warfield, now Mrs. Jenkins, who inherits the homestead.

Marcellus Warfield was a prosperous merchant of Sykesville, and a vestryman of his parish church. He married Miss Lawrence, daughter of Captain John Lawrence, of Frederick County, and left two daughters, Mrs. William Ward and Miss Ella Lawrence Warfield.

William Henry Warfield was a merchant at Laurel, and married Charlotte K., daughter of Dr. Mareen Duvall. He left no issue.

Harriet Warfield of Joshua and Ann, married Ralph Dorsey.

The daughters of John and Rachel (Dorsey) Warfield were Mrs. John Wayman (of Poplar Springs), Mrs. Sarah Griffith and Amelia, a maiden. They heired the homestead, which was later sold by Colonel Lyde Griffith to Jonathan Marriott.

Benjamin, Warfield of "Warfield's Range," married Rebeckah Ridgely, of Judge Nicholas and Sarah (Worthington) Ridgely. He built his cottage upon a commanding plateau, just north of his brother John. Its present owner, Mr. Samuel Hearn, has a picture of it. From its gateway an extensive view reveals a charming landscape. Surrounding the dwelling is a large grove, on the border of which stands one building over which the storms of many seasons have beaten. Benjamin and Rebeckah Ridgely had four sons, Captain Nicholas Ridgely Warfield, Captain Benjamin, Vachel and Elisha, and one daughter, Mary Ridgely Warfield, the wife of Thomas Dorsey, of Henry and Elizabeth Worthington. Captain Nicholas Ridgely Warfield, the bachelor, survived all his brothers, dying at an advanced age, in 1814. He was a tobacco inspector, of Elk Ridge Landing, and Captain of its militia; he held an extensive estate in both Howard and Montgomery Counties. Just across the road from the homestead was located his brother Vachel, upon a portion of the Range taken up later by his uncle Richard. This was recently the Groscup race-course. Still later, Vachel and his brothers, Benjamin and Elisha, removed to Upper Howard.

Benjamin Warfield Sr., married again Ann White and had one son, Caleb, and two daughters, Mrs. Charles Banks and Mrs. John Lansdale. After his death the homestead was bought by Vachel Yates, a relative. He resided there in 1774, as shown by a note from William Coale to him in 1774. It was found in the old cottage when torn down by Mr. Hearn.

Nicholas Ridgely Warfield, as heir-at-law, in 1810, confirmed the sale to Mr. Thomas Moore. It passed to Mr. Marriott and to Mr. Faire, who mortgaged it to Mr. Mason, and by the late John T. Mason of R. was sold to Mr. Hearn some twenty years ago. He has made it a model farm. The graves of Benjamin and Rebeckah Warfield are in the family ground.

DR. CHARLES GRIFFITH WORTHINGTON
OF "WARFIELD'S RANGE."

Removing from his birthplace in Anne Arundel, Dr. Charles Griffith Worthington (of Thomas) bought of Samuel Burgess and Leonard Sellman their interest in "Warfield's Range."

Here Dr. Worthington organized the first medical school in the Province. This embryo-medical college still stands.

Dr. Worthington acquired adjoining property and settled his sons upon it. His first wife was Mary Dorsey (of Amos). Their son and successor, Dr. Thomas C. Worthington, adjoined him on the north, and married a daughter of Ralph and Harriet (Warfield) Dorsey.

His patriarchal beard, handsome form and courtly manners are well remembered and give us a picture of those founders of many brilliant pages of Maryland history. Joshua Warfield Baxley holds his home. Nicholas Dorsey Worthington adjoined him on the north. His property is now owned by Ex-Sheriff James Hobbs. Charles Griffith Worthington, Jr., married Kate Stewart, daughter of Dr. Thomas Stewart, the surveyor, who built her a large brick house upon his estate. Mr. Harding has made a beautiful home here.

Brice Worthington, the bachelor, inherited "White Hall" upon the Patuxent, adjoining "Montpelier." This house has a history of two centuries and it still stands. It is a rough-cast brick, now showing its age. Five generations of Worthingtons are buried in its hill cemetery. By the light that comes from our Rent Rolls, its history goes back one century more. It stands upon a part of "Wincopin Neck." This was a joint survey by Benjamin and Richard Warfield, brothers.

It was heired by Mrs. Elizabeth Ridgely and by Alexander Warfield (of Richard).

The latter put his son Rezin and Honor (Howard) Warfield upon it. It came to their daughter Ann, wife of Major Richard Lawrence, who was known as "Major Lawrence, of White Hall."

It was from this "White Hall" Mrs. Rezin Warfield went out as the bride of her husband's cousin, John Davidge, to hand down her two celebrated sons, Dr. John and Henry Davidge, and afterward to die the widow of two more husbands.

"White Hall" finally passed to Dr. Worthington and his son Brice, and from Brice Worthington to his nephew, Dr. William Henry Worthington, a student of the first medical college, just in sight. Dr. William H. Worthington married Mary Ann Jones Dorsey, daughter of Ralph and Harriet (Warfield) Dorsey and left Mrs. Galena Hodges, of Ellicott's City. Achsah Worthington, his only sister, married Rinaldo (Warfield) Dorsey. Their son is Joshua Warfield Dorsey, of Ellicott City, who holds a beautiful and commanding estate adjoining "White Hall." His present wife is a daughter of Dr. Worthington by his last wife, Miss Cooke.

THE BURGESS FAMILY OF HOWARD.

The four brothers whose descendants make up a history of Howard were: John, West, Joseph and Caleb Burgess, sons of John and Matilda (Sparrow) Burgess, of South River.

Captain John led a company of militia. In April, 1776, Major Henry Ridgely and others protested against the officers made by the Company under command of Captain John Burgess, and it was resolved by the Council that they be rejected and commissions be made out of those elected by the people on the 9th of September last. viz., John Burgess, Captain; Davidge Warfield, First Lieutenant; Basil Burgess, Second Lieutenant, and William Simpson, Ensign. Captain John Burgess was also one of the justices of Upper Anne Arundel, and in 1778 was appointed Sheriff in the place of William Harwood. Captain Burgess was a brother-in-law of Colonel Thomas Dorsey, having married Sarah Dorsey, of Basil and Sarah (Worthington) Dorsey. Issue, Basil, John, Achsah and Sarah Burgess.

Basil became an officer in his father's company and later joined the Continental Army. He was a surveyor. He bought Edward Hall's interest in "Warfield's Range."   John Burgess removed to Frederick County.

West Burgess, brother of Captain John and Joseph, resided on the Severn, near Round Bay. He married Elizabeth Warfield, of Alexander and Thomasin (Worthington) of "Warfield's Range."

His brother, Caleb Burgess was Ensign in the Continental Army. He married Deborah, daughter of Alexander and Thomasin Warfield.

The descendants of these two brothers are named in the will of Alexander Warfield, of Frederick County, the bachelor brother of their wives.

"To my brother Brice Warfield, I leave a farm for life; to Rachel Burgess, wife of West Burgess and daughter of Brice, a legacy. To Matilda Simpson, wife of Joshua; To Matilda Spurrier and to to the daughters of my brother, John Worthington Warfield,viz.: Araminta, Ann and Sarah, similar legacies; To Samuel Burgess of West, my interest in "Warfield's Range."

"To Zadoc Warfield of Brice and to John Burgess of Caleb, my lands in New York with improvements lately made by Thomas Edmondston. To Arnold and Alexander Warfield, sons of brother John W. Warfield, the land I own in New York. To Caleb of Caleb Burgess, land bought of John Wampler. To Samuel, of Caleb, to Surrat D. Warfield of brother Brice, and to Alexander Burgess of Caleb, the remaining parts of my estate in Frederick County, to be divided by them."

West and Samuel Burgess held parts of "Warfield's Range;" they sold to Dr. Charles G. Worthington. Captain Joseph Burgess will be found at Triadelphia.

SENATOR ARTHUR PUE GORMAN
OF "FAIRVIEW."

Five miles northwest of Laurel, upon a nicely graveled road, made and kept yearly in repair by Senator Gorman, upon a ridge that commands an extensive view of a beautiful landscape, is the model farm of Maryland.

The present building stands upon the same site as the original, which was erected after the war and was burned several years ago.

The house stands upon a survey of 1686. "Fairview" farm embraces 500 acres of "Warfield's Range." The barren fields left by the old tobacco growers, by liberal dressings of lime and manure, aided by clover, are, to-day, producing corn, wheat and grass equal in quality and quantity to the limestone lands of Frederick County. Not a vestige can be seen of the old tobacco houses of the pioneers, but upon "Fairview" are extensive barns, and stables filled with grain, hay and high-grade stock. Over this extensive farm the Senator may frequently be seen on horseback directing its management. "Fairview" has a verandah from which the entire farm and neighborhood may be seen.

Three hundred yards west is the homestead of Mr. and Mrs. Peter Gorman, whose portraits, by Healy, now hang in the drawing-room of Fairview. The artist has represented Mr. Peter Gorman in early manhood, with an intelligent and striking face. His father, John Gorman married Miss McDonald, both of the North of Ireland. They came to Harrisburg, but later removed to Baltimore, where Mr. Peter Gorman was born. The latter in early manhood became the contractor and builder of the first section of the Baltimore and Ohio Railroad, from Ellicott Mills to Woodstock. Located at Woodstock, he there met and married Miss Elizabeth Browne, daughter of John Riggs Browne, of "Good Fellowship."

Mrs. Gorman's mother was Sarah Gassaway, daughter of Brice John Gassaway and Dinah Warfield, a sister of Major Charles Alexander Warfield. Senator Gorman was born at Woodstock, in 1839.

Upon the completion of his contract Mr. Peter Gorman bought the homestead of Dr. Charles Griffith Worthington, near Savage, and removed there, where his remaining children were born.

They are Mrs. Stephen Gambrill, of Laurel; Mrs. Thomas Marriott, of New York; Calvin Gorman, of Laurel, and William H. Gorman, of Catonsville.

Mr. Peter Gorman was one of Stephen Arnold Douglas' strongest supporters for the Presidency, in 1860, and, like Douglas, when the war came, supported the Union. Upon a trip South upon private business, during the war, Mr. Gorman was arrested and confined in Libby Prison.

The confinement weakened his nervous system, and, before a release could be secured from Governor Letcher, his health broke down. He died soon after his release.

His widow survived him several years.

Senator Gorman's career is an object lesson worthy of being perpetuated.

The idol of Stephen Arnold Douglas, United States Senator, he was made a page in the Senate. Even then he was a favorite with all who knew him. In 1861, when the war brought a Republican majority, his popularity again secured his retention and even his advancement to Postmaster.

Active in his opposition to the impeachment of Andrew Johnson, he lost his position, but through the efforts of Reverdy Johnson, Thomas A. Hendricks and Montgomery Blair, he was appointed Collector of Internal Revenue for the Fifth District. In this appointment several Republican Senators joined in his confirmation. At that time the Fifth District was not only an extensive one, but a difficult one to manage. Its accounts had never been settled up. Yet, Mr. Gorman in six months after the close of his term returned a satisfactory settlement.

In 1869 he was made a member of the House of Delegates and was returned in 1872, when he was made Speaker. Of his first experience in legislating for the still existing oyster interest, Mr. Gorman has given an interesting account.

When Speaker he came down from his chair to advocate an appropriation of $150,000 for the education of the colored people of the State. Appointed a member of the Board of Directors of the Chesapeake and Ohio Canal Company, he long remained an active member. When President of the Company, he made it, though previously unprofitable, to return over one million dollars; more than double the amount it had returned in twenty years previous.

In 1875 he was elected to the Maryland Senate to succeed Hon. John Lee Carroll, then nominated for Governor. As a member of that body his influence was always exerted in the development of the State's interest, and upon his individual efforts the Agricultural College was enabled to receive its appropriation. In 1877 he became Chairman of the State Central Committee. His personal popularity, success in organizing men, and in settling complicating interests, pointed him out as a leader able to represent the State in the Senate of the United States.

He was elected in 1882, and at once took a foremost rank as a leader. His force, calmness, cool courage, added to his well-equipped knowledge of men and measures in a critical era succeeding the Civil War, have made Senator Gorman a national leader.

His magnificent fight against, and defeat of, the "Force Bill," has been echoed and re-echoed in every journal of the United States. His splendid management of the New York Campaign, when he telegraphed to the *World*—"Cleveland is elected and will be inaugurated"—sent a thrill of satisfaction through the country.

Though not in sympathy with some of the later issues the Democratic Party was called on to face, Senator Gorman stood facing the storm until his party went down in defeat, and he went out of the Senate—because of that defeat. During the four years of his retirement all eyes turned to him as the leader of his party. In answer to the unanimous voice, he entered upon the State Campaign, was again successful, and in turn was honored by every Democratic vote of both houses of the Legislature as the next United States Senator from Maryland.

Senator Gorman took his seat at the Special Session, and at once held his former position as Democratic leader. His name had been prominently mentioned for the nomination upon the Democratic platform for the Presidency, but in throwing his influence to the support of Judge Parker, he was almost unanimously urged as Chairman of the Campaign Committee.

This honor he declined and urged a younger man for the arduous work.

Mr. Gorman was married in 1867, to Mrs. Hannah Donagan Swartz, of Reading, Pennsylvania. He has six children. His only son, Colonel Arthur P. Gorman, Jr., is an attorney, at present State Senator from Howard. His wife is Grace, daughter of James L. Norris, of Washington, D. C.

Senator Gorman's daughters are Mrs. Richard A. Johnson, Mrs. William J. Lambert, of Washington; Mrs. Stephen Gambrill, Jr., of London; Mrs. Ralph Hills and Miss Ada Gorman, of Fairview.

GAMBRILL.

The will of Augustine Gambrill, of 1774, is the earliest one on record at Annapolis.

To his sons, Augustine and Stevens, he left "Friendship" and "What You Please." Augustine was to hold the homestead. To these same two sons he left, also, a tract upon the Magothy, called "Young's Success." To his wife, Comfort, all of his personal estate, which at her death was to descend to his nine children, viz., William, Augustine, Benjamin, Stevens, Ann, Sarah, Martha and Comfort. To his daughters, in addition, he left several negroes. John Marriott and John Sewell were witnesses.

The will of John Marriott, of 1716, names his daughter, Ann Gambrill. This shows the family there much earlier than the above will. The will of Augustine Marriott, son of John, of 1716 probated 1729, shows a Joshua Gambrill as a witness and in 1791, Joshua Gambrill sold "Owen's Range" to Stevens Gambrill.

About the same time, Richard Gambrill bought of Richard and Sarah Marriott several tracts near Carroll's Manor.

In 1798 William, Mary, Augustine and John Gambrill sold their interest in their homestead on the Magothy.

In 1804 John and Elizabeth Gambrill sold to Mr. Ashley "Homewood's Forest," on Bodkin Creek.

In 1805 Joseph and Augustine Gambrill, sons of Benjamin, sold "Howard's Pasture" to Charles Waters.

In 1807 Augustine Gambrill sold to Richard Gambrill a tract called "Worthington." That same year, Lydia and Susannah Gambrill, daughters of Augustine Gambrill, granted to their brother

Augustine two tracts, "Friendship" and "What You Please." Richard Gambrill bought of Richard Warfield Jones "Lancaster Plains," willed him by Richard Warfield.

The following deed gives a further history of the family. Augustine Gambrill sold to Samuel Briant certain lands called, "Young's Success," held by Augustine Gambrill, who, dying in 1774, left it to his two sons, Augustine and Stevens, as tenants in common. About 1789 Augustine Gambrill died and by his will devised it to his son William, who possessed in common with Stevens Gambrill.

In 1803 William sold his part to his brother Augustine, who now sells to Samuel Briant his undivided part in 1812.

In 1805 Samuel Ridout granted Augustine Gambrill, according to a warrant of re-survey, several tracts, viz., "Wyatt's Hill," "Wyatt's Ridge," "Crouchfield," part of "Providence," now named "Gambrill's Purchase." The deed covers six pages of the record and the price was quite large. Augustine Gambrill married the widow of Captain Harry Baldwin. The sons were, Stephen and Charles.

The will of his father, Augustine, probated 1790, reads—"To sons Richard and Augustine, my dwelling and lands "Friendship" and "What You Please." To daughters Lydia, Susannah, Eliza, Margaret and Sarah the right of living in the houses in common with my sons Augustine, Richard and William." Witnesses, Lancelot Warfield, John Sappington and William Woodward. The will of Stevens Gambrill left all of his property to his nephew Stevens of Augustine and made the same his executor. Lancelot Warfield, Caleb Sappington and Richard Gambrill were witnesses, in 1808.

Mr. Richard Gambrill, of Columbia, Howard County, married Miss Iglehart. Their sons have all become prominent in the history of Maryland. The Gambrill Flour Mills of Baltimore, Howard and Frederick County were founded by these sons.

Mr. Stephen Gambrill, of Laurel, was formerly President of the Chesapeake and Ohio Canal. He married Kate, oldest daughter of Mr. Peter Gorman and Elizabeth Browne, his wife. She is a sister of Senator Gorman. They have two sons in the U. S. A., viz., George Thomas and Major William Gorman Gambrill, of the Philippines. They have written some interesting letters of devotion to parents and country. Stephen Warfield Gambrill married a daughter of Senator Gorman. He is the London representative of the Fidelity and Deposit Company, of Baltimore, of which Governor Edwin Warfield is President.

Arthur Pue Gambrill and his sister, Catherine Gassaway Gambrill, are with Mr. and Mrs. Gambrill in their handsome home in Laurel.

VENISON PARK.

Upon the east and south of "Warfield's Range," forming now a part of Savage Factory and extending west along Hammonds Great Branch, is the now almost forgotten tract of thirteen hundred and thirty-six acres of "Venison Park," marked out by Alexander and John Warfield. According to the arrangement of these brothers, some four hundred acres of this tract were surveyed for the two younger sons of John and the remainder for the two sons of Alexander.

The will of the latter, in 1740, shows his son Alexander, upon the "eastern limits of Warfield's Range," and extending to the mill site of Savage. About 1750 Alexander Warfield sold out his interest to his cousin Alexander (of John) and left no records at Annapolis.

Absolute Warfield, his brother, and executor of his father, sold another portion of Venison Park, to Thomas Sappington, who resurveyed it into "Sappington Sweep."

As executor of his father he completed the deeds for 200 acres each to Edward and Philip Warfield, younger sons of John. These tracts were west of "Sappington Sweep."

Absolute Warfield appears as a witness to several wills of his neighbors as late as 1777. He remained a bachelor.

The following interesting record from Mr. Frank Warfield, of Bellefonte, Pennsylvania, seems to point to a descendant of the above Alexander Warfield. I do not know where else to place him:

"My father Alexander Warfield was born in Maryland, in 1820, and died in San Diego, California, in 1893. He had a sister Adaline. He went to Kentucky when young; was afterwards President of a College in Georgia; was next in Missouri, and, in 1860, was in California as a mining expert. My mother was a descendant of John Quincy Adams. They were married in Missouri. Upon his return from California, in 1869, I was old enough to know him. He returned to Mexico to develop a silver mine.

"In 1884, after having made and lost three fortunes, with my mother and sister, he again went to the Pacific Coast, never to return.

"All I know of that noble man was gained while I was only a boy. I feel a just pride in being his son, for he was all that goes to make a man, and in all my travels I have found none quite equal to him. My oldest sister, Hattie A., married W. B. Ross, of Nashville, Tennessee. My youngest sister remains single."

The heirs of Alexander and Thompsy (Worthington) Warfield were, Thomas, the bachelor, of "Warfields Range;" John Worthington Warfield and Brice, twin brothers, of "Venison Park" and joint owners of the mill; Alexander Warfield, Jr., of "Venison Park" and three daughters.

Mrs. Alexander Warfield married again Francis Simpson, of Frederick County, who bought out the entire interests of the Warfield heirs. John Worthington Warfield then bought of Edward Dorsey's heirs, "Thomas' Lot," near Dayton. He there married Susannah Ridgely, who left a son Arnold Warfield, who married Margaret Browning and removed to Clifton Springs, New York, upon lands granted him by his uncle Alexander.

Arnold Warfield left several descendants in New York. Some of these have recently removed to Florida. One of them was the late Alexander Warfield Bradford, author of several legal works.

John Worthington Warfield left his Dayton farm to his brother Brice and removed to the Big Seneca, where he accumulated a large estate.   He married again, Mary Holland of Amos, and had John Holland Warfield, who married Mary, daughter of Amos Warfield, and lived at Scaggs' Corner.   Their son was Lorenzo Warfield, of Glenelg, whose old hostelry still stands.

Alexander Warfield, of John Worthington, inherited the Seneca homestead; married Mary Harwood, whose mother was Elizabeth Stockett of Thomas and Mary Noble, daughter of Captain Thomas and Mary Wells, whose father was Major Richard Wells of the Puritan Council.   Mrs. Stockett became the wife of George Yates, the surveyor, and had issue, George Yates, husband of Rachel Warfield, of "Warfield's Range."

Mary Warfield, of Alexander and Mary, married Ephraim Creager, of Frederick County.   Issue, Frank, George, Manilia Markey, Alcinda Savidge, Caroline Broadbent, Major Noble Creager, U. S. A., and Miss Virginia Creager, of Baltimore.

Caroline (of Alexander and Mary) married William Bantz. Their daughter was the late wife of Senator Henry G. Davis, of West Virginia, Vice-Presidential candidate.

John A. Warfield (of Alexander and Mary) married his cousin Henrietta, of Surrat D. Warfield.   Their heirs are living in Frederick County.

Brice Warfield (of Alexander and Thompsey) married Sarah Dickerson and lived near Dayton.   He had two sons and several daughters, all legatees of his bachelor brother, Alexander Warfield, of Unionville.   Surrat Dickerson Warfield (of Brice) was the chief heir and executor of his uncle Alexander, who in addition to several farms in Frederick County, held a large and undeveloped tract at Clifton Springs, New York, which he left to his Warfield and Burgess nephews.

Alexander Warfield's will also left legacies to the daughters of his brother John Worthington Warfield.

Surrat Dickerson Warfield inherited the estate near Unionville, and became State Senator from Frederick County.   His descendants are Dr. Brown Warfield, of Philadelphia; Surrat R. Warfield, and his sons, Guy and Frank Brown Warfield, of Baltimore.

The daughters of Alexander and Thompsey were wives of Caleb Burgess and of West Burgess, both brothers of Captain John and Captain Joseph Burgess, all engaged in the Revolution.   Their heirs held a portion of "Warfield's Range."   They sold it to Dr. Charles Griffith Worthington.   It is now the handsome estate of Senator Gorman.

GUILFORD.

Age, hoary and neglected sat many years upon the old stone houses of Guilford, but, built of the enduring granite found there, they will stand for centuries.   The site of the place is upon "Wincopin Neck."   Here Alexander Warfield and Mrs. Elizabeth Ridgely had a joint mill in 1750. It is upon the North branch of the Patuxent, to which the Baltimore and Ohio Railroad Company has now built a connecting road for the shipment of the output of the newly-organized Granite Company of Baltimore. Guilford has been renovated. Its neglected buildings have been restored. Its granite is acknowledged to be of the first order, and the only need was shipping facilities, which have been furnished. A macadamized road connects it with Savage Factory, and over this highway Mr. Penny's six-horse team did much of the delivery for market.

Charles Greenberry Ridgely, sixth son of Colonel Henry and Elizabeth (Warfield) Ridgely, inherited " Huntington Quarter" and "Harry's Lot," the most eastern division of the estate. He lived at the homestead, upon the hill east of Guilford. He was a member of the vestry of Queen Caroline Parish and married Sarah, oldest daughter of Rev. James Macgill, Rector.

Upon his estate stands, to-day, the Pattison homestead, the Commodore Barney house and the Cronmiller house. Charles Greenberry Ridgely, Jr., as executor of the estate, sold to Thomas Coale the property known as the Barney place. It was inherited by Miss Coale, the second wife of Commodore Barney. Archibald G. Ridgely, brother of the executor, his sisters Elizabeth, Ann, Mary received the home place.

Ann—Nicholas Griffith, youngest son of Colonel Henry and Sarah (Warfield) Griffith and became the mother of Sarah (Warfield) Griffith, wife of Amos Brown and mother of Colonel Ridgely Brown C. S. A.

Henrietta Griffith—William Penniman; Thomas Griffith—Elizabeth Griffith, daughter of Colonel Lyde. Their four sons, Captain Thomas, David, Festus and Frank Griffith were in the Confederate Army.

The homestead "Harry's Lot" descended to Archibald G. Ridgely, whose tombstone, now broken by the side of a hay barrack on the Pattison estate, reads:

"To my father, Archibald G. Ridgely; died November 21st, 1806."

His will reads: "To my daughter Emily, and unborn child, all my estate, but if the one born and the other unborn, should die, then I give to my wife all my estate to descend to Nicholas Ridgely Griffith, son of my sister Nancy, but not to deprive my wife of her third. Witnesses Richard Ridgely, John H. Dorsey and G. Watkins."

Emily Ridgely (of Archibald married Major Spedden, U. S. A., and held the homestead. By them it was sold to the Pattisons.

Close by this old family burying-ground, upon the edge of the wood upon the road to Savage, is an old brick and frame house, once the home of Commodore Barney. It is now Dr. Linthicum's. Still nearer Savage is another house of the family of Charles Greenberry Ridgely. It was known as the Cronmiller place.

This property is upon a commanding ridge overlooking the romantic centres of Savage, Guilford and Annapolis Junction.

SAPPINGTON FAMILY.

At Sappington station, Annapolis and Elk Ridge Railroad, stands a well preserved type of the cottage homes of early days. It was built by Caleb Sappington, son of John. On the Little Patuxent is "Sappington Ford," named for a kindred family. Both later had representatives in Howard County. Caleb Sappington's mother was Ann Everitt, who later became Mrs. Ridgely; his father, John Sappington, Jr., took up "John's Luck," near Savage. Caleb sold his interest in that tract to his sisters, Ann, Rebecca, Martha, Elizabeth and Caroline Sappington. It adjoined "Brown's Purchase," "Warfield's Contrivance," and "Food Plenty." Caleb of John— Margaret Gambrill, daughter of Augustine and Sarah Baldwin, widow of Lieutenant Henry.

Nicholas John Sappington, of Augustine and Mrs. Julia (Sewell) Worthington inherited the homestead of Sappington.

The Sappington estate on the Patuxent was sold by William Warfield, trustee to Dr. Anderson Warfield, both nephews of Caleb Warfield, who married into that family.

The will of Thomas Rutland in 1731 named Thomas Sappington, "his grandson." This Thomas Sappington removed to Howard County and bought of Absolute Warfield a portion of "Venison Park" and of Alexander Warfield a part of "Warfield's Range," which he resurveyed under the title of "Sappington Sweep." He married Frances Brown, daughter of Mark Brown, who bought of Neale Clark an adjoining tract to "Sappington Sweep," known as "Neale's Delight; this was given to his daughter, Frances (Brown) Sappington.

Thomas Sappington, Jr., Dr. Francis Brown Sappington and Mark Brown Sappington were the sons. They were all engaged in the revolutionary struggle. Thomas Sappington, Jr.—Polly Ridgely, daughter of Colonel Henry and Ann (Dorsey) Ridgely, of "Montpelier." In his will of 1783 he gave all of his estate to his son, Henry Sappington, and his three daughters, Frances, Henrietta and Ann. He appointed his brother, Dr. Francis Brown Sappington, trustee of his son Henry. Any dispute with Francis Simpson concerning lands bought of Absolute Warfield was to be settled by a commission, viz., Henry Ridgely, Jr., and Dr. Francis B. Sappington. He named his wife, Polly Sappington. In a neglected graveyard, just west of Thomas Sappington's old homestead, immediately upon Hammond's Great Branch, and within sight of the public road leading from Laurel to Senator A. P. Gorman's, I found tombstones to the memory of "Polly Sappington," "Frances Sappington" and "Henrietta Sappington."

The following transfers show the last heirs of this estate: "Zedekiah Moore and Anne Louisa, his wife, sell to Anne Prather, 'Venison Park,' 'Warfield's Range,' 'Sappington Sweep' and 'Two Sisters,' taken up in the name of Francis B. Sappington and Henrietta Sappington, conveyed by Francis Brown Sappington to said Frances, Henrietta and Louisa, daughters of Thomas Sappington."

Dr. Mark Brown Sappington inherited the upper portion of the estate adjoining Alexander Warfield; he was upon the committee of Observation for Anne Arundel County and witness to the will of Dr. John Warfield.

Dr. Francis Brown Sappington—Ann Ridgely, daughter of Greenberry and Lucy (Stringer) Ridgely, a cousin of his brother's wife. With her he removed to Liberty, Frederick County. Their son, Colonel Thomas Sappington, who was in the War of 1812, and six times senator of Frederick County, married Sarah Coale, sister of General James M. and Major Richard Coale, of Liberty. Issue, Dr. Thomas Sappington, late of Baltimore; Dr. Greenberry Sappington, of Frederick County; Dr. Sydney Sappington, of Liberty; Dr. August Sappington, of Liberty; William Coale Sappington, attorney-at-law, and Frank Sappington. The daughters of Dr. Thomas Sappington are Mrs. Caroline Davis and Sarah Sappington.

Martha, daughter of Dr. Francis Brown Sappington, became the wife of Dr. Richard Dorsey (of John and Margaret [Boone] Dorsey).

Harriet Sappington (of Dr. Francis Brown) was engaged to marry Dennis Howard (of Ephraim), a large land holder of Liberty. He introduced her to Dr. Peregrine Warfield as "the most beautiful woman in Maryland." Dr. Warfield must have thought so too, for Harriet Sappington became his wife and Mr. Dennis Howard remained a bachelor.

Nancy Sappington, her sister, married Mr. McSherry, grandfather of James McSherry, Chief Justice of the Court of Appeals of Maryland.

COLONEL HENRY RIDGELY'S "UPPER MONTPELIER."

Henry, second son of Colonel Henry and Elizabeth Ridgely, was born 1728. In 1752 he raised a company of volunteers in answer to the call of Governor Sharpe, and joined him at Fort Cumberland to resist the threatening Indians upon the western frontier. After a successful campaign, in which the Maryland forces were publicly complimented by Governor Sharpe, Captain Ridgely was promoted to Colonel in charge of the militia. He lived up to the time of the Revolution. The archives record the personal contest between Colonel Henry and his brother-in-law, Colonel Thomas Dorsey, upon the organization of the Elk Ridge Militia in 1775. In his letter to the Council of Safety, Colonel Ridgely, alluding to his former military service, and referring to the demand of his neighbors that he should again lead them, yielded his place to Colonel Dorsey and contented himself in offering his service as a private in the ranks.

Colonel Ridgely also wrote a protest against some of the officers in Captain Burgess' company of militia from Elk Ridge and succeeded in securing new officers under Captain Burgess.

Colonel Ridgely was located at "Montpelier," adjoining "Warfield's Range." A description of this homestead is elsewhere given. His wife was his cousin, Ann Dorsey, daughter of Joshua and Ann

(Ridgely) Dorsey. In the midst of his military career, and for that service he secured a large landed estate. His only son, Henry Ridgely, the bachelor, after the marriage of all of his sisters held the homestead until his death.

Elizabeth Ridgely (of Colonel Henry) married Dr. Charles Alexander Warfield, and upon her dower of several hundred acres of "Ridgely's |Great Park" was built "Bushy Park," elsewhere noted.

Polly Ridgely married Thomas Sappington, son of Thomas and Frances (Brown) Sappington, of "Sappington's Sweep."

Rachel Ridgely married Jesse Tyson, near Laurel.

Ann Ridgely married Major Thomas Snowden and transferred her residence further down the Patuxent in Prince George and presided over new "Montpelier," a still more magnificent home. Her record belongs to the Snowdens. She inherited "Summerville," near Annapolis Junction, and there lived and died her bachelor son, Thomas Snowden. Both "Montpeliers" have now passed into stranger hands.

Late in life, 1770, Colonel Henry assigned unto Brice Thos. Beale Worthington, his brother-in-law, fifteen tracts, negroes and black cattle, to pay a debt due Daniel Dulaney and Ann Tasker.

The homestead of Colonel Henry, as above described, is now the property of Mr. Wessel, who has restored it.

FULTON.

All the area around Fulton, south of Columbia road, upon the Patuxent, was embraced in "Snowden's Second Addition to Birmingham Manor."

North of Fulton, Colonel Henry Ridgely and Thomas Worthington took up "Partnership" and "Hickory Ridge."

Upon "Partnership," opposite Fulton, Major Thomas Gassaway was seated.

This later became the home of Brice John Gassaway. It is now the Moore property.

Fulton has a church and cemetery, a store, blacksmith shop and several residences.

A good road, now nearly macadamized, connects it with Highland.

THE GASSAWAYS OF HOWARD.

The Gassaways, of Howard, were decendants of Nicholas Gassaway (of John) and Nicholas Gassaway (of Major Thomas), both grandsons of Colonel Nicholas Gassaway, of South River.

Nicholas Gassaway (of John) sold his interest in his father's estate on South River to his uncle, Major Thomas Gassaway, and removed to the parish of Queen Caroline. His will of 1757 records:

"I Nicholas Gassaway, of Queen Caroline Parish, give to my deceased daughter, Ann Pierpont's heirs, Samuel Pierpont; to my daughter Susannah Mansill; to my son Nicholas, each one shilling: I bequeath to my three sons, Benjamin, Richard and Robert Gassaway, all my tract called 'Talbotts Resolution Manor.'

"I appoint my wife, Rachel Gassaway, executrix, and to her and my children, Thomas and James Gassaway, Hannah Porter, Mary Gassaway and Lucy Nicholson, Benjamin, Sarah, Richard, Robert and Rachel Gassaway, I give my personal estate."

The above testator was thrice married First, to Elizabeth Hawkins; second, to Sarah Shipley, daughter of Robert; third, to Rachel Howard, daughter of Joseph (of John) and Rachel (Ridgely) Howard. Witnesses, John Dorsey (of John) and Caleb Dorsey (of John). These locate the testator near the old Brick Church.

MAJOR NICHOLAS GASSAWAY
(OF MAJOR THOMAS AND SUSANNAH [HANSLAP] GASSAWAY).

Major Nicholas Gassaway (of Major Thomas and Susannah [Hanslap] Gassaway) married Catharine Worthington and resided also in Queen Caroline parish upon his wife's portion of "Partnership," between Highland and Fulton. Her father, Thomas Worthington, assigned to Nicholas Gassaway, husband of his daughter Catharine, 369 acres of "Partnership" taken up by Colonel Ridgely and himself. Major Nicholas' will, witnessed by Brice and Azel Warfield, was probated 1775, and reads:

"I give to my wife Catharine the whole of my personal estate. I give to my son Thomas what he already has from me, except his bond. To son Henry what he has already received. To daughter Susannah Rogers what she has already received and fifty acres to be laid out of a tract I bought of Richard Snowden, called 'Second Addition to Snowden's Manor,' to descend to grandson Nicholas Gassaway Rogers.

"To son Charles what he has already had. To son Brice John all the residue of 'Second Addition to Snowden's Manor,' and also the tract 'Partnership' on which I now reside. I give to daughter Ann Warfield, wife of Richard, what she has already received and also stock. Wife Catharine and sons Thomas and Henry executors."

Thomas Gassaway, executor of Major Nicholas, married, first, Sarah, daughter of Edward and Sarah (Todd) Dorsey, widow of C. Geist; second, Sarah Watkins.

Sarah Geist held "Uplands," near Triadelphia, from her first husband. As the wife of Thomas Gassaway she sold it to Wm. Cotter and rebought it. After her death Thomas Gassaway married Sarah Watkins, to whom he left his whole estate and made her executrix.

She sold "Uplands" to Jos. Dick, who later sold it to Captain Joseph Burgess.

Thomas Gassaway's son, Nicholas Gassaway, married Amelia Berry and held "Dorsey's Addition to Thomas' Lot," near Glenelg. His will granted his wife, Amelia, a life estate in "More houses Generosity" and "Dorsey's Addition to Thomas' Lot." His three sons, Hanson, John Gassaway and Berry Gassaway, were granted personal property, and upon coming to manhood were to receive their shares of real estate, including lands in Alleghany County. Witnesses, Chas. Alex. Warfield, Joseph Burgess and Deborah Berry. Probated 1806.

Their son John Gassaway—Eliza Dorsey (of Caleb and Mary [Gassaway] Dorsey), and will be later noticed.

Captain Charles Gassaway (of Nicholas and Catherine)—Ruth Beall, daughter of "Ninian, of Ninian." Issue, Charles—Catherine Noland, of Virginia, lived near Leesburg and left no issue; Thomas —Henrietta Dawson, of Virginia, no issue; Sally was engaged to Captain Samuel Dawson, brother of Henrietta; he died on their appointed wedding day; Rachel—Mr. Owings; Elizabeth—Mr. Darne, issue, Anne—Captain Smoot, U. S. N., issue Sidney Smoot; Maria Darne—Dr. Lacy; Cecelia—Dr. Beall; Louisa—Mr. Beall, issue, Ann, Mattie, Kate and Alexander, a lawyer of New York; Alexander Hanson Darne—Mary Gassaway (of John), a cousin.

Mary Gassaway (of Captain Charles and Ruth Beall)—Caleb Dorsey, only child of Caleb and Dinah Warfield (of Dr. Joshua and Rachel Howard, issue, Evelina A., Eliza and Deborah Lydia Ridgley —Evelina A.—first, William Prince, of Kentucky, issue, Cyeanne— Nicholas Dawson, of Montgomery County, issue, William, Thomas, Charles and Mollie; Evelina (Dorsey) Prince married, secondly, before twenty-one, her cousin, Amos Dorsey, of Howard County, issue, Napoleon, Pulaski, Judge of the Orphans' Court of Howard, Harrison, Ann Eliza Simpson and Ellen, wife of Otis Worthington, Kate and Laura, wife of Hammond Carr.

Eliza (of Caleb and Mary)—John Gassaway (of Nicholas and Millie Berry), her cousin, issue, Nicholas, John Hanson—Kate Armstrong, issue, John, Alexander—Bettie Miller, issue, John and Norman.

Mary (of John and Eliza)—Alexander Hanson Darne, her cousin, issue, John, William, Ella, widow of the late Thomas Anderson, Jane (of John and Eliza)—Alexander Peter, issue, Mrs. Beall, Mrs. Offutt, Mrs. Dr. Nurse, Evie and Willie; William (of John and Eliza)— Mary Farrow, half-sister of Bishop Cummings, issue, Sallie, wife of Rev. Mr. Griggs; Mary—Mr. Redding; Florence—Rev. McNair; William Gassaway, Jr.

Lavinia (of John and Eliza)—Hon. George Peter, son of Major George Peter, U. S. A., relative of General Washington; Mr. Peter was State Senator; issue, John, attorney; Sallie—Wm. Laird Dunlop, son of Judge Dunlop; issue, James and William Dunlop.

Mary (of George and Lavinia)—Thomas Dawson, Clerk of Montgomery; Edward (of George and Lavinia)—Mary, daughter of Judge Thos. Vincent—he was State's Attorney; Robert (of George and Lavinia)—a daughter of Judge Lowry, U. S. A.; Kate—Hugh Nelson (of Rev. Cleland K. Nelson); Arthur is a lawyer of Washington.

Laura (of John and Eliza)—George Bradley, issue, Thomas Gaither, of the "Rough Riders," complimented by Colonel Roosevelt; Harry, lives in the west; George—a daughter of Captain McDonald, late M. C.; Laura and Sadie Bradley.

Deborah Lydia Ridgely Dorsey (of Caleb and Mary), admired by both W. W. Corcoran and Richard M. Johnson—Dr. Charles Grey Edwards, son of Benjamin and Elizabeth Ellzey Minor, of Loudoun County, Virginia; issue, Benjamin, Caleb, Thomas Lee, Ann, Virginia Grey and Laura.

Ann—Dr. Richard H. Edwards, surgeon of Eighth Virginia Regiment, issue, Rachel—Dr. T. L. McGill, of Frederick; issue, Dr. Lloyd, Dr. Charles, William and Nannie, the young widow of Charles Hilfinstein. Dr. Charles Grey Edwards (of Dr. R. H. Edwards) served in the Loudoun Guards, 17th Virginia Regiment, and was badly wounded; removed to Louisville, Kentucky, where he married Ida, daughter of Dr. Edmund T. Perkins, the distinguished Rector Emeritus of St. Paul's; issue, Edmund, Ida, Harry and Margaret Grey. William Howard (of Dr. R. H. Edwards) served in Colonel Lige White's battalion, was torn to pieces by a shell; a comrade of young Edwards had a leg taken off by the same shell; upon Decoration Day he may be seen upon crutches, meditating, or decorating the grave of his companion. Thomas W. Edwards (of Dr. R. H. and Ann)— Lily S., daughter of Colonel Rush, of West Point, whose wife was Ida Lee, great-granddaughter of Richard Henry Lee; issue, William Howard and Ida Lee. Laura P. (of Dr. Charles Grey)—Dr. Richard E. Bland, of St. Louis, Missouri, descendant of Colonel Theodorick Bland, of Virginia, and relative of John Randolph, of Roanoke. She has one son, Richard Bland, of the West. John Randolph Bland, President of the United States Fidelity and Guaranty Company, of Baltimore, is the son of Dr. R. E. Bland by a former marriage to Miss Williams, of Norfolk.

Virginia Grey Edwards (of Dr. Charles Grey Edwards)—William Worsely, son of John Worsley, of Girton, Nottinghamshire, England, and Elizabeth Daniel, of Virginia. Their homestead, "Hedgeland," was named from the hawthorn hedge which separated every field. Issue, Lizzie and Nannie, of Leesburg, Virginia, and Thomas Lee Worsley, of St. Louis, who married Moselle, daughter of Judge Gustavus De Launay, of Columbus, Georgia. Issue, Corinne, William D., a student-at-law, Moselle and Charles Grey Edwards.

Henrietta Gassaway, daughter of Dr. Charles Grey Edwards, was the third wife of her cousin on three lines; Warfield, Dorsey and Beall. He was Nicholas Dorsey Offutt, whose mother was a daughter of Nicholas Dorsey Warfield, of Lieutenant Joseph and Elizabeth (Dorsey) Warfield. He was also the grandson of Zachariah Offutt and Ellinor Beall, of Ninian.

Henrietta Gassaway Offutt left no issue.

The children of Nicholas Dorsey Offutt by Rachel were Nicholas D. William Worthington, Lee. By a third marriage to Mary Anderson—issue, Lulie, Mrs. Dr. Campbell and Anderson Offutt.

Captain Charles Gassaway's homestead was "Pleasant Hill," near Darnestown. Its large rooms, high ceilings, carved stairway, perfect brickwork, may still be seen. Having ample means, his hospitality was proverbial. John Hanson Gassaway, near Germantown, now holds a part of the Beall estate, of Ruth, of Ninian.

Brice John Gassaway (of Major Nicholas) married Dinah Warfield, daughter of Azel and Sarah (Griffith) Warfield; she was a sister of Catherine, wife of Hezekiah Griffith, who died 1796.

Brice John Gassaway's estate was "Partnership" and "Second Addition of Snowden's Manor," at Fulton. His homestead is now held by Mr. John Moore. He also held the estate of his son-in-law, James Warfield, whose family removed to Tennessee. He was a leading member of the Baptist Church and bought of Rezin Hammond, in 1792, one acre of "Davis' Pasture" for a Baptist Church.

Having lost his estate through the failure of his sons, he removed to Brookeville, where he died, beloved by all, an active Christian. His heirs were George, Henry, Ann, Catherine, Sarah, Elizabeth and Mary—Thomas Gibbons. George—Miss Porter and removed to North Bend, Ohio; Henry—Rachel Griffith, daughter of Dennis. Their son Henry Charles—Elizabeth Allen, daughter of Rev. Ethan Allen. Henry Gassaway removed from Baltimore to Cincinnati. His son, Stephen Griffith Gassaway, a minister of the Episcopal Church, was killed in a steamboat accident on the Mississippi.

Ann (of Brice John)—James Warfield, of "Vension Park," son of Edward and Rachel Riggs. She married, second, Nicholas Worthington (of Thomas) and with him and her son-in-law, Walter Warfield Waters, joined her Warfield children in Tennessee.

Walter Warfield Waters was the son of Ignatus and Ann Warfield (of Azel). His brothers and sisters were Charles Alexander, Azel, Ignatus, Richard, Samuel, Elizabeth, Charlotte, Catherine and Louisa Ann—all grandchildren of Richard Waters, of Goshen, by Elizabeth Williams, sister, it is said, of General Otho Holland Williams.

Catharine Gassaway (of Brice John)—Colonel Charles Hammond and had issue, William Alexander, Evaline, Rezin, Gassaway, Lloyd, Annie, Mary, Sallie—Ephraim Carr, whose heirs are Hammond Carr, Henry and Mrs. Earp, who holds the commodious homestead upon "Brown's Purchase." Hammond Carr inherited and holds a portion of "Worthington's Addition," a part of "White Hall."

Sarah Gassaway (of Brice John)—John Riggs Brown (of Samuel and Achsah Riggs) who held the Brown homestead of "Good Fellowship." Her will of 1855 named her heirs, Henry G. Brown, Samuel John R. Brown; daughters Louisa Davis, Mary Ann Smith, Elizabeth Gorman, Kitty Ann Hood. (See Brown Record).

Elizabeth Gassaway (of Brice John) became Mrs. William Porter, of Sandy Spring. Issue, Charles and William Porter. The latter was a contributor to Edgar Allen Poe's journal. He married Mary E. Catlett, the daughter of Mary Dorsey by her second marriage. Mrs. Mary Porter established a successful school for girls, at Brookeville, which later became Briarly Hall, Poolsville. She, at an advanced age, has materially aided me in much interesting Gassaway data. Her tribute is—"They were cultivated, courteous and gentle." Four of them entered the Revolution as commissioned officers. John, Nicholas and Henry were with General Sullivan at Long Island, in that gallant charge.

Henry Gassaway was Lieutenant in the Fourth Maryland Regiment from 1781 to 1783; Brice John Gassaway rose from Lieutenant to Captain in 1780. He was taken prisoner at Camden and was paroled to the end of the war.

Charles Gassaway was Captain of militia.

The revolutionary claims entitled them to lands in West Virginia, which have never been located.

SIMPSONVILLE.

Upon the Middle Patuxent, nestled under hills on all sides, was an old-time mill, lately destroyed, which dates back to the earliest days of the settlers. In some of the Howard wills it was called "Dr. Warfield's Mill." In others, of later date, it was known as "Richard Owings Mill." It is now known as Simpsonville. Upon a southern hill stands the large and comfortable residence of the late Major Owings. Around this centre located Dr. Joshua Warfield, Ephraim Howard, Cornelius Howard, and his sons, the Howard Merchants, one of whom was Captain Brice Howard, commander of the Elk Ridge Militia, and here was Richard Owings, the merchant.

HOWARDS OF SIMPSONVILLE.

Two Howard families were in Upper Anne Arundel. Governor John Eager Howard invested in lands near Woodstock, in 1786, for his son George Howard, the Governor of 1832, but long before that Joseph Howard, son of Captain Cornelius Howard, of the Severn, had surveyed some four thousand acres upon both sides of "Doughoregan Manor," upon which he seated his three sons, Henry, Cornelius and Ephraim, one hundred years before Howard District was organized.

Joseph Howard and Margery Keith, his wife, lived upon the Severn homestead and there handed down a continued line of Joseph Howards, but following his neighbor Thomas Worthington into the neighborhood of Clarksville and Simpsonville, Joseph took up "First Discovery," "Howard's Passage" and "Joseph's Gift," between Simpsonville and Elioak, and then went west of Doughoregan and extended "Second Discovery" toward Glenelg.

To his oldest son, Henry Howard, he willed "Kil Kenny," "Howard's Passage" and portions of the First and Second "Discovery."

Henry Howard's descendants claim that he was "Sir Henry Howard, the British Commissioner, of 1706." He held a house at Elk Ridge Landing, which seems to confirm the idea that he was connected with that Port of Entry, but he was not born until 1708. No records to confirm the tradition have been found. He married Sarah Dorsey (of John and Honor Elder), of "Long Reach," and through her came into possession of a portion of "Dorsey's Grove" at Glenelg. This adjoined his "Second Discovery." At the time of his death he owned a greater part of "Dorsey's Grove" and had extended his surveys to Glenwood.

He also came into possession of 500 acres of his brother Ephraim's inheritance.

His will of 1773, shows him a man of marked intelligence, of determination, and an extensive landholder. At the time of writing it he seems to have resided at Glenelg, now the property of Frank Shipley's heirs.

He named his heirs, Ephraim, John Beale, Vachel Denton, James, Joshua, Mrs. Sarah Nelson, Mrs. Honor Davidge and Mrs. Rachel Warfield. Three of his sons, Dr. Ephraim, Dr. John Beale and Joshua, having inherited the Dorsey Grove estate, will be noted in Upper Howard.

Captain Vachel Denton, James and the daughters, holding lands near Simpsonville, will now be noticed.

Captain Vachel Denton Howard (of Henry) was with Colonel Richard Dorsey in the Revolution. He left Colonel Dorsey a memorial watch, which marked the hours by the twelve letters of his name. It was held by the late Richard Dorsey, of Glenwood, who handed it to his nephews.

Captain Vachel died a bachelor and left 500 acres of "Discovery" to his niece, Dinah (Warfield) Dorsey.

James Howard (of Henry) was the executor of his father and his brother-in-law, Dr. Joshua Warfield, of Simpsonville.

He was an attorney, but left no heirs that can be found.

Sarah Howard (of Henry)—Burgess Nelson, of Montgomery County. Issue, Henry, Benjamin, Rachel, Sarah—Vachel Dorsey (of Vachel); Elizabeth—Charles Griffith; Mrs. Nelson became the wife of Major Richard Green, of Montgomery County, and mother of Ruth, Mary, Amelia—Michael Dorsey, third, Israel and Mrs. John Cole.

Rachel Howard (of Henry)—Dr. Joshua Warfield (of Alexander and Dinah Davidge). Issue, Sarah, Dinah, Ruth, Rachel and Joseph Warfield.

Dr. Joshua Warfield resided at Simpsonville. His field of practice covered that whole section.

Sarah, his daughter, died single; Dinah—Caleb Dorsey; Ruth —Richard Owings; Rachel—Nicholas Worthington Dorsey and had Ezra, of Texas; Lloyd, Nicholas, Noah, Alfred, Reuben, Mortimer, Clarissa, Matilda and Joshua Warfield Dorsey, of Laytonsville. He married Miss Waters and Miss Childs. Issue, Mrs. Thomas Dorsey and Mrs John Warfield, of Laytonsville.

Lieutenant Joseph Warfield—Elizabeth Dorsey, sister of Nicholas Worthington Dorsey. Both families lived upon the Seneca, in Montgomery. Issue, Nicholas Dorsey Warfield, Eliza Offutt, Juliet Davis and Caroline, second wife of Major Richard Lawrence. Nicholas Dorsey Warfield and Mary, his wife, left Edwin Warfield, Mary Eliza Warfield and Elizabeth Ann Hawkins.

A grandson of Edwin Warfield is Professor Lodge.

CORNELIUS HOWARD (OF JOSEPH AND MARGERY).

Cornelius Howard (of Joseph and Margery) located upon "First Discovery" and "Howard's Passage." He married Rachel Ridgely Worthington, who inherited 369 acres of "Worthington Range," at Clarksville. The heirs of Cornelius and Rachel Howard were Thomas Cornelius, Brice, Joseph, Elizabeth, widow of Ephraim Davis and wife of William Gaither; Sarah Ducker and Rachel Hood. The three sons of Cornelius Howard were merchants with headquarters at Simpsonville.

Thomas Cornelius held the homestead just opposite the Catholic Church at Clarksville. It later became the home of Mr. Denton Miller, whose tombstone may there be seen. Joseph Howard held "Howard's Resolution" and "Poole's Desire;" Captain Brice Howard held the homestead near Simpsonville.

The will of Mrs. Rachel Howard, in 1801, named her "grandchildren, Thomas Worthington, Charles, Henry, Brice, Polly, Rachel Duval, Elizabeth Rowan, Rebekah Young and Anna Howard, children of her son, Thomas Cornelius Howard; her daughter Sarah Ducker; her granddaughters, Henrietta Poole, Martha Ann and Elizabeth Gaither, daughters of her daughter Elizabeth; grandson, Brice Howard; granddaughter, Ann Howard, of my late son, Brice Howard." Rachel Howard (of Cornelius and Rachel) became the wife of John Hood, Jr., of "Bowling Green." Her inheritance adjoined "Folly Quarter;" a part was bought by Charles Carroll Mac Tavish. Their daughter, Elizabeth Hood, married Nicholas Meriweather (of Reuben) and inherited the remainder, adjoining "Brown's Chance and Dorsey's Friendship." It was sold at public sale to John Hood, Jr., who resold it to John O'Donnell. It was again bought by Nicholas Worthington (of John) and by him deeded to John R. Clarke, who exchanged it with his father for lands at Columbia. The inheritance thus handed down to Rachel Howard is now known as "Hayland," the late homestead of William Clarke and the present attractive farm of Governor Edwin Warfield.

Joseph Howard (of Cornelius and Rachel) married Rachel Ridgely, of "White Wine and Claret," one of the eleven daughters of William and Elizabeth (Duval) Ridgely. Their son Joseph, Jr., married Mary, daughter of Thomas Cornelius Howard; Elinor Howard, their daughter, became Mrs. Azel Waters, and had issue, Mary Ann, Joseph Howard, Washington, Rachel Howard and Isabella Waters.

Captain Brice Howard commanded a company of militia in 1776, with Joseph Burgess, First Lieutenant; John Norwood, Second Lieutenant; Thos. Cornelius Howard, Ensign. He married Ann Ridgely, of "White Wine and Claret;" her will of 1801 named, "My daughter, Anne Howard, and son, Brice Howard," to whom she left money for their education. (The former married Caleb Dorsey, of Columbia, the latter became a lawyer in Cumberland.) "All the residue of the estate to be divided amongst all my children, viz., Willliam Cornelius (named for both ancestors), Harriet, Margaret,

George, Thomas Worthington, Jeremiah Brice Howard and my two younger children, Anne and Brice Howard.   George Howard, executor, sold a portion of Captain Brice Howard's estate, near Glenelg, to Samuel Owings.

Jeremiah Brice Howard held the estate of Colonel John Hammond Riggs at Brookeville, married Mrs. Harriet Watkins (nee Burgess) and left Brice Worthington Howard (who holds the enlarged and valuable estate) and Mrs. Harriet Mathews, of Glenwood. Brice Worthington Howard married Kate Orendorf; their sons are Brice Worthington, Jr., William Howard, of the south, Artemas, Thomas and Robert; their daughters are Miss Evie, Mrs. Kate Henderson and Miss Nannie Howard.

EPHRAIM HOWARD,
OF JOSEPH AND MARGERY.

Ephraim Howard (of Joseph and Margery) deeded his inheritance of 500 acres of "Discovery" to his brother Henry, held "Howard's Passage" and part of "Athol."   "Howard's Passage" is just west of "Oakland Manor."   In his will of 1770 he granted to his son Joseph lands on the west side of the Patuxent; to Ephraim, "my land in Frederick County called 'Lakeland;' to Henry, my lands in Anne Arundel on the south side of the Patuxent; to daughter Sarah and daughter Martha, personal property; to Margaret Mackelfresh, if she lays no claim to her father's interest, an amount of money.

"Son Joseph executor; wife Martha Howard, the homestead during life.   Witnesses, Thomas Dorsey, of Henry, Edward Gaither, Jr., and Wm. Selman."

Mrs. Martha Howard, his widow, in 1792, referred to her son, John Mackelfresh, son Joseph Howard, Ephraim, Henry, granddaughter Martha Mackelfresh, daughter Martha Howard, daughter Sarah Riggs; son Joseph, executor.   Witnesses, Vachel Worthington and Samuel Brown

Joseph Howard, son of the above testators, in 1792, gave to brother Henry and Ephraim £5 each; to Henry all my lands on the northwest side of the main road leading from the bridge near where my mother, Mrs. Martha Howard, lives, formerly called Ephraim Howard's bridge, to the mill commonly called Dr. Joshua Warfield's mill, at Simpsonville.

"I give to my three sisters, Margaret Mackelfresh, Sarah Riggs and Martha Howard, during single lives, my dwelling and all lands adjoining on the southeast or lower side of the aforesaid road leading from the aforesaid bridge to the aforesaid mill, and at the expiration of their single life or natural life, then to my brother, Henry Howard. My sisters are to have all negroes, houses, cattle, stock, furniture, plate, money in hand, bonds, notes and books.

"My brother Henry and sister Martha, executors.   Mr. Pue, Charles A. Warfield and Brice Howard, witnesses.

Henry Howard (of Ephraim) left his home place to his wife, Mary, during life.   It adjoined Samuel Brown, near a branch of the Patuxent, near Richard Owings mill.   "I give to George Howard (of

Brice) all my lands on which Patrick Donnahoo lives, near Thomas Cross, on the contemplated new pike. I give to Richard Owings, Sr., all the rest of my estate for a debt due him and make him my executor. John Garrett, Samuel Owings (of Richard) and Nicholas Watkins, Jr., witnesses."

Ephraim Howard, Jr., removed to Frederick County near Liberty. He married Elizabeth Dorsey, daughter of Basil and Sarah (Worthington) Dorsey, of "Troy Hill." Her silver key-holder, with name inscribed, is still in possession of Mr. Albert Jones, formerly of Mount Airy. She inherited "lands bought of John (of Gideon) Howard," just east of Liberty, Frederick County. Her sisters, Elinor Sheridine and Achsah Sollers, had their portions adjoining.

Ephraim and Elizabeth Howard had issue—Dennis Howard, who held the homestead and a large estate.

The will of Mrs. Sarah Riggs named her nephew, Dennis Howard (of brother Ephraim). She was the widow of James Riggs (of John and Mary Davis).

OWINGS.

Richard Owings, brother of Samuel Owings, of Owings Mill, Baltimore County, sons of Richard and Rachel Owings, of Baltimore County, married Ruth Warfield, daughter of Dr. Joshua and Rachel (Howard) Warfield, and settled as a merchant at Simpsonville. The foundation of his old store may still be seen there. Their sons were Samuel, James, Thomas, Joshua, Basil and Major Henry Owings. Samuel Owings married Sarah Ann Hatherly; he and his brother James were executors of their father's estate. James bought "Wincopin Neck" at Guilford; Thomas Owings—Ann Maria, daughter of Lancelot and Mary Warfield of "Brandy" and had issue, the late Richard Owings, of Friendship, Anne Arundel County, and Mrs. Eastwood, whose descendants are in Missouri. Joshua Owings removed to Missouri; Basil Owings was a merchant at Lisbon, married Eleanor Griffith; issue, Edwin U., Basil, Albin, Ulysses, Mrs. Laura Jessup, James. Amelia—Henry Owings and William W. Owings. James—Ann M. Carr; Basil—Mattie Massey; Ulysses G. Owings— F. Norris, and is a merchant of West River; Albin Owings—M. Plummer and resides at Woodbine as general agent of B. & O. R. R. Edwin U. Owings—Achsah Bradford and had William T. Owings, of Baltimore; Edwin U.—Miss Hall; Florence—Samuel Waters and resides at Parkton; Clarence, merchant of Lisbon,—Miss Henderson; Mary E. Owings, of Lisbon, now Mrs. Bradford.

Major Henry Owings, successor to his father, built his commodious home upon the southern hill of Simpsonville and still further increased his father's large estate; he was one of the first commissioners of Howard. His first wife was Miss Gist, whose son was Dr. James Owings, of Parkersburg, West Virginia; their daughters are Mrs. Alverda Dorsey (whose only son is Upton Dorsey, of U. S. Army), the late Mrs. Myerly, who lived at the homestead, and Mrs. Sally Pennypacker, of West Virginia.

Major Owings married, second, Elizabeth, daughter of John and Sally (Hammond) Dorsey; their sons are John H. Owings, Samuel Owings, Richard Owings; their daughters were Rebecca, wife of George Gambrill, and Susan, wife of Hon. John Ridgely Clark, former State's attorney for Howard. His estate at Columbia, and the Worthington property, near Simpsonville, are now well managed by his daughters.

John Hammond Owings, long clerk of Howard County Court, was his own successor for three terms. The Democratic party was defeated in 1895, and A. C. Rhodes, was elected to the office of clerk. Upon his sudden death, soon after, Judge Jones reappointed Mr. Owings, who held the office afterward by election. He was assisted by his son. Both were ready always to explain intelligently and courteously the workings of the office, which, in system and execution, is a model worthy of record.

Mr. Owings took his wife from the same Dorsey house out of which came his mother. She was Sally, daughter of Hammond and Lucretia (Brown) Dorsey. His son married a daughter of Colonel Thomas Hunt, of Ellicott City and resides there.

Mr. John H. Owings' estate is "Hazelwood," east of "Oakland Manor." Samuel Owings, his brother, lives near him. He married Miss Sallie Wethered, of Howard.

Richard Owings resides near Simpsonville; he married Caroline daughter of Hon. John Watkins. These brothers are model farmers.

SETTLERS NEAR THE BRICK CHURCH.

The neighborhood of this church was and is another Dorsey range. The church stands upon "New Years' Gift," a tract granted to Edward Dorsey and to Charles Carroll, of Annapolis, by their friend, the Proprietary, as a New Years' gift. The whole tract was bought by Caleb Dorsey, of "Hockley," who transferred it to his son John. It embraced a large and very rich body of land in one of the best agricultural sections of the county to-day.

One of the descendants of this family was William Dorsey, an attorney of Annapolis, whom Governor Sharpe honored by a consultation; another was Colonel Richard Dorsey, whose troop of horse was with General Washington in the North.

"John Dorsey, son of Caleb," located on "New Years' Gift." He held the land upon which Christ Church stands. He was a member of its vestry and signed, "John Dorsey, son of Caleb." He bought lands in Frederick County (now Montgomery), at Triadelphia; he also held property in Frederick City. He married his cousin, Elizabeth, daughter of Joshua and Ann (Ridgely) Dorsey; issue, Caleb, John, Richard, Elinor, wife of Richard Stringer, Elizabeth Burgess and Achsah, wife of Dr. Ephraim Howard (of Henry). His will was dated 1765; Caleb was made executor and inherited the homestead and lands in Frederick County. All of the remaining estate was left to John and Richard, who removed to their inheritance upon the Westminster road. Caleb, at the time of his will, held lands near

Shafersville. He married, first, Sophia Dorsey, of "Patuxent John;" issue, Elizabeth Dorsey; second, Rebecca Hammond; issue, George, John, Richard, William, Larkin, Caleb, Mrs. Sarah Lawrence, wife of Captain Levin, Mrs. Nicholas Owings, Mrs. Achsah Gwinn and Rebecca Dorsey. His will of 1790 appointed "his brothers, John, Richard and William Hammond, trustees" to divide his estate. To Caleb, Jr., he left the homestead upon "Israel's Creek." His grandson, Caleb Gwinn, was remembered.

Caleb Dorsey, Jr., granted his inheritance in Frederick County to his brothers, Larkin and Richard Dorsey, and the rest of his estate to Achsah, Caleb, Rebecca, Edward and Ann Gwinn, children of Edward and Achsah Gwinn. "To sister Achsah, all my negroes; to brothers John and William, my horses; to sister Rebecca, my silver plate."

George Dorsey removed to West Virginia. A recent Parkersburg paper thus refers to him: "Mrs. Ann M. Dorsey, aged eighty-seven, is one of the six "Star members" of the Daughters of the Revolution;" her father, Mr. Mathiah, having been a soldier in the Revolution; her second husband was George W. Dorsey, who was a large landowner and slaveholder on the Kingwood Pike, near Morgantown. The Dorsey home was noted for its hospitality, especially to Methodist ministers. The aged lady hopes to spend her days with her son, J. W. Dorsey, of this city. Two of her sons reside here, one in Morgantown and one in Dayton, Ohio."

Larkin Dorsey (of Caleb) built "Waveland," the late home of Mrs. Reuben M. Dorsey; he married Miss McCurdy.

In his will of 1837 he named his wife Jane, and appointed her, with James McHenry Boyd, his executors. He set his negroes free; they numbered twenty-two. His farm was to be sold and proceeds divided among Larkin Lawrence, Hammond Dorsey, William Baker Dorsey, Larkin Dorsey, Richard Dorsey and niece Caroline Owings, each to receive $1,000. All of the remainder of his estate, including that in Pennsylvania, to go to his wife, Jane Dorsey.

William Dorsey, his brother, was an attorney-at-law in Annapolis during the French-Indian war. He was consulted by Governor Horatio Sharpe concerning the right of the province to draft slaves for the war. Mr. Dorsey replied that "no such power existed without the permission of the owners." He was a bachelor. His will of 1802 devised the homestead left him by his father to brother Richard, but if brother John desires it, he gave his permission for an exchange. "All my law books to my nephew, Caleb Lawrence; my Illinois lands to Captain Levin Lawrence; my land obtained from Robert Dorsey, adjoining Price's place and Benjamin Dorsey's, I grant to my three brothers. My brother Richard executor, and, with John and Larkin, inheritor of my personal estate.

"Peregrine Warfield, Elisha Brown and John Hammond, witnesses."

Richard Dorsey (of Caleb) inherited the property immediately at the old brick church but resided in Baltimore; he married Mrs.

Sherlock, daughter of Robert Gilmor.   His will named his wife, Anne, and children, Caleb, Richard, Anne, Edward and Mary.   "To my brother, William Watson, my saddle horse; to my mother, Mary Watson, all my interest in the estate where she lives."

John Dorsey (of Caleb) exchanged with his brother Richard and held the homestead, through the permission of William, the attorney. He married Sally Hammond, the daughter of Colonel Charles Hammond, a neighbor.   The will of Mrs. Sarah (Hammond) Dorsey named her son Hammond, William Baker, Mary Bailey, Rebecca, Richard (died on the Eastern Shore) and Elizabeth—Major Henry Owings.   William Baker Dorsey, executor.   He came into possession of his uncle Richard's farm; he was one of the early commissioners of Howard County; his wife was Miss Wood.   He left no heirs and willed his estate to his nephew, Larkin Dorsey.

Hammond Dorsey inherited the homestead adjoining, married Lucretia Brown, daughter of Elisha of "Brown's Purchase," near, Guilford.   Their heirs were Hammond, Larkin, Richard and Sallie, wife of John Hammond Owings.

Hammond Dorsey inherited the homestead and married a daughter of Captain Pendleton, of "Walnut Hill."   They have a son, Hammond, and a daughter, who, with her mother, resides at the homestead.

The estate of Larkin Dorsey, immediately at the Old Brick Church, has become the property of Mr. Seiling.

The Old Brick Church stands upon the site of the first church of Queen Caroline Parish, organized in 1728.   It was an offshoot of St. Ann's.   Before it could be established it was necessary to secure the consent of the entire parishioners then living upon that immense territory.   Benjamin Gaither undertook this work.   Mounting his horse, he rode from Annapolis to Clarksville, over the entire area between the two rivers, and succeeded in this object.   The first church stood until 1806, when it was replaced by the present building, now nearly a century old.   Two of its latest building committee were Dr. Lloyd T. Hammond and Samuel Brown, Jr., long Register of Wills at Annapolis.

The following deed upon record at Annapolis, covers the ground upon which the church stands.   It was made in 1738, and reads: "To all Persons to whom these presents shall come greeting—know ye that we, Caleb Dorsey and John Dorsey, gentlemen, as well for and in consideration of the great love and affection we do bear to the Protestant religion, give and grant to Rev. James Macgill, Rector of Queen Caroline Parish; Richard Davis, Abel Brown, John Dorsey, Richard Shipley, Adam Barnes and Peter Barnes, present vestrymen, and to their successors, for the use of said Parish all those two acres called, 'New Year's Gift' on which the church now stands, as surveyed by Mr. Henry Ridgely, late surveyor of Anne Arundel, signed and sealed by Caleb Dorsey in the presence of Henry Ridgely, Edward Gaither and Richard Dorsey, and by John Dorsey in the presence of Henry Ridgely, Alexander Warfield (of John)."

The above granters were Caleb Dorsey, of "Hockley," surveyor of the tract and father of John Dorsey, who then held it, but could not give a deed without his father's signature. "Queen Caroline church has a handsome communion service dating from 1748, and a Bible presented by Commissary Henderson, who was sent to report on the church." (Old Brick Churches.)

The church has been recently painted and a memorial window has been added. The graves of Rev. Marbury Ogle and his wife, late of the church, are chief among the few buried in the old churchyard. This parish extended back ten miles or more west of the Landing at the Relay. Its territory was divided into Hundreds—each of which had its Captain, to look after the tobacco tax upon which the church was supported.

Some of its pew-holders in 1736, under Rev. James Macgill, were: Pew No. 1, Captain Henry Ridgely and Joshua Dorsey; No. 2, Basil Dorsey and three brothers, Henry Dorsey, and John Warfield; No. 3, John Dorsey, son of Edward; No. 4, Captain Nath Hammond, Benjamin Warfield and Alexander Warfield; No. 5, Edward Dorsey and William Ridgely; No. 8, Orlando Griffith, Captain John Howard and Nicholas Dorsey; No. 12, Nicholas Gassaway and Henry Howard; No. 17, Captain John Dorsey; No. 19, Alexander Warfield (of Richard); No. 20, Benjamin Lawrence, Lancelot Todd and his brother, John Todd; No. 23, Edward White, Joseph White, Edward, Philip and Alexander Warfield, Jr.; No. 24, Edward Dorsey, Jr., Reynolds Mackubin and Neal Clark; No. 25, John Elder, Sr., and John Elder, Jr.; No. 26, Joseph Hall and John Riggs; No. 29, Michael Dorsey.

West of the church looms up "Athol," the English castle of Rev. James Macgill, its rector. It was built in 1746, by English workmen transported by him. Its commanding site overlooks the old church in which he spent his life. He handed down from its threshold many fair daughters to be the comforters and helpmates to his parishioners. "Athol's" gray stone walls, high and massive chimneys and pitched roof are still well preserved, and though it has passed from the family, the old church has been remembered by a daughter of its rector. A part of the "Athol" estate is still held by descendants who have built upon it recently. Mr. and Mrs. Geaslin hold the old homestead.

OAKLAND MANOR.

North of "Athol," upon the Ellicott City and Laurel highway, was one of Hon. John Dorsey's surveys—"Dorsey's Adventure."

It was willed by him to his grandson, Edward Dorsey, son of his "deceased son, Edward Dorsey." Around it, later, arose "Oakland Manor" and Oakland Mills. There lived Luther Martin, Attorney-General of Maryland, when he broke to pieces John Randolph's charges against Judge Samuel Chase, another landholder in Howard. Following him came Robert Oliver, the English hunter, to build his English stables for his hunters, upon his own forest range of 2300 acres. From here, still later, Colonel Charles Sterrett Ridgely commanded his troopers as the bodyguard of General Lafayette, in 1825. Here was born Lieutenant Randolph Ridgely, a hero of the Mexican War.

From here George R. Gaither drove his four iron-grays to St. John's Church each Sunday. From here Colonel George R. Gaither organized his Howard Dragoons, successors to Colonel Charles Carroll's Dragoons, of earlier days. Colonel Carroll's reviews of Gaither's Troopers ended in a royal treat of Southdown mutton and its attendants. All this was after Howard had risen to the dignity of her county rights and before war had come to check her proud career.

The sixty young men of Gaither's Troopers, all relations and friends, with a future that seemed bright, soon were ordered to take up arms in defence of the State. They obeyed; with their Captain they crossed over the river, some to return not, some to go elsewhere, but few to remain. The Captain himself has passed on before.

The officers of Colonel Gaither's Troopers upon organization were:

Captain, George R. Gaither, of Oakland; First Lieutenant, Dr. Milton W. Warfield, of Lisbon; Second Lieutenant, John R. Clark, of Columbia; Orderly Sergeant, Benjamin D. Cooke, of the Brick Church neighborhood. The latter later took up the work of Dr. Warfield and was the drill-master for a long time.

The recent death of Dr. Warfield, of Lisbon, leaves Benjamin D. Cooke, of Colonial Beach, Virginia, the only surviving officer of that historic organization.

The author, as a high private of "Gaither's Troopers," here places a wreath of immortelles over the graves of his departed comrades.

"DORSEY'S ADVENTURE,"
HOME OF CAPTAIN EDWARD DORSEY.

This grandson of Hon. John Dorsey inherited two tracts, "Dorsey's Adventure" at Oakland and "Whitaker's Purchase," now the Stockett place. He was a witness to his brother's will, in 1761. He was not a surveyor and made no increase in his estate. His wife was Sarah Todd, daughter of Lancelot and Elizabeth Rockhold, descendant of James Todd, of the original site of Baltimore. Their son, Edward Dorsey, Jr., removed to the neighborhood of Hood's Mill and will there be recorded. Colonel John Dorsey held the homestead and became the Baltimore merchant; Lancelot Dorsey, Ely, Charles and Major Richard, of the Baltimore Artillery Company of the Revolution, were other sons. Their daughters were Elizabeth, first wife of Hon. Henry Griffith; Ruth, wife of Vachel Dorsey, near Hoods Mill; Sarah Gist, wife of Thomas Gassaway.

Captain Edward Dorsey, by exchange with his son Edward, of Hoods Mill, got possession of several adjoining tracts "Ely's Lot" and "Dorsey's Thickett," which he left to his sons, Charles, Ely, Lancelot and Richard, none of whom settled upon them. These were held by their brothers, Colonel John and Edward and their brother-in-law, Vachel Dorsey

Colonel John Dorsey and his brother Ely were the executors of their father's estate. They sold a portion of "Dorsey's Adventure" to Benjamin Howard, in 1768. Colonel John held a portion of "Dorsey's Adventure." He mortgaged it to James Russel, of London. In 1785 he sold it to Luther Martin, Attorney-General of Maryland.

As "Luther Martin's Elk Ridge farm" it embraced "Dorsey's Adventure," "Dorsey's Inheritance," "Good for Little," "Chew's Vineyard" and "Adam the First," covering 1100 acres.

In 1827, through a case in Chancery, in which Luther Martin and the Bank of Baltimore were defendants, it was sold by Judge Nicholas Brewer to Robert Oliver, an Englishman, who built Oakland Mills, (now a wreck by fire.) He increased the estate to 2300 acres and later sold it to Colonel Charles Sterrett Ridgely. It descended through Mrs. Elizabeth (Hollingsworth) Ridgely, to her son, John Sterrett Ridgely.

In 1838, Thomas Oliver, heir of Robert, who still held a claim, sold it to George R. Gaither. It then embraced "Dorsey's Search," "Dorsey's Search Resurveyed," "Felicity," "Talbott's Resolution Manor" and Oakland Mill, adjoining "Howard's Passage" and "Joseph's Gift." It bordered upon lands conveyed by Judge Richard Ridgely to James Sterrett, running to lands conveyed by Eleanor Dall to Robert Oliver, in 1825; adjoined lands conveyed by Nicholas Worthington (of John) to Charles Sterrett Ridgely, Richard Gittings and others and by them conveyed to Robert Oliver.

In 1785 Colonel John Dorsey, through speculation, became involved and sold his lands near Hood's Mill to his brother-in-law, Vachel Dorsey.

He sold to Robert Dorsey all the lands he held in common with John Sterrett, William Goodwin, Samuel Chase and others upon the Gunpowder. He sold to Colonel Thomas Dorsey and Samuel Chase another large tract bought for speculation. His interest in the Nottingham Iron Works led to a case in Chancery, in which the State brought suit. These investments caused the complete failure of himself and Colonel Thomas Dorsey.

Colonel John Dorsey was one of the first commissioners of Baltimore City. He was upon the reception committee to receive General Washington. He was a member of St. Paul's vestry and married Mary, daughter of Colonel William Hammond, the Baltimore merchant. Their daughter Elizabeth became the wife of Edward Dorsey, of "Belmont." Judge Walter Dorsey (of Colonel John) was elected Judge of the Court of Baltimore. His wife was Hopewell Hebb; issue, Anna Marie—Frank, son of Dr. John Beale Davidge and his wife, Miss Stuart, of the Fisgall estate of Scotland.

The issue of Frank and Anna Marie Davidge were William, Walter, Joanna, Robert Cunningham and Frank Davidge. William —Virginia Mason, of Virginia, whose son William married a daughter of Bishop Potter. Walter Davidge, the celebrated lawyer of Washington—Anna Washington. These were the descendants of John Davidge and Honor (Howard) Warfield, of "Warfield's Contrivance."

Judge Clement Dorsey (of Colonel John and Mary) married Miss Smith, of St. Marys.

Their daughter, Eliza became the wife of her cousin, Richard Brooke Dorsey, of Montgomery County, from whom descends Mrs. Vernon Dorsey, of the Congressional Library.

William Hammond Dorsey (of Colonel John and Mary) removed to Montgomery County; married a daughter of Richard Brooke, of Olney and was one of the first trustees of Brookeville Academy, in 1815. His heirs were William J., Richard Brooke, James M., Robert E., and Marie Dorsey, all holding portions of "Addition to Brooke Grove."

Richard Brooke Dorsey—Anne Eliza, daughter of Judge Clement Dorsey. Their son, Edward Bates Dorsey, was a Civil Engineer, living in Peru, Chili, California, Mexico, Nevada, British Columbia, South Africa, finally dying recently in London, having accumulated and lost several fortunes.

His brothers are Richard Brooke Dorsey and Vernon Dorsey, who married his cousin.

Mr. and Mrs. Dorsey have been long connected with the genealogical department of the Congressional Library. Their daughter, Miss Anna Vernon Dorsey, has made a mark in her imitation of Southern dialects.

Dr. Robert Edward Dorsey—Sarah Ann Duvall; their heirs are Dr. Grafton Duvall Dorsey and Mrs. George R. Coale.

Miss Cornelia Dorsey, of Baltimore, is a sister of Richard Brooke Dorsey.

Lancelot Dorsey (of Edward and Sarah Todd) sold "Lancelot's Lot" in Baltimore County to his brother Edward and lived for a time upon his inheritance, "Altogether," near Clarksville.

He married Deborah Ridgely, daughter of William and Elizabeth (Duvall) Ridgely, of "White Wine and Claret." They joined in selling their homestead to Thomas Dorsey. He left no will, but Dennis Dorsey, by case in the Court of Appeals brought suit against the estate. The heirs were Dathan Dorsey and Mrs. Elder. Dathan lived near Glenelg.

Charles Dorsey (of Edward and Sarah) sold his inheritance in Baltimore County to his brother Edward and removed to Frederick County. His brother-in-law, Thomas Gassaway, was appointed trustee of his estate.

Captain Richard Dorsey (of Edward and Sarah Todd) organized the Baltimore Artillery Company during the Revolution. His name appears frequently in the archives. With Captain Brown's Company he was in the North and later both were united to Colonel

Beales' Battalion in Virginia. His record has been mixed up with that of his namesake, Colonel Richard Dorsey, of "Happy Retreat." Captain Richard Dorsey remained in Virginia during the war and died there. In 1785 he deeded his land, house and lot in Elk Ridge, all land due him from the United States and State of Maryland, as Captain in the Maryland Line, to Thomas Gassaway, his brother-in-law. In 1795 he was Major Richard Dorsey and sold his lands near Fort Cumberland to George Golder. He was then living in Anne Arundel, but removed to Virginia later and married Mrs. Pierpoint (nee Hawkins), who bore him a son, Edward, and a daughter, Sarah, named for his father and mother. Edward died a bachelor and lies buried at Alexandria, by the side of his sister, who became Mrs. John Suter and left Mrs. Alexander Myers, of Havre de Grace; Mrs. Cornelius Jacobs, of Alexandria, Virginia; Mrs. Arthur Yeatman, of Warrenton, Virginia, and Mrs. George Emmerson, of Alexandria, Virginia.

It is claimed by his descendants that he bore the arms of the D'Arcys, of Kiltula House and of "Clifton Castle," Ireland—the same given by Burke—motto *"Un Dieu, Un Roi."*

The descendants of Ely Dorsey will be noticed at Poplar Spring.

"LONG REACH,"
HOME OF JOHN DORSEY, OF COLONEL EDWARD.

Adjoining "Patuxent John Dorsey" on the east, and by many of his descendants taken for him, was seated as early as 1708 another large surveyor.

He invariably signed himself "John Dorsey (of Edward)"—son of Colonel Edward, the surveyor of "Long Reach." At sixteen years of age he married Honor Elder, heir of John Elder, a large landholder upon the Patapsco, near Sykesville. Upon "Long Reach" was also located John Dorsey's brothers, Benjamin and Nicholas. A later survey of this tract is now known as "Chew's Resolution." It extended to and joined Patuxent, John Dorsey's estate. These two John Dorsey's even then had overreached Hon. John's surveys. Their combined tracts covered about one-third of Howard County. Nor did they stop in Howard, but reached out to Frederick, Carroll and Baltimore Counties, and left descendants in almost every family in the State.

"John Dorsey (of Edward)" married in 1708. He was a member of Queen Caroline Parish, in 1728, and in its vestry. He took up "Dorsey's Grove" in Upper Howard, 1080 acres, extending from Glenelg to Glenwood. By deed of partition, in 1735, this was divided among his four daughters, Hannah Barnes, Sarah Howard, Ruth Lawrence and Susannah Lawrence. With his brother Joshua, he took up "Brothers Partnership," in the neighborhood of Dayton. Upon this he put his son Michael.

His adjoining tract, "Good Range," was also given to Michael, and to Michael's son, John, was granted Thomas Brown's first survey in that neighborhood—"Brown's Chance and Captain Dorsey's "Friendship."

Captain John Dorsey (of Michael) married Ann Dorsey (of Captain Philemon) and had Vachel, Philemon, Michael and Ruth, who became the wife of Colonel Gassaway Watkins; Vachel (of Captain John) inherited his mother's survey upon the Patuxent, south of Florence. He married Ann Poole and left Harriet Dorsey, wife of Basil Crapster.

Mrs. Ann (Poole) Dorsey became the wife of Colonel Lyde Griffith. By a case in Chancery, entitled, Crapster vs. Griffith, the property descended to Harriet Crapster and thence to her sons, John and William. It is now the property of Joshua N. Warfield.

The homestead of Captain John Dorsey was left to his son Philemon, whose interest was bought by Colonel Gassaway Watkins and Ruth, his wife. By them it was named Walnut Grove.

Captain John Dorsey's daughter Catherine became the wife of Charles Warfield (of John), of Fredericksburg.

Michael Dorsey's wife, Ruth Todd, inherited from Lancelot Todd, her father, an adjoining tract, "Altogether." There was located Lancelot Dorsey, of Michael and Ruth, the heir of his grandfather, Lancelot Todd. He was sheriff, and like many other sheriffs, his estate was sold at Sheriff's Sale to his son, Darius Dorsey, whose mother was Sarah Warfield (of Philip), his neighbor.

Michael Dorsey, Jr., married the rich widow of three husbands, Honor Howard, and lived upon her estate, at Elioak. His record will be found in the Dorsey's of Elioak.

Michael and Ruth (Todd) Dorsey had daughters enough to occupy a whole pew in the parish church. They were Elizabeth, wife of Capt. Joseph Burgess; Sarah, wife of Richard Berry; Ruth, wife of Ely Dorsey (of Edward and Sarah Todd), her cousin; Honor Elder, Ann Elder and Lydia Talbott.

The will of "John Dorsey (of Edward)" in 1764, shows the advantage of namesakes. He especially remembered John Dorsey (of Michael), John Barnes (of Adam), John Elder (of Honor), John Lawrence (of Levin), John Howard (of Henry) and John Dorsey (of Nathan). He also honored his wife's namesakes, Honor Elder (of Michael), Honor Warfield, wife of Rezin, Honor Elder and Sarah Berry, all receiving negroes and money. Two of his daughters were twice married—Ruth Lawrence became Mrs. Tumey and Jemima, widow of Joseph Hobbs, became Mrs. Charles Elder.

Three of his sons, Vachel, Nathan and Edward were located upon his wife's inheritance and his own investments along the Patapsco. Vachel and Edward rivalled him in their continued surveys. Edward, who has been entirely lost sight of by his descendants, or at least mistaken for another, was the most noted man of all. He will be found at St. James Church.

NICHOLAS DORSEY OF "LONG REACH."

This son of Colonel Edward married Francis Hughes (of Thomas) and named his oldest son Thomas Dorsey, who was a partner of Benjamin Lawrence, of "Delaware Bottom." Benjamin Dorsey inherited the homestead and Edward the personal estate. His namesake, Nicholas, removed to an extensive survey, then in Baltimore County, but now in Carroll. He there was placed upon the Committee of Observation for that outpost, and when the war came, he was advanced from Ensign in Captain Godman's Regulars to Lieutenant in the Fourth Regiment of the Continental Army, which he held from April, 1777, to November, 1778. He was promoted to Colonel. He married Sarah Griffith, oldest daughter of Orlando and Katherine Howard.

Colonel Nicholas and Sarah (Griffith) Dorsey, of Eldersburg, left Mrs. Rachel Lindsey, Mrs. Lydia Dorsey, Mrs. Catherine Wood, Mrs. Achsah Warfield, Mrs. Lucretia Welsh, and Mrs. Frances Chapman, afterward Mrs. Elie Warfield. Their sons were, Nicholas—Ruth Todd; Charles G.—Catherine Welsh; Orlando Griffith Dorsey, heir of the homestead—second, Mary Gaither, daughter of Henry and Martha Ridgely. Their daughter, Mary Dorsey, rode from Eldersburg to Kentucky on horseback, to accompany her brother Beale, who went west for his health. There she met John Carr, of Jefferson County, Kentucky, and became his wife. In 1817 she joined her husband, brothers and sisters in the following deed: "To Nicholas Dorsey for $5,718, all the tracts in Baltimore County, on which Orlando G. Dorsey resided, known as 'Long Trusted Resurveyed' and 'Wilson's Meadows.'"

The signatures were Luke T. Dorsey, Beale Dorsey, Jonathan Norris, Deborah Dorsey, Henry C. Dorsey, John H. Dorsey and Mary Carr.

John and Mary Dorsey Carr had issue, Mary—John Fenley, now represented by Mr. William C. Fenley, of Crescent Hill, Kentucky.

Eliza Jane—Henry Hamilton Honore, now represented by Mrs. Potter Palmer and the wife of General Frederick Grant, U. S. A.

Laura Carr—Benjamin Lockwood Honore; Martha Carr—James T. Edmunds; Ruth Carr—Winchester Hall, a Dorsey and Lawrence descendant.

Mrs. Potter Palmer takes an interest in her Colonial ancestors. She visited Annapolis that she might see the original homes of them.

She saw the former site of Old Hockley and the city estate of Colonel Edward Dorsey in Annapolis; she walked through the corridors of "White Hall," which stands upon "Greenberry Forrest." She crossed over South River to the home of Colonel William Burgess, where his memorial tablet still reveals his masterly career; she visited Londontown and passed through its magnificent stone building, still silently pointing to its aged and courtly days. Though recently a visitor to the native homes of many of our founders, she comes back with renewed interest to study and honor the lives of those who were foremost in giving us our inheritance.

Nicholas Dorsey (of Colonel Nicholas) married Ruth Todd, granddaughter of Hon. Henry Griffith. Their daughter Elizabeth, as Mrs. Bayley, married John Hawkins. Issue, Ruth Dorsey Hawkins—Dr. Samuel B. Martin, an "Old Defender" of Baltimore. Frances McC. Hawkins—Rev. George Schaffer; John H. W. Hawkins, William Hawkins, Nicholas Dorsey Hawkins and Ann Grover Hawkins—all of Baltimore.

Charles G. Dorsey (of Colonel Nicholas)—Catherine Welsh. Issue, Edward Stanhope, Charles Nimrod Warren Dorsey, John Hammond, Sarah—Robert Crump; Ann Welsh, Lucretia Armstrong and Lydia Watkins.

COLUMBIA.

An expanded view here reveals a charming country. Off to the northwest is the Hammond Manor, bordering on Doughoregan.

Upon this Colonel Rezin Hammond of the Revolution placed his great nephews, Denton and Matthias, as recorded in Anne Arundel. Denton's estate adjoined "Dorsey's Search," the dividing lines of which were settled by the Court of Chancery.

Adjoining them was seated Dr. Lloyd T. Hammond (of Philip), both descending to Judge Edward Hammond and Colonel Mathias Hammond, whose families have been united by the marriage of Richard Hammond (of Judge Edward) to Grace, the only daughter of Colonel Matthias.

"Dorsey's Hall," home of Patuxent John Dorsey, is at Columbia. Adjoining it on the west is the residence of Governor Ligon—now held by his son. "Dorsey's Hall" is a splendid relic of the early settlement of Howard. It is a large brick house, now modernized by its present owner, Mr. Reuben Dorsey Rogers.

Columbia is the meeting point of roads leading from Annapolis, Laurel and Sandy Spring to Ellicott City.

PATUXENT JOHN DORSEY OF "DORSEY'S SEARCH."

This pioneer settler of Howard signed his name "John Dorsey, Jr." His wife and Dr. Joshua Warfield, the writer of his will, recorded him "Captain John Dorsey." His neighbors called him "Patuxent John Dorsey," because his estate was on both sides of the north branch of the Patuxent, which up to 1725 was the division of Baltimore and Anne Arundel Counties. Patuxent John Dorsey's substantial manor house, now held by Mr. R. Dorsey Rogers, is immediately at Columbia, Post-office. Patuxent John Dorsey's father was Edward Dorsey, oldest son of Hon. John and Pleasance Ely. In 1694 he was a mariner upon board of "The Good Hope," under the command of Captain Richard Hill. His wife Ruth was unknown, but she may have been the traditional "Lady Hill"— daughter of Captain Richard. Edward and Ruth had only two sons.

At the time of his father's will, in 1714, he was "Edward Dorsey deceased." She became, first, Mrs. John Greeniff and then the wife of John Howard, grandson of Matthew Howard, of the Severn. Her will of 1747 named "her two sons, John and Edward Dorsey, her executors." She was then residing in Queen Caroline Parish, perhaps with one of them. Patuxent John Dorsey was a progressive man. Holding the extensive tract of "Dorsey's Search," he enlarged it and then made the first surveys in the neighborhood of New Market and upon the Linganore. These were "Dorsey's Search," "Good Luck," Mt. Peasant," "Pleasant Valley." A view of him is in the following letter from a Baltimore merchant to his uncle in London.

"Mr. John Dorsey desires that I recommend your payment of his sons draft for £50. He has six hogsheads of tobacco in Captain Spencer's ship, and you will be right to pay it, as great umbrage to that family would be given, otherwise. Ely Dorsey desired that I would write that Robert Izard's draft for £10 and Benjamin Brown's for £9 be paid, which pray do. Ely and the old man are very serviceable to you, and you must be very careful to oblige them. In short, they are very powerful among the people." (Old Brick Churches.)

The above letter shows that Ely Dorsey, though not mentioned in Patuxent John Dorsey's will, was the son of the "old man," and not, as some of his descendants claim, the son of Edward Dorsey, a brother. Captain John Dorsey held a pew in the parish church.

His will of 1761, reads: "I, John Dorsey, Jr., bequeath unto my son Samuel, 450 acres of "Dorsey's Search," "Sam's Folly," and "Pleasant Valley." I give to my son, Benjamin, my tract called "Long Reach" and also, lands adjoining "Dorsey's Search;" also, a part of "Partnership," laid out by Plummer. To my son, John Dorsey, "Good Luck." To William Hall, of Elk Ridge, all the residue of "Partnership." To my daughter, Rachel Hall, ten pounds current money in full for her part. I give to my daughter, Lucy Dorsey, as much land as will make her part equal to my sons, Samuel and Benjamin. I have already given to my married daughters their portions. All the residue of my estate to be divided equally except Rachel Hall.

"My loving wife, Elizabeth Dorsey, and my son, Basil, to administer.   John Dorsey, Jr."

Basil Dorsey was then upon "Dorsey's Search," in Frederick County, and Ely Dorsey upon "Dorsey's Search Enlarged," in Anne Arundel, near Elioak; Lucy and Rachel's inheritance were near St. James Church. "Good Luck" was upon the Linganore, near New Windsor.

The will of Mrs. Elizabeth Dorsey, in 1775, named her children, Ely Dorsey, Basil, Benjamin, John, Samuel, Ruth Talbott, Rachel Ridgely, Deborah Dorsey and Lucy Dorsey.

Witnesses: Samuel Brown, Jr., Sarah Brown and Rachel Todd. Mrs. Elizabeth Dorsey has also been classed unknown. She was in the neighborhood of Browns, and her witnesses were Browns. She was likely a sister of Benjamin Brown, mentioned in Ely Dorsey's letter—heir of Samuel Brown, the Naval Officer, of Annapolis.

ELY DORSEY OF "DORSEY'S SEARCH."

St. Paul's record shows the marriage of Ely Dorsey to Mary Crockett, of Baltimore. She was the daughter of Colonel John Crockett, merchant. His widow, Mary (Coale) Crockett, married John Hopkins (of Gerard and Margaret Johns). Ely and Mary (Crockett) Dorsey had one son, John Crockett Dorsey. He was located upon a portion of "Dorsey's Search." It was mortgaged to Joseph Howard, but was redeemed by Ely Dorsey, who in his will left it to be sold for the children of his daughters, Mrs. Judge Richard Ridgely and Mrs. Eleanor Dorsey, wife of Captain Daniel. John Crockett Dorsey removed to his father's surveys in Frederick County. His wife, Elizabeth Robinson, held a tract—"Sandy Spring." Their heirs were Otho, Ely, Amos, Edward and Mary.

Ely Dorsey, in the interest of his second wife, Deborah Dorsey, surviving sister of Captain Edward Dorsey, of Annapolis, entered a case in Chancery against Caleb Dorsey, of Belmont, late partner of Edward, in the iron forges of Elk Ridge. The case had not been settled at the time of her will. His will of 1794, reads:

"To my grandson, Caleb Dorsey, my dwelling and all lands adjoining, consisting of sundry tracts, containing about 700 acres, together with all the personal property that did belong to his father, Caleb Dorsey, deceased. I give to my executors for the purpose of selling the tract called 'Dorsey's Search,' whereon my father lived, containing by patent about 479 acres, the same to be sold at public vendue to the highest bidder and the money to be divided between the children of my two daughters, Elizabeth and Eleanor. To my wife Deborah, one-third of my personal property and her thirds in my dwelling plantation.

"To Eli Dorsey, son of John Crockett Dorsey, and Eli Dorsey, son of Eli Dorsey, £100 each. The residue of my estate to be divided as follows: One-fourth to my son, Amos Dorsey; one-fourth to my grandson, Caleb Dorsey, and the remaining two-fourths to the children of my two daughters, Elizabeth Ridgely and Eleanor Dorsey. Executors—my wife Deborah, my son Amos and my son-in-law, Daniel Dorsey."

A second codicil announces the death of his son Amos; divides his interest among his four children; revokes the gift of personal property to his grandson Caleb, and makes his wife sole administratrix.

Her will claimed a large sum from the estate of Caleb Dorsey, the iron merchant, which, when recovered, she willed to her grandchildren. As the lands held by her grandson Caleb were in dispute, she granted him others.

The old homestead of Ely Dorsey, which stood upon the present estate of Napoleon Dorsey, was a brick-nogged frame with hipped roof, brick ends and high ceilings. It was upon the road leading from Elioak to Simpsonville.

Caleb (of Ely) married Dinah Warfield, daughter of Dr. Joshua Warfield, of Simpsonville. She inherited, also, 500 acres of "Second Discovery" from her uncle, Vachel Howard; their only son inherited the homestead of Ely Dorsey. His wife was Mary Gassaway. Issue, Evoline, Deborah, Lydia Ridgely and Eliza Dorsey. His widow Mary, married again her cousin, Grandison Catlett, and had one daughter, Mary, who became Mrs. Mary Porter. At an advanced age she is still living. Evoline Dorsey—first, William Prince, of Kentucky; issue, one daughter Cyeanne; second, Amos Dorsey (of Amos); issue, Napoleon, Judge Pulaski, of the Orphans' Court of Howard; Harrison, Anne, Eliza Simpson, Ellen Worthington, Laura, wife of Hammond Carr, and Kate Dorsey.

Napoleon Dorsey is upon the home tract of Ely Dorsey.

Judge Pulaski and brother Harrison reside with their sister, Mrs. Simpson. Both were members of Gaither's Howard Dragoons and with him joined the Confederate Army. Judge Dorsey is now Judge of the Orphans' Court of Howard.

Deborah Lydia Ridgely Dorsey—Dr. Charles Grey Edwards, of Loudoun County, Virginia, second cousin of Benjamin Edwards, who married Margaret Beall. Her inheritance, near Carroll's Manor, was sold to Lloyd Jones; Eliza (of Caleb and Mary)—John Gassawayr. Issue, John Hanson—Kate Armstrong; Nicholas, who died on his return from California; Louisa—George W. Peter, son of Major George Peter, U. S. A., and a member of Congress from Montgomery County.

Jane Gassaway—Alexander Peter; Laura—George Bradley; William—Mary Farrow, half-sister of Bishop Cummins.

Amos Dorsey (of Ely)—Mary Dorsey (of Nicholas and Elizabeth [Worthington] Dorsey). Issue, Amos, Mrs. Dr. Charles Carnan Ridgely, Mrs. Samuel Norwood Ridgely and Mrs. Dr. Charles Griffith Worthington.

"Ely Dorsey of Ely" was Captain in the Revolution and afterward resided at "Fruitland," near Unionville, Frederick County. He married Sarah Worthington, daughter of John—issue, as named in the will of 1821—John Worthington Dorsey, surgeon U. S. N. with Decatur during the Tripolitan War. He brought home the first tomatoes seen in this country; they were then used as mantle ornaments. He married Deborah Howard (of Joshua and Rebecca Owings), granddaughter of Henry and Sarah (Dorsey) Howard. Their residence was in Liberty, and their daughter, Matilda Dorsey, married Dr. Richard Dorsey. Both of their portraits are now in possession of Mr. Albert Jones.

Mary (of Captain Ely)—Sabritt Sollers; Elizabeth—Ignatius Waters; Anne—Otho Sprigg; Julia Anne—Richard Johnson (of Roger). Issue, Richard Dorsey Johnson—Nannie Simms, whose daughter Marion—Dr. Duvall.

Susan (of Captain Ely)—Joshua Howard. Issue, Sallie Rebecca, Lydia Moore, Deborah Ridgely, and Dr. Joshua Howard, who died, aged twenty-five years, Ely Dorsey, Jr.—Sarah Johnson.

Thomas Worthington Dorsey (of Captain Ely) had a son, Thomas Worthington Dorsey, Jr.

Eli Dorsey, the son of Thomas Worthington Dorsey, was born the 9th of January, 1826, and died the 8th day of November, 1877. He married Miss Nancy J. Gates; they had four children, Elizabeth Ann, born the 23d day of June, 1855; died July the 6th, 1897; Richard Worthington, born the 20th day of December, 1856; Daniel Howard Dorsey was born the 28th day of January, 1859; Walter Eli Dorsey was born the 30th day of October, 1864.

Richard Worthington Dorsey married Miss Emma Jane Campbell; they had no children.

Daniel Howard Dorsey married Miss Martha E. Umbarger; they had four children, Leroy H., born January 19th, 1887; James W., born July 17th, 1890; Elizabeth M., born August 7th, 1892; Maudie T., born August 30, 1896.

Walter Eli Dorsey married Miss Rosa M. Turley; they had one son, William, born October 12th, 1893.

Captain Ely Dorsey married again Araminta Cumming, sister of Mary Cumming, wife of his neighbor, John Dorsey, of "Good Luck."

In her will of 1823 she named her nephews, Samuel Thomas Dorsey and William Alexander Dorsey, sons of Basil Dorsey (of John), of "Good Luck," and grants them her inherited tracts, viz., "Howard's Chance" at Clarksville, "Mt. Gilboa," "Barnes' Luck," "Creagh's Enlargement," all resurveyed into "Cummings Farm," excepting the present graveyard, which is to be walled in with stone and never to be sold. To Clagett Warfield Dorsey and Basil Dorsey, sons of my nephew, Basil Dorsey (deceased), "Preston's March," commonly called Sugar lands in Montgomery County; To niece Mary Dorsey, $1,000; To nephew John Dorsey, $1,000; To step-daughter Anne Worthington Sprigg, silver spoons, marked A. C., (Araminta Cummings). To my step-daughter Julian Johnson, a gold locket; To granddaughter Elizabeth Ridgely Howard, $200; To grandson Joshua Howard, $200; To Margaret Clagett Hammond, daughter of George, $300; To Lucy Dorsey and Mariah Dorsey daughters of William Dorsey, (deceased) $300 each; To Harriet, widow of Basil Dorsey, my four-wheeled carriage; To granddaughter Sally Rebecca Howard, my bureau; To William Hammond (of George) $100; To the Methodist Preachers, $100; The remainder to Samuel Thomas Dorsey and Mary Dorsey. Mrs. Araminta Dorsey was the daughter of William Cummings, Sr., and Margaret Thomas.

From "Dorsey Hall" went out to "Dorsey's Search," in Frederick County, Judge Basil Dorsey, of the Frederick County Court and a member of its "Committee of Observation." By a daughter of John Crockett, merchant, of Baltimore, he had Evan Dorsey, whose wife was Susannah Lawrence. Evan Dorsey, Jr., married Julian Lawrence. They were daughters of John Lawrence, Sr., and John Lawrence, Jr., of Linganore.

Basil Dorsey, Jr.—Harriet Harris, daughter of Rachel Lawrence, widow of Captain Philemon Dorsey and wife of Nathan Harris; Cordelia Dorsey was the wife of William Downey, son of Captain John Downey, of Captain Nelson's Riflemen, of Philip Haas' Battalion in Canada, and was in Colonel Smith's Battalion on the frontier. Still later, Captain Downey was under "Light Horse" Harry Lee in the "Whiskey Rebellion." He cut down the pole erected by the rebels. His father was William Downey, the Scotch immigrant, and his mother was Ruhama Stocksdale, of Lancaster, Pennsylvania. Mrs. Cordelia Downey held 500 acres of woodland near Monrovia. When the Baltimore and Ohio Railroad was under construction, timber along the line had advanced so high the company could not buy. Mrs. Downey offered her tract to complete the road. The officers of the company tendered her a memorial cup—an acorn, on which was engraved, "Tall oaks from little acorns grow." The first engine, "the acorn," was succeeded by the "tall oak," the mammoth engine.

The late Mr. William Downey, of New Market, and his son, Dr. Jessie Downey, former Fish Commissioner, hold much of Mrs. Cordelia Downey's estate. Mr. William Downey's wife was Margaret Jane Wright, of Jesse. Their daughter is Mrs. Dr. Hopkins.

Harriet Downey, sister of William, became Mrs. Francis Sappington Jones, descendant through Abraham and Charity Stansberry, of Daniel Jones, who was the son of Deacon John Jones (of Piney Creek Church) and Hannah Crapster, of Sweden, progenitress of Basil Crapster (of Abraham.)

Albert Jones, former banker of Mt. Airy, John Dorsey Jones, William Downey Jones, Charles, Edward and Emma Jones are their heirs.

Upton Dorsey (of Evan)—Janette Hobbs whose brother William Hobbs—Susan Dorsey.

William Dorsey (of Judge Basil), through his son Corbin, was the progenitor of Senator Stephen Dorsey, of Ohio. Harriet (of William)—Colonel Thomas Gist, son of General Mordecai Gist. Evan, Basil, Vachel and Josiah Dorsey went West. Judge Dorsey married, second, Tabitha Richardson and had Tabitha, second wife of Hon. Upton Sheridine, member of Congress from Frederick. Mr. Albert Jones, of Baltimore, holds the seal and ring of Judge Dorsey.

Samuel Dorsey (of "Patuxent John") inherited "Dorsey's Search," near Columbia, and other tracts near New Market. His wife was Eleanor Woodward (of Henry and Mary Young). Their son, Henry Woodward Dorsey, was twice married, first, to Mary Maccubin, of Zachariah, whose daughter Achsah married Thomas Beale Dorsey, Jr., leaving a son, Samuel. Harry Woodward Dorsey's second wife was Mrs. Rachel Cooke (nee Magruder). They had an only son, Harry Woodward Dorsey, of New Market, whose wife was Sarah Waters (of Ignatius).

From them descend Vernon Dorsey—Miss Worthington (of Rezin); the late Dr. Harry W. Dorsey, of Hyattsville—Miss Waters (of Dr. William); Captain Ignatius Dorsey, C. S. A.—Laura Hobbs (of William); Pottinger Dorsey—Mollie Morris; Elizabeth—William Blunt, of Goshen.

Harry Woodward Dorsey's homestead descended to Harry Dorsey Waters. It stands upon an eminence overlooking the National Pike, east of New Market. From it an extended view of a beautiful country is presented.

During the Civil War, when Lee's army held that country, General Fitzhugh Lee spent an evening there.

Captain Ignatius and his late brother, Pottinger Dorsey, had adjoining properties.

Benjamin Dorsey (of Patuxent John) inherited "Long Reach," "Partnership" and lands adjoining "Dorsey's Search," in Anne Arundel County. He married Sarah Dorsey (of Henry and Elizabeth Worthington). Issue, Allen, Elizabeth, Ralph, Joshua, Sarah, Samuel and Rachel.

Ralph (of Benjamin) remained upon the homestead and married Harriet Warfield (of Joshua). Issue, Galen, Ralph, Joshua, bachelors; Benjamin and Rinaldo. Their sister, Mary Ann Jones Dorsey—Dr. William Henry Worthington; Benjamin—Henrietta Mathews. Issue, Samuel, killed at Greenland Gap; Louisa—Trusten Polk; Eliza Dorsey. Benjamin Dorsey was Register of Wills for Howard. His residence was the northern border of 'Warfield's Range." He held also a part of "Montpelier."

Rinaldo Dorsey (of Ralph)—Achsah Worthington, sister of Dr. William Henry. Issue, Joshua Warfield Dorsey, who still holds her inheritance, "Wildwood." He also holds a fine farm near it.

SHERIFF JOHN.

Sheriff John Dorsey, son of Patuxent John, inherited "Good Luck" and "Mt. Pleasant," near New Windsor, containing one thousand acres.

As there seemed to be no good luck for sheriffs in those days, his estate became involved, and by order of Chancellor Hanson, David Alexander Dorsey, a son, was made trustee. Harry Dorsey Gough held a mortgage which was taken up by Mrs. Rachel Hall, a sister of Sheriff John, and by Stephen West, father of Mrs. John Lawrence, of Linganore. Sheriff John Dorsey married Mary Cumming, daughter of William Cumming and Margaret Thomas, both of whom held a considerable estate in Howard. William Cumming also became involved and transferred his estate to William Cumming, the younger, of Frederick County.

Mrs. Margaret Cumming in her will of 1804, after having sold "Presley," near Roxbury Mills, to Henry Gaither, and by him conveyed to Captain Philemon Dorsey, left to her granddaughter, Margaret Dorsey, "Gosnell's Chance" and part of "Creagh's Enlargement" and to her daughter, Mary Dorsey, the other half of the same two tracts.

To daughter Araminta Cumming, "Howard's Chance," "Mt. Gilboa," "Barnes' Luck" and "Cumming's Bower." She made her daughter Araminta her executrix.

This daughter became the second wife of Captain Ely Dorsey, whose estate in Frederick County adjoined that.

The heirs of Sheriff John Dorsey were David Alexander, John, Samuel Thomas (named for his grandfather), Basil William, Elizabeth, Mary and Margaret Dorsey.

David Alexander Dorsey and his brother William assigned their interest in the estate through David Cumming, to their sisters. The sisters assigned their interest to their brothers, John and Samuel Thomas Dorsey, and to their nieces, Araminta Hammond, Lucy Dorsey and Maria Dorsey, daughters of brother William (deceased), and to their nephews, William Alexander, Clagett Warfield and Basil Dorsey, sons of brother Basil (deceased.)

Samuel Thomas Dorsey in 1836 held the present estate of the late Harry Peddicord, near Unionville, and left it to nephews William Alexander and Clagett Warfield Dorsey, sons of brother Basil, who married Harriet Jones, daughter of Westley Jones and Harriet Warfield, daughter of Colonel Charles Warfield, of Sam's Creek.

Their son, Clagett Warfield Dorsey, in 1843, granted to Upton Dorsey and Mary Forsythe a tract called "Cumming's Farm," a resurvey for Margaret Cumming, formerly sold to Philip Hammond. In 1843 Henry Forsythe and wife deeded the same to Upton Dorsey, son of John Dorsey, of Sheriff John.

Through Judge Thomas Beale Dorsey, Captain Ely and Araminta (Cumming) Dorsey, in 1817, deeded to Basil (of John) "Gray's Bower," and to Peggy Dorsey "Gosnell's Chance," on the old road leading from Hollofield to Frederick. In 1823 Mrs. Ely Dorsey left her mother's estate to her sister's children and their descendants. It finally came to John Dorsey, father of Upton and Mrs. Forsythe.

He held a large estate upon the old Frederick road. He died upon "Gosnell's Chance," which descended to his son Upton. His wife was Miss Cochran.

Mrs. Forsythe inherited her estate where she lived and died. It is now owned by Henry Forsythe, who, with his brother Arthur, holds a large and productive estate.

Upton Dorsey—Louisa Sophia Crawford and left John Cummings Dorsey—Alverda Owings; William Clagett Dorsey—first, Elizabeth Carr; second, Catharine Linthicum (of Lloyd); Upton Wallace Dorsey —Ella Waters (of James); Mary Virginia—William Clarke (of Thaddeus); Laura Lee—Samuel Cashell and Basil B. Dorsey, a bachelor; Howard Crawford—Miss Gartrell. Their estate, "Howards' Chance" and other tracts, is at Clarksville.

THE "MICHAEL DORSEYS" OF "ELIOAK."

Michael Dorsey, youngest son of Michael and Ruth (Todd) Dorsey, married Honor Howard, daughter of Henry and Sarah Dorsey, and removed to her estate at the junction of The Manor Road and Clarksville Pike. This property is now held by Quill, who tore down the old house, a long frame one, with dormer windows and porch, and rebuilt upon the site. Mrs. Michael Dorsey had an interesting career. She was taken from her birthplace near, if not the same, whereon she then resided as the bride of Rezin Warfield (of Alexander) down to "White Hall" near Guilford; as his widow with three children, she married, after 1767, Rezin's rich cousin, John Davidge; as his widow in 1773, with five children, she became Mrs. Joseph Wilkins, and with him administered upon the estate of John Davidge, and then, marrying Michael Dorsey, Jr., returned to her own inheritance. As his widow, in 1817, she named "her daughter Jemima Warfield, her daughter Oner Dorsey, and her son Owen Dorsey, her executors." But there was another son with a large family. Her son, Lloyd Dorsey, married Anna Green and had Mrs. Achilles Simpson; Honor, wife of Thomas Burgess, of "Prospect Hill;" Mrs. Annie Barnes, of Ohio; Michael Lloyd, Washington; William and Mary N. (Dorsey) Green, of Ohio.

Washington left Virginia Mitchell, Cecelia Lynch, Emma, Washington, Jr., Howard, Melvilla and Edward Dorsey.

William had issue: William Lloyd Dorsey, of Martinsburg, Nannie, Lucy and Mary Green, who married Charles W. Dorsey (of Hanson).

Judge Owen Dorsey (of Michael and Honor) was Judge of the Orphans' Court of Baltimore and made many sales of real estate in Howard. He built the present large brick house at Elioak, which he transferred to Michael Dorsey, the third, in exchange for other lands. Judge Owen Dorsey married Henrietta Dorsey (of Nicholas), of Annapolis Junction, and had Owen, Edwin, Elizabeth Duer and Lorenzo, who married Anna Hanson McKenney, the authoress, parents of Louis, Clare—R. B. Mohun, Angela—Major Eastman, Florence, and Ella Loraine Dorsey, of Washington, successor to her mother in literary work.

The daughters of Michael and Honor were Elizabeth, wife of William Dorsey Ball. Her son was Owen Dorsey Ball, who married Frances E. Boyd and was the father of Mrs. John William Hunter Porter, of Portsmouth, Virginia. Jemima Dorsey (of Michael and Honor) became Mrs. Alexander Warfield, of Sam's Creek. Honor married Joshua Jones, Cecelia—Daniel Dunn.

Michael (of Michael and Honor), of Elioak—his cousin, Amelia Green.

Dr. Hanson Dorsey (of Michael, third, and Amelia Green) graduated at University of Maryland, 1836, practiced his profession at Wickliffe, Park County, Virginia, until 1844; he then married Amanda Castleman, of Auburn, near Wickliffe, daughter of William Castleman, Jr.; he then removed to Front Royal, Warren

County, Virginia, where he spent the remainder of his life, respected and beloved by all around him; was learned and successful in his profession and a most intelligent and cultured gentleman of the old school; was remembered with love and gratitude by neighbors and friends; he died at Greenfield, near Front Royal, Warren County, June 21, 1903. Children of Dr. Hanson and Amanda Dorsey:

William Hanson, died in early manhood; Isabel, Louise, Rosalie, Owen, Warfield, dying in childhood; Charles Worthington, aged forty-four years, died March 10, 1898, in Baltimore. Living: Virginia, Howard and Caroline Hanson Dorsey, youngest of the family and unmarried. Charles Worthington Dorsey married his cousin, Mary Green Dorsey, only daughter of William Dorsey (of Martinsburg, West Virginia, and son of Lloyd) and Lucy Harrison, issue of Charles W. Dorsey and Mary G. Dorsey; Lucy Harrison Dorsey, aged twenty-one years; she and her mother are living in Washington, D. C. William Dorsey also left one son, William Lloyd, unmarried, in Washington, D. C.

Michael, the fourth, late of Elioak—Eliza, daughter of David Jones, late of "Cedar Grove," Baltimore County. Their daughter, Marion B. Dorsey, became the wife and widow of Mr. Louis Gassaway, Cashier of the first bank in Annapolis. The only son, Louis Dorsey Gassaway, fourth in line of his name, is the assistant cashier of the Farmers' National Bank of Annapolis, and Recorder of the South River Club. He married Miss Iglehart, a descendant of the distinguished family that has given the name to Iglehart Station in Anne Arundel. The only daughter of Mrs. Gassaway is the recent bride of Lieutenant Fisher, U. S. A. Mary Dorsey (of Michael, fourth) now resides in the handsome home of "Elioak" as the wife of Ex-Treasurer James T. Clark, of Howard. Their son, Louis T. Clark, attorney-at-law of Ellicott City, owns the historic house of "Walnut Hill." His bride is a daughter of Rev. Henry Branch, of Ellicott City.

HISTORIC CLARKSVILLE.

Rich in limestone, lovely in landscape, far-famed for its handsome daughters, this section was popular even before it had a name. To-day it is the centre of a progressive settlement.

A most attractive home is that of Mr. Nicholas Miller, son of Mr. Denton Miller, of Millersville, who lies buried upon his old homestead adjoining the former home of Thomas Cornelius Howard. Mrs. Denton Miller was a Miss Jenkins, aunt of Dr. William and Mr. John Hardy.

Clarksville has two attractive churches, two stores and several modern residences.

THE HARDY BROTHERS.

Southwest of Clarksville are the two substantial dwellings of the late Dr. William Hardy and his brother, Mr. John Hardy, now an octogenarian. Their father came up from St. Mary's County and settled across the Patuxent in Montgomery.

In 1875 Dr. Hardy was School Examiner of Howard and Mr. John Hardy was a School Commissioner of Howard. The latter also represented the county in the State Legislature.

The wife of Dr. Hardy was a Miss Speers, a niece of William Clark. The homestead is now held by Miss Jennie Hardy, who conducted for years a successful school near by.

Mrs. John Hardy was a Miss Rowles. Their daughter is Mrs. Thomas Clark.

Clarksville has for years been noted for its Rattlesnake Spring picnics and its tournaments. The Hardy brothers were always leaders in all social enjoyments. To these were added their long-distance fox-hunts over the Patuxent grounds. Mr. John Hardy can not resist a desire to follow his dogs even now.

Two roads leading across the Patuxent enter Clarksville. At Highlands was "Wall's Cross-Roads Tavern," long since lost to memory. It gave place to the wayside tavern at Clarksville, where the village pump still offers free entertainment, but the old hostelry is closed and its keeper, Mr. John Simms, with his fund of history, has passed away without recording it. Much of it was related to the author, but not for publication.

Long before Clarksville had a name or a tavern, three surveyors met at a corner stone in Mr. Nicholas Miller's field and determined to possess that entire country. The first was Hon. John Dorsey, who laid out "White Wine and Claret;" then Colonel Henry Ridgely and his brother-in-law, Major Thomas Worthington, came up. They surveyed, first, "Henry and Thomas," but later Mr. Worthington resurveyed it as "Worthington's Range;" still later, the Howard heirs of it resurveyed theirs as "Howard's Chance."

Colonel Henry and Major Thomas took up all the land north of "Snowden's Second Addition," up through Highlands and Clarksville, to the neighborhood of Glenelg. They put upon this long stretch an expanding line of descendants.

THE HOWARDS OF CLARKSVILLE.

Thomas Cornelius Howard, the merchant, son of Cornelius Howard, increased his mother's dower and left a large estate. His will makes no mention of his wife. It left to his son, Thomas Worthington Howard, "two tracts, 'Worthington Range' and 'Howard's Chance,' on the east side of the main road leading from Snell's bridge to Ellicott's; also a part of the said two tracts which lie between the main road leading from Green's bridge to Owing's Mill and the aforesaid main road from Snell's bridge to Ellicott's, which said part adjoins the lands of my son-in-law, Joseph Howard.

"To my son, Henry Howard, I give five shillings above his part; to son Charles Howard 'Brown's Chance' and 'Friendship,' commonly called 'Ryan's land,' whereon my son-in-law John Rowan now lives, provided the title shall ever be made good to my estate, but if not, then I give to son Charles a bond from William Taylor.

"To son Brice Howard all the remaining part of 'Worthington Range' on the north side of the main road, from Green's bridge to Ellicott's, provided my son Brice shall pay to my daughter Ann Howard, his sister, £150. To my daughter Mary Howard, wife of Joseph Howard, all she has already, as well as the account against her husband on my books, also, 'Poor Man's Beginning' and six head of horned cattle. To my daughter, Rachel Duvall, and her children a number of negroes named.

"To my daughter, Elizabeth Rowan, two tracts of 'Worthington Range' and 'Howard's Chance' in the fork of roads where a new house is built.

"To my daughter Rebekah, negroes and furniture. To daughter Anna Howard, negroes and furniture, horse and cattle. To my grandson, Thomas Howard, son of Charles, a grey colt; to grandson, Thomas Duvall, a colt. My son Brice and son-in-law, John Rowan, executors."

Thomas Worthington Howard (of Thomas Cornelius) named his wife Emma, nephew Thomas H. Howard, son of brother Charles: To Betsy Howard, daughter of brother Charles, be granted "White Wine and Claret," purchased of Charles Ridgely (of Charles); niece Nelly Howard, daughter of Joseph Howard. Test William Welling, Henry Welling and William L. Matthews.

Major Worthington's heirs at Clarksville were his daughter Rachel, wife of Cornelius Howard, who received 369 acres of "Worthington's Range;" Elizabeth Worthington, wife of Henry Dorsey, 369 acres; Sarah, wife of Basil Dorsey, 368 acres; Ariana Watkins, wife of Nicholas, received the remainder and 300 acres of "Altogether" adjoining it.

Thomas Cornelius Howard (of Cornelius) came into possession of his mother's portion, which embraced the whole site of Clarksville.

Thomas Worthington Howard—Eliza Ridgely Crabb, and their daughter Emily—John G. England, whose son is John G. England, of Rockville.

THE WATKINS OF CLARKSVILLE.

Nicholas Watkins, of Clarksville, son-in-law of Thomas and Elizabeth (Ridgely) Worthington, was a descendant of John Watkins, of Nansemond County, Virginia, who was one of the members who assumed to pay the church tithes of the Non-Conformist Church of 1642. Lower Norfolk records give the marriage contract of his widow, Frances Watkins, with Edward Lloyd, later commander of the Severn. She relinquished her dower in Virginia to Edward Lloyd and stipulated that her son, John Watkins, was to be paid his portion by Lloyd. This was carried out in 1658, when Edward Lloyd surveyed for John Watkins "his son-in-law" (step-son) 100 acres and "John Watkins demanded one hundred acres more in his own right." This was granted in "Watkins' Hope" surveyed in 1663. In 1675 John Watkins was living upon the Severn. His daughter Annie married John Watkins Lord; his widow, Ann (Watkins) Lord, married William Burgess, Jr., without issue. Her former husband's children inherited from William Burgess 1,000 acres in Baltimore County.

John Watkins, Jr., in 1688, married Ann, daughter of Colonel Gassaway. They were the executors of Colonel Gassaway in 1691.

In 1699 Ann Watkins took out letters upon the estate of her husband. Their son John Watkins, in 1715, conveyed as heir-at-law of his father, a tract of land located on Swan Creek, Kent County, to his brother, Nicholas Watkins, who was born in 1691. In his deed of conveyance it is stated that his father had so intended to devise this land, but died before the execution of his will. The third son of John and Ann (Gassaway) Watkins was Gassaway Watkins, to whom Colonel Thomas Gassaway left in 1739 "the farm on which he now lives."

Elizabeth Watkins (of John and Ann [Gassaway] Watkins) was born in 1693.

John Watkins and Mary Wárman were married in 1715. She was a descendant of Ninian Beall and held an estate in Prince George County. His will of 1734 left his Prince George estate to his sons John and Stephen, which, in the event of no heirs, was to descend to his son Nicholas. His wife, Mary Watkins, named her daughters, Hester Lane, Jane Smith, Sarah Keene and Frances Dorsey (wife of John Hammond Dorsey. She also named her grandson Nicholas Watkins (of Stephen) and her granddaughter Mary Smith (of Anthony).

Nicholas Watkins, Sr., second son of John and Ann (Gassaway) Watkins, in 1657, named his wife Margaret Watkins. His sons were Nicholas, born 1722; John Gassaway, Joseph, Thomas and Jeremiah; daughters, Elizabeth Hall and Ann Watkins.

Nicholas Watkins, Jr., married Ariana Worthington, daughter of Thomas and Elizabeth (Ridgely) Worthington, and removed to her estate near Clarksville. Their heirs were Margaret, Thomas, Elizabeth, John, Nicholas and Gassaway Watkins.

After the death of Nicholas Watkins, his widow became Mrs. John Ijams and with him administered upon the estate. In 1761 she deeded her estate of "Worthington Range" and "Altogether" to her sons.

Some of the marriages in the Watkins family after the Revolution were: 1778, Richard Watkins and Ruth Beard; 1778, Adam Richardson and Ann Watkins; 1787, Joshua Dorsey and Margaret Watkins; 1791, John Watkins and Ann Rutland; 1794, Benjamin Watkins and Anne Harwood; 1797, John Watkins (of Stephen) and Elizabeth Hall; 1798, Nicholas G. Watkins and Margaret Harwood; 1801, Rev. Nicholas Watkins and Rachel S. Watkins; 1805, Dr. William Watkins and Eleanor Harwood; 1806, Nicholas Watkins and Margaret Todd.

Margaret Watkins (of Nicholas and Ariana Worthington) married Benedict Dorsey, son of Thomas and Mary Warfield; she afterward became Mrs. Basil Gaither and was the mother of Nathan

Gaither, who was in the Constitutional Convention of Kentucky. Elizabeth Watkins, her sister, also became Mrs. Gaither. Thomas Watkins, their oldest brother, was High Sheriff of Anne Arundel, and, like many other sheriffs, lost his estate.

Gassaway Watkins entered the Revolution in 1776, and was mustered out with General Greene.

His Record in the Revolution.

The following partial sketch of his services during the Revolutionary War was found among his papers some years after his death. It is evidently incomplete, and no doubt the balance has been lost, as it is contained on one side of a sheet of foolscap-size paper, and stops very abruptly.

"I entered the Revolutionary Army with Colonel Smallwood's regiment in January, 1776, and was in the battles of Long Island and White Plains as sergeant. Was taken sick in November, and sent to and left at Morristown, Jersey. I put my clothing in the regimental wagon, and the driver carried all to the enemy. I traveled from Morristown to Annapolis without money or clothing, and got to Annapolis in January, '77, and lay confined to my room until the last of April. I was then inoculated for the small-pox, and remained in Maryland as lieutenant on duty until September. I joined the army a few days before the battle of Germantown and remained with the army and wintered at Wilmington, in 1778. I was in the battle of Monmouth and was attached to the command of General Scott's light infantry and after the battle, came to Bownbrook. Left camp the 24th of December, on furlough, and joined the army 26 of April, 1779. Continued in camp at West Point and wintered at Heck's farm. I was several times in the vanguard and was on Staten Island, in March, 1780, and was in Elizabethtown a few hours, after Major Egleston and his guard were taken. Was present when Colonel Hazen arrested Colonel Howard, for not keeping his men on the parade until they were frozen. I left camp the last of April for the South, and was in the battle of Camden. Was sent to a house by General Greene for information; was pursued by Tarleton's horse, jumped a fence eleven logs high and was two nights and days without eating and without seeing anyone and slept in the woods. Rejoined General Smallwood, at Elizabethtown. Was sent by General Smallwood, in September, with special despatches to General Marion. Joined the General at Hillsborough. Left Hillsborough under the command of Colonels Howard and Morgan. Commanded a company in the battle of the Cowpens, 1781. In February, the day General Davidson was killed, I left camp with orders from General Greene and was with the retreating militia, two miles from the battle ground. At twelve o'clock that night, I stopped at a house on the road, cold, wet and hungry, but got nothing to eat. There were at least one hundred persons in the house. My dress was noticed by an old man of the country, who asked to speak in private with me. He told me there were enemies as well as friends in the house and offered his services to me. I started in a few moments after, and told him what I wanted. He was faithful. We rode all night and got to the foard, about ten o'clock next morning. The trees came tumbling one after the other down the Yadkin. The old man said it was impossible to cross. I was satisfied there was nothing to stop the enemy and the wish of my general to bring his troops to a point near action, so I immediately pulled off my coat and boots, put the despatches in the crown of my hat, tied it on my head, took leave of my friend, who, with tears in his eyes, wished me well, and with difficulty crossed the river. My guide and friend expressed his joy by throwing up his hat and I returned it with gratitude. About seven o'clock I got to headquarters and was received by Generals Greene and Morgan."

Officers of the Revolutionary Army received from the United States government land warrants for their services, and the following was copied from the records in the Land Warrant Division of the Interior Department, Washington:

Gassaway Watkins, Warrant No. 2406 for 300 acres, located with others on lot 2, township 6, range 13, United States Military District, Ohio, Knox County. Patented to James Williams, March 21, 1800; warrant issued, May 11, 1790.

Mr. James Williams, being a son of General Otho Williams, of the old Maryland Line, was intrusted with the warrants of a large number of the old soldiers for lands, and located at the same time 4,000 acres of lands for them in Ohio, contiguous to the lot of Colonel Watkins. Captains received 300 acres, and privates, 100 acres. The possession of the warrant was the only requisite to carry title to such lands and authorized and empowered the holder to make the location. These lands were then considered of very little value by the old soldiers, and owing to the failure and subsequent death of Mr. Williams, and loss of papers, Colonel Watkins did not receive anything for his lot.

The State of Maryland, by an Act of the Legislature, passed November, 1788, ch. 44, granted to Colonel Watkins, in recognition of his services in the Revolutionary War, four lots of land in what is now known as Garrett County. The numbers of the lots are, 2244, 2245, 2246, and 2247, each containing 50 acres. These lots are now owned by his grandsons, Edwin Warfield and John Warfield.

Soon after the war Colonel Watkins married Sarah Jones, daughter of Captain Isaac Jones, of South River, and settled upon his inheritance, "Richland." His wife died within one year, without issue. He next married Ruth Dorsey, daughter of Captain John Dorsey, of "Brown's Chance." He continued at "Richland" until the death of Captain Dorsey, when he bought his heirs interest in the homestead and removed there.

The old pioneer house was the typical Queen Anne hipped-roof cottage. Colonel Watkins built the present commodious one of stone and, from the spreading walnut tree immediately at its door, named it "Walnut Grove."

His oldest son, Lieutenant Gassaway Watkins was in the War of 1812. He married Rebeckah Richardson, daughter of Richard and Elizabeth (Thomas) Richardson. Dying in 1817, he left a son, Richard Gassaway Watkins.

Bonaparte, second son of Colonel Watkins, died early; Thomas and Turenne went to Kentucky. The former left a son, Thomas, now a prominent merchant of Louisville,

Charlotte, eldest daughter, married Alfred Coale, brother of Mrs. Commodore Barney; Ann became Mrs. Lot Linthicum, leaving a daughter, the late Miss Eliza Linthicum.

In 1803 Colonel Watkins brought his third wife to "Walnut Grove." She was Eleanor Bowie Clagett, daughter of Wiseman and Priscilla Bowie (Lyles) Clagett, of Prince George County. She was a granddaughter of Edward Clagett and Eleanor (Bowie) Brooke—great-granddaughter of Richard Clagett and Deborah (Dorsey) Ridgely, who resided at "Croome." The immigrant and father of Richard Clagett, was Captain Thomas Clagett, of the British Navy, son of Colonel Edward Clagett, who held a Commission under Charles I. The mother of Captain Thomas Clagett was Margaret Adams, daughter of Sir Thomas, Lord Mayor of London.

Captain Clagett married Sarah Patterson, of London. "Goodlington Manor," "Greenland," "Weston," were his estates in St. Mary's County.

Reverend Samuel Clagett (of Richard and Deborah) was the father of the first American Bishop, Rev. Thomas John Claggett. His motto, handed down through the church, is "Gratia Dei Grata."

Colonel Watkins and Eleanor Clagett had eight daughters and two sons. The oldest daughter, Caroline, widow of Julius Watkins, died several years ago, aged ninety-two years, leaving an only son, Captain Richard Watkins, of California; Camsadel Watkins married Dr. Horatio Grieves (of Wales), leaving two daughters, Mrs. Eleanor Crapster, of "Ellerslie," and Mrs. Dr. Moorehead. Eleanor Watkins—William Ridgely Warfield; Amanda—Thomas Watkins; Elizabeth—William Watkins; Priscilla—George Kenly; Margaret Gassaway—Albert Gallatin Warfield; Albina—William Clark. In 1893 four of these daughters were living representatives of an officer of the Revolution.

Dr. William W. Watkins, oldest son of Colonel Gassaway and Eleanor (Bowie) Watkins resided at "Richland." His whole life was an official one. Sent as a delegate to the Legislature in 1838, he urged and secured a subdivision of the large county of Anne Arundel, and when Howard District, which he created, finally passed into a County, in 1851, he was chosen its first State Senator. Dr. Watkins was a graceful and eloquent speaker. His large and handsome form, added to his inherited perseverance, made him a popular leader. For twenty-five years he was successively chosen Clerk of the Court, and when he retired the honor was given to his son Lewis, whom he had brought up in the office—a worthy successor.

Dr. Watkins was twice married—first, to Laura, daughter of Thomas Watkins, and, second, to Eleanor Harwood, of West River. His oldest son, Thomas—Kate Welling. His namesake and successor in medical practice was Dr. William Watkins, Jr., who married his Watkins cousin.

Lewis J. Watkins held the office of Clerk during life; his widow resides on West River.

Harwood Watkins, youngest son, attorney-at-law, died in early manhood. He was editor of " The Times."

Ellen Elizabeth Watkins became Mrs. Joshua Warfield Dorsey. Issue, James Malcolm Dorsey, attorney of Howard; J. Worthington Dorsey, merchant of Baltimore; Benjamin Dorsey, attorney-at-law; William R. Dorsey, of Ellicott City.

Amanda Watkins, youngest daughter of Dr. Watkins, married Thaddeus M. Sharretts, of Baltimore. She is the only living child.

Hon. John S. Watkins, second son of Colonel Watkins, inherited the homestead, " Walnut Grove." He was State Senator of Howard at the outbreak of the Civil War. Genial, hospitable and popular, his home was an attractive centre of reunion. He married Amanda Linthicum and left two daughters, Mrs. Richard Owings and Mrs. John Bracco.

After the death of Hon. John S. Watkins the old homestead was sold to Edwin Warfield, grandson of Colonel Watkins, now our popular Governor of Maryland. He has made many improvements. His recent purchase of "Hayland," an adjoining estate of the late William Clark, with abundant limestone upon both, gives him some six hundred acres of the finest hay lands in Maryland. As elsewhere shown, these tracts cover the earliest surveys in Howard County.

"WHITE WINE AND CLARET,"
HOME OF WILLIAM RIDGELY.

Stretching out from Simpsonville to Clarksville is a beautiful tract of rolling, fertile land. Tradition records its history as follows:

After Hon. John Dorsey had selected a munificent inheritance for the descendants of his sons, he sent out surveyors with an abundant supply of White Wine and Claret to take up another body of good land for the sons of his daughter. When he saw the crooked outlines of their survey he thought White Wine and Claret had been the cause, and would be an appropriate name, and so it stands to-day. It embraced nearly 2,500 acres and was given to Charles and William Ridgely, sons of his daughter, Deborah Ridgely. A plat of it, now in the hipped-roof cottage of Irving Ridgely, of Clarksville, reads: "William Ridgely (of William) to hold 820 acres of the lower tract; John Ridgely (of Charles) to hold 930 acres of the lower tract; Charles Ridgely (of William) to hold 234 acres of the upper tract and John Ridgely (of Charles) all the remainder of the upper tract."

Charles Ridgely (of Charles and Deborah [Dorsey] Ridgely) was the founder of the Ridgelys of Hampton and never lived upon his inheritance.

William Ridgely, marrying his cousin Elizabeth, Duval, daughter of Lewis, made it their home, and from it sent out three sons and eleven daughters, viz., Samuel the bachelor, William, Charles, Martha—Henry Gaither; Margaret—Samuel Farmer; Deborah—Lancelot Dorsey; Elizabeth—Aquila Duval; Rachel—Joseph Howard; Anne—Captain Brice Howard; Mary, Sarah, Eleanor, Delilah and Assinah.

From the will of Miss Delilah Ridgely we learn that two more of her sisters were married, for she named, in 1798, "her mother, sister Sarah, brother Charles, brother William, nieces Harriet and Sarah Richardson, sister-in-law Ruth Ridgely, sister-in-law Mary Waters, brother-in-law William Simpson, niece Anna Howard, brother-in-law Thomas Richardson and brother Charles' daughter, Elizabeth Richardson."

William Ridgely, Jr., inherited the homestead and married Captain Philemon Dorsey's daughter, Elizabeth, which marriage united the two Ridgely families—the "blackheads," of St. Mary's, and the "lightheads," of Anne Arundel. Their heirs were William Pitt Ridgely, Samuel, Charles Greenberry, Philemon Dorsey; Elizabeth—Joshua Griffith; Sarah—Major Henry Welling; Rachel—Colonel George Dorsey; Amelia—Beale Warfield (of Captain Benjamin).

Charles Ridgely, known as "Black Head Charles," at seventeen years, built "Springfield" upon the upper tract, just north of Clarksville. It is a brick-nogged cottage, still well-preserved. He extended his surveys over "Hayfields" to the Frederick Pike at West Friendship. Later he made his residence near the Relay House. His brick house still stands near the quarantine yards of the B. & O. R. R.

He was twenty-seven years in the Legislature and was Speaker of the House during several sessions. His wife was Ruth Norwood, daughter of Samuel Norwood, who brought him her large estate. Their heirs were Samuel Norwood Ridgely, Dr. Charles Carnan Ridgely, William, Thomas P., Robert, John, Washington, Frank; Elizabeth—Robert Ridgely Richardson, of Prince George; Julia—Dr. Alexander Barron, of Towson; Ruth—Dr. John Baltzell, of Frederick.

Samuel Norwood Ridgely—Deborah Dorsey (of Amos). Issue, Amos Dorsey, Samuel and Lewis Ridgely.

Dr. Charles C. Ridgely inherited "Springfield;" married Elizabeth Dorsey (of Amos). Issue, Henry K.—Achsah Dorsey (of Colonel Richard) and had John T. Ridgely of the C. S. A., who married Sarah Jervis, of "Bowling Green;" Oliver Ridgely—Ida Hinkle; George Washington, Louisa Bradford and Carolina Bradford.

John R. Ridgely (of Dr. Charles)—Mary S. Ball; Charles Ridgely—Sallie Waters; Arthur P. Ridgely—Selah Waters; Elizabeth—John D. Alcock; Oliver D. Ridgely inherited "Springfield;" married Harriet Crawford, leaving an only son, Irving O. Ridgely, of Springfield, who married a daughter of the venerable William Brown, of Montgomery County.

Henrietta (of Dr. Charles)—Judge Deye Worthington; no issue. George W. Ridgely—Margaret Turner, of Virginia. Their daughter, Elizabeth—I. W. Hobbs, great-grandson of Luther Martin. William Ridgely (of Hon. Charles) located near Glenwood, married Elizabeth Dameste, niece of Colonel Bentelow. Issue, George K.—Martha Dorsey, leaving Mrs. Richard Lansdale, Mrs. Elisha Riggs, Mrs. Sheridine.

Gustavus Ridgely (of William)—Camille Hammond McKean. Issue, Ruxton Ridgely, attorney-at-law, Baltimore—Rebecca Gaither; Lieutenant Gustavus Ridgely, of Fifth Regiment and Genevieve—Ridgely Gaither, all of Baltimore.

William Ridgely (of William) died a bachelor; Thomas—Eliza Nally, of Virginia. Issue, William A.—Marie Offutt, of Baltimore County. He now holds the homestead of his grandfather.

WELLING.

Major Henry Welling inherited from his father, Peter Welling, a portion of "White Wine and Claret." He married Sarah Ridgely (of William and Elizabeth Dorsey), but had no heirs. His will of 1843 left his estate of "White Wine and Claret" to his wife Sarah. Upon it was a mill, which after her death was left to "my nephew, Henry Welling, and to my nephew, William Welling's son Henry. To wife Sarah, one-half of the "burnt-house" place. To nephew Henry Warfield, "Hearn's place," bought of Simpson. To nephew William Warfield, the place Cassidy lives on, to be shared, also, by my nephew, Richard Warfield.

"My lands purchased of the Warfield family, 314 acres, to go to George Dorsey Owings, son of my niece, Matilda Owings. The remainder of the "burnt-house" place to be sold and the proceeds to be divided equally among William Welling and my nieces, Elizabeth Young, Mary Iglehart and Rebecca Morris. "Harden's Place" to be sold and the proceeds to be divided among my sister's children, viz., Azel Warfield, George Warfield, Eliza Mercer, Mary Fisher and Nancy Dorsey.

"To Sarah Francis Richardson, I give a negro. Mr. Trueman Welling holds the old homestead."

From William Welling, brother of Major Henry, descends the Welling family of "White Wine and Claret." He had two sons, Henry and William. Henry's only daughter is Mrs. Kate Watkins, widow of Thomas Watkins (of Dr. William). Mr. Trueman Welling, upon the old homestead, and Mrs. Henry Forsythe are heirs of William Welling, Jr.

HIGHLANDS.

Highlands is the site of Wells Cross Road Tavern, which went down when Clarksville rose as a center for travel. The present village is becoming the literary centre of the county. Its fine hall and literary club attract visitors from several counties. Two stores and several shops are upon these cross roads. An Episcopal Church is near by.

Mr. Charles F. Disney, proprietor of one of these stores is a descendant of the large Disney family, of Anne Arundel, still prominent near Odenton. He owns several historic tracts at Highlands, viz., a part of "Hickory Ridge," "Partnership," and "Gaither's Chance." South of Highlands, leading to Snells Bridge, Benjamin Gaither located "Bite the Biter" and Richard Snowden stretched out his "Snowden's Second Addition." Upon this tract, near Snells Bridge was born the Continental Whig Major, who rode to Annapolis and ordered the "Peggy Stewart" to be burned. This was the home of Azel Warfield, whose descendants are world-wide. The Gaither tract has also passed to the Harding estate.

Mr. William H. Marlowe, recent Register of Howard County, holds two of the old pioneer cottages upon "Bite the Biter."

The estate of Azel Warfield descended to his son, who left it to a bachelor relative.

Just west of Highlands is Hickory Ridge, upon which Colonel Henry Ridgely seated his son Greenberry, who left a distinguished line of judges and patriots.

"GAITHER'S FANCY,"
HOME OF BENJAMIN GAITHER.

Benjamin Gaither, second son of John and Ruth Gaither, married, in 1709, Sarah Burgess, daughter of Captain Edward and Sarah (Chew) Burgess and located upon "Gaither's Fancy." He then surveyed estates upon the Patuxent which extended to Hawlings River. His heirs were Benjamin, the bachelor; John, Edward, Samuel, Henry, William, Elizabeth Davis, Sarah, Anne Hammond, Mary Long and Cassandra Linthicum.

Two old colonial cottages, with immense chimneys and dormer windows, still stand upon one of his estates, "Bite the Biter," between Snells Bridge and Highland. It is now owned by Mr. William H. Marlow, late Register of Wills for Howard. The Harding estate is also a portion of Benjamin Gaither's surveys, all upon the Patuxent.

"Gaither's Fancy," the homestead, was left to Mrs. Gaither during life. That was on the Patuxent. Benjamin Gaither was very active in establishing Queen Caroline Parish, in 1728. He canvassed the whole Parish of St. Ann's, which then embraced all of the settled area west of Annapolis and extending to Clarksville. He secured the necessary consent to establish the branch church upon the site of the present old brick church. He was an active buyer and seller of real estate. His name appears also as a witness to many wills of his neighbors. To each of his heirs he left a substantial inheritance in land and negroes.

Benjamin Gaither's will of 1741 left "my manor house to wife Sarah for life. To Benjamin "Pole Cat Hill." To John and Samuel, one-half each of "Bite the Biter." To Edward 350 acres of "Benjamin's Lot," (at Triadelphia). To Henry Gaither 350 acres of "Gaither's Chance" in Prince George County. To William Gaither 400 acres of "Gaither's Fancy," whereon I now dwell. To daughter

Elizabeth Davis, part of "Benjamin's Lot" in Prince George County. To Sarah, Ann, Mary and Cassandra Gaither, all the remainder, 710 acres of "Gaither's Chance" in Prince George County. Witnesses, Thomas Davis, Francis Davis and John Thompson."

It must be remembered that Prince George County at that time embraced all the territory north of Charles County, but after 1748 all the upper part of Prince George became Frederick County and after 1776 the same was attached to Montgomery. "Gaither's Chance," a large estate, was, therefore, upon Hawlings River, near Unity.

At Gaither's Rocks still stands, to-day, one of the pioneer houses of "Gaither's Chance." At Highland is another "Gaither's Chance."

Samuel Gaither (of Benjamin) was an attorney in Annapolis. He was a bachelor and left his estate to his sister, Sarah Sedgwick, and other sisters and brothers. His brother William inherited "Gaither's Fancy," the homestead, on the Patuxent, south of Millersville. He was also a bachelor, and in his will of 1782 appointed Lancelot Warfield, of "Brandy," his executor; granted him "Turkey Neck" and "Addition." To Mary Warfield, daughter of Richard and Sarah Gaither, he granted part of "Hammond's Forest." To sister, Mary Long, my tract "Gosnell," to descend to her daughter, Mary Norwood, and to John Norwood (of Edward). To Mary Berry (or Barrey), "Gaither's Tavern" and 100 acres of "Piney Grove."

Mary Warfield (of Richard) married Elijah Robosson.

Henry Gaither (of Benjamin and Sarah) married Martha Ridgely, oldest daughter of William and Elizabeth (Duval) Ridgely, of "White Wine and Claret." Henry Gaither was a progressive surveyor and held a large estate. His heirs were Beale (the bachelor); Benjamin—Rachel Dorsey; William, Colonel Henry, Daniel, Deborah Warfield, Amelia Holland, Mary Dorsey, Captain Frederick and Elizabeth Hood, wife of John Hood, Jr., of "Bowling Green."

William—Mrs. Ephraim Davis, daughter of Cornelius Howard and Rachel Ridgely Worthington. She was the mother of Thomas Davis and grandmother of Allen Bowie Davis, of "Greenwood." Her daughters by William Gaither are named in the will of her mother. Henry Chew Gaither, her son—Eliza, daughter of Major William Worthington. He built the handsome homestead near Unity, the late home of his son, Hon. William Lingan Gaither, the bachelor, afterward the property of Miss Lucy Worthington.

Major Ephraim Gaither (of William) built upon Hawlings River, near Gaither's Rocks, married Sarah Goldsborough and had Thomas Davis Gaither, Martha Washington, Elizabeth Worthington; Thomas Davis Gaither heired it; married Sarah, daughter of Frederick Gaither. Their only son Ephraim Gaither—Louisa Ross.

Martha Washington Gaither—first, Greenberry Gaither, and, second, Daniel Gaither, brothers; she left no heirs.

Elizabeth Worthington Gaither—Dr. William Magruder, of Brookeville and left one son Robert and two daughters, Mrs. Lieutenant Pierre Stevens and Mrs. Stonestreet.

Major William Gaither (of William) married Margaret Boone Dorsey (of John) and removed to his father's survey near Unionville, Frederick County. Issue, John Dorsey Gaither, Richard Dorsey Gaither (both bachelors), Henry Chew, George, Elizabeth and Margaret Dorsey Gaither.

Henry Chew Gaither—Juliet Maynard. Issue, Mrs. Norris, Mrs. Edward Hobbs and Thomas Gaither.

George Gaither—Kate Poole. Issue, Jesse, John, Lee, William, Fannie, Mrs. Colonel Washington Bowie and Florence Gaither; Elizabeth Gaither (of Major William)—Lot Norris. Issue, John Gaither, William Gaither, Richard, Henry and George Norris.

Margaret Dorsey Gaither—Thomas Ephraim Davis Poole, son of Dennis and Henrietta (Gaither) Poole. Issue, Mrs. Albert Jones, of Baltimore; Mrs. Albert Maynard, of Mt. Airy; Mrs. William Jones (deceased).

Mrs. Margaret Dorsey Poole died recently at the home of her daughter, Mrs. Albert Jones. Her heirs were her grandson, Poole Jones, Henrietta, Margaret Gaither, Nannie and Netty Jones, all of Baltimore, son and daughters of Mr. and Mrs. Albert Jones. She held many mementos of Major Ephraim and Major William Gaither, the ardent Federalists who accompanied Alexander Contee Hanson to Baltimore and defended his press during the mob of 1812. Major William Gaither had his hand pierced by an assailant 'as he lay a prisoner. He never flinched. His assailant, thinking he was dead, passed on, and thus his life was saved. Major Ephraim Gaither was also severely wounded.

Colonel Henry Chew Gaither, fourth son of Henry and Martha, was Captain of "The Flying Camp" and was later appointed by General Washington, Colonel of Third Regiment of United States Infantry. He was a splendid soldier and a strict disciplinarian. His portrait, formerly in possession of his brother, Captain Frederick, is now in possession of the family of Colonel George R. Gaither. Colonel Henry Chew Gaither was a bachelor; he lies buried in the Congressional Cemetery, Washington.

Daniel Gaither (of Henry and Martha)—Henrietta Riggs, daughter of Samuel. Issue, Henrietta, Henry Chew, Pauline, George Riggs Gaither, Samuel Riggs Gaither, Elisha and William Beale Gaither.

Henry Chew Gaither (of Daniel) removed to Ohio. His son Alfred Gaither, of Cincinnati, left Dr. Alfred Gaither, of Cincinnati.

Pauline Gaither became Mrs. Robert Ould, mother of Colonel Robert Ould, Confederate Commissioner.

George R. Gaither (of Daniel) the prominent merchant of Baltimore, married Hannah Bradley. He bought "Oakland Manor." His son Colonel George Riggs Gaither, of Howard County, organized "Gaither's Troopers" a few years previous to the war, and later it became a part of the Confederate Army. Colonel George R. Gaither was later in command of the Veteran Corps of Fifth Regiment. He married Rebecca Hanson Dorsey, daughter of Colonel Charles S. W.

Dorsey and Mary Pue Ridgely. Their son, George R. Gaither, was Attorney-General of Maryland; Colonel Charles Dorsey Gaither commands the Veteran Corps of the Fifth Regiment; Dr. Bradley Gaither, John Gaither and Ridgely Gaither are sons of Colonel George R. Gaither. His daughters are Mrs. Norris and Mrs. Ruxton Ridgely.

Thomas H. Gaither (of George R., Sr.)—Sarah Battaile Mayo, daughter of Commodore Isaac Mayo and Sarah Battaile Fitzhugh Bland of Chancellor Theodorick Bland. Their daughter, Mrs. Battaile, occupies the Peggy Stewart house in Annapolis. Thomas H. Gaither, Jr., is a capitalist of Baltimore.

The daughters of George Riggs Gaither, Sr., were Mrs. John Stewart and Miss Hannah Gaither.

Samuel Riggs Gaither (of Henry)—Maria Gaither, of Frederick, his cousin; Captain Frederick Gaither commanded a company of militia in 1814, held an estate upon the Patuxent, near Unity; married Jane Gartrell. Issue, Perry, Daniel, Greenberry, Frederick. Mrs. John Griffith, Mrs. Elisha Griffith, Mrs. Samuel R. Gaither, Mrs. Nicholas Warfield, Mrs. Fletcher Magruder and Mrs. Thomas D. Gaither.

Perry Gaither—Henrietta Hanson Poole (of Dennis). Issue, Dennis Poole Gaither, the late Kate A. Warfield, William Gaither and Charles Perry Gaither, of Boston.

Daniel Gaither and Greenberry, brothers, both married Patty Gaither (of Major Ephraim.) They left no issue.

Frederick Gaither, Jr., held the estate west of Unity; married Ann Gaither (of Henry Chew) and had one daughter, Henrietta Gaither.

Elizabeth Davis (of Benjamin and Sarah Gaither) became Mrs. Mark Brown. Her will of 1774, gave to her son Amos Davis, "Gaither's Chance" conveyed to her by Edward and Henry Gaither, in 1757; named her daughters, Mary Burgess, Sarah Norwood and Betsy Davis, to whom she left "Benjamin's Lot." Her grandaughter, Elizabeth Burgess, son Amos, and son-in-law, Edward Burgess, executors.

Mrs. Benjamin Gaither survived her husband and was honored at her death by the following notice in the Annapolis "Gazette": "On Tuesday last died in Anne Arundel County Mrs. Sarah Gaither, relict of Benjamin, formerly of the same county, in the seventy-ninth year of her age; a gentlewoman endowed with many good qualities and who performed the various stations of life with an unblemished character, having been a faithful wife, a kind neighbor, benevolent friend, and to her own sex an agreeable companion."

John Gaither (of Benjamin), of "Bite the Biter," married Agnes Rogers, daughter of Captain John Rogers, of Prince George County; issue, Evan, Vachel, Zachariah, John Rogers; Mary, wife of Seth Warfield; Sarah, wife of Richard Warfield; Susan and Agnes. Benjamin Gaither (of Benjamin) left his estate to his nephew Vachel (of John), who was a captain in the Revolution.

Zachariah (of John)—Sarah Warfield (of Edward and Rachel Riggs). Major Thomas Gaither, late of the Circuit Court of Baltimore, and his sisters, of Cincinnati, are descendants of James Gaither (of Zachariah). Greenberry Gaither's daughter, Mrs. Matilda Rawlings, has a son, James Brent Rawlings, of Falls Church, Virginia. Evan Gaither (of Zachariah) went to Cincinnati, married Mary Ann Hinkle and left Miss Caroline Riggs Gaither and sisters.

"Bite the Biter" was last held by Evan Gaither and Washington Gaither, who later removed to West Friendship.

Evan Gaither (of John) gave his one-third interest in 9,000 acres of military lands in Kentucky to his brother John; to his sisters Nancy, Sarah and Mary Gaither, "my right in 'Bite the Biter' and in a part of 'Second Addition to Snowden's Manor' and 'Gaither's Chance,' purchased of my brother Vachel; to Nathan Waters and my sister, Susannah Waters, a part of 'Snowden's Second Addition;' To Samuel and Zachariah and my sisters above all the remainder of my estate."

Edward Gaither (of Benjamin) married Eleanor Whittle. She was deeded 100 acres of "Gaither's Collections" by Edward Gaither (of Edward). Their sons all engaged in the Revolution, were Lieutenant Greenberry Gaither, quartermaster in Captain Briscoe's Company; Lieutenant Basil Gaither; Ensign Burgess Gaither; Lieutenant Benjamin Gaither, of Major Beall's Battalion. These brothers were all legatees of Benjamin Gaither, the bachelor son of Benjamin and Sarah Burgess.

Lieutenant Greenberry Gaither married Miss Anderson, of Rockville, and removed to Kentucky in 1813. Their sons were Dr. Edward and Greenberry Gaither. Dr. Edward Gaither was in the War of 1812 and was at the battle of Tippecanoe. His son Greenberry became Attorney-General of Arkansas. Horace was an attorney and so was his brother, James Anderson Gaither; Thomas was a physician; Brice Gaither, a merchant; John R. Gaither was a farmer. His son, James E. Gaither, was an attorney of Louisville, Kentucky. He holds still a memento of his ancestors—an old dinner bell, taken from the church bell of Rockville, upon which he had engraved its history

Greenberry Gaither (of Greenberry), the Kentucky settler, was Circuit Judge of Kentucky for many years, and left George Gaither, the bachelor.

Brice Gaither (of Edward of Benjamin) removed to Georgia.

Basil and Burgess Gaither, sons of Edward Gaither and Elinor (Whittle) Gaither, went to North Carolina, in 1781, from Maryland.

Basil Gaither represented Rowan County in the State Senate of North Carolina in 1788, and the House in 1790-91-92-93-94-95, and again in the Senate in 1796-97-98-99, and each year following until 1802. He married Margaret Watkins, of Maryland. Their children were Nicholas, Walter, Gassaway, Basil, Betsy, Nathan and Nellie.

Burgess Gaither represented Iredell County, North Carolina, in the House in 1792-95-96-97, 1800 and 1801. He married Amelia

(Milly) Martin, of Virginia, September 24, 1791.   Their children were
Alfred Gaither, born April 26, 1793, on Sunday, 3 o'clock, P. M.;
Martin Gaither, born December 20, 1794, on Saturday, 5 o'clock, P.
M.; Sarah Gaither, born October 19, 1796, on Wednesday, 4 o'clock
A. M.; Elvira Gaither, born August 1, 1798, on Wednesday, 10
o'clock P. M.; Forrest Gaither, born May 26, 1800, on Monday, 11
o'clock, P. M.; Lemira Gaither, born November 15, 1802, on Monday,
7 o'clock P. M.; Milly Maria Gaither, born December 20, 1803, on
Thursday, 8 o'clock P. M.; Burgess Gaither, born March 16, 1807;
Eleanor Emmeline, born April 6, 1810, Thursday, 10 o'clock; Charles
Cotesworth Pinkney Gaither, born May 31, 1812, 5 o'clock, P. M.
    This is an exact copy from the family Bible of Amelia Martin
Gaither.
    Of the children of Burgess and Amelia Martin Gaither—
    Alfred married Catharine Erwin, of Morganton, North Carolina,
and had one child, Julia, who died unmarried.
    Sarah Gaither married Robert Foster and lived in Lexington,
North Carolina. They had only two children, Alfred Gaither and
Amelia Emma Foster. Alfred Gaither Foster married Letitia Gray
and had five children—Robert Alexander, Alfred Gaither, Amelia
(Mrs. James A. Gwyn); Elizabeth, who is unmarried; Sarah Letitia
(Mrs. Robert Galloway). Amelia Emma Foster married Benjamin
Anderson Kittrell; of this marriage there were three daughters:
Louisa Melissa Kittrell (Mrs. James Wesson, of Estabuchie, Missis-
sippi), Amelia Eliza Kittrell (Mrs. VanWinder Shields, of Jackson-
ville, Florida), Sarah Letitia Kittrell (Mrs. Robert W. Lassiter, of
Oxford, North Carolina).
    Lemira Gaither married William Foster and left five children,
Laura, Sarah, Betty, Amelia and Julius.
    Maria Gaither married Phillip Pierson and left six children,
Gaither, James, Samuel, Susan, Sarah and Emma.
    Elvira Gaither married —— Reid and left four children,
Burgess, Oscar and two others.
    Emaline Gaither married Abram MacRee and left one child,
Emma, who married Chappel Hopkins.
    Burgess Gaither married Elizabeth Erwin and left one child,
Delia Emma, who married R. C. Pearson. Burgess Gaither had two
sons, who died before him. He married a second time and left one
son, Burgess Sidney Gaither, of Morganton, North Carolina.
    Forrest Gaither married a Miss Caldwell (sister of Judge
Caldwell, of Salisbury, North Carolina) and moved to Texas and died
there, leaving a large family.
    The brothers, Basil and Burgess Gaither, came to North
Carolina from Maryland in 1781.
    Nathan Gaither (son of Nicholas, son of Basil) had a son named
Edgar Basil Gaither, who was Captain of Third Dragoons in the
Mexican War. He was afterward State's Attorney for Kentucky
and died in 1855 in Kentucky.

Burgess Gaither, second, was a very talented and distinguished man, holding many prominent positions in the part of North Carolina in which he lived. There is a sketch of his life in a little book, "Prominent living North Carolinians."

GAITHERS IN NORTH CAROLINA.

A copy of my paper on the Gaithers and Burgesses, of South River, Maryland, having reached some descendants in North Carolina, Dr. P. F. Laugenour, of Statesville, North Carolina, has forwarded to me the following additional information of interest. Says he:

"I assume that our early settlers John and Benjamin Gaither were grandsons of John Gaither (of John) and Jane Buck; sons of John and Ann Gaither described by you in your sketch which reads.

"'John Gaither and Ann, his wife, were seatedon 'Left Out' (near Dayton, Howard County). Their issue were Benjamin, John, Elizabeth, Ann and Seth.'"

Soon after the close of the Revolution a number of Gaithers came from Maryland and settled in what then was Rowan County, but the territory is now embraced in the Northeastern part of Iredell and the part of Davis adjacent to it. Their lands lay on South Yadkin River, Hunting, Rocky, Dutchman, Little Dutchman, and Elisha's Creeks. This territory lies between Turnersburg, Houstonville and Mockville.

Those who were granted lands by the State from 1784 to 1787 were Burgess, Basil, Benjamin, Johnsie, brothers, Nicholas, Eli, brothers, Benjamin 2nd, Azariah, William and John.

Basil, in 1785, was granted 500 acres of land on Elisha's Creek, near Mocksville, in Davie County. He was wealthy for his day and community and was a member of the Legislature from Rowan County from 1792 till 1802, serving in both branches. (Davie County was cut off from Rowan in 1838.)

His children, according to his will dated 1802, were Martha (Jones), Walter, Gassaway, Nathan, Betsy and Basil. He gave from 200 to 250 acres of land to each of his sons and divided several negroes among his children. He has some descendants about Mockville through his son Basil.

Burgess Gaither was an important character in Iredell County a hundred years ago and figures on the records in land transaction, etc., rather conspicuously. He married Amelia Martin, who came from near Richmond, Virginia. He represented Iredell in the Legislature, from 1790 to 1801. His old homestead on Rocky Creek above Turnersburg, just opposite Tabor Church, is now owned and occupied by Columbus Hayes. On an elevated plateau near his old homestead, surrounded by a neat stone wall, repose the ashes of this pioneer of a family whose descendants are numerous, without a lettered stone to inform his posterity whose mortal remains were there laid to rest.

This solitary grave is now in the midst of a cultivated field; twenty-five years ago it was in an old field with a number of very old apple trees about it. There is a tradition that it was his request to be buried at that spot under a certain apple tree. He had a son Charles Cardsworth Pinkney Gaither, who, in 1836, lived in Morengo County, Alabama.

In 1829, Burgess S. sold to his mother his right and title in the old homestead devised to him by his father.

In 1836 his widow sold to Lebetius Gaither, son of Nicholas, the old homestead, "from which she recently moved" (to Morganton). He was the father of the late Hon. Burgess Sidney Gaither, of Morganton, an able and distinguished lawyer of his day and one of the prominent men of the State, who held many County, State and Federal positions and was a member of the Confederate Congress. He was born 1807, located at Morganton about 1830 and died 1893, leaving many descendants about Morganton, among whom are Burgess S., Gaither and Samuel Pearson.

Benjamin, brother of Basil and Burgess, in 1784, was granted land on Bear Creek. In his will, dated 1802, he names the following children, some of whom were small: Thomas, Johnsie, Beall, Basil, Brice, Bruce, Sallie, Henrietta, and alludes to his daughters, Margaret Howard, Elinor Varner and Ann Parker.

Johnsie, a brother of these, was granted land on Elisha's Creek, in 1786.

Of Azariah Gaither nothing is known, except that he was granted 400 acres of land on Hunting Creek, in 1786, adjoining John Gaither.

Eli Gaither, a brother of Nicholas, owned land on Little Dutchman Creek adjoining Jeremiah Gaither. His will, dated 1809, names Elizabeth, Bruce and William as his children, of whom I can learn nothing.

Nicholas Gaither, whose homestead was on Little Dutchman Creek, in 1793, willed lands on south side of South Yadkin River, to be sold after the death of his wife, the proceeds to be divided among his four sons, Edward, Libetius, Horatio, and Walter. In 1811 the land was sold and bought by Libetius and Horatio.

I know of no descendants of these in this country, except Libetius, born 1783, died 1860, who was father of David Burgess Gaither, who died an old man some fifteen years ago at Newton. Lawyer W. B. Gaither and Captain Junius R. Gaither, one of the leading business men of Newton, are his sons. Libetius had several daughters one of whom married Hall and one Donaldson. A son Junius died a bachelor. One daughter married J. A. Bell.

Benjamin Gaither, second, (in North Carolina,) whose will is dated 1788, died before 1804, that being the date of a sale of land under power of the will, left the following children: John, executor; Jeremiah, second, born 1771, died 1844; Zachariah, born 1772, died 1843; Basil, 1771—1844; Edward, Reason, Rachel and Ann.

Jeremiah, second, was father of Elam, who went to Tennessee and had four sons in the Confederate Army.

Zachariah has many descendants in the old neighborhood. His children were as follows:

Isham, 1809—1894, father of Enoch; Milton, 1812—1891, father of Spurgeon and Newton J.; Elijah, 1816—1863; Noah, 1819—1854, father of Tom, Zach., Yank., and others; Temperance, 1822, who married Casper Kinder; Asberry, 1824—1891, father of Wiley; Mrs. Dr. Ellis, 1827, mother of Milton; Wiley, 1829, killed in battle at Spotsylvania, May 9, 1864; Alexander Gray, 1832. The mother of all these, except Isham, was a sister of John Taylor, who being well off and having no children, willed his property to her and her children, embracing the old homestead occupied by the late Milton Gaither.

Basil, son of Benjamin, had five sons, Frank, Ivory, Bruce, Vincent and Azariah, all of whom went West, and three daughters, Nancy Maiden, Polly Forcum and Martha Mason. In 1805 he bought land on Hunting Creek, from Wilson Turner. His will is dated 1842. He died in 1844 and was buried near the residence of Mile Campbell. Of the other sons of Benjamin, second, I know nothing.

John Gaither was granted land on Hunting Creek, in 1786, near where Mile Campbell now lives, adjoining Azariah Gaither. His children were: Jeremiah, first, born 1762, died 1815; Greenberry, John, Sr., and three daughters of whom nothing is known. John, Sr., born 1766, died 1844.

Jeremiah Gaither, first, had two sons, Greenberry, second, who to distinguish him from his uncle, Greenberry, was called "Dockie," and Enos (Een Gaither) and some children by his second wife, who with her children went West after his death, in 1815. A daughter by his first wife also went West.

Enos, 1793—1877 had three sons, viz., Wiley Summers, 1822, who went to Georgia and died young, leaving a son, Wiley, and a daughter, who married Camp; Frank, 1824, went to Atlanta, left one daughter; Burgess, 1826, married in Richmond, Virginia, where he died. He had three daughters, viz., Lamira, who married, first, Robinson, whose children were John, who went to Alabama; Henry, who went to Tennessee; a daughter, who married Hay Powell; another who married D. A. Ratledge, both of Davie County. Her second husband was Jack Campbell, whose children were Tyson, who went to Tennessee; Amos and two daughters.

Elvira, daughter of Enos, married Marshall Turner, is the mother of Watt and Bill, of Cool Springs, besides one son, John Burgess, who died in the Civil War. She is still living at eighty-five years of age.

Darcus married Cam Powell, father of Frank and Jim, of Statesville.

Greenberry, son of Jeremiah, first, (Dockie) 1790—1860, was married twice; his first wife was Mary Tomlinson, daughter of John, who died 1826, about thirty-two years old. Her children were Ivey, father of William C., whose children are Mrs. Bena Houp, Charles, Frank, Oat, Robert, Will and Nellie (Carson) all of Statesville; Caroline, who married Robert S. Colvert, father of John E., Augustus A., Mrs. J. Wes. Nicholson, Mrs. C. W. Stimson, all of Statesville, and

Mrs. Johnsie, of Charlotte, all of whom are past middle age. Martin Gaither, father of Frank, of Harmony; Betsy, who married William I. Colvert, father of John G., Mrs. J. E. Stimson, and the mother of W. T. and Rev. Walter L. Nicholson, all of Statesville; Ellen, 1823—1854, first wife of Humphrey Tomlinson; mother of Mrs. Burt Owens, of River Hill; John M. Gaither, 1826—1874, father of Mrs. John Hayes, Lily who married H. F. Laugenour, 1877 and died 1878; Robert F., James and John, of Harmony.

The second wife of Greenberry Gaither (Dockie) was Joana Gray, who was born in 1801 and died July 9, 1857. Her children were as follows: Amos F., who died about 1884, leaving no children. He represented Iredell County several terms in the Legislature; Emily, married Oliver Henry, died 1903, children are Harvey, James F., Mrs. Newton J. Gaither, Mrs. Will Campbell, William S., and Robert; James went to Florida and died there leaving no children; Lavina, 1832—1859, married D. A. Ratledge and was the mother of Thomas Ratledge and Mrs. Dwiggins, of Davie; Emiline Juliana, 1840, only one now living, married J. Martin Turner, whose children are William S., who died 1901, leaving James, Thomas and Lonnie; Sallie, who married Dr. P. F. Laugenour in 1886; Cora, who married W. T. Nicholson; Lizzie, who married William Fraley; Eugene and Latona, all of Statesville; Sarah married Alfred Turner, died 1904, leaving Blanche (Clifford), Daisy (Foster) and Arthur, all of Statesvile.

Greenberry Gaither, first, son of pioneer John, has a number of descendants in Iredell. Four sons were: (Hostler) John, father of J. Alfred; Leander, father of Fry and William; William, Greenberry.

John Gaither, Sr., son of John, 1766—1844, was twice married. His children were as follows: two by his first wife, the others by his second, who was Drucilla Beall, who died September 29, 1872, in her eighty-ninth year. Elvira, married Samuel Albea; Sina married Elijah Campbell, who came from Maryland about 1790. Her children were Milus, Fry, Lewis, William, who was killed in the war; Elvira, wife of D. M. Campbell; Belt and David, all of whom are dead, or very old; Asa Burgess Friason, father of Dr. John B., of China Grove; H. Clay, of Statesville; Mrs. J. E. Colvert; William T., (Major Bill) 1826—1885, father of Turner, Dr. Beall, Ernest, Lum and several daughters. Mrs. Mary S. C. Morrison, of Jonesville, now eighty-seven years old, mother of James, Clay, Lum, Filmore and Mrs. Poindexter.

Descendants of the seventh generation from these pioneer settlers in North Carolina are now numerous in this country. Many members of the family went West, or South, as far back as seventy-five years ago.

GREENBERRY RIDGELY.

Greenberry Ridgely, heir-at-law of Colonel Henry, inherited "Hickory Ridge" and "Partnership," both adjoining each other at Highlands. There stands, to-day, just west of Highlands, his elegant old brick mansion, with its brick stables, near the brick-walled grave-yard of his family. It is now the estate of the late Samuel Hopkins. "Hickory Ridge" extends east of Highlands and embraces the present property of Mr. Ferdinand Pue. "Partnership" continues on east to Fulton.

Greenberry Ridgely was long a member of the vestry of Queen Caroline Parish. His wife was Lucy Stringer, daughter of Dr. Samuel and Lydia (Warfield) Stringer. She inherited a portion of "Warfield's Contrivance" at Guilford. Their heirs were Greenberry Ridgely, Jr., and Nicholas, who heired the homestead after the death of Mrs. Ridgely. Richard and Henry held "Baker's Quarter," Frederick heired "Ryan's Quarter." "To my four daughters, Ann, Lydia, Elizabeth and Sarah, £300 each." His will was probated 1738, with Azel Warfield, Launcelot Dorsey and Isaac Mayo witnesses.

Greenberry Ridgely, Jr., removed to Frederick County. Henry Ridgely, attorney-at-law and captain in the Revolution, married Matilda, daughter of Judge Samuel Chase, and resided in Baltimore; he became Judge; his daughter Emily became Mrs. Hollingsworth.

Nicholas Ridgely became the Baltimore merchant and married Eliza Eichelberger, whose daughter, Eliza Eichelberger Ridgely, married John Carnan Ridgely, son of Governor Ridgely, of Hampton. Elizabeth Ridgely—Dennis Griffith; Ann Ridgely married Dr. Francis Brown Sappington, and with him removed to Liberty.

Sally Ridgely died a maiden at the home of her sister in Liberty.

Frederick Ridgely became a noted surgeon.

Richard Ridgely, executor of the estate, became a distinguished attorney-at-law, advocate in the Court of Chancery and a Judge. His name appears in numerous transfers of real estate in Howard. He refused to stand for a seat in Congress. He married Elizabeth, daughter of Ely and Deborah Dorsey. Her inheritance was "Dorsey's Hall" upon "Dorsey's Search," which became the residence of Judge Ridgely. His will of 1824 records: "I desire no sermon to be preached at my funeral; the services to be held before a few invited friends; my body to be buried in the cemetery of my wife; to son Edward D. Ridgely I leave my library. To my sons-in-law, Robert Nelson and Richard Battie, and son, Edward D. Ridgely, I grant all my real and personal estate, in trust, with power to sell my plate, household furniture and divide the proceeds equally among my son Edward and daughters Betsy, Debby, Matilda and Sophia; their estates are not to be in the control of their husbands. To my granddaughter, Elizabeth E., daughter of my son, Daniel B. Ridgely, $2,000. To my son Richard's children, $1,500 each." He removed to Kentucky as an engineer, and in 1810 married Jane Price, daughter of Colonel John Price, of the Revolution, who settled in Jessamine County, Kentucky.

Captain Ridgely had two sons, Commodore Daniel Boone Ridgely, who married Joanna Clem and died in Baltimore, 1868, and Richard

Henry Ridgely, who married in Bowling Green, Kentucky, Martha Nantz, in 1838; issue, Richard and Jane, who married Mr. Peckover, of Cynthiana, Kentucky.

Daniel B. Ridgely (of Judge Richard) married Miss Hammond and left one daughter, Elizabeth Dorsey Ridgely.

Judge Ridgely's daughters were Mrs. James A. Sangston, Mrs. Deborah Neilson, Mrs. Matilda Chase Baer and Mrs. Sophia Battie. His granddaughters were Mrs. Dare, of Calvert, and Mrs. Dr. Joseph Graham Ridgely, of Cincinnati. Judge Ridgely's large estate included "Dorsey's Search." This was bought by Caleb and Charles W. Dorsey, who divided. The Stockett property was also held by Judge Ridgely's executors.

CECIL, OR CISSEL.

Arthur Cecil, of St. Mary's, died in 1690. He left two sons, James and John. The former went to Virginia, the latter had a son Zephaniah Cecil, who settled in Howard District, upon Snowden's Second Addition. Two sons, William and Samuel, and two daughters, Elizabeth Smallwood and Nancy Warfield, were his heirs. The Cecils, of Anne Arundel County, near Millersville, descend from William Cecil, who married Miss Pumphrey.

Samuel Cissel married, first, Susie Gartrell Belt and had one daughter, Susie, who married James Turnbull, and one son, Samuel, who married Margaret Belt. He spelled his name "Cissel." A notice of the death of his son, George Washington Cissel, states that he was born in Washington, in 1834, and that his mother was a niece of John H. Bell, of Tennessee. He was one of nine children, each inheriting a farm in Howard and Montgomery County. His farm was in North Laurel. He removed to Washington and went to milling. He was a Commissioner of the District of Columbia and Vice-President of the Farmers' Bank. His beautiful home was Oak Crest, with ample grounds in Georgetown. One son, S. Sewell Cissel, by his first wife, is now a member of the milling firm. The surviving widow is Mrs. Agnes Moore. The brothers of George Washington Cissel were John Bell, Benjamin Gartrell, Chas. Alexander, Thomas Bell, William H., John, Samuel, Nathan and Edwin G. The first Samuel Cissel married, second, Isabella Bell, by whom he had Osborn, Zephaniah, Benjamin G., Philip, James, Richard, Sarah and Margaret. Two of these sons, Osborn and Benjamin, went to Indiana. Philip purchased the other heirs' interest in "Hammond's Gist." Richard Cissel removed to Montgomery County and was County Commissioner for several terms.

Samuel Cissel, second, after purchasing a farm for each son, bought a home near Sligo, where he died in 1864.

Benjamin G. Cissel, of "Paternal Gift," married Mary Ann Childs and had issue: Mary Hortense Virginia Cissel, Samuel Nathan, a student at the Agricultural College, who died in 1880, William Washington Lee Cissel, physician and Clerk of Howard County Court, and Byron Vernon Cissel, Professor of Chemistry in St. John's College.

Dr. Cissel married Cordelia Bell Cissel and Professor Cissel married Mary Ada Cissel.

In Howard County to-day are children of Philip Cissel, of "Hammond's Gist," viz.: Wilbur, Claude, C. E. Marvin and Philip Cissel, all farmers; also, Harry G., Charles A. and Frederick W. Cissel, sons of Charles Cissel, of "Sappington's Sweep," all farmers.

ROBERT RIDGELY,
THE ELK RIDGE MERCHANT.

Hon. Robert Ridgely, of St. Inigoes, left to his oldest son, Robert, "Friend's Choice," 800 acres in Worcester County, "which, though at present in possession of the Duke of York, yet I doubt not, will be within the patent of Lord Baltimore." To Robert, also, a "tract of 600 acres in Somerset." Robert Ridgely, Jr., could not have secured the Worcester lands, for he made no reference to it in his will, but authorized a commission to sell his Somerset lands to pay his debts. He died in 1702, making no mention of his children. His widow became Mrs. Elizabeth Goldsmith. There were several children. Robert Ridgely, their son, was a merchant of Elk Ridge in 1728. His wife, Sarah, inherited "Freeborn's Progress," adjoining "Dorsey's Search;" it was conveyed by them to Thomas Howard for five shillings; still later, it was mortgaged to James Carroll, and in 1744 Robert Ridgely granted Charles Ridgely a bill of sale of all his growing crops.

William Ridgely (of Robert, second,) was a merchant at Elk Ridge in 1763. His will of 1779 named his wife, Margaret, and heirs, Rachel, Amelia, William, Zephaniah, Robert, Charles, Nancy Orem and Sarah Ridgely.

Charles Ridgely (of Robert, second,) held "Discovery," which he sold to Henry Howard and Philip Warfield. He left all to his wife, Hannah (Higgins) Ridgely, to descend to "nephew, Basil Ridgely, and sister, Sarah Ridgely." He named his brothers, William and Nicholas; nieces, Elizabeth Mercer, Susannah Warfield, Sarah Norwood, Mary Norwood, Hannah Spurrier; nephew, Joseph Hobbs (of Joseph); sisters, Mary Hobbs and Deborah Purdie. Wife and nephew, Thomas Hobbs, executors.

Amelia Ridgely (of William) remembered when the old Friendship Meeting House was built in 1800. This was located on the hill overlooking Rattle-Snake Spring.

Sarah Ridgely, widow; Nicholas R. Ridgely and Ruth, his wife; Dennis Dorsey and Rutha, his wife, sold a part of "Thomas' Lot," adjoining Vachel Warfield, to Beale Ridgely.

GLENELG.

This word spells the same from either end. It was given by General Tyson to his estate near by and was later adopted as the name of the post-office. The site is upon "Dorsey's Grove." The late Frank Shipley's modern house stands upon Sarah (Dorsey) Howard's part of "Dorsey's Grove." West of the post-office is Day's store, post-office, creamery and residence, the home of Mrs. Day, mother of Senator George Dorsey Day. Still further west is the home of Joshua Day. An attractive church and modern school complete this settlement. Along this extended line may be seen the heights of Poplar Spring.

Between Triadelphia and Glenelg are located the estates of former Commissioner Gillis Owings and the late Thomas O. Warfield, both progressive farmers. North of Glenelg, near Ivory post-office is the estate of the late Enoch Selby, near which was built, in 1750, "The Chapel of Ease." Mr. Selby's homestead was formerly Mr. Peter Barnes', one of the vestry of that Chapel of Ease. In sight of this was the home of Levin Lawrence, who sold the site of that Chapel. Peter Barnes and Henry Howard surveyed "Henry and Peter," upon which tract Judge William Day, of the Orphans' Court, now resides.

In a field of that tract lies buried Rebecca, wife of Dr. Henry Howard and mother-in-law of Colonel John Hammond Riggs.

Just south, upon "Round about Hills," is the home of Senator George Dorsey Day. His daughter is the wife of John O. Selby, School Commissioner of Howard, whose new dwelling near Glenelg is one of the attractions of that section. A daughter of Mr. Selby was crowned Queen at the Glenwood Farmer's Club Tournament in 1904.

Levin Lawrence was seated upon a portion of "Dorsey's Grove," on Poplar Spring branch, in 1741. He was the son of Benjamin Lawrence, the Quaker, of West River, and Rachel Mariarti (of Edward and Honor Mariarti), of Anne Arundel. Benjamin held "Benjamin's Fortune," which descended from his father, Benjamin, who married Elizabeth Talbott, daughter of Richard and Elizabeth Ewen. This Benjamin was the son of Benjamin Lawrence, of "The Deserts," whose wife was Ann Lawrence. It is now claimed that the original Benjamin was a brother of Sir Thomas.

Leaving the Quaker settlement of West River, Levin and his brother Benjamin came up to Upper Anne Arundel and both married daughters of John and Honor Elder Dorsey, who, in 1735, by deed of partition, granted them equal parts of "Dorsey's Grove," at Glenelg. Benjamin died childless. In 1741, Levin built a brick house on Susan Dorsey's estate. It has only recently been torn down by Mr. Hammond Grimes, now owner of it.

Levin and Susan Lawrence had four sons, all engaged in the War of the Revolution. Benjamin removed to "Delaware Hundred;" John removed to the Linganore; Richard was upon "White Hall," at Guilford; Levin Lawrence, Jr., remained upon "Dorsey's Grove."

As early as 1750, the new church of Queen Caroline Parish was too remote for the western members of the Parish, as seen by the following records:

"Christ Church, Queen Caroline Parish. At a vestry holden on the 1st day of May, 1750, were present the Rev. James Macgill, Mr. John Dorsey, son of Edward; Mr. Basil Dorsey, Mr. Cornell Howard, Mr. Henry Howard, Mr. Philemon Dorsey, Mr. Robert Davis, vestrymen. Mr. John Hood, church warden.

"The vestry having been applyed to by the inhabitants of the upper part of the Parish, requesting that, as they live at too great a distance from the church, a Chappel of Ease may be built in some place convenient to them, the vestry, thinking the proposal reasonable, agreed to go and look out for a place fit for it, and, after viewing several places, it was this day put to vote where it should be built, and, by a majority of voices, it was determined to be at a place known by the name of Poplar Springs, on a tract of land belonging to Levin Lawrence, upon which the vestry agreed to prefer a petition to his Excellency and the Assembly for a law to levy a tax of twelve pence per poll on each taxable inhabitant in the Parish yearly for the next ensuing three years."

The vestry met on August 20th at Poplar Springs and agreed to give Mr. Levin Lawrence fifty shillings for one acre, including the spring, on a part of which acre they proposed to build a chapel forty feet long and twenty-four feet wide.

On June 15th, 1751, the vestry, with Mr. Joshua Dorsey and Henry Ridgely, church wardens, met to let out the building. Mr. William Fee offered to do it the cheapest. He is to have one hundred and fourteen pounds, ten shillings, for building it according to the directions explicitly stated in the contract, "to be weather-boarded with good sound feather-edge plank, neatly planed and beaded, clear of sap and wind shakes, to be nailed on with twenty penny nails—to be completed by 1752."

In February, 1753, the vestry, then consisting of Mr. John Warfield, Mr. Philemon Dorsey, Mr. Greenberry Ridgely, Mr. John Dorsey, son of Caleb and Mr. Peter Barnes, considered the proposition to "Under Pinn the chapel and saw plank for flooring the same." Mr. Levin Lawrence undertook the job for £10. He also agreed to gett the sleepers, put in the "Lites," and finish the chapel for £39.10.

This delay was caused by an apprehension that Mr. Fee had not built the chapel according to contract. Mr. Joseph White was selected by the vestry to examine it and Mr. Robert Barnes was chosen by Mr. Fee. They must have decided against Mr. Fee, as the work was finished by Mr. Levin Lawrence.

This chapel was built about one century before Howard District was made into a county, and yet when I started out to locate the site on which it had stood, after consulting six of the oldest residents of that section, I found that three of them had never heard of it. One thought I was in search of the old election-house which came near being the county-seat.

An old lady (Mrs. Day) thought she had heard of some one hauling brick from the supposed locality and one, the late Mr. Enoch Selby, actually in sight of the location, pointed out "chapel road" and "chapel marsh," at the head of which was "chapel spring." It was close by Levin Lawrence's old brick house, which had been built in 1741, the ragged walls of which were still standing. Near by was the neglected burial ground, marked only by rude headstones. In sight were the storm-beaten brick houses of the former vestrymen of the "Chapel of Ease," but not a stone could be seen of the chapel itself. I was in the footsteps of F. Alden Hill, who had come from Boston in 1883 to trace the Lawrence, Dorsey and Townley families.

At that spring met, a century and a-half ago, many kindred families in Howard. To-day none are left to even know that such a place of meeting ever existed, and yet my notes record the pounds of twenty-penny nails used in its construction.

"JOHN LAWRENCE, OF LINGANORE HILLS."

The Archives of Maryland show John Lawrence upon severa committees of Frederick County, previous to the Revolution, but leading to it. He married Martha West, of "The Woodyard." Her family traces back to the English peer, Lord De La Ware.

Stephen West, the immigrant, son of Sir John of "Houghton," married Martha Hall, 1720. Stephen West, Jr.,—Hannah Williams, daughter of Captain Williams, of Wales, and his wife, Christiana Black, of Scotland. Captain Williams bought from his brother, Mr. Black, of London, the property called "The Woodyard," upon which Henry Darnall, brother-in-law of Lord Baltimore, had built a large brick house, but from reverses was not able to hold and sold it to Mr. Black, his creditor. It was inherited by Hannah Williams, wife of Stephen West, Jr. It was surrounded by a park in which was English shrubbery and was one of the most beautiful of our colonial homes. It is now a wreck by fire.

John Lawrence—Martha West, daughter of Sir Stephen. Issue, Colonel John Lawrence, Jr., of the militia of Frederick County, who married the only daughter of Peter Shriner, a wealthy farmer, of Frederick County. Issue, Josephine—Marcellus Warfield, of Sykesville. Their daughters are Mrs. Robert Ward and Miss Ella Lawrence Warfield.

Juliana Lawrence (of John and Miss Shriner)—Evan Dorsey, Jr., (of Evan, Sr.) and removed to Ohio.

Susannah Lawrence (of John and Martha)—Evan Dorsey, oldest son of Judge Basil Dorsey, of Frederick.

Their son, Evan, Jr.—his first cousin, Juliana Lawrence (of John Lawrence, Jr. and Susan Dorsey (of Evan and Susannah)—William Hobbs, Jr., (of William and Henrietta [Lawrence] Dorsey). Issue, Roderick, Ulysses, Edward, Mrs. Dr. Maynard and Mrs. Captain Ignatius Dorsey.

Mrs. Matilda J. Brent and Mrs. Barbara Compton, of Baltimore, descend from John Lawrence, of Linganore.

CAPTAIN LEVIN LAWRENCE.

The Archives of Maryland record Captain Lawrence, of "The Flying Camp," and his services during the Revolution. He inherited the homestead after the sudden death of his father upon the hunting field. Captain Levin Lawrence—Sarah, daughter of Caleb Dorsey and Rebecca Hammond.

Caleb referred to "his daughter, Sarah Lawrence, having already had her portion."

Captain Levin and Sarah (Dorsey) Lawrence had issue, Caleb Lawrence and Hammond Dorsey Lawrence, the executor of his father, who sold the homestead and removed to Baltimore. His son was the late France La Fayette Lawrence, of Baltimore, whose son is Warrington G. Lawrence, of the firm of Fornacon, Lawrence & Donnell, Architects, 111 Fifth Avenue, New York.

Caleb Lawrence (of Captain Levin) inherited the law library of his uncle, William Dorsey, attorney at Annapolis. Captain Levin inherited all of William Dorsey's lands in Illinois.

Major Richard Lawrence, of "White Hall," was born after the the sudden death of his father, Levin Lawrence. His official service in War of the Revolution is on record. He married, first, Ann Warfield (of Rezin and Honor Elder Howard), of "White Hall." Issue, Otho Lawrence, who studied law under Joshua Dorsey, of Frederick, and became an eminent attorney in Western Maryland. He married Catherine Murdock Nelson, only daughter of Roger and Mary (Brooke Sim) Nelson. Issue, Richard Henry Lee Lawrence, attorney-at-law, Baltimore, who married Rose, daughter of Judge Madison Nelson, of Frederick. Issue, Zulma Marcilly and the late Otho Lawrence, of Baltimore.

Ann Warfield Lawrence (of Otho)—Professor Samuel Humes Kerfoot, of the College of St. James, son of Richard Kerfoot of "Castle Blaney," Moneghan County, Ireland. Issue, six children; Mrs. Kerfoot is seventh in line from Richard Warfield, of the Severn, and for six years has been State Regent of Illinois in the Society of "The Daughters of the American Revolution," and for five years the president of the Society of Colonial Dames of America, of Illinois, being also a member of the Maryland Society of Colonial Dames of America. Mrs. Kerfoot has made investigations through "the county visitations" of the English office of Heraldry, and has proof of each link of two lines of her mother's ancestors (the Nelsons), reaching back to two Norman Barons, of William, the Conqueror. Mrs. Kerfoot's summer home is "Dawn in the Dells," Kilbourn City, Wisconsin. Her winter house is in Chicago.

Major Richard Lawrence—second, Charlotte, daughter of Lieutenant Joseph Warfield, of Smallwood's Battalion. Issue, Nicholas Otho Lawrence and Richard Joseph Lawrence, both under twenty-one years in 1857.

The daughters of Joseph and Elizabeth Dorsey Warfield were Eliza Offutt, Juliet Williams, Charlotte Lawrence. The only son was Nicholas Dorsey Warfield.

"DORSEY'S GROVE,"
LATER HOME OF DR. EPHRAIM HOWARD.

Dr. Ephraim Howard (of Henry) held "lands lying on Chapel road" and "Howard's Resolution." He married a daughter of John Dorsey, of Old Brick Church. He was also a large surveyor and a man

of prominence in business enterprises, including a mill and forge for
manufacturing steel.   He held several thousand acres in Kentucky.
Dr. Henry Howard, Brutus, Cincinnatus, Sarah and Elizabeth
Howard were his heirs.

Dr. Henry Howard resided near Glenwood, on property now held
by Judge William Day.   He married Rebecca Boone.   She named her
heirs Henry, Margaret, granddaughter Rebecca (of Henry); granddaughter Rebecca Boone Riggs; granddaughter Margaret, of son
John B. Howard; grandson Alexander Howard; grandson Augustus
Riggs; daughter Rebecca Riggs.

Dr. John Beale Howard (of Henry) held "Pheasant Ridge,"
"Windsor," "Safe Guard" and Levin Lawrence's lands.   His wife
was Elizabeth Gassaway (of Captain Thomas and Susannah Hanslap).
They had two sons, John Beale Howard and Henry Howard.   In
1783, Dr. Howard appointed Stephen Boone and John Dorsey
trustees to hold his lands for his wife and children, reserving 490 acres
purchased of Colonel Dorsey for paying debts and private use.   He
removed to Harford County.

Joshua Howard (of Henry) was a minor at the death of his
father and then resided in Frederick County.   The homestead
descended to him.   He purchased the interest of his nephew, Henry
Nelson, in "Dorsey's Grove."

Joshua Howard married, first, Rebecca Owings (of Samuel and
Urith Owings'.   Issue, Mrs. Sarah Winchester, Mrs. Samuel Thomas,
of Sandy Spring; Mrs. Rachel Robertson, Samuel Howard—Hannah
Dorsey (of Colonel Edward); Joseph—Lucy Colston; Deborah—
Dr. John W. Dorsey, of the Tripolitan War; Dr. Henry Howard, of
University of Virginia—first, Hannah, daughter of James Snowden
Pleasants.   The wives of Professor Courtney and Professor McGuffey,
L.L.D., were their daughters.   Professor Howard's second wife was
Eliza Elgars, of Virginia, and left Misses Eliza and Anna Howard, of
Charlottesville.

Dr. Marshall Howard (of Professor Henry)—Anna Norman
McCeney, of Anne Arundel County.   Issue, Mrs. Samuel Riggs, Mrs.
Elisha Riggs, Henry Howard, of Brookeville and Marshall P. Howard,
of Baltimore.   The second wife of Joshua Howard was Elizabeth
Warfield, widow of Colonel Charles, of Sams Creek.   Issue, John
Howard, of Baltimore—Juliet, daughter of Alexander Warfield, of
Sams Creek, whose daughter Jemima—Archibald Lamar, of Martins-
burg, West Virginia.

The children of Mr. and Mrs. Samuel Riggs, of Laytonsville, are
Samuel, Lawrence, Douglass, Bessie and Anna.   Mrs. Elisha Riggs
left a son, William, and several daughters.

Mr. Henry Howard, of Brookeville, holds the home of his grandfather, Dr. Henry, of the University, and is also president of the Board
of Trustees of Brookeville Academy, as was his grandfather.
He married Florence Jones, daughter of Josiah Jones, of Montgomery.

Marshall Howard, of Baltimore, married Betty Riggs (of John),
of Montgomery.

DORSEYS OF DAYTON.

Captain Philemon Dorsey (of Joshua) settled upon "Brothers Partnership," at Dayton. He married Catharine, daughter of Colonel Henry Ridgely, and succeeded him as District Surveyor. He was Captain of the Hundred whose duty it was to count the output of tobacco and to levy a church tax for its support. He was one of the builders of "The Chapel of Ease" upon "Poplar Spring Branch" and attended to its building in 1750. His homestead, as seen by one of his descendants, after it had been deserted, stood upon the west of the road leading from Glenelg to Dayton, nearly opposite the later homestead of Mr. Lloyd W. Linthicum. It was a large, square frame building, well built, with curious little closets, all the wood-work hand-carved. He not only surveyed his own estate, but located the heirs of his father-in-law. His surveys reached west of his homestead some ten miles. Philemon Dorsey Jr., was located on "Friendship" and "Sappington Range," near Roxbury Mills. He and his wife, Ann, corrected by deed some of the titles in the will of his father. Their son, Colonel George Dorsey, inherited the homestead, married Rachel Ridgely (of William Jr.) and left Philemon—Martha Warfield (of Azel), Julia—Henry Warfield (of Azel), Maria—David Clarke (of David), Matilda—Samuel Owings (of Samuel).

John Dorsey (of Philemon and Ann) held lands near Triadelphia; married Miss Stringer; issue, Samuel Dorsey, John, Mrs. Martin, and Mrs. Linthicum.

Some of the living heirs of Colonel George Dorsey are John O. Clarke, of Montgomery; James Clarke; heirs of the late George Clarke, Mrs. Dr. Thomas Owings, Mrs. Creager, George Dorsey Owings, William Owings, Gillis Owings, Mrs. George Ridgely, Mrs. Elisha Riggs, Mrs. Richard Lansdale, Mrs. Sheredine, Mrs. Dr. Owings and heirs of Henry Warfield.

The daughters of Captain Philemon Dorsey each received 400 acres of his estate. They were Ann—Captain John Dorsey; Elizabeth—William Ridgely, of "White Wine and Claret;" Sarah—Vachel Warfield (of Benjamin) and Rebeckah (Ridgely) Warfield; Catherine—Captain Benjamin Warfield; (of Benjamin and Rebeckah); Amelia—Samuel Riggs (of John); by a second marriage to Rachel Lawrence (of Levin), his daughter Henrietta—William Hobbs (of Samuel); Ariana—Samuel Owings (of Thomas).

Joshua Dorsey, attorney-at-law, of Frederick, only son of Captain Philemon and Rachel, married Janet Kennedy, of Phil. He held a large and valuable estate in and near Frederick. His only daughter, Elizabeth—Dr. Johnson, whose daughter Elizabeth—John Downey, of New Market.

Joshua Dorsey (of Joshua and Ann Ridgely) was a bachelor, holding "Locust Thicket" and "Anvil," near Waterloo.

Charles Dorsey held the homestead "Major's Choice." He left no descendants.

The living descendants of Captain Philemon Dorsey are in many States of the Union.

Vachel Warfield (of Benjamin and Rebeckah) sold his inheritance upon "Warfield's Range" and took up a large estate adjoining his wife's estate near Dayton. He bought of Nicholas Meriweather two tracts, "Good Range" and "Exchange." He bought of Lancelot Dorsey, sheriff, and his son Darius their part of "Brother's Partnership," adjoining Captain Philemon Dorsey's portion of the same tract. He bought of Lancelot Dorsey and Darius their part of "Good Range." He also held "Mother's Care," "Brother's Love," "Small Land," "Intervene," "Moorehouse's Generosity," "Anything," "Everything" and "Dorsey's Addition to Thomas' Lot," all adjoining each other in the neighborhood of Dayton, near the homestead of Captain Philemon Dorsey, his father-in-law. His will of 1815 was witnessed by Dennis Dorsey, Thomas Batson, Joshua D. Owings and Charles G. Ridgely. The sons of Vachel were Lloyd, Philemon Dorsey, Greenberry, Joshua, Allen. The latter alone married and left Greenberry and Allen.

Catharine Warfield (of Vachel) married Lancelot Linthicum and had issue, Vachel W., Lloyd W., Sarah and Mary Linthicum.

Mr. Lloyd Linthicum's homestead is a part of Captain Philemon Dorsey's homestead. Mr. Linthicum's wife was a sister of the late Aquila Jones.

TRIADELPHIA.

This little Patuxent village is named for three brothers-in-law, all Quakers. Its site is upon Colonel Richard Dorsey's tract "What's Left," which was sold by him to Caleb Bentley, Richard Thomas and Thomas Moore. They gave it its name, "Three Brothers," about half a century ago. This was a thrifty little manufacturing centre; its mill, stores, church upon the hill; its comfortable houses, in one of which were several handsome daughters, gave Triadelphia a far-reaching reputation, but a flood came and it was swept off. Under Mr. Miller it was a success, under Mr. Thomas Lansdale it was destroyed.

Just below Triadelphia was the homestead of Captain Joseph Burgess and his son, Captain Vachel Burgess, of the Revolution.

The survey was "Upland" or "Burgess' Look Out." It was bought from Mr. Dick, of Bladensburg. It is now the Underwood property.

At Triadelphia Benjamin Gaither took up "Benjamin's Lot." It was left to his daughter, Elizabeth Davis, widow of Thomas (of Greenwood), and later widow of Mark Brown.

Captain Joseph Burgess, commanded a company of Elk Ridge militia. He had six sons in the Continental army.

"On Tuesday, March 4th, 1777, it was ordered, That the Western Shore Treasurer pay to Captain Joseph Burgess one thousand dollars for recruiting service." On September 19, 1777, commission was issued to Thomas Worthington, son of Nicholas, in Captain Joseph Burgess' Company of Elk Ridge Battalion of Militia. Captain Burgess signed the protest against the removal of Captain Norwood for criticising General Smallwood.   About 1750 Captain Joseph Burgess married Elizabeth Dorsey, daughter of Michael and Ruth Todd. Their sons were John Burgess, born 20th November, 1751; Joseph, born 1753; Michael, born 1754; Vachel, born 1756; Richard, born 1757; Joshua, born 1760; Philemon, born 1761; William, born 1771; Joseph, Jr., 1780.

The younger, Joseph, was born and named after the death of Lieutenant Joseph Burgess, who died during the war.   He and his brother William were made executors of Captain Joseph's will in 1805, probated 1806.

After the war lots at Fort Cumberland were assigned to his sons who survived.

Michael Burgess, ensign, will be noticed at Marriottsville.

Vachel Burgess (of Captain Joseph) entered the army as ensign, in his nineteenth year, coming out as captain.   He died at his residence at Triadelphia in 1824.   Attached for seven years to the Maryland Line, he won the eulogies of his commanding officers at Guilford Court House, Eutaw Springs and the Battle of Camden, under Baron DeKalb.   He was an upright, hospitable, cheerful, kind-hearted man of intelligence, and a religious citizen who was deeply lamented by a large family and a still larger circle of friends.   Captain Vachel Burgess married Rebecca Dorsey, daughter of Thomas Dorsey (of Henry) by Mary, only daughter of Benjamin and Rebecca (Ridgely) Warfield. His sons were Perry, Thomas and Vachel, who removed to Kent County; the daughters were Anne, wife of Basil Burgess and mother of Arthur Burgess; Elizabeth became Mrs. William Hines, father of Vachel Burgess Hines, long of the Health Department, Baltimore; Harriet became, first, Mrs. William Pitt Watkins, and, second, Mrs. Jeremiah Howard; Mary became Mrs. Nicholas Owings, and Rebecca married Nicholas Dorsey Warfield (of Benj).   The living descendants of these sons and daughters are Vachel B. Hines and his wife, Henrietta, daughter of Thomas Burgess; Mrs. Minnie Gartrell, Oliver Watkins, Brice Worthington Howard, Mrs. Harriet Mathews, Mrs. Henrietta Henderson, Vachel Warfield, of Arkansas, Thomas and Alfred Burgess, (of Thomas) of Kent County, who bore many of the pleasing characteristics of their distinguished father.

Lieutenant Joseph Burgess (of Captain Joseph) died during the war in 1780.   A deed of conveyance of a tract of land, "Dispute Ended," from his grandfather, Michael Dorsey, was executed by Lancelot Dorsey, executor of Michael, in the name of Michael Burgess, older brother of Joseph, Jr., in 1783.

Lieutenant Joshua Burgess was under Colonel Otho Williams, of the First Maryland Regiment.

Philemon Burgess (of Captain Joseph) married Mary Ridgely Dorsey, sister of his brother Vachel's wife.   He resided upon a portion of "Worthington Range," near Clarksville.

Ruth Burgess (of Captain Joseph) married Elisha Warfield (of Benjamin and Rebeckah Ridgely).

In 1790 they removed to Kentucky and left a long line of distinguished sons and daughters.

ROXBURY.

An aged, dilapidated store-house, wherein Mr. James B. Mathews, three-quarters of a century ago, began business; a new store and post-office, a mill and a blacksmith shop, with its residence, all upon the Cat-tail River, with a modern building upon the site of "Roxbury Hall," make up this rocky and romantic settlement.

This survey of the Cat-tail was made by Colonel Richard Dorsey, of "Happy Retreat," or inherited by him from his father, John Dorsey, of the Old Brick Church. Mr. John Wolfe, present owner of "Roxbury Hall," in tearing down the chimney, after its destruction by fire, found a stone marked "R. D. 1776." This house was the home of Samuel Thomas, a minister of Friends, husband of Ann, daughter of Major Charles Alexander Warfield. It was sold by Colonel R. Snowden Andrews, of Baltimore, to Allen Bowie Davis, and by his heirs to Mr. Samuel Banks, from whom Mr. Wolfe holds.

South of Roxbury, upon the "rolling road," is the fine estate of Mr. George Washington Linthicum, descendant of Westley Linthicum and Mary Meriweather (of Reuben and Sarah Dorsey, of "Round About Hills").

Messrs. Linthicum and Sellman were the Anne Arundel electors of "the Glorious Nineteen" for Martin VanBuren, a full record of which will be found in the life of Governor Veazy.

Mrs. Washington Linthicum was the daughter of Mr. Thaddeus Clark and his wife, Miss Crawford, descendant of Colonel Truman Cross. The portrait of Mrs. Thaddeus Clark, now in possession of Mr. James T. Clark, of "Elioak," reveals a distinguished and stately figure.

Mr. Linthicum owns the homestead of the late Dr. John Hood Owings, where Rev. Dr. Jennings, for whom Jennings' Chapel is named, lies buried. His daughter, Mrs. Samuel Banks, adjoins him.

North of Roxbury, upon the Westminster Road, is Mt. Calvary Church, upon a site deeded to the vestry by Allen Bowie Davis and built by the efforts of Rev. Orlando Hutton, who lies buried there.

Just across the Westminster Road from the church was the homestead of John Dorsey. It later came into possession of Mr. Samuel Banks, son of Charles Banks by a daughter of Benjamin Warfield. He succeeded in embracing a large part of the Dorsey surveys into a splendidly-developed estate, placing his son upon a portion of it. His daughters became Mrs. Bartholow, Mrs. John A. Dorsey and Mrs. Dennis Gaither, who now resides upon the homestead.

The neighborhood has long been known as Bank's School House. This stands at the foot of the hill and has been a meeting-place for church organizations, literary societies and school purposes for many years. Near it, on the same road, is the Grange Hall, of a once well-organized order, now passed into history.

Just opposite, "Grange Hall," is the home of a progressive young farmer, political leader and twice a member of the Legislature, Hon. Humphrey D. Wolfe. From his homestead a magnificent view to the east still looks out upon a Dorsey survey. He now owns the property upon which Sarah Dorsey, daughter of Thomas Beale Dorsey and Ann Worthington and widow of Reuben Meriweather, built her home. Hon. Humphrey D. Wolfe is the son of Dr. John Wolfe and Lavinia Dorsey, daughter of Humphrey Dorsey (of John and Margaret Boone, who was the daughter of Captain John Boone, of Broad Neck, Anne Arundel). Her granddaughter, Miss Margaret Boone Dorsey, of the same old homestead, possesses many interesting links of history, and takes pride in helping to perpetuate them. Mr. Wolfe married Miss Margaret Griffith, of Montgomery.

THE DORSEYS OF ROXBURY.

John Dorsey and Colonel Richard, locating in sight of each other, took up a large body of land along the Westminster Road, from Glenwood to Roxbury.

John Dorsey built his house at Mt. Calvary Church, now the property of Dennis P. Gaither and his son Daniel Gaither. His estate extended east to Glenelg, and embraced a part of "Dorsey's Grove" and "Barnes' Purchase." He married Margaret Boone, daughter of Captain John, of St. Margaret's Parish; issue, Caleb, Charles, Stephen, Dr. Richard, Humphrey, Margaret Boone—Major William Gaither, of Unionville, Frederick County.

Caleb located in Glenwood—Ruth Griffith (of Colonel Philemon); issue, John A. Dorsey.

Charles held the present estate of "Longwood" and married Ariana Owings.

Dr. Richard held William Ridgely's homestead and married Matilda, daughter of Dr. Francis Brown Sappington.

Stephen went west.

Humphrey—Rachel Owings (of Samuel and Ariana [Dorsey] Owings) and held the present homestead.

His daughters are Miss Margaret Boone Dorsey and Mrs. Dr. Wolfe, whose sons are Hon. Humphrey D. Wolfe, of the House of Delegates, and John Wolfe, of Glenwood.

Stephen Boone Dorsey (of Humphrey)—Sarah Owings (of Joshua); issue, Humphrey, Mrs. Judge Charles Griffith, Mrs. Thomas Owings Warfield, Joshua and Stephen Boone Dorsey, Jr., who still holds the homestead near Mt. Calvary Church. He married a daughter of Mr. G. W. Linthicum.

"HAPPY RETREAT."

Standing upon the ridge upon which Mt. Calvary Church stands, and looking out to the northwest, over a landscape of surpassing beauty, there looms up the old homestead of Colonel Richard Dorsey, who, after the Revolutionary War was ended, built his "Happy Retreat" and retired there.

Receiving a personal request from General Washington to organize a troop of horse, Colonel Dorsey joined Colonel Moses Rawlings' Regiment of Riflemen, as shown by this old paper found among his records:

State of Maryland, To Richard Dorsey, Lieutenant in
   Colonel Moses Rawlings' Regiment of Rifle Men,
   1774, January 24th, To pay due.................................. £57   10s 9d
Credit amount paid at Phil.................................... 10   2   6

To 7 years, 8 months interest.............................. £47   8   3

     His silver spurs are now held by his grandson, Richard H. Dorsey,
of "Rockland." His sword was given to his son Caleb. Colonel
Dorsey was in the defense of Fort Washington, and, with many others,
was taken prisoner and paroled. Captain Dorsey's troop of horse is
on record in Washington's letters. His promotion came after the
war. Late in life he married Anne Wayman; issue, Mortimer, Caleb,
John, Hanson, Dr. Richard, Dr. Henry, and Dr. Septimus, who
resided upon the present Belvidere Avenue (Baltimore, Maryland),
between Roland Park and Mt. Washington.
     Colonel Dorsey's daughters were Mrs. Henry Ridgely, Mrs. Major
Charles Wayman Hood, Mrs. John Hood, Mrs. Dr. Warner Hobbs,
Mrs. Mary Guest, afterwards Mrs. Norris, of St. Louis. Their present
representatives are Richard H., William T., Mortimer, Mrs. Horatio
Griffith, Mortimer D. Crapster, the late Richard Dorsey (of Caleb),
Daniel and Richard Dorsey (of Thomas), Mrs. Robert Graham, Mrs.
Fisher (of Dr. Septimus), John T. Ridgely, Washington Ridgely,
Oliver Ridgely and Mrs. Luther Bradford.

NICHOLAS GREENBERRY RIDGELY,
ALSO OF ROXBURY.

     Nicholas Greenberry Ridgely (of Colonel Henry and Elizabeth)
inherited "Round about Hills," just south of Glenwood. Upon it
stands a house one hundred and fifty years old. Its high chimneys,
low dormer windows, hip-roof, irregular form and primitive masonry,
furnish abundant evidence of its age. Within the eye catches a
glimpse of Roman frieze along the bordered ceiling—a picture of the
prevailing pastime, a complete gilt representation of a fox chase. The
old entrance to this manor house was through a charming little
meadow, "Deer Park," backed by a sloping woodland. Upon a hill
in the rear is a graveyard, marked by a cluster of trees and headstones
that bear no tracings, yet within lie a family which goes back to the
days of heraldry.
     The will of a more recent owner gives this history. "I, Reuben
Meriweather give and bequeath to my youngest son, Thomas Beale
Dorsey Meriweather, my home plantation whereon I now dwell,
known by the name of 'Round about Hills,' laying upon Nelson's
branch, which I purchased of Nicholas Ridgely's executor, agreeable to his will and Greenberry Ridgely, as heir-at-law, by executing
a deed to me, confirmed the purchase. All the land joining 'Round
about Hills' I purchased of Henry Ridgely."
     This estate covered about one thousand acres.
     The will of Nicholas Greenberry Ridgely, in 1771, appointed his
wife Jane and her brother, Thomas Johns, his executors.

Mrs. Jane (Johns) Ridgely was the daughter of Richard and Margaret (Crabb) Johns. As executrix, she was required to sell the estate and reserve two-thirds for their daughter, Elizabeth Ridgely, who became the wife of John Threlkheld, of Georgetown.

The University of Georgetown stands upon a portion of the Threlkeld estate.

A great-grandson of this family is Captain John Cox Underwood, of Covington, Kentucky, Secretary of the Confederate Memorial Association and author of an interesting memorial of Confederate Generals.

The homestead of Nicholas Greenberry Ridgely was bought by Reuben Meriweather, of Virginia. His son, Thomas Beale Dorsey Meriweather, exchanged it for Mr. Thomas Cook's estate at Cooksville. A portion of it is still held by the heirs of Mr. Thomas Cook.

GLENWOOD.

This long-distance village is located upon the Westminster road. It is the outgrowth of a country store and post-office long kept by Mr. James B. Mathews. Two churches, one north and the other south of it, with a modern educational institution near its centre and a club house adjoining, warn the traveler that he is approaching a progressive people.

Union Chapel, on the north, is beginning to be classed aged. The first marriage celebrated therein was that of Dr. Benjamin Hood, father of our popular ex-president of the Western Maryland Railroad. The bride of that occasion was Miss Hannah Miflin Coulter, and the poetic reporter of the wedding recorded these words:

"Hannah's example cannot fail
 If followed to prove good;
 Whilst silly maidens take the veil,
 She, wiser, took a Hood."

In Oak Grove Cemetery, adjoining Union Chapel, are tablets, memorial stones and monuments, in many cases dating back to the original settlers.

The founder of Glenwood, his Griffith wife and distinguished son, Professor Lycurgus Mathews, organizer of Glenwood Institute, rest within.

Two popular physicians, Dr. Augustus Riggs, Sr., and Dr. Augustus Riggs, Jr., rest under a monument upon its hill.

"Longwood Chapel" stands upon the southern approach. This is a recent joint offering of the late Reverend Dr. Thomas J. Shepherd, his wife, Mrs. Emma (Warfield) Shepherd, and Miss Louisa V. Warfield, all of "Longwood," dedicated during their lives to Christian education. It stands upon the site of the first district school, erected seventy-six years ago.

"BUSHY PARK,"
HOME OF MAJOR CHARLES ALEXANDER WARFIELD.

Northwest of Glenwood, in sight of Union Chapel, stands a stately house now nearly a century and a-half in age. Its surroundings still bear evidences of culture and comfort. Its eastern lawn with playing fountains have disappeared, yet the building itself bids promise of another century of usefulness.

Surrounding it were thirteen hundred acres of Ridgely's Great Park, one-half of which was purchased by Charles Alexander Warfield; the other half was the marriage dower of Elizabeth, daughter of Colonel Henry and Ann (Dorsey) Ridgely, as the young bride of Dr. Charles Alexander Warfield, son of Azel and Sarah Griffith, both of whom were descendants on the distaff side of John Baldwin, of South River.

Dr. Charles Alexander Warfield had just graduated in medicine from the University of Pennsylvania; and was one of the organizers, still later, of the Medical and Chirurgical Society of Maryland. He took his young wife from her stately manor house of "Montpelier," upon the upper Patuxent, to the little cabin then standing upon "Bushy Park," and then commenced the erection of the present building in 1771. He was twenty and she was nineteen years of age.

Three years after their marriage the war cry of a revolution echoed throughout Maryland. The celebrated "Whig Club" had already made itself a power. Dr. Warfield was a member and a Major of Battalion. Parading his battalion in the vicinity of Carroll's Manor, he placed upon the hats of his men a label bearing the motto: "Liberty and Independence, or Death in pursuit of it." The venerable Mr. Carroll, father of the patriot, rode up to Mr. Azel Warfield, father of the Major, exclaiming, "My God! Mr. Warfield, what does your son Charles mean? Does he know that he has committed treason against his King and may be prosecuted for a rebel?" The father replied:

"We acknowledge no King; the King is a traitor to us, and a period has arrived when we must either tamely submit to be slaves or struggle for Liberty and Independence. My son Charles knows what he is about. His motto is mine and soon must be the sentiment of every man in this country."

The cry of "Treason against the King" ran along the line of the battalion, and in a few minutes not a label was to be seen in the hats of any of the men, except Dr. Warfield and Mr. James Conner, of Baltimore, who wore their labels home.

Shortly after this, hearing that the brig Peggy Stewart, loaded with tea, had arrived at Annapolis, Major Warfield placed himself at the head of the "Whig Club" and marched to Annapolis. Under the big oaks of Warfield's spring, upon "Warfield's Range," resting on the journey, these old pioneers determined to burn the vessel, not as disguised Indians, but in open daylight. When the club had arrived at the State House, Judge Chase, himself a connection by marriage of Major Warfield and who had been employed by Mr. Anthony

Stewart, owner of the vessel, to defend him, commenced to address the club in opposition to the destruction of the vessel. Major Warfield, finding that he was likely to make an impression upon his company, interrupted his speech, reminding Mr. Chase of his former patriotic speeches before the club which had inflamed the country, and now pronouncing it cowardice or submission, to stop short of their object, he called upon his men to follow him, that he himself would set fire to the vessel. In his hand he carried a chunk of fire. Stewart at first was bold and defiant. By way of intimidation a gallows was erected in front of his house. Major Warfield then said: "Mr. Stewart, we have come to offer you the choice of two propositions: You must either go with us and fire your own vessel or hang by the halter before your door." These words were spoken in a courteous, but determined, manner, and Mr. Stewart accepted the former, and in a few moments the whole cargo, with the ship's tackle and apparel, was in flames.

The writer of the above was in company with Judge Chase and Dr. Warfield a few years before their death, and heard Mr. Chase remark in a jocular manner, "If we had not succeeded, Doctor, in the contest both of us would have been hung, you for burning the ship of tea and I for declaring I owed no allegiance to the King and signing the Declaration of Independence."

The above facts were recorded in the "Baltimore Patriot," in 1813, shortly after the death of Dr. Warfield. They were also confirmed by descendants of Captain Thomas Hobbs, one of the club.

Mr. Mayer, in his recent painting of "The Burning of the Peggy Stewart," has followed the above record, placing Major Warfield, with torch in hand, standing beside Mr. Stewart as he fired his vessel. He is dressed in the Continental uniform, in early manhood, with kindred features of the handsome portrait by Peel, now in possession of Mr. Gustavus Warfield, of Glenwood.

Dr. Warfield's daughter, Eliza—Richard Snowden, of "Oakland" (see Snowden's); Ann—Samuel Thomas and resided at "Roxbury Hall;" Henry Ridgely Warfield was an attorney-at-law resided in Frederick and was a member of Congress, in 1820. He was also a witness to the will of Charles Carroll, of Carrollton. He died a bachelor. Dr. Peregrine Warfield was one of Hanson's Party of Defence, when the War Party of Baltimore forbade the publication of the "Federal Republican." He was severely wounded by the mob and was attended by his father at "Bushy Park,"which was the assembly hall for all sympathizing Federalists. Dr. Peregrine Warfield married Harriet Sappington, "the most beautiful woman in Maryland," and resided in Georgetown.

An eye-witness of the burning of the Peggy Stewart has been found. John Galloway's letter to his father, Samuel Galloway, of "Tulip Hill," West River, says:

"The committee then ordered the tea from on board the brig, but some of the mob called out that it should also share the same fate.

"The committee, then with the consent of Mr. Dick, declared the vessel and tea should be burnt. Then Dr. Warfield (a youth that practised under Dr. Thompson at the Ridge for sometime) made a motion that the gentlemen should make their concessions on their knees; there was a vote on it in favor of the gentlemen; they then came and read their concessions to the public, and then Mr. Stewart went on board of his vessel and set fire with his own hands and she was burning when I left."

Old Mr. Dick was the father of Mrs. Anthony Stewart.

Dr. Gustavus Warfield followed his father's profession and located near the homestead, and will be noted in "Longwood."

HAMMOND OF "BUSHY PARK."

This old estate passed some thirty years ago to Mr. Chadwick, of New York. He resold it to Mr. Nicholas W. Hammond, of New Market, a direct descendant of Major Charles Hammond and Hannah, his wife, daughter of Philip Howard. Mr. Hammond married Miss Wood, of New Market, who upon her mother's side goes back to Orlando Griffith, and through his marriage to Katherine Howard is doubly a Howard connection. Mr. Charles Hammond and Mrs. Effie Harban are the only heirs.

Mr. Charles Hammond married Hattie, daughter of Judge William Mathews. He is a member of the Glenwood Farmers' Club, and is not only a leading young farmer, but a genial and popular gentleman.

"GLENWOOD FARMERS' CLUB."

When Professor J. D. Warfield, the Principal of Glenwood Institute, had met the young, progressive farmers of that section he said to them:

"I was one of the organizers of "Vansville Farmers' Club," which proved to be a success. Now, I want you young men to come to the Institute and organize."

His proposition was accepted, and there, around the supper table, was instituted a club that has never had a break in its yearly work.

Out of it has grown a yearly picnic, sometimes agricultural and often running into a tournament and dance.

The Glenwood Farmers' Picnic is the meeting place for almost all of Western Maryland. The members of the Club are Mr. Gustavus Warfield, President; Mr. William Stinson, Governor Edwin Warfield, Marshall T. Warfield, Charles Hammond, Thomas C. Stewart, Samuel Musgrove, T. Musgrove, Harry Peddicord, Rowland Peddicord, Thomas Clarke, Hon. Humphrey, D. Wolfe, Shepherd Dorsey, Daniel Gaither, all large, progressive, intelligent farmers, who in one of the most cultivated sections of Maryland, in a garden spot of natural beauty, are continuing on in the good work organized at Glenwood Institute some ten years ago.

From Glenwood, also, was written "Historic Spots near Glenwood," which doubled the circulation of the "Ellicott City Times."

"LONGWOOD."

Back of the chapel is "Longwood," named in honor of Napoleon's exile home. It was built by Dr. Gustavus Warfield, son of Major Charles Alexander, of "Bushy Park," in 1820. When nearly ready for occupancy it was consumed by fire. Mrs. Dr. Warfield at that time was visiting her father, Mr. William Evan Thomas, near Philadelphia. Upon the very night of the fire, in her dreams she saw the house on fire and her husband consumed in it. Without waiting for confirmation, she started next morning for home. Dr. Warfield also started that same morning to convey the news to her in person. Reaching his destination and finding her gone he returned immediately. She had reached the tollgate opposite General Thomas Hood's home without learning anything to allay her fears. There General Hood met her carriage and assured her of her husband's safety and his departure for Philadelphia to meet her.

Taking her to his home and directing the gatekeeper to send the doctor to her upon his return, they there met in reunion after many hours of suspense.

Miss Louisa Victoria Warfield, who lately presided over the rebuilt "Longwood," was the first child born therein. Seven sisters went from there as brides. Martha Ann, born at "Bushy Park," in 1814, went as the bride of her cousin, Dr. William Gray Knowles. Born during the exciting war, when her uncle, Dr. Peregrine, had been brought to that same house wounded in defense of a free press, she kept during life a daily record of current history, embracing the still more thrilling events of the Civil War. Her death was the first broken link of her family. She died only a few days before the declaration of the Spanish War.

Elizabeth Ridgely Warfield, her sister, married Richard Nicholas Snowden, of "Oakland," at Laurel. Her daughter is Mrs. William Dorsey.

Emma Warfield became the bride of Reverend Dr. Thomas J. Shepherd, of Virginia, for years in charge of the First Presbyterian Church at Lisbon and the First Presbyterian Church at Philadelphia. He was the author of several standard church works.

Mary Warfield married Edward Snowden, of "Avondale."

Eugenia Gray Warfield married Dr. William H. Stinson, of Baltimore. Her son, William H. Stinson, now of Glenwood, is a member of "The Glenwood Farmers' Club" and owns the homestead of Mr. James Mathews, the first merchant. Mary, daughter of Mrs. Stinson, is the widow of Dr. Augustus Riggs, Jr. Her estate at Cooksville was the home of Thomas Beale Dorsey Meriweather. Isabella Stinson is now the wife of Dr. Macintosh.

Isabella Warfield went to "Bushy Park" as the bride of Charles D. Warfield. She died in Cumberland. Her family is elsewhere noted.

Adelaide Warfield married William Snowden, of "Birmingham Manor." He represented his county in the Maryland Legislature. He and his wife both died at Glenwood. His son-in-law, George

Addison Hodges, descendant of Governor Benjamin Ogle, is a resident of Glenwood. Her family is in the Snowden sketch.

Dr. Evan William Warfield, lately deceased, only son of Dr. Gustavus and only grandson of Major Charles Alexander Warfield, resided upon the northern border of Glenwood. His first wife was Sallie Warfield, of "Bushy Park," daughter of Charles D. Warfield and Mrs. Ruth (Griffith) Dorsey, his wife. Gustavus Warfield, former president of the Baltimore Cab Company, is the oldest son. His country residence is at "Inwood," opposite his father. His wife, Ella (Hoffman) Warfield, is a descendant of Patrick Henry. Mr. Warfield is now a purveyor of Springfield Asylum. Evan Warfield, Jr., and Charles D. Warfield, of "Clifton," are the remaining sons.

Mrs. Charles D. Warfield is the daughter of Nicholas Snowden, born at "Montpelier," who lost his life in the Confederate service.

Louisa, late daughter of Dr. Evan W. Warfield, was the wife of Charles Hook, civil engineer of Baltimore. Mary is the wife of Thomas Cockey, of Pikesville.

Dr. Warfield married, second, Julia Anthony, of Richmond, Virginia, and has one son, Gilmer Anthony Warfield. To Dr. Warfield is due the credit of giving to the world the true story of the "Peggy Stewart" episode, elsewhere related. His father heard many of the facts from the participators in that stirring contest. He was a writer of considerable note, and from his communications to the press were gathered the interesting story herein told. Dr. Warfield possessed a portrait of Major Warfield.

"KINGSDENE."

This imposing homestead of Judge William Mathews, merchant and postmaster of "Glenwood," stands upon a part of Captain Thomas Hobbs' surveys, which embraces the whole area east of the Westminster road to Cooksville. Judge Mathews succeeded his father, James B. Mathews, in his successful country store, the original site of which was just opposite the gateway of "Kingsdene." His present location is upon the original site of Glenwood Institute.

About the time of the organization of Howard County Judge Mathews married Harriet Howard, daughter of Jeremiah Howard and Harriet (Burgess) Watkins, both descendants of two Revolutionary captains.

"Kingsdene" has sent seven brides out of its threshold. Two of them went to Kentucky, viz., Mrs. Collins and Mrs. Dr. Norwood; two to Baltimore, Mrs. Dr. Thaddeus Clark and Mrs. Mary Griffith; one to New York, Mrs. R. McKean Barry, and two in Howard County, Mrs. Charles Harban and Mrs. Wheeler, leaving two still at "Kingsdene."

B. Howard Mathews, oldest son, is an attorney in Norfolk; William, Jr., is in business in Glenwood; Cleany Mathews has entered upon an actor's career, and Lycurgus, alone, remains as a Howard County farmer. He married Miss Pindell, of Howard, and located at Dayton.

Judge Mathews was for several years Judge of the Orphans' Court of Howard. Of the large family of sons and daughters of Mr. James B. Mathews, he and his brother Alfred are the only remaining ones in Howard. His mother was Catharine Griffith, daughter of Captain Samuel Griffith of the Revolution.

CRAPSTER.

Just opposite Union Chapel at Glenwood is a stone house of commodious proportions, which was built upon Captain Thomas Hobbs, survey by Basil Crapster nearly a century ago. He was the son of John Crapster and Susan Little. Basil married Harriet Dorsey, daughter of Vachel, son of Captain John Dorsey, of Walnut Grove.

Vachel Dorsey's mother was Ann, daughter of Colonel Philemon Dorsey. He inherited her dower upon the Patuxent, south of Florence. His wife was Ann Poole.

The issue of Basil and Harriet were, first, Abraham Crapster, who removed to Westminster, Carroll County, and married Alice Patterson, daughter of William, grandson of Nathaniel, of Ireland, who came in 1742. Issue, Ann M., Harriet, Basil Dorsey, Sarah J., William Woods, James, John J.

Ann—Captain John Gilleland, of Gettysburg, Pennsylvania, but now of Sabine Pass, Texas. Issue, William, of Texas; Ellen, of Gettysburg; Harriet E.—William Gillson, of Frederick, Maryland. Issue, Basil, of Emmittsburg; William, of St. Joseph, Missouri; Frances—Neil Zimmerman, near Frederick; Basil Dorsey, single (dead). Sarah J.—Mortimer Dorsey, of Howard County, grandson of Colonel Richard Dorsey, of the Revolution, who built "Happy Retreat." Issue, Harriet, William, Thaddeus, Alice Patterson, Clarence, late of Boston; Elizabeth, Anna, Richard, Harry, Adele. Thaddeus—Miss Donner, of Boston; Alice—R. Galt, of York Road; Annie—Mr. Barr, of Chicago.

William Woods Crapster—first, Elizabeth Morrison (of William), of Frederick County. Issue, William Bruce, of Washington; Alice Patterson—P. Jones, of Taneytown; Lieutenant Thaddeus Greaves, of the Revenue Service, now at Wilmington, North Carolina; James W. (deceased).

John J. Crapster—Mary O'Neal, daughter of Dr. I. W. C. O'Neal, of Gettysburg, Pennsylvania, whose mother was a daughter of John and Susan (Little) Crapster. Issue, Ellen Patterson, Anna P., John O'Neal, Basil Walter, Elizabeth C., all of Taneytown, Maryland.

John G. Crapster (of Basil) was seated upon the estate of Vachel Dorsey. He married Elizabeth Ann, daughter of Philemon D. Warfield; no surviving issue. Gustavus Crapster (of Basil) removed to Westminster. He is the only surviving executor.

Rhodolphus Crapster (of Basil) adjoined his brother John upon Captain Philemon Dorsey's survey. He married Elizabeth, daughter of Mortimer Dorsey and granddaughter of Colonel Richard, of "Happy Retreat." Issue, an only son, Mortimer Dorsey Crapster, who resides upon his father's homestead. He married Georgietta, daughter of William Ridgely Warfield, granddaughter of Colonel Gassaway Watkins. Issue, Rodolphus, Ernest, Eleanor, Mary Blanche, Thaddeus, Mortimer, Jr., Alice, Emma, Bowie, Robert Gordon.

Thaddeus Crapster (of Basil) inherited the homestead and married Eleanor Greaves, his cousin, daughter of Dr. Greaves, of Scotland. Her mother, Camsadel Watkins, was named for the Camden battle, in which her father, Colonel Gassaway Watkins, was engaged. There is no issue.

Rev. William Crapster, teacher and minister, succeeded his brother John and married Eleanor Amelia Warfield, daughter of William Ridgely. Issue, William Channing Crapster, Mrs. Emma Taylor and Mrs. Florence Shields, of California.

FLORENCE.

This village was named by Gassaway Watkins Warfield, now dead. Though present when it was named, I cannot remember the favorite lady thus honored.

Florence was started as a cross-roads store, later becoming a post-office; it is now a business centre for a large section of upper Howard. Hon. Walter M. Black, former delegate to the Legislature, adjoins it on the north and Joshua N. Warfield, of the Democratic Executive Committee and School Commissioner of the County, owns the whole village and adjoins it on the south. Both have converted old fields into productive farms, upon which are commodious houses upon the sites of their progenitors' primitive abodes. This whole section was a Welsh settlement.

Four brothers, John, Philip, Samuel and Henry Welsh, sons of John and Hannah (Hammond) Welsh, located north, south, east and west of Florence. Hon. Walter Black is upon a portion of Philip's; Joshua N. Warfield is upon Johns, and owns a portion of Samuel's and of Henry's. Three of the brothers married Griffith descendants. John married Lucretia Dorsey, a niece of Hon. Henry Griffith; Philip married Elizabeth Davis, a niece of Hon. Henry Griffith, and Samuel married Rachel, daughter of Hon. Henry Griffith. Lucretia Welsh (of Philip) became the wife of Philemon Dorsey Warfield, of "Locust Grove;" Rachel (of Samuel) became the first wife of Joshua Warfield, of "Cherry Grove," and great-grandmother of Mrs. Walter Black; Lydia (of John) became the second wife of Joshua, of "Cherry Grove," and grandmother of Joshua N. Warfield. The latter is upon her estate. He also holds the most western survey of Captain Philemon Dorsey, some ten miles west of Captain Dorsey's residence. It was the estate of his daughter Ann, descending to her son Vachel, then to Mrs. Basil Crapster and her sons, John, Rodolphus and William, and thence, by purchase, to its present owner.

Mortimer Dorsey Crapster (of Rodolphus) holds his portion and from his hillside home overlooks the Patuxent.

Joshua N. Warfield also holds another survey of Captain Philemon Dorsey, a portion of his great-grandmother's dower, and beyond that he now owns a survey of Hon. Henry Griffith, in all some 2,000 acres. He found much of it barren fields. By magnificent management, aided by generous liming, it now yields abundant crops of grass and grain.

"CHERRY GROVE," HOMESTEAD OF CAPTAIN BENJAMIN WARFIELD, OF THE ELK RIDGE MILITIA.

Upon the old rolling road, twenty miles west of "Warfield's Range," Benjamin, the son of Benjamin and Rebeckah (Ridgely) Warfield, seated himself and built, in 1768, the present hipped-roof house, "Cherry Grove." Over that road two generations, at least, rolled their tobacco to Elk Ridge.

Ten years after Benjamin had settled war was at hand. The city of Annapolis and all of its water inlets needed military protection. On Monday, March 2, 1778, a commission was issued, by order of the Council, to "Benjamin Warfield, Captain in the Elk Ridge Battalion of Militia." His assistants were Henry Griffith, first lieutenant, Robert Warfield, second lieutenant; Charles Warfield, ensign. These were all neighbors in upper Anne Arundel, now Howard.

Captain Warfield's wife was of a kindred branch of the same families as himself. She was Catharine, daughter of Captain Philemon Dorsey, and was a namesake of her mother, Catharine Ridgely. She brought him an estate about as large as his own, some 400 acres; it was immediately across the old rolling road.

Two sons, Beale and Philemon Dorsey Warfield, entered the next war—of 1812. They were called to defend Annapolis, but, when it was learned that Washington was in still greater danger, the Annapolis force was pushed on to Bladensburg. Before reaching it the bridge had been crossed by the British and the battle had been lost. In the midst of that war Captain Benjamin died, in 1814. His will placed Beale upon his mother's dower and his youngest son, Joshua, upon the homestead, whilst his son, Philemon Dorsey Warfield, was seated upon "Ridgely's Great Range," to the north of the homestead.

Beale built "Springdale" down by the spring. His wife was his cousin, Amelia Ridgely.

Philemon Dorsey built his brick house near the pioneer cottage of Charles Ridgely, from whom it was bought. His wife was Lucretia Welsh, daughter of Philip.

Joshua Warfield brought to the homestead, first, Rachel Welsh (of Samuel), and second, Lydia Welsh (of John).

These were daughters of three brothers. In the three graveyards just named a very interesting record might be made. Upon the marble slab, only recently erected to the memory of Captain Benjamin Warfield by the Governor and his brothers, might have been written the following: "Here lie descendant sons and daughters of twelve colonial leaders and friends," the history of whom fills a large portion of this volume. They were Colonel Edward Dorsey, Hon.

John Dorsey, Major John Welsh, Major-General John Hammond, Captain Philip Howard, Matthew Howard, Colonel Henry Ridgely, Hon. Robert Ridgely, Captain John Worthington, Colonel Nicholas Gassaway and Governor Nicholas Greenberry. In two of these graveyards are the remains of two daughters of a soldier of two wars, Colonel Gassaway Watkins.

CHERRY GROVE.

This hipped-roofed house was built in 1768 by Captain Benjamin Warfield, whose estate was "Fredericksburg." His wife Catharine Dorsey, daughter of Colonel Philemon and Catharine Ridgely, held her dower just across the old rolling road, which passed through the two estates.

Benjamin Warfield, their oldest son died in early manhood. The next two sons, Beale and Philemon Dorsey Warfield, were in the War of 1812 and were hurrying from Annapolis to Bladensburg to assist in its defense on that eventful day of retreat.

Beale was an intelligent man, a writer of deeds and wills, and he held the dower of his mother. Down by a spring he built his cottage and named it "Springdale." His wife was Emily Ridgely, daughter of William Ridgely, of "White Wine and Claret," at Clarksville, a descendant of Hon. Robert Ridgely, Lord Baltimore's Chief Officer.

Emily (Ridgely) Warfield's mother was Elizabeth Dorsey, daughter of Colonel Philemon, by Catherine Ridgely, granddaughter of Colonel Henry Ridgely, of Lord Baltimore's Council.

Beale Warfield's wife was a representative of both branches of Ridgelys, the "Black Heads" and the "Light Heads." The issue of Beale and Emily were George, the intelligent bachelor; 'William Ridgely and Catharine, wife of Warner Warfield, of "Bagdad," near Sykesville, Maryland.

SPRINGDALE.

William Ridgely Warfield held the homestead and married Eleanor, daughter of Colonel Gassaway Watkins. Issue, Rosalba, widow of Rev. Mr. Mosely, of Mississippi, who had one daughter, Bertha, now deceased. Beale A. Warfield, surveyor, married Cordelia England, of Abram; no issue. Bowie Clagett Warfield, horticulturist, of Sandoval, Illinois—Julia Gregory (now deceased). Issue, Alverta— Rodolphus Crapster and Alice Warfield, of Sandoval; Eleanor Amelia—first, Rev. William Crapster; second, Captain Richard Watkins, of California; children elsewhere named; Gassaway Watkins Warfield, the merchant, died in early manhood, unmarried.

Emma Warfield (of William and Eleanor), now desceased—John R. Kenley, former General Manager of the Atlantic Coast Line Railroad, now of New York. Issue, Edna and Nelly Kenly, the former a recent bride of Wilmington, North Carolina.

Camsadel—George England (of Abram). Issue, Elizabeth and Cordelia, the former a recent bride of Mr. Sollers, of Calvert County.

Alberta Clay—Samuel Sharretts and died a bride.

William Ridgely Warfield, Jr., is a hydraulic engineer and was in charge of the construction of the Harlem River Tunnel.

Georgietta, youngest daughter—Mortimer Dorsey Crapster, of Rodolphus and Elizabeth (Dorsey) Crapster.   Issue, Rodolphus, Ernest, Eleanor, Mary Blanche, Thaddeus, Jr., Alice, Emma, Bowie and Robert Gordon.   They can claim three Revolutionary ancestors.

Warner and Catharine Warfield, of "Bagdad," had issue— Marcellus Warfield, merchant, of Sykesville—Josephine, daughter of Colonel John Lawrence, Jr., of Linganore, whose mother was Martha West, of "The Woodyard;" issue, Mary, Joseph and Ella Lawrence Warfield; Mary Joseph—Robert H. Ward; issue, William and Warfield Ward; Manelia—Henry Jenkins (of Robert) brother of the late Colonel Stricker Jenkins.   She holds the old homestead, "Bagdad," and has considerable data of value to the family.

LOCUST GROVE.

Philemon Dorsey Warfield, third son of Captain Benjamin, of "Cherry Grove," was born at the beginning af the Revolution.

Returning from the War of 1812, he bought of Charles Greenberry Ridgely, Jr., the western part of "Ridgely's Great Range." Building his brick house near the log cabin of this pioneer outpost, he married Lucretia Griffith Welsh, daughter of his neighbor, Philip Welsh.

Leading his negroes he went into the forest and cut it down, raised tobacco, rolled it over the "rolling road" to Elk Ridge Landing and at his death held some 1,500 acres of fertile land.

Standing, to-day, in the centre of that tract the eye rests upon open fields of grain and grass; upon large modern barns; upon comfortable commodious houses; upon land all limed; upon a landscape of surpassing beauty, which to a returning exile is a revelation of agricultural development, for it must be acknowledged that the back country of Anne Arundel has come to the front.

Six daughters and five sons were born at "Locust Grove." To-day, only one son and three daughters remain.   Elizabeth Ann (now deceased) became Mrs. John G. Crapster (of Basil).   Their children died in infancy.   Lemuel Warfield, the oldest son (now deceased), inherited "Columbia," a large tract on the east of the estate.   He married Elizabeth Hood (now deceased), daughter of Dr. John Hood Owings.   Issue, Philemon Dorsey (deceased)—Carrie Dorsey.   Issue, Mary; John Hood O. Warfield—Annie Reed.   Issue, Stirling Custis, John H. Owings, Guy Trevelyn, William Howard, Bertha, Irene and Annie ˌElizabeth; Lemuel, Jr.—Vallie Burgess, daughter of Dr. Carter, of Virginia.   Issue LeRoy Carter, Edwin, Margaret Gertrude and Augustus Warfield; Guy Trevelyn Warfield, youngest son, is connected with the Ætna Life Insurance Company, of Baltimore.   He married Clara Pettes.   They have a son.   Amanda Lucretia, oldest daughter, became Mrs. John Willis Kincaid, of

Baltimore. No issue. Mary Boyle (now deceased) became Mrs. Dr. William S. Magruder, of Shepherdstown. Issue, Roy, Elizabeth Vandoran, wife of Professor Allen, of Missouri; Helen Augusta, bride of Samuel Emory, of Queen Anne County; Hannah Owings, next daughter, became Mrs. Andrew Denison Stanton, son of General David L. Stanton, of Baltimore. Issue, Beatrice Owings and Nellie Denison; Katherine Davis is the bride of Mr. Griffin, of Mississippi; Margaret Gertrude and Mattie Augusta are single.

Elizabeth Ann, wife of Thomas Emory, of Queen Anne County.

Clementine, wife of John Myron Adams, of Baltimore.

Amanda, second daughter of Philemon Dorsey Warfield, became the wife of Dr. Artemas Riggs, son of Colonel John Hammond and Rebecca (Howard) Riggs. Issue, Kate Riggs, wife of Frank Griffith, whose daughter Francis is the wife of Dr. H. G. Spurrier. Issue, Catharine; Artemas Riggs Griffith—Hattie Calliflower. Issue, Frank Riggs.

Catharine Dorsey became Mrs. Samuel Greenberry Davis. Their daughter Emma died in early womanhood.

Dr. Milton Welsh Warfield (now deceased), graduate of the University of Pennsylvania, settled at "Welwyn." His wife was Mary Elizabeth Dawley, daughter of John and Adeline (Cummings) Dawley, of Yorkshire, England, a lineal descendant of Lady Jane Grey. Issue, Benjamin Dorsey Warfield, graduate of University of Louisville Law School, adjusting attorney for the Louisville and Nashville Railroad, practices before the Court of Appeals of Kentucky. (See sketch elsewhere.)

Dr. Ridgely Brown Warfield, graduate of University of Maryland, was Surgeon-General upon the Staff of Governor Lloyd Lowndes. He practices in both Howard and Baltimore.

Milton Warfield was a member of the Fifth Regiment, Company D, in the Spanish War.

Anna, only daughter, is the wife of Dr. Archibald Harrison, of Baltimore. Issue, Mary Randolph, Julia Leigh and Alice Harrison.

Augustus Warfield (now deceased), who held the homestead— Kate A. Gaither (now deceased), daughter of Perry and Henrietta Poole. There was no issue.

Lucretia Griffith Warfield (deceased) married Dr. James S. Martin, "California Pioneer," son of "The Old Defender," Dr. Samuel B. Martin, by his wife, Ruth Dorsey Hawkins. Issue, Lizzie Blair, wife of Dr. William Mills, of Baltimore; Augustus Warfield Martin, of Baltimore—Annie, daughter of Captain Lay, U. S. N. Issue, Lay, Ann and Ruth Martin.

Dr. Frank Martin, of Baltimore, surgeon, graduate of the University of Maryland—Ann Coates, daughter of Dr. Coates, of Baltimore.

Avolina Warfield (of Philemon Dorsey) is the widow of Major Charles Wayman Hood, of Carroll County. Professor Joshua Dorsey Warfield, only surviving son, graduate of Dickinson College and for ten years Professor of English in the Maryland Agricultural College, married, first, Tonnie Dawley (of John and Adaline). Issue, Eldred Dudley Warfield, of the U. S. Army (elsewhere noted), and M. Serenah, wife of George Biglow Schley, of Cincinnati, Ohio. His present wife is Margaret, only daughter of the late Dr. S. J. Cooke, by Mary, daughter of Hon. James Duke Dalrymple and Christiana Clare, of Calvert. Issue, Mary Olivia, John Breckinridge, Bernard Dalrymple and Margaret Clare Warfield.

Joshua Warfield, youngest son of Captain Benjamin, of "Cherry Grove," heired the homestead. He married two Welsh wives. By his first, Rachel (of Samuel), he had Avolina Riggs, wife of Elisha, whose only living daughter is Mrs. Kate Dorsey, of Roxbury, already recorded in the Riggs family; and Nicholas Ridgely Warfield (of Joshua) married Eleanor Warfield and died without issue. She has only recently passed away. Joshua Warfield's second wife was Lydia, daughter of John Welsh, a brother of Samuel. From that marriage were Albert Gallatin Warfield, who built "Oakdale," and Catharine, late widow of Mr. James Baxley. She inherited the homestead which has now passed to her nephew, John Warfield, of Albert.

OAKDALE

In 1838 Albert G.' Warfield built "Oakdale," then a forest home. Many of its present attractions were his conception. He was a model man in every phase of life. As retiring as a child, he lived the calm, placid life of a typical farmer of the old school, refusing all attempts to draw him from his home life. In the interest of his children, whom he loved with manly fervor, he was induced to accept the position of School Commissioner. That office he filled with intelligent interest, but refused all others. He married early in life Margaret Gassaway Watkins, daughter of Colonel Gassaway Watkins. His life has thus been depicted, from which I quote:

Mr. Albert G. Warfield, one of the most prominent and respected citizens of Howard County, died at his residence "Oakdale," on Wednesday, after a brief illness. He was born February 26, 1817, on the plantation where he lived, in the old Colonial house built in 1768 by his grandfather, Captain Benjamin Warfield. He inherited from his father a large number of slaves and a portion of the home plantation, and spent there his long and honored life. His wife, who survives him, was Miss Margaret Gassaway Watkins, a daughter of Colonel Gassaway Watkins, of Revolutionary fame, and a sister of Dr. W. W. Watkins, of Howard County. Mr. and Mrs. Warfield would have celebrated their golden wedding on the 24th of August next. Mr. Warfield was a cultivated, refined and courteous gentleman of the old school, who dispensed at his beautiful home a generous hospitality. He was an indulgent master and, though one of the largest slave-owners of his section of the State, he believed that slavery was inconsistent with the character of our republican institutions, and acting upon that belief he manumitted his as they arrived at the age of forty years. Henry Winter Davis, who entertained in his early life similar views, was one of his boyhood companions and schoolmates. Mr. Warfield, though often solicited, never accepted public office but once, in 1869, when he served as president of the county school board. Since the war he has been identified with the Democratic party, and was one of Senator Gorman's first and staunchest political friends and supporters, and always noted with great interest and pleasure his success as a public man and citizen.

Two of his sons served in the Confederate Army—Gassaway Watkins Warfield, who died at Camp Chase, in 1864, and Albert G. Warfield, Jr., who after the war became a well-known civil engineer, went to Japan in 1873 as a member of the American Scientific Commission, of which Colonel Capron was chief, and died in 1883.

Four sons and two daughters survive him—Messrs. Joshua N. Warfield and Marshall T. Warfield, leading farmers of the county; Hon. Edwin Warfield, President of the Maryland Senate in 1886 and late Surveyor of the Port of Baltimore; Mr. John Warfield, member of the Baltimore Bar and editor of the "Daily Record;" Mrs. M. Gillet Gill, of Baltimore, and Mrs. Herman Hoopes, of Philadelphia.

By the death of Mr. Albert G. Warfield, Howard County has lost one of its most honored citizens. He has passed man's allotted threescore and ten years, and it was beyond human expectation that his days could be very many more. But still his demise falls as a heavy and sorrow-bringing blow upon all who were acquainted with the beautiful life which has been yielded up. The general respect and esteem accorded Mr. Warfield gives some idea of his character. He was the soul of honor, a man of quiet refinement, with a quick appreciation of the good and beautiful. He was essentially a man of domestic habits, loving his home and fireside. His declining years were happy in the contemplation of a life well spent and in the lustre added to an already honored name by the careers of his children.

Mrs. Margaret Gassaway Warfield, whose death occurred at the home of her daughter, in Pennsylvania, August, 1897, was the widow of Albert G. Warfield, of Howard County, and a daughter of Colonel Gassaway Watkins, of Revolutionary fame, who at the time of his death, in 1840, was president of the Society of the Cincinnati of Maryland, and the last surviving officer of the old Maryland Line. She was born at Walnut Grove, in Howard County, and since her marriage, in 1842, resided at "Oakdale," the old Warfield home, in that county. She was a woman of lovely Christian character, and made her home one of the most beautiful and attractive in the county, where her children, grandchildren and friends loved to meet and enjoy her sweet presence. She was loved by all who knew her, because her life was one of devotion to her family, friends and those in sorrow and need of sympathy.

Four sons and two daughters survive her—Messrs. Joshua N. Warfield and Marshall T. Warfield, prominent farmers in Howard County; Mr. Edwin Warfield, president of the Fidelity and Deposit

Company of this city, and Mr. John Warfield, editor of the "Daily Record;" Mrs. M. Gillett Gill, of this city, and Mrs. Herman Hoopes, of Philadelphia. Her oldest son was Major A. G. Warfield, Jr., a prominent civil engineer, who died several years ago. He, with Gassaway W. Warfield, served in the Confederate Army, the latter dying in prison at Camp Chase, Ohio, during the war.

Mrs. Warfield was a member of the National Society of the Daughters of the American Revolution, and was one of three daughters of a soldier who had served in the Revolutionary War.

A daughter of the Revolution, she leaves her credentials and her souvenirs as legacies, that she tried:

"To so live that when the sun of her existence sank in night,
Memorials sweet of mercies done might shield her name in Memory's light.
And the best seeds she had scattered bloom,
A hundredfold in days to come."

Alice Warfield, oldest daughter of Albert G. married M. Gillet Gill, senior member of Martin, Gillett & Co., the oldest importers of tea in Baltimore. Upon her wedding trip she visited Japan and was the first American lady in that now famous island. She is a member of the Colonial Dames of Maryland. They have three sons, M. Gillet, Jr., Howard and Royal and one daughter, Mildred.

The youngest daughter of Albert G., is Margaret G., wife of Herman Hoopes, of West Chester, Pennsylvania. Issue, Marian, Edward and Albert W.

John Warfield, fifth son of Albert G., and Margaret (Watkins) Warfield, of "Oakdale" is Editor of the "Daily Law Record," of Baltimore. He is a member of the Maryland Society of the Sons of the American Revolution. He and his brother, Marshall T. Warfield are engaged in farming upon the home estate of "Cherry Grove." Both are bachelors, but progressive farmers. The latter is a member of Glenwood Farmers' Club.

Elisha, fourth son of Benjamin and Rebecca (Ridgely) Warfield, was upon the Committee of Observation for Anne Arundel County, in 1775. He inherited his mother's dower in Dover. His first wife was Eliza Dorsey, daughter of Henry, grandson of Major Edward and Sarah (Wyatt) Dorsey. By that marriage he had three children, Polly, Sally and Nicholas, the last two dying in infancy. Polly, born December 13, 1772, married July 31, 1795, William Ford, of Fayette County, Kentucky, by whom she had three children, Charles, James C., and Eliza P., from whom are descended a numerous family. James C. Ford was one of the most prominent business men of Louisville, a man of large wealth and strong personality. He married Mary J. Trimble, a daughter of Justice Robert Trimble, of the U. S. Supreme Court. The second wife of Elisha Warfield, of Benjamin and Rebecca (Ridgely) Warfield, was Ruth Burgess, daughter of Captain Joseph, of the Elkridge Militia, of 1776. He was the son of John, of Captain Edward, of Colonel William

Burgess, Commander-in-Chief of the Provincial Forces and a member of the Quorum. Ruth Burgess' mother was Elizabeth Dorsey(of Michael and Ruth (Todd) Dorsey, of John and Honor (Elder) Dorsey, of Major Edward Dorsey, "Field Officer," in 1694; Judge of the High Court of Chancery in 1695. In 1790 Elisha and Ruth (Burgess) Warfield removed to Kentucky. Their sons were Elisha, Nicholas, Benjamin, Lloyd and Henry. Their daughters were Eliza, Sarah, Rebecca Ridgely, Harriett Burgess, Ann, Ruth and Nancy Dorsey. Their descendants, as far as have been given me, will be noticed in the order named.

Dr. Elisha Warfield held the chair of Surgery and Obstetrics in Transylvania University, Lexington. In 1809, he married Mary Barr, daughter of Robert and Rebecca Tilton Barr. Her mother was a Bourdenot. They lived at "The Meadows." Their children were Rebecca Tilton, Thomas Barr, William Pollock, Elisha, Anne Eliza, Mary Jane, Caroline Barr, Julia Genevive and Laura Ruth. Rebecca Tilton—Charlton Hunt, first Mayor of Lexington. Issue, Elisha, Mary, Catherine, Rebecca Charlton. Catherine—John Reid, of Maysville, Kentucky, and Rebecca Charlton was the wife of Ben Johnson, of Lexington. Thomas Barr Warfield—Alice Carneal, of Cincinnati. Issue, Sallie Carneal, Mary, Carneal, Thomas, Kate, Alice. Sallie Carneal—Sidney Clay, of Bourbon County. Issue. Alice, Isabel, Annie, Sidney and Katherine; Mary died early. Carneal was twice married—first wife, Alice Speed, of Memphis; second, Miss Nelson, of New Orleans. Thomas did not marry. Kate—J. Esten Spears, of Paris, Kentucky. Issue, Thomas Carneal, Henry, Esten, Warfield and Howell. Alice—Shelby Kinkead, of Lexington. Issue, William, Warfield, Carneal, Shelby and Sidney.

William Pollock Warfield married Maria Elizabeth Griffith, daughter of John T. Griffith, of New Jersey, who, when that State was made free, with his brother, William Thomas Griffith, moved their slaves to Natchez. They were direct descendants of Griffith *ap* Griffith, the last native Prince of Wales. John T. Griffith was a prominent lawyer of Mississippi and married Harriet Abercrombie, daughter of Dr. James Abercrombie, who was sent to the State of Pennsylvania by King George III., to establish the English Church. He was the younger son of Lord Abercrombie.

Mrs. William Pollock Warfield had a sister, Rosa Vertner Johnson, the poetess, also of Kentucky. The children of William Pollock Warfield are Harriet Griffith, who married Noah Davis Bell, of Lexington, Kentucky. Issue, Maria Griffith, wife of John Allen, of Boonville, Missouri, whose son is Henry Bell Allen. By a second marriage, to Mr. Joseph Binford, of Los Angeles, California, has one child. Clara Davis Bell—Henry Thompson, of Boonville. Issue, Henry, Noah and William.

Elisha, of William Pollock Warfield, married Mary Carson, of of Natchez. Issue, Lilly, Florence, Maria, Henry, Mary, Guey, Allen, Fairfax, Rosa and Vertner.

John Griffith, of William Pollock Warfield, married Henrietta Blackburn, niece of Senator Blackburn. Issue, John, Joe and Church. Thomas Barr, of William Pollock, married Mrs. Moore, of Mississippi. William Pollock, Jr., married Hattie Blackburn, niece of Senator Blackburn's second wife. Issue, Florence, Rosa and William.

Mary Barr, of William Pollock Warfield—first, Andrew Jackson Martin, of Grenada, Mississippi, nephew of President Jackson's wife. Issue, Maria Griffith; George W. Martin, First Lieutenant in Eighteenth Infantry, U. S. A.; William P. W., who—Montie Roberts, of Los Angeles, California; Hattie Warfield, who—Charles J. Meadowcroft, of Chicago. By a second marriage, to Colonel William C. Bayley, great-grandson of Lord Bayley, born in Melbourn—issue, Warfield Beal and Charles Abercrombie Dunbar. By a third marriage to Alvaro F. Gibbens, of Charleston, West Virginia, there is no issue.

Charles Abercrombie Warfield, of William Pollock and Marie E. (Griffith) Warfield—Miss Sellers, of Arkansas. They have three children, Dunbar, Warfield and Robert Barr Warfield.

Elisha Warfield, Jr. married Catherine Percy Ware, the authoress. Issue, Nathaniel Ware, Ellinor Ware, Percy, Mary Ross, Kittie and Lloyd. Nathaniel Ware—Miss Estel. Issue, Estel—J. Quitman Munce. Issue, Quitman and Warfield. Elinor Ware—first, Daniel Davis Bell; second, Erastus Wells, of St. Louis. Issue, Clara Davis and Henry. Mary Ross—Mr. Clemens, of St. Louis. Issue, Lilly and Bryon. Anne Eliza of Dr. Elisha—Major Edward Ryland; no issue, Mary Jane of Dr. Elisha—General Cassius M. Clay, U. S. Minister to Russia. Issue, Warfield, Green, Mary Barr, Sallie, Cassius, Brutus, Laura and Anne Warfield; Warfield and Cassius died unmarried. Green married Cornelia Walker, of Richmond, Kentucky; no issue. Mary—Major Herrick, of Cleveland. Issue, Clay, Frank and Green. Sallie—James Bennett, of Richmond, Kentucky. Issue, Mary, Elise, Helen, Laura and Warfield. Anne became Mrs. Crenshaw. Caroline Warfield (of Elisha)—Dr. Llewellyn Tarlton. Issue, Elisha and Llewellyn. Elisha—Gertrude Smith and had one daughter, Josephine. Llewellyn—Mrs. Hunt Reynolds, of Frankfort; no issue. Julia Genevieve (of Dr. Elisha)—Francis Key Hunt, of Lexington. Their daughter, Maria Barr—Dr. B. W. Dudley. Issue, Clara, Benjamin and William. Laura Ruth (of Dr. Elisha)—Christopher C. Rogers, no issue.

Dr. Nicholas Warfield, of Lexington, Kentucky, second son of Elisha and Ruth (Burgess) Warfield, married Susan Orr, of Bourbon County, Kentucky, by whom he had Mary Ellen, Rebecca, Ruth and Caroline, only one of whom is now living, Mrs. Rebecca Thornton, of Lexington, Kentucky, who has no children. Mrs. Sellers and Mrs. Gratz and their children are the only living representatives of this son.

Benjamin, third son of Elisha and Ruth (Burgess) Warfield, married, first, Sallie Caldwell, of Paris, Kentucky. Issue, Elisha Nicholas, William, Ruth, Sarah and Benjamin. Elisha Nicholas, of

"Forest Home"—Elizabeth Brand, of Lexington. Issue, Harriet and Sallie Sutherland Warfield. Dr. William Warfield was a noted stock raiser of the blue-grass region. He married Mary Breckinridge, sister of Mrs. General Wade Hampton. Issue, Sophia, Benjamin Burgess, Ethelbert Dudley, Ruth and Sarah. Sophia and Ruth died unmarried.

Professor Benjamin Burgess Warfield, of Princeton, graduate of Oxford University, England—Annie Kinkaid. Professor Ethelbert Dudley Warfield, graduate of Oxford University and now President of La Fayette College, Easton, Pennsylvania, married Miss Tilton, of Massachusetts. They have several children. Sarah—Dr. J. Rockwell Smith. Issue, Sallie, Amy, Ruth, Benjamin and J. Rockwell. Benjamin Warfield, Jr.—Clara Cochrane. Issue, John, Sallie and Mary.

The second wife of Benjamin Warfield, Sr., was Nancy Barr; no issue.

Dr. Lloyd Warfield, fourth son of Elisha Warfield and Ruth (Burgess) Warfield, was a practicing physician in Lexington, Kentucky, for fifty years and attained a high reputation in his profession. He married Mary Barr, by whom he had a number of children, only five of whom arrived at maturity. Rebecca Pollock, Mary Jane, Lloyd, Edward R., and Henry N.; Rebecca Pollock married her cousin, Dr. Lloyd Warfield Brown, of Jacksonville, Illinois, a son of Harriet Burgess (Warfield) Brown and Colonel William Brown. Three children survive her, William B. Brown, of Colorado, Edward Warfield Brown, of Morgan County, Illinois and Rebecca C., wife of Dr. E. J. Brown, of Decatur, Illinois. The second daughter, Mary Jane, married B. F. Bassett, of Missouri, by whom she had several children. Lloyd, Edward R., and Henry were never married and are no longer living. Each of them served in the Confederate Army with credit to themselves. Lloyd and Edward were under General Forrest, and Henry N., under General John H. Morgan, with whom he was captured on his Ohio raid and imprisoned in Camp Douglass, at Chicago. He escaped by digging out and was returned to prison by his brother-in-law and cousin, Dr. L. W. Brown, who then procured his parole by personal effort from President Lincoln, without, however, taking the oath, which he declined to do.

The second wife of Dr. Lloyd Warfield was Elmira Burbank, who descended from the good old English and Welsh families of Burbank and Church, from Old Town, Maine. Their children were Robert, Elisha, Charles Chase, Elizabeth Church and Burgess Barr Warfield. Robert Elisha Warfield, who is engaged in cotton planting near Tchula, Mississippi, married Laura C. Mosby, of Mississippi, by whom he has two children, Robert Mosby and Lloyd Burgess.

Charles Chase Warfield, who is engaged in the banking business in Fergus Falls, Minnesota, married Ellie C. Runyen, of Lexington, Kentucky, a granddaughter of Dr. Church Blackburn, a relative of the Kentucky Blackburns, by whom he had two children, Sallie R., and Lloyd Burgess. The second wife of Charles Chase Warfield is

Amy Rarey, of Ohio, by whom he has one son, Hunter Rarey. Elizabeth Church Warfield married Dr. W. C. Bedford, of Minnesota, but died without children.

Burgess Barr Warfield, who is engaged in the banking business in Battle Lake, Minnesota, married Grace Lane, of Manchester, New Hampshire, by whom he has two children, a daughter, Leela Howerton, and a son, Lane.

Henry Warfield, fifth son of Elisha Warfield and Ruth (Burgess) Warfield, was a promising lawyer, but died young. He married Eliza Millar, of Cynthiana, Kentucky, by whom he had two children, Henry Warfield, Jr., and Eliza (Warfield) Magee.

Harriett Burgess (of Elisha and Ruth [Burgess] Warfield) married Colonel William Brown, of Cynthiana, Kentucky, whose Cavalier ancestry traces back to James Brown, of Virginia, 1746, a successful lawyer, officer in the War of 1812, and colleague of Henry Clay in the National House of Representatives. They with all their children emigrated in 1833 to Central Illinois. Their children, all born in Kentucky, were James Nicholas, Ruth, Mary, William, Elisha Warfield, Rebecca P., Eliza Coleman, Lloyd Warfield and Harriett S. James Nicholas Brown, a noted breeder of short-horn cattle, was for several terms a member of the Legislature of Illinois, and was the chief founder of the State Agricultural Society, of which he was the first president,—Mary A. Smith. Their children are William, Charles S., Mary and Benjamin Warfield. Ruth Brown— James D. Smith, who was a member of the last Constitutional Convention of Illinois. Their children are William B., John P., Harriett B., James D., Patty, Ruth W., and Lloyd B. Mary Brown—Barton Stone Wilson, merchant of Boonville, Missouri. Their children are Rebecca, Joseph and John. William Brown, lawyer, judge, legislator and banker, married Susan, daughter of Rev. J. Finley, of New Jersey, one of the founders of the American African Colonization Society. Their children are Mary, Annie, William, Jr., and Susan.

Elisha Warfield Brown, merchant and banker, married Mary Brent. Their children are William, lawyer and Solicitor-General of the Chicago and Alton Railroad; Elizabeth, James N., Harriett, Wyatt, Mary and Washington.

Rebecca P. Brown married Charles W. Price, merchant and farmer. Their only child is Dr. William B. Price, of New Berlin, Illinois. Eliza Coleman Brown, now of Jacksonville, Illinois, married Washington Adams, late Chief Justice of the Supreme Court of Missouri. Their children are John, Elisha Brown, Harriett and James N. Lloyd Warfield Brown, physician—Rebecca Coleman, daughter of Dr. Lloyd (of Elisha and Ruth [Burgess] Warfield) and his first wife, Mary Barr. Their children are Harriett Burgess, William Barr, Edward Warfield, Rebecca Coleman and Lloyd. William Barr Brown, now of Manzanola, Colorado, married Frances E. McCoy. Their children are William Barr, Jr., May, Lloyd Warfield and Emiline. Edward Warfield Brown—Ruth Smith. Their children are Anna and Edward Warfield, Jr., Rebecca Coleman

Brown—Dr. Everett J. Brown, of Decatur, Illinois. Their children
are Rebecca, Alice and Lloyd Warfield. Harriett S. Brown —James
T. Johnson, merchant of Boonville, Missouri. Their children are
Harriett B., Caroline, Eliza and Ruth. Ann Warfield (of Elisha)
died single. Ruth—Dr. Joel Frazier. Nancy Dorsey—Dr. Samuel
Theobald, from whom comes Dr. Theobald, of Baltimore.

Eliza Warfield (of Elisha and Ruth [Burgess] Warfield) married
General James Coleman. Their son, Lloyd R. Coleman, of New
Orleans, is now represented by Miss Eliza Warfield Coleman, of New
Orleans. Sarah Warfield (of Elisha) became the second wife of
Colonel William Ford. Rebecca Ridgely Warfield—William Pollock.

WELSH.

One of the descendants of Samuel and Rachel (Griffith) Welsh
was Warner Welsh, who married Marab Scott and had issue, Luther
Warner, Elizabeth and Rachel.

Luther located in Upper Howard and married Juliette Moxley.
Their oldest son was Captain Warner G. Welsh, who was a dashing
soldier of the Confederate Army. He and his brother Luther are both
dead. Milton Welsh, their youngest brother, is a resident of and was
a candidate for Mayor of Kansas City, Missouri. His sisters, Rachel,
Ruth, and Elizabeth, are all dead.

Warner Welsh, brother of Luther, was a successful merchant
of Hyattstown, Montgomery County. His wife was Mary Ann Hyatt.
Their sons are William Wallace, Warner Wellington, Asa Hyatt,
Luther Warfield, Turner Wootten and Frank Welsh. One daughter,
Mary Ann Welsh (now deceased), became the wife of Mr. C. C.
Rhodes, attorney of Baltimore.

Mr. William Wallace Welsh is a successful merchant of Rockville and Warner Wellington Welsh a popular merchant of Olney,
Maryland. Professor Luther W. Welsh is the genealogist of the
family.

POPLAR SPRING.

Here the old Frederick Road crossed the National Pike and continued on a parallel upon the south of it. A large spring, surrounded
by poplars, here offered a halting-place for travelers, and when the
highway was completed, a road-side tavern, with extensive stables,
was opened. Two successive Allen Dorseys came into possession of
it. From it an extensive view, reaching down to Glenelg, may be
obtained. Poplar Spring Hotel afterward acquired a reputation as
a summer resort; picnic parties assembled in its groves and dances
were held in its large dining-room. It has passed to other owners.

Upon a long stretch of level land, a mile in length, upon
the Old Frederick Road, west of Poplar Spring, John Wayman
(of Leonard and Ann Rutland), coming up from Virginia at the
close of the Revolution, seated himself and built an extensive brick
house in the centre of his expansive survey. It became the resort

of eligible young patriots many miles distant, and on Sunday afternoons the fence along the Old Frederick Road in front had a horse standing at each corner.

John Wayman's daughters by Ann Warfield, of "Warfield's Range," were Mary, Rachel, Sarah, Amelia and Milcah Wayman.

Mary was selected by Joshua Crow, of Montgomery, and carried out West. Her descendants are now applying, from Pennsylvania and the West, for information of her progenitors; General Thomas Hood, Commander of the Militia of Howard District, captured Rachel and took her to his quaint brick homestead, still standing on "Hood's Manor;" Rev. Benjamin Hood, of Bowling Green, took Sarah to be a neighbor to her sister; Colonel Lyde Griffith bore Amelia to Montgomery, to hand down a line still there; Milcah could not choose a husband from her many admirers, and remained at home with her bachelor brothers, Henry Wayman and Charles. Her brother John married in the West and sent one of his descendants to the United States Senate.

The old estate, under Henry Wayman, was gradually reduced, by successive sales to Allen Dorsey and other neighbors, and after his death it was bought for a nominal price.

Messrs. Kuhn and Bunn came up from Baltimore, bought lime by the carload, and made it a valuable estate.

TRACEY AND WHALEN.

Opposite the Wayman homestead, upon the Frederick Pike, are seated two bachelors upon an estate worthy of record. They are Tracey and Whalen, cousins, descendants of Mr. John Stackhouse, of the Delawders, Welshs and Warfields, all pioneers in that immediate section.

Mr. John Stackhouse's heirs were John, Hammond, Mrs. Tracey, Mrs. Whalen and Miss Margaret Stackhouse, who presides over the bachelor home. His grandsons, by dint of persevering industry, have reached out and finally embraced in their estate all the Wayman property north of the Old Frederick Road. Lime, clover, grain, corn and cattle, aided by well-directed management, have made a beautiful estate that is an object lesson in farming.

John S. Tracey has for many years been a man of political influence in his district. He has made it a rule to stand by his promises and, therefore, he is a trusted leader. He never has cared for political honors, but prefers home life, and though he has several times yielded and become a delegate to the Legislature he has as often declined the honor. Mr. Tracey's last speech was made in nominating Governor Warfield. Open-hearted, charitable, always trying to do good, his home is a happy one.

DORSEYS OF UPPER HOWARD.

Nicholas Dorsey (of Henry and Elizabeth Worthington) took up lands in the neighborhood of Shafersville and Poplar Spring. He married Lucy Belt Sprigg; issue, Dr. Frederick Dorsey, of Hagerstown; Roderick, Dennis, and Samuel Dorsey.

Dr. Frederick—Sallie Clagett.

Roderick—Rachel Hobbs (of William). Issue, Mrs. Winder and William Roderick Dorsey, who married Miss Brashears and died from the result of a railroad accident, leaving Frank, Lucy, Henrietta Sprigg, Kate and William Roderick Dorsey, of New York. Henrietta Sprigg Dorsey—Benedict T. Keen.

Dennis Dorsey (of Nicholas)—Maria Owings (of Samuel). Issue, Samuel Owings Dorsey, Gustavus, Roderick and Nicholas Dorsey, the bachelor. Samuel Owings Dorsey—Mary Riggs Griffith; issue, Colonel Gustavus Dorsey, C. S. A.—Margaret Owens; Maria—L. J. G. Owings; Carrie—Richard Dorsey; Samuel and Mary G. Dorsey. Their homestead is upon "Griffith's Range," in Montgomery.

Gustavus Dorsey (of Nicholas) married Miss Buzzard, of Mt. Airy, and resided near there. The late Captain William H. Dorsey, of the C. S. A.; Byron Dorsey, Mayor of Mt. Airy, and his brother, Frank Dorsey, are his heirs. The daughters are the wife of Rev. Mr. Glover and Mrs. William Griffith.

Roderick Dorsey (of Dennis) resided in Carroll County. Nicholas Dorsey (of Dennis) died a bachelor.

Samuel Dorsey (of Nicholas) owned a large estate between Lisbon and Poplar Spring. He daily rode over his estate and seldom failed to visit Poplar Spring or Lisbon at least once a day. He rode splendid horses and was commanding in person, dignified and much esteemed. He died a bachelor. His estate has been greatly improved by James Warthen, Mr. Barnes, and others.

ALLEN DORSEY OF POPLAR SPRING.

After passing three-score and ten years, Allen Dorsey, commanding in person and popular with all, has made his last trip over the old National Pike. He died in Baltimore and left his estate to his stepson, Mr. Henry Holt, of New York.

Mr. Dorsey was the son of Allen Dorsey, born 1779, son of Ely Dorsey (of Edward and Sarah Todd). Ely married his cousin, Ruth Dorsey, daughter of Michael and Ruth Todd. They removed to Frederick County. Her will of 1815 named her children, Polly, Edward, Michael (of Baltimore), Allen and Edward. Allen settled at Poplar Spring and built the hotel, which still stands. His wife was Elizabeth Smith. His son John was a merchant of Lisbon, married Nancy Warfield (of Azel) and left Allen, of Washington; John W. Dorsey, of Baltimore; Hamner, of the West.

Presley W. Dorsey (of Allen) settled in Washington and married Mary H. Worthington; issue, Worthington Dorsey, Thomas Dorsey, Frank Dorsey, Virginia and Mary Eliza. William N. Dorsey (of

Allen)—Sarah Worthington and left one daughter, Henrietta.   Allen
Dorsey (of Allen), late owner of the Poplar Spring estate, married
Mrs. Holt, of Baltimore.   He was long connected with Baltimore and
Cumberland Turnpike Company.   Her sons are at the head of a
publishing house in New York.   The recent death of both Mr. and
Mrs. Dorsey leaves them executors in Howard County.

Edward Dorsey (of Ely and Ruth) removed to Waterford,
Loudoun County, Virginia; married Mary Klein.   Their son, Captain
Allen Dorsey, married Matilda Polton and in 1840 removed to
Maryland.   Their son is Charles W. Dorsey, President of the Manu-
facturers' National Bank, of Baltimore.   He married two daughters
of the late William J. Dickey, of Wetherdsville.   President Dorsey's
daughter is the wife of Rev. F. F. Kennedy; his son is Edgar A.
Dorsey, of Wetherdsville; they were litigants in a recent will case of
Mrs. Dickey.

LISBON.

The earlier surveys in this neighborhood were upon the Old
Frederick Road, a-half mile north of the village.   Here was located
"Warfield's Forest."

Caleb Pancoast built the first house in the village.   It still forms
the rear of the old hotel property in the centre of the place.

Judging by the street-like regularity of the houses on both sides
of the National Pike, which passes through it, the village must have
been laid out after the surveys of the pike were made.

In 1820 a deed was made by Caleb Pancoast, witnessed by
Samuel Hopkins and Edward Warfield, to Lloyd Selby, Beni
Warfield, Dr. Gustavus Warfield, Hammond Welsh and Nicholas D.
Warfield, to hold perpetually for public worship or education, as a
Union Church of all denominations.

It especially provided that any surviving member may call a
meeting of interested neighbors and appoint a board of succession.

Dr. Gustavus Warfield, as the last survivor, called such a meeting and perpetuated the board, but it is doubtful if such now exists.

A few years ago Mr. Cornelius Mercer was the only survivor, and
he was not then a resident.

Upon this grant was built a solid stone church, which fully
carried out its purpose, the only one, perhaps, of such so-called Union
Churches.   Here the Elder Plummer Waters long held his Baptist
Congregation, riding on horseback each month from Sandy Bottom.

Herein Reverend William Crapster organized his short-life Uni-
tarian Church; here the "old-side Methodists" held their meetings,
but all have now deserted it.   Even its lofty pulpit has tumbled and
its walls, which endured as a monument to the solid men who built
its solid foundation, have been removed.   Nearby a new Methodist
Church takes its place, close to the High School of the village.   Upon
the northern entrance still stands in good preservation a Presbyterian
Church, fully half a century old.

An Odd Fellows' Hall, more recent, stands in the village proper, close by the old Welsh homestead, wherein I early learned that it is not safe to tease a monkey. It was from this house, too, Mr. Ringgold brought out three chairs in answer to the call, "Three Cheers for General Lafayette," with the assurance he could have a-half dozen cheers.

Two stores and quite an avenue of substantial dwellings make up the present village, which now boasts of seven retired men of means. It, also, has an enterprising newspaper correspondent, several doctors and one or more ministers.

Bounded on the west by the Montgomery and Woodbine highway, now a macadamized road throughout, stretches out from Lisbon to Woodbine a well-developed and fertile body of land, once known as "Warfield's Forest." The National Pike and the Baltimore and Ohio Railway both pass through it. Its eastern limit is "Shipley's Adventure."

Five brothers, Seth, Beni, Bela, Elie and Azel Warfield, born on "Warfield's Range," came up the Old Frederick Road and seated themselves here to grow tobacco.

Not an original house stands, but upon their sites are modern homes of comfort and modern grain-growers of means.

They took for their wives a Welsh, three Dorseys and a Welling, and from their old pioneer cottages sent out descendants now in Philadelphia, Baltimore, Washington, Cumberland, Pittsburg and the West, with a few still remaining on their old camping-grounds. Many of them have become distinguished.

Seth has a grandson and a great-grandson of his name still residing in Howard and others in Philadelphia and Baltimore, one of whom is William Martin Warfield, of Hollins Street.

Beni, through his sons, Charles D., Daniel and Nicholas Dorsey Warfield, has numerous descendants in Howard County, Baltimore, Cumberland and Pittsburg.

Charles Alexander Warfield, of Pittsburg; Gustavus, Arthur, Peregrine, Miss Emma Warfield, of Cumberland, and Henry Ridgely Warfield, of Elkins, West Virginia, are the representatives of Charles D. Warfield, Jr., of "Bushy Park."

Daniel Warfield (of Beni) resided at White Cottage, afterwards the homestead of the late Thomas Rowles, long a political leader in Howard.

Daniel was residing there in 1825, and breakfasted with General La Fayette at Roberts' Tavern, Cooksville, that year. Removing later to Baltimore, he entered into the milling firm of Francis Mactier, the Scotch immigrant, and married his daughter.

Henry Mactier and Daniel Warfield, Jr., both became prominent in the history of the city. The former was the popular Reform leader and candidate for Mayor. His wife was Anna (Gittings) Emory, of "Manor Glen" on "My Lady's Manor."

The three sons of Hon. Henry Mactier Warfield are Richard Emory Warfield, of the Royal Fire Insurance Company, of London now at its head in Philadelphia, but owning still a homestead at Pot Spring, Baltimore County; his wife is Bettie Davies and his sons are Douglas and Henry.

Solomon Davies Warfield followed his father in active politics. He is a recognized leader, having just relinquished the office of Postmaster; he is President of the Continental Trust Company, on Baltimore and Calvert streets, and is also a director of the Atlantic Seaboard Railroad. He is still a bachelor. His mother lives with him on Preston street.

Henry Mactier Warfield, Jr., is the Baltimore representative of the Royal Fire Insurance Company. He is Colonel of the Maryland Fifth Regiment of Militia and was in the Spanish War.

His wife is Rebecca, daughter of Robert and Mary (Carroll) Denison. Colonel Warfield was upon the building committee of the Fifth Regiment Armory. Dr. Mactier Warfield is the representative of Daniel, Jr. His sister is Miss Mary Warfield.

Nicholas Dorsey Warfield (of Beni) remained upon "Warfield's Forest." His wife was Rebecca Burgess, descendant of the Provincial Commander-in-Chief and daughter of the Revolutionary Captain Vachel Burgess, of Triadelphia.

The late Alfred Warfield, Mayor of Westport, Illinois, now resting in Oak Grove Cemetery; Vachel Warfield, of Arkansas; Beni, Louis, both dead, and the late Mrs. Lucretia Dorsey and Mrs. Nicholas R. Henderson represent them.

Bela Warfield and his wife, Achsah Dorsey (of Colonel Nicholas and Sarah Griffith), left Nicholas Dorsey Warfield, who married Deborah Gaither, now represented by Mrs. Deborah Crowder, of Baltimore, whose son is Reverend Frank Warfield Crowder, of New York. Two daughters of Bela, Rachel and Achsah, married Reuben Warfield, the Lisbon surveyor and conveyancer, a man of marked ability, whose notes have given me many of the early grants herein recorded. His surveys covered nearly the whole country. Dr. Reuben Orlando Dorsey Warfield, of Lisbon, is his only son and Miss Fanny Warfield his only daughter. The recent wife of Dr. Warfield was a daughter of Dr. Francis Crawford, of Carroll County.

Elie Warfield, brother of Bela, married Frances (Dorsey) Chapman, a sister of Mrs. Bela Warfield.

From Elie Gaither Warfield (of Elie) and his wife, Ellen Bowie Magruder (of Dr. Jeffrey), descend Mrs. Fannie Engle, of Lisbon, and the late Magruder Warfield, of the Mechanics Bank' of Baltimore. His first wife was Mary E. Dorsey (of Caleb), of "Hockley." Mrs. Kate (Bridges) Warfield and her daughter, Ellen Bowie, survive him.

Augustus Warfield, of Washington, D. C., and Mrs. William Gaither, of Howard, are descendants of Rufus (of Elie), brother of Reuben the surveyor.

Louisa (of Elie)—James Henderson. Their heirs are Mrs. Dr. Gray, of Laurel; Seth Henderson, Nicholas R. Henderson and Gaither Henderson, who married a daughter of Joshua Burgess, of Lisbon. Their daughter is Mrs. Clarence Owings.

Nicholas R. Henderson married Henrietta Warfield (of Nicholas Dorsey and Rebecca [Burgess] Warfield). He holds the homestead of Elie Warfield, immediately upon the pike extending to Lisbon. He has long been a political leader in Howard.

Eleanor Warfield (of Elie), late widow of Nicholas R. Warfield, (of Joshua) long held his estate, now the home of William Gaither.

Azel Warfield, of "Warfield Forest," seated south of the National Pike; his estate reached to Lisbon. He married Elizabeth Welling, sister of Major Henry Welling, whose will of 1843 left a portion of his estate to her sons, "Richard, Henry, William, Azel, George, and daughters, Eliza Mercer, Mary Fisher and Nancy Dorsey."

Benjamin Franklin Warfield, of "White Wine and Claret" and his nephew, Nicholas Warfield, of Simpsonville, reside upon Major Welling's estate near Clarksville.

Henry Warfield—Julia Dorsey (of George and Rachel Ridgely). His sister Martha—Philemon Dorsey (of George and Rachel Ridgely).

William Warfield (of Azel)—Miss Lishear.

John (of William), formerly of "Warfield's Forest," is now in Lisbon. His wife was a daughter of Talbott Shipley. His brothers were the late Henry W. Warfield, of Baltimore, and the late William W. Warfield, of Washington, who left a son, William, of Washington, and others in New York.

Noah Warfield resides in Pennsylvania.

George W. Warfield (of Azel) held the homestead and left the late George Warfield, of Warfield & Rohr, and the late Thomas Warfield, of Hagerstown—Miss Mercer. Charles died in the West. Laura and Elizabeth, of Baltimore, are the only survivors of this family.

Charles A. Warfield (of Azel) married Ariana (Owings) Dorsey. The late Joshua D. Warfield, of Sykesville, was his oldest son. He married Elizabeth Polk. Issue, Howard, Nellie Dorsey, Annie Owings, Dorsey, Charles, Lee and Bessie.

Charles A. Warfield, Jr.—Carolyne A. Devries. Their only son is Wade H. D. Warfield, merchant and President of the Sykesville Bank. He married two sisters, Blanche and Ellen Waterhause. Issue, Josephine W., Helen and Blanche E. Warfield.

Thomas Owings Warfield, late of Glenelg, by his first wife, Susan Gosnell, had Mrs. Belle Runkles, of Mt. Airy; by his second, Laura Dorsey (of Stephen Boone), had Alexander, Owings, Dorsey, Alice Hebb and her sister, Mrs. Henry Clark.

Arabella Warfield (of Charles A.) became Mrs. Henry Banks. Issue, Samuel—Amanda, daughter of George W. Linthicum; Charles—Nettie Gaither (of Dennis) and left Charles and Louise; Thomas—a daughter of Dr. Crawford. Upon his death, she married his brother William Banks.

Mattie Banks, only daughter (of Henry), is the widow of Elisha Riggs Jones (of Evan A. Jones and Rachel Riggs), of Howard. She resides near Florence.

SELBY.

Two distinct families of Selby are in Howard. Upon the northern outskirts of Lisbon and extending to the village itself is the elegant estate of E. Greenberry Selby, descendant of Reverend Lloyd Selby, the organizer of our early church at Lisbon. Hon. E. G. Selby has frequently been called to represent his county in the Legislature. He is now the successor of the late Allen Dorsey as director of the National Pike. Thoroughly practical in every act, including political movements as well, Mr. Selby is a trusted and popular neighbor. He has converted worn fields into a model farm and upon his estate has erected commodious buildings, attractive and handsome.

The late Mr. Enoch Selby, who built upon the historic estate of "Dorsey's Grove," is now represented by Mr. John Selby, of the School Board. He has also made handsome improvements in Howard. His estate is near Glenelg.

COOKSVILLE.

Upon the completion of the National Pike leading from Baltimore to Frederick, then continuing on to the West, villages sprung up at almost every cross road. During the advance movements of our early pioneers of the West, long processions of primitive trains of covered wagons were to be seen almost daily on that road. The wayside tavern was then a necessity.

When the nation was honored by the return of General La Fayette in 1825, it was over this road he was conveyed to the West. At Mr. Joshua Robert's tavern, at Cooksville, General La Fayette sat down to breakfast with some of his admirers—General Thomas Hood, Mr. Joshua Hood, Daniel Warfield and others. The chair in which he sat is still preserved by the descendants of Mr. Thomas Cook, who then lived just opposite; his old residence, later the Meriweather homestead, was destroyed by fire, but the old Roberts' Inn is still standing.

Northwest of Cooksville is "Shipley's Adventure"; southeast of it is "Hobbs' Neighborhood;" and southwest is "Ridgely's Great Park."

Mr. C. C. Burton, merchant, is a descendant of Thomas Todd, the surveyor of "North Point."

The descendants of Mr. Walter Dorsey hold the Roberts' Inn, and Mrs. Dr. Augustus Riggs owns the handsome new residence upon the site of the Meriweather homestead.

HOODS OF COOKSVILLE.

The late Thomas Hood, whose old homestead still stands southeast of Cooksville, was three times elected a Commissioner of Howard. He was the only son of Mr. James Hood. Mr. and Mrs. Thomas Hood lie side by side in Glenwood Cemetery overlooking the present home of their oldest daughter, Mrs. Alfred Matthews, of Glenwood. Their oldest son, Mr. James Thomas Hood, of Missouri, named for both ancestors, holds the family records.

The only male descendent in Maryland is Mr. Stephen G. Hood, of Lisbon, the genial representative of the order of Odd Fellows. He married Miss Emma Turner, daughter of the late Hon. William Turner, one of the members of the House of Delegates which met at Frederick when Annapolis was filled with Federal soldiers at the beginning of the war. Several members of that Legislature were arrested and thrown into prison in order to prevent the passage of a Secession Act.

Mr. and Mrs. Stephen G. Hood have two sons, William and Stephen, and three living daughters, Kate, Lillian and Helen. Mrs. Alfred Matthews and Mrs. Eugene Buck are his only living sisters.

HOBBS.

The earliest Hobbs' will at Annapolis is that of John Hobbs, of 1731. His witness was Robert Browne. His wife was Dorothy and his four sons were Samuel, John, Joseph and William; he names one daughter, Margaret, and refers to his former wife Susannah's children. From an inventory of the above testator by Samuel Cootrall, executor, I learn that he was a member of Queen Caroline Parish and took up, in 1722, "Hobbs' Park" in that parish for his three sons, Samuel, John and Joseph, whilst the homestead, after the death of his wife, Dorothy, was to descend to son William; he also increased "Hobbs' Park Addition" for William. In 1743 "Hobbs' Park" was deeded by Samuel, Joseph and John Hobbs to Samuel Stringer, whose estate was not far from the Old Brick Church of the parish and lying upon the road from Laurel to Ellicott City; William sold his part also to the same.

Samuel Hobbs bought of Thomas Worthington a portion of "Altogether," near Glenelg.

John Hobbs bought of Thomas Worthington "Martin's Luck," taken up by John Martin. There was a marriage connection with the celebrated Luther Martin, for the Hobbs of lower Howard claim that descent. John Hobbs' wife was Elizabeth. He later sold his purchase, near Simpsonville, to Dr. Joshua Warfield and removed to Frederick County.

Samuel Hobbs sold his part of "Altogether" to Philip Warfield, who had come up from "Venison Park," near Laurel.

William Hobbs married Mary Ridgely and resided on the homestead. His descendants intermarried with Philip Warfield.

Joseph Hobbs came up to the neighborhood of Hobbs, where his descendants have handed down a family settlement extending from the Westminster Road over a considerable territory to the east.

John Hobbs, Sr., of Frederick County, in his will of 1768, names his sons Leonard, Nicholas and Greenberry Hobbs. The latter name is another evidence of the far-reaching reputation and connection of Colonel Nicholas Greenberry, of the Severn.

Nicholas Hobbs was upon the Committee of Observation for Linganore Hundred. He married Elizabeth Cummings, daughter of General William Cummings, of Liberty; issue, William Cummings

Hobbs and Brice Hobbs, of Maryland, and Basil Nicholas Hobbs, of Kentucky. He later married Mary Ann Dorsey (of Edward and Susannah Lawrence); issue, Edward Hobbs, father of Mrs. John Shirley, of Kentucky, whose homestead was the "Anchorage."

Joseph Hobbs—Jemima Dorsey (of John and Honor Elder). Their son Joseph—Elizabeth Higgins, daughter of Thomas and Dorothy Higgins. They bought of them "Dorsey's Friendship" and "Higgins' Chance" in 1742. Jemima (Dorsey) Hobbs, in 1770, left her estate to Joseph Hobbs, Jr. Through one of her descendants, Vachel Hobbs, who went to Kentucky, came Elie, Joshua, Joseph and John Hobbs, of Kentucky.

Hon. James Hobbs, delegate to the Constitutional Convention of Kentucky, in 1792, left two sons who were members of the General Assembly of Kentucky, viz., Hon. Joshua and Hon. Joseph Hobbs.

Joseph Hobbs, Jr., in his will of 1791, named his sons—Thomas, Henry, Cornelius, Joseph, Noah; daughters, Rachel Bissell, Hannah Spurrier, Elizabeth Hood. His lands were "Silence," "Poverty Discovered," Ridgely's Great Range."

Captain Thomas Hobbs was with Major Alexander Warfield at the burning of the Peggy Stewart. He was the surveyor who laid out a large tract now known as the "Hobbs' Neighborhood." In his will he named his heirs, Cordelia Barnes, wife of Adam, to hold Lot No. 1. William Peddicord, part of Lot No. 2 and after his death to descend to Sophia Musgrove, wife of Stephen; Nancy Warfield, wife of Richard; Eleanor Thompson, wife of Jacob; Gerard Peddicord, Sarah and Elizabeth Peddicord. To son Caleb Hobbs, Lot No. 3. Grandson Elias Brown Baker and his sister Sarah, Lot No. 4. Daughter Amelia Peddicord, wife of Jasper, Lot No. 5. Daughter Sarah Hood, Lot No. 6, one-third of which to descend to grandson Thomas Hobbs Hood, the residue to his sisters Harriet, Deborah and Mary Bissel Hood. To Hannah Sheets, Lot No. 8. To grandson Thomas Randall Hobbs, two tracts, First and Second Addition. Son Gerard Hobbs the remainder of First and Second Addition, except a portion adjoining Henry C. Hobbs. To Joseph, "Poverty Discovered." To Caleb and Gerard my theodelite and compass. Sons executors.

Henry Cornelius Hobbs (of Joseph) was the father of Henry and grandfather of Rev. James Hobbs and Charles Hobbs, who held "Hobbs' Camp Ground" and "Hobbs' Mill," now Rover. Their estates are still under the direction of their progressive and intelligent descendants, Mr. George Hobbs and his brother Harry, of Baltimore, and Mr. Albert Hobbs, of Howard, who made splendid agricultural developments in that section.

Noah Hobbs (of Joseph) married Rachel Warfield (of Edward and Rachel Riggs) and left Warfield Hobbs and his sisters Rachel and Nancy. His estate was near Cooksville.

Joseph Hobbs (of Thomas) married Ann Chew Randall and had eleven children; two of them, Captain George Hobbs and Peregrine, were in the War of 1812. Their sisters were Mrs. Harriet Barnes, Mrs. Mary Cassiday, Mrs. Matilda Howard, wife of Thomas, son of Brice Howard.

Peregrine Hobbs married Mary Howard (of Brice) and left Thomas Brice Howard Worthington Hobbs, an only son; his sisters were Louisa; Frances Ridgely Hobbs became Mrs. Porter; Kitty Hood, now Connell.

Captain George Hobbs' heirs were Alexander Brice Hobbs and Mrs. Nelson.

"HOOD'S FOREST."

Mention has already been made in Anne Arundel of John Hood, who settled near Herring Creek; and of his brother Benjamin, who settled at "Hollofields," upon the Patapsco.

The youngest son of Benjamin followed the Old Frederick Road back beyond St. James' Church and surveyed "Hood's Forest."

These early settlers were the younger sons of Samuel Hood, descendant of Lord Hood and of Lord North, whose estate descended to his oldest son, Samuel. The others came to America.

Benjamin died at "Hood's Haven." His son John built "Bowling Green" and married Elizabeth Shipley. Their combined estate covered some 5,000 acres. His will of 1786, written in 1785, when he was seventy-three years old, mentions five grandsons, "sons of my son, John Hood, Jr." His granddaughter, Sarah Hood, daughter of John Hood, Jr., by his first wife, Hannah (Barnes). To Elizabeth Hood, daughter of my son, John Hood, Jr., I give "Snowden's Cowpens" and "River Bottom." To his son he willed the remainder of his estate. Mrs. Elizabeth Hood, in 1795, mentioned her two grand-daughters, Sarah Worthington and Elizabeth Hood; her grandsons, James, John, Benjamin and Thomas Hood.

John Hood, Jr., heir of "Bowling Green" on "Hood's Forest," married, first, Hannah Barnes, daughter of Adam and Hannah Dorsey (of John and Honor Elder); he married, second, Rachel Ridgely Howard, daughter of Cornelius and Rachel Ridgely Worthington. Their daughter Elizabeth became Mrs. Nicholas Meriweather; her brothers are named above. John Hood, Jr., married, third, Eliza-Gaither, daughter of Henry and Martha Ridgely. His will bears the same date as his mother's, 1795, and adds to his other sons, Henry Gaither Hood, to whom he granted 859¾ acres. To his daughter, Hannah Hood, £300 and silver spoons. To Sarah Worthington, "exclusive of what I have given her" £50. To Elizabeth Hood £200, in lieu of the profits of her real estate left her by her grandfather.

The will of Mrs. Elizabeth (Gaither) Hood, in 1807, mentions her daughter, Hannah Owings, wife of Jesse Owings; her granddaughter, Elizabeth Hood Owings; her brother, Beale Gaither; her father, Henry Gaither, and Jesse Owings, her executor.

Hannah Owings became Mrs. Dr. Samuel Jennings.

Henry Gaither Hood died aged nine years.

James Hood (of John, Jr.,) located at "Hood's Mill." His estate extended into Carroll. By Sarah Howard (of Benjamin and Mary Govane) he had one daughter, Mary Govane Hood, who transferred her large estate to John Tolley Worthington; by them it was sold to Samuel Bentz, who renamed it "Bentz' Stock Farm." It is related that Mrs. Worthington, one day, in trying to cross Morgan's Run, after a heavy rain, had her carriage swept down the stream. Two slaves near by saw her peril and rushed to her, cut her horses from the carriage and rescued her. She went to their owner and tried to buy them in order to set them free, but, failing, set aside a fund for their support.

Rev. Benjamin Hood inherited "Bowling Green," and through his wife, Sarah Wayman, left Joshua, Charles Wayman, Benjamin and John. For forty-five years Rev. Benjamin Hood preached in neighboring meeting-houses; he died at seventy, and the text at his funeral was, "I have fought a good fight; I have finished my course; I have kept the faith; henceforth there is laid up for me a crown of righteousness." There are still some who remember his tall form, dignified bearing, commanding voice and fervent words.

Joshua Hood (of Benjamin)—Matilda Haughey; issue, James, Joshua, John, Mrs. Vansant, Mrs, Zadock Waters and Mrs. Joshua Baxley, of "Warfield's Range." Joshua Hood was one of the Committee to receive General La Fayette at Cooksville in 1825; he went to Baltimore to receive him and was also present at the ball given in his honor at Annapolis.

Major Charles Wayman Hood located north of "Hood's Mill" in Carroll. He was a surveyor whose lines covered much of that section. He always rode a fine horse, and when mounted, erect and handsome, was not unlike General Lee. From his intelligent record I have quoted much of the early history of the family. His first wife was Mrs. Catharine (Dorsey) Wheeler, who bore a son and daughter. His second wife and widow is Mrs. Avolina (Warfield) Hood.

"Bowling Green" descended to Dr. Benjamin Hood. His wife was Hannah Mifflin Coulter. Their son is General John Mifflin Hood, late President of the Western Maryland Railroad. His brothers were Wylie Mangum Hood, Civil Engineer of California; and Jennings Hood, who married Mary Sudler.

John Mifflin Hood completed a course of study at Rugby's Institute, Mt. Washington, in 1859; was engaged on the Delaware Railway and on the Eastern Shore Road; went to Brazil, but returned to Baltimore in 1862; ran the blockade and reported for service at Richmond; was at once assigned as topographical engineer and draughtsman of the Danville and Greensboro Road; after completing it he engaged as a private in Company C, Second Battalion of Maryland Infantry and was promoted lieutenant in the Engineer Troops, continuing until the surrender. At Spottsylvania he had his left arm shattered; wading the Potomac at night, he came to Baltimore and was treated by Dr. Nathan R. Smith, and returned with a large party of recruits. In 1865 he was upon the Philadelphia and Baltimore Railroad extension and upon the Port Deposit Branch. Becoming Chief Engineer of the Philadelphia and Baltimore Central, he constructed its line through Cecil County to the Susquehannah. In 1870 he was General Superintendent of the Atlantic and Gulf Railroad. In 1874 he was made Vice-President and General Superintendent of the Western Maryland Railroad, and in the following March was made President, including the office of Chief Engineer; in this work he has won an enviable and enduring reputation; not only has he well-conducted the road, but he has ably defended it through the press. Having recently been chosen President of the United Railway Company of Baltimore, he resigned the presidency of the Western Maryland and has been honored by a testimonial dinner in honor of his able management. President Hood married a daughter of Judge Hayden, of Virginia, and has Richard Hayden, Mary E., Florence M., John M., Alice Watkins and Mabel Douglas Hood.

After the death of Dr. Benjamin Hood, the estate, having no resident heir, was offered for sale, when it was bought by Mrs. Sarah M. (Hood) Jervis, wife of John Jervis, of Harford, sister of Dr. Hood. It was my privilege, when a boy, to visit her old long-drawn home at "Bowling Green," wherein six generations of noble men had lived. Their old English clock, with scriptural lessons, stood in the hall, and she was then the only representative of them. The old home has been replaced by "New Bowling Green," but a picture of the old one still hangs upon its walls; by its side is her handsome, genial face and form; her daughter, Mrs. John T. Ridgely, inherited it. Their heirs are Jervis, Mrs. Richard Dorsey, Mrs. Richard Hayden Hood, Nannie D., Charles H., Lourena, Ethel Lee, John T., Grace, Eloise and Benjamin H. Morgan.

Mary Hood Jervis became Mrs. Davis and, second, Mrs. Oscar Shipley, with a son, Oscar Carroll.

General Thomas Hood, brother of Benjamin, lived in sight of the National Pike. His brick house of quaint and curious design, is perhaps the oldest in that section. It was a resort for many distinguished men. General Hood was in command of the militia; a field nearby is still known as the "Muster Field." From 1814 to 1834 General Hood represented the upper district of Anne Arundel in the Legislature as a Whig. He was with General La Fayette at Cooksville in 1825. His wife was Rachel Wayman. Their son, John—Louisa Dorsey (of Colonel Richard) and left John Thomas Hood, of Alpha, who married Miss Perkins. Wm. Henry Forsythe owns the estate of John Hood.

Henry Hood (of General Thomas) adjoined his father on the north and married Kitty Brown (of Samuel). Elizabeth—Rev. Zadock Waters. Their daughters are Mrs. Washington Waters and Miss Eliza Waters.

General Hood died in 1849, seventy years of age. The tribute to him and his brothers by a contemporary writer was the quotation: "None knew them but to love them; none named them but to praise."

"Hood's Forest" covered pretty much all the land from the National Pike, near West Friendship, to the Westminster Road, and extending beyond the Baltimore and Ohio, reached up into Carroll County. It is now an elegant body of agricultural lands, upon which are seated such progressive men as Forsythe, Dorsey, Ridgely, Jones, Peddicord and Snyder brothers.

GRANT.

William Grant, of the Highlands of Scotland, during the Revolutionary period came over to Prince George's County, Maryland. Here he met Isabella Grant, also of the Highlands, who when fifteen years old, lost both parents on their passage over. She remembered they had considerable money, which the Captain seized, and actually sold her and her brother William and sister Rachel to some settler near Prince George's County. There she met her countryman, William Grant and three years later were married. Their issue were John, of whom nothing is known; Robert and Daniel, both single, and James, who married Elizabeth Madden. Issue, John, unmarried; Margaret— John Harrison. Issue, Peter, Richard, Margaret and Elizabeth.

James, Jr.—Margaret Thompson. Issue, Mary Ellen—A. H. Hobbs; Charles T.—Maude Hood. Issue, Walton and Maude; Charles—Mary Ann McKenzie and had three children; Mary Elizabeth—Minor Franklin Wells. Issue, Julia, Francis, Virginia, Anne, Emily, Charles and Benjamin.

The Grant homestead was upon the old Frederick road, near Alpha, the home of Thomas John Hood, grandson of General Thomas Hood, the old Whig representative of Howard District for many years.

The issue of Thomas and Julia (Perkins) Hood were Thatcher Hood—Ruth Shipley and had Edwin, May, Howard and Maude; Ellis—E. G. Jones. Issue, Ruth and Otis; Maude—C. T. Grant; Otis—Florence Whitey and Thomas—Daisy Maxwell. Issue, Alma and Mildred.

Walton Grant is a graduate of St. John's College and is now an officer of its faculty. His cousin, Howard Hood, is a student there.

HOOD'S HAVEN.

Benjamin Hood, son of Samuel Hood, of England, was the first known settler upon the Patapsco as far west as Hollofield's. My notes show that he was there before 1700. He built a mill at Hollofield's. He had two sons, James and John; James inherited the property. A flood came and washed the mill away. He held a tract of 157 acres and determined to rebuild the mill, and completed it one year before his death, in 1768. It was used in grinding corn.

Neither the wife of Benjamin, the father, nor James, the son, has come down to us, but James left sons, Benjamin, James, the Revolutionary soldier; Lucian, Thomas, and daughters, Nancy, wife of John Wooden; Sally, wife of Mr. Stevens.

Benjamin Hood, heir-at-law, in 1774, sold the mill and farm to Joseph Ellicott, reserving the burial-ground of his father upon the lowlands, north of the homestead. This was honored until the Baltimore and Ohio Railroad was built over the grave and nothing now marks the spot. Benjamin Hood later took up Hood's Hall, in the neighborhood of Elk Ridge. This became one of the estates of William Cumming. Thomas Hood, youngest son, married Margaret Crook, of the family of General George Crook, U. S. A. They removed in 1812 to West Virginia. From this family comes a long line, including Mr. James Hood, of Washington, who sends me the following:

"My great-grandfather, James Hood (brother of John), died about the year 1769 and lies buried near Ellicott's Mills, as I have been informed. I know nothing of his life or ancestry beyond the fact that he was a millwright and I have supposed that he was the same James Hood mentioned in the following extract from 'Biographical and Historical Accounts of Ellicott Family, Collected and Compiled by Charles W. Evans, Buffalo, New York (page 21):

"'Ellicotts upper mill was built by James Hood, in 1768, but was then only used to grind corn. It was conveyed to the Ellicott brothers, in 1774, by Benjamin Hood, eldest son and heir-at-law of James Hood for £1,700 Maryland currency. This property contained 157 acres and afterward 176 acres. The deed provides that the ground where James Hood, the father, was buried, should be retained as a family burying-ground. It was on the low ground north of the mansion. In after years the Baltimore and Ohio Railroad was constructed over it and obliterated all traces of it.'

"This James Hood had seven children as follows: Benjamin, James, Lucien, Nancy—John Wooden; Sally——Stevens; Thomas and another.

"Thomas Hood, my great-grand father, perhaps the youngest son of said James, was born May 16, 1763. He married Margaret Crook, who was born June 6, 1768. My grandfather's description of him is that he was tall and slender, dignified and stern. His wife Margaret was a woman of great force of character. General George Crook, of the United States Army, is descended from her family. It is related of her that when the spring floods of the Patapsco had in two successive seasons destroyed the milldam and otherwise caused great loss, in consequence of which her husband expressed his determination not to rebuild the dam again, but to devote his attention to the farm instead, she purchased the material and employed the labor necessary to build a stronger and better dam than ever, and herself superintended its construction almost to the finishing point before my great-grandfather yielded and consented to complete the new dam and continue milling. About the year 1812 they removed to West Liberty, Ohio County, Virginia (now West Virginia), where he died of a cancer in the face, on November 6, 1846. She followed him a year later, November 2, 1847 and both lie buried at Short Creek Meeting-House, Short Creek, Ohio County, West Virginia. On the stone above him is (or was) inscribed the following:

"Thomas Hood, died November 6, 1846. Aged eighty-three years, five months and twenty days.

'The voyage of life's at an end,
The mortal affliction is past,
The age that in heaven to spend
Forever and ever will last.'

"On the stone above his widow is (or was) inscribed the following:
"Margaret Hood died November 2, 1847. Aged eighty years, four months and eleven days.

'Called by her Lord to seek his face,
She joyfully obeyed
And eager flew to Christ's embrace
On whom her hopes were stayed.'

"The only relics of my great-grandfather which I possess are his family Bible, his cane, inscribed "T. Hood, 1763," some few pieces of silverware, probably presented at the time of his wedding, because inscribed "T. M. H." (Thomas and Margaret Hood), and a letter written by him on May 3, 1839, from West Liberty to his son James, my grandfather.

"The children of Thomas and Margaret (Crook) Hood were seven, as follows:

"Charles Crook Hood, born July 2, 1788—Frances Hammond; Priscilla, born November 28, 1792—Eli Green; Elizabeth, born September 30, 1799—Reverend James Taylor; Dr. James Hood, born April 10, 1802—first, Cordelia Pumphrey; second, Mary C. Jefferson; Rachel, born February 24, 1804—Joseph Brown; Sarah, born January 30, 1806—Jacob Bowman; Mary Ann, born July 17, 1808— Elzy Matthews.

"Dr. James Hood, my grandfather, was born in Maryland, but was taken in his childhood to West Liberty by his parents when they removed westward, as noted above. At the age of eighteen years he married Cordelia Pumphrey, May 25, 1820, and removed to Burgettstown, Washington County, Pennsylvania, where he began the practice of medicine. Here his children, Nancy and Elizabeth, were born. In a few years, he returned to West Liberty, continuing in the practice of his profession. His wife Cordelia was daughter of Beal Pumphrey, whose farm nearly adjoined the farm of his father, Thomas Hood, at West Liberty. Here his children, Thomas Beal and Benjamin Rush Hood, were born. He then removed to Flushing, Belmont County, Ohio, and afterward to Fairview, Guernsey County, Ohio. Here Charles and Adeline his two youngest children were born and here his wife Cordelia (who was born July 6, 1800, and was nearly two years older than himself) died, November 24, 1838, and there she lies buried. On September 3, 1839, he married Mary C. Jefferson at Fairview. Two years later he entered the ministry of the Methodist Episcopal Church and preached at Thornville, Gratiot, Johnstown, Somerset and other places on the 'Granville Circuit' for about five years, when continued ill-health, compelled him to discontinue his ministrations. I have the synopsis of many of his sermons in his own hand. He resumed the practice of medicine at Gratiot about 1846 or 1847 and here remained until 1851, when he removed to Newark, Licking County, Ohio. In 1864 he became a contract surgeon in the Federal Army and continued such until the close of the war; then returned to Newark, where he died March 1, 1874, and there he lies buried. He was much of an invalid all his life, although a large, fleshy man. His second wife, Mary C. (Jefferson) Hood, is still living and is now (February, 1896) in the eighty-fifth year of her age and in full possession of her faculties. No children were born of his second marriage. The children of James and Cordelia (Pumphrey) Hood were six, as follows:

"Nancy B., born August 21, 1821—Dr. L. J. Dallas; Elizabeth M., born February 24, 1823—Orlo Sperry; Benjamin Rush, born July 26, 1827—Edith Manley; Dr. Thomas Beal, born March 19, 1829—first, Margaret Hannah Winegarner; second, Mary E. Hyde; Charles F., born July 6, 1831—Anna E. Pickering; Adeline Cordelia, born September 14, 1837—first, Benjamin D. Evans; second, —— Gilmore.

"Dr. Thomas Beal Hood, son of Dr. James Hood, is my father.

"James A. Hood."

HOOD'S MILL.

James Hood, of "Bowling Green," inherited a large estate surrounding this mill. This descended to his daughter, Mrs. John Tolley Worthington, who sold it to Samuel Bentz. The mill was destroyed by fire, but has now been replaced by a modern rolling mill. This was run by the Dorsey Brothers. Hood's mill is the railroad terminus of the Westminster road. It is a busy shipping and receiving depot for a large territory. Messrs. Hammond Brothers conduct the store and depot.

Surveys were early made in this section. John Dorsey (of Edward) held large surveys here at the time of his death, in 1765.

Edward Dorsey (of Edward and Sarah Todd) was upon the northern border of Hood's Mill long before that. He sold "Dorsey's Thicket" and "Vachel's Purchase" to Vachel Dorsey in 1761, and Deborah Maccubin, his wife, joined him.

In 1764 Edward and Deborah sold to his father "Ely's Lot" and another part of "Dorsey's Thicket" in exchange for "Whitaker's Purchase." This he sold to Benjamin Scott.

In 1766 Edward and Deborah sold "Dexterity," on which "Hood's Mill" stands, to his brother, Colonel John Dorsey. This was sold by Colonel John to his brother-in-law, Vachel Dorsey. Edward and Deborah lived at the junction of the Westminster and Old Liberty roads. They sold a part of the homestead tract to Ely Dorsey, Sr.

Edward's will of 1782 names the following heirs: "To Ely 100 acres of 'Dorsey's Thicket,' upon which he now resides; also a part of 'Long Trusted,' on Piney Falls, near Gillis' Spring. To son Levin, all the remainder of 'Long Trusted,' excepting twenty acres and mill, which are to go to wife Deborah. To Edward ' Hawk's Nest Rebuilt.' To loving son, John Lawrence Dorsey, my tract 'Long Reach.' To my youngest sons, Benjamin and Rhesaw, all my lands where I now live, viz., a part of 'Dorsey's Thicket,' part of 'John's Chance,' 'Addition' to ' Kendall Delight' and part of ' Dorsey's Thicket Enlarged.' "In case of my wife's marriage, then I give to my three youngest daughters, Deborah, Sophia and Rachel, her portion. To son Levin, my tracts 'Folly' and 'Sumac Hill.'"

Mrs. Deborah Dorsey claimed her third.

The will of Mrs. Ann Maccubin, in 1798, tells us who Mrs. Deborah Dorsey was. She named "her stepson, Zachariah Maccubin, her stepdaughter, Deborah Dorsey and stepdaughter, Mary Dorsey; her husband Zachariah Maccubin." He was the son of John Maccubin, the immigrant, who claimed to descend from Kenneth II., the first King of Scotland.

The will of Mrs. Elizabeth Hood, sister of Deborah Dorsey, throws more light on this family of distinction. It was probated 1784 and named "her son, Zachariah Hood; her eldest daughter, Susannah Worthington; her daughters, Anne, Eleanor, Hester, Elizabeth and Mary." She refers to the confiscation of her son's estate. This was Zachariah Hood, the stamp distributor. Though his estate was confiscated, the English Government made him Governor of Turk's Island. He acquired an immense estate, died a bachelor, and no claim has ever been made to secure it.

Benjamin Dorsey (of Edward and Deborah) bought, in addition to his inheritance, all the rights of his brother Rhesaw in three tracts, "Dorsey's Thicket," "Dorsey's Thicket Enlarged" and "Brother's Discovery," in 1818.

He married Amelia, daughter of Jonathan Sellman, and had one son, Jonathan Sellman Dorsey. By a second marriage, to Catharine Perrin, of Hagerstown, he had a son, Benjamin Dorsey. His will of 1829 named his heirs: "Granddaughters Amelia Wade, Elizabeth Warthen, sons Jonathan and Benjamin." The latter's portion was land purchased of Campbell, intersecting the lands of Columbus O'Donnell. On the left of the road was Jonathan's, on the right was "Brother's Discovery," to be equally divided between them. Benjamin died a bachelor.

SELLMAN.

William Sellman, son of John Sellman and Elizabeth, his wife, was born January 22, 1689. He married the widow Sparrow, who was Ann, daughter of John and Matilda West, who was the mother of Matilda Sparrow, the bride of John Burgess, of Captain Edward and the mother of six Revolutionary soldiers.

William and Ann Sparrow Sellman had issue—John, born 1720; Charles, 1722; Jonathan, 1723; Ann, 1725. Jonathan Sellman was married by license September 16, 1746, to Elizabeth, daughter of Ferdinando Battee and Elizabeth, his wife. Their son, Jonathan,

born 1753, became the Revolutionary officer of the Third Battalion
of the Maryland Line and was promoted to Major and General. In
1783 he married Rachel Lucas, but without issue. He married next
Anne Elizabeth Harwood, daughter of Colonel Richard Harwood.
From his administrative account, rendered by his executrix, Mrs.
Ann Elizabeth Sellman, with Richard Harwood and Joseph Harwood
sureties, the distribution of his estate was made to herself and to
Alfred Sellman, Richard Sellman, John H. Sellman, Thomas Welsh,
Joseph N. Stockett and David M. Brogden.

A handsome portrait of General Jonathan Sellman now hangs in
the home of his Stockett descendants in Annapolis. Major Sellman
was at Valley Forge during that winter of discontent.

Other branches of the Sellman family moved to Elk Ridge. A
daughter of Jonathan Sellman (of William), Amelia, became the wife
of Benjamin Dorsey. Their son, Jonathan Sellman Dorsey, left
several sons, already noted among the Dorseys of Howard.

Jonathan Sellman Dorsey's homestead was at the junction of
the roads just north of "Hood's Mill." His daughter Ruth was the
wife of Julius Berrett, son of Joseph Berrett, of France, who took up
"Never Die," near Freedom.

Jonathan Sellman Dorsey's oldest son, Walter Dorsey, late
Sheriff of Howard, held the historic house wherein General La Fayette
was entertained, in 1825. His wife was Julia Forsythe, daughter of
Henry and Mary (Dorsey) Forsythe. The late Luther, Nimrod B.,
and Jonathan M. Dorsey, who held the homestead, were brothers.
The last surviving son of Jonathan S. Dorsey was Judge John R.
Dorsey, of "Oakland," who died recently. His commanding homestead is near West Friendship. To him I am indebted for several
historic records herein contained. His wife, Miss Whalen, was heir
to the old house wherein the first polls of the third district were held.
Their daughter Rose is now Mrs. Nicholson, of Baltimore, she has
several handsome daughters.

Reverend Wm. W. Dorsey and Harry C. Dorsey are the sons of
Judge Dorsey;

Anne Dorsey (of Edward and Deborah) though not named in
his will, was the wife of Philemon Dorsey Hobbs, who lived near
Poplar Spring.

Sophia Dorsey (of Edward and Deborah) married William
Dorsey (of Sheriff John), whose daughters were Maria and Lucy, heirs
to "Gray's Bower."

The descendants of Ely Dorsey (of Edward and Deborah
Dorsey) were Edward, Archibald and Sarah.

Edward married Miss Lunt, of Alexandria, Virginia. Their
heirs were the late Daniel Dorsey, of "Barnum's Hotel," Edward,
Augustus, Ezra, Sarah and Elizabeth, wife of Robert Hewitt.

Archibald married Lucy Dorsey (of William) and joined her
in selling "Gray's Bower" to John Dorsey (of "Sheriff John").

Daniel Dorsey, of "Barnum's Hotel," was the most popular man
in Baltimore. All agreed that he knew what Marylanders wanted,

and succeeded in rendering "Old Barnum's" the hotel of the day. His wife was a daughter of Mr. Barnum. His son Joseph was associated with him and was also very popular.

Dorsey Guy, grandson of Daniel Dorsey, former correspondent for the Baltimore "Sun," was with the Fifth Maryland Regiment during the Spanish war.

A daughter of Daniel Dorsey recently died in Washington.

Levin Dorsey (of Edward and Deborah) held for a time, his tracts near Freedom. After the death of his wife he left the homestead to his heirs and removed to the West. One son was Owen Dorsey, inventor of the Dorsey Reaper, whose son, Edmund Dorsey, has for several years been one of the County Commissioners of Howard. His residence is Gary Post-office. He has several sons, all progressive men of business. Mrs. Thomas Stewart, of "Round About Hills," is one of his daughters.

Rhesaw (of Edward and Deborah) sold three tracts north of "Hood's Mill" to Benjamin Dorsey, his brother, in 1818.

Edward Dorsey (of Edward and Deborah) inherited "Hawk's Nest Rebuilt." He married Sarah, daughter of General William and Sarah (Coppage) Cumming, of Liberty. He and his brother-in-law, Basil Nicholas Hobbs, sold their wives' inheritance, which was located near William Hobbs, at Ridgeville. Edward and Sarah Dorsey left no heirs.

DORSEYS OF ST. JAMES' CHURCH.

Vachel Dorsey (of John and Honor Elder) inherited "Belt's Hills," another tract of John Elder, which descended to Honor Elder and by her husband was deeded to Vachel.

Vachel Dorsey united the descendants of Colonel Edward and his brother, Hon. John, through his marriage to Ruth, daughter of Edward and Sarah (Todd) Dorsey. In addition to his inheritance of "Belt's Hills," 790 acres, he bought of his brothers-in-law, Edward and Colonel John Dorsey, "Vachel's Purchase," "Ely's Lot" and "Dexterity," all at and near "Hood's Mill." He also bought Nathan's property near Woodstock, which he later sold to Edward (of John). His will of 1798 reads: "To my son Levin I grant 'Dorsey's Interest,' 'Salophia' and 'Lost Sheep,' partly in Baltimore and partly in Anne Arundel. To son Edward I give 'Belt's Hills,' 790 acres, and a tract called 'Invasion,' in Anne Arundel County. To my daughter Ruth Owings I give 'Dexterity,' 580 acres; 'Vachel's Purchase,' 'Addition to Vachel's Purchase' and 'Ely's Lot.' If no issue, to descend to my two granddaughters, Ruth and Maria, daughters of my sons Elias and Vachel. I give to my granddaughter, Elizabeth Frost, a negro boy now in possession of my son, Johnsa Dorsey. The remainder of my estate to be divided equally among Johnsa, Elias, Vachel, Edward and Ruth Owings. My sons Johnsa and Elias joint executors." Johnsa had already been seated upon 500 acres in Baltimore County (now Carroll) and Elias had also received a similar estate in Carroll, both previous to his will.

The will of Mrs. Ruth Dorsey, in 1814, granted her son Johnsa "silver spoons." "To Ruth Owings, my wearing apparel. To granddaughter, Eliza Owings, a negro boy, in case her father will assist in the maintenance of my son Levin. To granddaughter, Ruth Maria Dorsey, a negro, in case her father, Johnsa Dorsey, will assist in the maintenance of my son Levin. To my granddaughters, Maria, Caroline, Mary and Rachel Dorsey, similar gifts, in case their father, Vachel, will assist in the maintenance of my son Levin. My granddaughter, Elizabeth Frost, residuary legatee. All money due me from Samuel Owings and all my property to be used by my executor in the maintenance of my son Levin. My son, Edward Dorsey, my sole executor."

Johnsa Dorsey married Sarah, daughter of Rezin Hammond, and had Rezin Hammond Dorsey, who died a bachelor in the West, and Nimrod Dorsey, who married Matilda Dorsey, daughter of his uncle Edward and Susannah (Lawrence) Dorsey.

Elias Dorsey married, first, Susannah Snowden, and, second, Mary, daughter of Benjamin Lawrence. (See Lawrence records.)

Edward Dorsey married Susannah Lawrence (of Benjamin). (See Lawrence records.)

Vachel Dorsey, Jr., married, first, Sarah Nelson, daughter of Burgess and Sarah (Howard) Nelson, and had the daughters named in his mother's will. He married, second, Elizabeth Dorsey (of Joshua and Elizabeth Hall), and had Essex Ridley Dorsey, late of "Hockley," and Elizabeth Hall Dorsey, wife of Caleb Dorsey, of "Hockley."

Vachel Dorsey, Jr., resided in Baltimore. He was engaged with Charles Carroll, of Carrollton, in surveying and selling vacant lands. Among the many interesting papers at "Hockley" is one containing a long list of vacant tracts in Anne Arundel and Howard, surveyed by Vachel Dorsey. (See Hockley record.)

Levin (of Vachel) passed his estate, through Edward, the executor, to Nimrod Dorsey, of Jefferson County, Kentucky, in 1814.

Edward (of Vachel), after selling most of his estate to Edward Dorsey (of Edward), removed to Kentucky with his daughter, Mary Ann Hobbs, wife of Basil Nicholas Hobbs. In 1809 Johnsa Dorsey, administrator of Edward's estate, sold "Belt's Hills" to Thomas Leach and named the heirs of Edward (of Vachel), as Sally, Matilda, Elias, Levin Lawrence and Urith Dorsey. These two sons became progressive stock-raisers in the West and left large families. Edward (of Vachel) was known as "Fuzzy Head Ned." He died and was buried at the "Anchorage," the home of his descendant, Mrs. John Shirley, of Kentucky. His will of 1808 named also Patience Lucket and Benjamin Lawrence Dorsey.

Elias Dorsey married a daughter of Benjamin Lawrence. He was in partnership with Thomas Dorsey and Benjamin Lawrence in milling. In his will of 1794 he ordered the mill to be sold; named his daughters, Mary and Ruth; if they die without issue, their portions to go to brothers, Johnsa and Edward, and nephew Charles (of Vachel). (This nephew was Captain Charles Dorsey, who was killed in the battle of North Point.)

Elias Dorsey, of Jefferson County, Kentucky, and Sarah H. Dorsey, his wife, sold "Selby's Lot" on the Severn to Mr. Tayman.

Edward Dorsey (of John and Honor) inheirited "Taylor's Park," situated on the Old Frederick Road and binding on the road leading from St. James' Church to Sykesville. It was taken up by John Taillor, descended to his daughter, Mrs. Higginson, who sold it to John Elder, and through Honor Elder, wife of John Dorsey (of Major Edward), descended to her son Edward, who was a large merchant of Baltimore, and acquired an estate equal to his father. He was upon the Committee of Observation for Anne Arundel in 1775, and built the brick house which still stands upon the Sykesville Road. Many of his descendants have erroneously classed him as Edward Dorsey, son of Edward and Sarah Todd. He married "Betty Gilliss," daughter of Ezekiel and Mary Hill, who was the daughter of Henry Hill and Mary Denwood.

Edward Dorsey (of John) bought two tracts in Baltimore County near "Soldiers' Delight" and 1,000 acres, known as "Small Beginning" from Charles Carroll, of Carrollton. In 1788 he and his son, Dr. Ezekiel John Dorsey, sold "Chaney's Neglect," in Baltimore County, to William Patterson. This later formed a portion of the Springfield farm of George Patterson, near Sykesville. He and his son, Dr. Ezekiel John Dorsey, also granted to Edward Dorsey, Jr., of Anne Arundel, three tracts "Progress," "Additional Progress" and "Dorsey's Dilemma." The signature of this son was "Edward of Edward." He held the homestead "Taylor's Park" and "Hay Meadows," patented to his father in 1785. He bought of Ely Elder the remaining part of "Taylor's Park." He bought of Edward Dorsey (of Vachel) 522½ acres adjoining "Taylor's Park" in 1801. He bought of Robert Shipley "The Last Shift" which, with other tracts on the road leading from Benjamin Lawrence's mill to Baltimore, he deeded to his son, Robert Dorsey. In 1825 he granted "Taylor's Park" to his son, Samuel Dorsey. In 1836 he sold to Joshua Barlow a part of "Taylor's Park" and a part of "Invasion." He joined his son Samuel in mortgaging a part of "Taylor's Park" to the Bank of Baltimore to secure a $4,000 loan to Samuel. It was redeemed by Mary Glenn, wife of Samuel. As guardian for Samuel, Edward (of Edward) loaned to Dr. Richard Hopkins, Samuel's inheritance, which was secured by a mortgage upon "Lockwood's Adventure."

In 1820 Edward Hill Dorsey, brother of Samuel, bought of James Hood, of "Hood's Mill," "Littleworth" and "Pleasant Meadows," beginning at "Ely's Lot" and "Vachel's Purchase." In 1830 Edward Hill Dorsey and Julia Ann, his wife, formerly Julia Ann Thomas, of Baltimore County, sold a lot in Easton, Talbott County, conveyed by Rev. Lott Warfield, of Easton, to Mary Thomas, mother of Julia Ann Dorsey. Other lots in Easton, belonging to the estate of James

Thomas, father of Mrs. Dorsey, were also sold by them.   In 1841, Samuel Dorsey made the following deed to Edward H. Dorsey and Julia Ann, his wife: "Whereas, Edward Dorsey, father of Samuel and Edward H. Dorsey, did, by his last will, bequeath unto Samuel a certain tract under the condition that Samuel should convey unto Edward H. Dorsey the same quantity of land which he had bought of Robert Dorsey (of Edward), he (Samuel) hereby conveyed to Edward H. Dorsey the three tracts, "Lucy's Lot," "Rachel's Lot" and 'Invasion,' adjoining 'Taylor's Park.'"   These same tracts were, that year, conveyed by Edward H. Dorsey and Julia Ann, his wife, to Henry Whalen.

The will of Ezekiel and Mary (Hill) Gilliss both name their daughter "Betty." She inherited "Withers Durand," which was sold by her and Edward Dorsey (of John) to Joseph Hill, her uncle. Their son, Dr. Ezekiel John Dorsey, of Baltimore County—Rebeckah Maccubin.   He left a tract "Nancy's Fancy" in 1822 to Rebecca Dorsey, of Edward.

Colonel Henry Dorsey (of Edward of John), clerk of the Circuit Court of Harford County, married Miss Smithson, whose daughter, Mrs. Farnandis, left the late Hon. Henry Dorsey Farnandis and his brother, of Harford.

Joseph Dorsey (of Edward of John) joined his father in bonding his brother, Dr. Ezekiel John Dorsey, in 1781.   He married his cousin, Amelia Gilliss (of Henry and Agnes Belt), of Curtis Creek, and removed to Washington County, Pennsylvania.   His wife's inheritance was "Rich Neck," on Curtis Creek, which they sold, while residing in Pennsylvania, to Mr. Pitcher.   Joseph Dorsey built a large stone house at Brownsville, Pennsylvania, upon 1,280 acres of land. Early in 1800 be bought Government lands in Ohio, now the finest in the State.   They are near Steubensville, Ohio, and are still known as "Dorsey's Flats."   The issue of Joseph and Amelia (Gilliss) Dorsey were Edward Gilliss, Ezekiel, Mary Hill, John, Rebecca, Ann, James, Elizabeth, Matilda, Harriet, Clarissa and Henry. Their daughter Ann married John P. M. Dubois, son of John Joseph Dubois, of Strasburg, France, brother-in-law of Isaiah Fox, constructor of the ship Constitution ("Old Ironsides").   The wife of John Joseph Dubois was Juliana Penn Miller, daughter of Peter Miller, the distinguished linguist employed by Thomas Jefferson to translate the Declaration of Independence into seven different languages.   Peter Miller's wife was Elizabeth Richardson, a descendant of Lord Aubrey, of Wales.

Joseph Dorsey Dubois, son of John P. M. Dubois and Ann Dorsey (of Joseph), is the Secretary of the Wheeling Steel and Iron Company.   His daughter is Mrs. J. J. Holloway, of Wheeling.

The daughters of Edward and Betty (Gilliss) Dorsey were Mrs. Betty Van Bibber, wife of James, to whom John Gilliss, of Baltimore County, granted his tract "Empty Bottle" in 1786, and Mary Hill Dorsey, to whom John Gilliss granted "Bachelor's Refuge" in 1789; she bought lands in western Baltimore in 1787; she became the wife of John Wilkins, whose daughter, Rebecca Wilkins, married Howell Williams. The brothers of Mrs. Betty Gilliss Dorsey were John Gilliss, of Baltimore County, and Henry Gilliss, of Curtis Creek. Her sisters were Mrs. Milcah Richardson; Sarah, first wife of John Davidge (of Robert), and Mrs. Pinkney.

SYKESVILLE.

This growing town was started in Howard County, but succeeding floods drove it into Carroll County. It takes its present name from Mr. James Sykes, the Englishman, who converted a flour mill, which had been carried on by Charles Alexander Warfield and others long before 1800, into a cotton mill and lived to regret it.

Mr. Sykes was the first to petition the erection of Howard District into Howard County in 1850. His old homestead on the Howard County side still stands, but his large cotton mill has stood idle since the last flood. It may yet rise from its ashes and be made to shed its electric light through the progressive town that now boasts of a bank, several progressive stores, several churches, a college and one of the handsomest station-houses along the Baltimore and Ohio Railroad.

As a shipping point for two progressive counties, this enterprising town will continue to grow.

In the triangle formed by two roads leading from Sykesville to the Old Frederick Road on the south were seated the following early settlers: Thomas Forsythe, Robert Shipley, John Hood, Vachel Dorsey, Edward Dorsey and Benjamin Lawrence, of "Delaware Hundred."

Old St. James' Church, upon the Frederick Road, celebrated for its camp grounds, stood near the present St. James.

Into this section progressive surveyors were early seated. Robert Shipley was nearest Sykesville.

"SHIPLEY'S CHOICE," 200 ACRES.

This tract upon the river side of the Severn is the earliest in the Shipley name. It was surveyed March 30, 1681, for Adam Shipley.

It was held later by Peter Porter and by James Barnes equally. Richard Shipley granted to his younger brothers, Adam, Robert and Peter, "Howard's and Porter's Range" and to his brother Robert lands on Elk Ridge. Adam was to hold the homestead of his mother, Lois Shipley, on "Howard's and Porter's Range." Peter Shipley, by will, left all of his property to his brother Richard, as heir-at-law.

Richard Shipley and Peter Porter sold 100 acres, in 1716, to Robert Freshwater. In 1720 Richard Shipley and James Barnes sold 100 acres to the same purchaser. Richard Shipley sold also to his sisters, Keturah Barnes and Lois Shipley, "Shipley's Choice." Richard and Adam Shipley sold "Howard's and Porter's Range" to Henry Sewell. This tract was the original survey of Captain Cornelius Howard and the first Peter Porter.

Robert Shipley (of Adam) was the inheritor of "Shipley's Discovery," upon the Patapsco, south of the Great Falls. This was laid out in 1724. It covered 250 acres. In 1742 Robert Shipley sold 140 acres of this to Nathan Barnes, and in 1744 he sold 110 acres more to Peter Porter, who named it "Porter." These same two families of the Severn followed him. Robert Shipley is next found upon his large survey at Sykesville. His inventory was returned in 1767, by his two sons, William and George Shipley, his executors. His daughters married John Hood, Upton Welsh, Howes Goldsborough, Dorsey and Gassaway.

Welsh and Goldsborough located upon his surveys. A large reserved graveyard upon his home marks many a resting-place. Dr. Howes Goldsborough and Captain Upton Welsh, with their Shipley wives, were neighbors.

From the large survey east of Lisbon, upon which Ex-Sheriff Nathan Shipley's descendants still live, a large family went out to many sections. Having failed to get some family data from representatives of the family in Howard, I can only name some of the descendants of these early surveyors in Howard and Carroll, as Judge Shipley, father of Mrs. H. O. Devries; Dr. Shipley, Mr. Oscar Shipley, Talbot Shipley, Samuel Shipley, Talbot Shipley, Jr., Bradley Shipley and Oliver Shipley, still upon the homestead. This tract was "Shipley's Adventure." Dr. Shipley, late Examiner of the Schools of Howard, and his brother, Rev. Ethelbert Shipley, are close upon the old surveys of Howard and Shipley.

FORSYTHE.

Thomas and James Forsythe came over from Scotland, in 1779. James went west. Thomas settled near Sykesville, now Howard County. He married, first, Miss Elizabeth Hasgood, of Devonshire, England, by whom he had one son, Henry Forsythe, who was born in 1804. Thomas Forsythe married, second, Miss Mary Warfield, daughter of John and Mary Chaney, and, third, Miss Amelia Gaither, having no issue by either.

His homestead, near Sykesville, was a part of Robert Shipley's estate. It descended to his son, Henry Forsythe, who married Mary Dorsey, daughter of John Dorsey and Ellen Cochran. Their heirs are Julia A. Dorsey, John T. Forsythe, Manelia, Arthur P., William Henry and Emily V. Forsythe.

John T. Forsythe heired the old homestead at Sykesville, now held by his son, John W. Forsythe. Mrs. Mary Forsythe heired from her father a tract upon the old Frederick road, known as "Lost by Neglect." This became the later residence of Mr. Henry Forsythe and is now held by his son, William Henry Forsythe. To this valuable property was added a handsome estate upon the "Hood's Mill" road, now the homestead of Arthur P. Forsythe.

Adjoining both is the late property of Mr. Nimrod Dorsey, who married two daughters of Henry Forsythe. This estate is now held by William Henry Forsythe, who holds an extensive property in a splendid state of cultivation.

These two brothers are among the first of our progressive farmers of Howard. Mrs. Walter Dorsey's estate, at Cooksville, and Mrs. Nimrod Dorsey's, east of her brother, are also well-developed.

Arthur P. Forsythe married a sister of Mr. James T. Clark, President of the Drovers' Bank of Baltimore. One daughter is Mrs. Hammond, of "Hood's Mill."

William Henry Forsythe married Miss Welling, of Clarksville. Their son, William Henry Forsythe, attorney-at-law, was a member of the Legislature from Howard, upon the Judiciary Committee of the House. Mr. William Henry Forsythe, Sr., has been a Director of Springfield Asylum since its removal to Sykesville.

DELAWARE HUNDRED,
HOME OF BENJAMIN LAWRENCE.

This oldest son of Levin and Susan Dorsey followed his brothers to the neighborhood of St. James' Church. He was upon the "Committee of Observation " for his section known as "Delaware Hundred." He built a mill, known later as Polton's, on Delaware Bottom.

In 1762 he married Urith, daughter of Samuel and Urith (Randall) Owings, of Owings' Mill. Mrs. Owings was the daughter of Thomas and Hannah (Beale) Randall. Benjamin Lawrence's heirs were Samuel, Levin, Mary and Susannah Lawrence.

Samuel Lawrence, in 1790, married Sarah Hobbs, daughter of Nicholas and Elizabeth Cumming (of General William and Sarah Coppage). Their daughter, Urith Owings Lawrence—James Brown, of Delaware, and left Caroline, wife of James Anderson, of Louisville, Kentucky, whose daughter Louisa became Mrs. Dr. Kemper, of Cincinnati, to whom I am indebted for valuable aid.

Benjamin Lawrence (of Samuel)—Susannah Howard (of Thomas and Ruth [Dorsey] Howard), whose grandmother was Susannah Lawrence (of Benjamin).

At the beginning of the Revolutionary War this section, known as "Delaware Hundred," became the centre of a busy settlement, after all available lands had been taken upon Elk Ridge. Benjamin Lawrence was a central figure of that settlement. His wife Urith Owings, was the daughter of Samuel Owings, whose estate covered a big section of Baltimore County. Their daughter Susannah married Edward Dorsey (of Vachel); their daughter Mary married Elias Dorsey (of Vachel), whose daughter Mary married-Levin Lawrence (of Benjamin).

Nimrod Dorsey (of Johnsa of Vachel) married Matilda Dorsey (of Edward and Susannah Lawrence).

Mary Dorsey (of Johnsa) had a daughter, Elizabeth Frost, whose daughter, Emily Childs, married Levin Lawrence Dorsey (of Elias), son of Edward and Susannah Lawrence.

In 1798 Benjamin and Samuel Lawrence removed to Jefferson County, Kentucky. The first stone house in the county, known as

"Eden," was built by them. Samuel Lawrence's wife rode in her carriage over the mountains of Maryland to join her husband, Edward, and his son-in-law, Nimrod Dorsey, soon followed.

The above marriages between the families of Vachel Dorsey and Benjamin Lawrence show some of the tangles we are called upon to solve.

"Two of Benjamin Lawrence's first cousins became his sons-in-law; his cousin's daughter became his daughter-in-law and aunt to her own first cousin; his cousin's granddaughter married his grandson."

Two of Benjamin Lawrence's descendants, Mrs. Dr. Kemper, of Cincinnati, and Mrs. John Shirley, of "The Anchorage," Kentucky, have spent thirty years of their intelligent lives in seeking to unravel the tangled threads of their Dorsey, Lawrence, Hobbs and Cummings relations.

My own researches of wills and deeds are herein added to their life-work.

MARRIOTTSVILLE.

The estate of General Richard Marriott, a descendant of John Marriott, of the Severn, gave the name to this little village of Howard. A magnesium limestone quarry is immediately at the railroad station.

The late Henry O. Devries was for many years the leading farmer of this section.

It was in this village he organized a Farmers' Grange. Upon "Prospect Hill," near by, lived Michael Burgess, oldest son of Captain Joseph. Coming out of the Revolutionary War, in which he fought as Ensign, he married Sarah Warfield, of Davidge, and handed down his estate to Thomas Burgess, Sheriff of Howard. The latter married Honor Dorsey. Their sons were Dr. Thomas Burgess, of Nashville, Illinois; Dr. Lloyd Burgess, of Sparta, Illinois; Joseph Burgess, of Nashville, Illinois, and William Burgess, attorney-at-law, of Orange Court, Virginia. The daughters of Sheriff Thomas Burgess were Mrs. Charles Hipsley and Mrs. Lucinda Day, mother of State Senator George Dorsey Day, of Commissioner William Day and of Joshua Day, of Glenelg. A portion of this estate is now held by the McEvoys.

William Burgess (of Michael), of "Prospect Hill," located in Baltimore. He began the business of Merchant Tailor. It has been followed by his son William and his grandson, William C. Burgess.

Joshua Burgess (of Michael) resided in Lisbon. His wife was Rebecca Mercer. They left three daughters, Sallie, Rebecca and Mrs. Gaither Henderson, and one son, William.

HENRY O. DEVRIES.

Henry O. Devries, the late President of the School Board of Howard County and long State Grange Agent, was born near Skyesville in 1826. His father, Saib Devries, came from Holland in 1803, where his family was prominent in the wars of Holland.

Mrs. Sarah Devries was of the Elder family, who took up a large estate upon the border lines of Howard and Carroll Counties.

In 1850 Mr. H. O. Devries married Ann E. Shipley, daughter of Judge J. H. Shipley, of Carroll County, and grandniece of Colonel Beale Randall, descendant of Thomas Randall and Hannah Beale, of Annapolis.

The Devries estate is a part of the property once held by Colonel John Eager Howard, near Marriottsville. Mr. Devries was Judge of the Orphans' Court of Howard; was a delegate to the Constitutional Convention of 1867. When the Grange movement was inaugurated he became an active supporter; was Master of the County Grange, and, still later, became the Master of the State Grange and General Manager of the State Agency, which he made a success. Mr. Devries also made a success of farming. He but lately retired from the Presidency of the School Board. Judge Devries' daughters are Mrs. Dr. Luke M. Shipley, Mrs. R. S. Maxwell, Cora and Martha Devries; Newton W., Alpheus C. and Rev. Benjamin F. Devries are his sons. After a long illness Mr. Devries died in the fall of 1902. The funeral took place from St. James' Church and was largely attended. Mrs. Devries survives.

WOODSTOCK.

A narrow valley, bisected by the rushing Patapsco, along which winds the Baltimore and Ohio Railway; a station-house, store and quite a hillside village on the south; a church and the magnificent Catholic College looming upon the north ridge of the valley, paralleled by a number of handsome summer homes on the south, constitute this charming resort.

Here were born two United State Senators; Senator Henry Gassaway Davis, of West Virginia, and Senator Arthur Pue Gorman, of Maryland.

Near by lived and died two of Howard's most intelligent and popular residents—Samuel Brown and his brother, John Riggs Brown; and here was born the brilliant editor of the "Ellicott City Times," John R. Brown, Jr., a relative of whom is still connected with it. Here, also, lived Dr. Herbert and his son, Brigadier-General James R. Herbert, whose estate was close to Governor George Howard's "Waverly."

Woodstock is also the home of Ex-Treasurer Frank Parlett, now Clerk of the Board of Commissioners. Woodstock's granite quarries are represented in the handsomest public buildings of Baltimore.

DORSEYS OF WOODSTOCK.

Nathan Dorsey (of John and Honor Elder) was located on the Old Frederick Road, near Woodstock. His tracts were "The Mistake," "Dispute Ended" and "Ranter's Ridge," the latter taken up by Thomas Browne. He bought of Benjamin Yates, two tracts, "Yates' Inheritance" and "Yates' Contrivance," on the Patapsco.

Nathan and Sophia, his wife, in 1764, sold part of "The Mistake" and mortgaged "Yates' Contrivance" and "Yates' Inheritance" to Hon. Henry Griffith.

In 1768 Edward and Vachel Dorsey, his brother, bought three tracts, "Mistake," "Dispute Ended" and "Yates' Contrivance."

In 1785 Vachel and Ruth Dorsey sold all their interest to Edward Dorsey, merchant of Baltimore.

In 1786 Edward Dorsey sold all of these tracts to General John Eager Howard for his son, George Howard, later Governor of Maryland.

Nathan Dorsey's homestead upon "Ranter's Ridge" was known as "Waverly." He left no will. His descendants are now in Louisiana, Georgia, Mississippi, Delaware and Maryland. His son, John Dorsey, was remembered by his grandfather, in 1764. Vachel (of Nathan), who lost a leg in the War of the Revolution, left a descendant, Dr. Nathaniel G. Ridgely Dorsey.

Edward Dorsey was known as "Curly Head Ned."

Nathaniel Dorsey was Secretary of the Society of the Cincinnati after the Revolution. In 1832 Nathaniel Dorsey, of Harford County, bought "Spring Garden" off James Kirk and others.

Dr. Samuel Dorsey, who graduated at the University of Pennsylvania, and Mrs. Priscilla Reid, have also been classed as heirs of Nathan Dorsey, of Waverly.

The record reads: "Nathaniel and Ann Owings Dorsey had seven sons and one daughter. Vachel lost a leg in the Revolutionary War and Edward was called 'Curly head Ned.'—Maria B."

"My grandfather was Vachel, who lost a leg in the Revolutionary War, and your father was Samuel, who studied medicine in Philadelphia. Both were sons of Nathaniel Dorsey, of "Waverly," which passed to the Howards and then to I. D. Judick.—N. G. Dorsey."

THE BROWNS OF WOODSTOCK.

I have studied three years to locate the Woodstock family. As there were eighty men and women bearing the Brown name, and seventy more spelling their names Browne, it is difficult to record with certainty the true family. I am aware of the tradition already published, that our Woodstock Brownes came from Captain Samuel Browne, who petitioned in 1692 to be restored to his position as naval officer. I am also aware that this Captain Samuel Browne is claimed as the nephew of Abell Browne, the ex-sheriff and ex-justice, whose will names his "nephews, Samuel and James, sons of my brother James, of Bermuda." The above testator was twice married, and yet he names in his will but one son, Robert, the namesake of Robert Harwood, who took up "Harwood," which Robert Browne inherited; but Abell Browne was also a brother-in-law of Michael Taney, and both were sons-in-law of Commander Samuel Philips. Abell Browne had a son Samuel, namesake of the Commander. He may be found as a witness in a contest over the title of "Harwood," and said Samuel was evidently the legatee of his grandfather Philips, and, as his legatee, became, without doubt, his successor and commander. This is strengthened by the fact that his father, Abell, left him no lands because he was a naval officer. This Samuel Browne (of Abell) took up no lands. He did not hold "Brown's Folly;" that was taken up by Thomas Brown, the ranger. He left no will or testamentary records and no lands.

I find a Samuel Brown upon the Bush River in Baltimore County; this was Abell Browne's estate. His will of 1713 left his lands to his three sons, Samuel, James and Absalom. The latter alone transferred these same lands still later. This shows that Samuel and James went elsewhere. The above testator naming his son James, appears to be the Samuel Browne, nephew of Abell; from his son Samuel could have come Benjamin, of "Good Fellowship," who handed down General Samuel Browne.

Benjamin Brown, of "Good Fellowship," was the brother-in-law of Patuxent John Dorsey, whose son Ely wrote to their London merchant to honor the drafts of Benjamin Brown and himself. Mrs. Elizabeth Dorsey, widow of Patuxent John, not only named her two sons, Samuel and Benjamin, in honor of father and brother, but her will of 1771 was witnessed by Samuel Brown, Jr., and by Rachel Todd, both representatives of Benjamin Brown, of "Good Fellowship." His will of 1768 names his wife, Susannah (Randall?) and his son Samuel, heir-at-law of "Good Fellowship." His remaining heirs were Rachel Todd, Ruth Todd, Joshua, Vachel, Susannah, Richard, Charles, Ephraim, Rebecca and Benjamin Brown, Jr.

Vachel Browne (of Benjamin) married Miss Hyatt and held her estate near New Market, Frederick County. His son, Joshua Browne, was President of the Elk Ridge Railroad and Mayor of Annapolis. Samuel Browne, several times Delegate to the Legislature from Frederick County, and the wife of Mr. Brashears, of Annapolis, are heirs of Joshua Browne. Samuel Browne, heir-at-law of Benjamin, held "Good Fellowship" at the outbreak of the Revolution. He married Achsah, daughter of John and Mary Riggs. The archives show his commission as lieutenant in Colonel Charles Hammond's Elk Ridge Militia in 1778. At the close of the war he was promoted to general. John Riggs Browne, Samuel Browne, Jr., Elisha, Vachel, Susannah and Achsah Riggs Browne were his heirs. General Browne left his homestead, "Good Fellowship," to his son, John Riggs Browne, and bought "Walnut Hill," near the Old Brick Church; here he spent his remaining days. His daughter, Susannah, became Mrs. Polton, of Guilford. Achsah Riggs, his youngest daughter, became the wife of Thomas Beale Dorsey, Jr., of "Gray Rock;" she was the mother of Achsah Riggs Dorsey, second wife of Reuben M. Dorsey, of "Arcadia," and of Sally, wife of Dr. Arthur Pue.

"Walnut Hill" is to-day one of the most attractive homesteads in Howard. It passed from Samuel Brown, Sr., to Samuel Brown, Jr., who was long Register of Wills for Anne Arundel County. It passed from him, a bachelor, to his brother Vachel. Upon the latter's removal to the city it was bought by Captain Pendleton, of Virginia, who restored it after the type of the Colonial houses of Virginia. It is now the property of Mr. Louis T. Clarke, attorney-at-law, Ellicott City.

Samuel Brown, Jr., also came into possession of the homestead of "Brown's Purchase," near Guilford. He deeded this to his brother, Elisha Brown, the surveyor of Anne Arundel. His wife was Ann Ray. It descended to their daughter Lucretia, who became the wife of Hammond Dorsey. By them the old homestead was sold to Ephraim Collins. Its handsome brick mansion is now the home of Mr. and Mrs. Earp In a graveyard, immediately in front of the dwelling, are well-preserved memorial stones bearing the names of Samuel Browne (of Elisha), who died 1826; Elisha Browne, 1832; James Browne, 1836; Anne Browne, 1836; she was the wife of Elisha Browne.

The deed from Mr. and Mrs. Hammond Dorsey to Ephraim Collins includes the adjoining tracts of "Warfield's Contrivance" and "Harry's Lot," and it joins the original homestead of Colonel Henry Ridgely.

Mr. Vachel Browne, of Baltimore, is a son of Vachel Browne (of Samuel) by his wife, a daughter of William Berry.

John Riggs Browne, of "Good Fellowship," married Sarah Gassaway, daughter of Brice John, of Fulton, whose wife, Dinah Warfield, was a sister of Major Charles Alexander Warfield; issue, Henry Gassaway Browne, Samuel, John Riggs Browne, Jr., Louisa, Mary Ann, Elizabeth and Kitty Ann Browne. John Riggs Browne was in the War of 1812 and died at thirty-two years.

Louisa Browne became the wife of Caleb D. Davis, of Woodstock, heir of Mrs. Ruth Randall and son of Robert Davis (and Ruth Gaither). Their son is Hon. Henry Gassaway Davis, Ex-United States Senator, late candidate for Vice-President, and President of several railroads in West Virginia, now a resident of Washington. Senator Davis and his cousin, Senator A. P. Gorman, of Maryland, both born at Woodstock, were in the Senate at the same time.

The late wife of Senator Davis was Catharine Bantz, of Frederick, granddaughter of Alexander and Mary (Harwood) Warfield, of the "Seneca." Their only son is John T. Davis, of Elkins. Upon the recent birth of his son, Henry Gassaway Davis, a telegram was received from Ex-Senator Davis, then a Delegate and Chairman of the United States Commission at the Pan-American Congress in Mexico, announcing a gift of $100,000 to his infant grandson and namesake.

The daughters of Senator Davis are the wife of United States Senator Stephen B. Elkins, of West Virginia; Mrs. R. M. G. Brown and Mrs. Arthur Lee. Senator Davis is President of the West Virginia Central Railroad. He and his brother, Major Thomas Davis, former Democratic candidate for Congress in 1900, are engaged in developing valuable coal mines in West Virginia. Senator Davis, with headquarters in Washington, has recently organized another railroad in West Virginia and has bee n made its president. In hi speech accepting the nomination for Vice-President he showed a conservative wisdom which has made him " The Grand Old Man" of the age.

Mary Ann Browne (of John Riggs Browne) became Mrs. Smith. Elizabeth married Mr. Peter Gorman, of Woodstock. Their oldest son, Senator Arthur Pue Gorman, was born at Woodstock in 1839. (See sketch of Senator Gorman.)   Kitty Ann Brown (of John Riggs) became the wife of Henry Hood, son of General Thomas Hood.

Samuel Browne, of "Good Fellowship," married Elizabeth Jenkins, of Richmond.   Issue, Henry, Thomas, Charles, Frank, Josephine and Ida Brown.

Thomas Browne (of Samuel) has been for several years one of the managers of Springfield Asylum.   Frank Browne bought the homestead and married Miss Davis.   He is a progressive farmer. John Riggs Browne, by his first wife had an only son, John Riggs Browne, Jr., for many years the brilliant editor of the "Ellicott City Times."   He died in early manhood, a bachelor.   The old homestead of "Good Fellowship" is still held by Mr. Browne's heirs.

THE DORSEYS OF ELLICOTT CITY.

The immediate settlers around the site of Ellicott's Mills, but long before this settlement, were the sons of Thomas Beale Dorsey (of Caleb of Hochley), who resided upon "Wyatt's Ridge," where "Belvoir" stands to-day.   This extensive tract was the inheritance of Ann Worthington (of John, the merchant, whose wife was Helen, daughter of Thomas and Mary [Heath] Hammond).

Thomas Beale Dorsey inherited from his father "two farms, bought of Thomas Higgins" twenty head of cattle, twenty head of sheep, the family silver and his mother's crest representing a stork; with this he sealed his will, now to be seen at Annapolis.

The only daughter was Sarah, wife of Reuben Meriweather, of a distinguished Virginia family recorded in Burke's Heraldry.   They settled at "Round About Hills," on a survey of Colonel Henry Ridgely.   Ann Meriweather became Mrs. John Worthington. Nicholas Meriweather, through his wife, Elizabeth Hood (of John and Rachel Howard), came into possession of parts of "Worthington Range" at Clarksville; to this he added other tracts.   Their daughter, Sallie Meriweather, married Reuben Meriweather Dorsey.

Sarah Dorsey Meriweather (of Reuben) became Mrs. Thomas Beale Dorsey (of Caleb).   Mary Meriweather became the wife of Westley Linthicum.   He was the Anne Arundel representative of the "Glorious Nineteen Van Buren Electors," and left descendants in Charles W. Linthicum, of Clarksville, and George Washington Linthicum, of Roxbury.

Thomas Beale Dorsey Meriweather (of Reuben) inherited "Round About Hills."   Through his wife, Miss Handy, he left Mrs. Dr. Augustus Riggs, of Cooksville; Mrs. Daniel Warfield, of "White Cottage," and Mrs. Dr. Lloyd T. Hammond, of the "Pine Orchard."   Their son, Edward Hammond, represented Howard in the Legislature and succeeded Judge Smith, the war judge of Howard, as Associate Judge of Howard County. Mrs. Dr. Wm. Magruder, of Brookeville, mother of Dr. William Magruder, of Sandy Spring, was a sister of Judge Hammond.

Mrs. Sarah Meriweather, after the marriage of her son, built upon property bought of Captain Philemon Dorsey. This estate was sold by her executors, Dr. Lloyd T. Hammond and Daniel Warfield, to Samuel Owings (of Thomas). It is now the property of Hon. Humphrey Dorsey Wolfe.

Thomas Beale Dorsey Meriweather exchanged his inheritance with Mr. Thomas Cook, of Cooksville, and resided there. It was later bought by Dr. Augustus Riggs, and is still held by his heirs.

CALEB DORSEY OF "ARCADIA."

Caleb Dorsey was a progressive surveyor; his signature, "Caleb Dorsey, of Thomas," appears upon numerous transfers in real estate, but he left four sons who surpassed him.

Caleb, of "Arcadia," married Elizabeth Worthington. Her mother was Susannah Worthington, nee Susannah Hood, sister of Zachariah Hood, the stamp agent of the revolution. Susannah Hood's mother was Elizabeth Maccubin (of Zachariah and Susannah Nicholson, daughter of Nicholas Nicholson and Hester Larkin and granddaughter of Sir John Nicholson, of Scotland). Zachariah Maccubin, son of John and Elinor Maccubin, claimed to descend from the McAlpines, who were descendants of Kenneth, first King of Scotland. Caleb and Elizabeth, of "Arcadia," had Mrs. Susan Brooks, Mrs. Sarah Waring and Mrs. Jacob Baer.

Caleb Dorsey, Jr., bought the homestead of "Patuxent John Dorsey" at Columbia, and married Ann Howard (of Captain Brice). Charles W. Dorsey bought the western part of the same tract. He built the old brick house upon the pike west of "Arcadia" and there resided. His wife was Mary Tolley Worthington (of Walter and Sarah Hood [of John and Hannah Barnes], of "Bowling Green"). Their daughters, Sally Ann and Mary Tolley, became wives of Governor Ligon; Comfort Augusta became Mrs. James Mackubin; Elizabeth became Mrs. William H. G. Dorsey.

John Worthington Dorsey (of Caleb) bought an elegant body of land near the Old Brick Church. He brought his wife from Major Philip Hammond's Manor, near Gambrill's Station. She was Mary Ann Hammond, who inherited the present property of Mr. Bond, near Millersville,. The late Judge Reuben M. Dorsey; Caleb, of California, Charles W. Dorsey, of the Confederate Home; Mrs. Levin Gale, Mrs. Dr. Mackey and Mrs. Benjamin Cook, of Virginia, were heirs.

Reuben Meriweather Dorsey, the richest of all, lived upon the old home tract, "Arcadia." He married Sally Meriweather, whose mother was Rachel Howard, whose mother was Rachel Worthington, whose mother was Elizabeth Ridgely. Reuben Dorsey's daughter, Ann Elizabeth—William Bose Dobbin, progenitor of Judge Dobbin and his son, Hon. Robert Dobbin, of Howard, late School Commissioner;

Josephine—Anthony Johnson, now represented by Thomas M. John son, of the present School Board; Sally Meriweather (of Reuben)—Dr. Samuel Owings Rogers. Their sons are Hon. John Gough Rogers and Reuben Dorsey Rogers. The second wife of Reuben M. Dorsey was Achsah Riggs Dorsey (of Thomas Beale and Achsah Riggs Brown).

COLONEL JOHN WORTHINGTON DORSEY OF THE REVOLUTION.

This second son of Thomas Beale and Ann commanded an Elk Ridge company in the Maryland Line, frequently mentioned in our archives. His estate was near the Old Frederick Road, north of Caleb Dorsey's. Colonel Dorsey married Comfort Worthington (of Samuel). Chief Justice Thomas Beale Dorsey, Caleb and Edward, of Kentucky; Colonel Charles Samuel Worthington and bachelor John Worthington Dorsey, Jr., were his sons.

The land records of Howard are strong evidences of the large practice held by Judge Dorsey. His signature in bold hand was "Thomas Beale Dorsey of John." An able jurist, his opinions were sought in leading contests. When called to preside as Chief Justice at Annapolis, he made the journey daily on horseback. He was a member of the Constitutional Convention of 1851. Through his efforts Howard District was erected into Howard County. Judge Dorsey's wife was Milcah Goodwin, a granddaughter of Caleb Dorsey, of Belmont. Their daughter, Rebecca Comfort, became Mrs. Allen Bowie Davis, of "Greenwood;" Samuel Worthington Dorsey removed to Louisiana and married Sarah Ann Ellis, of Mississippi. They lost heavily during the Civil War. Mrs. Dorsey presented "Beauvoir" to Ex-President Jefferson Davis; after his death Mrs. Davis returned the estate to Misses Comfort and Mary Dorsey, of Ellicott City, including rare household articles. They are the daughters of Attorney William Henry Goodwin Dorsey, who built the Macguire homestead, now owned by Mr. Richard H. Cromwell. Attorney William H. G. Dorsey married, first, Elizabeth Worthington Dorsey (of Charles Worthington Dorsey), and, second, Comfort Worthington Dorsey (of Colonel Charles Samuel Worthington Dorsey).

John Thomas Beale Dorsey, third son of Chief Justice Dorsey, was a candidate for Judge of Howard Circuit. He held the home-stead and during his absence in the Southern Confederacy it was sacrificed. He was three times married—first, to Sarah Ann Harrison; second, to Mary Campbell Harris; third, to Kate Mason, daughter of Judge James Mason, Confederate Commissioner to the English Court. Two daughters survive and reside in Washington. Mr. Dorsey was tall, distinguished looking, an accomplished talker with ready wit.

Caleb Dorsey, brother of Judge Dorsey, married Miss Taylor, of Kentucky, and died there.

Edward Dorsey, his brother, married Ellen Brown (of Moses) and in 1830 removed to St. Louis. His daughters were Mrs. Gilchrist Porter and the wife of Senator Broadhead, of Missouri.

Bachelor John W. Dorsey, Jr., conveyed "Rebecca's Lot" to Patrick Crowley. It began at the given line of a conveyance from his brother Edward W. Dorsey, at a corner between the lands of John G. Rogers and Mrs. Commodore Mayo, to a corner of John T. B. Dorseys. He sold another part of "Rebecca's Lot" at the tollgate to John Burgess.

Charles S. W. Dorsey (of Colonel John) married Mary Pue Ridgely (of General Ridgely) and left Comfort Dorsey and Rebecca Hanson, wife of Colonel George R. Gaither, Charles Ridgely Dorsey, attorney; John W. Dorsey, attorney and ex-member of the School Board, and Samuel W. Dorsey, of Baltimore, are sons.

Thomas Beale Dorsey, Jr., of "Gray Rock," located upon the south side of the Frederick Pike. His estate is Herbert's. He was twice married—first, to Achsah Dorsey (of Samuel), by whom he had Samuel; second, to Achsah Brown (of Samuel), by whom he had Achsah Riggs Dorsey, second wife of Reuben M. Dorsey, and Mrs. Sally Pue, wife of Dr. Arthur Pue. They had William, Ventress, Samuel, Ferdinand and Robert Pue. Three of these brothers removed to Texas. Ferdinand and Robert Pue remain in Howard. The former is a member of the vestry of Christ Church at Highland; the latter of the Episcopal Church at Poplar Spring. Thomas Beale and Achsah Brown Dorsey had one son, Thomas Beale Dorsey, Jr. "Gray Rock" was sold by Mr. Reuben Dorsey.

SETTLEMENT OF ELLICOTT'S MILLS.

Three years before the beginning of the Revolutionary War Joseph, John and Andrew Ellicott purchased lands on both sides of the Patapsco four miles in extent, including all water power two miles above and two below the mills. The exact amount of land covered cannot now be ascertained. These brothers were descendants of an old Devonshire family in England, who were in possession of their estate when the Conqueror came. They were sons of Andrew Ellicott, who came to Pennsylvania in 1730. Having journeyed over the middle counties of the province of Maryland to ascertain their adaptability for growing wheat, they were favorably impressed and concluded to locate upon the Patapsco. All of their stock and implements were put on board of a vessel at Philadelphia and were taken down the Delaware to New Castle and there landed. Wagons and carts forming a part of their outfit were then loaded and driven across the Peninsula to the head of Elk River, where they were again embarked on a vessel, which, by way of the Chesapeake and Patapsco, brought them to Elk Ridge Landing, then called Patapsco. There they were finally discharged; the wagons and carts were again landed, and moved over the rough and narrow country road to within one mile of their destination. Here they were obliged to stop on account of the rocks and precipices. Unloading their contents, parties of men with hand-barrows carried them to their journey's end, then known as "The Hollow."

By the harvest time of 1774 a house 100 feet long, with spacious chambers for storage, was finished, and with it a small village of comfortable houses had also been raised up. This first building was destroyed by fire in 1809. Upon the completion of the workmen's cabin, a saw-mill was the next object for securing the necessary lumber for the buildings. Quarries of granite immediately on the ground were next opened. All the implements, except some crowbars gotten from Dorsey's Forge, at Avalon, were brought from Pennsylvania. The whole valley was then a wilderness covered with great trees, centuries in age. The undergrowth was so thick a path had to be cut through to explore the ground. Small game of every kind dwelt therein, whilst upon the more open ground great herds of deer and flocks of wild turkeys frequently were seen. Shad and herring were caught in the Patapsco as far west as Elysville. Paths of the Indians were clearly traceable until 1828. Stone tomahawks, stone axes and arrow-points were so abundant where the Baltimore and Ohio Railroad office now stands, the presumption is that a great Indian battle had there been fought near the spring with its overshadowing trees.

In 1774 the Ellicott brothers were ready to grind wheat. Their books show that William Lux Bowly bought on December 4th, 1774, 100 barrels of flour, at seventeen shillings and charges; December 13th, 100 barrels, and on the 20th, 100 barrels more.

Bowly's warehouse was at Elk Ridge Landing, where beautiful residences, with handsome grounds, flower gardens and gravel walks were built immediately after the war.

The cost of living at that time may also be seen by Ellicotts' books. Bacon sold, per pound, at two shillings six pence; turkeys, four pence per pound; chickens, four pence; butter nine pence; beef and pork, three pence; wages, twenty pence per day. To grow wheat for their mill these pioneers had to cut down the forests upon the hills, clear out the stumps, plow and sow in order to set object lessons for their neighbors.

The "Elk Ridge" and "Upton" Hundreds were unwilling to give up their tobacco crops for wheat. They had their hand-mills for grinding corn for their negroes, and they looked with suspicion upon the Quakers and their new mills on the Patapsco, but the Ellicotts, believing that "a demand will create a supply," kept on offering a fair price for wheat.

Charles Carroll, of Carrollton, was then at Doughoregan Manor, and though the richest capitalist in the province, he saw that his revenues could be increased by cultivating wheat, and at once changed his methods upon both manors. He was ready, too, to encourage the new millers by loaning them money for the development of their enterprise. He was then about the only banker of that day. To his manor the Ellicotts built a road at their own expense. Beyond that, to reach the upper Manor of Carrollton, near Frederick, the planters along the route willingly helped them. A house on wheels was built for the workmen. It was drawn by horses from place to place. It had a kitchen for cooking everything but bread; this was supplied and forwarded from their mills.

The men who worked on this road were all from Pennsylvania. When the firm had completed their buildings and stabling which accomodated eighty horses, they next turned their attention to building a school for the neighborhood. The last building in the village before 1790 was their warehouse and store. This was located directly opposite the mill and immediately on the road from Baltimore to Frederick. This work was done by Maryland masons—the Spicers, of Harford County. Externally it remains as it was built, but it is now a dwelling for private families.

The Ellicotts sent agents to New York and Philadelphia, who bought goods and shipped them via Elk Ridge Landing. They dealt in linens, diapers, silks, satins, brocades, India china, dinner and tea sets, mirrors, glassware, mathematical instruments, ironware, groceries, liquors and wines. After our Independence they sent Samuel Godfrey, an English partner, to London for importation of their goods. Influential men for miles congregated at their store and postoffice. They brought their wheat in exchange for purchases. There political and even scientific questions were discussed, and there these intelligent Quaker brothers were always courteous with becoming gravity. They kept their roads in repair by means of "wheel-barrow men," men who had been convicted of minor crimes. These labored in small companies under an overseer, who wore his side arms and carried his musket. Depots, built of logs, were set up several miles apart, where their meals were prepared. At night they were locked up in their quarters. One of these depots, five miles from Baltimore, was standing in 1831. It was pointed out as the spot where an overseer, on two occasions, had been murdered by the men under charge.

Before 1783 the supply of wheat from Anne Arundel and Frederick Counties had so much increased the Ellicotts determined to export their flour. They purchased a lot and built their first wharf at Pratt and Light streets from logs cut at Curtis Creek. Daily communications between Ellicott's Mills and Baltimore were had by wagons loaded with flour.

The road made by the Ellicotts was the beginning of a still greater enterprise—the great highway to the West. This road is the only highway of its kind wholly constructed by the Government and was, says an interesting treatise upon it, what the "Appian Way" was to Rome. The conception of that gigantic work was by Albert Gallatin, the Swiss, when Secretary of the Treasury under Jefferson. Its cost was nearly seven millions of dollars, and when finished traversed seven States and extended eight hundred miles. One example of its value in building up the West, and thereby increasing the growth of the East, is shown in the fact that one single house in Wheeling, in 1812, unloaded 1,081 wagons, averaging 3,500 pounds each, and paid for the transportation of the goods the sum of $90,000. Another example of what could be done by a six-horse team was related by the late Johns Hopkins. In 1838 he engaged Daniel Barcus to haul a load of merchandise weighing 8,300 pounds from his store, corner of Pratt and Light streets, to Mount Vernon, Ohio. He delivered the goods in good condition at the end of thirty days from the date of his departure from Baltimore, the distance being 397 miles. Mr. Hopkins paid him $4.25 per hundred. On the return trip he loaded 7,200 pounds of Ohio tobacco, at $2.75 per hundred, in hogsheads.

Following the War of 1812 there was a great westward movement in Maryland. The war had brought disaster to many planters. Selling their lands for whatever they could get, they moved by wagons over the new road to richer lands of the West. Every cross-road had its wayside inn for the accommodation of the almost unbroken travel of the two decades from 1820 to 1840.

General La Fayette made his triumphal procession over it in 1825.

The Ellicotts also encouraged fruit growing by starting nurseries, which supplied trees to their neighbors free of cost. Practical irrigation was also taught by them. To keep their wheat fields moist in dry seasons they dug reservoirs, which by ditches carried the water to their fields.

When the war had ended in giving us a State Government these peaceful Quakers were ready to give advice to lawmakers.

Leaving the mills at night, they would ride on horseback to Annapolis, a distance of thirty-two miles, to breakfast. After spending the day they would return at night. When they came to Maryland the only passable public roads for wheeled vehicles were from Frederick to Baltimore and from Frederick to Annapolis.

The Old Frederick Road passed over the Patapsco, three miles above Ellicott's Mills, at Hollofields. It was used for an outlet for flaxseed and domestic produce of Frederick County as early as 1760.

A road from Sandy Spring touched the Old Frederick Road at Porter's Tavern, eighteen miles west of Baltimore. The Ellicotts by their enterprise changed the travel, after 1805, to the present bed of the pike. There were other "bridle-paths" and "rolling roads," very winding, to avoid the hills in getting their tobacco to market.

When they came to Ellicott's Mills the Quakers had a meeting-house near Elk Ridge Landing, about a mile from Ilchester. The Pierpoints, Haywards, Reads and Ellicotts were members.

To accommodate the people of their immediate neighborhood, as well as themselves, they built a meeting-house of stone on Quaker Hill, now in the centre of the town. This they presented to the Quakers of Baltimore. The deed covered four acres for a burial-ground and was dated 1800. Soon after that the old Elk Ridge house was abandoned. William Hayward an esteemed minister of the society lived for many years in walking distance of the old meeting-house at Elk Ridge. He was their only minister. There his daughter Elizabeth and her chosen partner, James Gillingham, rode on horseback to be married, and there assembled in silence, after his departure, the remaining members of the faith.

To the Ellicotts the County of Howard owes another debt. The cultivation of tobacco had discouraged many of their neighbors. The Dorseys, Worthingtons, Ridgelys and Meriweathers were seriously contemplating a removal to the more fertile soils in Kentucky and Tennessee, but when they saw the marked benefits shown in the experiments made upon the Ellicott's estate, by using plaster, they decided to give it a trial. The Ellicotts built a mill for grinding the Nova Scotia stone which they imported and prepared for their neighbors. This led to increased crops of clover and restoration of worn-out lands. In 1808 they sold nearly nine hundred acres, two miles in extent, to the Union Manufacturing Company of Maryland. A large manufacturing village grew up.

A tanyard was erected by Samuel Smith upon another site purchased of them. They leased lands to Joseph Atkinson in 1804 for an oil mill. They established in 1806 iron works for rolling and slitting bars, making rails on a large scale. To this was added later other mills for sheathing copper. The skilled laborers were mostly people from Wales.

In 1825 the population of the different manufacturing plants reached three thousand. In 1774 Joseph Ellicott withdrew from the firm and purchased the old Hood Mill at Hollofields. This he tore down and put up another with the latest inventions of his own. He built a storehouse for merchandise, stables for horses, houses for his laborers and a dwelling for himself. This was a model of comfort. He filled his garden with rare and beautiful plants, in the midst of which he placed a fountain, which sent a stream ten feet high, falling into a pond filled with fish. His four-faced clock, his own invention, represented on one face the sun, moon and planets moving in different orbits. On another were hands designating minutes, hours, days, weeks, months and years. On a third face twenty-four tunes of ante-Revolutionary music were played. It was constructed in 1769 by Joseph Ellicott and his son Andrew, afterward Professor of Mathematics at West Point. Another clock was placed in the gable of his house, to serve as a guide to travelers on their way from Frederick to Baltimore.

Over this road that passed Hollofields goods were first carried on pack-horses. It was followed later by immense wagons drawn by eight horses. A glance at Hollofields to-day shows no signs of its past advancement.

The site of Patapsco Institute was a free gift from the Ellicott's for an educational institution, which for a number of years shed its commanding light into many Southern homes. Upon Quaker Hill rest these sturdy settlers who gave life and form to the wilderness. For years the old Quaker Meeting-House had been deserted, but recently a descendant has rescued it and preserved its honored remains. All of these enterprises were organized whilst this section was still a part of Anne Arundel County.

CHARLES CARROLL, OF DOUHHOREGAN.

Charles Carroll, the emigrant, came to Maryland October 1, 1688. The Protestant Revolution was at hand, which resluted, next year, in the overthrow of the lord proprietor who had appointed him his Attorney-General. When Sir Lionel Copley was Governor, representing the King, who had taken possession of the province, he charged Mr. Carroll with disloyalty and still held him in prison. After the restoration of the Protestant Charles Calvert, in 1715, Mr. Carroll was appointed Judge and Register of the Land Office, succeeding Colonel Henry Darnall, his father-in-law. The position was higher than that of Governor Hart, who, also, represented the youthful proprietor.

Mr. Carroll was granted an extensive estate, consisting of "Carroll's Forest," 500 acres in Prince George's County, in 1689; "Ely O'Carroll," 1,000 acres in Baltimore County, in 1695; "Litterlouna," 400 acres in Baltimore County; "New Year's Gift," 1,300 acres, at Elk Ridge (afterward held by Caleb Dorsey [of Hochley] upon which tract the Old Brick Church stands to-day).

In 1701 he resurveyed his tracts of land in Baltimore County, which then embraced 1,969 acres. In 1707 he added "Clynmalyra," of 5,000 acres, and that same year was granted his princely domain of 10,000 acres of "Doughoregan Manor." He also owned "Enfield Chase," in Prince George's, and still later increased his estate to 60,000 acres. In one of Lord Baltimore's grants he wished Mr. Carroll to locate "as near as possible to my manors for the benefit of his society," and to enable Mr. Carroll to be of service in the province. A small brick house and two lots in the port of Annapolis were granted him; this was the property of a widow, whom Mr. Carroll paid for her claim.

Charles Carroll was temporarily Surveyor-General. His commission, in 1716, included also Naval Officer. He married, first, in America, Martha Underwood, daughter of Anthony, of St. Mary's County; she died in 1690. In 1693 he married Mary Darnall, the fifteen-year-old daughter of Colonel Henry Darnall, of "Portland Manor," by his wife, Elinor Hatton, widow of Major Thomas Brooke, of "Brookefield." Five of their ten children survived, three sons and two daughters. Their oldest son, Henry, died at sea on returning from school at St. Omers. Charles Carroll, Jr., born 1702, became the heir-at-law. His younger brother, Daniel, born 1707, married Ann Rozier, of "Notley Hall" and became the progenitor of the Carrolls, of Duddington, Prince George's County, now in Washington City. The old mansion was torn down some years ago.

Charles Carroll, the immigrant, was in England at the time of the death of Lord Baltimore, the second, and became the attorney of Lady Baltimore. On returning, in 1718, he made his will, which was probated in 1720. His three sons, Henry (then living), Charles and Daniel, were made executors. During the absence of the two remaining sons in Europe the estate was managed by James Carroll and Madam Mary Carroll. In 1729 Charles and Daniel Carroll sold sixty acres for the site of Baltimore City.

To distinguish him, Charles Carroll was known as Charles Carroll, of Annapolis. His only son was Charles Carroll, of Carrollton, born in 1737, whose mother was Elizabeth Brooke, daughter of Clement Brooke and Jane Sewall, daughter of Colonel Nicholas and Susannah Sewall. He was the stepson of the second Lord Baltimore and she was the daughter of Colonel William Burgess by Mrs. Ewen. Mrs. Carroll was, therefore, a relative of her husband on both sides.

At ten years of age young Carroll was sent to school at Jesuit College, of Bohemia, on "Herman's Manor," in Maryland. His cousin, John Carroll, later Archbishop of Baltimore, was a student there with Robert Brent, who married a sister of John Carroll. The two Carrolls, in 1748, went to St. Omers, in French Flanders, thence to the College of Louis le Grand, at Paris. In 1757 Charles entered the temple to study law, remaining three or four years.

There was, also, in Annapolis, in 1731, Dr. Charles Carroll, of an older branch of the Irish house. He and his cousin, Charles Carroll, of Annapolis and of Doughoregan, became partners in the Patapsco Iron Works, founded in 1731. This was a very valuable enterprise.

Daniel Carroll, of Duddington, died in 1752, and Charles Carroll, his brother, made an arrangement with Charles Carroll (of Daniel) to divide the estate of the immigrant. Charles Carroll (of Charles) was to hold "Doughoregan" of 10,000 acres, and "Chance" of 969 acres, whilst Charles, Jr. (of Daniel), was to hold "Clymalyra," "Vale of Jehosophat," "Ely O'Carroll" and "Litterlouna" and parts of two tracts in Frederick County, in order to give "more than an equivalent for the exchange." "Carrollton," in Frederick County, was patented in 1733 by Charles, Daniel, Mary and Eleanor Carroll, being the half of 20,000 acres granted them in 1723 by their father. It was then in Prince George's County. Daniel, in 1734, after the death of Eleanor Carroll, left his claim to his sister Mary. In 1764 Charles Carroll, of Annapolis, wrote to his son at school, and gave him the following estimate of his estate:

"40,000 acres of land, two seats alone containing each upwards of 12,000 acres, would now sell at 20 shillings sterling per acre..........................	£40,000	
"One-fifth of an Iron Work, with two forges built, a third erecting, with all convenient buildings; 150 slaves; teams and carts, and 30,000 acres belonging to the works; a very growing estate, which produces to my fifth annually at least £400 sterling, at twenty-five years' purchase.................	10,000	
"20 lots and houses in Annapolis..................	4,000	
"285 slaves on the different plantations, at £30 each..	8,550	
"Cattle, horses, stock of all sorts on my plantations, with working tools............................	1,000	
"Silver household plate............................	600	
"Debts outstanding at interest in 1762, when I balanced my books...................................	24,230	97
	£88,380	97

"You must not suppose my annual income to equal the interest of the value of my estate. Many of my lands are unimproved, but I compute I have a clear revenue of at least £1,800 per annum, and the value of my estate is annually increasing.

"I propose, upon your coming into Maryland to convey to you my manor of "Carrollton," 10,000 acres, and the addition thereto of 2,700 acres, now producing annually £250 sterling, not one-half of which is let. Also my share of the iron works, producing at least £400.

"On my death I am willing to add my manor of "Doughoregan," 10,000 acres, and also 1,425 acres called "Chance," adjacent thereto, on which the bulk of my negroes are settled. As you are my only child, you will, of course, have all the residue of my estate at my death. Your return to me, I hope, will be in the next fall."

Mrs. Elizabeth (Brooke) Carroll was then dead.

In 1765 "Charles Carroll, Jr.," arrived at his father's house in Annapolis, after about sixteen years from his natal country at his studies and on his travels. He came home at twenty-seven years, an amiable, upright, accomplished young man, with the polish of European society and the social acquirements of studious culture. Debarred by his religion from political honors, he came to occupy, in ease and comfort, his manorial estates, but he was not long to rest in retirement. In 1768 he was married to his cousin, of the same name and family into which his grandfather, the immigrant, had married. She was, also, Mary Darnall, daughter of Henry and Rachel (Brooke) Darnall.

His first appearance in the political arena of that eventful era was his answer, under the name of "The First Citizen," to "Antilon," who proved to be the distinguished Daniel Dulany, Jr. Reference, elsewhere in this history has been made to that memorable debate through the "Maryland Gazette." Young Carroll was unknown, but his courage in meeting so able an antagonist, and the ability with which he met and vanquished him, amazed the people and carried their sympathies with him. The thanks of the Assembly, through two of its members, were tendered the unknown writer through the press, and when it finally became known that the able defender of the people was the young student many sought him to express their hearty appreciation. Thenceforth Charles Carroll, of "Carrollton," was foremost in popular favor.

The Revolution was at hand. In 1775 he was one of ten members of the Council of Safety which met that year at Chestertown.

His associates from Anne Arundel were Charles Carroll, barrister; Thomas Johnson and Samuel Chase.

He was next one of the agents to secure the assistance of Canada. His religion and influence peculiarly fitted him for that mission, and his notes upon that adventure are very interesting bits of our Revolutionary history, but the mission proved a failure. During his absence the Maryland Convention had sent delegates to Congress with instructions not to urge independence.

Upon his return, finding the delegates thus hampered, whilst the whole Congress was ready for the declaration, Mr. Carroll and Samuel Chase went to Annapolis, ably represented the necessity for a withdrawal of those instructions, succeeded in convincing the representatives that the hour for action had arrived, and returning as a delegate, carried back the glad news that Maryland, too, was in line for independence. And when that vote had been taken and the Declaration of Independence was to be signed he wrote his name Charles Carroll, of "Carrollton."

From Rev. M. Hayden, son of the first clerk of Howard County, I quote:

"So much of the mythical has grown up around that remarkable scene, the "Signing of the Declaration of Independence," that it becomes a duty to separate the history of the event from the fiction. It must have been a moment of solemn stillness when John Hancock stepped forward to the table on which the Declaration lay to affix to it his bold signature. And as each signer, whenever it was done, followed his example there was doubtless now and then a word of cheer or of wit to relieve the tension of the hour."

But the story of Charles Carroll's signature has varied until truth has been lost in imagination. Lossing says that at the signing "Charles Carroll" to enable the British minister to identify him as an arch-rebel, and not mistake his cousin of the same name, added 'of Carrollton' to his signature on that great instrument."

General Bradley T. Johnson, in Appleton's Cyclopædia of American Biography, writes, "on the 2d August, 1776, . . . he signed the Declaration of Independence. It is said that he affixed the addition 'of Carrollton' to his signature in order to distinguish him from his kinsman, Charles Carroll, barrister, and to assume the certain responsibility himself of his act." Both these writers give the impression that the suffix was used August 2, 1776 for the first time.

Hon. Robert C. Winthrop in his Centennial Oration at Boston, July 4, 1876, gives another version thus:

"'Will you sign?' said Hancock to Charles Carroll. 'Most willingly,' was the reply. 'There goes two millions with the dash of a pen,' says one of those standing by; while another remarks, 'Oh, Carroll, you will get off, there are so many Charles Carrolls!' And then we may see him stepping back to the desk and putting that addition, 'of Carrollton,' to his name, which will designate him forever, and be a prouder title of nobility than those in the peerage of Great Britain, which were afterward adorned by his accomplished and fascinating granddaughters."

None of these stories have more than a shadow of truth for a basis. It is barely possible that when Carroll stepped forward and affixed to the Declaration the name that he had invariably signed since he had first learned to write, that of "Charles Carroll, of Carrollton," some such conversation as Mr. Winthrop records may have occurred. But it is not possible that Carroll signed his name at this time by instalment.

His biographer, J. H. B. Latrobe, Esq., now dead, wrote me in 1877: "I have a bond signed by him as 'Charles Carroll, of Carrollton,' dated and filed many years before the Declaration. In Maryland the 'pretty story' of the signing was long, long ago dropped, and I am a little surprised that the correction escaped Mr. Winthrop's notice." Again he wrote me in 1889: "I have no recollection of having heard the reason given in Appleton for attaching the 'of Carrollton' to the signature of Charles Carroll, to the Declaration of Independence. No such reason was given to me by Mr. Carroll in my conversation with him during the preparation of his biography."

It can be readily seen that if Mr. Carroll had invariably signed his name with the suffix until he appended his name to the Declaration and then omitted it, adding it only as a second thought after the suggestion that the king could not identify him by so common a name as Charles Carroll, this act would at once have stamped him as a man void of independence and lacking in that high sense of honor which his history proves him to have possessed to a marked degree.

In the numerous mention of Mr. Carroll in Force's Archives, 1774–1776, which record his various public actions in the Maryland Convention and the United States Congress, he is invariably named as "Charles Carroll, of Carrollton."

"Doughoregan Manor," now in Howard County, Maryland, the home of Mr. Carroll, is a very extensive estate which Mr. Carroll devised to his grandson, Colonel Charles Carroll, and to his male heirs forever. It is now owned by Hon. John Lee Carroll, great-grandson of the "Signer,"Ex-Governor of Maryland and President of the General Society of the Sons of the Revolution. The Manor house is a large and very handsome residence of the old style, with chapel annexed, built about the year 1717. "Carrollton Manor" was divided among Mr. Carroll's daughters. He owned, in various parts of Pennsylvania, 27,691 acres of land, part of which lay in Bradford County. His autograph in my collection is a power of attorney, July 5, 1815, to George Dennison, Esq., of Wilkes-Barre, relating to the Bradford County land, of which he owned 1,038 acres, bought of Josiah Lockhart. It is entirely in Mr. Carroll's handwriting and is signed, as is his will, "Ch. Carroll, of Carrollton."

I have a distinct and delightful recollection of a visit to Doughoregan Manor in my boyhood, with my father, who was an invited guest of Colonel Charles Carroll. The occasion was a tournament which, as far as my knowledge of tilting extends, was unique. The gentry of the neighboring counties, with their families, were present, and the display of beauty and fashion was such as made a lasting impression on a youth of ten years. The joust was out of the ordinary way of such entertainments. Instead of the conventional ring suspended in the air, through which the knights at full gallop were to thrust the spear, the object of their skill was a lay figure of wood, representing a man, life size, caparisoned as a knight and so nicely balanced on a pedestal that a blow in the face from a well-poised spear would "unhorse" the figure, while a stroke against the body was calculated to shiver the spear, or unhorse the knight.

Against this figure each knight, handsomely attired and mounted, with heavy spears, about twelve feet long and one to three inches thick, with strong, brass point, was to dash himself at full speed. One knight was dismounted and another had his spear shivered, but no injury occurred to man or horse. The victor who overthrew the lay figure three times and so won the right to crown the queen of honor was an officer of the United States Cavalry; but his name, with that of the queen, I have forgotten. After the joust followed the crowning of the queen and then the "menu," and the departure of the many guests.

"The Life of Charles Carroll, of Carrollton," was written and published in 1824, eight years before the death of the "Signer," by the late J. H. B. Latrobe, Esq., of Baltimore. It was submitted to Mr. Carroll for examination before it was printed. But a more extended memoir of this eminent statesman has been prepared by Miss Kate M. Rowland, author of the "Life of George Mason, of Virginia."

Throughout the contest succeeding he was always a leader. In 1783, when peace was declared in the very city of his birth and Congress was sitting in the city of Annapolis, it was on "Carroll's Green" the festivities were held and a "grand dinner on Esquire Carroll's grounds offered a whole ox, sheep and calves, besides a world of good things, including liquor in proportion, concluded with illuminations and squibs, ushered in the new Statehood of Maryland."

Charles Carroll, barrister, died soon after, but Charles Carroll, of Carrollton, was destined to be a guide through the perils of that critical era. He was elected President of the Senate, in the place of Matthew Tilghman, then sick. Congress was put into possession of the State House, public circle, Governor's house and thirteen dwelling-houses for the use of its Thirteen States' Representatives. In the historic Senate Chamber of the State House the final act of Peace was solemnized, when General Washington came to resign his commission. Two of his generals, Gates and Smallwood, went out to meet him and attended by all the principal inhabitants, the conquering hero was conducted to Mann's Hotel, where room No. 9 was set apart for his accommodation. Formal addresses, a public dinner, illumination of the State House, a ball by the General Assembly, all preceded the final act that has rendered the name of Washington immortal. When that was accomplished "he arose, bowed to Congress, withdrew from the chamber, leaving beauty's eye dimmed with affection's tear."

Smallwood, who led from Annapolis the Maryland Line which followed him to victory, was spared to accompany the retired general to South River and witness his departure to Mt. Vernon.

Charles Carroll, of Carrollton, as a State Senator, helped to draft the Constitution of Maryland, and under that Constitution was the first United States Senator serving two terms. Nor did his honors cease there. Called to adjust the boundary line of the State, he was ever prominent in its industrial development. At ninety years of age, in 1822, before an immense concourse of his admiring people, he laid the corner-stone of the Baltimore and Ohio Railroad. Though he had retired from public service in 1800, as a leader of Federalists, when in the Senate, his political influence attended him in his retirement. He and Samuel Chase were copartners in the work of Independence, but when it came to making a Constitution for the State, Carroll was the Federalist and Samuel and Jeremiah Chase, William Paca, William Pinkney, John Francis Mercer and Luther Martin were Anti-Federalists. To this list may, also, be added General Smallwood. These were then known as Federal Republicans.

Charles Carroll, of Carrollton, was always an able opponent of all measures that were not democratic. He opposed high salaries, titles and kingly fawnings. He favored bringing the Capital to the Potomac. Mr. Carroll's own record of his correspondence is of interest. "Though well acquainted with General Washington, and I flatter myself in his confidence, few letters passed between us. One, having reference to the opposition made to the Treaty concluded by Mr. Jay, has been repeatedly published. That letter is no longer in my possession."

In 1825 John Quincy Adams wrote to him:

"Mr. Warfield came to see me. He said he had not expressed his determination for whom he should vote in the House on Wednesday. His friends, Charles Carroll, of Carrollton, and Roger Brooke Taney, of Baltimore, had urged him to vote for General Jackson, under the impression that if I should be elected the administration would be conducted on principles proscribing the Federal Party. I said I regretted much that Mr. Carroll, for whose character I entertained a profound veneration, and Mr. Taney, of whose talents I had heard high encomiums, should harbor such opinions of me."

In 1820 the estate of "The Signer" included 27,691 acres in Bradford County, Pennsylvania, which he devised to his two daughters and four granddaughters of his only son, Charles Carroll, of of "Homewood." A resurvey of Doughoregan, in 1820, with the additions to the original tract, shows 13,361½ acres. The beginning was at a stone, heretofore planted near the east side of a public road, leading from Baltimore to Rockville, marked with the following inscription, to wit: "There stand the Beginning Trees of Doughoregan, Push Pin and the Girls' Portion."

It is said that the Mansion upon Doughoregan Manor was built in 1717 by Charles Carroll, to whom it was granted. It was 300 feet in length, with a wide paneled hall leading to the library, where Charles Carroll, the signer, held his headquarters, among the portraits of the family, beginning with the handsome face and form of Charles Carroll, of Annapolis.

The Chapel on the right was built by "The Signer." Within it he lies buried. It is kept in excellent repair by Governor John Lee Carroll. Charles Carroll, of Carrollton, lived long enough to build magnificent homes for his children and even for his grandchildren.

His daughter Mary, at seventeen years of age, was married, in 1787, to Richard Caton, an English gentleman, who settled in Baltimore in 1785. He was a cotton merchant and geologist. Her marriage gift was the magnificent old homestead around which is the suburban town of Catonsville. Her portrait reveals a handsome attractive woman, distinguished for her elegance of manners. She was the mother of three beautiful women, still remembered as "The American Graces," all married into the distinguished families of England. A fourth married in her own country and was the only one who left descendants.

In 1800 the only son of "The Signer," Charles Carroll, of "Homewood," married Harriet, daughter of Hon. Benjamin Chew, Chief Justice of Pennsylvania. Upon this estate, north of Baltimore, was built the stately brick mansion of "Homewood," now the country school for boys upon Charles-Street Avenue and the future site of Johns Hopkins University. One mile south of it was "Homestead," wherein Jerome Bonaparte and his brilliant American bride, Miss Patterson, lived for one short year.

In 1801 Catharine Carroll, second daughter of "The Signer" was married in Annapolis to Robert Goodloe Harper, of South Carolina. This gentleman, eminent in law and statesmanship, was in Congress in 1794, and was a leader of the Federalists. Removing to Maryland, he became United States Senator, in 1815. His country home was "Oakland."

The granddaughters of Charles Carroll, of Carrollton, the Caton beauties, were the attraction at a grand ball given at Hampton in 1807.

Mary Caton became the wife of Robert Patterson, who was a brother of Madame Jerome Bonaparte.

Louisa Caton married Colonel Sir Tilton Bathurst Hervey, who had fought under Wellington in Spain and was his aide at Waterloo.

Mrs. Robert Patterson became a widow in 1822. She and her two sisters, Mrs. Hervey, afterwards Duchess of Leeds, and Elizabeth Caton, who became later Lady Stafford, were together in England at the country-seat of the Duke of Wellington, where they were visiting. The fair widow met the Duke's elder brother, Marquis of Wellesly, a widower of sixty-three. They were married in Dublin, where the Marquis was then living in vice-regal state as Lord Lieutenant of Ireland. Here the Marchioness of Wellesley presided at a grand ball in 1826, seated on a throne under a canopy of scarlet and gold.

At a banquet given the next year in Charleston, South Carolina, Bishop England, in alluding to these granddaughters of "The Signer," gave this toast: "Charles Carroll, of Carrollton—in the land from which his grandfather fled in terror, his granddaughter now reigns a queen."

To Emily McTavish, wife of John McTavish, British Consul, was given 1,000 acres of the western portion of Doughoregan Manor, and in his declining years Charles Carroll, of Carrollton, commenced and, perhaps, finished another magnificent home, popularly known as "Folly Quarter." On the map of Howard County it is known as Carrollton Hall.

"FOLLY QUARTER."

Deserted, yet magnificent in its isolation; its splendid apartments, where once gathered the aristocracy and the beauty of Maryland in revel; dismantled and scourged by the tempests that have swept through the paneless windows; a shelter for tramps and wayfarers, and its far-stretching grounds the roaming-place for hogs, there stands, within two hours' drive of Baltimore city, the mansion of "Folly Farm."

The old manor house—by no means a ruin, for its granite blocks would to-day withstand an army of besiegers—is the most prominent of the group of buildings that rose seventy years ago in the midst of as beautiful a tract of land as any of the many held by Charles Carroll, of "Carrollton." It crowns the proudest, loftiest hill of all its thousand acres, regal in beauty and sturdy as the mountains of adamant. It stands there silently guarding the history of its past splendor, calmly resisting the lashings of the wind and the beatings of the snows and rains. Its grim desolation is pathetic and absolute, but it seems to say, "They will come back; here I will be found."

When and how this splendid home was deserted is not absolutely clear, but after a week's research "The Sun" presents as complete a tale as appears possible.

"Folly Farm," or "Folly Quarter," as it is more generally called, lies in Howard County, about seven miles west of Ellicott City, off the Old Frederick Road. It is now owned by Mr. Charles Carroll, son of Ex-Governor John Lee Carroll, of Doughoregan Manor.

"Folly Quarter" has not only a historic interest of its own because of its connection with the long history of the Carroll family and the special attention given it by Charles Carroll, of "Carrollton," the last signer of the Declaration of Independence to survive, but about it cluster local traditions and pleasant memories that have made the name familiar to all in that section of the country.

"Folly Quarter" farm is as fair and beautiful to look upon as that "Garden of the Lord" whose vistas enraptured the Confederate hosts as they gazed first upon the lovely valley encircling Frederick town. Billows of round-topped hills guard fertile valleys, and these in turn clasp leaping, sparkling streams in their embrace. One thousand fertile acres of rich agricultural promise spread around the visitor to "Folly Quarter." Spacious farms indicate the ample harvests, and sleek, fat cattle contentedly munch fodder in large stable-yards.

"Folly Quarter" is part of the original tract granted to the ancestors of Charles Carroll by Charles Lord Baltimore. They were given a grant of 10,000 acres in Frederick County, with liberty to select the best land they could find. They first fixed on a spot beyond Frederick town, according to Charles Browning's "Chief Explanation," but finding the land better on this side of Frederick, changed to the country surrounding the present "Doughoregan Manor," in Howard County. This land was not seized, as was so frequently done, but was purchased from the Indians, who were paid in merchandise selected by them. Mr. Browning, in his book published in 1821, has this to say further:

"The grant of this land first appears to have been made April 10, 1723, to the Carroll family, some of whom dying, there were different assignments from time to time, up to 1734, but I understand the land was not taken up till just before the Revolution by the present Charles Carroll, of "Carrollton," for his father, and the only money that appears to have been given for the land was a rent of $20 per annum, which the present Mr. Carroll got rid of by the act for the abolition of quit-rent, 1780."

Charles Carroll, of "Carrollton," took a deep interest in the management of his splendid estates, and gave to this labor of love as much time as he could spare from the important services he was called upon to render to his State and nation. A large part of his closing years were spent at "Doughoregan Manor." A loving attendant was his granddaughter, Emily Caton, who married Mr. John McTavish, British Consul at the port of Baltimore. Desiring to bestow a fitting testimonial of his appreciation and affection, the venerable Carroll gave her 1,000 acres of the finest farm land in Howard County—the tract known as "Folly." In order that she might live there in a style conforming her position and wealth, he began, a few years before his death, the erection of a palatial mansion.

The site selected was a lofty hill, from three sides of which the eye beheld the waving grain fields and fine old forests of the farm. Great blocks of granite were quarried from the rocky hillsides of "Woodstock," and slowly the stately mansion grew under the busy and skillful hands of the artisans. The massive walls took shape as the months went by, and woodworkers and carvers busied themselves on the interior, plasterers plied their trowels and painters their brushes. Plumbers were proud of a chance to install the mostmodern sanitary features of the day and decorators eagerly applied their art to the finishing touches. Other buildings were erected about the new mansion and for months the favored hilltop seemed a beehive of industry.

The builders' art in those days was not the same as now. There were no immense steel girders, weighing tons, to be hoisted high in air; no complicated calculations to insure the correct holding of joints and frames; and yet as great, or greater, skill, perhaps, was required of builders then. The problem of transporting and shifting heavy building material had not the ready aid of steam in its solution, nor had mechanical ingenuity come very far toward lessening the wear of physical labor. One cannot look upon the massive pile at "Folly Quarter" without feeling admiration for the men who builded so strongly and well in their time.

It is difficult to learn just when the buildings were begun, but they were finished in 1832. Charles Carroll, of "Carrollton," died in Baltimore, November 14, 1832, and it is probable that, owing to the feebleness of great age, he was not permitted to look upon the finished structure at the "Folly."

How and why "Folly Quarter" received its name is a question that seems to be considerably clouded by the mists of time. In the surrounding country is a tradition currently believed to the effect that Charles Carroll, son of the signer, had accumulated a considerable sum of money from his allowances. In looking about for a good investment his attention was called to a fine tract of land several miles west of "Doughoregan Manor." He was pleased with it and purchased it. When he informed his venerable and distinguished father of the fact the latter, according to the story, exclaimed:

"That is folly; we have enough land now."

And so, the tradition has it, the farm was known ever afterward as "Folly Quarter," or "The Folly."

This would be a very interesting explanation of the subject but for the anachorism that this is at once in evidence. In his will the signer refers to the farm as though it had been for some time a part of his property. He does not devise the estate in his will, indicating that he had transferred it to Mrs. McTavish, his granddaughter, before his heath. He does, however, bequeath to his son Charles, slaves "on the farm known as 'Folly.'"

The word "Quarter" seems to have been applied generally to sections—perhaps quarter sections—of large tracts of land.

Not far from "Folly Quarter" was a large estate known as "Mike's Quarter."

The present visitor to "Folly Quarter" who goes out from Ellicott City drives west along the Frederick Turnpike through a picturesque, rolling country. On either side are comfortable farmhouses, surrounded by fertile fields, with great, large-doored barns, telling their story of the generous soil. Here and there are handsome mansions—some of attractive modern architecture and others recalling memories of a time long dead. Many of these are summer homes of wealthy city families, who fly to the cool, pure air of the resplendent hills when the heated term draws near. Streams ripple and sparkle in the sun, dash merrily over rocks and whirl in cool, deep eddies on the lower side, where anglers steal to kill the speckled trout. Out past St. Charles' College and the lodge-house at the gates of "Doughoregan Manor," standing opposite each other, the visitor drives. Then over through stretches of woodland, over hills and through open valleys, until the "Vineyard" road is reached. Turning to the left a drive of about three miles brings one through a long piece of forest to the top of a hill, and "Folly Farm," in all its beauty, lies before the eye.

The original entrance to the mansion has not been used since
the old house was deserted, fifteen years or more ago; now one must
drive half a mile or more farther on to the farm-house, occupied by
Mr. Christian Broseener, tenant of the place. From the roadway
only parts of the old mansion can be seen, because of the tangled
growth and the unkempt surrounding trees, some of which, being
evergreen, obstruct the view at all seasons.

To reach the place one has to drive through the yard of Mr.
Broseener and cross a field and part of another, encountering several
somewhat obstinate gates on the way.   This is the most direct route.
Another entrance is from the south, through a piece of woods—that
is the "longest way 'round," and is not often used.

After climbing a steep hill, the lower edge of which is rimmed
by a granite wall, the visitor reaches the open space surrounding the
old mansion and pauses in admiration, almost in awe.   It is like
coming upon the decaying mausoleum of a dead and gone race.

It is the rear of the building that is first seen, and because of a
larger open space there a better view can be had of it than from the
front.   Desolation is everywhere.   The very air seems somnolent
and the bare tree branches are quiet.   Gleams of sunshine breaking
through the overhanging tanglewood play fitfully over the granite
walls and peep in the open windows.   Traces of a winding roadway
may be seen in the yard, and there are long rude tables showing that
picnickers make merry under the trees during the summer.

The house fronts nearly east.   It is plainly but very substan-
tially built of large granite blocks that average in size thirty-five
inches long and nineteen inches deep; many are considerably
larger.   Surmounting the two stories is a commodious attic.   The
front and rear are almost identical in appearance.   In the centre of
each is a massive porch, with six solid granite columns.   These columns are seventy-one inches—nearly six feet—in circumference at
the bottom, tapering slightly as they rise.   A large window on each
side of the porch lights the lower rooms, while three windows light
the second story.   Two windows are in each side of the house.   These
would seem inadequate to brighten the great extent of interior, but
because of the arrangement of halls and rooms are sufficient.

From the first floor front windows balconies project, protected
by iron framework.   Dormer windows, one in front and one in the
rear, are placed in the center of the roof to light the attic.   Two tall
chimneys stand like silent sentinels on top the venerable pile.

That cost was little object is shown by the fact that copper rain-
spouts carry water off from the metal-sheathed roof and the massive
doors are of mahogany, plainly but handsomely carved.

It is not difficult to enter the building.   The doors and windows
stand open, as though glad to welcome the light and fresh air.   Entering at the front one finds a splendid hallway the width of the
porch.   Its lofty ceiling bends in a graceful arch.   The floor is of
finest hardwood, closely fitted and polished like that of a ballroom.
Near the western, or rear, entrance the hall narrows, the projections

on each side being guarded by a graceful Corinthian column.   A stair hall, running at right angles to the main hall, divides the southern half of the floor and leads to the Colonial stairway, constructed of oak, with a mahogany handrail and newel post.

The north side of the first floor contains two stately apartments, with high ceilings and plain white walls.   They can be thrown into one, making a magnificent ballroom.   Few modern ballrooms have better floors for dancing.   Open fireplaces indicate that festive occasions in the old house were made cheerful by the blaze and splutter or burning oak logs.   One can readily imagine that the genial glow thus given fashionable gatherings of that day could not have been improved by the sultry steam-heating fixtures of modern times.   It is said that artistically carved marble mantels adorned these open fireplaces, but there is no trace of them there now.   This ballroom is even now a noted place for jollity in Howard County, as dances are frequently given there, and the polished floor kept smooth by the feet that follow the music of the two-step instead of the stately minuet and the rollicking Virginia reel.   These modern visitors seem to delight in having their visits known, as the walls are covered with names and inscriptions of various kinds.

In the hall are long rough pine tables, where refreshments are served.   In fact, the picnickers and dancers who visit the place now appear to lay considerable stress upon the importance of fortifying themselves with food.   Not only are there tables in the rear yard and in the main hall, but in the upper hall and the basement as well.

On the south side of the first floor, beside the stair hall, are two large well-lighted rooms, evidently used as dining-room and library.   These two have open fireplaces, but no mantels.   Indeed, open fireplaces are in nearly every room in the house, but whatever adornments they may have had have long since disappeared.

The second floor is also traversed by a wide hall, ample enough to accommodate a score of patrons at a seaside hotel.   There are six large chambers, enticing even in their present bleak desolation— dreams of luxurious comfort in their days of use.   There is also a smaller chamber containing the wreck of an old-fashioned bathtub, partly set in the wall.

It is said that among the appointments of the mansion when it was left new and beautiful by the builders was a magnificent marble bathing pool, costing many thousands of dollars.   It is not known where this pool was located.   A local tradition has it that the pool was some distance from the house and connected with it by a subterranean passageway.   There is no trace of any such thing now, and Mr. Broseener, who has lived on the farm a number of years, says he has never heard of it.

A gentleman who knows a great deal of the old place says that a marble bathing pool existed at one time, but he does not know its location.   It is probable that the pool was demolished at the same time the marble mantels were taken away.

Two cross-halls and five rooms of good size take up the space in the attic.   The hallways in the centre extend upward to a square elevation or cupola on the roof, where a skylight lets brightness through to the floor below.   This cupola is not noticed from the outside of the building because of its stunted form.   The rooms of the attic have sloping ceilings, conforming to the slanting roof, which fact somewhat diminishes their area.   Above them, in a kind of half attic surrounding the cupola and skylight, are three small rooms, or large closets; they were probably used as storage-rooms.

A remarkable thing about nearly all the rooms in the second story and attic is the number of large closets they contain.   In some rooms these extend around three sides.   They are long, shallow affairs, filled with shelves, giving the rooms somewhat the appearance of abandoned country stores.

The builders were liberal in their ideas of space.   Even the basement has a large hall running through it.   This portion of the mansion contains four large rooms, one evidently having been a kitchen, as its old-fashioned ovens and range, set well in the chimney wall, show, and they suggest the good cheer that such an equipment, in conjunction with a well-filled larder, could provide.

There are no indications of the uses for which the other rooms were intended—probably as servants' quarters, storage-rooms and serving-rooms.   Two smaller rooms, more or less secluded from the light of day, and two vaults of good size, but dark interiors, suggest that ample provision was made for wine cellars.   One of the smaller rooms may have contained the bathing pool, already referred to.

The old house has outlived a substantial marker of the passing hours in the yard.   On the slope of the southern hill stands a stout granite post, hewn in one piece, about four feet high.   This was the pedestal for a stone sun-dial, considered a necessary adjunct to almost every old homestead.   It can yet be plainly seen where and how the dial-plate was fastened to the pillar, but the plate is gone.   Parts of it may be seen lying on the ground.   On three sides of the base are the following inscriptions:

"MDCCCXXXII," "NICOLLET," "POSUPT."

The fourth side is blank.   The date marks the completion of the mansion.

Not far from the site of the old sun-dial are the ruins of an extensive hothouse, built against the southern retaining wall in such a way that it caught the warm rays of the sun from early morning until late in the afternoon.

It was not intended that guests at "Folly Quarter" should find themselves without means of amusement.   About fifty yards west of the mansion is a large stone building that in itself would be a comfortable home for entire families.   It is a two-story structure, built on the slope of the hill.   The upper floor, which is practically the first floor when approached from the mansion, is entered from a porch, the distinguishing feature of which, like the porches of the mansion, is large, solid granite columns.   This opens into a spacious billiard-room. It is a well-lighted apartment, and, with a wood fire burning in the open hearth, must have been a delightful resort when wintry winds blew across the hilltops.

Here is the same sad scene of desolation that the old mansion presents. A dismantled billiard table stands in the room, covered with broken plaster and autumn leaves that have blown in the open doors. There is no cue-rack and the only closet in the room is empty as the cupboard of Mother Hubbard. The table belonged to Mr. Charles M. Dougherty, who owned the property a number of years ago. There were two, but when Mr. Dougherty sold the place he sent the best one to St. Charles' College. Adjoining the billiard-room is a large apartment and still another considerably smaller. The floors of these are now covered with corn.

Below are rooms that may have quartered servants. A carriage-house occupies the centre of the lower floor and the eastern end contains the stable, with eleven comfortable stalls. These are not now occupied by spirited hunters and stylish carriage horses, but seem to be regarded by a drove of fine Berkshire hogs as their own special lounging apartments.

A little farther away from the mansion, northwest, is the chapel erected for the use of the family and servants. It is nearly as large as many country churches of the present day and is surmounted by a belfry and small steeple. The interior is devoid of furnishings. At one end is the altar platform, back of which is a small apartment designed for the priest's robing-room. The building is simple in design, but stands with a quiet dignity of its own upon a small elevation. Sturdy oak trees partly surround it, and in that peaceful retreat one can feel that the worshipers, during the solemn hours of service, could truly lift up their hearts " through nature up to Nature's God."

Cool comfort during summer days came from a cavernous ice-house, built of huge granite blocks and banked over with dirt several feet thick. The distance from the top of the arched ceiling to the bottom is not far from thirty feet, and this great, walled hole-in-the-ground will hold enough ice for a medium-sized hotel. A passageway like a tunnel, eight or ten feet long, leads to the pit.

Set in the granite slab that covers the entrance to the pit is the iron pulley used to haul up the blocks of ice. A diminutive kind of cupola rises from the roof of the structure, probably having contained a skylight. Ivy and moss cover the roof and through the broken cupola hangs a slender, shivering spray of green that seems to have unwittingly fallen in and has resigned itself to its fate in that dark, damp grave.

Traces of the landscape gardening that beautified the old place in its palmy days may be seen on every side. The immediate surroundings occupied several acres crowning the hill and extending back to the west. The stone retaining wall previously mentioned at the base of the hill ran around two sides of it, bringing the attractive lawn out in bold relief. A wooden fence, ruins of which are yet here and there, divided the front lawn from that in the rear. In the front lawn were flower beds with trim boxwood borders, and boxwood lined the walks and drives.   Tall button trees alternate with spruce, hemlock and arbor vitae.   Farther away are pines and cedars.   Tangle growths show where roses flourished.

Standing on the front porch and looking out through the mass of twisted, interlaced boughs, a scene of rare beauty is presented— the rolling hills, the valleys, the winding stream, the far-away forests and the fields, some green with a rich growth of newly-sown wheat and others studded with shocks of corn.   But "silence, prolonged and unbroken" wraps the old mansion in its embrace, and the only living things about are a score or more of grunting hogs.

It is said that the buildings on "Folly Quarter" cost Charles Carroll, of "Carrollton," $100,000.   To further enhance its beauty he caused a massive granite and marble bridge to be constructed across the stream that ran through the farm between the dwelling and the main road.   This stream is a branch of the Upper Patuxent River, and it is said that trout may be found in it on "Folly Farm."   The entrance gate was then directly in front of the house, the private road sweeping in a curve through a pretty valley.

The bridge is now used only in crossing from one part of the field to the other.   Its foundations, piers and floor are of granite blocks as substantial and enduring as those in the mansion.   The bridge springs from each shore of the narrow stream to a central pier, thus having two spans.   The thick side walls, nearly shoulder high, are of marble, with two square marble columns at each end extending a short distance above the walls.   Storms, rain and time have given the structure a dingy appearance, and marble and granite look much alike.   It is said the bridge cost considerably over $10,000.

Persons driving along the front of "Folly Farm" notice a large barnyard, in which are new buildings and other of great age.   At the gate are two great square pillars, or towers, of granite, which lead many to suppose it to have been the original entrance to the mansion's grounds.   This is also thought to have been the site of the first buildings on the estate.   Some of the queer-looking old barns were built in 1790.   One of the features is an ancient old blacksmith shop and forge.

The farmhouse occupied by Mr. Broseener is an interesting structure in its way.   It has the spacious porch, with immense pillars, that seemed to characterize architecture of that day, but the ravages of time have exposed a clever deception.   Instead of being of solid material they were constructed of laths and plaster, and the plastering has fallen off in places.   In the bathroom of this house a large bathtub was constructed.   Water was piped from a neighboring spring and poured into the tub through a finely carved marble lion's head.   The tub has long since passed the stage of usefulness, but the lion's head is still in place.

Mr. and Mrs. John McTavish made their home at "Folly Quarter" for many years.   Their son, Mr. Charles Carroll McTavish, inherited the property and resided there with his family a number of years. Mr. McTavish finally decided to dispose of the estate, and it was sold through Messrs. Alexander Yearley & Son, of this city, to Mr. Charles M. Dougherty, a Baltimore merchant, who paid $100,000 for it. Mr. Dougherty made the place a summer home for some time, until he removed to New Orleans, about twenty years ago. He took great pride in the place and kept it up handsomely. Shortly after his removal he sold it to Mr. Royal Phelps, of New York, father-in-law of Ex-Governor John Lee Carroll, through whom it passed into the possession of its present owner, Mr. Charles Carroll.

Mr. Carroll renamed the place "Carrollton Hall," but it continues to be known far and wide as "Folly Quarter" and "Folly Farm," and will probably never shake off these names.

It is known as "Folly Quarter" to the persons who pass along the road and catch a glimpse of the stately old pile through the surrounding trees, and "Folly Quarter" it is to the merry young folk who picnic in its shady groves and dance the evening hours away in its fine old rooms.

Charles Carroll, of Homewood, and Harriet Chew, his wife, had issue—Charles Carroll, heir of Doughoregan Manor, born 1801; Elizabeth—Dr. Aaron Tucker; Mary Sophia—Hon. Richard Bayard; Benjamin Chew; Harriet Julian—Hon John Lee, of "Needwood; Louisa—Isaac Rand Jackson.

Colonel Charles Carroll, of Doughoregan, in 1825—Mary Digges Lee. Issue, Mary—Dr. Eleazer Acosta; Charles inherited Doughoregan—Caroline Thompson, of Virginia; Louisa—George Cavendish Taylor, of England, nephew of Lord Waterpark, an Irish peer.

John Lee Carroll, born 1830—first, Anita, daughter of Royal Phelps, of New York; second, Mary Carter Thompson, sister of Mrs. Charles Carroll. (His biography will be found in the Governors of Maryland.)

Albert Henry—Mary Cornelia, daughter of William George Read. He was in the Confederate States Army and died at Martinsburg in 1862. His widow—Colonel James Fenner Lee.

Robert Goodloe Harper Carroll—first, Ella Thompson; second, Mary Digges Lee. He was, also, in the Confederate States Army.

Helen Sophia Carroll—Charles Oliver O'Donnell.

In 1826, when all the signers of the Declaration had passed away, except the venerable Charles Carroll, of Carrollton, a committee waited upon him to obtain from him a copy of the document, and when again signed by him this copy was to be deposited in the City Hall. After he had signed the paper he wrote the following supplemental declaration:

"Grateful to Almighty God for the blessings which, through Jesus Christ our Lord, He has conferred on my beloved country in her emancipation and on myself in permitting me, under circumstances of mercy, to live to the age of eighty-nine years, and to survive the fiftieth year of American Independence, adopted by Congress on the 4th day of July, 1776, which I originally subscribed on the 2nd day of August, of the same year, and of which I am now the last surviving

signer, I do hereby recommend to the present and future generations the principles of that important document as the best earthly inheritance their ancestors could bequeath to them, and pray that the civil and religious liberties they have secured to my country may be perpetuated to remotest posterity and extended to the whole family of men.   CHARLES CARROLL, OF CARROLLTON.
          "August 2, 1826."
       Charles Carroll, of Carrollton, was a liberal patron of St. Charles College. He gave the ground on which it stands and laid the cornerstone.
       A historian thus records the death of "The Signer." "It was toward sundown in November. The weather was very cold. In a large room, his bedroom, he sat in an easy chair before an open fireplace. On a table were blessed candles, an antique bowl of holy water and a crucifix. By his side, Rev. John C. Chance, President of St. Mary's College, in rich robes, offering the last rites. On each side of his chair knelt a daughter and grandchildren. In the rear were three or four old negro servants kneeling in reverence.
       The assembly made a picture never to be forgotten. The venerable patriot went through the ceremony with evident pleasure, and refusing nourishment said: "This supplies all the wants of Nature; I desire no food." He was then placed on the bed. It was after midnight when he passed away.

THE HOME LIFE OF OUR EARLY SETTLERS.

       Having now traced the families who left the attractions of Annapolis, the only town where pleasure and luxury then centred, to live the almost secluded life of the frontier, it will be well to look in upon them in their forest homes. As has been already shown, nearly all the families thus located were allied by marriage ties. The large estates taken up in the beginning were subdivided among succeeding heirs who located upon adjoining tracts. They thus became little communities of relatives, and as such each had its attractions.
       From the assurances of recent survivors whose experiences and inherited information covered more than a century there is every evidence that the social life of our pioneers in Howard was most enjoyable. Dress was not then the chief feature of country gatherings. Ladies could and did appear upon many occasions in the same gown. As riding horseback was the chief means of reaching neighboring settlements, dress was made a subordinate consideration. Though our ancestors were in many cases well up in Latin, their far-famed dinners and suppers were not announced in French. The chief feature of all gatherings was the dinner or supper, always fit for a king. Maryland biscuits were then in order. They were made in this way: "A section of a tree was firmly and permanently placed in a corner of the kitchen and the dough placed upon it and usually hammered or beaten until both the block and dough were 'blistered.' Then the latter was fashioned into round, chubby shapes, like unto small, flattened oranges, pierced with a fork and placed in a 'dutch oven,'

with live coals above and underneath, whence they came forth golden in color. These were not raised with baking powder nor as hard as stone, but light, beautiful and wholesome." (From one of Mr. W. T. Riggs' contributions upon the days of good eating.)

Country life consisted then, as now, in social gatherings, horse-back parties, sledding parties, surprise parties, sometimes covering long distances, but always ending in a social dance, card party and supper.

Every extensive plantation was in itself a storehouse of supplies, and the chief pleasure of the planter was in entertaining. The wealth of the province was then chiefly in the country, and, up to the Revolution, the fashions of the plantation were true types of social life in the province. Of that life we gather from portraits, still extant, the elegant dress of the lords and ladies of the manor, and from their wills come good views of the accumulated wealth in many of their homes.

City life was then but a repetition of the styles of the plantation. From Hon. John P. Kennedy we have a humorous view of the styles in Baltimore just subsequent to the Revolution, from which the following quotation is taken:

"Market street (now Baltimore street) had shot like a snake out of a toy box up as high as Congress Hall, with its variegated range of low-browed, hip-roofed houses, standing forward and back of the line like an ill-dressed regiment.

"Some houses were painted blue, some yellow, some white, and here and there a more pretending mansion of brick, with windows after the pattern of a multiplication table, square and many-paned, and great wastes of walls between the stories; some with court-yards in front, and trees in whose shade truant boys and ragged negroes 'skyed coppers' and played marbles.

"This avenue was enlivened with matrons and damsels, some with looped skirts, some in brocade luxuriantly displayed over hoops, with comely bodies supported by stays disclosing perilous waists and with sleeves that clung to the arm as far as the elbow, where they were lost in ruffles that stood off like feathers on a bantam. And then such faces, so rosy, spirited and sharp, with hair drawn over a cushion tight enough to lift the eyebrow into a rounder curve, giving pungent supercilious expression to the countenance, and curls that fell in cataracts upon the shoulders. Then they stepped away with such a mincing gait, in shoes of many colors, with formidable points at the toes and high tottering heels delicately cut in wood, and in towering peaked hats garnished with feathers that swayed aristo-cratically backward and forward at each step as if they took pride in the stately pace of the wearer.

"In the train of these groups came the gallants, who upheld the chivalry of the age, cavaliers of the old school, full of starch and pow-der, most of them the iron gentlemen of the Revolution, with leather faces, old campaigners renowned for long stories—not long enough rom the camp to lose their military brusquerie and dare-devil swag-

ger; proper roystering blades who had not long ago got out of harness and begun to affect the elegancies of civil life, all in three-cor-
nered cocked hats and powdered hair and cues, and light-colored
coats with narrow capes, long backs and pockets on each hip; small
clothes and striped stockings, shoes with great buckles, and long steel
watchchains, suspended on agate seals in the likeness of the old
sounding-boards above pulpits.

"It was a sight worth seeing when one of these weather-beaten
gallants accosted a lady.   There was a bow which required the width
of the pavement, a scrape of the foot and the cane thrust with a
flourish under the left arm and projecting behind in a parallel line
with the cue.   And nothing could be more piquant than the lady's return of the salutation, in a courtesy that brought her, with bridled
chin and a most winning glance, half way to the ground."

Having now traversed the upper section of Anne Arundel and
noted the chief settlements that had been made whilst still a part of
the mother county, attention will be directed to the efforts made to
secure better accommodations for this settlement.

Nearly a century and a-half had passed since the surveyors had
first marked out the advance of settlement.   Those old settlers had
all passed into an unwritten history.   Several generations of their
descendants had rolled their tobacco to Elk Ridge Landing; had
subdued forests; built magnificent homes, and had passed with their
fathers to the great beyond—and still there was no place, short of
Annapolis, for the transaction of legal business.   At length, in 1838,
a progressive man was sent to the Legislature.   Dr. William W.
Watkins, son of Colonel Gassaway Watkins, presented and ably defended the following bill, which now forms Chapter XXII of the Laws
of 1838:

"An Act for the establishment of a municipal jurisdiction over
a part of Anne Arundel County and to alter and change the Constitution of the State, as far as may be necessary, to effect the same.

"Section 1.   Be it enacted by the General Assembly of Maryland,   That after the confirmation of this Act there shall be established in Anne Arundel a district included within the following boundaries, to wit:

"Beginning for the same at the intersection of the west shore of
Deep Run, with the southern shore of Patapsco River, at or near
Ellicott's Furnace (Relay), and running thence southerly with said
Deep Run until it reaches the Baltimore and Ohio Railroad, and
thence with said railroad, and including the same, until it reaches the
southwestern line of Anne Arundel on the Big Patuxent River, and
thence with said river and the lines of said county until it intersects
the northwestern point of said county, and running thence with the
lines of Carroll and Baltimore Counties to the place of beginning, as
above mentioned; and that the said district shall be called Howard
District of Anne Arundel County.

"Section 2.   And be it enacted,   That to aid in administering
justice and providing for the peculiar wants and necessities in civil

and political matters of the people of said district, there shall, from time to time, as occasion may require, be appointed or elected therein, as the case may be, a Register of Wills, a Sheriff and a Clerk of the Court, to be established therein, which said officers shall have the same qualifications, hold their offices by the same tenure and be appointed or elected therein in the same manner with similar officers in the several counties of this State.

"Section 3.   And be it further enacted,   That upon the confirmation of this Act, it shall be the duty of the Executive of this State to issue writs for the election of a Sheriff by the people of said district within thirty days thereafter, who shall serve until the time of the next general election of this State, and the citizens of Anne Arundel County, now inhabitants of the Fourth Election District thereof and residing in said Howard District, shall, until otherwise provided by law, vote at all elections at the Fifth and Sixth Election Districts of Anne Arundel County as now established by law, in all their future elections and until regulated by law according to the Constitution of the State.

"Section 4.   And be it further enacted,   That upon the confirmation of this act a court shall be established and styled the Court of Howard District of Anne Arundel County; that the judge of the Third Judicial District of the State shall be judge thereof, and presentments, indictments, suits and actions at law may be removed to and from the Court of Howard District of Anne Arundel County in the same manner as if it were one of the County Courts of the State.

"Section 5.   And be it further enacted,   That if this Act shall be confirmed by the General Assembly after the next election of Delegates, at the first regular session after such new election according to the Constitution and form of government, that in such case this alteration and amendment of the Constitution and form of government shall constitute and be valid as a part thereof, and everything therein contained repugnant to or inconsistent with this Act be repealed and abolished.

"Section 6.   And be it further enacted,   That all charges and expenses growing out of the subdivision of Anne Arundel County shall be assessed solely on the property within Howard District."

Chapter 55, Acts of 1839, provides that the seat of justice in Howard District be selected by the voters of the district; judges to make returns and to certify the selection of the seat and to publish the same.

Chapter 60, Acts of 1839, authorized the judge to administer the oath to the clerk, and the ratification of said election of clerk, provided such returns be made and filed with said clerk within three days after his qualification; that the State Librarian be authorized to furnish certain laws for the use of the Court and Orphans' Court of Howard District.

Chapter 98, passed March 4, 1840, provides for the election of Commissioners in the same manner and by the same persons who hold the election for delegates to the General Assembly.   The Commissioners to lay off the district into three election districts; to designate the place in which to hold elections; to deliver to the clerk of Anne Arundel County a description in writing, under their hands and seals, of boundaries and numbers of each, and the place where the election is to be held, to be recorded respectively; to cause copies of said description to be published and set up. Voters qualified to vote for delegates to vote at their respective places, for one person resident of such district. Commissioners to remain in office one year; to have all the power and subject to the same liabilities as Commissioners of Anne Arundel County; to appoint constables and tax collectors as in Anne Arundel to appoint nine Commissioners of Public Schools, and not exceeding eighteen persons who, with the Commissioners, to be inspectors, and said bodies to act as in Anne Arundel; the same laws to be in force as in Anne Arundel. Two-fifths of the tax levied in Anne Arundel for the purpose of colonization to be paid by Howard District and three-fifths by Anne Arundel. The Commissioners to fix upon the sites for public buildings; to purchase land not exceeding in cost $20,000, and not to levy more than $4,000 any one year; to borrow money not more than $4,000 in any one year to be due; no compensation except per diem.

To provide suitable buildings for the Court purposes until the erection of proper buildings. The Governor to appoint coroners, and the district judge to appoint electors.

All deeds of land lying in, after the appointment and qualification of the Clerk, to be recorded by said Clerk.

The laws of the State in regard to wills, after the appointment of Register, to apply to said district. The Commissioners of Anne Arundel to levy, including Howard District, a sum sufficient to defray all liabilities up to the time of passing this Act. The sessions of the Court to be held on the second Monday of March and third Monday in September. Ellicott's Mills was chosen.

Howard District existed for a decade. At the Constitutional Convention of 1851, Judge Thomas Beale Dorsey, of Howard District, a delegate thereof, on January 29, 1851, presented the petition of James Sykes and others, praying that Howard District of Anne Arundel be made a separate county to be called Howard County. The petition having been read, Mr. Dorsey moved its reference to the Committee upon Representation. Mr. Bowie moved its reference to a select committee, which was adopted. The committee was Messrs. Dorsey, Bowie, Smith, Harbine and Ricaud. Mr. Dorsey spoke in favor of the petitioners. The report of the committee, through its chairman, reads: "That part of Anne Arundel County, called Howard District, is hereby erected into a new county, to be called Howard County; the inhabitants thereof shall have, hold and enjoy all such rights and privileges as are held and enjoyed by the inhabitants of the other counties in this State; and its civil and municipal officers shall continue in office until their successors shall have been elected or appointed, and shall have qualified as such; and all rights, powers and obligations incident to Howard District of Anne Arundel shall attach to Howard County." This report having been read, Mr. Dorsey moved it be printed and made the order of the day for Wednesday next. Mr. Sellman, from Anne Arundel, stated that no objection had reached him from any citizen of Anne Arundel.

When the appointed day had come Mr. Dorsey called for his report; it was, however, postponed under a motion of Mr.Merrick, of Charles County, for the report on legislation. On Friday, March 7, 1851, Mr. Dorsey again called for his report, when it was adopted. At an election held Wednesday, November 5, 1851, Thomas Brice Hobbs was returned by the judges of election as Register of Wills for Howard County and was duly commissioned as such, having paid the tax fixed by law upon said commission. A contest was carried to the Legislature, when the House of Delegates decided that a tie existed between said Thomas B. Hobbs and Thomas Jenkins and issued a warrant for an election to fill the office. On the 7th of April following said election resulted in the return of Mr. Thomas B. Hobbs, who was commissioned without a demand for his commission tax by order of the Assembly

By Act, Chapter 110, the Treasurer of the County was ordered to be chosen by the people.

Dr. William W. Watkins was elected the first State Senator of Howard.

By Act, Chapter 364, George B. Dobbin was appointed Visitor from Howard County to the Maryland Hospital and John K. Longwell for the new county of Carroll.

The first voting place in Howard was the "Old Election House," on the "Old Rolling Road," which divides the third and fifth. It still stands under a hill just west of the Tyson Mansion, which was built about the time of the organization of the county. This once splendid estate, upon which one hundred thousand dollars were expended in its equipment, bears a name which reads the same both ways. It was the invention of General Tyson, now adopted for the neighboring post-office of Glenelg.

General Joseph Tyson served under President Tyler as Assistant Postmaster-General and as Commissary-General of the United States Army. He was also president of a mining company. His son, Henry H. Tyson, was a member of the Maryland Legislature in 1877. Tyson's Manor house has been the scene of the most brilliant entertainments in Howard. This estate is now held by Mr. Knox.

Upon that same rolling road, leading toward Elk Ridge, is "Carrollton Hall" or "Folly Quarter," upon which another one hundred thousand dollars were spent.

In connection with Doughoregan Manor, an excellent review of this home has been given from the Baltimore "Sun," of December 20, 1900.

The first statistical correspondent of Howard County for the Department of Washington, under Horace Capron, Commissioner of

Agriculture, was Dr. Horatio Lawrence. He was assisted by Hon. James Morris, Judge H. O. Devries, Hon. John R. Clarke and Aaron Chadwick.

Dr. Lawrence was a descendant of Sir. Robert Lawrence, of Ashton Hall, Lancashire, England; knighted during the Crusades. His grandson James married Matilda Washington. Dr. Lawrence lies buried in the Friends' Cemetery at Sandy Spring. His son, Dawson Laurence, was the chief actor in getting up an excellent map of Anne Arundel and Howard Counties, in 1870, to which I am indebted for some data and locations of estates. From him also, comes the curious genealogical note concerning an old Howard County schoolmate, "Thomas Peddicord, son of Jasper, oldest son and his grandfather's oldest grandson, was born in November and married Rebecca; Washington A. Peddicord, son of Thomas, oldest son and his grandfather's oldest grandson, was born in November and married Rebecca; Thomas J. Peddicord, son of Washington, oldest son and his grandfather's oldest grandson, was born in November and married Rebecca."

Mr. Thomas J. Peddicord left Howard in early manhood and is now a prominent lawyer of Washington County.

THOMAS BRICE WORTHINGTON HOBBS.

Thomas Brice Worthington Hobbs, the first Register of Wills of Howard County, at an advanced age, now resides in Baltimore.

There was a contest over his first election, and it was again placed before the people, who confirmed his election by an increased majority. Mr. Hobbs is an intelligent, genial gentleman of dignified bearing and pleasant address. His record was most excellent. He was succeeded by Mr. Ely Peddicord, whose successor was Benjamin Dorsey, who died in office.

Hon. Edwin Warfield, now Governor, followed Mr. Dorsey, and his successors were Messrs. Maclin, Scaggs and Marlow.

Mr. Hobbs is the son of Peregrine Hobbs by his wife, Mary (Howard) Hobbs. Mr. Peregrine Hobbs was in the War of 1812. His father, Thomas Hobbs, was the surveyor who took up the large estate extending to the east of the Westminister road from Cooksville to Glenwood. A further history of this surveyor will be found elsewhere in the history of Howard County.

EDWIN PARSONS HAYDEN.

Edwin Parsons Hayden, first Clerk of Howard County Court, 1847–1850, was born in Baltimore, Maryland, August 7, 1811. He was the son of Horace H. Hayden, M. D., an eminent geologist of Baltimore and a Founder and President of the Baltimore Dental College. Dr. Hayden was a soldier in the War of 1812, serving in the battle of North Point, 1814, and as Assistant Surgeon in the Military Hospital. His father, Adjutant Thomas Hayden, Continental line, served through the Revolutionary War. The original ancestor, William Hayden, of Connecticut, was a soldier, and the first one to receive honorable mention for gallantry in the Indian Wars of New England. He received land in 1642 for his services, which land, as well as his sword, the family still own after 260 years. Edwin Parsons Hayden was educated at Baltimore College and studied law at Yale College, where he was a classmate of Governor Thomas Watkins Ligon, of Howard County, during the years 1831 and 1832. In 1832 he was admitted to the bar in Baltimore and continued his studies under Hugh Davy Evans, L. L. D., of that city. In 1836, he moved to his farm at Catonsville and began the practice of law at Ellicott's Mills, where he located in 1840, building the handsome stone residence at "Oak Lawn," near the Court House. This home his family occupied until it was sold in the seventies to Henry A. Wooten, Esq., whose widow now lives there. Mr. Hayden is described by one of his contemporaries as "a lawyer of more than ordinary ability, a successful pleader at the hustings and a decided Whig. He was a man of handsome features, pleasing manners and an easy and graceful speaker." He was nominated by the Whig party for the Legislature of Maryland in 1846, and in October, 1846, was elected by a large Democratic vote. He took his seat in the House of Delegates and served until March 10, 1847, when he was appointed by the Governor to the office of Clerk of Howard County Court for the usual term of six years. He was a member of the Howard County Dragoons, Charles Carroll, Captain, and a communicant of St. Peter's Protestant Episcopal Church. He died of congestion of the lungs, May 10, 1850, aged thirty-nine, leaving his widow and six children. One of his sons, Charles L., served in the United States Army in 1861, and another, Rev. Horace Edwin Hayden, served in the Confederate States Army, 1861–1865. He is now Secretary and Librarian of the Wyoming Historical and Geological Society of Wilkes Barre, Pennsylvania; member of the Southern Historical Society and Pennsylvania Historical Society.

Rev. Mr. Hayden is the author of "Virginia Genealogist," most accurate in data and most comprehensive in scope and material. He is also the author of a sketch of Charles Carroll, of Carrollton, and a history of "The Massacre of Wyoming." He resides at Wilkes Barre, Pennsylvania, and has charge of a church in addition to his editorial labors.

Another son of Mr. Edwin Parson Hayden is a prominent merchant of Baltimore.

WORTHINGTON.

Dr. William Henry Worthington, successor to Mr. Hayden, was born January 30, 1812, died January 5, 1886; was twice married—first, to Mary Ann Jones Dorsey; second, Ellen Dall Cooke. He was son of Thomas Worthington and Eliza (Baldwin) Worthington, he was born at his paternal home, situated near the locality known as "Rising Sun," in Anne Arundel County. His parents both died, leaving him and one daughter, Achsah, very young children.

Achsah—Rinaldo Warfield Dorsey, and they had one son, Joshua Worthington Dorsey, whose mother died leaving him about two years old. Rinaldo Warfield Dorsey afterwards married Margaret Ann Stockwell, by whom he had Christiana Wilton Dorsey, who married Lieutenant Edwin S. Jacob, United States Navy.

Dr. Charles Griffith Worthington became guardian for his brother Thomas's children, and with him William Henry Worthington studied medicine. He graduated at the Maryland University at the age of twenty-one. Inherited from his uncle, Brice Worthington, the old homestead, situated on Middle branch of Patuxent River, adjoining "Montpelier." The old homestead was known at that time as "White Hall;" in later years the name was changed to "Glenburnie." A part of this same property now belongs to Joshua Worthington Dorsey, known as "Wild Wood." In 1858 William Henry Worthington sold the old home, reserving the graveyard, with a right of way to it, for the benefit of any of the family who might care to be buried there. Up to that time, 1858, there were five generations buried there, and many of the inscriptions on the old tombstones were scarcely legible. After the sale of the place William Henry Worthington went to Ellicott City with the intention of moving there, thence to St. Paul, Minnesota. He spent the winter of 1858 in St. Paul; made some investments in town property; but on his return changed his mind about taking his family there, thinking the climate too severe to be endured by women tenderly raised. From early manhood, to and up to the time he left the old home, he was a member of Christ Church, Queen Caroline Parish, holding the position of vestryman, warden, register and delegate to the convention of the Diocese. While a resident of Ellicott City he was a member of St. Peters' Church, holding like positions. He was County Commissioner at the time Howard district became Howard County, and was one of the committee appointed to select the site and direct the building of the Court House in Ellicott City, then known as Ellicott's Mills. He was appointed Clerk of the County Court by Governor Philip Frances Thomas to fill an unexpired term, at the expiration of which term he was elected by the people for the usual term of six years. He afterwards held a position in the Custom House, Baltimore, during the administration of James Buchanan. In 1885 he was obliged, on account of failing health, to give up the practice of medicine, and he then moved to Baltimore, where he died.

JUDGE ISAAC THOMAS JONES.

Born in 1838, Judge Jones, of Howard, is just in the prime of his judicial career. Cares rest lightly upon his genial life. He is a combined son of both Anne Arundel and Howard. His progenitor lived upon the Patuxent, near Queen Anne, in Prince George's. By his wife, who was Miss Knighton, of Anne Arundel, he had sons—Isaac, Edward, Henry and Samuel.

Isaac Jones—Miss Hopkins, of the Gerrard Hopkins family, and their issue were, Edward, Elizabeth, Henry, Samuel and Sarah, Rebecca, Mary and Richard Jones.

Edward Jones resided upon the road leading from Owingsville to Mt. Pleasant, on the Patuxent. He married Miss Croxall, a descendant daughter of Richard Croxall, by the sister of James Carroll, of All Hallows Parish. She was a great-granddaughter of Robert Morris. The issue of her marriage to Edward Jones is our present Judge Isaac Thomas Jones, Mary Elizabeth, Augusta, Ida E., Anna M. and Arthur L. Jones.

Judge Jones married Mary, daughter of Richard Gambrill by Miss Iglehart, daughter of Richard Iglehart, of the neighborhood of Atholton, Howard. Mrs. Jones is a sister of Mr. Stephen Gambrill, of Laurel. Judge Jones removed to Howard in 1864, was elected a member of the Legislature in 1868; was chosen Judge of Howard District, in 1882, and re-elected fifteen years later, in 1897, without opposition. In 1899 he was made Chief Judge of Fifth District and Judge of the Court of Appeals. His Howard County estate is near the Old Brick Church. A granite quarry of excellent stone has recently been developed upon it. Mr. Samuel Jones, the merchant of Annapolis, who bears a striking likeness to Judge Jones, is the son of Henry Jones, an uncle of the Judge.

"HON. JOHN GOUGH ROGERS, OF HOWARD."

Chairman of the "Ways and Means" Committee of the House of Delegates, in the Maryland Legislature, of 1902, Hon. John Gough Rogers, Ex-School Examiner, Ex-State Senator, Ex-Candidate for Congress and one of the foremost men of Howard, not only legally, but as a man of business, has an interesting fund of information for the historian concerning the ways and means of his ancestors.

His progenitor was Nicholas Rogers, Major in the Continental Army under General La Fayette, coming over with him from France. His history is a part of the history of Baltimore. His son, Philip Rogers, was one of the leading merchants of Baltimore, in partnership with Samuel Owings. These partners became brothers-in-law. The wife of the former was Rebecca, daughter of Henry Woodward, only son of Amos Woodward and Achsah Dorsey, first daughter of Caleb Dorsey, of Hockley.

The wife of Samuel Owings was her sister, Mary Woodward, widow of William Govan.

The mother of these two sisters was Mary, daughter of Colonel Richard Young, of Calvert County, and Rebecca Holsworth, who came up to Anne Arundel and settled at "Primrose Hill," two miles out of Annapolis, near the Severn. She became the wife of Henry Woodward, heir of Amos Woodward and of Amos Garrett, the Annapolis merchant of great wealth. Henry Woodward died at twenty-three years of age, leaving a young and handsome widow with four interesting daughters, two of whom have already been noted. Harriet, another daughter, became first the wife of Edmund Brice; second, Mrs. Alexander Murray; Eleanor became Mrs. Samuel Dorsey, son of Patuxent John Dorsey, of Howard County. They came into possession of "Dorsey's Search," and their only son, Harry Woodward Dorsey, by his Maccubin wife, leaving one son, Henry Woodward Dorsey, was the father of Achsah Dorsey, first wife of Thomas Beale Dorsey of " Gray Rock."

Upon the early death of Mr. Henry Woodward his widow became the wife of John Hesselius, an artist of note, son of Rev. Samuel Hesselius, of Sweden. To her husband we are indebted for her existing portrait, now in possession of the wife of Commodore Daniel Ridgely, and of the family of Dr. William Ridout, of Annapolis, copied in " One Hundred Years Ago," by Elizabeth Hesselius Murray, of West River. Elizabeth, daughter of Mrs. Hesselius, became the wife of Rev. Walter Dulaney Addison.

Charlotte Hesselius became the wife of Thomas Johnston (son of the Governor). She had for bridesmaids Miss Sarah Leitch, daughter of Major Leitch, aid to General Washington, afterward Mrs. John Addison; Miss Murray, afterwards wife of Governor Edward Lloyd; Miss Maria Murray, afterwards Mrs. General Mason, and Miss Cromwell, afterwards Mrs. Lee. These weddings took place at "Primrose Hill," to which Mrs. Hesselius had removed from "Bellefield," after the death of her husband. Though loyal to her own church, Mrs. Hesselius, having heard the thunder tones of Whitfield, opened her doors for the worship of the young Methodist Church, and her name has come down the corridor of time as an intellectual, earnest believer, brilliant in conversation, idolized by all who knew her. Whitfield said her house was open to the word of God and closed to everything else. She has also handed down a poetic description of her coterie of daughters and their Colonial dress, so well described in "One Hundred Years Ago." These daughters were frequent visitors at the home of Philip Rogers, her son-in-law.

John Gough Rogers (of Philip and Rebecca) married Sophia Gough Owings (of Samuel and Mary Woodward Govan), and his son, Dr. Samuel Owings Rogers, was the father of Hon. John Gough Rogers and Reuben Dorsey Rogers, of Howard.

Down upon West River, in the neighborhood of "Cedar Park," "Tulip Hill," "Joy Neck," among the Chews, Galloways, Murrays, Mercers, Richardsons and Chestons, was the Rogers homestead, some seven miles south of ancient Londontown. The locality was formally known as "Red Miles" and "Butler's Tavern." "Greenwood" and "Druid Hill Park" were also the homesteads of this family in Baltimore County.

Edmund Law Rogers, owner of " Druid Hill," married a great-granddaughter of Governor Plater. Their daughter is the charming wife of Professor Smith, of Johns Hopkins University.

The late Henry W. Rogers, of Charles Street, whose wife, Fanny Dennis, is one of the leading officials of the Colonial Dames, is also a descendant of Philip Rogers of Major Nicholas.

Dr. Frank Rogers, brother of Samuel Owings Rogers, married Eleanor Johnson, daughter of Elisha and Eleanor (Worthington) Johnson, last daughter of Samuel Worthington and Martha Garretson, of Baltimore County.

COLONEL THOMAS H. HUNT.

Colonel Hunt has been identified with Howard County since its organization. He was born in Frederick City in 1832. His mother was Miss Jones, and both father and mother were of English parentage, coming over about 1810. He is a cousin of Mr. German H. Hunt, of Baltimore. His wife is a Linthicum and Warfield descendant. Colonel Hunt has kept closely to his business as a merchant, but he has long been an active Democrat and upon the Executive Committee of his county. He served as a director in the board of the House of Correction, and was the treasurer of the board until the Republicans gained control in 1896, when he resigned. Colonel Hunt is one of the directors of the Patapsco Bank at Ellicott City. His oldest daughter is the wife of Mr. Harald Hardinge, cashier of the Patapsco Bank.

Mr. Hardinge was born in Missouri. His mother, Henrietta Cristine Kemp, was a daughter of Colonel Louis Kemp, the famous Baltimore merchant, who married Miss Buckey, of Buckeystown, Maryland. Mr. Hardinge was a resident of Frederick. He has been connected with the Ellicott City Bank since 1888.

Another daughter of Colonel Hunt is the wife of Assistant Clerk W. Owings.

JOSHUA N. WARFIELD.

Joshua N. Warfield, member of the Democratic Executive Committee and present School Commissioner of Howard County, has long won a reputation as one of the best political organizers in the county. With the same energy with which he manages one of the largest landed estates in the county, he enters into the public service to succeed. He is now holding the only office his father, the late Albert Gallatin Warfield, ever consented to hold.

His residence at Florence is upon the site of his ancestor, John Welsh, and he holds, in addition, a portion of the estate of Samuel Welsh, from both of which houses his grandfather selected his wives. He holds the most western surveys of Captain Philemon Dorsey, out of whose house came his great-grandmother, Catharine (Dorsey), wife of Captain Benjamin Warfield. Out of barren fields left by the old tobacco growers he has demonstrated, as did the Ellicott brothers, that lime, grass and grain restore not only worn-out lands, but increase the revenues of the land-holders. Some twenty years ago he married Lucy, daughter of the late Enoch Hutton, of Montgomery County, and sister of Hon. J. J. Hutton, of Brookeville. Two sons and one daughter bless their union. Both sons intend to remain in Howard as successors of their father.

TALBOTT.

West River was the abode of Richard Talbott in 1649; he was a Quaker. His wife was Elizabeth, oldest daughter of Major Richard Ewen, who that same year brought his wife, Sophia, five children and three servants at his own charges, for which he demanded and received, in 1650, a patent for 1,000 acres. The issue of Richard and Elizabeth were Richard, Edward, John and Elizabeth, wife of Benjamin Lawrence. "Poplar Knawle" was left by his will of 1663 to Richard; "Talbotts Ridge" to his sons, Edward and John, jointly; to Elizabeth his personalty. Richard Galloway was a witness.

Edward Talbott married in 1679 the widow Coale (nee Elizabeth Thomas), daughter of Philip Thomas. They had issue, Richard, Edward, Elizabeth and John Talbott, of West River, who married— first, Elizabeth Galloway; second, Mary Waters, of West River, and had Cassandra, Lucy, Elizabeth, John and Edward, of West River; born 1723. This Edward married Temperance Merryman in 1745 and had John, Benjamin, Vincent, Mary, Temperance and Edward. Edward the elder was a witness to the wills of Major Welsh and Benjamin Laurence.

Benjamin removed to Baltimore County and married Sarah Wilmott. Their daughter Harriet became the wife of Greenberry Ridgely.

John Talbott, above, surveyed in 1732 "Talbott's Last Shift." This is on the Patapsco, adjoining "Moores Morning Choice," "Chews Vineyard" and Edward Dorsey's estate, near Columbia. It contained 1,120 acres. He sold it to Edward Talbott, Richard Talbott, Richard Galloway and George Ellicott.

The Ellicott part was bought by Benjamin Dorsey, in 1741. Edward Talbot resurveyed his as "Talbotts Vineyard" and increased it to 1,031 acres.

The muster roll of Maryland shows the following Talbotts in the Revolution: Benjamin R. Talbott was with Thomas Lansdale Company, in 1776; Elisha Talbott was in the artillery at Annapolis, in 1776; John Talbott was enlisted by John Eager Howard, in 1776; John Talbott, enrolled by Thomas Burke, was passed, in 1776.

Richard Talbott, ensign in Anne Arundel County, was passed by John Dorsey, in 1776. He was in Captain Edward Norwood's Company in 1776. He was a son of Richard Talbott, of "Talbott's Vineyard." Richard Talbott married Ruth, daughter of Patuxent John Dorsey. (Mrs. Elizabeth Dorsey named in her will of 1777 her daughter, Ruth Talbott.) They resided near Jonestown. The old graveyard was removed to St. John's Church. Their son, John Lawrence Talbott (1784—first, Henrietta Phillips; second, Mary Porter (1799). Issue, Richard, John, Providence, Jefferson of Laurel, Madison, George Washington, Charles, Allen and Mary.

Richard—Mary Fairall. Issue, Henrietta Phillips Talbott— Richard Harden; Mary, Drusilla Coale, Sarah, Stephen, killed in the Mexican War; Edward A., of Ellicott City—Mary Jane Wareham.

Issue, Hattersley Worthington Talbott, Elizabeth A., and Rebecca; Edward A.—Georgiana Laney; Mary C.—John L. Clarke, son of James.

Mr. H. W. Talbott is the Immigration Agent of Maryland and attorney-at-law and Mayor of Rockville. He married Laura Williams Holland, daughter of Zachariah, a Lieutenant in United States Navy, son of Solomon Holland, Register of Wills. Her mother was a daughter of Captain Ely Williams, brother of General Otho Holland Williams.

THE GAMBRILL BROTHERS.

Two sons of Mr. Stephen Gambrill are in the United States Army. The letters of William, when in Honolulu, in 1898, before annexation, give an interesting insight into the foreign provinces. He writes from the "Officers Club of Hawaii," of the very lavish entertainments given by the people, in which champagne was one of the ordinary beverages and interesting young ladies considered it an honor to wait upon them. He met the Prince, who invited him to tea to meet his daughter.

On August 13, 1898, he writes again: "We are now in possession of Manila, which surrendered at 2.30 this P. M. This could be made a pretty city. I do not know of but one place hotter than this. It is not to be found on a map. Major Gambrill, of the Pay Master's Division, was with the fleet which sailed from San Francisco July 3, 1898. About 5,000 soldiers were with the fleet. Generals Merritt and McArthur were among the officers. We had as rough a night on the Pacific as has ever been experienced, and all were sick."

BENJAMIN DORSEY WARFIELD.

Benjamin Dorsey Warfield, of the Louisville and Nashville Railroad, was born in Howard County, in 1862. He is the oldest son of Dr. Milton Welsh Warfield and Mary Elizabeth Dawley, his wife. His early education was given him by his mother, a very cultivated woman. He attended Glenwood Institute, then in charge of Professor Lycurgus Mathews. Entering the service of the Baltimore and Ohio Railroad, he remained till 1882, when he removed to Louisville, Kentucky, in a similar position with Hull & Co. In 1885, he entered the service of the Louisville and Nashville Railroad as Secretary of Judge Houston, Chief Attorney. He was chief clerk of this law department until 1891, when he was advanced to Adjusting Attorney, having been admitted to the Court of Appeals of Kentucky, in 1890, as a graduate of the Law School, of Louisville. In 1901 he was appointed District Attorney for Kentucky for the same company, in charge of the entire litigation of the company.

Out of twenty cases he won all but one. Upon this record Judge Bruce, the general counsel of the company, declared it was unparalleled by any lawyer of any age so far as he knew.

In 1898 he married Selenah Cecilia Barret, second daughter of James Samuel and Elizabeth Bullitt (Middleton) Barret and great-great-granddaughter of Captain Chiswell Barret, of Colonel Baylor's Regiment of Dragoons. Francis Barret immigrated to Kentucky. His son, Dr. Lewis Barret located in Hart County. From his second wife, Miss Garvin, came James Samuel, the father of Mrs. Warfield. Her mother was Elizabeth, eldest daughter of Craig and Mary (O'Bannon) Middleton, of Henry County, Kentucky.

DR. RIDGELY BROWN WARFIELD.

Dr. Ridgely Brown Warfield, second son of Dr. Milton Warfield, of Howard, was named in honor of Colonel Ridgely Brown, who, leading the Maryland Battalion, lost his life at Ashland Gap, in the war between the States, and now lies upon his native soil upon the border of Howard and Montgomery.

Dr. R. B. Warfield, like his brother, was educated chiefly by his talented mother and by Professor Mathews, of Glenwood Institute. Having read medicine with his father, he graduated at the Maryland University and commenced practice with Dr. Ridgway Trimble, a descendant of the Lloyds of "Wye House."

The latter when asked by Governor Lloyd Lowndes, a relative, to recommend a young physician of good standing for his staff, Dr. Trimble said: "I know a gentleman who can fill the bill, but he is a Democrat." The Governor replied: "I don't care anything about his politics; ask him to serve me." Dr. Warfield accepted the staff appointment and with the Governor was present at the inauguration succeeding.

Dr. Warfield, though a bachelor, bought a house on Park Avenue, into which he has brought a library of choice reading and articles of household adornments that have won him the title of "a gentleman of perfect taste." Dr. Warfield has spent several vacations in Europe and Mexico. In consultation with his father, he has frequently been called to practice in his native country.

CAPTAIN ELDRED DUDLEY WARFIELD.

Captain Eldred Dudley Warfield, of United States Army, is the son of Professor J. D. Warfield by his first wife, Tonnie Dawley, sister of Mrs. Dr. Milton Warfield. He was a student of the Maryland Agricultural College when his father held the chair of English Literature there.

Entering the service of the Baltimore and Ohio Railroad, he was several times promoted. At the time of the Spanish War in Cuba he was then captain of Company D, of the Fifth Maryland Regiment of Militia, and with that regiment was enrolled in the service of the Government. While at Huntsville, Alabama, he was made Provost Marshal of the Fourth Army Corps, and his entire company was encamped in the city as permanent guard. This service was performed with such complete satisfaction the citizens joined gladly in an address of thanks to Captain Warfield. Returning at the close of the war all Baltimore turned out to welcome the boys of the Fifth. Captain Warfield, with many others of the regiment, was even then suffering with typhoid fever. Recovering, he offered himself to the government and was appointed second lieutenant in the regular army.

During his present service he has spent three years in Porto Rico, where he also received the thanks of the people and a handsome sword as a mark of appreciation for his services, and one year in the Philippines as first lieutenant. He is now at Fort Rheno, and last September entered the staff school at Fort Leavenworth to pass the examination for promotion to rank as captain.

Captain Warfield, upon a recent trip East from his army post at Fort Leavenworth, at the request of Governor Warfield, wrote in the Log Book of "Oakdale" the following outline of his official life in our foreign provinces:

"SUNDAY, August 13, 1905.

"On April 10, 1899, I was commissioned second lieutenant in the regular army. Within one month I was on duty at Fortress Monroe, Columbus Barracks, Jefferson Barracks and Fort Hamilton. On May 14th I was assigned to the Eleventh Infantry and was ordered to Porto Rico.

"For nearly three years my work was both diversified and attractive in tempering force with gentleness among our new-found wards.

"Promoted first lieutenant on February 2, 1901, I was transferred to the Twenty-third Infantry, and for a year was at Fort Ethan Allen and Plattsburgh Barracks.

"Ordered then by cable to Manila to fill a vacancy, my lot fell among friends in the famous Island of Mindaro, wild and untrammelled in its natural beauty. I was among the military prisoners and around the garrisons of Manila.

"Coming back by way of Japan and Honolulu at the dawn of a bright and happy year, only those who have been absent from home can appreciate such a home-coming. I bring back to old Howard the floral offerings of countless lakes and rivers of Florida. I bring back the memories of many pleasant wanderings among the Danish West Indies and St. Thomas; among the historic scenes of Cuba, Porto Rico and the Philippines or the Flowery Kingdom of Japan, or the balmy islands of Hawaii. Yet, here among the foot hills of Howard I find a home life, a hospitality and a greeting dearer than all."

JAMES CLARK.

James Clark, president of the Drovers and Mechanics' Bank of Baltimore, is one of Howard County's sons, born about the time of its separation as a district; he is the son of James Clark, a farmer of Howard, who was the son of John Clark, one of three brothers, John, James and David, who came over from the North of Ireland just subsequent to the Revolution.   These brothers settled in Anne Arundel and founded a carding wool business on the manor.   Those mills have now been changed to grain mills.

James Clark, Sr., married Jemima Ward, of London, then living with her father on "Carroll's Manor."

Mr. James Clark, Jr., began his business career in Adams' Express Company, at Richmond, Va.   In 1862 he went into Confederate service, resuming it after its close with the Southern Express.   Accepting employment in the Virginia and Tennessee Railroad Company under General Mahone, he continued for five years its purchasing agent.   In 1872 he came to Baltimore and embarked in the live stock business at Calverton Stock Yards.   He was, during fifteen years, eminently successful.   Retiring to Lynchburg, Virginia, he became President of its national bank for five years.   In 1892 he was called to the presidency of his present bank.   He is a director in a cigarette company's works at Salem, Virginia.   He married in Lynchburg, in 1865, Miss E. R. Booker, who died in 1885, and in 1887 he married Miss E. V. Lumpkin, daughter of Robert Garrett Lumpkin, of Baltimore.   Mr. James Booker Clark, a farmer of Howard, is a son by his first marriage.   Mrs. Arthur Forsythe and Mrs. Albert Thomas, both of Howard, are sisters of Mr. James Clark, the banker.

DR. THADDEUS WATKINS CLARK.

Another Howard County physician, now in Baltimore is Dr. Thaddeus Watkins Clark.   He is a son of the late William and Albina (Watkins) Clark, of Clarksville.   His mother was the youngest daughter of Colonel Gassaway Watkins, of "Walnut Grove," a soldier of two wars, whose wife was of the family of Bishop Claggett, the first Episcopal Bishop of Maryland.

The late William Clark was an extensive farmer of the limestone section of Clarksville.   He was a son of David Clark, one of the three brothers who came from the North of Ireland after the Revolution, and married Rachel, daughter of John and Mary (Chaney) Warfield, of Anne Arundel.

Dr. Clark studied under his uncle, Dr. W. W. Watkins.   He was graduated from the Maryland University in 1880, and was later Demonstrator of Physics, Chief of Clinic and Nervous Diseases and Clinical Lecturer at Bayview Asylum.   He is a member of the Medical and Chirurgical Faculty of Maryland and of the Neurological Society of Baltimore.   He is upon the Medical Staff of the Fifth Maryland Regiment and was with them in the Spanish War, under the title of Captain, remaining with the regiment until the close of the war.   In 1885 Dr. Clark married Florence C., daughter of Judge William Mathews and Harriet Howard, his wife, of Glenwood, Howard County.   She is a descendant of Captain Brice Howard, of the Elk Ridge Militia during the Revolution, whose wife was one of the eleven Ridgely daughters of "White Wine and Claret," great-granddaughters of Hon. John Dorsey, of the Provincial Council.

Thomas Clark, brother of Dr. Thaddeus, was formerly editor of the "Ellicott City Times." He married the only daughter of Mr. John Hardy, and has several interesting children. He resides in Howard, but has for some years been an official in Washington, D. C.

POSTMASTER-GENERAL GARY, OF PRESIDENT McKINLEY'S CABINET.

Mr. Gary was born in Connecticut in 1833. He was only six years old when, in 1839, his father established The Alberton Cotton Mills. In 1861 he became a partner. Nine years later his father, James S. Gary, died, and the management of the mills and counting-room descended to him single handed until 1885, when his son, E. Stanley Gary, was given an interest.

Mr. James A. Gary was, first, a Henry Clay Whig. In 1858 he was nominated for State Senator, but was defeated. He was a delegate to the Union Convention in 1861; a delegate to the Republican National Convention of 1872; Chairman of the Maryland delegation; ran for Congress in 1870, but was defeated; was in the reform movement of 1875 and a delegate to the National Convention of 1876. In 1879 was defeated for Governor by William T. Hamilton; opposed Blaine in 1880. In 1884 he was for Arthur and in 1888 for Sherman, falling into line on General Harrison. In 1892, for the sixth time a delegate, he helped to nominate General Harrison. In 1896 he was a Maryland member of the Finance Committee.

His business interests embraced a general supervision of his own large plant, with its extensive offices on German street. He is President of the Citizens' National Bank, President of the Board of Trustees of the Enoch Pratt Free Library and Vice-President of the Consolidated Gas Company; was for several years President of the Merchants and Manufacturers' Association. He is a Director in the Baltimore Trust and Guarantee Company, of the American Fire Insurance Company and of the Savings Bank of Baltimore, and Chairman of the Board of Trustees of Brown Memorial Presbyterian Church. He has made a handsome little village surrounding his cotton factory at Alberton.

"CHANTILLY" AT THE RELAY.

Within sight of the Relay in 1797 stood "Chantilly," the homestead of Horatio Johnson, who was, for a number of years, Inspector of Tobacco at Elk Ridge Landing.

Horatio Johnson was the second son of Thomas Johnson, often referred to in our Archives as an authority on the manufacture of guns. He was of a kindred family to John W. Johnson, father of Reverdy Johnson.

His homestead at Pikesville, Baltimore County, now replaced by the modern one of Mr. McHenry (lately consumed by fire), stood near Sudbrook. A pen and ink drawing of it upon the old surveyor's maps, made by Cornelius Howard for Mr. Johnson in 1799, is now in possession of a descendant daughter, Mrs. H. Johnson Niedringhaus, of St. Louis.

"Rockland," the homestead of William Fell Johnson, in Green Spring Valley, was another portion of the Johnson estate, which included an extensive survey, also along the Patapsco.

Thomas Johnson married, in 1752, Ann Risteau and had issue—Rinaldo Johnson, who married Ann Eilbeck Mason, daughter of Hon. George Mason, of Gunston Hall, Virginia; Horatio Johnson, of "Chantilly," married, first, Sarah Norwood; second, Elizabeth Warfield, daughter of Colonel Charles Warfield, of Sams Creek; Rachel Johnson—John Woodward; Mary Johnson—Lieutenant Adam Jamison and Mr. Goldthwaite; Elizabeth Johnson Fox; Dr. Thomas Johnson—Joanna Giles and resided at "Rockland;" William Johnson, bachelor, of "Pleasant Green;" Captain Caecilius Johnson, bachelor, of "Pleasant Green;" Ann Johnson—Thomas Beale Owings, and John W. Johnson—Mrs. Lucy Gooding, of St. Louis.

Horatio Johnson, of "Chantilly," was ensign of the Anne Arundel Militia under Captain Edward Norwood, and later under Captain Elisha Riggs. His first wife was Sarah Norwood, whose daughter, Sallie Norwood Johnson, became the second wife of Dr. Abram Barnes Hood, of Virginia. By his second wife, Elizabeth Warfield, there were Charles David Warfield Johnson, Major of Militia, who resigned his commission to go West in 1834; he married Eliza McKonkey, of Baltimore, and had issue: James Thompson Johnson—first, Harriet Smith Brown; second, Henningham Brown, a descendant of Haden Edwards and James Brown, of Kentucky—issue, H. Johnson, Niedringhaus, James T. Johnson, Joseph B. Johnson, George B. Johnson and Edwards Johnson.

Arthur Livingston Johnson (of Horatio)—Margaret Smith, daughter of Judge John Smith, of Baltimore, and granddaughter of Conrad Smith, whose name appeared in the first directory of Baltimore; she was a sister of Rebecca (Smith) Norris, second wife of George W. Riggs, of Baltimore. The living issue of A. L. Johnson are Mrs. Caroline O'Donnell, Mrs. Laura Campbell and Mrs. Ella James.

Thomas Rinaldo Johnson (of Horatio) was a surgeon in the Seminole wars.

Eliza Ann Johnson (of Horatio)—James H. Preston, of Baltimore, and had issue: Frances Preston, Wysong, Caroline Preston and James H. Preston, of Harford, whose two sons are James H. Preston, of Baltimore, and Walter Preston, of Belair.

Caroline Johnson (of Horatio) died single, at "Rockland."

Evalina Johnson (of Horatio)—her cousin, Joshua Warfield, and had issue: Horatio Johnson Warfield, Elizabeth Warfield Reed, Caroline Warfield, Thomas, David Warfield, Evalina Warfield and Joshua Warfield.

OFFICIALS OF HOWARD COUNTY.

COMMISSIONERS.

1847.
Theodore Tubman,
Chas. R. Simpson,
Wm. Hughes,
John Hood,
George Howard.

1848.
Theodore Tubman,
Littleton Maclin,
Thos. Hughes,
Wm. Hughes.

1849.
David Fielmyer,
Saml. Brown,
Saml. Nichols,
David Clark.

1850.
David Fielmyer,
David Clark,
Geo. Bond,
Theodore Tubman,
Slingsby Linthicum,

1853.
Stephen B. Dorsey,
Slingsby Linthicum,
George Bond.

1855.
Wm. J. Timanus,
Thos. H. Hood,
Chas. D. Worthington,

1857.
Amos Earp,
Thos. H. Hood,
Martin H. Batson.

1859.
Theodore Tubman,
Wm. Hughes,
Chas. G. Linthicum.
(Records do not show
list of 1861 and 1863).

1865.
Jas. Garretson,
Saml. Hopkins,
John L. Lane.

1867.
Anthony Johnson,
Thaddeus S. Clark,
John S. Tracy.

1869.
John S. Tracy,
John T. Harvey,
C. M. Roberts.

1871.
Samuel Gaither,
Dennis P. Gaither,
Anthony Johnson.

1873.
Jerome C. Berry,
Joseph Barlow,
Saml. Brown.

1875.
Saml. Brown,
Jerome C. Berry,
Wm. Rowles.

1877.
Saml. Brown,
Jerome C. Berry,
Wm. Rowles.

1879.
Thos. H. Gaither,
N. S. Childs,
J. D. Warfield.

1881.
J. H. Toomey.

1883.
Ephraim Collins,
Benj. Sunderland,
John T. Ridgely.

1885.
Benj. C. Sunderland,
Wm. J. Harding,
Wm. H. Forsythe.

1887.
Benj. C. Sunderland,
Wm. J. Harding,
Wm. H. Forsythe.

1889.
Benj. C. Sunderland,
Benj. F. Hess,
Edmund Dorsey.

1891.
Benj. F. Hess,
L. J. G. Owings,
Henry Mollman.

1893.
Patrick L. Smith.

1895.
Edmund Dorsey. 6 yrs.

1899.
Thos. O'Neill. 6 yrs.

1901.
Jacob J. Weiner. 6 yrs.

1903.
Benj. F. Hess. 6 yrs.

1905.
Henry A. Penny. 6 yrs.

CLERKS TO COMMISSIONERS.

Littleton Maclin,

John A. Denton,
Frank Parlett.

Wm. J. Robinson,

SHERIFFS.

1848.	1869.	1889.
Chas. G. Haslup.	Claudius Stewart.	Stephen R. Hobbs.
1853.	1871.	1891.
E. A. Talbott.	John S. Tracey.	Wm. G. Owings.
1855.	1873.	1893.
Joshua McCauley.	Walter Dorsey.	Gilbert E. Flower.
1857.	1875.	1895.
John Quinn.	G. Washington Carr.	Greenbury Johnson.
1859.	1877.	Succeeded by Frank
Thos. Burgess.	Joseph Hunt.	Oldfield.
1861.	1879.	1897.
J. P. Ijams.	Joseph McCauley.	Chas. D. Picket.
1864.	1881.	1899.
David E. Hopkins.	Edward A. Talbott.	Lewis E. Philps.
1865.	1883.	1901.
David E. Hopkins.	N. T. Hutchins.	Jas. E. Hobbs.
1867.	1885.	1903.
Edward McCauley.	Frank Shipley.	John F. Kyne.
1867.	1887.	1905.
Wm. A. Webb.	Geo. D. Day.	Joseph Hunt.

TREASURERS.

1897.	1899.	1903.
Frank Parlett.	Jas. T. Clark.	Saml. C. Musgrove.
(For 2 yrs.)	1901.	1905.
	Jas. T. Clark.	Saml. C. Musgrove.

REGISTERS OF WILLS.

1857.	1874.	1887.
Thos. B. Hobbs.	Edwin Warfield appoint-	Isaac Scaggs.
1867.	ed to succeed Benj. H.	1893.
Eli T. Peddicord.	Dorsey, deceased.	Isaac Scaggs.
1867.	1875.	1899.
Benj. H. Dorsey.	Edwin Warfield.	Wm. H. Marlow.
1873.	1881.	1905.
Benj. H. Dorsey.	Thos. L. Maclin.	Richard Davis of W.

CLERKS OF THE CIRCUIT COURT.

	1885.	1895.
Dr. Wm. Henry Worth-ington.	Lewis J. Watkins.	A. C. Rhodes.
Dr. Wm. W. Watkins.		1896.
	1888.	John H. Owings.
1873.	John H. Owings.	1897.
Lewis J. Watkins.		John H. Owings.
1879.	1889.	1903.
Lewis J. Watkins.	John H. Owings.	Wm. W. L. Cissel, M. D.

JUDGES OF ORPHANS' COURT.

1855.
John Quinn,
Henry H. Owings,
H. Baker Dorsey.

1857.
Thos. Burgess.

1859.
Henry O. Devries,
H. H. Owings,
John A. Dorsey.

1864.
Jas. B. Mathews,
Samuel Waters,
J. T. Ijams.

1867.
Hy. H. Owings,
Thos. J. White,
A. P. Amoss.

1869.
Jas. F. Gordon, appointed 1869 vice H. H. Owings, resigned.

1871.
Jas. F. Gordon,
Martin H. Batson,
Dye W. Worthington.

1875.
Dye W. Worthington,
Wm. Mathews,
Jas. Harban.

1877.
Anthony M. Johnson.

1879.
Anthony M. Johnson,
Reuben Dorsey,
Geo. M. Buckingham.

1883.
John W. Hepp,
Anthony M. Johnson,
Reuben Dorsey.

1887.
Anthony M. Johnson,
Reuben Dorsey,
John R. Dorsey.

1891.
John McShane,
Reuben Dorsey,
Laurence W. Hobbs.

1895.
Jas. A. Curtis,
Edmund Dorsey,
John H. Herker.

1899.
Wm. T. Day,
Pulaski Dorsey,
Henry Mollman.
(Elected again in 1903).

STATE'S ATTORNEYS.

1855.
Geo. W. Sands.

1859.
John R. Clark.

1864.
Geo. W. Sands.

1867.
Henry E. Wootten.

1871.
Henry E. Wootten.

1876.
Henry E. Wootten.

1883.
Joseph D. McGuire.

1887.
Joseph D. McGuire.

1891.
Joseph D. McGuire.

1895.
Joseph D. McGuire.

1899.
Martin F. Burke.

1903.
Martin F. Burke.

SCHOOL COMMISSIONERS.

1868.
Saml. H. Henry,
David Burdette,
Wm. H. Hardey,
Hy. O. Devries,
Edward A. Talbott,
Joshua W. Dorsey.

1870.
Albert G. Warfield,
Joseph Barlow,
Chas. G. Linthicum,
Zedekiah M. Isaacs,
Amos Earp,
Joshua W. Dorsey.
John H. Hall vice Joshua W. Dorsey, resigned.
Wm. H. Hardey vice Chas. G. Linthicum, resigned.

1872.
Rev. J. Avery Shepperd,
Wm. Clark,
Dr. Jas. T. Williams.

1876.
Wm. Clark,
Dr. Jas. T. Williams,
Jno. G. Rogers.

1879.
N. S. Childs,
Jno. J. Donaldson,
John G. Rogers,
Dr. Jas. T. Williams.

1880.
John W. Dorsey,
Saml. K. George,
Dr. Jas. T. Williams.

1881.
John Lee Carroll.

1882—1884.
Dr. Jas. T. Williams,
John W. Dorsey,
John Lee Carroll.

1885.
W. Mackintosh,
N. A. Childs.

1888—1890.
W. Mackintosh,
N. A. Childs,
Marion A. Brian.

SCHOOL COMMISSIONERS.—Continued.

1892.
W. Mackintosh,
L. Page Cronmiller,
Wm. B. Gambrill.

1893.
Robt. A. Dobbin,
John T. Hardey,
John W. Hebb.

1894.
Henry O. Devries,
Rev. Henry Branch,
Grovesnor Hanson.

1896.
Jas. E. Shrieve.

1898.
John Q. Selby.

1901.
Thos. M. Johnson,
Joshua N. Warfield,
John W. Selby.

SCHOOL EXAMINERS.

Saml. K. Dashiell,
Dr. Wm. H. Hardey,
John G. Rogers,

John E. Hill,
Dr. Luke M. Shipley,

Philip T. Harman,
Woodland Philips.

SURVEYORS.

1854.
Wm. A. Loder.

1855.
Nathan Shipley, Jr.

1859.
J. B. Winbigler.

1867.
Nathan Shipley.

1869.
A. C. Rogers.

1873.
Henry Lucy.

1876.
Luke M. Shipley.

1877.
John A. Denton.

1881.
John T. R. R. Carroll.

1883-5-7-9.
John T. R. R. Carroll.

1891.
John T. R. R. Carroll.

1893.
Beale A. Warfield.

1895.
John T. R. R. Carroll.

FIRST OFFICERS OF HOWARD COUNTY.

Judge of the Circuit Court............HON. NICHOLAS BREWER.
Clerk of the Circuit Court ....DR. WILLIAM H. WORTHINGTON.
Sheriff.................................JOSHUA MCCAULEY
Crier...................................GEORGE W. ISAACS.
States Attorney.........................GEORGE W. SANDS.
Auditor................................THOMAS DONALDSON.

JUDGES OF THE ORPHANS' COURT.

WILLAM BAKER DORSEY,   HENRY H. OWINGS,   JOHN OREM

REGISTER OF WILLS.

THOMAS BRICE HOBBS.

COUNTY COMMISSIONERS.

WILLIAM J. TIMANUS,   CHARLES G. WORTHINGTON,
THOMAS H. HOOD.

TREASURER.

LITTLETON MACHIN.

THE NEW YORK DESCENDANTS OF
MARYLAND WARFIELDS.

Since my book has been in type I have learned of many very worthy descendants of Maryland progenitors, which I will give in the words of my correspondent in the following addenda:

John Worthington Warfield, of "Big Seneca," and Brice Warfield, a Revolutionary soldier, were twin brothers, sons of Alexander Warfield, of "Warfield's Range," whose homestead is now a part of Senator Gorman's estate. These twin brothers had another brother, Alexander Warfield, the bachelor, whose estate, at Clifton Springs, New York, was given to his nephews, Arnold Warfield, son of John Worthington Warfield, by Susannah Ridgely, his wife, and Zadok Warfield, son of Brice Warfield, by Elizabeth Dickerson, his wife.

Arnold Warfield, his wife Margaret Browning, and children were the first to remove to Clifton Springs. One of his eight sons, Thomas Worthington Warfield, built a $35,000 block of houses in Clifton Springs. He was a bachelor. Lewis Warfield (of Arnold) had three sons in the Union army and one in the Confederate army. I have no other data of them.

My correspondent is Zadok Warfield 3rd, son of Zadok 2nd, son of Zadok 1st, the oldest son of Brice, the Revolutionary Maryland soldier, whose tomb, in Warfield Cemetery, Frederick County, Maryland, is marked by a Scotch granite monument. His son, Surrat Dickerson Warfield, once State Senator of Frederick County, lies beside him. Zadok (of Brice) removed to his inheritance, at Clifton Springs. My correspondent records the following: "Alexander Warfield, brother of Brice, was a bachelor. At his death, in 1812, aged sixty-two years, he left a property worth $100,000. He held four farms of 200 acres each, improved by substantial stone houses. He held over 400 acres in and around Clifton Springs, and $20,000 of personalty, which he gave his nephews and nieces. I have a speech he made here in 1804. By his will my grandfather, Zadok (of Brice), inherited a part of "Clifton Springs." Caleb Warfield Burgess, John Burgess and sister, Susan Burgess, were also heirs of his New York property. One descendant of this family is Benjamin Burgess, bookkeeper of the Baltimore daily "Sun." Zadok Warfield's wife was a daughter of William and Dorcas Chambers, whose family came to the Genesee country in covered wagons in 1828, after a travel of sixteen days on the road. They erected a log dwelling with no floor. Snow sometimes offered them a covering at night. Back-logs were drawn into the house by horses. Wolves and wild hogs often visited them.

Zadok Warfield's children were: Nathan, born in 1802; William, 1804; Susannah Dickerson, 1806; Zadok, 1808; John, 1810; Rachel, 1812; Mary Anne, 1814; Surrat Dickerson, 1816; Leweyar, 1818; Evan Jones, 1820; Elizabeth Anne, 1822; Brice, 1824. Two of these—Brice and Surrat Dickerson—died in Frederick County, Maryland.

Upon his arrival in New York the family Bible was missing, and "Pilgrims Progress" had to record the subsequent births. Nathan, the oldest son, married Catherine Worthington Burgess, the heiress of her uncle Alexander. William Warfield married Lucinda, daughter of Leonard and Mercy Ann (Brown) Knapp, oldest sister of my mother, Chloe (Knapp) Warfield.

Evan Jones Warfield's widow, Caroline Bale Newton, lives in Orlando, Florida. The remains of her husband are at Fernandina, Florida, where he died twenty years ago, a successful merchant, of $45,000 capital, of Clifton Springs. His only son, Carl Warfield, is engaged in banking at Orlando, Florida. He married Miss Hutchins, of Palmyra, New York. Their daughter Zelda took a musical prize, and will graduate this year.

My uncle, John Warfield, left an estate of $35,000. He was well-beloved, well-informed and accommodating. Upon his estate handsome buildings may be seen. His maiden sisters have ample means.

My father, Zadok 2nd, had a farm of 212 acres, with splendid buildings. He was very successful.

My brother Eugene owns a part of it, and he is an up-to-date farmer.

I have also farmed, but, my health failing, I retired with a competence.

We are all of light complexion, with hair snow-white. A Baptist minister who saw Governor Edwin Warfield thinks there is a striking resemblance.

My wife is of the Ferguson family, descending from the Scottish line.

My brothers and sisters are all living, viz.: Leonard Knapp, a resident of Ocean Beach, California, whose late wife was Mary Elvira Antisdate, and his daughter, Ida Elvira Warfield, is an excellent business woman, successful in real estate investments. My sisters are: Mary Elizabeth, born 1835; Clementine Lincoln, born 1838; Louisa Jane, born 1840; Isabel Chloe, born 1852.

I was born in 1843, and my brothers, Henry Jerome, in 1845, and Emerson Eugene, in 1848.

My own son is Herbert Douglas, and my only daughter is Mary Estelle Beach, wife of Stephen, of Bristol. They have two daughters.

My brother Henry is now of Mason, Michigan. His wife was Sarah Lavinia Jacques. They have a farm. Their children are Frank Milton, who has two sons, Eugene and Arthur. They have a farm. Eugene is in Lansing. Elmer, wife and daughter have removed to Denver, Colorado. Walter went with them for his health.

Sister Clementine's children are: Henry Carlton Lincoln and Zadok Carson Lincoln, twins; Mattie, Mary Alice, Ida Clementine, Chloe Lania, Ira James, John Burton and Nellie Artimicia.

There are fifteen grandchildren in this line.

My brother Eugene married Ann Maria Corey.   Their issue are Anna Corey, Ina Maud, Earl Emerson.

Anna Corey is now the wife of Wm. D. Power, of Syracuse. They have Ruth and Winfred W. Power.

Wm. Warfield, my uncle, left a daughter, Susan Warfield Jones, wife of John Jones, and Wm. Henry Warfield, now seventy-one years of age.   He holds a large estate.   He has been president of Canandaiqua, New York, for five years.   He is secretary and treasurer of the Ontario County Agricultural Society.   He writes many wills, and is ofter executor.

INDEX.

Caution!—The reader is advised to read each page carefully, as, although a name may occur several times on a page, there is but one reference to a page in the index.

A

D

F

G

H

K

L

N

xxxvi

INDEX.

P

S

T

xlviii INDEX.

U

V

W